Europe Ablaze

An Analysis
of the History of the European
Resistance Movements
1939–45

Odense University Press · 1978

Published in Danish May 1976

Printed by Andelsbogtrykkeriet i Odense

ISBN 87-7492-237-8

nificance for the general development of the war. Provokingly he challenges historians to do their job, and he defines, what he calls "the kind of study that is needed: that is to say, by studying Resistance as an integral part of the total history of the war, and by doing so on a comparative basis over all the countries in which Resistance took place".

The aim of this exposition therefore is to contribute towards solving the above mentioned task. But it is made without any illusion, that it can cover the whole ground, or even in any way be entirely complete. The reader is asked to accept it as it is meant: As a contribution to answering a question, that ideally can never be fully answered. But nevertheless one should endeavour to do so, in trying to understand the totality.

The Resistance Movements in the occupied countries of Europe were so many, so complicated and so diverse in their forms of actions and gallery of personalities, that no general survey can do full justice to either country, movement, group or person. In addition to this the most decisive factor is, that most Resistance activity naturally must be incompletely documented, as a direct consequence of the secret and diffuse character of the actions, and that the separate effect of the actions is lost in the course of the millions of parallel actions, which singly are only small particles in the great entirety. In principle the historian who occupies himself with the traditional warfare is in the same position. He devotes himself to the separate battles of the war and their outcome and only rarely with the contribution of the individual soldier or officer. But he can at least determine the result of the battle and estimate its significance. Here, however, it will be only in exceptional cases one can speak of tangible operations, where the place, time, plan, execution, achievements and results can be determined. Here it is a question of an unceasing and growing fight, which day after day, night after night, made unnoticeable traces in the development, but even so in their combined efforts they noticeably influenced the ultimate result. This, in principle, is also the case even if many para-military operations can be fixed in place and time, in plan and execution. A reception of arms and a sabotage can thus be determined, but to define the ultimate consequences is often impossible, as much resistance-activity cannot be either sufficiently documented nor the after-effects measured.

It is the historian's task to reveal, through existing documents, the unique course of events. The more comprehensive and genuine the documents are, and the more the historian narrows down his field of investigation, the better chance he gets to come to a positive conclusion. But nevertheless it must also be a historical assignment to give a survey

Contents

Preface

The Russian historian, E. Boltin, has stated the following about the Resistance Movements during the Second World War: "History has never known a popular fight of such huge dimensions as was apparent during the 1939–45 war. Furthermore the masses had never before taken so directly part in the military combat, as was the case in the last war in Europe. The Resistance Movement against German fascism has, in some way or other, affected all the countries and people that were subjected to Hitler's occupation, but at the same time the Movement's concrete manifestations, the forms of campaign, were of an unusual variety".

This view is also shared by the French historian, Henri Michel. He stresses the global character of the Resistance, indicating especially China, but he also emphazises, that it was in Europe, however, that the Resistance most clearly manifested itself as part of the fight against the common enemy but at the same time as an element in the struggle, the significance of which for the continued existence of the occupied countries as free nations it might be difficult to appreciate fully. "Thus to study the European Resistance Movements, is to understand the principal characteristics of the Resistance during the war". Having pointed out the universal character of European Resistance Michel concludes: "As far as Europe is concerned, this form of fighting was not completely unknown, but the complex form it took, gave it nonetheless a distinct originality". The universal and complex character of the movements, in connection with their nature as underground movements, which are normally difficult to comprehend, means that the Resistance and its results, from a historical point of view, is often seen in isolation from its intimate connection with the total development and result of the war. All the same the case is clear, as stated by the Belgian historian, Henri Bernard: "It is only by studying the European Resistance taken as a whole, that one can fully appreciate the significant part it played".

The English historian, C. M. Woodhouse, adopts the same theme, when he calls for an attempt to make a total survey of the Resistance Movements in their complexity, and in their relationship to, and sig-

directed towards the comprehensive, the typical and the syn with a proportional resignation towards a description of the indiv regional course of events. In this particular case, where it is a questn surveying mass-activity in the greater part of one corner of the wo, during 6 years, where everybody in different ways were the victims, and where millions took part, then this resignation is close to powerlessness.

In view of the considerable dimensions and character of the resistance-activity and considering the extensive litterature, that through the years after 1945 have seen the light of the day about the developments in the countries involved and about resistance-groups or individual efforts, as well as co-operation between the Resistance organisations and the free world, it is with the greatest reservations for unavoidable gaps and omissions of even the most important details that an attempt has been made to give a comprehensive account of the Resistance Movements' development, organisation and significance. The account is made without any illusion that it will prove tenable confronted with detailed analyses, but with a hope that it may all the same be useful as a contribution towards the comprehension of the nature of the Second World War and also towards a better understanding of the further development in the post-war years.

Reservations are not, however, taken from the standpoints expressed in the exposition. This is especially the case when referring to the fundamental point of view: That the Resistance Movements, seen in their entirety, deeply influenced the course of the war, psychologically, militarily and politically. The same applies indeed to the viewpoints expressed in the various chapters. Irrespective of the acknowledged gaps and omissions there might be in the foundation of the survey and its argumentation and course, no standpoint can plead immunity because of the dimension and complications of the work. They are all made to withstand documentary trial and both critical and constructive correction.

The survey is limited to the occupied countries and areas in Europe. Omission has been made of the opposition/resistance in Germany and in the countries, which were Germany's political axis-partners with Italy after 1943 as the only exception. Leaving out Asia as well, is probably leaving out the greatest Resistance Movement of them all, that of the Chinese under the leadership of Mao-Tse-Tung.

This is an acknowledged shortcoming, that stems solely from the necessity of defining a limit for the survey.

During the working out of this survey I have received valuable and comprehensive information from the Russian historians Julia Kudrina and A. A. Kurnosov, from the Norwegian historian, Berit Nökleby, as well as from the Belgian "Centre de Recherches et d'Etudes Historiques de la Seconde Guerre Mondiale". I am most grateful to all the above mentioned.

I extend my gratitude to the Odense University Library for the valuable help in obtaining the necessary litterature. I also thank professor Tage Kaarsted for his inspiration and encouragement during the work, and also stud.mag. Flemming Madsen, for the technical help of compiling the literature lists and notes.

But first and foremost I owe my deepest gratitude to my fellow colleague, the University Rector, Aage Trommer, for his numerous encouragements, critical comments and advice, as well as generous help with the Russian texts. I thank him for the incentive to the work, his assistance and criticism during the elaboration.

I also thank Mrs. Alison Borch-Johansen for an excellent translation.

My warmest thanks, though, go to my wife, Mrs. Gudrun Hæstrup.

Sct. Klemens January 3th, 1976.

Jørgen Hæstrup.

1. A Survey of problems

"THE FOURTH ARM". The Resistance Movements of the Second World War have been characterized as "the Fourth Arm", on a level with the traditional Arms – the Army, Navy and Air Force.

This expression – and the claim which it implies – was launched by the British Minister of Economic Warfare, Hugh Dalton, who used it as the title of a memorandum dated 19 August 1940, marked "Secret", addressed to the British War Cabinet. In this he argued energetically and enthusiastically for the idea that subversion behind the lines of the Axis Powers, and British co-operation with existing and future Resistance Movements, held great possibilities for supplementing the British war effort; and he urged that these possibilities should be promoted and exploited with full respect for the equal status of the executive organs involved, in the British military hierarchy. In his memorandum Dalton states: "Subversion should be clearly recognized by all three Fighting Services as another, independent Service." It was Dalton's idea, further, that the new arm was so important that the political responsibility for its development should be in the hands of a member of the British War Cabinet; and he suggested that Clement Attlee was the right man to undertake this political responsibility for the development of subversion, which in the summer 1940 could only be a vision of the future.[1] It was Dalton himself, however, who was to have charge of this development up to 1942,[2] as Minister of Economic Warfare – and as such, without a seat in the War Cabinet. Thus, no formal equality was established with the three regular Arms. On the other hand, practical co-operation was started and would constantly increase, between the Special Operations Executive (SOE) – as the organ in charge of the development of resistance possibilities was designated – and the three Services, particularly the Royal Air Force.

The designation "the Fourth Arm" can be a matter for discussion. But it is the purpose of this exposition to try to analyse to what degree it is reasonable to state that the European Resistance developed during the Second World War into a fighting weapon which psychologically, militarily and politically was to intervene deeply and perhaps even decisively in the whole course of the War. The first claim in this sentence – that the Resistance was to intervene deeply in the course of the War – seems indisputable. On the other hand it must be admitted that it will be difficult to analyse the question as to how decisive the Resistance was to the course of the War. The Resistance Movements won no military victories, but they influenced the course of events in the different war theatres, in varying degree, and several of them achieved marked political influence. It seems evident, however, that the Resistance Movements and a great many strongly differentiated forms of subversion, from psychological warfare to guerilla warfare and terrorist actions, would play a conspicuous rôle in the post-war world. The Second World War left an inheritance and a sum of experience which could not simply be shaken off.

THE HIDDEN WAR. Since this is the case, one may find it surprising that up to now, the various works on the Second World War, including a very extensive literature of memoirs,[3] only deal marginally with these Resistance Movements and their influence on the course of the War, and this applies particularly to accounts of the actual military course of events. The Resistance Movements are mentioned in the majority of these books, but often only in subordinate clauses or foot-notes, and never with any attempt on the part of the authors to evaluate them or their collective effect, in reasonable ratio to the rest of the material. There are implications and hints throughout, and now and then a few direct mentions, but as a rule there is no more than a respectful intimation, and at best a few general remarks. If it is true that the Resistance Movements collectively constituted an important fighting arm during the Second World War – and on closer examination, this seems highly probable – then the history of the War and its course has yet to be thoroughly dealt with in depth, in spite of the fact that so many books have been written on the subject of this world conflict.

Just as there are usually explanations for everything on this earth, so it is with this phenomenon. One explanation is mainly technical. Whilst every historian of the Second World War – and there are many authoritative works, from Chester Wilmot's in 1952 to Liddell Hart's in 1970 – had knowledge and the possibility of evaluating the developments on the "open" fronts, the situation was far more diffuse as to knowledge and evaluation of the continuous "little war", which developed everywhere in the countries and areas occupied by the Axis Powers. No historian of the Second World War could be unaware that this was active and important, but an evaluation of it, and particularly an evaluation of its importance in relation to the chief developments on the "open" fronts was impossible for some years. It was, if not a simple, at least an obvious task to establish the importance of the Battle of Britain in 1940, of Moscow in 1941, Midway in 1942, Stalingrad in 1942–43, the battles in the Libyan Desert or the Invasion in Normandy in 1944; and the importance was equally obvious of the great conferences in Moscow, Casablanca, Teheran, Yalta or finally Potsdam. It was quite another matter to assess to what extent a sabotage action here, an intelligence report there, or an escape organised by the underground somewhere else influenced the outcome of the War. The fact is that in this area, practically no action had self-evident importance. This is true even in cases of very striking Resistance achievements, such as the sabotage of the Gorgopotamus viaduct in Greece in 1942, General Giraud's escape from France the same year, or the Polish Intelligence report on a captured V.2 missile in 1944. Even where there is a question of such aggressive forms of resistance as the partisan movements in the Soviet Union or Yugoslavia, or of the influence of the French Resistance Movement on Allied strategy and policies, most writers have shown a clear, if understandable, tendency to avoid any evaluation of the Resistance Movements as a whole. In the first round, they have used the pages of the atlas, not of the ordnance map.

In this connexion there is an even more clearly technical explanation. For obvious reasons, documents relating to the Resistance Movements' activities formed the most inadequate group of archive material from the War, and they were the last to be examined. Before the study of these Resistance Movements could begin, a work of investigation had to be carried out in all the countries involved, to unearth the documents which – in spite of everything – had survived underground existence; and as far as possible, valid eye-witness material had to be obtained from Resistance members still living, before expositions could be made of the Resistance history of the various countries. The political developments could be roughly described, country by country, but it was a far more demanding task to undertake a thorough and precise description of the hidden history of these countries, although in several of them this was the most important – and also the most complicated. Before this hidden history could be uncovered, scattered fragments of material needed to be dug up, many of them of almost archaeological character.[4]

General de Gaulle's "Mémoires de Guerre", which appeared about ten years after the cessation of hostilities, can serve as an illustration of the problems indicated here. De Gaulle's large two-volume work deals in

e general course of the War, and with the Free French
'ements in the joint Allied war effort. De Gaulle gives a
)f the political and military connexion between the Allies
nce which he and his movement claimed to represent. He
_strates, with deep and expert insight, the contribution which the
Free French land, sea and air forces made to the common struggle on the
open fronts, although these forces were extremely modest, at least up to
the autumn 1943. However, as far as any description of the French
Resistance Movement at home is concerned, and its development into a
mass movement, with approximately three million men and women more
or less attached to the various Resistance organisations by 1944,[5] it is
only the roughest outline that de Gaulle is able to give his readers. It is
only in glimpses and thumbnail sketches that the exile politician de
Gaulle can report on the decisive Resistance developments which took
place in the various departments of the France which he claimed to
represent. Out of the sixteen long chapters of the books, one single
chapter is devoted to "la France Combattante", and even this chapter
gives no impression of any thorough insight into the mass movements
which developed and became organised during the occupation in France.
The subject is touched upon in the first half of the chapter, but attention
is concentrated chiefly upon General Koenig's fight at the head of the
Free French Forces in the desert battle around Bir-Hakeim, and on the
creation of the Free French Forces in general, outside the occupied
areas. The book is mainly experienced from the outside, from London,
Cairo, and the French Empire, not from Auvergne, Brittany or Lyons.
What happened here would only be brought to light in detail and as a
whole, after many years' laborious, detailed study of the French Resistance Movement's extremely varied history.

How historians in the various countries started more or less systematically to obtain the material which had been hidden during the Occupation, and the supplementary eye-witness accounts needed for expositions
of the Resistance Movements' history, is a chapter of its own. In one
country after another, it was necessary to uncover myriads of details,
often minute, and then gradually to piece the single items of information
together into larger or smaller collected mosaics – stories of individual
actions, of individual organisations, individual districts, and sometimes
of individual men and women. In putting the mosaic together there was
only exceptionally any decisive date, and even more exceptionally any
epoch-making single event, but there were millions of detailed facts

which together made up the pattern of events which formed the history of the Resistance Movements.

THE IMMEASURABLE CHARACTER OF THE RESISTANCE MOVEMENTS. Here there appears a further explanation of the phenomenon that the importance of the Resistance Movements has been largely overlooked, in the accounts of the history of the Second World War as a whole. This explanation lies in the unmeasurable character of these movements, and the often quite incalculable importance of each single item among the millions which made up the Resistance Movements. How important was a partisan poster, stuck up on the wall of a house in Kharkov, or for that matter, the distribution in the Ukraine of about 400,000,000 leaflets, newspapers and brochures?[6] Or the appearance of an illegal newspaper in Holland? The derailment of a train in Poland? Shelter for a British pilot shot down over France? A partisan attack on an Italian sentry post in Greece? A Norwegian courier, crossing the frontier into Sweden with dispatches? The questions could be piled up in millions, and the standards of measurement are difficult or impossible to set, because a single event in itself seldom represents more than the value of a particle. Added to this, there is the most imponderable of all the factors – the psychological factor. This factor had its effect upon the peoples of the occupied countries, upon the Occupying Powers, and upon the Allies, who registered and followed these activities with lively attention.

The way to a recognition of the collective weight of these movements, which have left only scanty, and often fragmentary traces in the form of archives – in countless cases none whatever – then becomes long, tortuous and full of blind alleys. The research worker soon finds himself in a jungle of items of information, few of which have immediate illustrative value in the question as to the Resistance Movements' collective influence upon developments. No item of information, on whatever Resistance activity, is unimportant, however, since it must be fitted into its organic context with activities of a similar kind, somewhere or other in the "non-system" of Resistance activities in every area where the Occupation was of long duration. This is the case wherever the impulse to resist was aroused in the occupied territories and almost regardless of which type of impulse we are considering. An activity in Holland could have influence on a situation in Poland; an activity in Norway could affect dispositions in the Soviet Union, Yugoslavia or France. Effects were seldom immediate, in the sense that one heard in one place of activity in the other, and could be inspired by it. This did occur, but it was the exception.[7] Effects were, on the contrary, long-term, in that activity in one place could force the Occupying Powers to make dispositions which could affect the other, and often in such a way that these projected experience and reactions from one area to another. Regardless of the geographical diffusion of Resistance activities, and the almost total lack of direct connexion in the atomized Resistance mass, invisible and often untraceable ties did exist between what happened in one place, and what the reactions were in another.

What was true, geographically speaking, was also true in the field of Resistance functions. Resistance activity was composed of a great many different functions: the formation of groups with more or less clearly defined aims; protests; demonstrations; strikes; illegal news services; illegal propaganda; intelligence services; the establishment of escape routes; the creation of postal or radio communications; the organisation of help to the many categories of people threatened with political persecution; the organisation of weapon manufacture or the reception of weapons parachuted down or landed from the sea; sabotage; assassination activities; partisan warfare; large- or small-scale political co-ordination of the scattered initiatives; and corresponding attempts to co-ordinate fighting activities on the home fronts with the battles on the fronts abroad.

The more successful the efforts at co-ordination and organisation were, in the various countries, and between these countries and the nations openly at war, the more marked was the collective weight of the Resistance Movements in the general course of the war. But there could never be any question of popular revolt with revolutionary leaders in the traditional sense, for the revolts were the result of the coincidence of millions of impulses and components. On the outside fronts, the fighting units were mobilised, organised and sent into action according to dispositions and orders from above. On the inside fronts, the numerically large Resistance units found their own way to action, without any possibility of a correspondingly consistent direction. On the outside fronts, the individual knew his place, his tasks and his importance. On the inside fronts, the individual often had to content himself with the expectations of faith or of desperation, that his or her pin-prick efforts served a common, meaningful purpose.

No assertion is intended here that no organisation took place within the heterogenous masses of the Resistance. On the contrary, organisation was carried out everywhere within the individual Resistance branches, in the mutual relations between them, and to the degree that this was possible, also in the relations between the more or less co-ordinated Resistance organisations and the military and political organs which led the fight on the open fronts. The higher the level of organisation these movements achieved, the more effectively they were able to function, and therefore to influence the collective war situation.[8] If the Resistance Movements had only distinguished themselves through a more or less accidental coincidence of individual or local initiatives and actions, their effect would probably have been relatively unimportant, but just because this situation forced extensive and complicated organisational efforts upon them, within the individual areas of activity, an interplay gradually arose between them. Interplay also arose between the Resistance organisations, closely interlinked as they gradually became, and the support organs directly involved in the free world: the exile governments, exile politicians, the B.B.C., Radio Moscow, the British SOE's various headquarters and the General Staff of the Soviet Partisan Movement in Moscow, from 1942 the various branches of the American sister organisation to SOE, the Office of Strategic Service (OSS), and all the military and political organs outside the occupied areas which would and could support Resistance activity. Close links were forged here between activity on the inside fronts and the military, political and psychological offensives which were set in motion from outside.

THE DEMAND FOR ORGANISATION. If we now turn to the efforts at organisation within the various and multifarious Resistance Movements behind the lines of the Axis Powers, it must be reasonable to establish that practically no active Resistance group could exist without creating its own internal organisation, or seeking co-operation with parallel Resistance groups, and later also with groups specializing in other types of activity. It must be obvious that Resistance activity, of whatever kind, itself created the need for organisation. Every illegal newspaper, and every decision for sabotage contained in itself the seed of an organisation, and no demonstration or strike took place without an organising factor existing behind it, or developing in the course of action. Precisely the same is true – but in higher degree – of the more advanced forms of resistance, such as intelligence services, radio communication, weapon reception, the creation of escape routes, etc. Examples can here be more illustrative than generalisations.

A person or group undertaking the publication of an illegal paper had to make sure of their sources of information, editorial treatment, paper, printing and distribution possibilities, and – as the background for the publication – money. Even in the most simply conceived instances, a minimum of organisation was needed, from the moment the decision was taken. The more a function expanded, the more the demand increased for differentiated organisation. If a local paper aimed at becoming regional or national, the demand for organisation increased progressively with such ambitions. Precisely the same applied to the groups which decided to take up sabotage. Here too, the demand for organisation presented itself. It was necessary to obtain information in advance on the objective and its surroundings; it was necessary to plan the course of the action, ensure access to the means of sabotage – incendiaries or explosives – and it was necessary to make sure that there were possibilities for cover, when the action had been completed. If such an action was not to remain an isolated and unimportant single event, but was to become a more meaningful link in a chain of actions, the decision for sabotage must inevitably entail extensive organisation. This applied especially to the procurement of explosives and hand weapons, which in the course of time led to co-operation with groups specializing in weapon reception. It was also important that understanding of the importance of sabotage should be promoted, and contact with the illegal Press could therefore be desirable, or necessary.

Where there was a question of demonstrations or strikes, the problem was slightly different from those mentioned above, but here too the necessity for organisation is evident. The difference lies in the fact that behind the demonstration or the strike, an element of spontaneity must come into the picture. No demonstration or strike could be carried out successfully without a latent accumulation of feeling and atmosphere existing behind the action, among the larger or smaller groups or sectors of the population taking part in actions of this kind. This accumulation was by no means always the result of any organised influence, or any specifically directed propaganda, but could just as well be the outcome of general conditions, brought about in the first place by the Occupation situation itself, and the evils which it brought with it. But having said this, one should add that the actual explosion was very often caused by a more or less organised initiative, and that its course was most often directed as regards length, extent and method by organised groups, in countless cases set up with the *ad hoc* purpose of achieving the most effective action possible, and perhaps also later of bringing the action to a stop, where and when this was considered most expedient. The great mass movements which arose in most areas called upon organising forces which could direct and control, now stimulating, now moderating.

Where there was a question of more complicated Resistance functions such as the establishment of intelligence networks, weapon reception, radio communication, courier or escape routes, etc., detailed and extremely complicated organisation was an absolute condition for a successful course of action. This must be obvious, and only one example will be given, therefore, in illustration. The group which stood ready somewhere in Europe to carry out weapon reception must of necessity be closely woven into an organisational pattern, which on the one side included the actual recruitment and collection of the group, its procurement of means of transport and depots, its orientation as to codes and signals, and on the other side included contact with radio or courier organisations, superior distribution organs, and in the final instance with the free world from which the operation started.

To sum up, it may be claimed that all Resistance activity depended upon an extremely high degree of organising ability, and that the effectiveness of Resistance work increased proportionately with the capacity of the movement and its possibilities for developing a high level of organisation.

ORGANISATIONAL FORMS. These remarks on the Resistance Movements' organising ability cannot end here. Some comments must be added on the forms of organisation which the situation forced upon these movements. These were, and had to be, different in principle from the forms of organisation on the open fronts. Here, organisation was carried out according to directives and orders from above. Governments, ministries, military staffs, etc. established the complex of organisation which the conduct of the war necessitated. The initiative came from the State, and the traditional State machinery, supplemented with the organisational additions, demanded by the fighting, which were made available for the conduct of the war. The total complex of organisation had the form of a vast pyramid, the base of which consisted of the private soldiers who were all fitted into the system according to decisions and orders from above. Regardless of how complicated this pyramid system could be, with its myriads of intermediate authorities, good or poor co-operation between the individual links and the organisation, or friction between these links, where it was a question of issuing orders, competence, use of resources, etc.,[9] this was a system which in the final instance was built up on a centralized form, with a centralized command, where the leaders at the top of the pyramid always had the possibility of intervening with adjustments or orders. The system could be more or less complicated, and function more or less satisfactorily – depending upon which country we are considering – but in principle there were a number of factors which differed fundamentally from the forms of organisation under which the Resistance Movements had to work.

In the first place, the system was built up especially for war conditions, with decisions working their way downwards according to orders from above. Next, the various members in the system knew each other or could at least obtain information about each other, and each member of the organisation received his duties from superior organs. The system did not exclude initiatives from the ranks, but the decision as to whether these initiatives should be promoted or stopped was taken on the basis of overall considerations, by the higher organs, and in the last instance by the Heads of State. In this system, a free bird's eye view which allowed for the survey of the whole field was the ideal, at least, and to a great extent the reality.

Compared with this firmly constructed centralized system, the conditions of organisation and the organisational forms under which the Resistance Movements had to work were certainly very different, if not diametrically opposite.

First of all, if one excludes the partisan movement in the Soviet Union, the Resistance Movements' form of warfare was not the product of a State decision, nor did the fighting methods which were taken into use arise from a State decision, and nor were they under State direction. It is true that several of the Resistance Movements could to some extent work in harmony with the exile governments, which had their seat in London, or in the case of the Soviet partisans, in harmony with the Soviet Government in Moscow; but the situation of the Occupation, and purely technical considerations, even in cases where the Resistance Movements were loyal to such State authorities, made any completely centralized command impossible. It should be added that there was a clear tendency for differences in views and standpoints between the exile governments and the Resistance Movements at home to increase proportionally with the duration of the Occupation. In spite of all the information which reached them, exile entailed an isolation for the exile politicians which debarred them from fully understanding the conditions of life and the developments at home. In exile, one received news of developments. At home, one experienced them. It should also be mentioned that a number of the Resistance Movements not only refrained from working under the aegis of a State authority – they worked directly against the State authority. In this field, conditions were extremely varied, with a wide spectrum of possibilities. There were movements which recognized the distant State authority in principle, regardless of the fact that it only had meagre possibilities, or perhaps no possibilities whatever, for intervening in the direction of the movements' growth and actions. For the exile governments in London, the situation was that any intervention depended upon Allied sanction and upon the technical assistance of the supporting organisations set up by the Allies in support of the Resistance Movements, which stood between the exile governments and the home movements as intermediary links. This applies, for example, to the Polish, Norwegian, Dutch and to some extent the Belgian Resistance Movements,[10] whereas it applies less to the partisan movements in German-occupied Russia, which acknowledged the authority of the Soviet State unconditionally, and co-operated with it, under its orders, without intermediaries. There were other Resistance Movements which turned directly against their own State authorities, because they did not recognize their legal right to represent the State. This was the case, for example, in France and Yugoslavia, and it was also true of important sections of the Greek and Italian Resistance Movements. The French Resistance organisations, and as their exponent in the Allied world, de Gaulle and his movement,[11] never recognized the legality of the Pétain regime, and nor did the Yugoslav partisan leader Tito recognize the legality of the exile Yugoslav Government.

In the Greek Resistance Movement, there were important factions which turned categorically against the prospect of the restoration of the exile Greek Government after the War. And in the Resistance Movement which arose in Italy after the creation of the Badoglio Government in 1943, there were also strong factions which denied that government's right to represent the Italian State authority, and in addition they both turned against their monarchy. Denmark was a different case. Here the Resistance Movement turned against the State policy vis-à-vis the Occupying Power, without actually challenging the legal right of the government to represent the authority of the State, until in August 1943 the government resigned. After this, the Resistance Movement was exempt from consideration for any State authority, since such an authority no longer functioned. It was a common feature for them all, that in their choice of fighting methods and in the extension of their forms of organisation, the Resistance Movements were quite independent and often acted without any State directives.

The fundamental fact should also be mentioned in addition to the above, that all Resistance activity was based upon volunteers, and this, at least in theory, excluded the issue of orders in the normal sense of the term. This assertion that all resistance was based upon volunteers is only valid, however, with certain modifications, although these do not affect the basic fact that the volunteer system was the underlying principle in the construction of the Resistance Movements' forms of organisation, and in their preparation of the systems of command which had necessarily to be made to function, if the Resistance Movements were to acquire striking power. The modifications arose in connexion with the very large groups which were forced into resistance by the Occupation situation, in some cases so that participation in the Resistance became the natural choice, in others so that participation in the Resistance was chosen as the lesser evil. The European Communists can be cited as exponents of the first of these groups. Up to the German invasion of the Soviet Union on 22 June 1941, they were not active in resistance, even if they prepared for the likely possibility that the German-Soviet Pact could break down. After this date, however, they joined the Resistance organisations already existing, consistently and in strength, or led in building up such organisations. One could also mention among this category the groups of officers for whom the path to the Resistance ranks was opened up in a situation of compulsion, as was the case for a large group of French officers in November 1942, when the Armistice Army from 1940 was dissolved and the alternatives were either German imprisonment, passivity or participation in the Resistance groups.

As exponents for the second group, one can mention first of all the European Jews, who in the given situation had no other choice than to join the Resistance, or at least seek the shelter which was available through the auxiliary organisations of the Resistance Movements. In this group one should also include the many who evaded forced conscription to work for the Germans by joining the Resistance, and this group provides countless examples of persons who fled from the terror campaigns started by the Occupying Powers or their henchmen in many places in the occupied countries. It should be sufficient here to mention the German SS Sonder Commandos in the East, Joseph Darnand's militia in France or the Ustace movement in Yugoslavia.[12] Lastly, this group includes a conglomeration of homeless people, refugees, deserters, etc. "The Boys in the Forest" in Norway, large sections of the Maquis in France, the partisan groups in the Soviet Union, Poland, Yugoslavia and Greece received considerable numbers of recruits for the above reasons, and throughout Europe there were countless men and women who went underground and were then absorbed into the Resistance groups or the circles friendly to the Resistance, regardless of whether they came to make larger or smaller or even no direct contribution to the work of resistance.

Quite apart from the circumstances of recruitment, however, it seems to be a valid statement that the Resistance work and therefore the work of building up and expanding the Resistance organisations was founded upon volunteers, whether they were individual volunteers or groups of volunteers. This could not but affect the construction of the Resistance organisations decisively.

The voluntary system which was the underlying principle in the construction of the Resistance did not in any way exclude willingness to receive and obey orders. But this willingness did not spring from any sense of duty towards a State or other established authority. It was based upon a sense of loyalty of one kind or another, loyalty to comrades, loyalty towards organs whose use one accepted, or loyalty towards the common cause to which one had consecrated ones strength and life. Loyalty was first of all attached to what was at hand – the group or guerilla unit to which one belonged – but willingness to subordinate oneself to more distant and perhaps anonymous command authorities also made itself felt, in spite of all formal difficulties. It was simply a condition, that every authority which issued orders within the Resistance organisation had to live with, that they could suggest and persuade, but not order or command. Every Resistance authority had to work under the pure democratic law that they must win their authority by their words and deeds, day by day, situation by situation. Directives, not concrete and unassailable commands, were the rule and the Resistance groups could usually be trusted to obey directives, with the addition of their own independent initiative and the adjustment of the general instructions of the directives to local conditions and personal possibilities. All this contained a certain weakness for the Resistance organisations, but it also contained a strength. Instructions were sent out in the illegal world with the knowledge that there could be doubt as to their course, but there could also be a probability of their being followed with all the elasticity which unknown and incalculable circumstances could demand.There was neither accepted authority in the illegal world nor paralysing anarchy.

TENDENCIES TOWARDS CENTRALIZATION. All resistance was based upon initiative, and there were countless scattered initiatives, some of them very deliberate, with an immediate purpose, others uncertain as to their purpose and marked by indecision as to what possibilities there might be for action. As long as uncertainty remained, and as long as the person or group taking the initiative did not realise that any concrete tasks lay open, so long – even with the best will in the world – did the initiative remain "floating". In many places in the Occupation areas, very many small, varied initiatives were taken locally. One hid weapons, copied and passed on leaflets, collected in groups to listen in to the wireless, exchanged information and cursed the enemy, or one met to discuss how one could grope ones way to some meaningful action or other. One made a note of ones neighbours' reactions, or those of ones comrades at work. Very few had the imagination or the possibility for realising a concrete plan immediately, as did, for example, the Belgian engineer Walther Dewé. As Chief of the Belgian telephone and telegraph network, he established an effective intelligence service, "Le Corps d'Observation Belge" immediately after the capitulation of the Belgian Army.[13] Quite a different example can be given from the little French island of Sein, where all the 130 male inhabitants capable of bearing arms went on board the fishing fleet of the island and sailed to Cornwall, to join de Gaulle's Free French Forces.[14] On the local level, many plans were discussed, and many initiatives taken, but the first weeks and months of the Occupation had to be a period of leavening, where initiatives could only be isolated, scattered in character and vague as to purpose. In the countries in the North and West, there were no traditions for illegal activity to build upon. In Poland there were long traditions of this kind, but even here, the Resistance began with scattered initiatives. In the winter 1939–40, a number of officers met in Warsaw[15] on the orders of the Polish Head of State and Minister of Defence, General Sikorski, to consider how to obtain control of the many independent groups which they knew had been or were being created in many places in Poland. Here as elsewhere, the unification of their forces and the firm establishment of organisational forms was a necessity if the movements were to achieve striking power. Isolated groups must themselves feel this necessity, and seek contact to all sides, upwards and outwards. In the first place, whatever sphere of action they might have marked out for themselves, they had to consolidate themselves in limited, closed internal organisations. But as soon as this process was finished, it was seldom long before the group sought contact outside its own circle, either with like-minded circles within the same field of action, or with groups working in other fields. The establishment of contact became a central function, both because the individual groups' actions were meaningless if they were not supplemented by and co-ordinated with corresponding actions in other circles and other fields, and because the possibilities for action within one field could depend upon those in another. Isolation became synonymous with impotence.

The possibilities for an isolated group to find its place in a larger system must of necessity be few, however, and many small groups could look in vain, for months, for the desired contacts. A well-knit organisation depended therefore also upon initiatives from above, which aimed at creating effective organisations, co-operating within and between the various fields of action, as well, finally, as between these organisations and the Allied world.[16] Initiatives of this kind could proceed from individuals with special possibilities for seeing a way through the chaos, from political parties, from trades unions, from military circles or from illegal groups which undertook tasks of organisation which went beyond their own needs. Where there was a question of establishing co-operation between illegal organisations and the supporting organisations of the free world, initiative often, and naturally, came from instructors dropped by parachute or smuggled in by some other way, from SOE, OSS or from the Central Staff of the Partisan Movement. Such organising and unifying parties, organisations or special groups, having an overall view as well as the possibilities for making the right contacts, gradually made their presence felt and found their way to the resistance-minded. The latter were then channeled into larger systems, and thus unified organisations arose – at widely different tempi – often with specific functions: newspaper groups, sabotage groups, intelligence groups, reception groups, military groups etc. Organisation then continued, branching out continually, and expanding as long as the Resistance Movements were in action. An organisation which expanded step by step was noticeably a living organism, constantly adjusting itself to the varying situations and possibilities, without ever stiffening in a fixed scheme decided from above. The groups functioned under general directives, and on the basis of complicated individual agreements, but they added their own improvisations and ingenuity to the work, with such flexibility that general agreements were adjusted to the special, local, individual possibilities. Underneath all the changeableness, there was a noticeable tendency towards establishing superior organs, which increasingly sought to co-ordinate the scattered forces, and to a great extent succeeded . This tendency came into being within all kinds of Resistance functions, and sprang partly from technical necessity and partly from political intention. In the long run, all the Resistance Movements found their way to a joint national command, which could both give the movements a political image, inwards ensuring the national organisation of the common but many-stringed fighting activity, and outwards promoting the best possible co-operation with the Allies. It should be added, however, that it was never possible to create a stiff, unified command or an authoritarian leader over the flexible and constantly changing organisations which the Resistance Movements built up. As far as the purpose was to establish full control and total expediency in operations, the purpose remained an illusion. To the extent that the purpose was to make the individual Resistance branches capable of functioning, these efforts were very largely successful.

This applies most clearly to the organisations of a technical character, which the Resistance Movements had to build up, in order to create a certain amount of unification and co-ordination between the countless local and even individual actions. Here there was a question of organisations for the promotion of the intelligence services, internal and external communications, all kinds of supply services, as well as organisations to promote the best possible co-ordination between the many direct action forms which the Resistance Movements took up – whether they were demonstrations or strikes, sabotage or assassinations, the creation of military groups, or actual guerilla activity. For all the fields of endeavour indicated, such co-ordination of forces was desirable, and for the great majority it was directly necessary, in spite of the risks which all co-ordination involved. Generally speaking, every expansion of an organisation for the promotion of a common purpose involved a considerable risk, but this had to be accepted if effectiveness was to be achieved. The Polish Resistance leader, General Bor-Komorowski, has stated this categorically in a commentary on the Polish courier service.[17] He stresses that there even existed a direct ratio between willingness to take risks, and effectivity. Where safety precautions went too far, tempo and effectivity decreased, whereas effectivity increased where safety precautions were slackened. This observation covers all Resistance work.

The need for organisation was not equally acute for all types of Resistance work, and the need was only acknowledged as Resistance activity gradually expanded. The remnants of a guerilla group which had been broken up could carry out minor harrying operations, for a time and to certain extent, just as an isolated sabotage group could achieve minor results on their own.

Similarly, an illegal newspaper group could exercise some local influence without much contact with other newspaper groups or other illegal organisations, just as individual escapes to neutral or Allied countries could occasionally be arranged on the basis of completely private initiatives, coupled with daring, ingenuity and a certain amount of luck. But groups which had been broken up or isolated had little real importance. It was only when initiatives approached each other, and co-operation was brought about, that local and individual actions were transformed from symptoms to important parts in a larger, meaningful whole. The guerilla struggle swelled and became dangerous to the degree that units joined each other; sabotage received increased striking power where it was co-ordinated with the supply organisations of the Resistance Movements, so that its logistics were put in order; the illegal newspaper world gained the capacity really to form public opinion when the breakthrough of co-operation occurred, and the stream of information became abundant and reliable; and the individual escape, with all its dangers, became superfluous as organised escape and courier routes were made to function. Leaders of the various technical functions were established, and in the midst of the volcanic landscape which was the product of the explosive Resistance activity in many fields, various national liberation councils, committees etc. arose. Their work aimed unceasingly at co-ordinating the scattered efforts around them, at giving their Resistance Movements political programmes and images, and at creating the best possible co-operation with the Allies abroad – sometimes in co-operation with their own exile organs, sometimes in sharp opposition to them. Among such bodies were the Polish home army, "Armia Krajowa", which co-operated with a political directing committee; the Norwegian "Hjemmefrontens Ledelse" (HL); the Danish "Danmarks Frihedsråd"; the Dutch "Raad van Verzet"; the Belgian "Front de l'Indépendance"; the French "Conseil National de la Résistance"; the Yugoslav provisional government, with its military command firmly in the hands of Marshal Tito; the political resistance council EAM in Greece; and from 1943, in occupied North Italy, the liberation committee, "Comitati di Liberazione Nazionale di Alta Italia" (CLNAI).[18] Conditions and circumstances varied from one country to another, but the main pattern was generally the same: every Resistance function received its independent organisation with its own secrets and its centralized command – or something approaching a command – and above all technical leaders stood the national committees, councils or commissions, with varying possibilities as to competence. Common to them all was the tendency towards centralization.

CLOSED SYSTEMS. The Resistance function which was most in need of a solid, but discreet, organisation was perhaps the least noticed, although it may have been the most important of them all – the Intelligence Service.[19] The fact that this particular function more than any other called for organisation – and an extremely fine-meshed organisation – was connected with its character as what can be described as an atomized organism. This organism received life only in the degree to which its individual elements were linked together in phased series of chains. The extremities in these chains – the observer/reporters – had few possibilities for assessing the value of their observations, and it was only in the higher organs, where observations could be filtered and evaluated, that the impression came through of the importance of each single observation in the pattern of the whole. In other words: the observer, whether he or she was an officer, a lighthouse keeper, a stationmaster, a waitress, a lorry driver, a camp follower, a fisherman, or conscript worker, and whether he or she was a private person or a civil servant with more or less insight into the actions and dispositions of the Occupying Power, could only have a hint, at the most, of whether an individual observation was valuable. It was only when the collection of information gradually became systematized that the value of the countless single observations was sucked up into the system, the observers instructed and the information channeled upwards into the "machine", that the single observations began to form the mosaic where their value was evident, and only if the treatment of these observations was carried out with minute attention to detail, and took place at higher levels. This is precisely what occurred.

Over all the vast occupation areas, intelligence organisations developed which followed and registered the doings of the Occupying Powers, with more or less skill, partly for the internal use of the Resistance organisation, and partly for the external use of the Allies, with whom the intelligence organisations came into close co-operation. Specially trained officers came naturally to play an important part in the creation of a number of European intelligence networks. This was true of Poland,

Czechoslovakia, Norway, Denmark, Holland, Belgium and France, but it was also a decisive factor in the construction of these services that the professional, traditional services in the occupied countries received a great and unique supplement of volunteer recruits. This occurred particularly among the observers, but it also occurred in the illegal staffs, where a mass of information was converted into orderly, clear intelligence. In the Soviet Union, the partisan organs worked closely with the General Staff of the Soviet Armies, and with the Central Staff of the Partisan Movement.

In the sphere of intelligence, the situation changed radically for the belligerents, from what it had been previously, for example during the First World War,[20] or even during the first year of the Second World War. During the First World War, the French Army Command misjudged or was ignorant of the German Schlieffen Plan, and in the spring 1940, the German armoured break-through in the Ardennes took them by surprise. From the autumn 1940, this situation altered completely. The enormous size of the Axis-occupied areas and the degree to which the Occupying Powers were dependent upon the conquered peoples for guard duties, transport, production and manpower, resulted in a huge stream of information from these regions on enemy activity – much of the information in edited form. This meant that at least from 1942, the Allies could plan their conduct of the war with increasingly detailed knowledge of the troop movements of the Axis Powers, their defence installations and their instruments of aggression, their conditions of production, etc. The dispositions of the Axis Powers were everywhere watched by vigilant, expert observers, organised in a fine-meshed network, and it was impossible for the Axis Powers to free themselves from ceaseless observation. It can be said, without much exaggeration, that the Axis Powers were surrounded by millions of potential spies, and the task for the Resistance was therefore simply to organise observers, create organs for filtering and evaluating information, and establish the necessary contact organs to forward the collected data, either to their own organisations or to the Allies. The word "simply" must not be misunderstood. It is intended to indicate that the task was clear-cut, but certainly not that its solution did not entail endless toil, elements of great danger, minute attention to every detail and, as the result of all the experience gained, the creation of extremely competent directing organs.

The Allies naturally maintained traditional spy networks with air photography, signal reports, planting of agents from outside, and the systematic study of all available sources of information. The planting of agents was greatly facilitated by the Resistance Movements, and the results which they achieved in this way were supplemented by the continuous stream of mass information, collected as described, by the Resistance organisations. In his work on the Second World War, Winston Churchill repeatedly touches upon the question, for example in a chapter in Volume IV on the British air offensive and the German countermeasures in the field of radar.[21] He applauds the "friendly neutrals" and the information they obtained from the German-occupied areas, and then adds: "In speaking of agents and friendly neutrals it would be fair to single out the Belgians for special mention. In 1942 they provided about 80 per cent of all agent information on this subject, including a vital map, stolen from the German Officer Commanding searchlight and radar equipment for the more northerly of the two sectors of the German night fighter line in Belgium".

Many other statements of a similar nature could be cited. The Allies waged war with their eyes open as to enemy movements and possibilities, and seldom allowed themselves to be taken by surprise. The most outstanding successes in this area were perhaps the intimate knowledge which Great Britain had of the experiments with the V bombs in Peenemünde and in Poland, and the production of heavy water in Rjukan, and the Soviet Supreme Command's usually very reliable information on German troops movements and preparations for offensives, when once the war in the east had begun, and the partisan organisations' intelligence service was established.

The situation is all the more remarkable when one compares it with the fact that the German leaders were generally speaking unaware of the Allies' plans, misjudging the relative strengths again and again, and so allowing themselves to be taken by surprise. In spite of the myth of the German Fifth column, and its effectiveness,[22] the German Government and military leaders, both in victory and defeat, acted on the basis of extremely befogged impressions. They misjudged the French Army's sudden collapse in 1940, and allowed it to take them by surprise; they misjudged the situation at Dunkirk; and they misjudged the strength of the R.A.F. in the autumn 1940. Further, they misjudged the resources of the Soviet Union in 1941; they overestimated their own possibilities in the campaign in the Soviet Union in 1942; they were unaware of the Allied landings in French North-west Africa in 1942; they were taken by surprise by the Allied landings in Sicily in 1943; and they were utterly confused in their reactions to the Invasion in Normandy in 1944. They grossly underestimated the potential strength of the U.S.A., and they misjudged the attitude of the American Heads of Government. One can easily find other examples. Behind all this lay, amongst other things, a fundamental difference in the intelligence situation between the warring powers, and it was here that the Resistance Movements came to make an essential contribution. That the Allies by no means always exploited this advantage fully is another matter, which can be explained quite simply by the fact that nothing man-made is perfect, least of all in war.

The intelligence service is here mentioned as an example of how an individual Resistance function created its organisational forms with a foundation of elementary components and the necessary superstructures, which could vary from one country to another, and from one organisation to another.[23] At the same time, two fundamental features have been lightly touched upon which were common to the organisational forms which the Resistance Movements had to utilise. One of these concerns the isolation of the function, which had to leave its mark on the working form. The other concerns the reverse – the co-operation with other Resistance forms which arose in all Resistance activity as an absolute necessity. For quite obvious reasons, this particular service of espionage had to be carried out as discreetly as possible – and a considerable degree of screening from all other Resistance work was maintained. The work proceeded best and with the greatest security when the participants were not involved in direct action, where the danger of arrest and the round-ups which followed were considerable.

The situation where the activities of one individual Resistance function were sealed off from the others was not confined to the intelligence service, however. On the contrary, this situation was typical of all kinds of Resistance work. On grounds of security, and because the Occupation situation ruled out open activity, every link in the jungle of organisations must in principle be isolated behind a network of secret arrangements, and as a basic rule, in such a way that as few as possible had knowledge of as little as possible. In theory, the shutters could not be closed too tightly, and in theory this took place both vertically and horizontally. Where there was a question of contact upwards to superior organs, it was best if only the leaders were initiated, and most often the arrangers of the contact remained anonymous, establishing it through unknown couriers who passed on unsigned directives or orders from above, or enquiries or reports from below. Even those partly in the know could normally only be aware of the existence of superior organs, without having exact knowledge of the structure of these organs. It was a system, but a system which, in its entirety, worked in the dark, even as regards those who carried or created it. Practically no one had full overall knowledge of the whole system. For example, for a member of a courier or escape route, the whole structure and method of cohesion was a mystery – and a mystery which in principle should not be investigated. Courier messengers or refugees could travel the pathway in question without divulging his or her identity or past, and passing on a message depended only upon ones knowing the next link in the chain – but nothing of its further progress. To the extent that there was a system, it was a system which deliberately avoided question and answer. On the lower levels one received messages, packages of newspapers or explosives, without asking where they came from. On the higher levels one delivered them without checking their use.

On the horizontal plane, also, the same situation held. A number of groups could turn out the same night for weapon receptions over a large area, without having the least idea of each others parallel actions. Similarly, both newspaper groups and sabotage groups could be active in the same town or the same region without any form of direct contact between them.[24] A partisan unit in the Ukraine could fight its own fight, without either connexion with or knowledge of similar units in action in White Russia and the Baltic regions, or the much more distant Savoy, Montenegro or Greece. A sabotage group could decide to sabotage a factory without knowing that a weapon reception group in the same district had chosen the cellar of the same factory as safe storage for explosives received. The basic principle was that groups and units shut themselves in with their secret knowledge and their mutual agreements.

THE DEMAND FOR CO-OPERATION. The insulation and lack of orientation on what was happening in other fields and other regions was inevitable, and was rooted in the demands of illegality and the impossibility of allowing information to circulate within the various countries. The principle of watertight compartments had to be followed. In practice, however, the principle had to be adapted to the needs of the situation. Insulation, however desirable it might be on grounds of security, could not have become total. On the contrary, as the Resistance Movements developed, a great deal of bridge-building took place within the various Resistance functions, and common superstructures joined many of them to each other. The reason for this is quite obvious. The groups needed each other, and had little effect so long as they were scattered elements. The sabotage group, or the partisan group, needed the information and propaganda which the illegal newspaper world provided; strikes were often set in motion as the result of the accumulation of public feeling and opinion, roused by that same newspaper world, and perhaps with a sabotage action and the reprisals which followed it as the immediate incitement. All the groups needed the various kinds of material which arrived by sea or air for the Resistance organisations, whose work depended upon close co-operation with the communications organisations, whether radio communication or courier communication, while the intelligence service had a corresponding need for knowledge of the groups' activities and for co-operation with the communications services. At the top of this complex of multifarious organisations, the various national councils or committees wished to have insight into, and if possible control with, the activities of the groups.

In addition to all this, there was the labyrinth of lines of communication, running from the Resistance Movements out to the Allies in the free world, with whom the Resistance made common cause, and on whose direct or indirect support they depended.

The result was a hotch-potch of organisations in perpetual motion, where connexions criss-crossed each other, often deep into an apparently normal, loyally functioning society, which was thus illegalised to a degree which it is impossible to measure directly in numbers of members of illegal organisations or volume af activity. Great numbers of illegal groups profitted by some form of support from the sector of the population which did not take part in resistance, or from sympathisers in the production, transport or administrative sectors, etc. Such support is inclined to fade into obscurity, but it belongs to the total picture of a number of organisations, where plans, arrangements and contacts were changed from one situation to the next, sometimes from hour to hour. The most surprising part about it is probably that this jumble, on close analysis, turns out to consist of extremely well organised elements in a whole, which – in spite of all the difficulties – succeeded in functioning so effectively in the popular struggle which took place behind the lines of the Occupying Powers, and which to an important extent helped to mark and influence the course of the struggle.

COMMON FEATURES. It may seem a rash undertaking, to try to point out the common features in a large number of popular movements, which included both widely different functions and even more varying conditions as regards the geographical, political and social situations of the Resistance Movements, and their positions as to international law and entire structure. Nevertheless, it must be stated that there were dominating common features, even though one must freely admit that it is just as easy to stress the differences between these movements as being characteristic, as it is to postulate their similarities.

The Occupation was common to all, and thus there was a common enemy, and the defeat of the Axis Powers was a common purpose. There was therefore a common will to place oneself in the Allied camp.

To a great extent, the work was also common to all. Most of the functions mentioned above,[25] with the sole exception of partisan activity, are to be found in one country after another.

Another feature common to all the occupied countries was that all the organisations started from zero. No co-ordinated resistance reaction against the Occupation had been foreseen or planned in North and West Europe, and one can only speak of such foresight in East Europe and the Balkans with considerable reservations. Generally speaking, the Resistance Movements started with improvisation, when resistance actually arose. The exception to this rule can perhaps be found in the situation after 22 June 1941, when the Germans attacked the Soviet Union, and Communist organisations joined or started national Resistance Movements in a war which they had stamped as imperialistic and capitalistic.[26] These organisations were both by tradition and by situation prepared and partly equipped to bring organised cadres to the Resistance work.

Too much weight should not be attributed to this last factor, however. Wherever we look in Europe, we find that a Resistance struggle of the dimensions and in the form which it took was neither foreseen nor planned. The earliest groups were isolated, and at a loss as regards their first actions, which were haphazard and unplanned. To some extent, the fact that the Resistance struggle had to begin in a vacuum can be explained by the circumstance that in spite of all the omens and direct warnings, the Occupation took the countries involved by surprise. This was the case in Poland, where neither attackers nor defenders had foreseen such a rapid collapse of the Polish State as actually occurred. It is true of Denmark and Norway, where the surprise was almost complete, and it is true of Holland and Belgium, which clung as long as they could to the hope that their neutrality would be respected, or at the worst that help from the Great Powers in the West would be effective in support of their own defence. The Dutch "fortress" held for five days, and the occupation of Belgium was complete after less than three weeks of fighting. It was particularly true of France, whose total defeat and partial occupation was sealed within a period of five to six weeks. In 1941 it was true of Yugoslavia, whose fate was decided within a period of two weeks, and Greece was defeated soon after. The Germans also took the Soviet Union by surprise, with the occupation of immense areas of the country in the summer and autumn 1941. None of these countries had calculated with the picture of Europe being turned upside down so suddenly, and none of them had been able, or had had the imagination to make preparations for the total resistance struggle, which would grow up with greater or lesser speed and strength as soon as the Occupation was a fact.

Nevertheless it did occur, and here we find a further common feature. The resistance struggle became universal.[27] All the occupied countries reacted alike, in that they all established an underground struggle which, in spite of all the differences, had certain common features, although their possibilities varied greatly: they used almost identical fighting means and methods, although these varied according to geographical and political conditions. One may say of some of these countries that the struggle which was raised after the Occupation had begun was a greater military and political problem for the Germans than their traditional military forces could have inflicted. It is a matter for assessment, to what extent this was the case, but it is certainly true of two countries so far and so different from each other as Yugoslavia and Denmark.

A further common feature of the European Resistance Movements was that they all achieved their results in close co-operation with military, para-military and political organs in the Allied world, outside the occupied territories. Their groups and organisations strove, as a first priority, for the vital contacts with the fighting Allies on the other side of the fronts. It was from them that help must come, in the form of instructors, information, money and material of every kind. It was from them that the organisations could draw encouragement, advice and recognition of their efforts. Both psychologically and materially, the consciousness of support from outside had decisive importance, for material support was also a psychological stimulus. One was not forgotten, and one had joined the struggle. "I remember feeling a strange, emotional excitement", writes the Polish Resistance leader, Bor-Komorowski, describing his experience of a weapon reception.[28] "These men brought with them the very breath of liberty." Tens of thousands all over the continent of Europe came to share his experience.

But people, groups and organisations could have cried for contact in vain, in a vacuum, if the organs had not been created on the other side of the fronts, which could send back an echo. Here too, initiative from outside was the necessary condition for the establishment of the co-operation which gave Resistance work enlarged meaning. And this initiative was taken – with especial consistency in the Soviet Union, where traditions existed for partisan warfare, and where partisan formations were already in action a few weeks after the German attack. As quickly as this could be done, the effort was made to co-ordinate activity in the enemy hinterland with the fighting on the regular fronts, and to encourage and support all kinds of partisan activity. During the retreats in 1941, suppport had to be improvised, but in May 1942 it assumed a more definite form, when a special organisation was established – the Central Staff of the Partisan Movement,[29] whose field of activity was the occupied territory of the Soviet Union, and whose task became both technical and political. The Central Staff's technical task was to bring the instruction and materiel they needed to the partisans. Politically it was to see that the leadership of the movement was firmly in the hands of the Soviet State, and that the Communist ideology pervaded the movement. However, the Soviet Union was hard pressed, its fronts had already been pushed back many hundreds of kilometers to the east, and right up to 1944, any support activity from the Soviet Union had to be confined to Soviet territory. In addition to this, the nearest resistance countries, Czechoslovakia and Poland, had exile governments established in the West, and none of these governments felt themselves ideologically attached to the Soviet Union. The exile Polish Government, and with it the largest Polish Resistance Movement, regarded the Soviet Union with fear and anger, after the Russian invasion in East Poland in 1939, and pinned their hopes to an early Allied victory, with the possibility of a strong Western Allied influence when Poland's fate was decided after the War. The Czechoslovak Government under President Benes worked for a *modus vivendi,* which would give influence to both East and West, when Czechoslovakia's future was decided after the War. In Yugoslavia, the Partisan Movement led by Marshal Tito tried to make contact and obtain support from the special Soviet organs in aid of the Yugoslav Partisan Movement, but here co-operation was prevented both by technical and political difficulties, until the Soviet Armies reached the Yugoslav frontier. Cool, sterile exchanges of telegrams in 1942, between Tito's Partisan Headquarters and Moscow[30] did not lead to any form of co-operation.

The Russians were far away at that time, and had enough to do to support their own partisan formations and, in addition, recognized the exile Royal Yugoslav Government, so that Tito and his movement, on Soviet instructions, had to appeal for material and political support from a different place.

LONDON. The place was London. Great Britain, after the fall of France in June 1940, went very deliberately into the work of establishing connexions with potential resistance movements in Europe, bringing them moral and material support, and seeking later to co-ordinate their many-sided actions with each other and with Great Britain's own conduct of the war. This was done more or less regardless of the ideological orientation of these movements, and the decision was taken principally on military grounds, while political considerations received a lower priority. British operations on behalf of the Resistance Movements included, obviously, extensive weapon deliveries, and the advantages of the whole of this underground activity were reaped equally by the Resistance Movements and the Allies, Great Britain included.

Great Britain's decision to take up a task of this kind was part of her strategic planning with the final purpose of attack, which was prepared in co-operation with American Staff Officers from the summer 1940 to March 1941, under the designation ABC-1.[31] The plan, which was clearly stamped by British influence and British views of the future as it appeared in the summer 1940, included continuous propaganda, which for the B.B.C. alone was to reach a total of 160,000 words in foreign languages per day;[32] total blockade of the Axis Powers; sustained bombing; minor military raids where opportunity offered; the capture of starting-points for later offensives; the creation of offensive forces for later action; and the undermining of enemy morale and production possibilities through close co-operation with exile governments and through them – or without them – with Resistance Movements in the territories occupied by the enemy. The actions of these Resistance Movement should, in the first place, increase the effects of blockade and bombing by passive resistance, strikes, and particularly by sabotage, and in the long term, underground armies should be built up, supplied with weapons from Great Britain, and organised in such a way that at a later date they could form the background and give support to the offensives planned. With this offensive purpose, fixed at a moment when she stood alone, and with her back to the wall, but nevertheless had the surplus capacity to think in offensive terms, Great Britain could not but be the natural centre for all efforts to co-ordinate the existing and coming European Resistance Movements, and to bring their millions of small and great actions of multifarious kinds in, as far as possible, under joint Allied command.

In the summer 1940, such plans could only be visions, with countless built-in hypotheses. The Resistance Movements did not yet exist. They were still – perhaps with the exception of Poland – only hopes and assumptions. But if the plans were to be lifted up from the level of visions and into the world of realities, an instrument was needed which could translate thoughts into facts. This was already clear at the end of May, during the evacuation from Dunkirk. In a memorandum of 27 May to the War Cabinet, from the British Chiefs of Staff,[33] the latter were dealing with the possibilities – almost invisible at that stage – of defeating Germany. Here we already find several of the basic elements of the ABC-1 plan mentioned above. In an introductory summary it is stated: "The defeat of Germany might be achieved by a combination of economic pressure, air attack on economic objectives in Germany and in German morale and the creation of widespread revolt in her conquered territories".

These possibilities are then examined in detail, and on the last of them – subversive action – we read: "The only other method of bringing about the downfall of Germany is by stimulating the seeds of revolt within the conquered territories. The occupied countries are likely to prove a fruitful ground for these operations, particularly when economic conditions begin to deteriorate.

In the circumstances envisaged, we regard this form of activity as of the very highest importance. A special organisation will be required and plans to put these operations into effect should be prepared, and all the necessary preparations and training should be proceeded with as a matter of urgency".

It was on this background, and based on these ideas, that the British War Cabinet in July 1940 set up SOE as the instrument which was to stimulate and support a general European revolt – whatever character this might take. In the summer 1940 there was no room for political worries. Quite logically, the organisation was placed under the Ministry of Economic Warfare, with the Labour politician Hugh Dalton as Minister. The organisation was an improvisation and an experiment, but it should be added that as far back as 1938, study groups in several ministries had been examining the idea of an organisation and an activity such as those which were now realised. The previous history of the plan is long and complicated, and will not be dealt with here.[34] It will be pointed out, however, that the British had experience which made it understandable that they, especially, saw the possibilities of irregular warfare – experience from the Boer War, from Lawrence's achievements in guerilla warfare in the Arabian Desert during the First World War, from Ireland in 1919–22, as well as from knowledge of the Chinese partisan war which was going on at the time, against Japan. Past experiences from

Wellington's campaigns in Spain during the Peninsular War were also remembered. In a memorandum from Dalton[35] during the negotiations leading up to the creation of SOE, we find these experiences and visions, as he saw them: "We have got to organize movements in enemy-occupied territory comparable to the Sinn Fein movement in Ireland, to the Chinese guerillas now operating against Japan, to the Spanish Irregulars who played a notable part in Wellington's campaign or – one might as well admit it – to the organizations which the nazis themselves have developed so remarkably in almost every country in the world. This democratic international must use many different methods, including industrial and military sabotage, labour agitation and strikes, continuous propaganda, terrorist acts against traitors and German leaders, boycotts and riots". Dalton goes on to argue for an organisation of this kind being fired by "a certain fanatical enthusiasm, willingness to work with people of different nationalities, complete political reliability".

He stresses that the work must be done in absolute secrecy, and suggests that for that reason the organisation must be completely independent of the British Civil Service and the War Ministry machinery. One senses the Labour politician behind the words, but since the words are addressed to Lord Halifax, who approved the idea, including the suggestion that the Foreign Office should be by-passed, one senses also the resolution in the face of the unorthodox which stamped the Churchill government in those days.

In a conversation with Churchill on 16 July Dalton was urged to undertake the creation of the new organisation,[36] and on 22 July the War Cabinet formally recognised the existence of SOE as an independent organisation, with an independent strategic rôle on a line with the Army and Air Force. The task was two-fold. In the first place, systematic sabotage and information was to be organised, enemy morale was to be undermined through propaganda and other means, and the enemy's grip on the occupied areas was to be slackened, by diffusing his watchfulness and his forces. Parallel with this, underground armies were to be created and supplied with weapons everywhere where this should prove to be a practical possibility. The idea of such underground armies was not that they should rise in open and immediate rebellion – and in this the British theory differed fundamentally from the views of the Soviet Union as to their Resistance organisations – but that they should be ready to intervene in places and times where the enemy was weakened and the situation was ripe, particularly as auxiliary forces during Allied offensives on the Continent, at a time in the future which was unforeseeable in

1940. In such a situation, but only then, it was considered that underground armies could be of real strategic importance. This was the concept in 1940, it was the concept which was developed in careful detail in a memorandum in June 1941,[37] and it remained the concept which held right up to the actual invasion in 1944.

A short comment must be made here on the theory that SOE was an independent organisation. It contained a truth and an illusion. The truth was that SOE maintained a considerable degree af autonomy in its dispositions. British military and political relation with the European countries were largely channelled through SOE, which became the permanent connexion between Great Britain and the European Resistance Movements, with the sole exception of the Soviet Resistance. The illusion was that SOE was independent, for SOE depended completely, in its technical dispositions, on the resources which the other Services were willing to put at its disposal. Here it was particularly decisive to what extent the R.A.F. would spare the bombers for transport, when every single bomber used for SOE purposes must be taken out of the programme for the high priority strategic bombing. Here was a question of weighing up the practical effects of bombing versus sabotage, the results of which in the first years of the War were not in SOE's favour. Similarly, SOE had to adjust its directives to the underground armies in accordance with the wishes and plans of the High Command. Lastly, particularly in the later phases of the War, SOE had to adapt its political activities to the wishes and assessments of the Foreign Ministries of the Western Powers, as well as those of various exile governments, etc. Altogether, SOE had to run the gauntlet between many opposing interests, but it became a powerful instrument in the Western Allies' conduct of the war, nevertheless, from 1943 integrated with the American sister organisation, the Office of Strategic Service (OSS), which brought SOE both strength and complications.

From the start, the idea was that propaganda should also come under SOE, and Dalton placed great weight upon the unity which could be created in the work vis-à-vis the European peoples and their Resistance Movements, and which could justify his demanding expression "the Fourth Arm".

In the late summer 1941, this work was divided, however, after a considerable amount of internal conflict and departmental jealousy. It was then placed under a special organisation, the Political Warfare Executive (PWE) led by the British Ambassador to the exile Czechoslovak

Government, Bruce Lockhart. The latter sums up his task briefly as follows:[38] 1) To undermine and to destroy the morale of the enemy, and 2) to support and foster the spirit of resistance in enemy-occupied countries. The weapons for this were the radio, and propaganda material dropped by parachute or smuggled into the various countries in other ways. After this, SOE had to reconcile itself to the division, but it could, on the other hand, devote itself to operational missions. These became great enough.

In 1940 and thereafter, close links were forged between London and Cairo[39] on the one hand, and the Resistance Movements of Poland, Czechoslovakia, Denmark, Norway, Holland, Belgium, Luxembourg, France, Yugoslavia, Albania, Greece and Italy on the other. It is a matter of opinion, what degree of weight should be attributed to the British share in these Resistance Movements – its importance varies from one country to another – but it is beyond discussion that Great Britain's initiatives were appreciable everywhere. Further, it is a fact that the movements had little or no contact with each other, but that with London/Cairo as the forwarding centre, they acquired some degree of mutual contact. Lastly it can be established that their co-operation with the Allies, first of all with Great Britain, forced the Resistance Movements to develop the organisational forms which made co-operation technically possible. The functional form which the movements took on was in high degree stamped by the demands of this international co-operation and of the possibilities which it made available.

TECHNICAL CONDITIONS. When examining the possibilities for co-operation one is immediately struck by two decisive technical factors which clearly show the difference in conditions between the First and the Second World Wars. Large areas were also subjected to German/Austrian occupation during the First World War – Serbia, Rumania, Poland, some Baltic and Russian areas, Belgium and several departments of North-east France. In none of these areas was there any attempt to create closely knit Resistance Movements, although one can register sporadic instances of espionage and illegal newspaper activity, particularly in Belgium[40] and North-east France, and some weak attempts to form military groups on the periphery of the occupied parts of Serbia. The phenomenon of the Resistance Movement never became a problem for the Central Powers, but Turkey had to face an Arab guerilla rebellion, inspired by the co-operation between T. E. Lawrence and a number of Arab princes.

It was a different matter during the Second World War. Here, as has been pointed out, the phenomenon became universal, and its rise calls for an explanation. One fundamental reason for it is certainly to be found in the ideological situation, the universal hatred of Fascism and Nazism, which was intensified by the incredibly primitive and barbaric Occupation policy conducted by the Occupying Powers, especially Germany, which resulted in violent ideological polarisation. Although the Occupation policy varied from one country to another, even in its mildest form it was so crude that it called forth violent reaction.

Technical factors can also supply an explanation, however. During the First World War, a conquered territory was a closed area, which the conquerors controlled. But during the Second World War, although a conquered territory could serve to some extent as a base and production area, at the same time, the Occupation created great military and political problems for the Occupying Powers, for example because the occupied countries were not so isolated from the surrounding countries as in earlier days. The radio and aircraft on the one hand and a higher level of organisation on the other precluded the spiritual and material isolation from the outside world which had characterised the situation of conquest in the First World War. The radio was perhaps the most decisive medium in this new situation, and the radio had a two-dimensional effect. First of all the population as a whole could listen to foreign stations, and thus escaped from isolation both as regards information and propaganda. The fact that listening to foreign broadcasts was forbidden or interrupted by jamming stations, made no difference to this situation, for it proved in fact that the prohibition could not be enforced, even where and when confiscation of radio sets was begun. On the contrary, the effect of the prohibitions was a further psychological incitement, and what the Axis Powers achieved by their prohibition was rather to cut off their own possibilities for influencing the populations through this new medium. Prohibition and confiscation, as far as it was possible to enforce them, prevented the Axis Powers' own information and propaganda from reaching the people. And the prohibitions entailed in particular that everything broadcast officially was felt to be untrue and misleading propaganda, whilst everything that was gleaned from abroad was regarded as absolute truth. Added to this, the hindrance of listening-in was compensated by intensified distribution of news material. Europe set her bush telephones in action during the Second World War. The prohibitions precluded the Axis Powers from being believed, even when their information was correct, whilst on the contrary it was possible for the free world to achieve credibility, even when an objective listener could have questioned it.

In this whole war of the ether, the B.B.C. played a decisive rôle, not only in North and West Europe, but also in East Europe and the Balkans, and Radio Moscow played a similar rôle in Russia. But the game did not end there. Throughout the occupied territories, people listened in to the neutral stations such as those in Switzerland and Sweden. It is impossible to assess the collective effect of this, but there is no doubt that it was considerable.[41]

However, this was only one of the dimensions of the radio. In addition to the one-way listeners, there were the hundreds of individuals engaged in two-way communication, with radio receivers and transmitters, who gradually engaged themselves in this service throughout the occupied areas. These stations with their two-way communication brought the illegal groups into close and rapid contact with governments and staffs outside the occupied territories, and they became the vital nerve for a great deal of illegal activity. This was of utmost importance for the intelligence service, for all arrangements for deliveries of weapons, for political information, and indeed for arrangements of every kind, where co-operation was established between the open and closed fronts. The war of the ether thus led not only to a propaganda struggle, but also to a bitter war waged by the Axis Powers against illegal transmitters, and here too, it was the telegraphists and their assistants who gained the upper hand, in spite of severe losses. In the face of the ever-expanding and often sophisticated attempts of the Axis Powers to liquidate the illegal transmitters with the use of direction-finders of various kinds, mobile as well as stationary, the illegal radio organisations replied with indomitable energy, setting up efficient security systems; and transmitting techniques, code systems and radio sets were constantly improved. How vital this whole struggle became can best be illustrated with the situation which arose in Holland in 1942-43, where the German counter-espionage, after the arrest of a Dutch radio telegraphist, succeeded in gaining control over the radio communications between Holland and SOE, with the catastrophic result that the Dutch Resistance Movement was temporarily infiltrated and was not only partly nullified, but actually came to function under German direction.[42] In this instance more than in any other, it proved that illegal radio communication was and continued to be a vulnerable vital nerve for all organised resistance. The final result of the struggle was, however, a convincing victory for the illegal radio stations,[43] which made ever closer co-operation possible between the

Resistance Movements and the Allied supporting organisations. The Axis Powers' hope of isolating the occupied areas remained a threadbare illusion.

The radio was only one of the media in the co-operation between the open and closed fronts. Air traffic was the other. Thanks to aircraft, and increasingly improved navigation technique, it was possible for the Allies to give the Resistance Movements considerable support of various kinds. Specially trained instructors, propaganda material, money, explosives and other sabotage material, various articles in short supply, and – particularly – weapons and ammunition were sent over in ever greater quantities, throughout Europe. Normally, personnel and/or materiel were dropped by parachute, but in certain areas, where Resistance Movements had won sufficient terrain and had cleared improved air strips, this could also be done by direct landings behind the enemy lines. This also made it possible to fly out specially chosen personnel, couriers, wounded, Resistance leaders on political missions, Resistance members who were to receive special training, etc. Here too it proved impossible for the Axis Powers to stop this illegal traffic, which increased, if not every month, at least every year. Here again, the Resistance Movements' reply to the counter-measures of the Occupying Powers was a constantly expanding and improved technique and organisation. Their percentages of losses were periodically high in certain places, but in favourable circumstances they were, on the contrary, very low,[44] and both the Allies who delivered equipment and the occupied countries receiving it gradually developed such improvements in technique that the losses showed a tendency to decrease. Improved navigation technique contributed in high degree to this development, and the "S" telephones and "Eureka" devices came to play especially important rôles. The S telephones made it possible for pilots and reception teams to speak to each other during the approach, within a radius of approximately 90 kilometres, also allowing for the pilots to fly in on the radio beam. Stationary and mobile Eureka stations[45] also made it possible for approaching aircraft to take their bearings from them within a radius of 150 kilometres. The limits in this field lay not so much in the counter-measures of the Occupying Powers as in the fact that suitable aircraft were in short supply during the first phases of the War, and in the limits as to distance which the aircraft could cover, even up to 1945, when load capacity had to be taken into consideration, as well as the long detours which pilots often had to make to avoid enemy anti-aircraft batteries. This last problem was particularly serious in the case of distant countries such as Czechoslovakia and Poland, whereas deliveries to North and West Europe and to the Balkans could be carried out more easily, from bases in Britain and the Middle East, and from 1943 in South Italy.

In this connexion, a mention should be made of the use of fishing boats, small coasters, and submarines, which now and then operated in suitable areas such as off Norway, in the North Sea, off Brittany, the South of France, in the Adriatic and among the Greek islands. The importance of this was marginal, however, in comparison with the communication by air.

The attraction of and the co-operation with the free world was thus one more fundamental feature of all Resistance Movements, and this co-operation, both inwards and outwards, continued and led to the development of strongly differentiated as well as quite similar forms of organisation. Here differences presented themselves yet again. There was an enormous difference between the solutions which were workable and possible in countries such as the Soviet Union, Yugoslavia and to some extent Greece and France, where large areas were geographically suitable for actual guerilla warfare, and the forms of organisation which had to be used in small, densely populated countries such as Belgium, Holland and Denmark. In all these areas, co-operation was based upon a combination of communication services with the organisation of reception and distribution groups, but in the first group of countries more direct co-operation was possible. The enemy was farther away, and had fewer possibilities for direction finding or for intervening directly in the increasing deliveries of weapons. In the smaller countries, and in closely built-up areas, co-operation with the free world demanded an extremely high level of organisation.

ACCELERATING GROWTH. Almost everywhere, the development of resistance was characterized by accelerating growth. As mentioned above, development towards effective resistance started everywhere from zero. But from this zero, Resistance Movements generally developed in continuous growth, as regards both numbers and results. This took place in spite of the efforts of the Occupying Powers to combat it with every imaginable counter-measure, from propaganda and counter-espionage to police actions, arrests, raids, deportation, executions and random terror as the well-known means, which have often been described. The struggle of the Occupying Powers against illegal Resistance Movements, with its drastic methods, required considerable manpower to carry out, and the results of this ruthless campaign against all resistance cannot be and need not be disregarded. In certain places and periodically it did achieve considerable results. Through preventive measures, infiltration, by informers, methodical police activity and blind terror, the Axis Powers succeeded again and again in rounding up illegal groups and activities of every kind, and thousands upon thousands of Resistance members were brought to prison, concentration camps or the firing squad.

Nevertheless, there is practically no region in Europe nor field of activity in the illegal work which could not register progress in the long run, and increased recruitment to the ranks of the Resistance.[46] In general, there was growth in the numbers of illegal publications, of receptions of weapons, in the size and numbers of illegal groups, frequency and effects of sabotage actions, quantities of telegrams and dispatches, dimensions of strikes and desertion from labour conscription, amount of guerilla activity and the stream of intelligence to the Allies abroad. What began in 1940–41 on a small scale, and as an irritating phenomen which could be held in check, by 1944–45 had grown to a considerable military, psychological and political phenomen. The general graph of activity rises steadily and sometimes steeply, as do the individual graphs of activity in the individual areas. Sometimes and in some places there are minor breaks and perhaps even an evident drop in the upward progress of the graph, but taken over a longer period and over larger areas, constant and accelerating growth can be proved.

The claim might even be made that the counter-measures of the Occupying Powers, especially where they took on the character of terrorism, had a clear tendency to promote recruitment and activity. It is indisputable that terror was a weapon, but this weapon was a boomerang. It struck, but it also struck back.

Acceleration in the growth of the Resistance Movements naturally occurred at the same pace as the Allies ' advances and the defeats of the Occupying Powers, and a clear connexion existed between the course of the war on the actual fronts and the development of resistance behind the lines of the Occupying Powers. This was a matter of course, and is stated here without any intention of casting a slur of opportunism on either the Resistance Movements or the populations who increasingly backed up these movements. Obviously in certain and even widespread circles, an opportunist evaluation could have its effect, but this makes no difference to the fact that Resistance activity was started, and in growth, long before the defeats af the Axis Powers could be seen as the writing on the wall; and that participation in the work of the Resistance, or simply support for it, remained an extremely dangerous affair also after the

Occupying Powers began to meet reverses. It should perhaps be added that the measures against all resistance, and especially the use of terrorist methods increased violently when the defeats of the Occupying Powers resulted in their growing desperation. The fact that the Allied victories meant increased growth for the Resistance Movements can be interpreted with good will or bad, as the sign of increased solidarity or of opportunism. But one comes nearer to the truth if one remembers a number of other factors. On the one hand, these victories gave inspiration to the work of resistance, and on the other, they made the work more meaningful, and at the same time, the increased strength of the Allies made possible increased support to their comrades under occupation. As long as the Axis Powers retained the palms of victory, and it was the general opinion that the Occupation would last for many long years, perhaps decades, so long was the incentive, at least to armed resistance, less urgent than it became, as the Occupation Colossus staggered and the possibility of liberation approached.

The War had to be won, and was won, through the course of the battles on the outside, open fronts, and Resistance activity could only be a bonus and not a substitute. Resistance men and women regarded the situation thus all over Europe, but adapted their pattern of activity according to the general course af the War, and when the defeats of the Axis Powers began, they were able to intensify their demands upon themselves and their efforts. Their contribution must be seen in relation to the general developments, but it cannot be explained simply as the product of these developments.

2. The Emergence and Background of the Resistance Movements.

THE RESISTANCE SPECTRUM. When and how did the Resistance Movements emerge, and what were the features that characterized them and qualified them to the name? These are obvious questions. The answers are far more complicated.

To the question as to when these movements emerged, it must be said that it is hardly possible to establish their start in any country at a specific point in time.[1] As indicated above, the movements germinated and grew, and it is a matter of opinion, at what moment one will assert that, in one country or another, definite Resistance Movements existed, recognized as such at home, and acknowledged abroad. For a very few men and women, the resolve to exercise and organise resistance came almost immediately after occupation, but this resolve did not create a movement, at most it formulated the call or prepared the conditions which, sooner or later, led to the realisation of the resolve. The outbreak of war and the battles that followed can be marked precisely in the calendar, but not the Resistance Movements. Nor is it a simple matter to decide how these movements arose. They grew up because of the coincidence of scattered initiatives, organised efforts, and influence from abroad, most rapidly and with most assurance in countries where there was a tradition to build upon, and where the Occupation situation and the country's political position motivated acts of defiance most strongly. Regardless of pace and form, however, it is important to emphasize that even major actions, if they were isolated, did not qualify the participants to the designation of Resistance Movement. Combination, growth and organisation had first to establish the entirety which became the hallmark of the Resistance Movements. An assassination or a strike, or a combination of both did not create a Resistance Movement, however much or little such actions might injure or alarm the Occupying Power. Nor did a demonstratively hostile attitude, possibly expressed in symbols, or perhaps coupled with an effective passive resistance to the wishes or will of the Occupying Power, create a Resistance Movement. Nor did the existence of an espionage network. Even violent guerilla activity in an isolated mountain or forest district – if it stood alone – could hardly be called a

Resistance Movement. A quite isolated conspiracy of one kind or another would probably receive the stamp of "Resistance Movement" just as little. When, then, can one speak of "Resistance Movements"? What criteria must be met? Once more: the question is easier to put than to answer. There is no chemical formula or mathematical equation which can permit one to state that here a Resistance Movement exists. There is no fixed political definition which can unequivocally determine the framework and content of the movements. We must embark upon an analysis of an extremely complicated phenomenon, which contains numerous elements, both civil and military, of which practically none are in themselves the decisive component or components. It is a collective designation.

All the occupied countries cast up movements during the Second World War which are designated with the common name, "Resistance Movement", although the movements in question developed very variously, in situation, geography, fighting methods, political conditions and organisational forms , etc.

The names "Resistance Movement" – "Résistance" – "Mod-standsbevægelse" – "Resistenza" – "Dvisjenie soprotivljenija" – "Wi-derstandsbewegung"[2] – made their appearance in the terminology of this war, and remained in the general post-war vocabulary.

It may be advisable to consider two opposite poles within this group of heterogenous movements, which are covered by the same terms. There is a wealth of difference between the frontal, open partisan war which developed in for example Yugoslavia's waste, lonely mountain regions, and the more diffuse underground activity which grew up in a small, thickly populated country such as Belgium. In Yugoslavia, direct fighting with the temporary liberation of larger or smaller parts of the country was already a reality a few months after occupation, and this continued with growing intensity as long as the occupation lasted. The struggle began in July 1941, with ambushes, derailment of trains, attacks on isolated garrisons, sabotage, assassinations, etc., and in its first phases, special guerilla tactics were employed, consisting of hitting the enemy where he was weakest and then withdrawing to bases in inaccessible areas, to prepare new attacks. Only a few weeks later, however, Tito's organised partisan forces could claim at least temporary control of certain country districts. In a radio message from Zagreb to Moscow on 23 August 1941, Tito reported his self-confidence to the Communist leaders there:[3] "The partisan operations in Serbia are assuming to an ever greater extent the character of a national uprising. The Germans are only holding the larger towns while the villages and hamlets are in the hands of the partisans." This was only the beginning, however. Gradually partisan forces were created which grew to brigades and divisions, and by 1944 had reached a total of nearly 400,000 men, all of them directly involved in military confrontation with the Occupying Powers, which carried out one unsuccessful offensive after another against this open but volatile enemy. In Belgium, the means of action and the possibilities for functioning were of a totally different kind: espionage; the illegal Press; help to Allied pilots and Belgians capable of bearing arms, who made their way via France, Spain and Portugal to the free world and the fighting duties awaiting them; the creation of a widespread illegal network to absorb the men who evaded forced conscription to work in Germany; and the secret creation and arming of underground forces, which would not be sent into military action until the final phases. Similar differences, and many others, are to be found in whichever European country one may choose to take up to closer analysis.

Here, however, it is not the differences but the likenesses that we must examine – and the similarities behind all the dissimilarities. First there are the quite fundamental facts that all Resistance Movements were in the same situation, in the sense that they shared a common enemy; that all their destinies were inseparably linked to the hope of an Allied victory; and that all had to seek moral, political and material support in that part of the unoccupied world to which they were attached, geographically, ideologically or perhaps simply strategically. Next there is another fact of equal importance: any local activity whatsoever was meaningless, and could not create a Resistance Movement, so long and in so far as it remained purely local. For all the Resistance Movements the rule applied that they had to extend their activity to the whole Occupation area, and that they had to gain a considerable amount of support at least amongst the majority of the populations. This last circumstance went without saying, for technical reasons alone. Whether it was a question of large-scale partisan warfare, or of the establishment of espionage or escape networks, such activities had to extend beyond the neighbourhood of – shall we say – Stavanger, Dinant or Serajevo. The Resistance Movement – in whichever country we are dealing with – had to base itself upon a wide popular backing; and regardless of whether the first initiatives started from this or that locality, from individuals or from political or professional organs, every Resistance activity forced its participants to create illegal networks, which stretched over the whole territory, and in many cases beyond the territory, to co-operation with illegal activities in other national regions, and finally in co-operation with neutral or Allied nations outside the Occupation area. Sweden, Switzerland, Spain, Portugal and Turkey all offered more or less slippery stepping-stones on the jungle paths to the free world, which was the final target for many, and became a refuge for others. The help given in Belgium to Allied pilots and crews brought about 1500 Allied flying personnel back to Britain[4] to renewed action in the struggle, whilst others were kept hidden in Belgium; and this help depended upon a close but vast co-operation with illegal networks which streched through Belgium, France and Spain to Portugal. In the same way, it was both natural and necessary that partisan forces in Montenegro or Bosnia sought co-operation with like-minded forces in Croatia and Serbia, or in Macedonia, Albania or Greece. Here too, particularly from 1943, the lines of communication stretched farther to the Allies, in Egypt and South Italy.

Here the dissimilarities are so striking that it may seem absurd to speak of common features, and yet these appear when one looks closer. They present themselves when one deals in more detail with the Resistance Movements' possibilities for functioning, and the organisational demands involved. Here there is a question of an enormously wide spectrum of possibilities. One country would be capable of realising certain parts of the spectrum, whilst other opportunities were open in other areas of Europe. The great majority of Resistance functions reappear, however, in country after country. Regardless of how much or how little the individual movements were able to make use of their potential, no movement confined itself simply to one function. In all cases there was a question of a combination of possibilities. We must go through the whole spectrum before we can attempt to establish the extent to which the different countries exploited the opportunities available.

Two characteristics appear, then, for the Resistance Movements: they embraced extensive geographical areas, and their functions were many-sided.

EXILE GOVERNMENTS AND "FREE" FORCES. It will be reasonable, however, to point out the not unimportant fact that practically all the occupied countries had essential values outside the occupied territories to place at the disposal of the Allies. First, there were the moral and political values which the gathering of exile governments and national councils in London represented. These stood for the assurance that Occupied Europe was in a state of protest against the ideas of the Axis Powers for the "New Order" in Europe; that they expected liberation; and that they would contribute to this liberation with the means which they still possessed. Next there were the larger and smaller contingents of "free" forces, which the occupied countries could mobilise from the elements from their populations that poured in from overseas, or gradually leaked, drop by drop, from the occupied territories by the escape routes which were established in all these territories. Forces of this kind were by no means negligible, particularly from Poland, France, and to a lesser extent Greece. In the case of Poland, the existence of free Polish forces was already a reality in 1940, before the fall of France. These were recruited under the leadership of the Prime Minister, Sikorski, for example from Polish foreign workers in France, and later considerable contingents were added after the German invasion of the Soviet Union, when the Polish General Anders carried out extensive recruitment among Polish prisoners of war in the Soviet Union. Three Polish Divisions were formed and assembled in Persia,[5] and were later sent into action on a number of sectors of the Western Front. This kind of growth was even more marked in the Free French Forces, even if the Western Powers, in political consideration to the Vichy Government did not give their leader General de Gaulle the best conditions for recruitment.[6] Immediately after the fall of France, these forces were still diminutive. De Gaulle makes some bitter remarks as to this in his memoirs:[7] "On 24 August (1940) King George VI visited our little army. When one looked at it, one could see that our sword would be sharp, but my God, how short it was! At the end of July our forces hardly numbered 7,000 men. This was all that we could enroll in Great Britain itself." This would change, however. As Frenchmen from overseas gradually rallied to de Gaulle, and some leakage occurred out of France itself, these Free French Forces increased steadily, and they increased explosively whenever a territory of the French Empire was liberated by the Allies.[8] Then the measurement was no longer a Brigade, but Divisions and Army Corps. The contribution of free forces from the other occupied countries was of lesser dimensions, and generally had only symbolic value.

All exile governments, and with them most of the "free" military forces, were established in the West. But when the Soviet Union was drawn into the War in 1941, and was on the offensive from 1943, "free" Polish and Czech forces were also formed there. Recruitment took place among refugees from the two countries and among prisoners of war in the Soviet Union of Polish and Czech nationality.[9] A Polish Infantry Division, "Tadeusz Kościuszko", under the political control first of the organisation, "the Association of Polish Patriots", and later the "Polish

Committee for National Liberation", with its headquarters in Lublin, became the nucleus for a "Polish People's Army" which quickly developed into a considerable military force, particularly after the Soviet conquest of the East Polish regions. After this extensive recruitment, and by the end of 1944, the free Polish forces reached a total of about 300,000 men, under the Soviet High Command. One of its main difficulties was to recruit trained Polish Officers, with the result that a considerable number of Russian Officers – a little over 50 % of the whole Officers Corps – were posted to these "free" Polish forces, which were politically, operationally and organisationally outside the control of the exile Polish Government.

The original Chief of these forces, the Divisional Commander, General Zygmunt Berling, was replaced in October 1944 by the Soviet General Korczyc, amongst other reasons because of Berling's criticism of the lack of Soviet support to the uprising in Warsaw in August-September 1944, and from then until the end of the War, these forces were placed under the First White Russian Army under Marshal Rokossowskij. These Polish forces became the counterpart to the 300,000 Free Polish Forces which were fighting in the West under General Anders, exemplifying the political split between Western democratic conduct and the Communist conduct which made its mark on both the Polish war effort and Resistance contribution.

A similar formation of "free" Czechoslovak forces on Soviet soil took place, although on a smaller scale and in different political circumstances, in that the Soviet Union recognized the exile Czechoslovak Government under President Benes, but not the exile Polish Government. In 1943, a Czechoslovak Battalion was set up in the Soviet Union, which increased the same year to first one and later several Brigades, after which the Czechoslovak forces grew until in 1945 they constituted an Army Corps of about 60,000 men, fighting side by side with the Soviet forces, formally under the exile Czech Government's instructions, but in reality more or less independent of it, and operationally under the command of the First Ukrainian Army. The differences between the Czech forces' Commander-in-Chief, General Svoboda, and the Defence Minister of the exile government, General Ingr, were very marked, and the development of the Czech forces was considerably weakened because of the losses suffered during the Soviet-Czech attempt to come to the relief of the partially unsuccessful rising in Slovakia in August 1944.

The "free" military forces were by no means the most important values which the occupied nations could contribute to the Allied cause, even after the Occupation had begun. As mentioned already, it was essential, politically, that a number of exile governments established themselves in the free world, first and last in London, and from here declared themselves resolved to continue the struggle, or that exile national councils, committees, etc. undertook a similar rôle. The liberation of Occupied Europe, which was the declared objective of the War, would obviously be meaningless if both Occupied Europe and its exile representatives did not demonstrate, through the continuation of the struggle, that the occupied European countries ardently desired liberation from the yoke of the Axis Powers, and were prepared to make whatever contribution they could. This objective of the struggle was maintained and constantly documented by exile representatives, whose numbers grew, and whose character became somewhat mixed.

An exile Polish Government was reconstituted under General Sikorski's leadership after Poland's military defeat in the autumn 1939, and after the fall of France in June 1940, it established its seat in London. Here too the exile governments of Norway, Holland, Yugoslavia and Greece settled, in each case with both the Regent and the Government choosing exile and its conditions, and they retained international recognition as the legal representatives of their countries. The situation was rather more complicated in the case of Belgium. Here King Leopold III, as Supreme Commander of the Belgian Army, chose to capitulate on 28 May 1940. This decision was taken in opposition to the Belgian Government, which under Hubert Pierlot regarded King Leopold as a German prisoner, and chose exile and the continuation of the struggle from the Belgian Empire, without the King. In the case of France, the formal situation was more complicated still. Here General de Gaulle, who in June 1940 was Under-Secretary in the French War Ministry, chose exile in London, where he formed a French National committee, under whose leadership France's struggle should be continued. It was de Gaulle's obstinate assertion that he, and the forces which rallied to him and the National Committee, alone represented the French Republic,[10] that the armistice which the Vichy Government under General Pétain had agreed with the Axis Powers was invalid, and that the French Republic had at no stage laid down its arms. On the strength of this claim, he and his National Committee were recognized on 28 July 1940 by Great Britain, as leaders of a free France, still at war with the Axis Powers. Czechoslovakia's case was again different. The Czechoslovak President, Eduard Benes, formed a Government Committee in December 1939 in London, and in July 1940 Great Britain recognized this committee as the

Czechoslovak government, and Benes as President, the U.S.A., the Soviet Union and China also giving their recognition from 1941.

In the case of Denmark, the formal situation was anything but clear. A legal Danish Government, with the King at its head, continued its governmental functions, so that in spite of occupation, protest against it, and sporadic fighting, the country did not attain the status of belligerent, and therefore Ally.[11] The situation seemed to exclude any initiative in the direction of a Free Danish movement. Such a movement did arise, however. The Danish Minister in Washington declared himself "free", involving that he would not obey direct orders from the Government, but would act on his own judgement of what he saw to be Danish interests. He was joined by other Danish Ministers, from November 1941 by the Danish Minister in London, and in 1942 a leading politician escaped to London and joined the Free Danish movement. A Danish Council had been formed in London in 1940, and an awkward, lame Danish movement grew up, based more upon practical arrangements than upon any formal clarification of a situation which was hopelessly undefinable.

The stranded exile governments, national councils and committees had other assets than a policy of hostility to the Axis to offer the Allies. The free military forces only constituted the least of the values which the exile world could put at their disposal. The far-flung territories with possibilities for bases, the vital total tonnage available, were the most important assets in this sphere. Almost all the occupied countries had important contributions to make to the conduct of the War. Norway brought her large modern Merchant Navy, which included tankers which perhaps were indispensable for Great Britain's survival in the Battle of the Atlantic. Denmark had a not inconsiderable free Merchant Navy available, and in April 1941, the Danish Minister in Washington made an agreement with the American Government which gave the U.S.A. the right to set up air bases in Greenland. Holland also had considerable tonnage available, and her colonial Empire in Indonesia and the West Indies. Belgium contributed with the colonial areas in the Congo, and their considerable production of copper. De Gaulle was disappointed in his hope that the whole French Empire would rally to him, but he could register support from French Equatorial Africa, some naval units and a certain amount of tonnage. Yugoslavia and Greece also had tonnage available. Altogether, the decisions of the exile organisations not to give up, even after the loss of their national territories, was far from unimportant.

It is hardly possible to evaluate what had the greatest weight in this situation, the political decision, the additional tonnage, the possibilities for bases, or the deliveries of important raw materials from the colonial territories. But it is reasonable to state that the exile world taken as a whole certainly laid obligations and a certain burden upon the Great Powers, first and last Great Britain and the U.S.A., but that it also brought the Allies indispensable assets. Apart from this, the exile organisations naturally also had importance at home by virtue of the political and psychological influence they exercised upon their peoples in the occupied areas, and of the complicated organisational co-operation which developed in the triangle between the front abroad, the home front and the Allies. The above remarks regarding the exile organisations are to be considered introductory to the study of developments in occupied Europe.

THE COMPOSITION, FUNCTION AND AIMS OF THE RESISTANCE MOVEMENTS. The men and women of the European Resistance were a heterogenous mass. People of many languages, people of all ages, people from every imaginable trade and profession, irreligious people and religious people, from many faiths, people with widely different political views, townspeople and country people, military people and civilians, intellectuals and illiterates, people of different races, royalists, republicans and socialists – a sociological register which contained every imaginable shade of difference. Ones nearest approach to a definite statement must be to say that there can hardly be any variety in professional, political, religious, cultural or other respect which cannot be found in this register. One may then ask what it was that united the kolkhos peasant in a forest in the Ukraine with the Polish Officer in Warsaw, with the Jutland landowner, with the assistant manager in Oslo, with the fisherman in Stavanger, with the journalist in Amsterdam, with the manufacturer in Liège, with the docker in Marseilles and the prelate in Rheims, with the lawyer from Zagreb, with the clan chief in Albania, and with the mountain peasant in Epirus. The answer must be in the first place, that they all had certain things in common: Occupation, and the will or necessity to oppose it with all the means still available to them. It may seem difficult to accept that there was a connexion between a leaflet in Cracow, a strike in Utrecht and a fierce guerilla engagement in Bosnia, and yet such a connexion did exist. The Occupation Powers experienced it. They faced unexpected enemies everywhere, with unexpected and incalculable reactions of an extent and kind that were not included in the military appreciations. It is for this reason alone that one can permit oneself the overall designation:

European Resistance. The Occupation gave rise, throughout Europe, to conspiracy which did not reach everyone – fortunately, since no Resistance Movement could exist without a certain degree of normality in the community – but was sufficiently massive for its force to take the Occupying Powers by surprise. Their mastery over the conquered territories was superficially an advantage, but under the surface, it was also a burden.

Another remarkable characteristic was also common to all the Resistance Movements. When normal political life came to a halt or faded away, and when the normal political leaders disappeared more or less voluntarily from the political arena because they took the road to exile, were dismissed or imprisoned, and were replaced by impotent marionettes, or when they lost the trust of their people, either because they negotiated or because they co-operated with the Occupying Powers,[12] the leadership of the improvised underground, which decided the developments in the occupied countries, was taken over by persons who under normal conditions were not chosen to play leading political rôles. It was new people, and largely young people, who now intervened in their countries' destinies. In general, they were all to work in a situation where they could not use the normal means of agitation, election or other usual ways of rising in the hierarchy, to gain political mandate for the weighty and often fateful decisions they took. Voluntary support for their varied illegal initiatives would come to determine to what extent their actions would have military or political consequences. None of the European governments, before the Occupation or even in the moment of capitulation, had made arrangements for a continued struggle against the Occupying Powers, and a Colonel Bor-Komorowski in Poland, a President of the High Court, Paal Berg in Norway, a Master of Philosophy, Frode Jakobsen in Denmark, a Colonel Bastin in Belgium, an editor, Frans Goedhart in Holland, the Prefect of a French province, Jean Moulin, the editor Ferrucio Parri in Italy or the Communist Party official Josef Broz (Tito) in Yugoslavia, and the Conservative but Republican Colonel Napoleon Zervas in Epirus,[13] all had to begin their illegal activity without support in the traditional ruling organs of society, and without any state organ appointing them to the posts of leadership which they earned by their own efforts. Everywhere in the occupied areas it proved that below the traditional political apparatus there existed a reserve of talent, of politically and nationally conscious persons who were able to formulate an unorthodox and often revolutionary political standpoint. One might have expected a waiting, resigned, static situation in the occupied areas, but in fact there was a dynamic, almost explosive development, led by people who until the Occupation took place were little known, unpretentious citizens, to whom the situation suddenly assigned a task which they had neither expected nor angled for. When the Occupation gave way to the Liberation, the political picture in Europe had altered radically and fundamentally. The result of the War was here the decisive factor, but the development of Resistance was a contributory factor.

If the Resistance men and women constituted a heterogenous mass, the word "heterogenous" can also apply to the far-reaching set of functions which in one or another context were to form the framework of the various Resistance Movements. Here there was a question of a long series of combinations, from the cold shoulder policy, through passive resistance and symbolic demonstrations, to sabotage and militant partisan warfare. How an individual country chose to link up the various elements into a meaningful activity depended less upon inclination than upon necessity. The choice was not free, but had to be made with regard to the possibilities of the various countries, particularly as to geography. What was possible in the thinly populated forest districts of White Russia was not possible in the Dutch agricultural areas, and agitation which was natural for a Parisian journalist of Gaulist views would not have the same degree of effect in Croatia, ravaged as it was by the terrorism of the Ustace bands.[14] And it was not only geographical conditions which affected the character which the various Resistance Movements might take. Political, national and cultural conditions were just as decisive. In countries such as Norway or Yugoslavia, where the war with the Occupying Powers was declared, the enemy revealed himself in his true colours, whilst conditions were more complicated in countries such as Denmark and France, where legal governments, although under pressure and – for many leaders – of bitter necessity, entered into negotiations and even into direct co-operation with the Occupying Powers.[15] Here differentiated and difficult deliberations were needed before it was established who the enemy was – the Occupying Power, the home Nazi or Fascist movement, the legal Government or simply some of its Ministers, or perhaps even the Allies. After the British attack on the French Fleet at Mers-el-Kebir in July 1940, the last possibility might seem, to many Frenchmen, to be the most reasonable answer.[16] And if this was the end of the complications. If one could simply divide the countries into two blocks, those who had declared war and those who had not. But there, as almost always in the world of realities, every attempt at systematisation breaks down.

Norway and Yugoslavia are quoted as two countries where the war was declared, but the political conditions and therefore the political aims of the Resistance Movements in the one country were almost the diametrical opposite to those in the other country. When the Occupation took place, Norway was a constitutional monarchy, with a parliamentary government firmly rooted in the consciousness and political will of the people. The aims of the Resistance Movements were therefore to hinder the Quisling regime and restore the pre-war political situation, by throwing off the yoke of occupation. Further, Norway was a national state without inner national contradictions. No particular differences arose between the Norwegian Resistance Movement and the exile government, whose return the movement was fighting for – at the most there could be tactical disagreements. In the case of Yugoslavia, the situation was quite different. Here the Resistance Movement came very quickly to represent a total change in the political and social conditions in the country, and here resistance had both to scale the national barriers which separated the single components of the Yugoslavian State from each other, and at the same time fiercely oppose any idea that the pre-war situation should be re-established. Here there was a clear breach between the Resistance Movement and the exile government. Both countries were thus in a declared state of war, both countries raised Resistance Movements, both countries had an exile government and a common enemy, but as regards form and content, here ends any similarity between the two Resistance Movements.

The situation is no simpler, if we turn to the other two countries mentioned which, at least from June 1940, were not in a state of declared war against the Occupying Powers: France and Denmark. Here the differences are obvious and need no further elaboration. But there was a similarity between the Resistance Movements of the two Countries which deserves to be pointed out. In both these countries the first task for the two Resistance Movements was to turn their fire against the policy of negotiation and co-operation,[17] which the legal governments were engaged in, with varying emphasis, and to agitate for the possibilities and rightness of resistance. This meant that the first enemy of the Resistance was the home policy of concession to the Occupying Powers, and that the Resistance only gradually acquired respectability, as its possibilities began to take form in concrete results. Here there is probably a close connexion between the possibilities and the gradual recognition of the rightness of the Resistance standpoint. In both countries at the beginning of the Occupation a certain paralyzing apathy prevailed, with widespread acceptance of the political dialogue with the Occupying Powers, in which the respective governments engaged. And in both countries any initiatives in the direction of resistance against the Government and the Occupying Power were condemned as criminal acts, whether the initiative came from the exile world, or from persons or circles within the area of occupation. The French exile leader de Gaulle was condemned to death *in absentia*, and the Danish Minister in Washington was dismissed, and legal proceedings taken against him. And in both countries, Resistance agitators at home were energetically hunted by the police and prosecuted by the legal authorities. The similarities are between a great and a small country, but the presentation of problems is the same. The legal Government clung as long as possible to the law of the land and its formalities, whilst the Resistance Movements acquired general recognition, by stages, by virtue of the realities of the struggle. In both countries the apathy of 1940 was replaced by an energetic Resistance Movement, designed according to the resources in the two countries; and the possibilities of resistance promoted both a stronger will to resist and an accelerating acceptance of the demand of the two Resistance Movements, that they and they alone represented the political will of the people.

FORMATION OF GROUPS. Both while the many varied Resistance Movements were being built up, and during the further development of what became their very differentiated activities, the formation of groups was one of the supporting elements in the construction of the Resistance organisations which emerged. From the start there was no superior organisation or authority which could appoint an individual to his or her place in a system which did not yet exist, and which no one could foresee would arise. Only the communists had a developed system of cells at their disposal – especially in countries where the Communist party was forbidden – a system which could be activized immediately, if and when the party leaders might find it expedient to give the word to the rank and file. On the other hand, the leaders could then be fairly certain of discipline in the party and loyalty to the word given. In addition, many Communists were familiar with illegal activity. However, the Communists were under the pressure of the German-Soviet pact from August 1939, and were not active in the Resistance until after the German invasion of the Soviet Union on 22 June 1941 – even if party leaders were preparing in many places for the possibility that this pact would break down, and with it the German-Soviet co-operation. When this happened, the strength of the Communist cell system became obvious at once. After this the Communists came to play a dominating rôle in a number of countries,[18] partly directly, because of the striking power of their own organisations, partly because of their indirect influence in co-operation with national Resistance organisations.

For everyone else, the situation after the Occupation was quite different. By far the greatest number of Europeans were organised in political parties, trades or professional unions, religious, national and cultural associations, etc., but these forms of organisation were not adapted to the task of proclaiming resistance or establishing illegal networks. The organisations, where they were not dissolved, were legal, open and under the check of the authorities and the Occupying Power. The illegal growth had therefore to start from rock bottom, with the gathering of like-minded men and women who looked to each other, with a common purpose, when some suitable situation arose. When this occurred, the group became a closed unit within which one could debate or act in relative confidence, and at the same time it became an instrument enabling its members to undertake actions which were beyond the possibilities of an individual alone. Groups, cells and circles began to form with the one common purpose of finding ways and means to excercise resistance against the Occupying Powers, to the extent and with the means which might be available locally or within a specific sphere. This situation, where the movement began on a small scale, without precedents for what such group formations might develop into, was more or less general. But here all similarity ends. In the actual partisan areas such as the Soviet Union and Yugoslavia, quite large, regular fighting detachments soon formed, where groups were absorbed into larger units, and where actual warfare behind the enemy lines became the predominant fighting form, side by side with extensive sabotage activity. Here the group might well consist of a whole village or a dispersed army unit, or both combined. But here too, the movement began with local revolt, and without any connexion between the locally inspired reactions.

If the formation of greater or lesser groups, with more or less clearly defined purposes, was the underpinning factor in the construction of the Resistance Movements, this characteristic feature was by no means confined to the phase where Resistance organisations were being built up. As the organisation of the movements developed, and presented one differentiated task after another for solution, the need continued and increased to form groups which could undertake to carry out the tasks which arose at an accelerating pace. The groups remained, although as they developed, they merged together in larger organisational bodies, and their numbers increased with the increasing functional demands. Even where the organisational construction had long been a reality, a specific task was often entrusted to a special, separate group. Regardless of all differences between East and West, North and South, or between one function and another, it may be claimed that the group element remained one of the most essential fundamentals in all Resistance organisation. This was due to considerations both of security and technique. Inside the group, the members knew each other and could trust each other, the division into groups could serve to limit possible round-ups, and the small, often specialized group was particularly well equipped technically to carry out the tasks which the war on a small scale presented to the Resistance Movements.

The actual creation of groups thus became a fundamental function for the Resistance Movements. One should add that even though most groups were formed, as the time went on, with clearly defined aims, determined by the demands of the developing Resistance, there existed parallel group formations where the aim could be unknown to the participants, hidden in the fog banks of the future. The very need for contact with each other could be typical for a world in chains, and the possibility that the contact could later be exploited in some more specific function was always present. The prison psychosis of the Occupation called forth a symphony of tapping signals, and in families, circles of friends, places of work or in every gathering, people listened intently for the character and strength of the signals.

When organised initiatives began to penetrate society from above, people in many places were ready to catch the signals from these initiatives, and their demands. One knew whom one could depend upon.

AGITATION FOR RESISTANCE. If the formation of groups could therefore be an end in itself, at least in the beginning phases of the Occupation, where ideas were still vague as to the future development of resistance, it naturally became primarily a means for promoting the more purposeful functions which the Resistance Movements might take up, and which would come to characterize the movements, in different combinations. First among these functions was probably the promotion of information and agitation. Here it will not be adequate simply to mention the illegal Press, which became the most important tool of the information service. Listening-in to Allied and neutral radios played a part, as has been said, as well as both rumours, which were an extremely effective if unreliable source of information, and the mouth-to-mouth information which flourished in circles of friends, at places of work and at more or less closed meetings, where apparently innocent remarks could be heard and understood. It should not be forgotten that echoes reverberated far and fast in the enclosed spaces of the Occupation and this intensified sharply, even as regards the most unreliable rumours. What a rumour might lack of truth was richly compensated by the fact that it circulated in a world which was dominated by desperate willingness to indulge in wishful thinking. All supplies of information – true and untrue – had extremely favourable conditions in such circumstances. It is hardly too much to say that the censorship itself created a tropical climate for the growth of the political "facts" which one wished to hear.

This was a part of the background for the illegal Press, which became the most important instrument in the establishment of the internal information services. Practically everywhere, it served the double purpose of spreading news, particularly good news, and as the weapon of the Resistance Movements in the struggle against enemy propaganda and in agitation for the movements' political and technical fighting programmes. The illegal Press did not itself constitute a resistance movement, but it proclaimed the fight and in every area it reached, it created the background for the development of a more concrete resistance, through the combination of the possibilities for action which were available to the various movements. The illegal Press was thus the spearpoint of these Resistance Movements, and it contributed to paving the way for all other activities. In most occupied countries this free Press became quite indispensable in the struggle, just as it became a basic component of the collective Resistance activity.

In addition to this, the illegal Press promoted organisation to an exceptional degree, and often the newspaper groups themselves became the nucleus of later formations of a more militant character. People who had engaged in agitation for resistance at an early stage, and had become accustomed to illegality, were often to be found among those who took the consequences of the agitation. Lastly the illegal Press became both a link between the Resistance groups and the driving force behind their multifarious activities. Quite apart from its informative function, it could both form public opinion on the long term, and in acute situations help to whip up feeling and give directives for a desired action or series of actions. And it addressed itself in both instances not only to the convinced Resistance members, but also to the doubters and the waverers among the broader strata of society. For the early Resistance groups, the issue of illegal messages was naturally a primary task, whether in chain letters, notices, leaflets, or actual papers, and whether these were primitive type-written or duplicated sheets, or more advanced printed publications. In the first months of the Occupation, the Resistance-minded, who knew nothing of the many-sided, explosive Resistance development to come, could be doubtful and confused with regard to which activity they ought to engage in. They could meet in groups, but a group which had no specific purpose easily went to pieces. Here, the publication of illegal printed matter was the most obvious and most visible task, and here it was that the illegal Press became the creator of organisations. The production and distribution of even the simplest publication demanded a certain amount of organisation, and once a start had been made, the expansion of the activity was a natural consequence, both in the main stem and in the end in the side shoots of auxiliary groups, which followed the original initiative.

Illegal publications made their appearance as one of the first omens of what was to come, when the snowstorm of free speech would spread over Europe and continue as long as the Resistance Movements were active. Less than two weeks had passed after the fall of Warsaw when the first illegal Polish paper, "Polska Zyje" (Poland lives) appeared in the bombed-out city.[19] It would be the forerunner of no less than approximately 1300 illegal publications in Polish territory, with editions which for certain publications reached a total of about 200,000 copies.[20] But none of the conquered countries would have to remain long under the censorship of the Occupation before illegal papers made their appearance, and took up their part in the joint campaign. Even in countries such as Yugoslavia, where the Resistance soon took on more militant forms of warfare, the revolt was started with illegally distributed proclamations, leaflets and news sheets. At the end of April 1941, the Communist Central Committee under Tito's leadership gathered in Zagreb, and decided upon armed revolt against the Occupying Powers and the collaborating government set up by the Occupying Powers. The news of this decision was spread through the country in a special edition of the paper, "Proleter" as well as in various news sheets and leaflets, and news sheets in German, Italian and Bulgarian were printed for distribution among the rank and file of the invasion troops.[21] In June the same year, the young Communists went into action repeatedly and over a broad front against the Belgrade newspaper kiosks which distributed the official Yugoslav newspapers, containing propaganda directed by the Germans.

But then, the illegal forest of papers was already in tropical growth, in

North and West Europe, lastly in Denmark, where for a time people managed with imported Swedish papers, chain letters, listening-in to the B.B.C., and the anti-German hints which the official Press could indulge in under the milder Occupation conditions. In Norway, Holland, Belgium and France, the first illegal publications were already appearing in the summer 1940,[22] at first with primitive duplicated printed matter, and soon with more professionally produced papers with fairly regular publication and distribution. Put briefly, and by a posterity with "hind sight", this all sounds simple and obvious, but for those times, when there was no precedent for such a process, the appearance of this first sign of resistance represents not only a breakthrough to illegal new thinking, but also the mobilisation of ingenuity, courage and will, and it demanded a considerable, and later an enormous effort of a purely technical and material character. During the whole process, difficulties and risks piled up, in connexion with obtaining news, paper, printing possibilities, the organisation of distribution and the constant procurement of badly needed money. These were papers without subscribers or advertisers, and when the editions ran into tens of thousands – as they often did – the postage alone was a problem. Sheer hard work was needed, and the fact that there was also room for inspiring talent will only be mentioned, remembering for example the millions of envelopes that were written all over occupied Europe. The illegal European newspaper world is rich in literary pearls, and the political and ideological debate in the illegal Press was lively and meaningful in the acute situation of the Occupation. Malraux, Camus, de Beauvoir and Sartre are world-famous names from the French Press. Vercors' "La Silence de la Mer" was published illegally. The authors behind the nom de plume Vercors, Jean Bruller, founded an illegal publishing concern, "Edition Minuit". These authors were writing in a world language, and became famous outside their own country, but they are only examples to underline the fact that the challenge of the Occupation called forth literary and journalistic talents almost everywhere in the occupied areas. Each of the occupied countries can point to talents which came to their maturity at the very time when the normal Press was crushed by propaganda and the trivialities of the censored news.

Inspiring tones from abroad also made themselves heard through the illegal Press, in pamphlets and in book form. Speeches and articles by Churchill and Stalin, books of collected articles by world-famous journalists such as Ilja Ehrenburg or Walter Lippmann, and political commentaries – also often in book form – by such well-known political names as Harold Laski, Lord Vansittart and Wendell Wilkie. Poets, too, lifted their voices. A Nordahl Grieg had to write from exile, but he was read illegally wherever the Nordic language was understood, and from the other side of the Atlantic, a Steinbeck received impulse in the Occupation situation for his "The Moon is down", which was widely distributed in translation. Even German voices joined in the illegal chorus – first of all Hitler's own. It was an obvious job for journalists to put together a series of "Führerworte" which revealed his unscrupulous plans and his inconsistencies; and Germans in exile with special insight into the inner character of Nazism such as Herman Rauschning and Fritz Thyssen also contributed their confessions to the illegal information.

Altogether, the printed sheet became an integral part of the total sphere of function of the Resistance Movements, but it goes without saying that the importance of this side of the Resistance struggle was to vary considerably from one country to another. The differences could spring from many causes. Geographical, ideological, cultural conditions and fighting technique could play their parts, and the need could be more or less outspoken; also purely technical possibilities could be determining factors for whether distribution was large or small. For the Partisan Movement in the Soviet Union, which decided from the start upon militant action, and where weapons, explosives, food and boots were the first necessities rather than printed matter, an advanced illegal Press had to take second place. The partisan had no address, and delivery of messages to his helpers in the village had to be made under the noses of the Germans. Propaganda material was flown in to the Russian partisan areas from the central Government in Moscow, and was also produced locally in the urban districts, so that placards made their appearance on the walls of houses, where any were still standing, whereas in the partisan camps in the forests, marshes and mountains, the ideological message was less important than sub-machine guns and bombs. In addition, the incitement to resistance was in one sense a gift to the population. It sprang more from the visible brutality of the Occupying Powers and from a simple will to survive than from any proclamations of agitation or national or ideological persuasion. There was a somewhat similar situation in the Balkans, where the fight against hunger and the fight against the enemy were equally remorseless. It was therefore the populations of North and West Europe and of Poland, accustomed as they were to the influence of the written word, that had the greatest need of a rousing Press, and acquired such a Press.

The number of illegal papers amounted in these countries to several hundreds, and some papers reached editions of over 100,000 before the end of the Occupation. The practical difficulties in getting hold of reliable news, of paper – which was in short supply – money and possibilities for distribution as well as expert editorial commentaries were the same everywhere, as was the field of activity: the supply of news, countering of enemy or collaboration propaganda, agitation for Resistance actions, issue of directives for these actions, etc. The papers received the double task of working up a permanent standpoint and intervening in acute situations. Neither of the two tasks could be completed without the leaders of the newspaper world working their way into or being accepted in the collective illegal organisational network, and this was what occurred. The newspaper world became a vital centre for the illegal organisations with contacts to many sides, and in its unifying function it reached a perfection which no one could have foreseen in 1939–40. In many places, illegal news agencies[23] ensured rapid and reliable information, large organisations stood behind production and distribution, and the newspapers received a hearing among the masses. The most difficult task was to reach the agricultural communities, for example in a country like Norway, where distribution to the many small, isolated hamlets raised almost insuperable difficulties. But the problems of distribution were generally greater than those of production.[24]

Illegal papers, whether they were large or small, had one fundamental attitude in common: they agitated for resistance and turned against the Occupying Powers and all forms of collaboration. Both parties were exposed to a bombardment of aversion and hatred from a Press which in this respect was united. In other respects, however, one must register great differences on many levels between the many publications. There were large papers which covered whole countries, and there were small local organs. Very often the local papers were special editions of the large illegal newspapers, spiced with local news and able to intervene with directions in local developments, often with hastily produced leaflets. But athwart unity as to essentials, the various papers developed their independent standpoints in political, religious, national or otherwise ideological matters, although this did not apply to the Soviet publications, whether they were produced locally or were flown in. These acknowledged only the Communist ideology and were without differentiation. Yugoslavia was in a somewhat similar position. But otherwise, the illegal Press was not only the hotbed for the struggle against the Occupation, it also provided the soil for an extremely vital spiritual debate. It is hardly too much to say that when censorship smothered the traditional and very often party political exchange of views, this exchange became even more alive and vigorous than in normal circumstances. Here where it was a matter of life and death and national survival, political view-points became a vital matter for far wider circles than in normal condi-tions. The barriers created intensity, where the purpose of the barriers was to create paralysis. One might have expected a resigned, apathetic Europe, but what emerged was large groups of societies in lively movement, in open resolve, and with the will to continue the war with other means and with new purposes.[25] The fact that in a certain sense problems were very much simplified contributed to this development. For more and more people there was only a question of black and white, without light and shade. Even in areas such as unoccupied France and Denmark, which existed in relatively tolerable conditions, the will to take part in the struggle manifested itself. In Vichy France the movement grew of those who wished for renewed French participation in the War, and in Denmark a slogan was taken up to the effect that rather than the legal Government's actual protection, one would prefer what were called "Norwegian conditions".

Just as the papers could be divided in their political views, so long as the great common purpose – to fight external and internal enemies – was clear, so could there also be marked differences in style, tone and theme. Many were primitive fighting organs, whilst others had a more sophisti-cated literary character. Often this depended upon to whom the paper addressed itself. There were local papers, there were publications which addressed themselves to specific professional groups or to a public which was limited in some other way,[26] and this could be reflected in the agita-tion for definite political, religious, national or reformatory outlooks. An internal ideological debate went hand in hand with the general discus-sion, and in the midst of what was common to all, there was also plenty of room for special interests. Altogether it must be stated, however, that special interests were generally subordinated to the common line, and the mood of a popular front which had been so difficult to establish in the thirties became the general guiding line, at least for the leading Resist-ance papers. The will for this was expressed again and again by the leader-writers of the papers and the fact that the papers often found each other in more or less formalised co-operation also contributed to unity. The actual situation of occupation obviously promoted a relieving and, for people of those days, abnormally certain feeling as to what was black and what white. There were naturally, then as always, many nuances in political viewpoints, but Italian Fascism and particularly German

Nazism were nevertheless such extreme and inhuman challenges, that atheist and prelate, worker and director, officer and conscientious objector in decisive situations could find each other in common hatred and rage. When the time came, and with all reservations as to the erring and misled, to the passive and the opportunist, it may be claimed that the two dictatorship movements showed a surprising ability to gather the great masses, not as they expected, under them, but unexpectedly, against them. The illegal Press had much of the credit for the achievement of this final result.

It had an easy run. The Axis Powers and particularly the German Occupation policy was stamped by a strange primitiveness, which particularly in the East, but also elsewhere, in the North and West, included the belief that military victory followed by the military and police use of might, leading to the most cold-blooded terror, would also solve all political problems. All conquests were therefore based upon detailed military planning, after which a vacuum arose. In practically no instance had the Axis Powers any clear political plans in their support.[27] In particular there was no acceptable political alternative to offer the conquered – only submission under the will of the Occupying Powers, which to the surprise of the conquerors never came. This resulted in *ad hoc* solutions, direct military government in certain areas, appointment of politically impotent puppet governments and administrations in other areas. Solutions of this kind, based irresponsibly and short-sightedly upon a conviction of the ability of might to solve all problems, was increasingly marked by the use of force, where pressure begat counter-pressure. The result of the political vacuum was also a constant internal strife between the Axis partners and between their many political organs, as to the correct Occupation policy. The consequence was inarticulateness, typically obvious in regard to policy towards the Soviet Union, which will be mentioned here simply as an example. Here Ribbentrop and "Auswärtiges Amt" wanted one thing, Rosenberg's "Ostministerium" a second thing, Himmler's SS a third, and Goebbels' Propaganda Ministry a fourth, whilst the Army was divided as to views, which varied from one General to another, until the final decision could end up in Hitler's Headquarters, where Borman intrigued with and against Lammers and Keitel as to influence with the Führer, who noticed with satisfaction what he thought was the opposing forces keeping each other in check; and these – lacking any independent thoroughly studied policy – usually ended up with the simplest solution: violence and increased violence. Out in the conquered territories, the local Gauleiters could play upon these differences and to some extent decide their own policy. However, for the reasons already given, these never became real policies but were loose single decisions without perspective, which quickly lost any political meaning, and acquired the one purpose of keeping down defiance and opposition – with the use of violence and terror.[28] In this connexion, however, the Soviet Union is only one glaring example. Everywhere in the occupied countries, the Occupying Powers lacked a meaningful Occupation policy, and everywhere the internal struggle for power in the German hierarchy was marked, so that this policy became uncertain and unsteady, and soon had effect only when it was a question of demonstrations of strength and the use of violence.[29] The Occupying Powers had their conquests, but no political purpose connected with them apart from the sterile and hopeless belief that they, alone and without visible friends, could maintain these conquests for their own gain. It was this background that gave the illegal Press an easy, or at least an easier run.

There is a certain irony connected with the astonishing growth of the illegal Press in numbers, distribution and quality. The first primitive duplicated or type-written sheets, often in tiny editions, were read and re-read, copied and passed on. Their contents were discussed again and again, word for word, in the circles where people could talk to each other in a beginning illegal world. The primitive form itself was enticing, because it was a sign of the secret conspiracy for which it was presumably the messenger, and perhaps also because it came at a stage in the War where a special need existed for good news, for encouragement and for the hope that something might turn up in the midst of all the misery. At a much later stage, when illegal papers poured out in many places, and became everyday things, the intensity of reading weakened correspondingly. The main message of the papers was then accepted, and its repetition in another or several papers could only have a dulling effect. The heirloom's value lies in the very fact of its uniqueness, but when receiving the paper was a routine matter, it easily became trivial. For the same reason, one must probably take care not to measure the influence of the papers according to distinguished appearance or number of copies. These were the expression more of the capacity of the organisations and their means, than of the involuntary subscribers' views. In a normal society, numbers of copies are a reliable measurement for the capacity of a paper to form public opinion. In an illegal society, it was perhaps often the small local paper with a small circulation, or a leaflet in an acute situation, which had the strongest effect.

THE POLITICAL FIASCO OF THE AXIS POWERS. The information and views of the illegal Press also found their way to the Press and radio of the free world. For the free world they were a proof of the occupied peoples' ardent hope and cry for liberation, and were therefore a stimulus for the decision to come to the relief of Occupied Europe. In the psychological war, the illegal Press therefore had effect both inwards and outwards. In the beginning phases of the War, it was only to a modest degree that the messages of the underground Press reached the news media of the free world, but as it gradually became clear that the occupied countries carried on their desperate struggle according to their abilities and possibilities, behind the enemy lines, the actions of the Resistance Movements drew more and more attention in the free world. In addition, the underground Press gradually expanded its lines of communication to the neutral and Allied world more and more. Illegal actions could then become front page news far outside the countries' own frontiers.[30] They became symptoms which were registered, quite apart from the contribution they added to the common struggle. Resistance actions were also good material. They could contain not only elements of excitement but dramatic tones, which could help to spice the official military bulletins which also bore witness to the military and political difficulties with which the enemy had to struggle on the other side of the Front. They were therefore encouraging, and could therefore contribute to stimulating morale in the whole Allied camp.

The publication of an illegal paper was not, however, a military action, regardless of the paper's proclamation of active struggle, and in differentation between civilian and military activity within the sphere of action which the Resistance Movements developed the underground Press belongs to the civilian sector, on a line with, for example, demonstrations, protests, and strikes or – where this can be proved – passive resistance. Nevertheless, the underground Press lies in a sort of intermediate position in the frontier area between the two types of activity. The newspaper people sometimes went out on sabotage actions, or took part in weapon receptions, and the men from the sabotage groups could often be active in the publication of an illegal paper. This was neither right in principle nor technically defensible, but it happened, particularly in the childhood days of the movements. It would therefore be incorrect to draw all too sharp dividing lines. The Resistance Movements, even after all the organisational segmentation, consisted of series of units, where one function inevitably overlapped the next. Sabotage groups needed the calls which went out from the illegal Press, and the papers' agitation for sabotage and other forms of direct struggle, and they had support in the appreciative publicity of successfully accomplished actions, which the illegal Press could give them. Sabotage groups needed the weapon reception groups which perhaps never fired a shot, and the illegal Press, through the weapon deliveries, received important information material from the free world. All illegal functions depended upon the secret communication network which was built up, and intelligence reports could serve to promote the outside world's willingness to increase weapon deliveries. Altogether, functions and people in the Resistance world were interwoven so closely and inseparably that it is unwise to speak of systematization, if one does not immediately mention the exceptions to the rule.

Seen in a wider context, the illegal paper was a fighting instrument, even though the newspaper groups' fight was fought mostly with words. The Occupying Powers and their collaborators, who resisted with all their strength the political influence which the free Press gradually won, treated the illegal journalists and type-setters with the same brutality that they accorded the members of more militant groups. Prison, deportation, and death sentences hung over this work as it did over the other Resistance activities. Nevertheless, this struggle of words increased constantly and fought its way from the primitive beginner stage to the final situation where speech was free for those who would bear the risk. What began as a symptom of an attitude ended as a massive statement of this attitude. During this development, Axis propaganda was miserably shipwrecked. In reality this was astonishing.

The military conquest of large parts of Europe had taken place with relative, surprising ease. In the first two years of the World War, the well-greased German military machine seemed almost unconquerable, and it could look as though Europe's fate was sealed – and apparently for many years to come – after an unbroken series of German victories. Only in the Battle of Britain did the German leaders fail to get their will, even though Great Britain, here too, was forced on to the defensive and suffered under the destroying hail of bombs, and the still more dangerous submarine warfare. On this background of all-conquering German military superiority, one could have expected at least an opportunist submission or adjustment to a situation which, up to December 1941, appeared as a concrete *fait accompli,* which hardly left room for wishful thinking. There were certainly also opportunists and those who were resigned, but even during this period, the early Resistance groups worked their way forward to win a hold on public opinion, and the number of important Axis sympathisers was surprisingly small.

The reason was political. German military effectiveness was, as we have seen, inseparably coupled with political barrenness, approaching folly. Even after June 1941, when Germany entered a politically ideal situation, in that in the invasion of the Soviet Union it could proclaim a European crusade against Bolshevism, and therefore could appeal to the not inconsiderable anti-Communist circles, both in Poland and North and West Europe, the Axis Powers were only able to acquire a minimum of sympathy and assistance on ideological or opportunist grounds. Finland and Roumania joined the Axis Powers, but in the occupied countries the crusade appeal aroused only a faint echo. The effect was rather that even arch-enemies of Communism softened their views of the Soviet Union and the home Communists, and for many the new aggression against yet another state led to Resistance co-operation athwart all ideological barriers; and the Soviet Union's struggle and sufferings also came to set a wave of sympathy in motion, for the country and the party, far outside the Communist ranks. Even if no brotherhood arose on these grounds, at least there was a question of an ideological armistice, as long as the common enemies – Fascism and Nazism – were in power. Poland was the only exception in this respect, but even here there was an outspoken will to co-operate with the Communists in the exile government and among the leaders of the Resistance, until the Katyn affair in 1943, and the formal break between the Polish and the Soviet Governments. Even after this, both the exile government and the Resistance leaders made approaches to the Communist circles, in recognition of the wishes of the Western Allies, and of the fact that the struggle at least was common to both parties, even if the final political aims were not.

Even Poland, with her century-old anti-Russian traditions, refused to allow herself to be mobilised in any anti-Bolshevist crusade. There was no question of it in Czechoslovakia. Nor in the Balkans. But nor was there any support in North and West Europe. Developments in France were typical, where the de Gaulle movement, before 22 June 1941, refrained from any anti-Communist pronouncements, and after that date both wished for and realised the establishment of co-operation with the Communists. Maurice Schumann, de Gaulle's spokesman on the B.B.C., was the first to express this, saying[31] that the Free French Movement still maintained the principle not to say anything against the Communists which could one day stand in the way of their return to the patriotic camp, convinced as General de Gaulle was, that Germany would one day declare war on the Soviet Union. When this declaration of war came, a Communist representative, Fernand Grenier, was co-opted on to de Gaulle's National Council in London, and later in the Provisional French Government in Algiers; [32] and in de Gaulle's entourage the hope was that the French Communist Party, under the influence of the struggle, would change character and become French first and Communist second. The French Resistance leader, Gilbert Renault, Chief of the Resistance organisation "La Confrérie Notre-Dame", who accompanied Grenier on his illegal journey to London, expressed this in the words:[33] "Out of the struggle, a French Communist Party has been born which will never again separate itself from France." Renault was not alone in cherishing such hopes. Another French Resistance leader from the de Gaulle camp, Pierre Brosolette, expressed the same thought: "Perhaps the Communist Party after the War will survive in a fundamentally changed form? Perhaps the whole political chess-board will look quite different."[34] These and other similar remarks were the expression of an ardent French desire for unity in the struggle, and in spite of all ideological differences – which remained, in spite of the good intensions – this unity was a reality as long as the struggle lasted, and the Axis Powers succeeded just as little in France as in other western and northern countries in working up any crusading spirit with their propaganda. Communists and non-Communists found each other in co-operation, and saw only one enemy – the Occupying Power.

In this situation, the occupied areas were not the prize which had been expected, but a burden in at least as high degree. Everywhere in the occupied areas the conquerors met a dull, obstinate aversion, approaching horror and hatred. And psychologically, the Occupation did not succeed in bringing with it an atmosphere of submission, but rather one of protest, in which the occupied peoples gradually mobilised a stubborn will to fight on, even after the traditional military means had been taken from them. This was clearly expressed in France, where the defeatism and panic of 1940 was replaced by a newborn will to continue the fight with new and limited means, but the same tendency showed itself everywhere. Yugoslavia is another clear example, where the real war – for the Axis Powers a war of attrition – did not begin until the traditional military machine had been smashed to pieces after a campaign of only two weeks. Norway is yet another example, where the will to fight broke through in earnest and proved its vigour after the country's weak military forces had been defeated. The same thing occurred in the case of Poland, whereas the will to fight was very evident in Greece both before and after the Occupation began. Even in Denmark, where living standards and Occupation conditions were bearable for a long time, and could have remained so if the population had kept quiet, the will to take part in the struggle won through. In one place after another, a glaring contrast appeared between the military triumph of the Occupying Powers and their almost total political fiasco. The fiasco was so much the more striking in that Germany had made a point of raising propaganda to a main instrument in the political struggle, with its own Ministry and plenty of money for use both in Germany and elsewhere. In Germany the instrument proved useful but in the Occupation areas, money, persuasions and threats were wasted on the heavy mass of defiant fury, felt by millions who had one thing in common – that in the Occupying Power they came to see one common foe, who must be fought with all the means available. In this heavy mass, political, social, economic and religious differences were largely obliterated. To an extraordinary degree, every pronouncement which were issued from official quarters came to excite repudiation, rage, hatred and combat.

This does not imply that the Axis propaganda did not win proselytes, but simply that these were relatively few, and they soon became isolated and proved unable to contribute anything of importance to the fulfilment of the wishes of the conquerors. Of them too it can be said that they often became a liability, in just as high a degree as they were an asset. The reason naturally lay in the actual situation of occupation but by no means in this alone. A decisive cause of the universal growth of resistance – apart from the technical reasons mentioned – may be found in Fascism's and particularly Nazism's total disrespect for all human dignity, and the inhuman occupation policy which resulted from it, particularly in East Europe, manifesting itself equally in brutality and folly. To this challenge, all the occupied areas reacted sooner or later with an unequivocal and demonstrative "No!"

3. Forms of Civil Disobedience

Demonstrations

Demonstration was one of the first signs of resistance, and one of its first weapons, used in countless variations at an early stage of occupation, where other more outspoken measures were not yet available, or practicable.[1] It reflected a natural – often naive – urge to do something, of some kind, and it was the expression of a state of mind which had to find some outlet. Demonstrations could take every imaginable form, and it was difficult to combat them by prohibition, since only the demonstrators themselves had the imagination to devise their varying and often seemingly quite innocent forms, and since a demonstration could take the authorities by surprise, as a spontaneous action at a chance opportunity. In the early phases, symbolic demonstrations thrived. Even something as innocent as a flower could play a part. In Norway, thousands of people carried flowers on King Håkon's birthday, and had the satisfaction of seeing Quisling's henchmen tear the flowers out of the demonstrators' hands. In Holland, thousands of people wore white carnations – Prince Bernhard's favourite flower – in their buttonholes on the prince's birthday, 29 June 1940. This resulted in countless clashes and a German proclamation on 1 August 1940 forbidding all demonstrations in favour of the House of Orange, a prohibition which was flouted in all sorts of ways – in laying wreaths, cultivating flowers in the national colours, christening babies with the names of the Royal Family, etc. – bringing a further prohibition in March 1941.[2] In the French districts occupied by the Italians, many people demonstratively wore a more prosaic buttonhole – a piece af macaroni. Everywhere, flowers were laid on national memorials, and on national holidays, and flying the national flag, also at half mast, was obviously symbolic. National anthems became fashionable, and in many places the national – or Allied – colours and symbols appeared in every imaginable variation: clothing, melodies, flower arrangements, etc. Manifestations of this kind covered a richly varied spectrum, from grim humour, via baiting, and national sentiment, to genuine pathos.

The possibilities for symbolism were endless and unpredictable.

Inscriptions appeared on the walls of houses and at cross roads. In Norway, the sign H7, for King Håkon VII, flourished, as did the Cross of Lorraine in France.[3] In Denmark it became quite common to wear a special royal badge, and in Warsaw and Prague, signs went up at night, rechristening streets and squares with names of national or international celebrities, Kosziusko, Wenceslas, Churchill and Roosevelt.

A demonstration of quite elementary character[4] was the wide-spread refusal to understand a single word of the language of the occupying troops, and the consequent apparent inability, for example, to show the way or serve foreign customers, were elementary forms of demonstration, not to mention the excuse of language for failing to obey the orders of the Occupying Power. Connected with this there was the more obvious action of leaving the premises or public transport when an occupation soldier or a collaborator in uniform appeared. This "cold shoulder policy" was met, to a greater or lesser extent, throughout all the occupied countries, but it was organised in Holland, and it was also widespread in Norway, where the authorities in Oslo had to put up notices warning people that such demonstrative acts were punishable offences:[5] "It is regarded as a demonstration to change places when one finds oneself beside an NS member or a German, or to refrain from sitting down beside an NS member or German, when this would otherwise be natural." A comic parallel can be mentioned from Denmark, when a newspaper, with ill-concealed irony, could publish the following official appeal:[6] "As it has occurred several times recently that irresponsible persons have shown a conduct, for example by ill-timed spitting, which can be construed as expressions of contempt for the German Army, it must be pointed out in all earnestness that such ill-considered actions can have the most serious consequences, not only for those involved, who commit them, but also for others." Here it is comedy, and baiting, which predominate. A more severe form of demonstration was the boycott of German newspapers, which was started for example in Czechoslovakia and Poland, where buyers could be exposed to stigmatization with a placard announcing the crime in unmistakable terms; and subscribers, advertisers and buyers of papers friendly to the Axis Powers were stigmatized everywhere in the occupied countries.

In many of the instances mentioned here, the demonstrations would not have been possible if they had not been prepared via the "bush telephone". The white carnation would have had no effect, if it had only been worn by a few, but it was effective when thousands wore it. If one person left a restaurant or a tram, when a German soldier came in, this could be accidental, but it became more than an accident, when it recurred incessantly, and people flocked out of the pest-ridden places. The fact that demonstration became quite an effective weapon was due to its uncovering a latent implication of enmity, which cannot be traced today, but to which the Occupying Power and its collaborators were bound to be sensitive, simply because it was the proof of a treacherous under-current which could not be controlled. Just how sensitive to this attitude the Occupying Power could feel is shown, for example, by a new Polish penal law of 18 December 1941,[7] which went so far as to make the death penalty possible, even for persons under sixteen years of age, for anti-German statements, provocation or simply "hostile mentality". Demonstration was not dangerous in itself, but as a symptom it had to be countered with the most severe measures. Even well-meaning attempts by the Axis authorities to show a conciliatory attitude of neutral character could lead to unintended results. When the Austrian football club, "Admira", came to Copenhagen in June 1941 to play a friendly match, this gesture from the Axis side led to violent demonstrations, followed by fights, after which both German soldiers and Danish onlookers had to be treated in hospital, whilst the Danish Minister of Justice became the scape-goat of the day, and had to resign on German demand.[8] The same sort of thing happened when the Berlin Philharmonic Orchestra was to give a concert in Lyon on 18 May 1942. The visit of the orchestra led to violent demonstrations. An enormous crowd of demonstrators blocked all access to the concert hall, and the German orchestra found an empty auditorium, and had to leave the town without giving the concert.

Here as in many other instances, demonstration emerged as a clear, direct confrontation with the Occupying Power. This occurred, for example, when French students on Armistice Day in November demonstrated at the Unknown Soldier's Grave in Paris, by swinging two sticks, and shouting, "It is two sticks (deux gaules) we need;" or when Belgian demonstrators the day before filed past the monument to Belgian independence, the "Congress Pillar" – a demonstration which was repeated the following year on the anniversary of the German invasion, 10 May 1940; or when the citizens of Marseilles, on the news of the coup in Belgrade on 28 March 1941, gathered round the monument to the murdered King Alexander of Yugoslavia.[9] These were examples of demonstrations on national remembrance days. An unmistakable demonstration of this kind took place in Denmark, which was mildly treated, when every chick and child in the capital turned out in September 1940 to celebrate the King's seventieth birthday, in a beflagged city, and in an atmosphere of newly polished patriotism and royalist fervour. Here the Occupying Power had to make the best of it, in a mixture of astonishment and grim irritation over the implied elements in the phenomenon.

Very wide-spread demonstrations took place in France in 1942. De Gaulle appealed from London for demonstrations on May Day that year, and the call was followed very generally, especially in the unoccupied zone, and particularly in the towns of Toulouse, Nice, and Avignon, and in Marseilles where 30,000 responded to the summons. An even greater wave of demonstrations followed the same year, on July 14th, when a corresponding call was followed in all the larger towns such as Lyon, Grenoble, Limoges, Toulon, Marseilles – with 100,000 demonstrators – Toulouse, Nice and Avignon, and many other towns in the unoccupied zone.[10] In the occupied zone, demonstrations were confined to the laying of wreaths. These demonstrations underlined the growing influence which the Free French movement now exercised in France, and was thus a sign of unrest of considerable importance, particularly on the background of similar appeals in 1941, which had not had the same breakthrough – for instance, an appeal for a five-minutes silence all over France in memory of the hostages shot down in Nantes and Bordeaux.[10]

In reality these visible demonstrations had symbolic character, however, and the symbolic demonstration, which was one of the earliest features in the fermenting resistance, became a catalysator which continued as long as the Occupation lasted. The "V" sign campaign, launched from London and the B.B.C. had the greatest success.[11] The suggestion came to the B.B.C. from a Minister of the exile Belgian Government, de Laveleye, and the B.B.C. seized the idea at once,[12] combining the appeal to plaster the walls of Europe's houses with the "V" sign, with a new pause signal – four notes, or simply four beats of the drum, from Beethoven's Fifth symphony, which gave the rhythm of the Morse code's V sign: ...–! Churchill, who was not an enthusiastic propagandist, otherwise, even though his speeches in 1940 must be among the best propaganda achieved, seized the idea, pointing two fingers up in a "V" sign, which was thereafter inseparably connected with his person, and with Great Britain's struggle. Hardly had the B.B.C. launched its "V for Victory", before the sign turned up all over Europe, very often painted over German placards and side by side with the initials RAF, or short slogans with local significance. The speed with which the "V" sign spread everywhere was alarming for the Occupying Power, for the sole reason that it showed to what an extent Europe listened to the BBC, and how much a great, but unknown number of people were ready to follow orders from London. If it could happen with the "V" sign, it could also happen in other more dangerous matters. In Germany, Goebbels felt himself forced to an impotent attempt to make the "V" sign into a German symbol, but this failed completely. The "V" sign remained the symbol for victory for the Allies, and it contributed to establishing the BBC's absolute sovereignty over all German propaganda. This was significant, because the psychological climate was of decisive importance, both for the growth of the Resistance Movements and for the course of the war.

With this success alone, the BBC had put the cartoonist, David Low's words to shame, from the text to his world-famous sketch showing a self-satisfied Goebbels in an effective radio studio, and a Colonel Blimp with a toy balloon – a reference to the British attempt in the first months of the war to influence the German population with propaganda sent in over Germany, for example in balloons. Low's text was:

"The worst cause in the world and the best propaganda.
The best cause in the world and the worst propaganda."

His words might perhaps have been valid up to the time when Mr. Chamberlain, as Prime Minister, in a moment of irresponsibility and before the war had started in earnest in April 1940, had been so unfortunate as to declare that "Hitler had missed the bus". It was not valid after a great deal of Europe had been steam-rollered by the German military machine, and in spite of all prohibitions, had learned to listen intently to the BBC's more sober and realistic reports, and in a great many situations were prepared to follow instructions from the radio studios in London. The "V" sign and the "V" demonstrations were just two – very significant – expressions of this fundamental fact.

The urge for demonstration in Occupied Europe did not confine itself, then, to symbols. In spite of the fact that demonstrations were forbidden, they were used as opportunity offered, both in the positive form, where great masses of people gathered on national holidays and at national memorials, or – just as often – in the negative form where people left their work for minutes, hours, or occasionally days; left the streets empty; or refrained from carrying out acts which were either compulsory or normal. If the omission was general, the demonstration was clearly underlined. Obviously, demonstrations could only be used outside the actual partisan areas, and were only a poor supplement to other and more dangerous forms of activity, but they also had their place in the collective resistance. We meet the demonstration in a very well organised form in Norway, where a number of Trades Unions found each other in civil resistance, when the political organisations were put out of action. This work was aimed directly against Quisling, and the "Norwegian Unity Party", and its efforts to single-track Norwegian society in the corporate Nazi pattern; but indirectly, resistance against the Occupying Powers' marionette movement was naturally also a clear protest against the Occupying Power itself. In 1941, this co-operation, which was led by a co-ordinating committee, included no less than 43 organisations, with about 750,000 members, and every attempt to nazify a specific group – the medical services, education, the Civil Service, sport, etc. – was met by compact resistance and refusal.[13] Threats, arrests and deportations did not succeed in breaching this wall of demonstrative and outspoken aversion, and refusal of all co-operation, and the civilian Resistance in Norway became an important counterpart to the military resistance which developed.[14] It can be mentioned that in Poland, also, an organisation was created to arrange civil resistance, a Directorate for Civil Resistance,[15] as it was called; but this was closely connected with the Command of the military Resistance, and functioned mostly as an auxiliary organ for promulgating directives from the military Command out to the people. Demonstrations also took place in Poland, but here they had only quite secondary importance. On the other hand, demonstration was often used as a weapon in Denmark. When the legal Government signed the Anti-Commintern Pact in November 1941, there were serious open demonstrations against the Government in Copenhagen, and later in the Occupation, demonstrative strikes of longer or shorter duration became a favourite means of expression of the attitude of the population.

It is obviously impossible to assess the value of demonstration as one of the range of resistance forms. But it is possible to establish that they were effective in various ways. First of all, they had domestic effect. They both registered and strengthened solidarity and hope, and people from all levels of society and from all parts of the country, perhaps to their surprise, could find themselves belonging to a hidden fellowship which became stronger with every manifestation. For the active, the sight of the "V" sign alone could be a confirmation that others besides themselves were in action, and for the passive, the same sign could be a reminder that forces were fermenting, which had not passively reconciled themselves to the situation of occupation. For the Occupying Powers, demonstration was both an irritating and nerve-racking provocation, to which it could be difficult to decide how severely they should react. In themselves, demonstrations could be harmless phenomena, not worth more than a shrug of the shoulders, but as a symptom they were ominous. As the State Authority, the Occupying Power had to react, to make an example if for no other reason. But it had to do so with the knowledge that any violent reaction would let loose new waves of anger, which at any moment could explode in new and incalculable demonstrations, or something worse. Added to this there was the psychological effect on the individual soldier in the Occupation forces, or their uniformed collaborators. Was he the victor, or was he simply surrounded? Uncertainty and fear were manifest in the German or Italian soldier of the Occupation, who received orders to enter and clean up a partisan district – "Bandengebiet" – where ambush was certainly lurking behind every cliff, or in every piece of scrub. But the feeling of being an undesirable, or an object of hatred, was also implanted, with varying degrees of intensity, in the Occupation soldier who found himself in so-called pacified areas of Europe. It is quite believable that this could have an effect on the morale of some of them. Signs of hostility were everywhere present.

Even in comparatively quiet occupied areas, the signs of aversion and hostility could cause uncertainty. The feeling of uncertainty could haunt individuals or patrols everywhere in occupied Europe, but it was only in the great Partisan areas that it could be felt throughout whole garrisons. Regarding conditions near the Russian Partisan areas, the German historian Erich Hesse remarks:[16] "The German garrisons and gendarmerie posts were held in constant uncertainty and nervous tension. Among the soldiers posted there the feeling spread of personal powerlessness and despair."

For members of the Occupying Powers' satellite parties and auxiliary corps there was no doubt. They were outcasts from the fellowship, and with the Allied victories and ever-increasing and intensified Resistance actions, they had to face the vengeance which they knew awaited them. Regardless of their form or extent, demonstrations therefore became a phenomenon which was registered in both camps: an encouragement for some, for others a warning, for all a reminder. But the demonstrations were also registered outside the occupied territories. They helped to stress the attitude which could be expected from the peoples whom the Allies were to relieve.

Protests

Protest was another form of civil action, and it is not unreasonable here to differentiate between demonstration and protest. A demonstration was of course a protest in itself, but a protest could also be made without its being combined with the participation of demonstrating crowds, and instead depended upon the weight which lay in its objective arguments, its psychological force, or the strength behind the person or organisation making it. Protests came from many quarters, from organisations with professional, economic, cultural or religious backgrounds, from local or central authorities, from individuals, and even from collaborating organs and governments, when these felt themselves forced into concessions or standpoints which separated them all too clearly from the population in the society in which they had to operate.

It was part of the philosophy of collaboration, that it was through collaboration, and collaboration alone, that one could hope to obtain favours from the Occupying Power. It was therefore an obvious argument in negotiations with the occupying authorities that these should make the situation easier, through concessions, for their assistants and for themselves. Examples of this are legion, and here, where the exposé is not concerned with collaboration, but with the Resistance struggle, one or two typical examples only will be given in illustration. On 11 or 12 May 1941, the French Prime Minister at the time, François Darlan, negotiated with Hitler and Ribbentrop in Berchtesgaden. The negotiations were on the question of French assistance in German military actions in Iraq, via French bases in Syria.[1] Darlan gave in and thereby brought France perilously near to active French participation on the side of the Axis Powers but he then inserted his wish for a German quid pro quo:[2] "France has already manifested her wish for co-operation in the economic and military domain, by giving her effective support in Syria. France will continue to follow this policy, but it would be opportune if from the German side one would kindly make concessions to France." The key word here was "opportune", and what lay behind it came out more clearly when, a few days later, after negotiations with General Warlimont, Darlan made the concrete agreements in the so-called Paris Protocol. He there obtained a political supplementary protocol, which contained the words, in the final paragraph: "The German Government, through political and economic concessions, will supply the French Government with the means which, vis-à-vis public opinion in the country, can justify the possibility of a conflict with England and the USA."

Collaborating authorities required concessions for domestic use, and had regularly to beg for them, as well as now and then to come near to protest and threats, in order to keep the policy of collaboration from collapsing. Often, however, nothing came of the idea of protesting. This

was the case when in October 1941 the Germans took to extensive shooting of hostages in France.[3] Pétain, in real desperation, conceived the idea
of going to Paris to declare himself as Germany's prisoner and hostage.[4]
Sole hostage! The idea was not realised. His Ministers did the old man a
bad turn by dissuading him from his purpose, and not even an official
protest was sent from Vichy, which perhaps contributed more than anything else to accentuate the divorce between public opinion in France
and the Vichy Government. But the collaboration administrators in
Europe, both on opportunist grounds and for more noble motives,
needed now and then to make objections and to protest. This was the
case with the Vichy Government in the first months of 1942,[5] when
Pétain could use hard words on the radio of the "deserters" who both in
London and Paris, in the Press and on the radio, engaged themselves in
contemptible efforts to create disunity, and therefore strangle France.
Here he aimed his fire equally against the Free French and the extremist
collaborators in occupied France, and at the same time, the Vichy Government bombarded the German Occupying Power, during the first quarter of the year, with a stream of protests. That the Occupying Power took
no notice of the protests, and that they were usually only pious wishes
and empty promises, and that the stream of protests led to Darlan's fall
and replacement by Pierre Laval is another matter.

It should not be forgotten when the policy of the Axis Powers is examined, that the Occupying Authorities, and especially the Central State
organs in Berlin showed little sympathy for the difficulties of their collaborators. Perhaps it was unfortunate for them that the first victories
were so easy and complete. This increased the arrogance of the Occupying Authorities, and reduced their sense of long-term political
perspective.[6] Objections, proposals and protests from collaborating services and persons were easily brushed aside. In the examples cited
above, it was the French Government that was hit, but so were Quisling,
Mussert, Nedic and their like. The goods were ordered, but support for
the possibilities of the suppliers to deliver the goods was forgotten.

Protests came from many sides, however, and here we are thinking of
the protests from legal organs, not of the voices which were raised from
abroad and through the organs of the Resistance Movements, particularly the illegal Press. Protests came particularly from the Churches, and
here both Germany and Italy were extremely sensitive to criticism and
opposition, and at least in Northern and Western Europe they were
relatively careful in their reactions. An open struggle with the Churches,
in view of the enormous influence exercised by the Churches and Chris-

tan communities, was the last thing that the two Axis Powers desired. Nevertheless, there were sharp confrontations with the Churches in Norway, Holland, Belgium and France, and to a certain degree also in Denmark after August 1943, whilst developments were somewhat different in Poland and the Balkans.

In Poland, open Church opposition was strangled at birth. The reason for this was the German Occupation policy, which was based upon the barbaric pretence that the Polish population was a racially inferior group which should be deprived, as slaves, of any possibility for cultural influence. All universities, institutes of higher education, and grammar schools were closed, as well as museums, libraries and theatres. Books could only be published with German permission, and this excluded all literature which had even the faintest connexion with Polish cultural life, history, geography or other national themes. National monuments were destroyed. All this obviously hit the culturally dominating Catholic Church, and if this were possible, hit it even harder than any other institution of society.[7] Churches were closed, cathedrals, religious societies, religious orders and seminaries were dissolved, Church property was confiscated, and any religious influence in elementary schools was forbidden; and at the same time, thousands of priests were imprisoned and deported, some to concentration camps in Germany, some to camps in Poland itself. Many were executed. Even before the end of 1939, the number of priests deported had passed 1000, and it grew rapidly, until practically all Catholic priests and bishops and other clergy were imprisoned, deported, executed or otherwise debarred from rendering the services of the Church to the population. The Evangelical Church, also, was oppressed and decimated, and the final aim was the total abolition of the Church as an element in society in all Polish territory. In these circumstances, the Vatican could and did protest, and protests, accompanied by shocking proofs could be made from abroad.[8] The Polish clergy was debarred from protest.

It was otherwise in Northern and Western Europe.

In Norway, the Primate of the Norwegian Church, Bishop Berggrav, who had originally been in favour of a reserved attitude to the political situation from Church quarters, took the initiative in October 1940[9] in creating a "Christian Council for the Norwegian Church", including practically all Norwegian Church and missionary societies, and in February 1941, the confrontation with the Quisling movement started with a letter signed by the seven bishops of the country. This letter, addressed to the Church Minister, asked the question, as to how far the Quisling administration recognized the Word of the Bible and its ethics; and a few days later, a pastoral letter followed, signed by the Norwegian bishops, and was read from all the pulpits in the country. The pastoral letter definitely condemned the Quisling government and its interference in Church matters. With this, the Church had taken its political stand, and had given directives for the people, and in October the same year, this line was followed up. The Quisling administration, which in February had established the supervision of Church services to hear how the individual clergy openly or covertly expressed themselves, demanded a Church appeal to the Norwegian people, directed against Bolshevism and for Germany's war against the Soviet Union. This demand was refused by the Norwegian Church collectively, after all Norwegian bishops, at a General Assembly in Oslo, had categorically refused to have anything to do with such an idea. This time the refusal led to the dismissal of two bishops, and the struggle between the Church and State began in earnest. In February-March 1942, the Church struggle reached its climax. On 24 February, all the bishops resigned their offices, and the deans refused to take their places, if this were demanded, in a joint letter to the Church Ministry. On 22 March this was followed by a new pastoral letter, read out in all churches, containing a protest against the supervision of education by the State. The State was forced to react to this, and Bishop Berggrav was placed under house arrest, with the result that all the clergy in the country resigned their offices. An attempt by the Quisling administration, to get laymen authorized to maintain Church services, and also an order to the clergy to resume their offices, under the threat that their conduct was a revolutionary act, miscarried completely; and when the German Gauleiter Terboven intervened, the Quisling administration had to give in, and let the clergy function, although these maintained their unchanged protest against the State and its conduct. It was not possible in Norway to break the Church standpoint of protest, and the Church struggle, severe and intense as it was, became an important part of the Norwegian civil resistance, more than inopportune for both the Occupying Power and the Quisling administration, in view of the vast membership which the religious communities could muster throughout the country.

In Holland also, the Occupation and its consequences met protests from Church quarters, even though here too, the attitude of the Church in the first months of occupation was hesitant. From 1941, however, the Church declared itself in definite opposition to the actions of the Occupying Power.[10] Here the three most important religious denominations – the

Roman Catholic Church, the Dutch Reformed Church and the Reformed Church, which together included 80 % of the population – were in a-greement with each other, just as in the occupied countries generally there was a clear tendency towards joint action by previously competing re-ligious groups. In January 1941, the Catholic Church promulgated a pas-toral letter repeating an earlier prohibition against any Catholic joining any National-Socialist movement, and the Protestant Churches took the same stand. A preliminary reply came in the form of a ban against the Catholic newspapers, "De Maasbode" and "De Tijd". The conflict had begun, and it became more acute in 1942. On 25 July 1942, the Church protest was stressed in a pastoral letter from the Dutch Catholic bishops, read in all Catholic churches, with a severe warning against all Nazi threats against Christendom and Christian institutions, and in September 1942, the country's five Roman Catholic bishops joined in an appeal to the 200,000 workers in the Catholic Trades Unions, to keep away from all Nazi organisations – an appeal which ran parallel with a correspond-ing appeal from the Dutch Reformed Church Synod. In February 1943, the Church went a step further, and – under the impression of the perse-cutions of the Jews, which were just beginning – enjoined their congrega-tions to practise civil disobedience towards the authorities, and in no circumstances take part in any co-operation connected with the persecu-tion of the Jews, those who avoided forced labour, or others wanted on political grounds. Protests from the Dutch religious bodies took the form of pastoral letters, which were both read out in the churches and distri-buted illegally; instructions during confession; and a direct approach to the Reich Commissar, Seyss-Inquart, including a meeting between him and the leaders of the united Churches in February 1942, where Church representatives protested jointly against anti-Jewish measures, random arrests and every attempt to force the National-Socialist ideology upon the Dutch people; and the Roman Catholic Church procured a special fund, through collections in the churches, to support anyone who was in need because of their Christian faith, also including persons who resigned their office or in other ways found themselves in financial difficulties owing to their Christian conscience. The Church also rejected every attempt at interference by the State in Church services. For example, the churches maintained the traditional prayer for the House of Orange generally, and Queen Wilhelmina in particular. The result of this Church struggle was on the one hand the arrest of hundreds of clergy, although not within the highest Roman Catholic hierarchy, and on the other, a clear definition of the stand which the Dutch should take against National-Socialist ideology, and with that, an important strengthening of civil resistance in Holland.

In Belgium it was the Primate of the Roman Catholic Church, Cardinal van Roey, the Archbishop of Malines, who opened the Church struggle in March 1942.[11] This was done in a sermon in the Church of Our Lady in Wavre, during which he declared hostilities, in harsh terms, against both the Occupying Power and its Flemish and Walloon collaborators under the leadership of Staf de Clerq and Leon Degrelle respectively. The Church, declared Archbishop van Roey, could not keep out of politics. Its task was the defence of the Catholic faith in all facets of life, and for that reason he rejected all co-operation with what he designated as "the enemy" – the reference in the sermon to earlier Belgian history made it quite clear who was "the enemy" – and stated that the Church must refuse to co-operate with those who supported "the enemy". Here the acute hostility between the Catholic Church and the forces of collaboration was highlighted, and this enmity intensified when priests refused to pray for the fallen in the Flemish Legion on the East Front, and the Church refused to make its schools or other precincts available for Nazi meetings. In July 1942 this hostility was intensified still further by a pastoral letter, which the Archbishop ordered to be read from all the pulpits in the country, in which the re-establishment of a free and independent Belgium, including both Flemish and Walloon, was emphasized as the aim of the Church, and refusal to pray for the fallen on the East Front was maintained. The demand for the re-establishment of a free and independent Belgium was in clear opposition to the plans of the Occupying Power, for incorporating Belgium in the Great German Reich, but was allowed to go by default, and a bitter strife then developed between the Belgian Nazi Parties which were not particularly influential, and the Church, which was attacked in the Nazi Press for sowing hatred and contempt among the Belgian population towards Nazi-orientated Belgians – a claim which was undeniably valid. Belgium was under direct German martial law, however, and the Occupying Power found it wisest to refrain from engaging in an actual Church struggle, and the Church was thus able to maintain its negative attitude and its important influence in the Belgian community.

In France, at first, the position of the Church – and here it is a question primarily of the Roman Catholic Church – was quite different. Here, since the armistice in June 1940, a national government had existed with its seat in the unoccupied zone, and a government programme, which the Leader of the Government, Marshal Pétain, formulated in rather vague terms with, for example, the motto on "Work, family, fatherland", as the basic civic virtues, could not arouse any immediate protest from the Catholic Church. On the contrary. As late as November 1941, an assembly of bishops and archbishops in the unoccupied zone, with Cardinal Gerlier in the Chair, in Lyon – his seat – could make a joint declaration which expressed support for the work of national regeneration under the leadership of Marshal Pétain.[12] The Vatican had diplomatic relations with the Vichy Government, with Valerio Valeri as Papal Nuncio. A similar declaration had already been published in September of that year by the Church leaders in the occupied zone, and the Vichy Government had long been able to claim the support of the Church. As the Vichy Government developed, however, with increasingly far-reaching compromise, not only with the Occupying Power, on questions of material concessions, but – especially after Pierre Laval took over the real power of government in april 1942 – with concessions on the ideological and human plan, this Church attitude was somewhat impaired. A watershed was reached in September 1942, after conflict had arisen with the Church in August, when the Laval government began the arrest of Jews of foreign nationality in the unoccupied zone of France, and they were transported across the demarcation line, and on to concentration camps in Germany. When this happened, protests poured in.[13] They came from the occupied zone in the form of a joint protest to Pétain from all the cardinals and archbishops, and they came from the unoccupied zone in the form of pastoral letters, read out in all the churches, against all forms of anti-Semitism. Cardinal Gerlier, who led the protest movement, refused to celebrate mass for the fallen from the "Légion Tricolore" on the East Front. The Primate of the Protestant Church, Pastor Boegner, joined in these protests on behalf of his Church. The Vatican also intervened through the Papal Nuncio in Vichy, but its protest was rejected by Laval, and a number of priests were arrested, after which the Roman Catholic Church withdrew the support it had originally given to the Vichy Government, to an increasing degree. A great many priests joined or supported the Resistance, and Catholic organs such as "Jeune République" and "Démocrates Chrétiens" came to play an important rôle in the whole Resistance Movement; and a number of Roman Catholic newspapers such as "Cahiers du Témoignage Chrétien", "Défence de la France" and "Résistance" saw the light of day.[14] All in all, the Catholic Church and especially very many of its members moved further and further away from Vichy during the Occupation, and over to the Resistance Movement, where they obtained influence in the co-ordinating organs, corresponding to the tremendous influence of the Catholic Church in the population.

In Denmark, where 97 % of the population, at least formally, were members of the Protestant State Church, there was no actual struggle with the Church. In the period up to August 1943, a legal Danish Government retained power, and negotiated with the German Occupation Authorities – although this was always under German pressure – and the Church lived its normal life without interference from the State, and without qua Church, interfering in political developments. But after August 1943, when the government resigned, and the German seizure of power became increasingly glaring, the situation altered considerably. This took place to an especial degree in October 1943, when the German Occupying Power tried to arrest the Danish Jews – an action which failed, in that about 95 % of the Jews were brought to safety in Sweden.[15] Here the Church had to protest as a Church, on a line with many other institutions, and this also took the form of a protest from all the Danish bishops to the German Reich Commissar. Added to this, from now on, the clergy created their own illegal organisation and joined the existing illegal organs in considerable numbers. A bishop was for instance a Member of the Resistance Movement's supreme organ, Denmark's Freedom Council. Although no actual Church struggle broke out, it was obvious, here too, that both the Church as a Church and individual clergy[16] closed ranks in the face of the Occupying Power's violations.

In the Balkans, as has been mentioned, conditions were different from those in Northern and Western Europe. The Orthodox Church in Greece remained largely passive towards the Occupation and its political problems, but in Yugoslavia the situation was more complicated. Here the population, in so far as they subscribed to any particular faith, were split up in three religious groups, Roman Catholic, Orthodox and Mohammedan. When a Croat vassal state was created in the spring 1941, under the exiled Croat politician, Anton Pavelic,[17] and bands from the Ustace Movement which supported him, attacked the populations of Croatia, Slovenia and Bosnia with barbaric cruelty, amongst other atrocities practising forced conversion to the Catholic faith, in campaigns during which tens of thousands and sometimes whole village populations were butchered if they refused, the question arose of the Catholic Church's attitude both to the actual massacres, and also to the recognition of the "conversions" which took place.[18]

The Primate of the Catholic Church in Croatia was the Archbishop of Zagreb, Stepinac. This did not make him the supreme authority for the attitude of the Catholic Church in the country, but his views set up a standard, and were of enormous importance for the rest of the clergy in deciding their standpoints. When the vassal state was created, Stepinac gave unqualified approval to the new state and its patent zeal for the advancement of the Catholic cause, by every means, even when the Education and Church Minister of the Pavelíc regime publicly declared the government's will to kill, exile and convert by force, and concluded a tirade on their intentions in this respect, with an answer to a journalist, who enquired as to its aims for the national and religious minorities in Croatia: "For them we have three million cartridges." Nevertheless, Stepinac praised the new state, and in a pastoral letter in April he enjoined the Catholic clergy to serve it loyally. It was also a well known fact that he looked with hatred on the Orthodox Church, and its influence in the country. No one could be more zealous than he, when it was a question of missionary work in favour of the Catholic Church, and if this could be done through the Pavelic Government, he welcomed it. He shared this attitude with the other bishops in the area, particularly with the Bishop of Serajevo. The attitude he had to take to the mass conversions, as the ravages of the Ustace bands gradually became known was another matter. According to Canonical Law, he could not recognize mass conversions by force, and without preliminary religious instruction of the converts; nor, according to the same Canonical Law, could he recognize such conversions when it was obvious that they were motivated by opportunism alone, based upon well-founded fear; and lastly he had to take the Catholic Church's long-term reputation into consideration. The fact emerged, from the reports he received from his subordinates in the area, and spoke in no uncertain terms of the bestial cruelty and indescribable violations, that the Church's reputation was being seriously undermined by the terror which the Ustace bands were committing everywhere.[19] In November 1941, under the impression of this and after conferring with his fellow bishops, Stepinac made a cautious retreat as regards Pavelic, in the form of an appeal to him. He emphasized that the process of conversion must lie in the hands of the Catholic clergy and not with the State, and on realistic grounds he opposed "political conversion". On the other hand, he refrained from accusing the Pavelic Government itself, blaming the notorious atrocities upon "irresponsible" elements in the Ustace circles. He continued to fill his high office, in full awareness of what was going on, and carried out all the functions attached to it. He accepted high decorations from the Pavelic Government, and he also accepted the post of religious leader of the armed Croatian forces. It cannot be denied that Stepinac made objections, even if they were tame, at what had happened, but he did not take the clear consequences of his knowledge, and here, therefore, no Church struggle took place, but the attitude of the Church towards the Pavelic Government, originally positive, later became lukewarm. The atrocities continued, although to a lesser extent, when the first savagery had spent itself, and when large sections of the population had sought refuge in Tito's partisan camps. Another side to the question is that some priests joined the partisan movement,[20] in horror at what had happened, and in protest against their Primate and his attitude, and they came to do both religious and military service in its ranks.

Strikes

The strike as a weapon in the resistance struggle. Demonstrations and protests were two of the means which civil resistance could take into its service. In addition, strikes were another means of resistance which could be considered, and which were also taken into use by the unarmed masses in the occupied territories. The use of this method of struggle was all the more obvious in that the strike, in most of the occupied areas, was a familiar and normally completely legal tool in the economic and social struggle, although it was only used exceptionally in national or political questions. However, it had been clearly demonstrated earlier in the century that strikes could also be used as political instruments, and that they were both effective and dangerous, particularly when they developed into general strikes. The earliest examples had been in Russia and Finland, in 1905 and again in 1917, in Germany during the Kapp coup in 1920, and during the French occupation of the Ruhr in 1923. In Denmark in 1920 it had been proved that the threat alone of a general strike could compel a fundamental change of policy, whereas on the other hand, strikes in Italy in 1920 and in England in 1926 had failed, and had given a political backlash. Nevertheless, strikes, especially for the socialist ideological mentality, must seem a logical fighting weapon, where the military possibilities were exhausted, and enemy occupation followed.

In the front ranks of the agitators for striking stood the Communists, when after June 1941, they joined the resistance activities. For them, the strike not only impeded production – depending upon the extent of the strike and the importance of its object – it could also contribute to cementing large sections of society together, and acting as catalysator for other resistance activities.

But if the strike could seem an obvious weapon – particularly for the established, strong labour organisations and trades unions – for the occupying powers, the dangerous nature of the strike was just as obvious, not only as regards the maintenance of production but also maintenance of law and order and political calm. The quite natural consequence of this was that strikes, in particular, were absolutely forbidden throughout the occupied countries, and participation in or even encouragement to strike was punished with the most severe penalties and reprisals, military intervention, imprisonment, deportation or, in the final consequence, the death penalty.

The only exceptions were the unoccupied French zone and Denmark, where Occupation decrees could not be put into force as a matter of course, but where the Occupation Authorities had to negotiate their wishes and demands with national governments; but here too, the strike as a weapon must appear weak in comparison with its strength in normal conditions. In France, the Vichy Government led the reorganisation of the State machinery, creating corporate organs for both business and cultural life, and completely subordinating industry to State control.[1] This was done by a law of 16 August 1940, and even though some so-called "organisation committees" were set up by this law as links between the State and production, it turned out in practice that the State ensured its total command over production and distribution by this law and a number of subsidiary laws. This applied to appointments and the engagement of personnel, leadership of production, distribution of raw materials, wages and salaries, hours of work, working conditions, sales and prices, etc. Everything was subordinated to the Ministry for Industrial Production and Work. Added to this, the great traditional organisations of the labour market were abolished in November 1940. It applied also to the great employers' unions, especially in coal and steel production; it applied to the French industrial leaders' unions just as it applied to the trades unions, both the Christian unions and the socialist orientated and dominated trades unions. It goes without saying that the possibilities for striking were reduced under such conditions, and in April 1941, strikes were officially forbidden. In the case of Denmark, the laws were not changed in principle, as far as conditions of work were concerned,[2] but the political truce and the attempts to freeze wages and control prices, as well as the uncertain economic situation and doubt as to how the Occupying Power, and therefore the Government, would react to wide-spread industrial conflict, contributed in the first phase of the Occupation to damping any urge for striking. Obviously, the Government had to take an increasingly serious view of labour unrest, and the climate for strikes worsened.

France and Denmark were exceptions, however. Everywhere else, the will of the Occupying Power was law, without any possibility of intervention by conciliation institutions with even a minimum of manoeuvrability. It was only under these conditions that strikes could be included in the Resistance struggle as a whole, and they had an exceptional position among the weapons employed, in that by their very nature they could not be hidden in illegality. Other resistance groups such as illegal newspaper editors, saboteurs, radio telegraphists and many others from the underworld of the Resistance, lived and worked underground, and were nameless and without address, whilst workers, office staff, tradesmen or civil servants who went out on strike were registered and vulnerable, if and when there were reprisals, as was inevitably the case where the Occupying Powers were in complete control. This circumstance, that strikes would be met with immediate and drastic measures, such as executions, deportation or random shooting of participants at their places of work or in the streets, was bound to reduce the possibilities of the strike weapon very considerably. And if there was evident danger in taking part in a strike, the danger was no less for those preparing and organising it. At the important preliminary stage, where feeling was to be worked upon, and instructions given, as well as at the no less important stage, during the strike, where its course needed to be organised, the restrictions of the times placed almost insuperable obstacles in the way. If a strike was to become a reality under such conditions, there must at least be such desperation present that the cost was no longer counted, in addition to a formidable solidarity.

Both these elements appeared, however, under the stress of occupation and the unwise measures taken by the Occupying Powers, and so, in spite of all coercive measures, the strike became one of the weapons to which the peoples of the occupied territories resorted, often egged on by illegal agitation. Desperation could be caused by many different situations: general want, the conscription of forced labour, the deportation of the Jews, the shooting of hostages or other acts of terror in connexion with the Occupying Powers' coercive measures and the collaborating authorities' concessions. The Occupation itself produced a latent desperation, in the long run, which only needed an excuse or flagrant provocation to burst out in violent reaction. If the atmosphere was sufficiently electric, organisers' orders to strike could have their effect. The excuses could be manifold, and more or less genuine: insufficient wages, insufficient rations, unreasonable working conditions, lack of shelter during bombing raids, military occupation of factories and many others. Often, little was needed, and if the preventive and punitive measures had a restraining effect on the one hand, on the other, if a strike did occur, there was correspondingly deep gravity in the action, and there was always considerable danger of demonstrations in sympathy, and of uncontrolled waves of strikes. An extreme instance occurred in Copenhagen in June 1944, when a wide-spread general strike, which went quite out of control[3] spread to practically the whole city, with its million inhabitants. In this instance, after a decree of martial law, which shut the people in their hot flats from 1800 hours, factory workers stopped work in the middle of the day, ostensibly to look after their allotment gardens before the hour of the curfew, an excuse and a reason which had been formulated by an inventive journalist in the illegal Press, and was immediately seized by the strike leaders and the population. The ironic element in the situation was intensified by the fact that the people of Copenhagen by no means kept indoors after the curfew, but on the contrary, swarmed and demonstrated in packed, defiant crowds, on the streets which the Germans had ordered to be emptied. In answer to random shooting, the people of Copenhagen built barricades and lit bonfires in the streets.

But if desperation was essential for strikes, solidarity was no less so. A strike succeeded best where it covered large areas and great masses of people, and where the risk for the individual was therefore reduced, because it was impossible for the representatives of the Occupying Power to hit more than a fraction of one per thousand implicated. Here solidarity came into its own, and most effectively when it included all ranks of society. Indeed the strikes which took place during the Occupation usually changed character, from being traditional economic confrontations between workers and employers to becoming political or national actions, where it was not only the workers who demonstrated, but where countless others, students, office personnel, factory owners, businessmen and civil servants could rally around the strike or at least sympathise with it and give it more or less tacit support. Faced with a large town, a whole province, a whole provincial group, or a whole population, the Occupying Power was often forced to yield to some extent, and embark on concessions or negotiations which were dangerous in themselves, because they could very easily create precedents and lead to new outbreaks of popular national pride. On the other hand, strikes, as the obvious acts of defiance that they were, were extremely dangerous tools for those who organised them or rallied to them, and this must necessarily limit their use in the resistance struggle. The astonishing thing is that they were used at all as weapons, under the conditions of occupation.

Strikes during the years of occupation, then, took on a different character from that of the ordinary type of strike. In normal conditions, a strike was usually a question of interests, where the strike was directed against the employers and aimed at obtaining concessions as to wages, hours of work, working conditions, etc. Such strikes were often connected with sympathetic strikes in related industries, and their extent and duration depended upon the course of the strikes and the results achieved. Strikes of this type also took place in the occupied territories of France and Denmark, where the Occupying Power could not intervene directly, but even strikes of this kind inevitably acquired a more political character than normally, because in the special circumstances, the strikes were not so much directed against the employers involved, as against the conditions which the country's authorities, the Occupying Power, or a combination of both had dealt out for the possibilities for production, and where the employers were just as restricted in their arrangements as their opponents on the strike front. The confrontation between employee and employer did not come to a stop, but it was just as often a question of a confrontation between the factories, the State and the Occupying Power, where there could even be a question, as was often the case, of a latent or declared solidarity between the strikers and the managerial staff. Protest strikes, however, had more importance for the Resistance Movement, in that they sprang from the urge to manifest general dissatisfaction with the conditions of occupation or to react against a political situation, whether a strike was directed against the national authorities or against the Occupying Power, perhaps in the person of the local Commandant. The protest strike had a clear tendency, to an even greater degree than in normal circumstances, to inspire sympathetic actions; and it was typical for the course of strikes during the Occupation, not only that they acquired far greater national and political character, but also that they showed an evident propensity to spread, and they could reflect solidarity between groups which were traditional opponents. It was also typical for protest strikes that they were often limited in time, without for that reason losing much of their effect. A stoppage of work of an hour, a day, or even two minutes, could contain a protest which could not be misunderstood, and where its extent more than its duration could be decisive for the strength of the protest.

It is hardly possible to differentiate between demonstrations and strikes, under the conditions which the Occupation engendered. Demonstration, protest and strike! The three concepts merged into each other, and the strike contained all three elements. It is true that there was a marked difference between the three forms of action, and that neither demonstrations nor protests constituted a concrete attack on the Occupying Power in its exploitation of the resources of the occupied territories, whereas strikes did contain a real assault on the production apparatus, and its effect therefore had direct influence on the Administration of the Occupying Power. In this respect, the strike was a grassroots supplement to two of the important weapons which the Allies took into use against their Axis opponents, blockade and bombing. This is particularly true of the invisible strike, that is, the strike which consisted simply in reduced tempo or shoddy production, and it may have been this form of strike in particular that the Minister of Economic Warfare, Hugh Dalton had in mind, when in 1940 he spoke of strikes as an aid to the Allies' economic warfare.[4] This is of course the explanation of the Occupying Powers' extreme sensitiveness to strikes, and especially to their ultimate form, the general strike. They had to react with constant and justified suspicion, and – where a strike flared up – with the most severe sanctions. Occupied Europe never "pulled its weight", and never fulfilled the production standards which were possible. Production and distribution were carried out under compulsion, with the limitations, delays and evasions which resulted from this. In this lay the difference. Demonstrations and protests were irritants which threatened danger, but strikes were an actual lurking danger, which must at least be prevented from developing openly. The fact that, nevertheless, one cannot differentiate clearly between the three forms of action, is due to their interrelation. This is apparent simply from the fact that strikes themselves were demonstrations and protests, carried to their conclusion. It is also apparent, however, that strikes were normally accompanied by extensive demonstrations and disturbances, and spread far beyond the strike area in question, involving elements in the population which would not normally dream of resorting to the strike weapon. The student strikes in Delft and Leyden[5] in 1940, in connexion with the dismissal of Jewish professors, can serve as clear examples of both strike and sanctions. This was one of the instances of a strike which had the character of a demonstration, and where the strike was carried out by a group which did not normally resort to this form of action and where the German sanctions – the closing of Leyden University and the Technical High School in Delft – expressed the Germans' correct assessment of the fact that the strike aroused sympathy in far wider circles than those of the university or the Technical High School themselves, and that therefore they must make example of them. Besides this, these episodes followed a written protest, prepared by a group of professors and addressed to the German Reich Commissar, Seyss-Inquart, and spread illegally over the whole country, so that these university events had nation-wide effect upon public opinion, far beyond the circles immediately involved.

Strikes had therefore considerable repercussions, particularly in psychological effect. Not only could they, as already mentioned, assume the character of a violent demonstration, or take shape as the most severe and desperate instruments in a wave of popular demonstrations, but they also served in high degree to show up and cement a solidarity which perhaps until the wave of strikes began and demonstrated this solidarity, had been hidden to those who took the risks of striking, or more or less wholeheartedly rallied in its wake. The masses involved could look around them in wonder: Are there really so many of us? Do we, at the bottom of our hearts, think and feel so alike? How much power do we really possess? This was obviously the case to a special degree, where a strike spread, not only from factory to factory, and from region to region and perhaps to a great city, but where it infected the local community, and made it clear to both friend and foe that the strike, and with it the concept of resistance, had support and sympathy far beyond the circles which were normally strike-conscious, and used to striking, or were resistance-minded. Through this effect alone, the strike – quite apart from all the evident but often limited damage it could do to the production plans of the Axis Powers – was a catalysator for growing national self-respect among the peoples of the occupied countries. And as a symptom and a threat, strikes became the writing on the wall for the Occupying Powers. Open strikes could be painful facts, which could be combatted, but was there also a hidden strike in the daily course of production? How deep did the hatred go, and how wide? To what extent was the aversion organised? Added to this, after a strike, it was a shorter step than before, from striking to joining direct illegal activity, often, and perhaps particularly when a strike was crushed with brutal means. In the special circumstances, strikes had, on the one side, less elbow room than under normal conditions, but on the other, they had far greater perspectives than normally.

The conditions of occupation, and the measures with which the Occupying Power found itself forced to block all possibilities for calling strikes – and here it was a question of measures for prevention, control and punishment – must inevitably check or hinder a great many of the preparatory processes which normally led to strikes and carried them through to conclusion. Open agitation before the strike, its organised start, its well planned course, with posting of strike pickets, payment of subsistence money, support from sympathetic actions, organised negotiations between the parties concerned, and finally the conclusion of the strike through the Trades Unions and the enterprises hit by the strike – all these actions were unthinkable in the special circumstances, where police and armed forces were constantly on the watch, and prepared for immediate intervention, and both at the outbreak of a strike and at its conclusion, the parties groped for each other or for some agency which could mediate. The situation could often develop in such a way that both parties wished to stop, but were cut off from any direct contact. On the other hand, the Occupation itself supplied intense motivation for the reaction of striking. The War, the Occupation, the cost of living, the restrictions and oppression, hit the whole population, but their effects were undeniably greatest in the towns and industrial spheres, and for the working classes for whom the strike was a traditional tool in the economic and political struggle.

There were incentives enough: the suppression of the Trades Unions, the constant rise in prices accompanied by the depreciation of wages, lack of elementary necessities, increasing working risks, longer hours of work, the risk of conscription to forced labour and many more evils piled on the top of the general burden of occupation. For these reasons alone, the constant danger lurked everywhere in Europe of an explosion of strikes, which could quickly spread and get out of the control, both of the Occupying Power and of the strikers. For that very reason, the Occupying Powers were relentlessly and ruthlessly on guard against any signs of strike mentality, and for that very reason, although there were a number of outbreaks, the weapon of the strike never had an effect which could be compared with the potential danger of the weapon.

The dream of a General Strike, which could bring the Occupying Powers' exploitation of the occupied territories to a stand-still, was easy to conceive, and the tactics of agitation were just as obvious for the Communists, who were almost inevitably in the vanguard in the appeal for strikes. The effectiveness of the strike weapon was urged again and again, both when it was a question of small individual pin-pricks in the production process, and where the agitation could be for major collective strikes, preferably a general strike, where all became responsible and were therefore equally in danger of reprisals. In agitation, the constant appeal was for action for the everyday things, of which war and the Occupation produced a lack: more bread, more milk, more elementary necessities of life, less pressure of work and better protection of workers, etc. This was the case, for example, when a strike broke out on 27 May 1941 in the mining districts in the French departments of the Nord and the Pas de Calais,[6] and quickly spread to the whole mining area, with its French, Belgian and Polish miners. Work was not fully resumed until 9 June, and only after both the French authorities and the Occupying Power had yielded and complied with the economic demands of the strikers, at least partially. This strike was carried through on the demand for everyday things, but behind the tactically worded appeal to strike for apparently elementary and non-political demands, was the hidden latent dissatisfaction with conditions, and the fact that every demand therefore implied opposition to these conditions, which consequently could lead to subversion, dissolution and revolution. The stripping of the occupied territories was also causative here. Every material improvement achieved must mean a corresponding reduction of the Occupying Powers' exploitation of the meagre resources of a Europe under blockade. A statement based upon these facts was issued in the form of illegal instructions by the Communist-inspired French Resistance organisation, "Front National", in the spring 1944:[7] ". . . one must realise the fact that not all Frenchmen are convinced as yet of the necessity of joining the FTP ("Francs-Tireurs-Partisans-Français") immediately. But this vast mass is ready to act to protect the necessities of life . . . We cannot therefore with one stroke lead 300 peasants from a village out into the armed conflict, but they can resist requisitioning, or they can struggle to obtain paraffin for lighting. We cannot with one stroke lead 150,000 French miners of the Nord out in armed conflict, but they can carry out a heroic strike to get soap, free Sundays. These demands unite the most important classes of the French population in action."

The wheels of Europe did not come to a stop. The Occupying Powers made sure of this, with their intervention, as did the day-to-day demands upon the individual to obtain work, wages and the necessities of life. The heroic strike was the exception in a world of heroism. One feature of the situation was that the Communist Party, which more than any other advocated and was expert in the anatomy of the strike, in theory as in practice, stood under the shadow of the German-Soviet pact until 22 June 1941, and was therefore uncertain and in doubt as to its views of the European revolt which was emerging. It was not until July 1941 that

"L'Humanité" made a clear statement:[8] "It is our duty to help the Soviet Union with all means." Both before and particularly after this turning point, however, the threat existed of a more or less declared "go slow", and this became a strain on the Occupying Powers, both psychologically and materially. It is a fact that any demand, even the most innocent, contained an element of resistance, and it is also true that every delay, omission, mistake, or absence, not to mention the rarer open strike, contained elements of an undermining nature in relation to the grip in which the Axis Powers held occupied Europe. How far the pin-pricks reached, it is idle to speculate. The same may perhaps be said of the psychological effects of the open strikes which broke out. One thing is certain, however – the strike, both hidden and open, became one of the many weapons which the Resistance Movement dreamed of using, and which, when opportunity offered here and there, they did use.

The most dangerous strikes were those which broke out in connexion with the Allied offensives and contributed to compromising military dispositions in an area under attack. Then they had tactical importance, as was the case in France in the summer 1944, or in North Italy in the spring 1945. The danger of this became a factor which all Occupation authorities had to take into consideration, and the risk alone contributed to creating uncertainty. Both in military and civilian staffs, the Occupation authorities had to calculate with the possibility of an explosion – a wave of strikes, a wave of sabotage, revolt – and they had to look over their shoulders with the knowledge that incalculable actions, of incalculable dimensions and incalculable character could be organised by a central command, or even co-operated with an attack coming from outside. Experience must point to the conclusion that this was no imaginary risk, but a reality. There could be variations from staff to staff as to how alarmingly their experience was interpreted. No staffs were quite impervious.

HOLLAND. In Holland the use of the strike weapon became a characteristic feature in the history of Dutch Resistance. This was logical, in view of the geographic and demographic nature of the country, and the structure of its society. The possibilities for resistance were extremely poor, but the weapon of the strike could be used to mark the standpoints of the population. A forewarning came with the demonstration, already mentioned, by students and their professors in two Dutch university towns in the winter 1940–41, against the dismissal of Jewish professors; and it was the Jewish question which started the first major Dutch strike soon after.

In February 1941 there were serious disturbances in Amsterdam,[9] which at that time had become a centre for considerable political unrest and nervous tension. The background was made up of many different components: the brutal German attack in May 1940, with the barbarous bombing of residential areas, the rapid, humiliating Dutch capitulation, the fortunate result of the Battle of Britain, and the British winter victories in the Mediterranean, as well as the daily propaganda which was broadcast with great effectiveness from London over Radio Orange. These were the background and influence from abroad. But internal factors had an even greater effect: first of all the provocations practised by the Dutch Nazi Party (NSB)[10] under the leadership of Anton Mussert, and particularly of its storm troopers section WA ("Weer Afdeling"). These tried to force hotel owners in the capital to put up notices forbidding Jews admittance, and tried to stop Jews by force from using the tramways in the city; uniformed members of the WA also took to violence against Jews in a number of the restaurants in Amsterdam – behaviour which must make a particularly deep impression in Dutch society, where the Jews constituted quite a considerable section of the community, in which they were integrated to a great extent. The first results were disturbances which spread to the whole town. There were more violent developments, when young Jews from the Jewish quarter of the city formed action groups for defence ("Knokploegen"), who made contact with the left-wing groups in the neighbouring slums, and when, on 11 February, direct fighting broke out between members of the WA who, contrary to the wishes of the Germans, had forced their way into the Jewish quarter and the Jewish action groups, a fight which ended in the WA men receiving such a beating that one of them died from his injuries. The atmosphere in the town was tense already, and the affair led on 15 February to mass demonstrations. Worse was to come, however, when the German police intervened with a raid on the Jewish quarter, during which acid bombs were thrown by the Jews, and a single shot was fired against the German police, after which the Germans proceeded to arrest 425 young Jews.

In this situation where the indignation in the city had reached a climax, agitators and organisers intervened energetically.[11] On 17 and 18 February they had succeeded in forcing a strike through in the shipyards of Amsterdam, to obstruct German plans to deport workers to Germany, and when the news of the German arrests spread through the town, the strike broke out in earnest. Duplicated leaflets called for a general strike, and for demands for higher wages, and appealed to Christian families for help for the oppressed Jews, and on 25 February the strike took on a really extensive character. The trams stopped running, civil servants in the local administration stopped work, and factory after factory shut, as workers, office staff and businessmen went out in support of the strike. Everywhere there were demonstrations and clashes in the wake of the strike. Trams which tried to drive out were stopped by demonstrators, and the life of the city came to a standstill. The strike was proclaimed as a twenty-four-hour protest strike, but in the conditions of occupation it was just as difficult a process to end a strike as it was to start one, and the strike continued the following day, and also began to spread to other Dutch towns.

The strike, the disturbances and the demonstrations took the German authorities by surprise, but when they realised the seriousness of the matter, they resorted to drastic action. The country was immediately placed under the authority of the Commanding General, and he at once proclaimed martial law, under which 1000 strikers were arrested and deported. In the face of the massive use of force, and the threat of further reprisals, the wave of strikes had to ebb away. The German measures also included a fine on the city of Amsterdam of fifteen million guilders, as well as corresponding collective fines to the towns of Hilversum and Zaandam. The civil authorities in Amsterdam were temporarily deprived of their authority. The fact that the strike made an impression in Berlin became apparent when an appeal was broadcast over the Berlin radio to the Dutch people. The appeal was not without concessions. It declared that Germany was "deeply shocked", and complained at the "provocative attitude and increasing resistance" of the population, and it pointed out that if the German population had dared behave in such a way during the Occupation of the Ruhr, the French reaction would have been one of rigorous counter-measures. The tone of the appeal was defensive, offended and apologetic, and revealed deep uncertainty at the first serious outbreak of an occupied people's unforeseen reactions.

The short, but sharp strike naturally had no decisive material importance, but it was a reminder to the German authorities that their hold over the country was based upon their military presence alone, that the Nazi propaganda was a complete fiasco, and, especially, the strike showed the deep gulf which yawned between the population and Mussert's little Nazi Party, which proved itself to be completely dependent upon the German military power. After the strike, if it had not been so before, it was obvious that this party was quite unsuited to play any important rôle in the German Occupation policy in the country. It was especially against this party's conduct that the strike had been aimed, and the Germans were taught the lesson that for the future, here as elsewhere, they could only count upon their own strength.

The next major strike in Holland was directed, to a greater degree than the first, against the Occupying Power itself. It came in April-May 1943. By then, the foreign political situation had altered completely. The Soviet Union and the U.S.A. had entered the war, and the Axis Powers had suffered their first decisive defeats on the East Front, in the Mediterranean, in the Atlantic and in the air over German towns. All this created an optimistic atmosphere, and an atmosphere of defiance, which now came to a nation-wide outbreak in the form of a far-reaching wave of strikes.[12] A strike broke out this time in the industrial town of Hengelo, caused by a German military decree of 29 April 1943 that Dutch ex-soldiers should report with a view to internment in Germany. The Germans claimed that many of them had shown a hostile attitude, and had therefore failed the trust which had been shown them in May 1940. In reality, Germany was needing foreign workers. The immediate reply was a spontaneous strike, without factories making any attempt to stem the strike wave, and when the news was telephoned to other parts of the country, the strike was followed up, as instructions got through, for example in the mining district of Limburg and in the Philips works in Eindhoven, but also in many other places.

During the days that followed, the wave of strikes spread, especially in the frontier provinces of the country, and at its climax it included several hundred thousand men. Strangely enough, the strike also reached the country districts, where the farming community, which had no strike tradition whatever, stopped deliveries of milk, dairy products and other articles of food. The strike, as in 1941, was underpinned by mass demonstrations, and in one district by open revolt. On 30 April the exile Government appealed to all involved to refrain from obeying the German orders, evade registration and go underground.

This time, also, the strike took the German authorities by surprise. Also this time, they had to resort to violent reprisals to re-establish calm in the country, a course which, as always, involved the dilemma that even if the reprisals had the effect intended for the moment, on the longer term, they only increased bitterness against the Occupying Power. All over the country, summary police courts pronounced and executed summary sentences of death, for example at the Philips factories, which were important for German production, but in spite of the rapid and ruthless German intervention, calm was not re-established – superficially

– until after about ten days. This time the strike had been directed against the Occupying Power, and it was a serious reminder to the German military authorities that the Dutch people, in certain situations, such as in the event of invasion, would be an incalculable factor, whose probably hostile reactions were to be taken into account. There could be no question of secure, unchallenged possession and exploitation of the country, conquered by force of arms, and it was impossible to foresee where, when and how similar revolts could manifest themselves. A complete show-down with all agitators was impossible, and in a talk on the B.B.C. on 19 May, the Dutch Prime Minister Gerbrandy sounded this theme, giving a warning against revolt at too early a stage – revolt which could be suppressed – whilst on the other hand, he encouraged widespread passive resistance, against which it would be impossible for the German authorities to defend themselves – a resistance of this kind being based upon a population of about nine million people.

Both in 1941, when the Axis Powers stood victorious, and in 1943, when they were forced on to the defensive, the Dutch strikes, among others, illustrated that fermentation was going on behind the victors' lines, and no one could judge with certainty how strong the fermentation was, or what its consequences could prove to be. Both strikes were pin-pricks, and nothing more than pin-pricks, but their psychological and political effect reached a great deal farther than their material importance.

In 1944 it would prove that the German military power, in the event of actual fighting on Dutch soil, had to face the fact that the population would be prepared, in such a situation, to put every available obstacle in the way of the German Army. When in 1944, the Allied Armies, after the invasion in Normandy and the break-through in the German lines in France, reached South Holland in September, and attempted a blitz panser movement combined with the dropping of parachute troops at the Rhine bridges in Nijmegen and Arnhem[13] – an operation which, had it succeeded, might have led to a quick conclusion to the war – the Dutch Exile Government broadcast an appeal on the evening of 17 September for the Dutch railway personnel to go on strike immediately, to support the British parachute troops who had been dropped that day at the Arnhem bridge-head.[14] The plan for an all-inclusive railway strike, synchronized with the Allied troops' operations, had been discussed since the strikes in 1943, in which scattered groups of railway personnel had also taken part. The plan had been suggested by the central Dutch Resistance Council ("Raad van Verzet") and then discussed between groups of the Dutch Resistance Movement, the Exile Government in London and the Allied Staffs, as well as with the top leaders of the Dutch Railways in Utrecht. During the Occupation, these leaders had maintained correct relations with the Occupying Power, although they had resisted Nazi infiltration into the service. Now, in connexion with a possible final battle, they were not unwilling to consider releasing a centrally directed strike, which could have tactical importance, as had been the case in France, during the invasion battles that year. The plan had thus received support in principle from all sides, on the condition that the order came at the right time, and that it was given by the leader of the Dutch Exile Government, Gerbrandy. During the spring 1944, the plan was worked out in detail, as regards both a centrally directed release of the strike, and also the financial arrangements for what might be a long strike, in consideration of the strikers.

The carefully prepared plan did not work out altogether as intended, however. The failure took place in London, where both on this occasion and on various others, it proved difficult to achieve sufficient co-ordination between the Allied Staffs' decision and the Resistance Movement's adjustment to these decisions. This was also the case here. At the critical moment, when operational and weather conditions suddenly made possible the Allied decision to get possession of the bridges over the Upper and Lower Rhine,[15] it proved difficult to contact Gerbrandy, and inform him. For that reason, the strike did not start before the parachute troops landed, as had been planned, but several hours after the attack had been launched. The first parachute troops had landed near Arnhem at about midday, and it was not until the evening that Gerbrandy made his appeal to the Dutch railway personnel, to carry out a total stoppage of all railway traffic, and a similar appeal to the population to support the strike, and give the railwaymen all possible help. The delay in the start signal for the strike was bound to reduce its effectiveness and tactical importance, and what was perhaps more serious, the word to strike could not reach the personnel through the central channels by which it was intended to formulate a joint strike order. There was thus no possibility for creating the situation, "one for all and all for one", which contained both solidarity and pressure.

Nevertheless, the strike became a reality, as, in spite of the ban on listening to London, and the forced surrender of all radiosets,[16] Gerbrandy's words did come through and were known, and personnel, regardless of the increased danger caused by the absence of common instructions, acted on their own initiative in a large part of the country.

Where the higher echelons of the service did not give the signal, the lower echelons acted on their own, and started the strike. It proved most effective in the central and western parts of the country, and in the provinces of Friesland and Overijsel. It was less effective in the north-eastern provinces, and in the south, where the fighting actually took place. Nevertheless, the strike was sufficiently extensive for railway traffic practically to come to a halt, and at least it could only be kept going by the hasty use of German personnel.

The strike was started on the expectation that the war, or at least the occupation of Holland would be over in a short time, a few weeks at the most, perhaps only a few days. This was not what took place, as we know. The British attempt to capture and hold the bridgeheads north of the Lower Rhine failed, and the Allied advance against Germany from the west ground to a halt for the winter 1944–45. It should be mentioned that the British officer in command of the Arnhem operation, Major-General R. E. Urquhart, in his retrospective conclusions[17] on the course of the battle, puts forward as a contributory cause of reverse – among many – the fact that the British had not based themselves sufficiently on the Dutch Resistance Movement while the battle was in progress. But the Arnhem defeat was a fact, and the war, and with it the occupation of Holland, continued for many more months.

The strike therefore became long and obstinate. The Dutch Government renewed its appeal to continue the strike in October 1944, and again in January 1945; and the Dutch Resistance Movement maintained the demand for the continuation of the strike to the bitter end – a demand which the Allies supported as regards the northern and eastern provinces, which had strategic importance for the Allied concentrations of troops. In one sense, the strike lost its character as a strike, and became more of a resistance action than was originally intended. A contributing factor was that the question of the continuation of the strike or its conclusion contained numerous political, economic and practical problems. The railwaymen had gone underground, and could only report for duty again at the risk of their lives, so that there was something final about this action. Added to this, there was a complex of problems connected with their continued subsistence, when they were no longer in the railway service. A further problem was that the traffic stop was a two-edged sword, which prevented the delivery of elementary necessities of life from the northern and eastern provinces to the central and western provinces, which were already hard hit by that winter of starvation.[18] The result was greatly reduced traffic, maintained partly by the Germans being forced to use reliable German personnel, amounting to about 5000 men, to look after the most essential traffic, where German interests were naturally given first priority. On the other hand, Germany had to produce this personnel at a time when trained railway personnel were in scarce supply. The strike therefore hit both the Occupying Power and the occupied area.

The importance of the strike is a controversial question. The danger of over-estimation is probably more likely than that of under-estimation. But to the extent that an estimate proves to be chiefly negative, it must be emphasized that the basis for assessment would without doubt have been quite different, had the British advance succeeded. When this did not occur, the strike lost its tactical importance, and became the two-edged sword we have considered. The situation underlined the importance of co-ordination between Allied operations and the use of the strike weapon in the event that this was intended to be used for tactical purposes.

The German reprisals were considerably less severe than one might have feared. A few railway men were arrested and executed, or sent to concentration camps, but no systematic search or pursuit of the striking personnel was launched by the German security authorities, who already had their hands full with more pressing problems, and who were less zealous than they had been, in the shadow of the German collapse. They may also have reasoned that the strike also hit the Resistance Movement's communications, and the supplies for the whole Dutch population. Here the problem of this strike is lifted from the particular to the general: no Resistance Movement could achieve full effectiveness without a certain amount of normality in the surrounding community, and what, here and there, could seem to be improper and culpable collaboration with the Occupying Power could now and then cover behaviour which, also from the point of viev of the Resistance, must be considered desirable or even necessary. The recognition of this does not make the study of the Resistance Movements any less complicated than it is already.

ITALY. Strikes in an occupied area were a serious problem, but they were perhaps even more serious when they occurred inside an Axis Power's own territory, as happened in Italy, from March 1943, when strikes had been abolished for twenty years as instruments in the economic and political struggle. Here too, the wider political background was decisive and obvious. From the moment of her entry into the war in 1940, Italy had gone from defeat to defeat, and the war, which had been unpopular from the start, was a drain both on the material plane and as regards the general feeling among the Italian population. In the spring 1943, the atmosphere was one of unalleviated gloom.

After the capture of Tripoli, and the landings in North West Africa, the Allies were engaged in mopping up the Axis Powers' last pockets of resistance in Tunisia. The blockade, which made Italy completely dependent upon the meagre deliveries from Germany, hit Italy even harder than Germany. Bombing attacks on Italian towns, particularly the industrial towns in the north, were constantly increasing in numbers and strength, and the threat of invasion hung over the Italian peninsula. War fatigue and depression in the Italian population created the best possible conditions for a revival of the old, but not forgotten, political methods of struggle. Now the strike came to Italy, as a forewarning of the energetic and diversified Resistance Movement which was soon to rise, also here.

Opposition to Mussolini's Fascist Regime had apparently been extinct for many years. What opposition had survived was in all important respects an "exile opposition",[19] and to the extent that oppositional ideas were kept alive in cells and circles in the country itself, these had few possibilities to manifest themselves. Any tendency towards republican or Communist agitation was smothered at birth, in arrests and executions. This applied to the creation of a Republican Movement, led by Carlo Roselli[20] and it applied to Communist agitation led and inspired by Palmiro Togliatti. During the Spanish Civil War, an Italian Brigade of volunteers was raised and sent into battle on the side of the Spanish Government, and slogans appeared on the walls of Italian towns, such as "Today Spain, tomorrow Italy". But in 1940, opposition was still weak and revolt against the regime was still in embryo. Now, the war with its sacrifices of human life and the growing want among the people, changed this apparent apathy on the home front. There were demonstrations, when troop trains were to leave for the Eastern Front, and there were sporadic strikes, particularly in the industrial towns in North Italy, where the workers could point to the fact that food prices had nearly doubled, without wages keeping pace with them. Intensive Allied bombing of the North Italian towns contributed to the growing dissatisfaction and defeatism.[21] The bureaucracy of the Fascist Party was well aware of the danger, but waited fatalistically – a situation which can also be explained by the feeling of discouragement, impotence and scepticism towards the country's leaders which had crept into the party machine itself. A number of purges and replacements among the party leaders did not help, and it helped just as little, that severe punishment was introduced – even the death penalty or life imprisonment – for disobedience to the laws on rationing, failure to deliver, etc. Both internally and externally the hopeless conditions had to be admitted, with public attacks upon the "unwilling", the "defeatists" and the "doubters".[22] Mussolini himself had no illusions. After an unsuccessful propaganda tour in May 1942 of a number of provinces, where he had only met evasiveness, gloom and signs of wide-spread corruption, he declared uncompromisingly, at a meeting with the top leaders of the party:[23] "I have no longer any doubt in regard to the lack of discipline, sabotage and passive resistance all along the line. The Régime is exhausting itself, wearing itself out, and literally consuming scores of comrades in the Party organisation and the Ministries, and we are almost back where we were". Mussolini was particularly disappointed that the Party Youth did not fulfil the expectations of twenty years of Fascist education, and that a new generation had not grown up which could zealously bear the Fascist ideas onwards. In a speech to the Party Secretaries in Umbria and Tuscany he struck this theme:[24] "The youth of Italy has been softened from too many favours from Fascism, and in the main the intellectuals have contributed by their abstentation from the régime". Mussolini had no illusions. And with good reason.

On 5 March, there came a sudden and violent explosion. At 10 o'clock in the morning the workers at one of the Fiat factories in Turin stopped all work, and during the day the strike spread to other big factories in the city. The following day the strike spread to other towns in the Piedmont region and soon included 100,000 strikers.[25] When the authorities hesitated to intervene, either administratively with better wages, or by sending in the police or the Fascist militia, the strikes continued, and spread on 24 March to Lombardy, where over 130,000 workers in Milan came out in support of the strike. The strikes hit key industries in Italy's war production, and were therefore not only an Italian but also a German concern.

The strike was carefully planned, and while it lasted, skillfully organised. Behind both the start of the strike and its course stood, first, the Communist groups. The basis of the strike was apparently the demand for higher wages and better rations, but behind this "official" demand was the much more far-reaching hidden political intention, to force Italy out of a hopeless war, and to hit the actual Fascist Regime, which in the eyes of the population was responsible for the war.

For this regime, the eruption in North Italy came by no means as a bolt from the blue. Both the local authorities and the leaders in Rome were perfectly well aware of the fermentation in the population, and realised that this fermentation had even penetrated the Fascist Party itself, where distrust of Mussolini's personal dictatorship over both State and Party was increasing ominously, in spite of repeated purges and changes among the leaders. The local police had been able to register an increasing circulation of illegal newspapers during the months before the strike, including the publication of the Communist paper, "Unita", ever since June 1942; and in addition, it had recorded the creation of a National Action Front, including not only Communists, but also a number of other anti-Fascist parties and groups – Socialists as well as Liberals. This was the People's Front from the 1930's, which elsewhere in Europe was being resuscitated with the Communists taking the initiative, and on 27 December 1942 this National Front stepped forward with a call from "Unita", addressed to the population as a whole, to the armed forces and, characteristically enough, also to "honest Fascists". The call appealed both for Italy to abandon the war, and for the Fascist dictatorship to be abolished. With an appeal on these lines, the Communists could count on a strong response, both from the population and within the Army, and this was clearly demonstrated by the strikes in March 1943, and the lack of fighting spirit during the Sicilian campaign. As far as the strikes were concerned, these included thousands of participants outside the quite small organised Communist cells.

The reactions of the Regime were noticeably weak. Effective preventive measures were not carried out, either by the local authorities or by the State, and during the strike these had to register, with bitterness, that workers from the Fascist organisations also took part in them. The punishments which followed were also moderate. They were confined to arrests, which in Milan amounted to about 300 men, and in Turin to about 150, of whom quite a number were released again, whilst others were sent to the front in Sicily. The local Chiefs of Police realised with anxiety that the Communist Party was now established in the industrial milieu of Northern Italy, and probably also in the Army, but reports of this state of affairs were marked more by resigned acceptance than by the will summarily to intervene. Under the pressure of the war and the defeats, the Regime was marked, both at the top and in the lower echelons, by vacillation and confusion approaching dissolution. In Germany – and for Hitler – the strikes, and the tame reaction of the Italian Government aroused bitterness and deep distrust of the government's ability and will to keep developments under proper control. In Hitler's eyes, the actions were "unthinkable", and it was unforgivable that "no one dare to intervene", and Hitler also lectured on his well-known recipe for "radical measures". "If one shows the slightest weakness in such a matter, one is finished. That is what I have said the whole time."

From the point of view of his philosophy of power, Hitler was right. Developments would demonstrate it. He was so much the more right in that the March strikes were to contribute not only to accelerating the formation of anti-Fascist groups in the Northern region, but also to sowing doubt as to reliability within the Fascist ranks. The first countermeasure on the higher levels was the choice of the Chief of Police for the whole country, Carmine Senise, as scapegoat. He was dismissed in the middle of April, under pressure from Germany.[26] At the same time, Mussolini issued more rigorous directives to the Police. From now on, strikers would be fired upon – a measure which must presumably be considered logical for a dictatorship in a state of emergency.

The strike weapon would be used again in Northern Italy, however. This occurred next in November 1943, and again in Turin. By then the political situation in Italy had altered fundamentally.[27] After a stormy meeting in the Fascist Great Council, at the end of July 1943, the Fascist Regime had collapsed. After a vote of "No confidence" in Mussolini, in the Great Council, King Victor Emanuel had seized the opportunity to appoint General Pietro Badoglio as chief of a new Italian government, which had sought and obtained an armistice with the Allies, after which the liberated Italian regions had joined the ranks of powers waging war on the Allied side. As a counter-measure, Hitler, after a dramatic rescue of Mussolini from the new Italian regime, had established him as the leader of a neo-fascist government, with seat in Salo in north-east Italy; and Italy was now in a state of bloody civil war, combined with German occupation.

In this deteriorating situation, where groups of partisans were establishing themselves in the Alpine regions of the north and north-west, and in the Appenines, and where assassinations of leading Fascists were the order of the day, civil resistance broke out again in Turin.[28] At the end of November 1943, over 50,000 workers in the Fiat factories went out on strike. Here again they were inspired by Communist underground cells, but with the support of non-Communist Labour groups; and here again, economic claims for higher wages and better rations were used as the lever for the real object: an end to the war, the occupation, and the Salo regime. Resistance against the neo-Fascist regime and all it stood for had thus spread from the partisan groups in the mountains to the urban population, and it proved that neither Mussolini's new regime nor the German Occupying Power had anything approaching sufficient forces available to send in against this or future disturbances in the important industrial areas. The consequence had to be a further drain upon the German resources in men and material, already strained, either by German forces intervening directly or by Mussolini's reorganised police and militia being reinforced at the cost of German manpower. Added to the problems of material and men, there were political and psychological problems. The strikes, as well as a long list of symptoms of a still more disquieting character, demonstrated that the new Fascist regime had no solid foundation in the population, but on the contrary, that the population was directly hostile to it. At the end of November, simultaneously with the Turin strike, twenty-eight leading Fascists were assassinated outside the actual partisan regions. Mussolini took the opportunity to beg Berlin for weapons, and for the release of Italian prisoners of war interned in Germany, so that the Fascist militia could be reinforced. The answer was in the negative, however. The Germans no longer had any illusions as to Mussolini's ability to control developments in northern Italy. The Germans would have to rely on their own efforts, and in reality they had no need of Mussolini and his puppet government, except as an instrument to justify the fact that Italy was now under German occupation.

The picture was not altered when Mussolini, under the pressure of the German opinion that private interests were not valid during a total war, resorted to nationalizing all Italian industry,[29] a measure which in different circumstances might perhaps have aroused support from the factory workers. There was no support for the measure, however, when the nationalization was carried out in the name of the Salo government. On 1 March a new strike broke out in the Fiat factories, a strike which spread to Milan, Genoa and other industrial cities, this time accompanied by a wave of sabotage, partly of the transport system. This time, both the extent of the strikes and their duration were greater than before. It is calculated that a total of 200,000 workers went out on strike. The link-up of the strikes with sabotage of the transport network – so that workers quite simply could not get to their work and were covered by that excuse – was the proof that now, co-ordination was being achieved between the various forms of Resistance organs and actions. This co-ordinated action was actually planned by the "Comitato di Liberazione Nazionale", which included the whole of German-occupied Italy, and worked through local action committees which in the industrial areas were largely dominated by Communist influence. If the strikes were more severe on this occasion, however, the measures taken against them were no less so. These measures were in fact so severe that for a time they must appear prohibitive, even for those who agitated most for the use of the strike weapon. The Germans resorted to mass deportations of striking workers to Germany, and the action committee, in the face of these measures, found itself forced to call off the strikes, which were therefore only a qualified success.

Nevertheless, from the Resistance point of view the strikes were valuable. They showed the workers' opposition, also to the project for nationalization as a product of the neo-Fascist regime; it revealed the connexion between the illegal organs; and it did not pass unnoticed that during the strikes, there had been an evident, tacit understanding between the strikers and the factory leaders and owners.

In the following months, this tendency towards mutual understanding became more and more noticeable, particularly because of German plans for moving the factory machine park away from the disturbed industrial areas, and if possible also away from the areas threatened by bombing. Here both parties had common interests, and when the German plans became known and removal began, new strikes broke out, in June 1944,[30] still with the Fiat factories as the starting point, and again with the demands for material improvement as an excuse, but now with the additional demand that the machine park should not be removed.

If the machine park was removed, the workers' livelihood would also disappear, and the logical consequence must be their forced transfer. In the face of this new action, and considering the whole atmosphere in the region, both the Fascist and the German administration recoiled from intervening too severely. On the contrary, recourse was now made to concessions, as regards both wages and assurances that the machine park would remain where it was. The Resistance in the whole of Northern Italy had by now taken on a far more militant form than previously, and first priority was given to combatting the partisan movement. On this background, the strikers had a stronger position than before. If it came to massive reprisals, the road to the Partisan Movement was not long, and there was a stronger motivation for taking this road. Both the strikers and the authorities had experience of this kind, and hesitated. Another reason for the Occupying Power's relative moderation was the growing recognition of the fact that defeat in the war was not far off, and with it, an increasing unwillingness to take the responsibility for further drastic reprisals. The population which was baited today would be the victors of tomorrow. Unfounded ideas had emerged that winter even in the top SS Command, as to the possibilities for coming to some agreement with the Allies,[31] and thus possibly salvaging some fragments from the approaching shipwreck.

As the Resistance struggle developed in Northern Italy during that long winter, the strike ceased to be its chief weapon, but in April 1945, the struggle culminated in a combination of partisan attacks, strikes in factories and in the transport sector, and open revolt, which, together with the Allies' offensive in the Po Valley led to the liberation of Northern Italy. In this final phase, all the factors were important, and it is hardly possible nor fruitful to seek to specify the importance of each individual factor. Here, however, the strike received a tactical role which it had not had previously.

FRANCE. Much the same can be said of developments in France, where paralysing strikes, in connexion with an open revolt in Paris in July 1944, were important for the Allies in working out their strategic plans.

It must almost be a foregone conclusion that the strike would become a weapon in the French Resistance struggle. The French working classes were well organised, and the right to strike – also with political intention – was deeply rooted in the tradition and history of the country. On the other hand, the working classes in France were in an extremely difficult position, as was the whole population. First, they must recover from the "débacle" of 1940, and with it the dissolution which lay over the country, with several hundred thousand refugees, the collapse of production and transport, confusion in administration, 1.8 million prisoners of war in the hands of the Germans, and the many craters and bloodstains from the German bombardments. After the military collapse followed the psychological collapse, of which the repercussions stretched far into the future. Large sections of the population, understandably enough, felt great bitterness against their political leaders, against the Army Command, and to a high degree against Great Britain, who in the eyes of many Frenchmen had not only failed them with regard to immediate military support, but who after the French armistice had also attacked the French Fleet at Mers-el-Kebir. The bitterness was also directed against the Communists, who up to 22 June 1941 had been against the war, and who under the impression of the German-Soviet pact encouraged Franco-German fraternisation in their newspaper, "L'Humanité". The expressions used in this and other Communist papers were clear enough:[32] "Whilst English capitalistic henchmen wish to orientate the

French people in the direction of chauvinism, we Communists wish to orientate them towards brotherhood with the German people, whom we do not confuse with their present rulers," or "the French people do not want war, either for Hitler's or for Churchill's blue eyes." While the Communists turned against the Vichy regime and its domestic policy, they had a passive attitude to the war, and until June 1941 were in temporary isolation. In the bitter, apathetic atmosphere which dominated France long after the collapse, large sections of the French population pinned their hopes to Marshal Pétain and the Vichy Government. These new leaders claimed to stand for France's rebirth, introducing corporative State forms in its name, abolishing the great Trades Unions in October 1940,[33] and taking all control of economic life into their own hands. But Vichy was completely bound by engagements under the German Occupying Power, and to a great extent at the mercy of its pressure.

Added to all this, economic difficulties now arose, created by the British blockade and the German plundering of the country, which reduced the legal rations to a point near or under starvation level, and which created a black market which, with its exhorbitant prices, was a closed country to those who had nothing but a weekly wage to live on – if a weekly wage was obtainable at all. Unemployment lay, as yet another fact of life, on the top of desperation and fatigue, and its burden was heaviest in the urban and the industrial areas. Other burdens included direct German control of a great deal of French economic life, particularly the metal industry, 85 % of which was placed under German control; the total annexation of Alsace-Lorraine; and the control of the important mining districts in the departments of the Nord and the Pas de Calais by the Ministry of Industry and Labour, which was itself controlled by the German military administration in Belgium/North France. For the first year of occupation, there was thus little background for resistance in general, and strikes in particular. The background would be created gradually, as the fortunes of war changed, and as the German regime of terror brought a desperation which finally overshadowed even the relentless problems of daily life. When this occurred, and when it was combined with the illegal re-establishment of the trades unions, and particularly when the Communists began their agitation for resistance, including agitation for disturbances in the factories, the picture changed radically. The Communist standpoint was then clear. It was a question of creating a popular front, including the whole French population without regard to age, party, occupation or religion.[34] Even earlier opponents, even erring fellow countrymen were welcome in the fight, in the name of the Father-land: "As our forefathers united under the call to arms: 'The Fatherland is in danger,' so let us unite, young Gaullists, young Communists, young Catholics," or an even clearer call among many: "Fight to unite the French masses, the workers, the peasants, the tradesmen and artists, the intel-lectuals, the housewives, the old, the veterans and victims of two wars, the young," or the quite common: "All patriots without exception." In the Communist vision of the creation of a "Front National", no one was forgotten, and no one excluded: "The Fatherland opens its arms to all its children, even to those who yesterday were led astray . . . The Com-munists stretch a brother's hand to all Frenchmen who in an hour of decision rediscover the way to the Fatherland."

Recruitment was prepared, and the aims were clear: immediate com-bat on all fronts, also on the strike front,[35] small strikes as well as the final great strike, the General Strike, to be started at the decisive mo-ment. "Every effort, every manifestation, every strike is a step on the way to the practical preparation of the national rising. As we raise the degree of the French people's will to fight, the fight for improved living standards show everyone that better wages, improved supplies, all this, in the final analysis, will have as its first foe the invading enemy and his toadies." The strikes, the small as well as the great, were therefore proclaimed as weapons against the enemy: "The workers in the indus-trial centres should develop the strike movement until the moment where the General Strike can become a reality . . . It is not necessary to wait . . . If the conditions for a General Strike are not present, this does not mean that they will be realisable during the waiting period." Here too, we meet agitation for struggle for daily needs, in order to reach a political objective, clearly expressed in slogans such as "to fight to de-fend ones bread is to fight against Hitler, who is starving us".

The Communists were not alone on the field, when it was a question of agitating for the use of the strike weapon. The possibility was obvious to others. Nevertheless, it was probably the German interference in the French Labour market more than the agitation which produced the most serious reactions.

Ever since 1940, the Germans had tried to entice French labour to Germany.[36] They held out promises of permanent employment, good wages and good working conditions, and they could appeal to a labour market suffering from considerable unemployment. Nevertheless, it was only to a very limited extent that French workers applied at the German recruiting offices. Up to 1942 the problem was not acutely pressing for the German State Administration, but as the enormous losses of men on the Eastern front made themselves felt, and Germany was forced to drain the factories of manpower which could be mobilised, the problem became urgent, and heavy German pressure was brought to bear. In March 1942, the Reich Commissar Fritz Sauckel was given full powers in the use of labour[37] within the framework of the four-year plan, and together with the Chief of the German Labour Front, Robert Ley, he was appointed leader of the Central Inspectorate for Foreign Workers. The neutral titles are euphemisms for the reality, which was shortly to be expanded by force: the organisation of millions of foreigners as slave labour.

It was not an unqualified success. Vis-à-vis Hitler Sauckel had undertaken to procure millions of foreign workers from the occupied territories, and even though he succeeded to some extent as to numbers, Sauckel's policy was to prove itself a two-edged sword. The German Armaments Minister, Albert Speer, who was more dependent than anyone else upon Sauckel's results, gives the following assessment of the final consequences:[38] "Sauckel's promises . . . were not fulfilled. Hitler's expectations of being able, without difficulty, to fetch the workers needed in Germany from a population of 250 million inhabitants, stranded just as much upon the German executive authorities' weakness in the occupied areas as upon the inclination of the workers in question rather to flee into the forests to the partisans, than to let themselves be deported to Germany. Our industrial organisation informed me, in addition, that the enemy spy and sabotage organisations found it easy to reach their objectives, when their agents sneaked into Sauckel's columns . . ."

In June 1942, Sauckel came to Paris. His demand to the French Government under the leadership of Pierre Laval[39] was precise, unequivocal and had the character of an ultimatum: France must immediately place 250,000 workers, of whom 150,000 must be metal workers, at Germany's disposal. If the demand was not met without delay, the German masters would resort to forced conscription and deportation. In this situation, and after a stormy meeting with Sauckel, in which the latter modified the immediate numbers, Laval gave in and, what was more, believed that he had found the Columbus' egg, which could save the situation. He proposed "la Relève", a bargain by which for every three workers who would undertake work voluntarily in Germany, the Germans should release one prisoner of war. In a great radio speech on 22 June he described this vision in connexion with a strong appeal to French workers to understand Germany's situation, and to show their solidarity with Germany as the country which, with the sacrifice of the blood of her sons, was fighting Bolschevism, and thereby saving Europe. It was in this speech that Laval challenged his countrymen with one of his most revealing remarks – one of the most damaging to his position among the French people:[40] "I desire Germany's victory, because without it, Bolshevism will gain a footing everywhere." The speech was followed up on 8 July by Pétain, with another radio appeal to French workers to mitigate the lot of French prisoners of war by their efforts.

The appeal could have an effect on the background of increasing unemployment in French industry, suffering as it did from shortages in raw materials. On 16 June the Vichy Governmant decided to shut 1300 factories in the unoccupied zone, claiming lack of raw materials, coal, energy, and irrational production as their reasons. The men now out of work were forced to look for employment in agriculture or by going to Germany. Neither Laval's nor Pétain's appeals, nor the German agitation had the effect which the Germans had made a condition, however. At the beginning of July, twenty-seven recruiting offices in all could report c. one thousand volunteers, and the situation did not improve greatly, so that on 20 October Laval had to go to the microphone again.[41] Now the background was not only that French workers were boycotting the arrangement, but also that direct disturbances such as strikes were reported. On 2 October, the workers at the Renault factories in Paris stopped work for three hours, and only resumed after a German threat to shoot fifty hostages. Here there was a question of the beginning of a strike in the occupied zone, where strikes could be nipped in the bud. It was another matter in the unoccupied zone. On 13 October, a strike broke out in the Gnome-Rhône works in Lyon. Only 15, out of a total of 700 workers selected, had reported for departure to Germany, and when the remaining 685 were dismissed, all 3000 men at the works came out on strike. After this, the strike spread rapidly. In spite of the French Mobile Guard being sent in, and in spite of rumours of the Gestapo's arrival in the town, the wave of strikes spread further to the towns of St. Etienne, Grenoble, Annecy and Chamberry, and strikers from the Trades Unions, which were now working illegally, agreed upon the wording of a protest to the Government, threatening a General Strike on 17 October, not only in the unoccupied, but also in the occupied zone. The explosive development of the strike bore witness to the desperation of the workers, and the form of the address indicated that there was organised contact, reaching in over the unoccupied to the occupied, and most threatened area. German threats to set up military tribunals, aimed at the strike leaders, did not make the workers yield, and the Germans brought pressure to bear upon the Vichy Government, to get it to negotiate that the strikes be called off, so that a General Strike could be avoided, and also to obtain an increase of labour for Germany. The Vichy Government gave in to all this, and after a government meeting under Pétain's chairmanship on 16 October, promised that only volunteer workers would be sent to work in Germany – a promise which, however, could only be valid if the number of volunteers reached the minimum figure of 150,000 men, to which Sauckel had reconciled himself for the time being, in the negotiations with Laval. This was the background for a renewed, pathetic appeal from Laval on 20 October. This followed precisely the same lines at that of June, and contributed further to widening the gulf between himself and the population in general – the working classes in particular. The strike became particularly remarkable in that at its conclusion, the Vichy Government resigned itself to negotiating with representatives of the French Trades Unions, which although they had been formally abolished, were thus accepted as existing. The episode contributed to strengthening the workers' self-confidence, and to weakening the prestige of the Vichy Government appreciably.

Both on the German and on the French side, the threat of a General Strike had to be taken seriously. Only a few weeks before, a General Strike had become a reality in neighbouring Luxembourg.[42] On 30 August, the Chief of the German Administration in the Grand Duchy, the Gauleiter Simon, officially announced the annexation of Luxembourg in to the German Reich, and at the same time the details of rules and timing for conscription of the male citizens of Luxembourg to military service or forced labour in Germany. Violent attacks upon the Grand Duchy's dynasty, and upon the population's unwilling attitude had accompanied this announcement. The immediate response was a country-wide General Strike, which broke out in the mining districts of the Esch region, but then spread to the whole country and the whole population, high and low. Before the General Strike, there had been a period of passive resistance against the German Occupation, during which the iron and steel production in the country had dropped from about 2½ million tons in 1939 to about ¾ million tons in 1941. The General Strike in this little country, with only 300,000 inhabitants, was the first mass revolt of a whole population which the German Occupying Power met in the occupied territories, and must serve as a warning symptom of the climate surrounding the victors, even though Germany naturally had little difficulty in quelling the revolt. This was done by the introduction of martial law, the shooting of hostages, deportations, and mass transfer of the population. The measures were followed by a threatening radio speech by the Gauleiter Simon, in which he produced the grotesque remark, that Luxembourg constituted a constant, if minor danger to the life of the German Reich. The remark did not escape the attention of the exile Government, and the B.B.C. "What an admission!" said the Luxembourg Foreign Minister, Joseph Bech, in a radio speech to his people, and to the world. "The German colossus trembles under the threat from Luxembourg! Eighty million members of the master race are afraid of a handful of Luxembourgeois!" It was obviously revealing that there was a question of a colossal over-reaction from the German side, both in the treatment of Luxembourg and also in dealing with the General Strike. In the psychological war, the Occupying Power came off worst, in the dress rehearsal for the coming mass risings, even if the material loss from the few days' stoppage of work could have little importance.

In the wider perspective, this General Strike was to serve as a reminder, but undeniably a reminder to both sides. For one party – the Occupying Power – the strike called for caution as to the incalculable consequences which could follow, where the violent use of force overstepped the threshold of desperation. For the other party – the strikeminded – the experience gave rise to consideration of the equally incalculable total of reprisals which the use of the strike weapon entailed. Both parties had reason to think again, and both parties played upon threats, with well-founded hesitation as to carrying out their threats. While both parties kept watch on each other, the threats themselves became a not unimportant factor behind their considerations.

The Franco-German question of manpower could not be solved in the long run by volunteers, and on 15 February 1943 the Vichy Government decided to introduce forced labour service for all those born in the years 1920–22. An announcement made it clear that out of these three classes a section of the manpower conscripted would be employed in Germany.[43] One of the reasons given was the "shocking insufficiency" of the results of "la Relève". But this time, there were no longer two zones in France. In November1942, the Allies had landed in French North-West Africa, and one of the consequences had been an immediate German and Italian occupation of the hitherto unoccupied zone. The French decree included the whole of France, therefore, and the decision came after severe German pressure. The pressure to come could be foreseen from a declaration of foreign policy, which had been published on 2 January from

Berlin:[44] "France finds herself at the cross-roads. France must choose between joining Europe without reservations, or it will disappear completely from the world arena." The concrete pressure came in the person of Sauckel, who met Laval in Paris in the middle of January, and brought an order from the Führer to procure a further 250,000 French workers before March, including 150,000 skilled specialists; and now there was no question of either voluntary recruitment, "la Relève", or political considerations of French interests or of the French Government. Faced with this pressure, Laval capitulated, and with him the French Government, and forced conscription of the classes mentioned was put into the hands of a new organisation, "Service Obligatoire du Travail", which had the duty of carrying out total mobilisation, first of the classes 1920–22, but without any guarantee whatever that the demand would stop there.[45] The decision was immediately sharply criticised by the Free French Movement under de Gaulle's leadership, and it was the movement's National Commissar for Home Affairs who expressed this condemnation over the B.B.C., and the appeal:[46] "This is no longer 'la Relève', it is the beginning of unmitigated deportation of an increasing section of our people. Do all you can to avoid or delay this." This was followed by a number of political instructions as to how the appeal could be followed: refusal to register; sabotage by the Administration of the decisions of the decree; appeals to go underground; and appeals to all, particularly the agricultural community, to hide those threatened with deportation; appeals to doctors to give certificates of unsuitability for hard labour, etc. The appeal was followed to a great extent. The simplest way out for the young men called up was to seek shelter in the Maquis, which now began to form in earnest in the mountainous districts of the country and other suitable regions. Other ways were to go underground; to obtain false papers including the doctors' certificates; to find convincing excuses; to get assistance from an Administration which was becoming more and more resistance-minded; to seek help from militant groups to destroy files and registers; and lastly, to ignore or sabotage the work which they were ordered to perform, in spite of all, at home or in Germany. It is clear that a certain work force was mobilised after the new decree, but it is just as clear that it was an unwilling, hostile and inefficient work force. The advantage to the Axis Powers cannot be measured simply by the numbers of those who were forced to work in the French factories, on the Atlantic ramparts or in Germany. Bad work, slow work, all forms of scamped work, carelessness, swindle or direct sabotage and espionage form part of the picture, without it being possible to assess their importance; and the by-product – increasing unrest in the whole French community and an ever more solid organisation of resistance – must also be taken into account.

In November 1943, another strike broke out, this time among the miners in the departments of the Nord and the Pas de Calais, and in Lyon.[47] Seventy thousand men in all stopped work, and with the usual but also justified demand for higher wages and better rations as official reasons, although this strike, also, clearly had political undercurrents. All the enterprises hit by the strikers were working for German interests, and the two-sided German reaction showed a certain caution. On the one hand, the Germans resorted to arrests and deportations, and on the other hand they gave in as regards wages, and tried to damp down the ominous unrest by conceding to the official demands of the strikers.

Up to the end of 1943, this and other scattered strikes had only had the character of extremely modest supplements to the main, violent Resistance activities, in the form of assasinations, sabotage and partisan actions. They had only constituted the prologue to the real objective of the strike ideology: to paralyse society completely, at the right moment, by a General Strike combined with wide-spread sabotage, with the partisan movement's final show-down with the Occupation, and with an allembracing popular rising. The right moment came, when the Allies landed in France, and the actions of the local Resistance forces could rely upon and co-ordinate their actions with the regular Armies' conduct of the war. Up to then, strikes had had secondary aims: to stress the latent dissatisfaction, to make material demands in order to improve everyday conditions, as much as possible[48] – and maintain an atmosphere of dissatisfaction; to create and demonstrate a broad front of solidarity, and thereby consolidate self-confidence and trust in the potential possibilities of the strikes; and to keep the authorities – the French as well as the German – in a state of general uncertainty. For the illegal trades union leaders, who were in touch with each other and who from May 1943 had entered into direct agreements with each other, these secondary aims became important. With every partial strike, opposing standpoints were intensified, and with every partial strike it was confirmed that the General Strike, when the moment arrived, could be a real possibility, which could be started by a common order. On the one side of the strike front, the partial strikes stimulated a growing belief in the usefulness of the actions, on the other side growing anxiety. Both camps were psychologically prepared and warned of what was to be expected.

The right moment came in June 1944, when the invasion began in

Normandy. From now on, the scattered attempts became a wave of strikes, which portended the final storm, when the strikes would also have strategic importance. Strikes could be registered in many places in France, on 29 and 30 June, and on 8, 14, 15, 16, 18, 21, 24, 25 and 26 July. These strikes, in addition to the other and far more serious actions of the French Resistance forces,[49] were the introduction to the decisive out-break of strikes in the Paris region in the middle of August, as the Allied breakthrough from the beach-heads in Normandy, and the rapid advance of the American Panser Divisions approached the Paris region.

Under the impression of this, and while about four hundred sabotage groups were in action in the Paris districts alone – districts of utmost importance to the German High Command in the West[50] – a strike broke out among the railway personnel on 12 August.[51] This strike quickly spread to the whole Parisian transport network, and paralysed all transport and production, and it was the prelude to total paralysis in the great city, and to open revolt. The Paris Police, too, went out on strike. They had maintained their normal functions during the Occupation, but had in secret formed three illegal organisations, with the object of organising revolt: "Honneur de la Police", "Police et Patrie", and "Front National de la Police", the first two being non-political, while the third was directed by the Communists.[52] On 15 August, the three police organisations sent out a joint call to carry out a strike throughout the whole Police Force, and on 16 August, about 98 % of the Paris Police found themselves on strike and therefore in open and, if necessary, armed conflict with the Occupying Power. In the wake of these events, armed Resistance forces entered the city, and in spite of their numerical inferiority and meagre supplies of weapons, and regardless of the scepticism and opposition of de Gaulle's representatives as to immediate revolt,[53] went into open action. The city was brought to a standstill, and revolt was a fact. Street fighting broke out, and the situation in Paris quickly became critical, both militarily and as regards supplies.

Developments in the French capital forced the Allied Supreme Command to alter their strategic plans. Their intention had been to by-pass Paris, and cut it off at the Seine bridges south and north of the city, in order to avoid destruction, but now these plans were changed. The Supreme Commander of the Allied Forces, General Dwight D. Eisenhower has summed up the situation with the following words:[54] "In this matter my hand was forced by the action of the Free French Forces inside Paris. Throughout France the Free French had been of inestimable value in the campaign. They were particularly active in Brittany, and on every portion of the front we secured help from them in a multitude of ways. Without their great assistance, the liberation of France and the defeat of the enemy in Western Europe would have consumed a much longer time and mean greater losses to ourselves. So when the Free French forces inside the city staged their uprising it was necessary to move rapidly to their support."

Eisenhower did move rapidly, and hard pressed by de Gaulle, but in any case under the pressure of events,[55] he sent the Second Free French Armoured Division, under the command of General Le Clerc, by forced marches against Paris, followed and supported by the 4th American Division. Two more American Divisions passed through the city over the Seine Bridges, which were still intact, and on to further fighting east of the Seine. Here, as in North Italy, the strike was thus an auxiliary factor in the overall strategy of the final struggle.

SCANDINAVIA. The strike could also have political consequences. This was the case in Denmark. Here it was a question of a so-called "peaceful occupation" ("occupatio pacifica"), that is to say, the occupation was carried out ostensibly in order to "protect" Danish neutrality, and without an actual state of war arising between Denmark and Germany. Some scattered fighting, and the Danish protest on 9 April 1940 did not alter this state of things. The Germans promised to respect Danish integrity and sovereignty, and although this was a fiction after the actual occupation and in view of Denmark's total dependence upon Germany, this meant that politically the Danish Government maintained the administration of the country up to 29 August 1943, with full parliamentary backing, and that the apparatus of society, including the trades unions, functioned, at least formally speaking. Here strikes could be called, with demands for higher wages, better working conditions, etc., without this automatically leading to German intervention, and in the shelter of this situation, numerous strikes were actually carried out in the years 1941 and 1942.

From the summer 1943, however, strikes had quite a different perspective. The friction between large sections of the population and the Occupying Power, and particularly between these groups and the Government, which had been forced, in one affair after another, to make compromising concessions to the Occupying Power, had become so acute that in August 1943 a long series of strikes broke out in large and small provincial towns all over Denmark.[56]

The background for this unrest was naturally, in part, the military situation, which was by then becoming unfavourable for the Axis Powers, but its main cause was the illegal activity of the groups which were hostile to the Government, and the growing support which the illegal actions, supported by a "free" Danish movement in the Western Allied countries[57] enjoyed in the population as a whole. The result was what the Danes called "people's strikes", that is strikes which included all strata of the population in the towns on strike, and were directed against the Occupying Power and its interference in the internal affairs of the country. These strikes, combined with a wave of sabotage and extensive disturbances, took on such extreme dimensions in August that they had political consequences in two directions. They had political consequences in the Führer's Headquarters, where Hitler ordered that an ultimatum be given to the Danish Government demanding amongst other things the death penalty for sabotage. And they had political consequences for the Danish Government, which was forced to recognize that the population's stand did not permit the fulfilment of this demand.[58] The German ultimatum was refused, and the "people's strikes" in August 1943 led thus to the resignation of the Danish Government, and with it to the end of the politically compromising policy of negotiation with the Occupying Power, which had previously dictated conditions in the country. There was no declaration of a state of war between the two countries, but in reality the growing Resistance groups regarded themselves as actually at war with Germany. And the Resistance groups now became organised more firmly under the leadership of a "Denmark's Freedom Council", which both at home and abroad decided Denmark's illegal course, and in fact came to act as an anonymous and self-appointed government.[59] On the other hand, the administration of the diminishing possibilities for action on domestic matters remained in Danish hands.

After 29 August 1943, a total ban on strikes was proclaimed here as in other occupied countries, with threats of incalculable reprisals, but this did not result in the strike weapon disappearing from the arsenal of the Danish Resistance. In June-July 1944, unrest came to a head in a total strike in Copenhagen, which awakened echoes around the world because of its extent, its duration, and its stubborn character, with barricades, shooting in the streets, etc. This strike was only brought to an end after complicated negotiations and German concessions, and thereafter strikes of limited duration were used repeatedly as demonstrations and protests, for example after German deportations, and when the Germans dissolved the Danish Police Force in September 1944. All in all, the strikes became one of the most effective forms of action in the Danish resistance struggle.

In Norway, a peculiar form for obstruction and strike, with a special psychological effect, became a characteristic of the thoroughly organised Norwegian civil resistance struggle. A "normal" strike broke out in September 1941 in the Oslo region, and led to the introduction of martial law and the execution of two of the Norwegian Trades Union leaders.[60] All tendencies towards strikes were to be put down from the start, and a German declaration made this plain: "Communist and Marxist elements in the trades unions, and particularly in their administration, have recently disturbed work in criminal fashion by preparing strikes." The declaration then decreed a total prohibition against preparing or participating in strikes. At the same time, the German Chief of Police announced that the two Trades Union leaders had been executed, and that a number of other Trades Union leaders had been sent to prison with from ten years' to life sentences. One more Trades Union leader was condemned to death, but the sentence was commuted to life imprisonment. The reason for all these sentences was said to be that the men had prepared a General Strike. In spite of this extreme reaction, it was in Norway that a particular form of strike was developed which can perhaps best be described as an "organisation strike", or "organisation avoidance".

The underlying cause of this was the attempt of the Norwegian Nazi Party, the "National Unity Party", under the leadership of the "Führer" Vidkun Quisling, to seize power in the country, to the sometimes very limited extent to which the German Occupying Power permitted this experiment. One method of seizing power was to be by the party introducing corporate State forms, and by this means gaining control of the whole, very complete Norwegian complex of organisations, in order to influence and control the population in the spirit which the "National Unity Party" considered the right one for the Norwegian people. When full control was achieved, a "State Parliament" was to be set up on the foundation of the corporation system, and this was later to enter into a peace agreement with Germany, by which the way would be paved for a possible Norwegian entry into the war at the side of the Germans. This was the vision which would be swept away by the storm, protests, and boycott which the plans met in the Norwegian population.

The details of this tug-of-war for the Norwegian people's support are omitted here, but a few features will be mentioned briefly, because, in a quite peculiar way, they contain factors of manifest obstruction or strike activity.[61] One, but only one of the first trial moves was an attempt by the "National Unity Party" in 1941 to bring all Norwegian athletic organisations into a "Norway Athletic Union", under party leadership. This field was chosen as an experimental sector, because it was a seemingly neutral and non-political area. An alert public immediately reacted politically, however, even in this apparently innocent field. The idea of the party was quite simply that obligatory membership was to be imposed upon all Norwegian atlethic organisations under the proclaimed party leadership. The result was just as simply what has been called an "athletic strike". The athletic organisations were emptied of members, and all athletics came to a halt, which lasted throughout the war.

This was only an introductory episode in the prelude to the head-on collision between the party and the population which was to come. The actual conflict broke out in the years 1941–42. In May 1941 a number of the larger organisations – forty-three in all – sent an energetic joint protest against the plans of the "National Unity Party" to the German Gauleiter, Josef Terboven, and the latter summoned the organisation leaders in June 1941 to a "Besprechung" in Oslo. This "Besprechung" consisted of a thundering rebuke from Terboven, some arrests, and the announcement that political commissars from the "National Unity Party" were appointed to a great many of the most important organisations. This counter-measure ended in fiasco. A "strike" now took place, in which representatives and officials in the organisations involved resigned their offices, while resignations streamed in from the ordinary members. In a great many of the forty-three protesting organisations, this wave of resignations reached about 90 % of the total membership.

It was perhaps typical of the situation that on one side, Terboven allowed the "National Unity Party" to attempt this fruitless "putsch" through the organisation system, but on the other side he refrained from appointing political commissars to the most important of the 43 organisations, the "Workers' National Trades Union", which, with its 300,000 members was the organisation with which the Germans were most unwilling to quarrel. The situation is perhaps illustrative of the attitude of Terboven and the leaders of the German Reich. If open strife with the well organised Trades Unions could be avoided, it should be avoided. The strike was a weapon which could be countered by brutality, but which one was unwilling to provoke unnecessarily.

The first round failed, therefore, in the "National Unity Party's" attempt to seize power over Norwegian society, by obtaining commissar posts in the national organisations. The organisations did not dissolve but acquired renewed vitality with the illegal leaders who joined together under the direction of the Co-ordination Committee, which covered the whole country, and from about the New Year 1942 took over the illegal command of the Norwegian civil Resistance. After the mass resignations, the "National Unity Party" conceived the obvious alternative idea of making membership compulsory in all areas of society, in the sense that no one could exercise his trade without being a member of the state-controlled trade organisation. This attempt also stranded on the mutual loyalty which was welded together under the Co-ordination Committee's leadership, right to the most outlying villages in the country. Representatives were chosen with connexions up to the Co-ordination Committee, and down to the towns and villages, and a courier system was established so that a joint and united reaction could be organised.

A test case, which will be mentioned here as an example, and which aroused attention all over the world, was an attempt to force compulsory membership upon the Norwegian teachers. This offensive took the form of a law of 5 February 1942, which set up a "Norway's Teachers Union", with a leader for the whole country appointed by Quisling, and with compulsory membership for all teachers in the country. This offensive on the educational front was intensified by the fact that another law was decreed the same day, aimed at the youth of Norway, creating a "National Youth Service". The two laws together aimed at establishing state control of all education, both in and out of school. The affair was now not only a matter for the teachers, but for parents, and therefore in reality a matter which affected society as a whole. The question was now, how the 14,000 teachers involved should react. It was a test case on a matter of principle, and there must be a joint order in reply, common to all, and formulated in such a way that it could be the pattern for other future orders, if and when it was the turn of other professional fields. After hectic and exhaustive discussions among the teachers, in the Co-ordination Committee and among representatives of other professions, on the right procedure, an order was issued that every single teacher should send the following letter to the Church and Education Department: "I find myself unable to co-operate in the education of Norway's youth on the lines which are laid down for NS's youth service, as this conflicts with my conscience. As membership in Norway's Teachers Union, according to the national leaders' statement, imposes upon me the duty, among others, of assisting in such education, and in addition makes other demands which conflict with the conditions of my appointment, I find that I ought to state that I cannot regard myself as a member of Norway's Teachers Union."

The ball was now in the opponents' court, and they hit hard. The teachers had a short time-limit within which they were to join the union. The alternative would be dismissal without salary or pension. Both Quisling and, a few weeks later, Terboven, described the teachers' conduct as "a strike", and when the teachers did not yield under their pressure, arrests followed. On 20 March over one thousand teachers were arrested and deported to forced labour in North Norway. The attempt to get the schools running again with "loyal" teachers failed, however, and in the end the attempt to force the union upon the teachers had to be abandoned, and the schools were re-opened without the teachers' acceptance of the new decree.

It is a matter of opinion, whether this sensational conflict with the teachers can be, or must be, regarded as a "strike". It did not affect the production apparatus of the country directly. Nevertheless, it did affect the Occupying Power quite perceptibly. Terboven made this clear in a speech in Oslo. The teachers' action, he said, was a strike, which meant a threat to the interests of the German power of defence, for which reason it was not a question of an internal Norwegian matter. The words contained a threat, but they also contained a somewhat surprising admission. There was a background for Terboven's words, however, which was more serious than the problem of the teachers' conditions. That spring, 1942, the "National Unity Party" was working on urgent plans for creating a "Norway's Labour Union", which, with the incorporation of "the Workers' National Organisation", "the Employers' Union" and "the Craftsmen's Union" with various other groups would include practically the whole Norwegian labour market. The idea was that the corporate creation of this new body should be proclaimed on Labour Day, 1 May 1942.

Nothing came of this carefully prepared plan. After the experience of the "teachers' strike", Terboven shelved the "National Unity Party's" great idea. The "teachers' strike" was a bearable, if irritating affair, which hit Germany's prestige and propaganda. A labour strike would be quite another matter, since it would affect German military interests directly, and at that particular moment the Germans believed that important military interests might be at stake in Norway. After the first period of war with Russia, Hitler thought that North Norway might be invaded by the Allies, in order to cover deliveries to Murmansk, as well as to stop the deliveries of Swedish iron ore. He therefore designated Norway as a "Schicksalgebiet" – an area of decisive importance – and the country was therefore fully garrisoned with troops and naval forces[62] – at the very moment when Sauckel was engaged in preparing an offensive to mobilise every possible form of manpower and develop all feasible production possibilities in the occupied territories.

In this situation, the idea of baiting the Norwegian workers by setting up a "Norway's Labour Union" became quite irrelevant, and on this background, the "teachers' strike" had consequences which justify the use of the word "strike". In effect it saved the Norwegian labour market from the measures which, if one projects the developments on the one plane over to the other, as Terboven did, would have let loose disturbances in the factories which would have greatly intensified the German authorities' anxiety at developments in this frontier area – and this was serious enough already. It would undoubtedly also have set serious reprisals in motion, in a country which was already ravaged by reprisals.

OBSTRUCTION. In Poland and the Soviet Union the German regime was so ruthless that the strike weapon never became a real possibility, and in the areas of the Soviet Union, Jugoslavia and Greece which were suited to guerilla warfare, resistance turned immediately into partisan war, which left no room for the strike weapon. On the other hand, strikes were used in Czechoslovakia,[63] where in 1940 there were strikes in both Bohemia and Slovakia; and after the German invasion of the Soviet Union in 1941, there was renewed strike activity which led, on Communist initiative, to the creation of a revolution committee which undertook the co-ordination of resistance, strikes, and sabotage, and preparations for armed revolt.

The recognized strike was one thing, the unrecognized strike, in the form of slow or ineffective work, obstruction or direct sabotage during work was another, which it is not only difficult but often plainly impossible to establish, because here we have to deal with hypothetical and imponderable questions. It is not only probable, however, that strikes did occur in this form, we actually glimpse it occasionally in calculations and in scattered documented examples. In Belgium, obstruction and "go slow" tactics seem to have influenced production to an important extent. Obstruction appeared when the Occupation Authorities dissolved the existing Trades Unions, and ordered all workers to join an "Union des Travailleurs Manuels et Intellectuels".[64] This organisation was boycotted, and condemned by the illegal Press as being contrary to the Constitution, and the leaders of the Trades Unions maintained the traditional unions as far as possible illegally, and organised frequent strikes, worked against the conscription of forced labour, and organised help for all those who in whatever way avoided the decrees of the Occupation. The consequences were noticeable in production. During the winter 1941–42, the exile Belgian Government could report noticeable "go slow" tactics,[65] particularly among the miners. Coal production fell by 36 %, and this had repercussions in limited production and temporary production stoppages in the factories still working. In addition, there was a documented instance of serious obstruction, when the German authorities discovered that 1½ million cartridges had been delivered from the arms factories in the town of Herstal without gunpowder, a discovery which led to many random arrests, as it was not possible to identify those responsible. A parallel instance of "go slow" tactics occurred in Denmark,[66] where a German mine-sweeper from a Danish shipyard which would normally have taken nine months to build, and of which the keel had been laid in May 1941, was not ready for delivery until July 1943 – that is after 26 months – and this in spite of the fact that there had been no shortages of material nor labour problems. Just before the delivery, the mine-sweeper was sabotaged, which again delayed its delivery and the picture is complete when one adds that the ship was sabotaged again several times, and never went into action.

As we have seen, it is not possible to give the statistics for this combination of hidden strikes and sabotage. It cannot be denied, however, that these were widespread throughout all the occupied territories and included the forced labour camps in Germany; and at best, the Occupying Powers in all these areas had to reconcile themselves to the fact that manpower was either motivated by opportunism or was refractory to the point of hostility. This involved a political defeat and an economic weakening. It involved a definite reduction of the value which, under other political circumstances, the great occupied territories, with their resources and productive capacity, could have contributed.

Passive Resistance

A mention of the non-militant resistance in occupied Europe is not complete if it only indicates some of the demonstrations, protests and strikes which were aimed against the Occupying Powers, or the collaborating governments and administrations. It must also include what can be described with a common designation as passive resistance in all its multifarious forms: the policy of the "cold shoulder"; slow deliveries; leakages of information; spreading of rumours; conscious or unconscious evasion of obedience to orders and decrees; and most important, administrative resistance, which could take every imaginable form, from dilatoriness, circumlution, passivity, falsification, quibbling, faulty or slow service, tinkering with statistics, to direct evasion of or opposition to the wishes and demands of the Occupying Power. Month-long filibuster negotiations aiming at delaying affairs come into the picture in this connexion. The difficulty in mentioning this passive resistance – for there can hardly be a question of more than a mention – lies first of all in the fact that these actions, or absence of actions, often disappeared from the historical point of view, in the sense that they left no trace in any archives, and were therefore wiped out as far as later research was concerned. But there is little doubt that passive resistance flourished, and supplemented the declared Resistance. Both the Occupying Power and those occupied operated with this as a reality, which was more or less obvious, and the European Resistance Movements could to some extent link up with a resistance-minded population, with the personnel of the government services, or with regional or state administrative organs.

It is well known that those in the German camp lived in an atmosphere of suspicion towards their own people, towards their allies, and towards their collaborators. One or two quotations from Goebbels' diaries are quite illuminating in this respect.[1] He refers to the German Generals: "We certainly must be on the watch as to the older Generals in the Armed Forces, only a few of them are our friends. They try to play the one of us off against the other . . ." Of their Axis partner, after the collapse in September 1943 he writes: "This Italian defeat has been good business for us, both the expropriation of their weapons and the use of their manpower." On their allies: "As far as the possibilities for treachery from the other 'Yes'-men are concerned, Horthy would like to back out, but the Führer has already taken measures to prevent this. Kally, his Prime Minister, is certainly a swine, but he does not forget himself, he is too cautious to give himself away. We must therefore make the best of a bad job for the moment. One can trust Antonescu, as far as one can trust anyone from the Balkans." On the French collaborators: "Now both Pétain and Laval are waiting to see which way the wind blows, in their heart of hearts, of course, they are both opponents of the Reich and its interests, and we cannot therefore trust them a yard."

These are some glimpses of Goebbels' views on Germany's friends. As to her enemies in the occupied countries he had no illusions.

The basic fact was that the Axis Powers dominated most of Europe until the tide turned in 1942, either occupying large European territories or controlling vassal states such as Finland, Roumania, Hungary, Bulgaria, Slovakia and Croatia, which were allied to the Axis Powers, and lastly with Spain, which observed friendly neutrality vis-à-vis the Axis Powers. Only Sweden, Switzerland and Portugal remained outside the conflict, with completely neutral status, and in these three countries, considerable activity hostile to the Axis Powers developed as the fortunes of war turned against them. The occupied region was by far the largest, both as regards territory and population, and here the situation was that the Axis Powers were invaders, and therefore both by definition and in fact found themselves in hostile country. In principle, every single inhabitant in the occupied regions was a potential enemy, and the advantage in holding such enormous areas diminished in the ratio that hostility made itself felt, either openly or under cover, or even simply in the form of stubborn passivity. The situation can perhaps best be illustrated if one imagines what would have happened if the occupied countries had lived up to the propaganda dream of the Axis Powers as regards production, work and military assistance, and had acted as the idealistic champions of Europe's happy future in the fight proclaimed against British imperialism and Russian Bolschevism. In 1941, particularly when the German campaign started against the Soviet Union, there might have been grounds for wishful thinking in this direction. Considerable aversion did exist towards the Soviet Union and the Communist system, both in Western and Eastern Europe, and it was not unthinkable that even in the Soviet Union an opposition existed against the Communist regime to which Germany could have made a cunning appeal. But this campaign aroused opposing currents to a special degree, not only among the Communists but also among liberal and conservative circles, and the volunteer military contingents which were called for from the occupied countries in this situation were of minimum dimensions, and at best had only symbolic and propaganda value. It should be added that the aim in the Axis camp was not a mass mobilisation of auxiliary troops. One reason for this was that the German leaders underestimated the Soviet Union's military strength and counted upon a quick victory in Russia by their own efforts – a repetition, if on a larger scale, of the campaign in the west in 1940. Another reason was that there was no desire to arm large forces from the occupied countries. And lastly, Germany had not the weapons or equipment to supply other forces than those of the Axis Powers themselves. When they appealed in the north and west, therefore, for the creation of auxiliary corps in a European crusade against Bolshevism, the appeal was coupled with deep distrust, which resulted in limits being set for the auxiliary corps which they professed to want. The limit[2] for the French "Légion des Volontaires Français contre la Bolchévisme", for example, was set at 10–15,000 men – a precaution which was unnecessary, however. In February 1942, recruitment had in fact only reached about 3,500 men. No crusading spirit was aroused in 1941,[3] and besides this, the small forces proved to be a cause of bitterness in their respective home lands, both against them and against the Occupying Power which had recruited them. The local police and gendarme auxiliaries, which appeared here and there in the pay of the Axis Powers, were no less detested. The Axis Power had to live with the law that in the eyes of Europe they were ruthless invaders, and had to accept the conditions of invaders.

Among these conditions was the dilemma that the captured territories were so vast, and the captured communities so complicated that the Occupying Powers had to seek support to a great extent in the machinery of society in the defeated countries, regardless of how reliable or unreliable they believed it to be. This applied to state as well as regional administration; it applied to the production apparatus; it applied to the transport system and communications network; and it applied to the forces of law and order. In principle, the Occupying Powers had to regard every citizen of an occupied country as a potential enemy, or at best a friend motivated by opportunism, who must therefore be spied upon and deprived of any influence, but in fact the Occupying Powers had to rely upon the assistance which, in spite of everything, was to be had from these citizens. In the military, police and administrative sectors, the enormous conquests entailed spreading the forces of the Occupying Powers far beyond the capacities of their available manpower – particularly qualified manpower – and in addition, they faced difficulties caused by differences in language, technique and tradition. The disparity in numbers between occupied and occupiers was obvious, and was stated fairly and squarely after the liberation of Corsica in the autumn 1943 by the French Communist paper, "L'Humanité":[4] "There are 300,000 inhabitants in Corsica, and there are 30,000 Germans, that is one Boche for every 10 Corsicans. In continental France there is not even one Boche for every 100 Frenchmen. The lesson can be deduced." At all events, this illustrated the fact that collaboration with co-operative partners in all the occupied territories was an absolute necessity, and the strength of collaboration was decisive for the degree of reliability and efficiency which the Occupying Powers could count upon. It became a problem to decide how far they could count upon the good will and possibilities of the collaboration. But if it was a problem for the Occupying Powers, it was also a problem for the people of the occupied countries. No community and no group in the community, however much it hated the Occupation, could allow itself to refuse a certain amount of co-operation. Daily life and its material requirements made quite simple demands upon the community, in spite of the war and occupation, to go on functioning, and although total dissolution would certainly hit the Occupying Powers, it would hit the community itself even more. This problem was intensified for the occupied communities by the fact that in every situation of acute lack it was the Occupying Powers which, simply by the use of force, could supply themselves and ensure that their needs were covered. We have seen that the Belgian coal production was reduced by 36 %, and it should be added that the first consequence of this was severe rationing of gas and light. Paradoxically enough, even the most militant resistance organisation was interested in and directly dependent upon the community maintaining a certain amount of normality, at least until the hour struck for the final reckoning. Production, the supply services, the intelligence services and the communication services were not only tools of the legally functioning citizens in the community, but in high degree also of the growing illegal groups. Even the partisan groups needed deliveries and contacts. The question for the occupied peoples, and particularly for their leaders at many levels, was not whether one should co-operate with the Occupying Power, first of all by maintaining production – for this type of co-operation was an absolute necessity – but rather to what extent and in what form, and particularly with what motives this co-operation should be maintained.

When deciding upon forms of administration in the various countries and regions, the Occupying Powers must have realised that internal order and control would be easier, if orders and instructions could be promulgated by governments and administrations which could count upon a certain degree of authority in the areas in question, preferably with the intermediate authority placed between the Occupying Power and the population consisting of nationals of the country in question. Instructions from the Occupying Power inevitably had the character of commands, and for that reason alone must appear to be motivated by the Occupying Power's interests, whereas similar instructions promulgated by the country's own nationals had a little more hope of appearing as measures motivated by the community's collective interests and needs. This was naturally qualified by the amount of confidence enjoyed by the intermediate authority in the population. In this field, the Axis Powers were in a weak position, and it was here that the political weakness behind their captures showed itself. In by far the largest sectors of the occupied regions they had either to disregard the possibility of appointing credible national intermediate authorities, or to engage in doubtful experiments with nationally compromised Nazi parties without numerical strength among the population, and directly detested by them – a detestation which increased with the parties' co-operation with the hated Occupying Powers.

It was only in two countries, France and Denmark, that the Occupying Power could negotiate for a time with governments with qualified authority in the population, and in both these countries the negotiations, with concessions to the demands of the Occupying Power, contributed to wearing down this authority. It was only a question of time, therefore, before the Occupying Power had to intervene, and here too be confronted squarely with an unwilling population or a hostile Resistance Movement. In both countries the Occupying Power had to register the glaring fact that the more concessions the two governments made, the more their authority was undermined, and the more their political value deteriorated. Here too there was a dilemma, and here too it was two-sided. The Occupying Power had to beware of forcing concessions through so brutally that the local authority was weakened to the point where its co-operation became useless, and on the other hand the two governments had to make every effort to obtain such useful results from their negotiations that they could retain the maximum confidence and authority among the population. For both parties this was a question of a difficult balancing act, and in both cases, in the long run, the attempts at negotiation collapsed.

In the other occupied territories things were no better. In the Soviet Union, German military control was set up in the front line regions, while the occupied hinterland behind them, which was devided up into state commissariats, came under the control of the SS. No serious attempt was made to appeal to or co-operate with possible anti-Communist elements, even in the Baltic countries or the Ukraine, where possibilities existed for appeal to national feeling. In Poland, large territories to the west, with an area of about 70,000 km^2 and a population of about seven million, were annexed as part of the Great Reich, whilst parts of Central Poland were organised as a "Generalgouvernement" under a German governor-general. Czechoslovakia, as early as 1939, was divided into a German protectorate, in the case of Bohemia and Moravia, and a German satellite state – for a short time – in the case of Slovakia. In Norway and Holland, experiments were made with Vidkun Quisling and Adriaan Mussert and the small Nazi-orientated parties as possible intermediate authorities between the Occupying Power and the population, but in both countries the experiments failed, and probably created greater problems than they solved; and the real power had to remain in the hands of the two German Reich Commissars, Josef Terboven and Arthur Seyss-Inquhart. Belgium was placed under a German military government, led by General A. von Falkenhausen, who also had the direct control of two northern French departments. Parts of Yugoslavia were incorporated into Germany, and other parts into Italy, Hungary and Bulgaria, while a puppet government, without any possibilities or influence, was set up in the remaining Yugoslavian state, while Croatia was separated as a satellite state, with as short-lived an existence as Slovakia. In Greece also, a puppet government was set up with no more influence than that which the presence of the Axis Power could give it.

All in all, one must conclude that the political ability of the Axis Powers to exploit the conquered regions of the continent and their resources, with even an approximately normal fulfilment of the demands made by the Occupation and the requirements of the War, proved inadequate. On the short term, it proved possible militarily to conquer enormous areas, but when the War dragged on and became global, the great territorial conquests, although they certainly had great value both economically and strategically, became just as great burdens – in some instances proving fatal. As a whole, European territory became enemy country, with mounting opposition even in the few states allied to the Axis, and the conquerors of 1940 and 1941 found themselves surrounded by enemies in 1943 and 1944, depending to a great extent upon the inhabitants of the "European fortress" proclaimed by the Germans, but which in reality only existed so long as the German war power was able to hold the outer bastions. Even before these fell, however, the defence of the fortress was crumbling away. Many circumstances contributed to this, among them the actions of the Resistance Movements, and within the framework of these actions, passive resistance played a part, even though this must unfortunately be said to have its place among the imponderabilia of the War.[5]

Passive resistance created no organised resistance movement, but it could serve to supplement and support such movements. If it had had to stand alone, with its incalculable possibilities for pin-prick activity or simply stubborn obstruction, it would probably have been able to restrict but not seriously injure the Occupying Powers; and these would have been able to ignore it, even though it both sprang from and underlined the hostile atmosphere which existed in administrative organs and services, and which the bailiffs of the Axis Powers had to report on all sides in Europe, sometimes with irritation, sometimes with disquiet, and now and then with alarm. But passive resistance was not simply a symptom of an attitude, it was also the first form of spontaneous reaction against the Occupation, which could come into being without organisation; and it was important both in the first phase of the Occupation and in later phases, when it became increasingly active and merged with the organised Resistance. Both in Rome and in Berlin the conquerors were forced to register the unpleasant fact – both psychologically and materially – that they had conquered most of a continent, and this functioned because it was in its own interest to function, but it functioned with inertia, resistance and open hostility against the visions and interests of the Axis Powers. These dragged the continent along. They were not carried forward by it. The vitality and the dynamics which remained in the occupied communities were mobilised far more to outspoken resistance than to support of the conquerors. Their true friends were few, and generally dependent upon the support they could obtain from the Occupying Powers, and even the support of the friendly camp was often motivated by opportunistic expectations. As the fortunes of war gradually turned against the Axis Powers, the effect of this situation was intensified. In the stock-taking after the military triumphs of 1940 and 1941, the ideological and political fiasco had to be taken into account. The importance of most of the Resistance Movements lay in accumulative effect. The independent action was often only a microscopic molecular fraction of a whole, which acquired meaning and effect through the accumulation of fractions. This must be particularly true of passive resistance, regardless of what form it took. Primarily, this type of resistance was marked by its quite untraceable and therefore disquieting character. The authorities were forced constantly to operate from the supposition that measures which they must regard as essential or decisive for their interests would be met with aversion, obstruction, delay or counter-proposals. The Occupying Powers' course, when they were faced with this attitude, became unsteady. Sometimes they tried to force their way through, and this constantly increased the aversion and the possibilities for resistance, and sometimes they tried to ease their way through, and this inevitably placed a certain amount of influence in the hands of their opponents who, even if they were ready to co-operate, had their own national or economic interests to consider. Where the latter solution was attempted, it must be obvious from the start, that the Occupying Power would have to reduce its original demands and accept the partial solution which could be achieved through compromise.

The possibilities for passive resistance clearly depended upon the importance of the trade or professional sector within which it developed. It could, for example, be a question of obstruction which only involved factors of irritation, as when Norwegian actors, in the summer 1941, refused to appear on the Norwegian radio, which was directed by the Germans.[6] This led to the arrest of some of the actors and then to a blockade by actors of all the Norwegian theatres. Passive resistance of this kind was limited, and could be borne, although, undeniably, it showed how deeply passive resistance was affecting society. This obstruction was also visible, and could be contained. It was more dangerous, for example, when the Danish State Radio appointed a speaker who carried out the normal duties of a speaker, but who in reality was there to make a code announcement when a certain situation arose, which would give the necessary information on the position in the country.[7] Here the camouflage was impenetrable, and counter-measures therefore out of the question. The problem became more serious, however, in the degree that day to day production, the labour market, the transport system, the communications network or the administrative organisation in all its branches were affected. Here the consequences could be lack of or delay in deliveries, leakages, the issue or assistance in the issue of all kinds of false papers, and administrative circumlution or omissions, sometimes open refusal of administrative co-operation, with all the risks such refusals entailed. The very awareness of this must be a burden to the Occupying Authorities, and must influence their attitude and actions.[8]

We have already considered how passive resistance merged into the organised Resistance at a later stage in the War. To put it more precisely, this occurred when the organised Resistance infiltrated the apparently normally functioning community, and exploited it. A condition for organised Resistance in the form it took was that it could operate in a society which was not in a state of total chaos. Production, transport, communications and the administration were tools of the Occupying Power, but these and other functions of society also became tools of the organised Resistance, which succeeded, with great skill, in using the possibilities of legal society. The village, or simply the independent farm contributed with supplies contrary to wartime rules; the fisherman fished, but also sailed illegally; the factory contributed with "go slow", or more important still, with information on production, on guard rotas, technical instructions for saboteurs; the transport system carried both legal and illegal goods; personnel in the communications network had abundant possibilities for funneling important information out to the active Resistance members, and thus also on to the free world; and the personnel in the administrative organs had opportunities both to prevent, delay and inform. In all the areas mentioned and in all sectors of society, it was a condition that good will and sufficient courage were present, but in all imaginable sectors this proved to be the case. To some extent this was due to the course of the War, so that good will actually increased in proportion to the defeats of the Axis Powers. In this respect, the Axis Powers entered a vicious circle. As time went on, it was less and less a question of passive resistance. This was not because passive resistance ceased. On the contrary, it is possible – and here we can only operate with possibilities – that it intensified, gradually changing its character as it merged into the active Resistance, and positively supported it. As this infiltration increased, any dividing line between passive and active resistance disappeared.

A brief mention of passive resistance must necessarily touch upon the attitude of the forces of law and order in the community, particularly the Police Force, whose position was the most exposed and difficult as regards the problem of collaboration, or passive resistance, or active resistance, but which could also be an important tool for the passive resistance. Where the maintenance of law and order was in the hands of the Occupying Powers' own men,[9] there was no problem. But the spread of the Occupation over the most of Europe meant that the Occupying Powers were not in a position to raise enough men – and particularly qualified men – to cover the Police service throughout the occupied territories, and were therefore forced to rely upon some co-operation with the national forces of law and order. For these forces, and particularly for the Police, the Occupation posed acute and quite extreme questions of conscience. It was the duty of the Police in co-operation with the courts to maintain law and order, and guarantee that the law of the land was kept, but in addition to this, the Police had a great many administrative functions, from traffic control, supervision of essential areas, such as the Health Service, the Passport Office, price control, air observation service, etc. etc., to guard duties, where it should be remembered that these were questions of equally vital importance for the occupied communities as for the Occupying Powers. It was of the utmost importance that "normal" criminality was kept down, and here, a group of foreigners with no knowledge of the language or local conditions, and without technical information, could do little or nothing, quite apart from the fact that such a group had no interest whatever in anything but combatting the active Resistance and rigorously carrying out the summary coercive measures of the Occupying Power. The situation arose where it must be in the interests of the occupied community that the established Police was able to continue its functions; but the situation entailed that these functions included the duty for the Police that, willingly or unwillingly, they must superintend and ensure the execution of the decisions which the Occupying Power forced through, either by direct decree or with the assistance of collaborating organs. In many instances, such as the decrees as to the fate of the Jews, or of political fugitives, and especially in all cases relating to combatting the active Resistance, the decisions of the Occupying Powers conflicted directly with all traditional law in the territories in question, often even with constitutional rights whether these decisions were promulgated by decree or had been negotiated. In such cases the Police must see themselves as the executive organ for decisions which not only conflicted with the letter and spirit of the legislation in force before the Occupation, but also conflicted with their national, religious and human conscience. The personnel of the forces of law and order, more than any other group in society, found themselves in a deep conflict of conscience and an utterly insoluble dilemma.

It can be maintained that the forces of law and order could have freed themselves from this dilemma by refusing to function, but quite apart from the fact that this would immediately have called down the well known drastic reprisals, and at best have meant farewell to their accustomed profession and an extremely uncertain future for the recalcitrants, such a refusal was a two-edged sword, for several reasons. Their refusal would not only hit the community which would find itself without its own Police Force, it would also lead to their immediate replacement by newly recruited police, who at all events would be more willing tools for the Occupying Powers than the former corps. There were enough men, in spite of all the bitterness and all the national solidarity, who were willing to run the errands of the Occupying Powers, for the sake of gain, of opportunism, ambition or political convictions, and the occupied communities where this choice arose at all, were hard hit by such refusals. In addition, a newly formed ad hoc corps would be completely devoid of normal police technique, and among potential recruits to a new corps the presence must be feared of fanatics, political deviators, and criminal elements. In all the occupied countries, the fear of corps of this type could only be compared with the fear of members of the German SS Corps, or the Gestapo. Added to this, these corps, such as Quisling's "Hird" in Norway, the "Schalburg Corps" in Denmark, the "Schalkaar Corps" in Holland or Darnand's "Milice" in France were regarded as traitors, and because of their knowledge of local conditions had better possibilities for infiltrating the organs of the community or the Resistance organisations than anyone coming from a foreign country. Members of such corps showed a brutality towards their countrymen, in their actions, which could exceed even the brutality of the forces of the Occupation. The most extreme example of this was in Yugoslavia, where Pavelic's Ustace Corps carried out unheard-of atrocities in an extermination campaign against Serbs, Jews, Orthodox Christians, and all others who gave so much as a hint of opposition to the Pavelic regime. The massacres began in June 1941, and included countless murders, rape, burning down whole villages, mass murder and every imaginable form of terror, so extreme that they aroused horror even in the Axis camp. "To kill became a cult, a mania," writes the British authority, Fitzroy MacLean,[10] describing this terror, carried out by terrorists who had been trained for years in special camps in Italy and Hungary.

For many reasons, but especially under the impression of the danger of terror corps, and in spite of all the humiliation, conflict of conscience and doubt as to the rightness of obeying orders of the Occupying Powers, it must be in the clear interest of the occupied countries that the traditional police continued to function as long, and as extensively as possible. Any alteration could only be for the worse. The situation in Norway, as early as December 1940,[11] was an object lesson. Here the High Court protested to the Reich Commissar Terboven against a number of decrees which interfered directly with the Norwegian legal system, and which were contrary not only to the Norwegian Constitution, but also contrary to the Hague Convention of 1907 on the powers of occupying authorities; and the High Court also protested against the arrest of one of its members. The protests were ignored, and a new protest against new violations only led to a written instruction from Terboven that the High Court had no juridical authority in these political matters. At this, all the High Court Judges resigned their offices. The result was foreseeable. A new High Court was appointed by Quisling, and this decided in February 1941 that it had no authority as far as statutes promulgated by Terboven were concerned, and also that its decisions were entirely subject to the approval of the German Reich Commissar. Parallel with this, there was a purge of the Norwegian Police and an attempt – on the whole fruitless –

to get its members to join Quisling's "National Unity Party". The affair seems to illustrate the underlying fact, that any surrender of authority necessarily played into the hands of the Occupying Power and its collaborating organs. Other countries such as Denmark, Holland, Belgium and France had similar experiences. On the other hand, in Norway the clear lines were drawn, which characterized the Norwegian civil resistance, and which aroused respect throughout the world.

Refusal to carry on ones functions might ease personal conscience, but it seldom hindered those functions. When in August 1942 the Vichy Government began the mass arrest of Jews not of French nationality, the Lyons Governor of the French Armistice Army, which was the foundation for the Vichy Government's forces of law and order, General de Saint-Vincent, refused to obey orders to place troops at the disposal of the Government.[12] He was immediately dismissed and placed in house arrest. A great many members of the Police, also, refused to obey the inhuman orders, and preferred arrest. None of this hindered the function. By the end of the month, 30,000 Jews had been deported.

There were others who were willing, and the refusal to function had to lead to greater latitude for those who were willing.

To the very limited extent to which the traditional forces of law and order continued their functions, their members had extensive possibilities for passive resistance. In this respect, there was probably no other service which had greater possibilities. In their co-operation with the Occupying Power, the Police had insight into their methods and intentions, and could give warning, remove evidence, act slowly or carry out ineffective interrogations, and also leak information of great importance particularly to the active Resistance organisations.[13] It must be emphasized, however, that such activities cost dear, and that the freedom of movement of the Police was not unlimited. First of all, the Police, if it was to be maintained, had to show certain results in order to preserve their credibility, which was in any case under the constant and often justified suspicion of the Occupying Powers; and secondly the possibilities for the Police to exercise passive resistance depended upon initiatives within its ranks, or often the initiative of individual policemen who had to use their own judgement and act on their own responsibility. In the very nature of things, the top leaders could not promote subversive activities or passivity, but in their orders had to demand loyalty and effective police work, quite regardless of what those top leaders might think or perhaps hope. The result had to be an impossible and – in view of the seriousness of their functions – a painful dilemma for the individual policeman; and it is just as true that the Police came to execute deeply compromising actions in accordance with the demands of the Occupying Powers, as it is true that the possibilities for passive resistance were exploited to an important degree. It is striking, however, that whilst police actions to the advantage of the Occupying Powers and their collaborating political organs were obvious and recognisable, passivity and, especially, direct support of the Resistance organs took place in obscurity. This situation could only lead to the undermining of the reputation of the Police, even though circles in the know were in a position to acknowledge the true facts, and even though help from the Police when the opportunity arose was very often given in extremely precarious and critical situations.

In one country, Denmark, a total dissolution of the Police was carried out, because the German authorities clearly recognized the unreliability of the Police. The dissolution took place on 19 September 1944,[14] and resulted after a period without any police, in establishment of an obedient but criminal and politically compromised auxiliary corps, which immediately brought the population's hatred upon its head, while those police who had escaped arrest and deportation went underground and formed an illegal police corps under the command of the Resistance Movement's central organ, Denmark's Freedom Council. This illegal corps was joined by practically all the police who had avoided the German raids on 19 September – about 7,000 men in all.

In one corner of Europe, the British Channel Islands, passive resistance was the only form of resistance, which was feasible. The historian, who has dealt with the history of the islands during the occupation,[15] leaves us in no doubt as to the impossibility of open resistance: "It is manifestly impossible that there should have been in the Channel Islands anything like the resistance movements which developed in the larger countries occupied by the Germans." The author analyses in great detail the many negotiations, which the occupation necessitated between the local and the German authorities, and he comes to the conclusion, that these negotiations and the form they took on the whole were justifiable: "There is a broad spectrum stretching from passive resistance to active collaboration, and the intermediate bands – passive resistance, reluctant co-operation, and so on – shade into one another with all the delicacy of the colours of the rainbow. There is no doubt that according to their own standards the Island administrations never went beyond passive co-operation, but sometimes they give a false impression of willingness to co-operate . . . But on the whole the official attitude was correct and unforthcoming. If the Island administrations seem occasionally to have leaned too far in the direction of collaboration it was their judgement that was at fault and not their loyalty". Many examples of passive resistance are mentioned in the quoted work on conditions in these islands. These conditions were, indeed, of a special nature.

From a historical point of view it is an unfortunate fact that when considering passive resistance, one is deprived of statistics of any kind, and to a great extent forced to confine oneself to general statements, random documented examples, and probabilities. In such circumstances, one could ignore the phenomenon, but in that case one would do violence to the truth of the realities of those times. Passive resistance was latent and built in in the Europe hostile to the Axis, and exercised its influence and was acknowledged by friend and foe. In the nature of things, its size and importance cannot be assessed, but this does not relieve posterity from mentioning the phenomenon, just as it did not relieve the contemporary period from taking it into account. This was what the German authorities did, when in December 1941 in Poland they introduced new general legislation,[16] decreeing long penal sentences and even the death penalty, and even for children, for a great number of extremely vaguely defined crimes, such as provoking conduct, anti-German remarks, or simply hostile mentality towards Germany; and in the premises for these statutes the argument was used that the Polish population, including the Polish-Jewish population, had shown themselves stubborn opponents of Europe's New Order. These statutes and numerous others in reality outlawed the Polish population, but they also showed to what an extent an unspecified resistance was effective in the country. Statutes of this kind could only aim at hindering and punishing passive resistance. For open resistance, there were already penal statutes enough.

4. Intelligence Service

Latent Resistance Possibilities

Before we attempt a description of the more advanced forms of resistance, it will be practical to make a few introductory remarks.

The first remark refers to the relationship between passive resistance and spontaneous reaction on the one hand, and the systematic organised Resistance on the other. As previously mentioned, it is impossible to draw a sharp dividing line between them with any certainty, even though one may consider it practical from a schematic point of view. The transition and overlapping between the two forms of resistance is so obvious, however, and will become even more so in our account of the systematically organised Resistance, that the boundary must be regarded as a practical arrangement for the purposes of our study, but not as any assertion that the sharp and clearly defined boundary actually existed. The spontaneous protest action and participation in passive resistance were often only the introduction to engagement in cadres of systematic Resistance, and in addition, the two forms of resistance were so infiltrated in each other that the boundary remained a fiction. Lastly, no organised resistance was possible without considerable support from the section of society which "only" practised civil and passive resistance; and these forms of resistance, which underlined the general attitude both psychologically and practically became an indispensable foundation for those who undertook the development of the forms of struggle and the construction of the organisations which would bear the burdens of systematic, organised Resistance.

The next introductory remark refers to the fact that in 1939–1940 absolutely no one could have imagined, with even reasonable certainty, how such active resistance should be constructed and structuralized, what forms of action could be considered, and in what circumstances and conditions such active resistance might develop. There were absolutely no precedents for what happened on this front in 1940–45, and those who took up the struggle had long to grope their way towards a solution of its problems, without any clear idea of the operational possibilities which a new era would make available, especially in the field of communications and advanced technology. Retrospective inferences from what took place in the Spanish Peninsular in 1808, in France in 1870–71, or from conditions during or just after the first World War could give few or directly misleading conclusions, in view of the tremendous developments of the modern industrial system, with its changed possibilities and its vulnerability, which had come into being since the cannons fell silent in about 1920. Flying, radio technique, new explosives, sophisticated photographic technique, etc. were only one side of the matter; another side was the vulnerability of modern industry as regards raw materials, technically skilled personnel, unrestricted transport, and particularly intensive research and changed patterns of society. When the War ended, it was easy to survey the enormous operational possibilities which a well organised resistance movement could exploit, but this was wisdom after the event which the Resistance pioneers of 1940 did not possess. They began their work in the dark, from desperation and with hope. To this, as the months passed, they added the imagination which gradually bore much unforeseen fruit, but only after untold bitter experience had been gained, and only after extremely close co-operation had been established across the closed frontiers of the Occupation with corresponding imaginations in the free world. As this co-operation developed and gathered momentum, the technical means and the practical arrangements were found which made the close co-operation possible.

Naturally, those involved were not completely inexperienced. If that had been the case, there would have been no vision, and there would have been no initiative. The men who created SOE in 1940 had vision, and as we have seen, they based their vision partly upon dear-bought experience. But in 1940 they could not know what technical aids would be developed and put at their disposal with the purpose of translating vision into reality, nor could they have been sure how strong would be the resonance on the other side of the front. They could not have known with what imagination, self-sacrifice and ardour their coming partners on the Continent would seize their initiative, nor with what skill these partners, in one country after another, would build up the organs which would make effective resistance possible. A new approach to problems would be needed, here as in other fields, and as in all new ways of thinking, there would be a need for hope, which might endure or fail. It would be useful to make a comparison between the original thinking in this field, and the original thinking behind the Western Allies' decision to carry out the invasion of the European continent with combined operations between all existing types of arms – original thinking which failed

Germany, when in 1940 she was confronted with her only chance of invading Great Britain. The British author Peter Fleming writes on this subject:[1] "The need for inter-service planning when a combined operation is being mounted is to-day axiomatic. It requires an effort of the imagination to remember that in 1940 this was a novel conception, untried and scarcely recognised on either side of the Channel or the Atlantic".

Similarly, it was also an obvious truth in 1945 that resistance movements could be drawn into the struggle with great effect, and here too, it requires an effort of the imagination to remember that in 1940 this too was a new idea, untried and only recognized as a possibility by few, on either side of the Channel, and not at all on the other side of the Atlantic. It was not recognized on the European continent by the man in the street who, in only a matter of months, would stand in the midst of the struggle and the co-operation.

It was more obvious in Moscow, when in June 1941 the Soviet Union was drawn into the War. Here there was a tradition of partisan warfare; here the size of the country invited resistance in the hinterland behind the enemy lines, as a part of the conduct of the war; and here the Russians were prepared from the beginning of the War to develop partisan activity into an integral part of the collective war effort, even if here, too, it was necessary to experiment and to gain experience.

In 1940, a central starting point for any realistic ideas of resistance must be that first of all it must give support to the only power which at that time still stood in the way of the Axis Powers' total and final victory. This power was Great Britain. It was obvious that no continental European power had or would acquire the strength to free itself by its own efforts. Only a military defeat, achieved either by the British Commonwealth alone or through the war spreading, to global dimensions, and drawing other great powers into the conflict, would make possible the restoration of some form of independence to the occupied countries. It would be the military developments, in the last resort, which would decide the fate of the occupied countries, and their efforts in the various forms of resistance could only have the character of supporting operations. In Czechoslovakia and Poland in 1939–40, all hope of freedom must be pinned to a Franco-British victory, but after 17 June 1940, when France withdrew from the struggle after a paralysing armistice, all hope for the two East European countries and for the occupied countries of North and West Europe depended solely upon the possibilities latent in the British Commonwealth's continued fight, and in the British

Government's solemn declaration that it was the Commonwealth's historic duty to free Europe from the yoke of the Axis Powers.

With this, an immediate task and an immediate adjustment of the compass was indicated to the few who, in the hour of defeat, were capable of seeing beyond the difficulties of that hour, to a future situation where the victory march of the Axis Powers would be halted. It was they who engaged in more or less concrete plans to revive occupied Europe to a continuation of the struggle. Such personalities existed, but they were few. Their importance was so much the greater.

The most outstanding man among these personalities was the French General and Deputy Minister of Defence, Charles de Gaulle, who, the day after the French armistice, on 18 June 1940, in a flaming speech on the B.B.C. addressed the French people with an ardent appeal to continue the struggle.[2]

De Gaulle saw clearly that the war with the Axis Powers was global, and that it had not ended with the German victories in Poland and Northern and Western Europe: "For France is not alone . . . She has a vast empire behind her. She can unite with the British Empire, which controls the seas – and is fighting on. Like Britain she can call on the huge industrial resources of the United States. This war is not confined to the luckless soil of our country. This war has not been settled by the Battle of France. This war is a world war." Here was true vision. But de Gaulle's instructions of the moment, which few heard and fewer were able to follow, were still primitive in regard to resistance policy: "I, General de Gaulle, now in London, call on French officers and men who are on British soil, or may find themselves on British soil, with or without their weapons, and on engineers and skilled munition-workers who are on British soil, or may find themselves on British soil, to get in touch with me".

What de Gaulle had in mind, here, was the formation of a Free French force on traditional lines, which does not embrace any vision of what would perhaps be a more important struggle, raised behind the lines of the Axis Powers. But perhaps an opening in this direction was contained in his concluding words: "Whatever happens, the French flame of resistance must not be and will not be extinguished." It was the task of the French and other European pioneers in resistance work, however – pioneers who had no possible chance of reaching British territory, or who believed that they had greater possibilities if they remained in the mother country – to find the way to the methods by which, on home soil and with support from abroad, they could create an effective resistance against the Axis Occupying Powers, and thereby rally behind Great Britain's struggle.

It is this search for possibilities and the struggle to release them that we shall examine in the account which follows:

It is reasonable to begin in France, even though Polish individuals, especially, and also Norwegians and a very few Danes were already grappling with possibilities, and the first speculations had begun in Holland and Belgium. Let us retain the word, speculation, with stress on the fact that in the first phases of the Occupation, there could only be a question of speculation as to the future, rather than concrete plans. The possibilities for resistance were still undiscovered. But the structure of the future Resistance began to take shape, as soon as the first resistance pioneers undertook the study of the tasks before them. Inspiration accompanied the work, and the practical solutions appeared at a pace corresponding to that with which the concrete tasks presented themselves. One of these resistance pioneers was the French Major, Henri Frenay.

The Intelligence Service
FRANCE. On 25 June 1940, Frenay was taken prisoner with his unit in one of the many "pockets" which the French collapse created for the French Army Units. Five days later, on 30 June, he escaped from prison, and after fourteen days of wandering through the Vosges, he reached the demarcation line on 23 Juli. During his wanderings he had acquired civilian clothes, and he succeeded without much difficulty in slipping through the control and into the unoccupied zone of France, where he was attached to a unit of the Armistice Army in Marseilles.[3] Here began Frenay's work of building up one of the French Resistance organisations, "Combat", which would rise in France in the following months and years, and permeate French life during the Occupation. It is chosen here as an example, not because the organisation became typical – it was too large and too important for that – but because it contains all the typical elements, in intention, developments and problems, which were to mark the development of French Resistance.[4]

The general atmosphere which Frenay met in Southern France horrified him. Masses of people apparently resigned themselves to the situation, took comfort in having avoided direct occupation, and with naive trust looked to Pétain as the idolised national figure who would know how to regenerate France, in the belief that he was simply playing a clever double game vis-à-vis the Germans, which after the impending

German victory would be to the advantage of France.[5] Faced with this type of feeling, the far-seeing Frenay revolted. For him the demand upon every Frenchman was for continued struggle and immediate action. For Frenay there was no question of dream-like notions or indulgence in wishful thinking. This trained General Staff Officer soon had his plans ready. He would raise a national liberation movement ("Mouvement de Libération Nationale"), which would be organised in three sections: propaganda, intelligence service and attack. The three sections would not have equal priority as to timing. The intelligence service came first, in one sense, because it could be established more quickly than the other two sections, and because the free world and particularly Great Britain could not be supplied too quickly with the fullest possible information on conditions in France in general, and German troop movements in particular.

The work of the other two sections was certainly to be started at once, but they both required time and changed conditions, as well as material possibilities, which it was still impossible to visualize in the summer 1940. Frenay created a special organisation to solve the first task, the "ROP" (Recruiting, Organisation, Propaganda) and his idea was that these three functions must precede the last of the tasks envisaged, the attack in the form of sabotage, assasinations or armed resistance which were to be directed against the Occupying Power.

Here we shall examine Frenay's efforts to solve the first of his ambitious aims, the establishment of a French Intelligence Service.

It was an advantage for Frenay, both as to objectives and execution, that he was a trained General Staff Officer, who had passed through both the Saint-Cyr Academy (1924) and the French École de Guerre (1935), and had been posted to the French Army Centre in Strassbourg for the study of the German Army methods, just before the War. On the strength, amongst other things, of this experience, he was from November 1940 to the end of January 1941 attached to the Armistice Army's Second Bureau in Vichy itself, and here he made contact with a number of officers in the French Army's Second and Fifth Bureaux, which included intelligence duties.[6] This was the case with officers from the Second Bureau, who worked in the Army's "German Section", which – contrary to the terms of the armistice – had continued their functions, although in a camouflaged form, and with illegal offices in Lyons. Even before his short but fruitful stay in Vichy, Frenay had begun to build up his own intelligence, however, and he continued with this after his Vichy period; and in his relations with the French military bureaux he thus became both supplier and receiver. It now became his task to arrange for sorting, assessing and forwarding the important military, political and economic information which his organisation collected in increasing quantities. Information was made available to the public in the form of duplicated illegally distributed publications ("Bulletins d'Information" and "Bulletins de Propagande"). It was also sent to the illegal French organisations, and, particularly, to Great Britain. In this last respect, Frenay had already found the way, during his stay in Vichy, to a forwarding agent. Via the Chief of Police in the town he had made contact with the American Embassy,[7] which was able to forward his information.

Frenay's activities were not confined to the "free" French zone. He was also determined to build up his National Liberation Movement in the Occupied Zone, and here too his stay in Vichy was to have importance. He renewed an old acquaintanceship with a colleague, Major Robert Guédon, who like himself was on a short stay in Vichy, and the two now divided the work between them. Guédon was to build up an intelligence network in Normandy, in co-operation with the Armistice Army's Intelligence Department, whilst Frenay was to extend his efforts in organisation to other areas in the Occupied Zone. Both men succeeded in achieving important progress. Guédon managed to build up a very extensive intelligence network, which was not only to cover Normandy, but most of the coastal areas of North France, where he came in touch with a number of other intelligence networks which had grown up independently of his. The details of this work would burst the bounds of this account, but a single detail can illustrate to what an extent it was possible to penetrate normally functioning society, and obtain important information. Frenay had put Guédon in contact with a social worker in a factory in Vierzin on the actual demarcation line, and she used her position to arrange possibilities not only for Guédon but for many others to pass through the demarcation line controls, and she used her position to put Guédon in touch with the principal of a training school in Paris for factory inspectors. Through her position, she in turn had contact with many colleagues and former pupils in posts in a great number of factories in the northern zone, and thus the way was open for Guédon to obtain information on manufacturing programmes in many of these factories, which had been requisitioned by the Germans or were working partially to German requirements. This may serve as just one example to illustrate to what an extent the Occupying Power's dispositions could be watched through the co-operation of the organised Resistance with a passively observing but hostile people.

In addition it became evident that the atmosphere in the occupied parts of France was quite different from that prevailing in the south. Here the enemy was omnipresent, and although this created problems of security, it also created a feeling which was soon translated from dissatisfaction and anger into opposition and illegal activity. This last step had its own logic. When there was no possibility for the opposition to speak out, illegality was the alternative possibility. Another logical factor also emerged. When people's aim was to struggle, and the means for winning the struggle were not present, there was only one way open – to help the only opponent of the Axis who was still fighting, Great Britain. The task at hand was then to obtain information for the Staffs in London. It was on this background that Guédon and the information network co-operating with him came to work. It was also on this foundation that Frenay's work was based.

His organisation quickly penetrated the Occupied Zone, where, for example, he created a great number of groups, preparing for the attack which he had in mind as the final goal; and as one of his first steps, he organised the publication of an illegal paper, "Les Petites Ailes de France", later re-christened with the names "Résistance" in the north zone and "Vérités" in the south zone. Both papers gained enormous influence, as long as they existed, and were distributed in every imaginable milieu side by side with other papers which soon appeared, such as "Voix du Nord", "Véritas", "La France Continue", "Libération" – with an edition in both zones – and many more. These papers reached practically all sectors of society, and there was even an illegal publication for the German soldiers – "Unter Uns" – edited by one of Guédon's collaborators from Alsace.

Parallel with Frenay's efforts in organisation in the north and south, the consolidation of an intelligence service, with headquarters at Lyons, continued. There were two enemies, the Occupying Power and the Vichy Government. As regards both of them it was important to obtain information on their strengths and weaknesses, and on both fronts there was a need for military, political and economic information. The collection of intelligence was not the main problem. There was detailed information enough, both as to the situation of the Vichy Government and as to German dispositions. Within the Vichy Government administration and until the end of occupation, there were many patriotic informers with outspoken or hidden Allied sympathies,[8] and as far as the Occupying Power was concerned, this was forced to co-operate with the French administration – a situation which offered possibilities for all kinds of leakages and warnings. The French historian, Henri Michel, mentions the importance of the forced co-operation which the Germans had to have with the transport sector, the post and telegraph services, the Agricultural Ministry, the Trade Ministry and the various industrial enterprises, the leaders of the administration in the departments and towns, as well as the Police and the Corps of Gendarmes. Frenay saw it as his task to exploit the possibilities which this offered, and with this in view he created a special organisation, "NAP" ("Noyautage des Administrations Publiques"), whose job was systematic infiltration of the public and private sectors. Added to this, every Frenchman could in principle be an observer and could obtain information on German troop garrisons, movements, fortification work, etc. Often all that was needed was the naked eye and a little primitive instruction. Every participant in Frenay's ever-expanding organisations was instructed – and it became a routine matter for countless other Frenchmen in other Resistance networks – to report, by the channels laid down, every observation which might seem interesting either for the illegal French organisations, for de Gaulle's Free French Movement or for Great Britain; and it also became a natural duty to give warnings when anyone had the scent of danger which could threaten members of one or other of the organisations.

The collection of all this information required organisation, and this was built up under the leadership of the chemical engineer Jean Gemahling, who made his headquarters in Lyons, where he gathered the threads together. In time, information poured in, from NAP and from all levels of society, fishermen, lorry drivers, workers on the fortifications, engineers, railway officials, etc. etc.; and Intelligence Officers, shorthand typists, photographers, draughtsmen, code men and other specialists were attached to the office in Lyons – or rather the offices, for Guédon, for reasons of security, set up five offices in all. One of the main problems was to obtain a sufficient number of trained intelligence staff, who knew the compulsory security rules, and were familiar with the Intelligence Service methods, and who were able to help with the filtering and sorting of the material before the final reports were prepared for forwarding. Such reports were prepared about every ten days in 1942, and consisted of about 30 pages – by 1944 about 200 pages – of which a good many were enclosures in the form of plans, diagrams, drawings, etc. When the movement had found its organised form, such main reports were sent to London, to de Gaulle's central bureau there, the BCRA (Bureau Central de Rénseignements et d'Action); to Switzerland; to de Gaulle's chief delegate in France; to the leaders of NAP; and also to the leaders in Frenay's organisation. This organisation was first merged with the organisation "Combat", which in its turn, in the summer 1943, merged with an even more extensive fusion, "MUR" (Mouvements Unis de Résistance). A good deal of intelligence material also found its way to the illegal Press.

It was one thing to collect and edit the material, it was another matter to smuggle it out of the country. Various channels were built up for this: that already mentioned, with the American Embassy in Vichy – as long as it existed; a channel to Geneva; the long, vulnerable illegal route through Spain to Portugal; and the normal flights to Switzerland and Madrid were also used, by camouflaging material in every imaginable way. The technology of this time opened a number of possibilities here, which could be used, although they were dangerous. The Achilles heel of the service, however, was and continued to be the forwarding of express messages. The only solution here was the use of radio, but in this domain the organisation we are considering had to make the best of the radio channels put at its disposal by the agents whom the BCRA sent to France, and also by the agents whom the British sent across the Channel independently of de Gaulle's organisation.[9] A great many agents of both categories worked in France, but their presence, and occasional connexions with them, did not change the fundamental weakness, that right up to the liberation, "Combat's" intelligence service had no independent radio connexion of their own.

It did not help matters that in January 1942, Frenay achieved a meeting with de Gaulle's most trusted man vis-à-vis the homegrown Resistance Movement, the former Prefect of Chartres, Jean Moulin.[10] Frenay was handed the considerable sum of 250,000 francs, for which the movement had sore need after the explosive growth which had taken place since 1940, but both this and later meetings between the two men made it clear that de Gaulle and his Free French Movement, for whom Moulin was spokesman, wanted a hierarchial construction of the Resistance Movement, with the command and control situated in London, and not out in the Field. This concept was the precise opposite of that of the homegrown Resistance, which was based upon experience. The difference between the underlying concept of the London Staffs, both the Free French and the British, and that of the man in the Field – a difference[11] which reappears in other occupied countries and in other resistance activities –

was due, fundamentally, to the difference in outlook of a military staff, with its traditional thinking, who wished to have centralised control, with isolated groups screened from each other and therefore having maximum security, each with its special tasks, and the illegal organisation actually at work, with the pragmatic experience that it was possible to build up nation-wide organisations with considerably greater striking power than London was able to imagine. The result, in the case of Gehmahling's organisation, was that they had to forward their information, gathered with such difficulty, either through the organisation controlled by de Gaulle, "SOAM" (Services des Opérations Aériennes et Maritimes), or through British agents' radio channels. It should be added that there was a high degree of political intention in this, de Gaulle wished to obtain the political leadership of the homegrown Resistance through his control, and with this, a broader backing for his claim that he and he alone represented Free France, both abroad and at home. This wish was far from being shared by these organisations, where there could well be divergent political views, even if the overriding aim – the fight against the Occupying Power and the collaborators – united them in spite of political differences or shades of difference. In the case of "Combat", the situation was that this organisation was not unwilling to accept de Gaulle as the supreme leader of Free France. Here the argument was solely concerned with the views of the command in London on the technical set-up.

The situation has been touched upon in this short description of the Intelligence Service, that this was a single component of a much more widespread Resistance organisation, and that a considerable amount of other intelligence activity ran parallel with it. Guédon was not the only officer whom the Armistice Army planted in the north. The officers of this army carried out extensive espionage,[12] and civilian Resistance organisations did the same thing. Guédon could therefore draw upon the knowledge and initiative of others to a great extent, and both de Gaulle's organisation and the British, independently of him, sent a great many missions to France with duties of sabotage, organisation and intelligence. All in all, France was honeycombed with espionage activities. Information leaked out of the country in a steady stream, and in all the Germans' economic, political and military dispositions unfolded almost like an open book for the Staffs in London. Thanks especially to the activities of the Resistance organisations, espionage acquired an effectiveness and an extent which was unknown in earlier times, when espionage was supplied by professionals, often highly paid agents, who had to be smuggled through the front lines, and at best try to obtain information and try with considerable difficulty to get it back to the Staffs expecting it. Here, there were spies in thousands, already in position, and often in key positions, and they were voluntary and unpaid. The espionage of the Resistance became a valuable supplement to all the other intelligence. The only problem here, as in all the occupied countries, was to get the information collected, edited and – what at first was the most difficult stage – forwarded. Where this could be done by radio – and radio was a novelty in this connexion – the information was especially valuable, and the radio service therefore became the bottleneck and the most vulnerable link. It functioned, nevertheless, with increasing effectiveness and to an increasing extent. In April 1944, 2600 radio messages were sent from France to London. In May 1944 their numbers was 3700.[13] About 150 illegal W/T operators were posted in France by SOE in June 1944.[14] The Allies were well supplied with information.[15] When they landed in Normandy on 6 June 1944 they were already informed on the numbers, armaments and positions of the German Divisions, on the character of the fortifications, and the range and bearing of the coastal batteries, on the positions of the anti-aircraft batteries, on the consistence of the beaches, on dikes, ditches, roads, mine fields, and on a great many other matters which could be of importance in planning an operation. Only the American forces landing on the "Omaha" beach-head met serious surprises, because units of the 352nd German Division, which General Eisenhower described as "alert", had been brought up to the front line just before the invasion,[16] whereas it normally lay in reserve in the hinterland, and this was known. Sufficient information on the movements of this Division and its position had not reached the Allied Staffs, and its presence in the landing area, which the Americans had expected to be relatively lightly manned, was a surprise. On the other hand, the surprise was the exception that proves the general rule: that the Allies were supplied with massive information. This was naturally not due to the work of the French Resistance organisations alone – air photographs, routine intelligence, signal intelligence and messages from special missions, for example, played decisive roles. But the Resistance organisations' work was an important factor. "Combat", for example, had about 1200 trained agents in action in 1944, supported by thousands of local observers.

A striking example of the vital importance of concise information from the Resistance organisations' ranks can be given from the Allied landings in the South France on 15 August 1944. The invasion here, with the code name "Anvil", was under the supreme command of General Alexander

Patch, and was to be carried out partly by American and partly by Free French forces. The strategic plan included the establishment of bridge-heads on the French Riviera, with the capture of Toulon and Marseilles, and an advance through the strongly fortified Rhône Valley to Lyons, followed by the fusion of these forces with the Allied Invasion Armies in the North. This plan was radically changed at the last moment and the alteration was due to intervention from French Resistance circles who were able to lay military information of decisive character before the Allies. The information came through a Colonel Zeller,[17] who was Chief Delegate in Southern France for "COMAC" (Comité d'Action du Conseil National de la Résistance), which again was the military executive organ for the central Resistance Command "CNR" (Conseil National de la Résistance), which Jean Moulin had established in the early summer 1943.

Zeller was well aware that while the Germans were relatively strongly entrenched in the Rhône Valley, and an advance here would be costly, the Alpine roads from the South of France to Grenoble and Lyons, and in fact the whole Alpine region was practically speaking in the hands of the French Resistance Forces "FFI" (Forces Françaises de l'Intérieur). An American advance, even with modest forces by this route – the "Route Napoléon" – would not meet much resistance, but it would have extensive support from the French Resistance Forces. An advance upon Lyons by this route, cutting off the German forces in the Rhône Valley, would be far more rapid and demand less men than the original plan. Zeller's intelligence reached its destination in time. He flew from the Alps to Algiers[18] on 2 August 1944, where he first had talks with the Gaullist leader, Jacques Soustelle, who directed the secret Free French operations in the home country from Algiers. He was then received by de Gaulle, who both on political and military grounds favoured Zeller's plans and therefore arranged for him to be flown immediately to Naples, where on 5 August he had a decisive conversation with General Patch. The result of this conversation was that Patch was convinced by Zeller's information and arguments and ordered the revision of his original plans. In these plans he had operated with the capture of Grenoble on D Day + 90, but in fact the town fell on 23 August, that is on D Day + 8, and Lyons fell on 2 September, after the Germans had had to make a hasty retreat out of the Rhône Valley, giving up their fortified positions, and leaving their heavy materiel behind them. Zeller's information and assessments had proved correct. This is one of the clearest examples from the Second World War of the importance of precise intelligence and of co-operation between the Resistance organisations and the Allied Armies.

From the day of the French armistice on 17 June 1940, the French ports from Dunkirk in the north to Bordeaux in the south-west were in German hands and at least until 22 June 1941, the threat of invasion menaced Great Britain unceasingly from the French Channel ports. There was obvious British interest in being informed as accurately as possible on German activity in and around these ports, and in these circumstances the Intelligence Service from the Channel ports received very high priority. But what applied in the case of the French Channel ports, applied also as regards the possible German approaches in Belgium and Holland, and to a lesser extent Denmark and Norway, where the Norwegian aerodromes in particular posed a threat to northern England. Here too, the Intelligence Service had to be given high priority, and with considerable emphasis on the contribution which the people of the occupied countries could make. The British Government's interest in this situation is clearly reflected in two memoranda which Churchill wrote in the critical summer months. On 6 June he took up the problem in a memorandum to General Ismay with the words:[19] "We have got to get out of our minds the idea that the Channel ports and all the country between them are enemy territory. What arrangements are being made for good agents in Denmark, Holland, Belgium and along the French coast?" And, summing up: "A proper system of espionage and intelligence along the whole coasts." He developed similar ideas on 23 July 1940 for the War Minister, Anthony Eden:[20] "It is of course urgent and indispensable that every effort should be made to obtain secretly the best possible information about the German forces in the various countries overrun, and to establish intimate contact with local people and to place agents. This, I hope, is being done on the largest scale, as opportunity serves, by the new organisation under "MEW" (Ministry of Economic Warfare)." Here Churchill referred to the newly created SOE organisation, of which the purpose was to support European resistance movements and which in many connexions was to play a dominating rôle in the creation of these movements. The above quotations show that in the first hasty rounds it was the Intelligence Service which had top priority, and that it was the countries bordering the Channel and the North Sea which were considered first, and here Belgium and Holland shared the most important position with France. Anxiety as to sufficient expansion of the Intelligence Service was not only a matter for Churchill, however. It was a matter for all British Staffs and for the British Government's Defence

Committee, and led to the request of the Navy's Intelligence Service for the creation of a "Combined Intelligence Committee",[21] which received the task of working out daily reports on the situation across the water.

It is a measure of the extent of British unpreparedness that the Prime Minister himself had to point out the necessity of what must appear a purely routine matter, but Churchill's starting point – that these areas were not hostile but friendly territory – held, even if an effective Intelligence Service could not be raised up from scratch from one day to another. With the good will of those involved it was at least soon in progress.

BELGIUM. In Belgium the first steps were taken[22] by the Belgian Chief Engineer of the country's telephone and telegraph service, Walthère Dewé. He had extensive contacts with people in key positions, from his many years' service, and in addition he had experience from the first World War, where he had led a Belgian intelligence organisation, "La Dame Blanche". Immediately after the capitulation of the Belgian Army on 28 May 1940, he began the work of collecting information from engineers, administrators and businessmen with errands in Germany, and all others who could give him information on German industry, the German Army's armaments, German troop positions and movements, etc., and he created an intelligence organisation under the cover name, "Cleveland". This work continued until, in January 1944, he was shot down in the street, in Brussels. But Dewé was not unique. There were others who created similar organisations, under the cover names "Zéro", "Luc", "Benoit", "Tegal" and several others. Here as in France, espionage by the population was organised at a very early stage, and here as in France it was a problem for the Occupying Power that it must reckon with its slightest dispositions being closely observed by a hostile people, sometimes in areas where the results of espionage might seem small. For example, the organisation "Luc", noted in January 1941 that the German Army had ordered many thousands of tropical uniforms from the textile factories of Hainaut. After making sure that the order really had been given by the German Army, and not by the Italian Government, the organisation sent the news to London, confirming the impression there that German troops were preparing to embark for North Africa. The Belgian Intelligence organisations' uncovering of the fact that the German radar system was being built up in the country has already been mentioned.[23]

A characteristic feature of the Belgian Intelligence organisations' activities was their close co-operation with parallel networks and groups in Luxembourg and North France. Co-operation with the northern French groups, especially, grew up so to speak organically, because the northern departments of France, the Nord and the Pas de Calais, were placed under the same administration as was Belgium – that of the German General Falkenhausen. This was of vital importance. Because of the compact German occupation of the country, and particularly because of the close watch which was kept upon the whole stretch of the Belgian coast, which lay so near to Great Britain, the Resistance here was at an extreme disadvantage as regards contact, both with the exile Belgian Government, and with the British Staffs. In the early days, the Belgian Intelligence network had to be attached to the long, dangerous courier service through France and Spain to Portugal; and it was when this route was established – further complicated by the demarcation line in France – that co-operation with the northern French groups became indispensable. The long routes across four frontiers were laid through this co-operation, but the first Intelligence Service certainly found itself repeatedly in the frustrating situation where they possessed information which they could not get sent direct to London, or at once. In addition they had no certainty that information reached its destination in time, or even at all. Here as in France, the main problem was never the collection of intelligence, but the forwarding of it; and here as in France, the only real solution to the problem must be the establishment of a permanent radio service. This problem was obvious both to the groups at home and to the Staffs in London.

In London the question was raised by the exile Belgian Government, in running consultation with the British Staffs, and the work to create contact with the Belgian Intelligence organisations, both as regards the difficult courier routes and as regards the establishment of radio communication, was put into the hands of the Counterespionage Service of the Belgian Government,[24] ("Sureté de l'Etat"), which itself was under the Ministry of Justice. The 35-year-old judge, Fernand Lepage, was put in charge of this, and he came to work in close co-operation with the British Secret Service – SIS – as well as with SOE; and he also established co-operation with French and Dutch Intelligence organs in London. Co-operation with the British was not without friction, as Lepage maintained connexions both with the Belgian Intelligence organisations and with the Resistance Army which was being built up for future action, whereas the British – both SIS and SOE – claimed, with a good deal of justification, that Intelligence work should be kept quite separate from other illegal activities, and reproached Lepage and the Belgian Government for not strictly observing the separation. Friction of this kind was not unusual in the shadow world of secret British and Allied organisations, which were working to link up the European Resistance organs to the struggle of the free world, since their starting-points, standpoints and situations were utterly different. For the Belgian Government it was a cardinal point that control of the Belgian Resistance groups as a whole should lie in the hands of the exile Belgian Government as far as possible – an opinion which was also based upon the hostile relationship between the exile Government and King Leopold, but was not shared either by the British Staffs or by the groups at home. There were similarities between this situation and that in France.

This friction did not prevent the Belgian Intelligence Service from quickly becoming effective, however. The first Belgian wireless contact was established with London from November 1940, when agents with Intelligence missions, supplied with radio sets, were sent across the Channel. From that time, the number of agent missions grew steadily, most of the men being dropped by parachute, although a smaller number got through by the long route through Portugal, Spain and France, or occasionally were landed on the coast. The number of agents engaged solely in Intelligence missions reached 108 before the Liberation, and added to this number, 115 were sent over on other missions.[25] The agents in question established a considerable spy network, either on their own, or more often co-operating with existing Intelligence groups. There were quantities of cover names for them – "Bayard", "Mill", "Bouclé", etc., and their work of obtaining information was not confined to Belgium, but also penetrated Germany itself, as did that of several other European information organisations, such as the Polish and the Danish. At the end of 1942, the Belgian-British Intelligence groups had about 25 illegal transmitters at their disposal, and by 1944 the number had increased to about 40 – some active transmitting stations, some reserve stations.[26] It was with good reason that the Belgian Prime Minister, Hubert Pierlot, could state, before the Invasion of Normandy began, that for the Allied Supreme Command, Belgium was like a glass house.

As in other countries, the situation also arose in Belgium where a number of Intelligence groups and organisations succeeded in penetrating the heart of German activity, because of the Germans' dependence upon local Civil Services, and because of the predominantly hostile feeling towards the Occupying Power. And this penetration was achieved in fields which were of vital importance for German troop movements. For instance, the organisation "Mill" succeeded in tapping Belgian railways' telephone and telegraph network, which was also used by the German transport service, with the result that the Resistance was able to acquire exact knowledge of the German transport arrangements, and in addition could do so with illegal radio telegraphists operating at a considerable distance from the closed telegraph network, so that they were protected against the German counterespionage. This last point was important. There can hardly have been any other illegal group which was hunted with more determination by the German counterespionage than those illegal radio telegraphists, who were in constant danger from the German direction-finders.

HOLLAND. Holland, like Belgium, lay quite near to Great Britain, geographically, but as far as courier services were concerned, desperately far away. As regards communications, Holland was even more isolated than Belgium. Here there was no co-operation with French groups, and where the Belgians had to operate with four frontier crossings on the long route to Portugal, the Dutch had one more frontier to cross, and one which was tightly closed. Holland was sharply divided from Belgium as far as administration was concerned, when Arthur Seyss-Inquart was appointed Reich Commissar, and the Germans made no secret of their long-term aim of incorporating Holland in the German Reich. Holland thus probably became more completely cut off, for several reasons, than any other country in the north or west. The problem grew more serious in the spring 1941, when the North Sea coast of Holland, which was already closely guarded, was in addition isolated from the rest of Holland, as the Friesian Islands, the provinces of South Holland south of Rotterdam, and the whole province of Zeeland, became forbidden territory for all but the local population. This added one more "frontier" line, with the demand for special exit permits. In April 1942, the whole coastal zone between Helder and the Hook were put out of bounds. During the whole war, only about 200 Dutch nationals succeeded in reaching Great Britain by crossing the North Sea.[27]

In spite of all the difficulties, however, intelligence activity was also established here.[28] On 19 July the exile Dutch Government, which was then completely cut off as regards information on developments at home, set up an Intelligence Office under the name "Centrale Inlichtingendienst", with the duty of establishing intelligence contacts in the occupied areas, and of obtaining both military and political information, also including reports on feeling and standpoints, for the use of the B.B.C. and its special department, "Radio Oranje". In the previous pages, particular emphasis has been laid upon the value of the work of intelligence organisations in obtaining military intelligence for the use of the British and Allied Staffs, but it should also be mentioned that the British Government, the "Political Warfare Executive", and particularly the exile governments were hungry for information which could keep London up to date as regards information of all kinds in the occupied territories. Such knowledge was a condition for effective propaganda, and the technical preparation for resistance movements, and for the exile governments' policies and reactions; and even details such as the character of rationing, local restrictions and all the restrictive decrees of the Occupying Powers were of interest. No exile politician came to London without – only a few days later – feeling himself isolated and out of touch with feeling and conditions at home. The exile Dutch Government's initiative must also be seen in this light.

The leader chosen for the "Centrale Inlightingendienst" had been a high-ranking member of the Hague Police – F. van't Sant. As long ago as the First World War, he had co-operated with the British SIS, and he therefore had good connexions with this organisation. In collaboration with SIS's expert on Holland, Colonel Rabagliatti, he took up the work of repairing the broken threads of contact across the North Sea. This work was started on 28 August 1940, when a Dutch Naval Lieutenant, van Hamel, was dropped by parachute with a radio transmitter near Leyden, and he succeeded in the course of a few weeks in getting four information groups set up, and in addition acquired three more transmitters of Dutch make. Van Hamel himself was arrested in October and later executed, but three of the groups he organised were able to continue working throughout 1941, and one of these into 1942, until they too were torn up. Although it was extremely meagre and sporadic, the first intelligence leaked out by this channel to London. Van Hamel's pioneer work was followed up by another agent, who was dropped in November 1940, but his contact adresses turned out to be unworkable, and his mission had no results. Van't Sant and Rabagliatti made a further attempt in June and again in July 1941. The first agent made contact, and a little military intelligence material was sent out of the country, but he was arrested after six weeks, while the other agent succeeded in working for a year before he too was arrested.

From London's point of view the situation in the years 1940–42 was far from satisfactory. The intelligence received was scattered, slow and quite insufficient, and information on political and practical conditions, especially, was far from adequate, so that both the exile government and British Staffs were still groping in the dark as regards the situation and feeling in Holland. There was a lack of quite elementary knowledge as to such things as the form of identity cards, the withdrawal of silver coins, the clothing situation – all of them details which in one way or another would come to affect possibilities for equipping the agents sent over sensibly and realistically. In addition, there was disagreement in London. Van't Sant withdrew from the work in the summer 1941 after criticism from exile Dutch circles of his combining his intelligence work with his work as Queen Wilhelmina's Private Secretary. His successor, a Naval Officer, de Bruyne, quickly came into conflict with Rabagliatti, and he too withdrew from the work in the spring 1942, after he had, however, sent over four more agents.

Just how desperate was the need to obtain information from the closed country was demonstrated by one of the methods which were attempted. A young student from Leyden, Hazelhoff Roelfzema, succeeded in escaping to London with a group of comrades. Roelfzema could give the information that there was a curfew in Holland between midnight and 4 a.m., but that every Friday evening and night, German officers held a noisy party with guests at a beach hotel in Scheveningen, directly overlooking the promenade. The plan, which was carried out after eight unsuccessful attempts, was that a fast gun-boat should come in to the coast and land an agent dressed in a dinner jacket, covered by a watertight suit, who should wade the last few metres and later mix with the guests. In addition, the agent was well supplied with cognac, and smelled strongly of it. Two men, one a radio telegraphist, van der Reyden, who was an excellent telegraphist, but had no experience in intelligence work, were smuggled into the country in this way. On the other hand, an attempt failed to smuggle out a Social Democrat, Doctor Wiardi Beckmann, who was to have had a seat in the exile Dutch Cabinet,[29] by this dangerous back door. The hope had been to achieve a blood transfusion of competent political information for the exile government on developments at home, through him. He was arrested, however, during the attempt in January 1942.

An attempt to promote the intelligence service in Holland with the help of a Belgian agent, Gaston Vandermeersche, who was sent over in September 1942, also stranded. He did succeed in getting a few reports prepared and sent to London, but poor communication there between the Belgian and Dutch Headquarters prevented the reports from reaching the exile Dutch authorities until well into 1943. "It is sad to relate", notes the

Dutch historian Louis de Jong,[30] "that the reports gathered dust on the shelves of the Belgian Intelligence Service in London until, about a year later, they were discovered there by the Dutch".

Added to these more or less unsuccessful attempts, from March 1942 the "Englandsspiel", as it was called, began. This was the German infiltration of the whole Dutch-British Resistance apparatus, which paralysed large sectors of this apparatus completely up to the end of 1943, with catastrophic effect, but which will be described in detail in another context.[31]

To sum up, it must be recognized that the intelligence work carried out in Holland during the years 1940–1942, in spite of determined efforts, tragic losses and intense need of it, had but few and scattered results, and that accidents, political and personal differences, and extremely difficult conditions stood in the way of effective work. On the other hand, a decisive change for the better was to come, with finally, excellent results in the later years of the Occupation.

The change followed initiatives in London, in neutral countries, and at home. In London the Dutch leadership was completely reorganised at the end of 1942. A fresh start was made, with an entirely new office, "Bureau Inlichtingen", under the command of a Major J. M. Somer,[32] who was familiar with conditions in Holland from personal experience, as he had himself taken part in the work of the Intelligence groups which the various agents had tried to establish up to 1942. Somer worked in close and smooth co-operation with SIS, and he showed excellent judgement in his choice of men for the work. From March 1943 and thereafter he sent 43 agents in all to Holland, with the mission either to build up independent networks or to co-operate with networks already in existence. Seventeen of these Resistance men lost their lives during the dangerous work, but in spite of these inevitable losses, the radio contact now increased very rapidly, so that all German troop movements and other important military dispositions, as well as general conditions in the country, were known in London with minimum delays, often only a matter of hours. Information which both here and in Belgium was particularly important and which was repeated in the case of Holland four times a day, on weather conditions and therefore flying possibilities, and here too, with the help of local technicians, the Dutch telephone network was successfully tapped for information on German dispositions of every kind, and this was done behind the Germans' back. Somer also achieved close co-operation both with SOE and OSS, as well as establishing connexions with a British organisation for building up escape routes for

British pilots, escaped prisoners of war, or soldiers who in other ways were cut off from their units. This last group was especially important after the Arnhem operation in September 1944, where Parachute Troops who were hidden by the local population north of the unsuccessful Rhine bridge-head, were smuggled back in their scores to the Allied Lines.[33] Somer's work was in full progress from 1943 and gradually intensified as the months passed, particularly in the period following the Normandy Invasion in June 1944. When the Allied troops reached South Holland in September 1944, and occupied, among other towns, Eindhoven and Nijmegen, a new tool was taken into use. One of Somer's Intelligence groups, "Groep Albrecht", led by the parachutist de Jonge, noticed that a private, closed telephone network existed, belonging to one of the Dutch electricity companies, and through this telephone network, which was unknown to the Germans, information was telephoned daily direct from occupied Holland to a branch office which Somer had set up in Eindhoven. Similar telephone contacts, even occasionally over the normal telephone service, were taken into use for communication between the Resistance groups in North Holland and an Allied Intelligence centre in Nijmegen. This became especially important during the Allied offensives in March and April 1945.

This was the London initiative. It was concentrated on military intelligence. But from 1942, a wider political information service was set up, forewarding material via Sweden. A certain amount of shipping plied between Holland and Sweden, based upon the harbour of the town of Delfzijl in Groningen, in the north-east corner of the country. Ships crept along the coasts and through the Danish waters, carrying chemicals on the outward voyage and returning with timber, and these offered an open door which had to be used. After this had been used as an escape route, and one of the refugees thoughtlessly boasted of it to a reporter from an American radio station, the ships were strictly guarded and searched, but a number of the skippers using the route undertook nevertheless to smuggle microfilm material out; and one of the town doctors, Oosterhuis, formed a local intelligence group, collecting material from the whole of Holland, which the Dutch Consul in Stockholm undertook to forward to the Allied embassies. The route became effective and it was particularly political and other material, of less urgent character than military intelligence, that came out in this way, until Doctor Oosterhuis was arrested in July 1943, and this traffic was brought to an end.

By then, however, another courier route had been opened. In the summer 1942, a young girl, Miss Kohlbrugge, who was a member of a

Resistance group which published the Resistance paper "Vrij Nederland", and who had previously studied in Switzerland, obtained permission to travel to Switzerland. The reason she gave was study, but her real
purpose was to set up a courier route through Belgium and France to
Switzerland. In Geneva she contacted the Dutch General Secretary of
the World Council of Churches, Doctor Visser't Hooft. Shortly before –
in the spring 1942 – he had been in London, where the Dutch Prime
Minister, Gerbrandy, had urged him to obtain information on conditions in
Holland. Now the two initiatives and two "men of good will" met, and a
courier route became a reality from the autumn 1942 until the summer
1944, when the situation rendered it unnecessary. The route became
thoroughly organised with the help of Dutchmen in Brussels and Paris,
and with the formation of a special committee in Holland, "De Switserse
Weg", which itself was in contact with a special committee in Paris,
"Dutch-Paris". It was of decisive importance that "De Switserse Weg"
had regular contact with reliable chiefs of administration throughout the
whole of Dutch society,[34] and that the committee had close contact with
the most important illegal organisations in the country.The fact that it
now became possible to establish contact, in spite of the closed frontiers,
illustrates the situation, where Resistance groups in West Europe had
now succeeded in organising and uniting to an extent which was unthinkable in the pioneer phase in 1940.

A steady stream of military, political and economic information now
passed along this route towards Switzerland, all of it naturally in microfilm and with the use of every imaginable form of camouflage packing,
as was the case all over Europe, when it was a question of forwarding
illegal material: microfilms in tooth paste tubes, in soap, in tooth
brushes, fountain pens, book bindings, etc. From Geneva the deliveries
were forewarded to Stockholm or Lisbon which, unlike Geneva, had
direct air routes to London.

All in all, it was probably Holland which had the greatest difficulties of
any country in northern and western Europe in building a bridge to the
free world and delivering intelligence material. But in spite of all the
difficulties and reverses, both the military Staffs in London and the exile
Dutch Government came into possession of an ever-increasing amount of
vital information on developments and conditions in the country.

DENMARK. In the list of occupied countries which could give Great Britain important military information, Denmark must necessarily take a
key position. Most of the German transport to Norway, and to some

extent also from Germany to Finland across the Øresund and through Sweden, went through Denmark, and German shipping movements could largely be registered in Danish waters.

In addition to this, there was naturally interest in the German troops' positions in Denmark itself, German fortifications there, and German use of Danish economy. This last question had no great importance in 1940, but became increasingly important as the War developed, whereas German shipping movements in Danish waters and in the Baltic were of intense interest throughout the War. Denmark was not at war with Germany, however, and Denmark was not an Ally. The question arose as to how Denmark or Danish Intelligence organs would react to the very special situation which existed.[35] A democratic Danish Government was negotiating with the Occupying Power, although with no liking for it. It was directly on guard against any risk of Nazi influence in the country – apart, of course, from the all too real influence which the physical presence of the Nazi Occupying Power constituted, and its ability in the event of Danish unwillingness to negotiate, to enforce its will. The Germans could do this as they did in Norway and Holland by operating with the small Danish Nazi Party which, although it had no influence in the country, could in a given situation be pushed into place by German bayonets. This threat seemed realistic in 1940, and had considerable influence on the decisions of the Government.

It is clear that the Danish Government could not take any steps in support of the Allies – from June 1940, of Great Britain. But the existence of a Danish Government and the conditions of the capitulation of 9 April 1940 meant, nevertheless, that the Danish Army was maintained, even though in extremely reduced strength, and with it, the Army Intelligence Section. The officers in this very small and therefore closely knit section were in a very favourable position to obtain military and other intelligence of value to the Allies, and the temptation was not only obvious, it was so to speak built into the actual Intelligence functions. The officers were in the possession of important information, and were constantly receiving more, but this had no value so long as it simply piled up in the section's archives in Copenhagen. From a functional point of view, such information could have but one logical destination – the British and later the American Headquarters in London. Added to this, Denmark, unlike Holland and Belgium and to some extent also unlike France, had few problems as regards forwarding possible intelligence material. Neutral Sweden lay within sight of the Staff Offices in Copenhagen, and the connexion between Denmark and Sweden was not quite cut off, nor particularly strictly guarded, for one reason because the guard duties were in the hands of the Danes, although under German supervision. This opportunity must be and was exploited.

In the summer 1940, the Danish newspaper editor Ebbe Munck, who had close contacts and friendships within the British world from the Greenland expeditions of the thirties, and from a four-year period as correspondent in London (1931–35), negotiated with the Danish Intelligence Officers on the question of how a Danish Intelligence Service could be established on behalf of Great Britain.[36] The plan was very simple. Munck would take up residence in Stockholm as correspondent for one of the leading daily papers based in Copenhagen, and the officers would simply send him microfilms of their information. Such microfilms could be sent over quite easily, by varying couriers on official legal errands in Sweden, and with the co-operation of the Passport Police. The couriers were handpicked from Munck's and the officers' circle of friends. The first delivery came through in October 1940, and from then on until the Danish Army was disbanded in August 1943, delivery after delivery crossed the Øresund. From February 1941, this contact was further consolidated by SOE posting a permanent representative, Ronald Turnbull, in Stockholm. He thereafter maintained a running correspondence with the officers in Denmark, in close co-operation with Munck. This co-operation led to the supply of such a vast amount of comprehensive material that from the spring 1942, an official agreement was made, whereby the British, with the authority of the British Government, refrained from carrying out intelligence activity in Denmark themselves. In the autumn 1941, SIS had tried to send their own agent, a Danish Flying Officer, Thomas Sneum, to Denmark,[37] but his attempt to establish his own network stranded. After the above agreement had been reached, all intelligence activity in Denmark was solely in Danish hands – up to 29 August 1943, the circle of Intelligence Officers working formally in co-operation with SOE. This vast material had a purely static character at first, since before 1943 the officers had no possibility of sending urgent messages by radio. However, the material was often of great importance, particularly when it referred to German shipping movements, and for example, in the spring 1943, when it made correspondence possible between the British nuclear physicist Lord Chadwick and the Danish nuclear physicist Niels Bohr; and also in 1943 when information was sent through on an unexploded V.1 missile which had landed on the Danish islands of Bornholm during trials.[38]

On 29 August the Danish Government resigned, and the Army was disarmed and dissolved. The circle of officers who had carried on this service sought safety in Sweden, where they set up an information office, in co-operation with the Swedish Intelligence Service and the Allied authorities in Stockholm. All this had been foreseen, however, and the Intelligence Officers had made arrangements before leaving with a young Lieutenant of the Reserve, Svend Truelsen, that he should re-establish the service in Denmark. With this possibility in view, he had already been given special staff training. Truelsen's re-establishment of the Intelligence Service succeeded beyond all expectations,[39] and from November 1943 material was again flowing via Stockholm to London. The stream swelled rapidly, and the Danish editing and digesting of the material was now so thoroughly organised that the information became easier to grasp and to handle. From March 1944, Truelsen had his own direct independent radio contact with London, so that thereafter, urgent messages could be sent over without delay.

It did no harm to this work that Truelsen had to leave Denmark in the early summer 1944, and go to London via Sweden. Here too, others were ready to assume the work in Denmark, and when Truelsen was taken on to SOE's Staff in London in July 1944, he had the opportunity, in a leading position, of editing the material received. This was then passed to the Staffs interested – first of all SHAEF, the Admiralty, the War Office, the Air Ministry, and the Foreign Office, and to the American Staffs – in the form of summarized and complete reports on the position of German troops, fortifications, etc. It was also concentrated into weekly surveys, and, lastly, in daily messages on alterations during the preceding 24 hours. Also, the Allied Staffs could send and often receive answers to questions of special interest.

In the years 1940–43 the Danish Intelligence Officers had regarded their work as so vital that it must be considered Denmark's most important contribution to the Allied war effort, and all other Resistance activities – including SOE's plans for sabotage and the formation of an underground army – should be subordinate to the maintenance of the Intelligence Service. The British, particularly the Admiralty, could accept this point of view up to the autumn 1942, but no longer. During the whole Occupation, however, the Danish Intelligence Service was highly valued as an important contribution to the common struggle, and the Danes themselves jealously guarded their monopoly of the service, so that it remained in Danish hands and was staffed and financed solely by Denmark.

NORWAY. British Intelligence, led by the Secret Intelligence Service (SIS) was established in Norway as early as the winter 1939–40, and was expanded at the beginning of the spring 1940, simply in consequence of the Franco-British plans for a Franco-British military intervention in North Norway.[40] After the occupation of Norway, SIS set up secret radio stations in many places in Norway, particularly along the coast and in the ports. But in addition to this, after Norway was occupied, a purely Norwegian Intelligence Service[41] was established and expanded, which functioned under the designation "XU". This service had its main contact with the free world via the Norwegian Legation in Stockholm, which set up a special office for intelligence, known as "Mi II", that is to say, the Second Military Office , which again had contact with the exile Norwegian Government and its intelligence organisation, under the Defence Department's E-Bureau, and the Defence High Command's Second Office (FO II). XU worked chiefly with defensive intelligence, that is, they collected material for use during a possible invasion of Norway – maps, reports, sketches and photographs. Towards the end of the War, XU also obtained radio contact in co-operation with SIS, which maintained its independent intelligence work in Norway. The work of SIS in Norway must be regarded as part of the Norwegian Resistance work, as SIS worked closely with the Norwegian Foreign Department and the Norwegian Navy as well as with FO II. For this work, agents were trained in Great Britain and then sent in by SIS in co-operation with the Defence Department's Intelligence Section or – towards the end of the War – by FO II. In the actual work there was a clear-cut separation from all other Resistance work, beginning with the first radio contacts in June and July 1940. The number of SIS stations increased considerably, consisting in 1940 of two stations, in 1941 six stations, and in the years 1942–45 increasing to 16, 28, 58 and 47. One of the principal tasks of the service was continuous orientation on German shipping movements, and particularly information on the positions of German warships, the "Bismark" and the "Tirpitz" in particular, and also the German U-boats. All in all, intelligence from Norway was both comprehensive and rapid. XU mapped the development of "Festung Norwegen" continuously, and German shipping movements were closely followed and quickly reported to London. Static material was normally sent via Stockholm by courier, but the information on shipping went through the radio channels established. From 1942 the radio stations together covered the whole of the long Norwegian coastline, and formed the background for the British attempts to neutralise the German Fleet operations from Norwegian ports.

POLAND. Intelligence material from the occupied countries of northern and western Europe went to the West alone – to British and later American Headquarters. This was also the case with the Polish Intelligence Service, although after the German Invasion of the Soviet Union on 22 June 1941, it found itself in quite a different situation from that in North and West Europe, in that, unlike intelligence from the North and West Polish intelligence had immediate relevancy for the Soviet Union, increasingly so through the years 1942–45. This created quite special problems for the Polish Resistance organisations' Intelligence Service, and these problems grew to almost catastrophic proportions in April 1943, when the Germans uncovered a group of mass graves at Katyn near Smolensk, containing the bodies of about 4500 Polish Officers, taken prisoner after the Soviet invasion into East Poland in September 1939, and executed and buried in the Russian occupied area.[42] Although, when the Germans published this discovery, the Soviet Government repudiated all responsibility or guilt, and accused the Germans of having carried out the massacre, the Polish Government under the leadership of Wladyslaw Sikorski, who in December 1941 had signed a pact of friendship and mutual support with the Soviet Union in the hope of a Polish-Soviet understanding, immediately demanded a Red Cross investigation. This resulted in the Soviet Union breaking off diplomatic relations with the exile Polish Government. Poland thus found herself in the exceptional situation of being an Ally without an alliance or even diplomatic relations with the warring Great Power to which she was, both geographically and strategically, inextricably bound. This inevitably influenced the Polish Intelligence Service, which primarily and, in the situation, strategically speaking illogically, was West-orientated, although Poland lay within the Soviet operational area, and quite outside the area where the Western Powers could exercise any decisive influence.

Poland's political situation must be summed up briefly here, in explanation of the specific situation in which Poland and the Polish Resistance now found themselves. Poland was an ancient nation, and a young state. The old, powerful Polish nation had been split apart when Poland was carved up in the eighteenth century – Russia, Prussia and Austria-Hungary each seizing a share of a country in internal dissolution. But the Polish people lived on, and during the nineteenth century they carried out a number of rebellions against the Russia of the Tzars – the central division of Poland and her capital of Warsaw having fallen into the hands of Russia. All these rebellions failed, and the Russian autocracy became firmly established during the century. The consequence of this became a tradition of strong anti-Russian feeling in large sections of the Polish people,[43] and an exile Polish movement kept alive the hope of restoration of the Polish State.

This hope was fulfilled at the end of the First World War, when the treaty of Versailles ensured the establishment of the Polish State, at the cost of Germany, Russia and Austria-Hungary. The new state became larger than foreseen, however, as the new Poland, in a war with the Soviet Union, ravaged by civil war, took large areas of White Russia and the Ukraine. Thus the foundations were laid for serious Polish-Soviet tension, which was maintained through all the years between the wars. Thus Poland had a good deal of responsibility for the fact that no alliance was signed between the Western Powers and the Soviet Union in 1939, when there was an acute threat of German aggression against Poland. The anti-Soviet Polish Government did not want Soviet troops on Polish territory. The results was a Polish alliance with the Western Powers, who in 1939 were cut off from bringing aid to Poland. Another result was theNon-Aggression Pact between Germany and the Soviet Union, and an agreement on the liquidation of the Poland of Versailles.

When in the middle of September 1939 Poland collapsed under the German Army's onslaught, Soviet troops advanced into East Poland on 17 September, and seized the large territories which Poland had captured in 1920, taking 250,0000 prisoners, of whom about 15,000 were officers. The fourth partition of Poland was a fact. But a consequence of this was that the exile Polish Government and the Polish Resistance Movement it created, as long as they desired the restoration of an unchanged Versailles Poland[44] must turn to the Western Powers – from 1940, Great Britain, as the United States was not involved in the Polish question – in the hope of a Western Allied victory which could re-establish the Versailles Poland which the Soviet Union neither could nor would recognize in any circumstances. A deep aversion against the Soviet Union, and unwillingness to co-operate with her eastern neighbour went hand in hand with hatred of the German Occupying Power, and the early Polish Resistance Movement, which worked with the exile Government, found itself held in a vice of ambivalence, to put it mildly. They desired a German defeat, but not an all-conquering Soviet victory – and this was precisely what they got.

In the two years of occupation from 1939–41, the problem was not acute. During that period, there was only a question of a purely British struggle against the Axis Powers. The Soviet Union was not involved. But after the German aggression against the Soviet Union in June 1941, problems began to present themselves. Great Britain and later the U.S.A. became allies of the Soviet Union, and the Western Powers could easily pay more consideration to the Soviet Union than to national Polish interests.[45] In 1941 and 1942, however, the situation had not reached an acute stage. The German Armies were then far inside Soviet territory, and no one could foresee with any certainty how strong Soviet dominance would be in eastern Europe when the war was over. From 1943, however, the picture changed on the East Front, with the advances of the Soviet Armies, and the Polish Resistance Movement had to adjust themselves – with hope or fear – to the idea of liberation from the east. From then on, the ambivalence of Polish feeling became serious. On the one hand it was in the Polish interest and also a Polish duty to fight against the German Occupying Power and thus support the Soviet Army. On the other hand, the Polish Resistance Movement which was attached to the exile Polish Government desired a Polish, and not a Soviet, liberation. A liberation by the Western Allies was out of the question. And just at that moment, the Katyn massacres came to light, followed by the break-down of diplomatic relations between the exile Polish Government and the Soviet Union. The strong attachment of the Poles to the Western Powers thus lost much of its realism. It was maintained, nevertheless – with modifications. In reality, two Polish Resistance organisations emerged. The eldest of these, and by far the largest, was loyal to the exile Government and its policies. But from the end of 1942 a Communist-orientated Resistance Movement regarded it as a duty to pin all hopes on a Soviet victory, and to assist it in every possible way. This ambivalence in principle in the Polish attitude must be stressed, while at the same time it must also be stressed that in this résumé the problem can only be presented in black and white. There were countless nuances in the picture, for example in the local co-operation between groups orientated to the exile Government and Communist groups, and also in that the fight against the German Occupying Power was and continued to be the paramount consideration for all Polish patriots, in whichever camp they stood.

The fact remains, in this connexion, that most of the Polish intelligence work, at least for a long time, was orientated to the West.

A Polish Intelligence Service was established immediately after the Polish military collapse in September 1939, and it became an important department of the Polish Resistance organisation which, after several reconstructions and changes of name, was united in the "Armia Krajowa" (Home Army). The Commander of this army was first General Rowecki, later – after Rowecki's arrest in 1943 – the Chief of Staff, General Bor-Komorowski. In the operational plan of this organisation the Intelligence Service figured as a special and important department.[46] Both in the first years of the War – when the war effort which could be made by the scattered and under-equipped Polish Resistance forces in the common struggle was still extremely limited – and also later, when actions increased in numbers and were very useful, intelligence work received great importance in the Polish Resistance as a whole.

Before the collapse of France in June 1940 there were no insurmountable difficulties in establishing connexions between occupied Poland on the one side and the exile government in Paris and the Western Powers on the other side. From the autumn 1939 the West was extremely well informed on conditions in Poland. Great numbers of Poles were able to escape, by many different routes, and to reach the West, there to join the Free Polish forces;[47] and these refugees brought a great deal of information with them on great and small matters. The courier and escape routes went through Roumania and on to Turkey, or via Hungary, Austria and Switzerland to France, or they went through the Baltic countries to England. As early as the autumn 1939 there was direct contact between Sikorski's exile Government and Resistance groups in Poland, and it was possible, for instance, for the exile Government to transfer considerable sums of money to the leaders of Resistance in Warsaw, most of them officers who had gone underground. The exile Polish Government believed that in the end the Polish Home Army would become the nucleus of the Polish fighting forces, regardless of the creation of a considerable "Free" Polish Army outside the area of occupation; and that this Home Army, which immediately after the defeat of Poland consisted only of scattered groups,[48] should be gathered under a united command, and that it should be under the orders and the political leadership of the exile Government. Directives from Sikorski on these lines were discussed by leading officers in Warsaw during the winter 1939–40, and in May 1940 there was a meeting in Belgrade between representatives of the exile Government and the Polish Home Army, the organisational framework and international communications of which were now being set up under the command of General Rowecki.

Sikorski, and with him the military leaders of the Polish Home Army, now visualized three phases in the Polish fight for freedom: a first phase

("Mucha" = "Fly"), where emphasis must be given to organisation, intelligence service and sporadic sabotage with the means available; a second phase ("Burza" = "Storm") which would be characterised by major sabotage activity and diversionary attacks by partisan groups in connexion with Allied offensives, for which a condition must be supplies of materiel; and a third phase ("Powstanie" = "Rebellion") which would consist of a nationwide people's rebellion at a moment where Germany's collapse was believed to be imminent. When this plan was conceived, its creators foresaw Western Allied offensives into Germany, not the situation which actually arose, but which could not be taken into their calculations in the spring 1940. In accordance with this rough outline, the Intelligence Service was the function which could be and was put into action immediately; but naturally it was implied in the plan that this service should function as long as the Occupation lasted, both because there would be a need for intelligence on the short and on the long term, in the Allied world, and because each of the three phases depended upon the Polish Home Army being in possession of exact information. It should not be forgotten that although intelligence activities were intended for the free world, they were intended just as much for internal consumption.

After the fall of France, Sikorski and his government moved their seat to London, and clear agreements were made with the British authorities on Polish-British co-operation. This was based upon close collaboration between SOE and the Polish General Staff's Sixth Bureau – the Intelligence Department – under the command of General Sosnkowski. The exile Government together with SOE thus had sole responsibility for communications with the Home Army and therefore supreme authority in regard to its organisation, operational plans, supplies and communications – all of which had naturally became much more difficult after the fall of France, and became even more so after the Italo-German occupation of the Balkans in the spring 1941, but which nevertheless was of vital importance for the Intelligence Service. Contact was successfully maintained, however. The Polish Resistance leaders in the mother country made use of two methods. First, they succeeded in keeping courier and escape routes open in three directions: through Germany, France, Spain, Portugal; through Sweden; and through the Balkans to Turkey. Secondly and most important, from the autumn 1940, radio contact was established with London.

The first contact, established by technicians in Warsaw, was somewhat fragile, but from December 1940 the Sixth Bureau and SOE began attempts to send parachutists to Poland with radio sets, men and weapons. These attempts were extremely dangerous, owing to the long flying distances and the lack of sufficient, and sufficiently good British aircraft at that time, but in February 1941, the first parachutists reached their destination.[49] It is true that they landed in the Polish territory which had been directly incorporated into Germany, that is about 100 kilometres west of their destination, the "Generalgouvernement" as it was called. The team had lost the weapons they had brought. However, the most important thing was that they reached Warsaw with radio sets and money. Now a start had been made, and from now on, Poles from Great Britain got through, at shorter and shorter intervals, particularly after the British were able to put four-engine Halifaxes at their disposal. In all about 350 parachutists reached Poland, many of them W/T operators.[50] The number of Morse letters transmitted increased steadily and for August 1944 added up to about three million letters, sent by telegraphists whose numbers periodically reached about one hundred. It was typical for the situation that contact between the provinces and Warsaw was often more difficult that between Warsaw and London, so that London became the relay station in internal communications.[51]

A considerable part of the material transmitted consisted of information on the military, political and economic situations. Thanks to the detailed intelligence they received, the B.B.C., which set up a "secret" station in England in 1942 under the control of the exile Government ("Swit"[52]), could give comprehensive information on conditions and developments in Poland, and often bring the news of events the very day they occurred. This added to the credibility of these programmes, and stiffened morale in illegal circles. In addition it had a depressing effect upon German listeners, that a poster had hardly been pasted up before its contents – perhaps of quite a trivial nature – blared out in "Swit's" broadcasts. The "Swit" stations' broadcasts, sent with powerful transmitting effect, gave many listeners the impression – as was intended – that the station must be operating from Polish territory. Important military intelligence also reached London by the same channels, however. And it was military information from Poland that was particularly important, especially from the spring 1941. Poland was the concentration area for the German troops before the invasion of the Soviet Union on 22 June 1941, and in the spring 1941 the Polish Intelligence sources supplied London with weekly – in June daily – information on the German troop concentrations. This information together with other indications of imminent aggression were forwarded to Moscow, where, however, they were ignored. Also after 22 June 1941, Poland remained an important concentration area for the German Army which was fighting in the Soviet Union, or which was reorganising and regrouping on Polish territory before and after battles, and from the outbreak of the German-Russian war, the Polish Intelligence organs had important tasks to fulfil, both for the West and for the East.

And both West and East received intelligence. The question is simply by whom and in what way this was done, and here we must briefly consider developments in Resistance policy in Poland. As mentioned earlier, the Home Army, or "Armia Krajowa" was the first and by far the largest of the Polish organisations. In Polish circles it has been referred to as an organisation which included "the more conservative forces in the nation",[53] created by and loyal to the exile Government in London, and rallying to high-ranking officers of undoubted conservative views. The leader of the organisation, from 1943, and including the rising in Warsaw in 1944, General Bor-Komorowski, has a different opinion as to its roots in the population.[54] "I do not think that it has often occurred in history that the leaders of a people could be so completely certain of fulfilling a nation's will . . . No dictator, no leader, no party and no class had inspired this decision (to continue the struggle). The nation had done it, spontaneously and unanimously." This last statement is supported at least to some extent by the numerical size of the movement. In 1941, according to Bor-Komorowski's information, the Armia Krajowa reached a total of about 380,000 organised members, and this corresponds very closely to the German calculations on 1 March 1944 of a total of about 350,000 men.[55] The organisation had its political roots in four political parties,[56] the Peasant Party, the Socialist Party, "Freedom, Equality and Independence", which constituted the right wing of the pre-war Socialist Party, the National Party and the Labour Party – all of them parties which had been in opposition to the government in Poland before the war. But regardless of its composition and roots in the population, the Armia Krajowa, as we have seen, was strongly attached to the policies and directives of the exile Government, and for that reason alone it was hardly suited to supplying intelligence or to any other form of co-operation eastwards. It had no direct connexion with the Soviet Union Government or Staffs, and any possibility for creating such a connexion was seriously reduced after the Katyn affair and the Polish-Soviet rupture. But with good or ill-will, both intelligence contacts, and later tactical agreements etc. had to take the round-about route via London – if this was ever possible. During the Warsaw rising in August 1944[57] it proved fatal that the organisation had no established contacts eastwards, or that they did not use them or did not react to them.

Besides the Armia Krajowa a parallel organisation began to build up from the autumn 1942 – the People's Army, or "Armia Ludowa"[58] founded and developed by the Communist Labour Party, and allegedly supported by "certain radical groups in the agricultural community and the Left Wing in the former Polish Socialist Party".[59] With this, Poland and the Polish Resistance struggle acquired a different character from that typical of the North and West. Here developments did not lead to the creation of a Resistance-minded people's front, but to two Resistance organisations, co-operating with each other very often locally, but now and then competing with each other, and at all events with very different political aims. The Soviet Union's orders for a people's front quite evidently did not apply in Poland, although one cannot state definitely whether this situation was caused by the lack of diplomatic relations, by the Soviet state's distrust of the leaders of the Armia Krajowa – a distrust which must, logically, be mutual – or by more long-term political considerations. But when the Armia Ludowa came into existence, and co-operated on the local level with units of the Armia Krajowa, and its groups co-operated with Polish and Russian agents and Polish and Russian partisan formations,[60] the possibility arose for sending a stream of detailed information eastwards; whereas it remains an open question to what extent the Armia Krajowa, with its intelligence network links to the West, could contribute here, or in fact did so. The information stream concerned the constant German troops transports through Polish territory, and re-direction of German units, the positions of airfields and depots, and the character of German armaments as these were gradually altered. Here as everywhere, the Occupying Power ran into the problem of having to operate through enemy territory and be watched by unknown numbers of spies who could not be identified, because every railwayman or builder's mate, or in fact anyone at all could be and often was a potential spy. The Polish Resistance has pointed out[61] that this Intelligence Service eastwards made its greatest contributions in 1942, when, on the basis of German troop concentrations and transports, Polish groups foresaw and reported that the pivot of the German 1942 offensive would be in South Russia, and that its direction would be the oil fields in the Caucasus; and in 1944 and 1945, when the Soviet Army

Command was informed of the character and depth of the German defences, before they began the great offensives into White Russia and across the Vistula river.

While Polish intelligence was flowing to the Soviet Supreme Command or other Soviet Staffs, a similar service was continuously expanding westwards, and this Intelligence Service was not confined to Polish territory. Many Poles lived outside Poland's borders as forced labour, for example in the mining districts of North France where Polish Intelligence groups were active and co-operated with French groups, and Poles were also active in Denmark and Sweden. But it was most decisive that Polish workers and technicians were sent in great numbers to forced labour in Germany, where Polish espionage became possible in the heart of the German arms industry. It was here that the Polish Intelligence Service achieved its most important results. In the spring 1943, Polish technicians succeeded in establishing that experiments with V missiles were taking place near Peenemünde, and in getting hold of plans and drawings of the experimental area. This led to increased British attention to these experiments[62] and to intense air photography of the area, and in August 1943 to destructive bombing of the installations.[63] The bombing delayed the German experiments considerably, and resulted, for instance, in the experimental stations and trial grounds being moved back to Polish territory, out of reach of the R.A.F. This gave the Poles a new opportunity, which was exploited with sensational results. New detailed reports came through to London, from the start of the experiments in January 1944, and in May 1944 Polish Resistance men succeeded in getting hold of an unexploded trial missile,[64] which had landed in a marsh and was then "drowned" in the Bug river, after which, when the Germans had given up their intense search, Polish experts were able to measure, photograph, and describe it in complete technical detail. This find resulted in a special operation "Crossbow",[65] where a British Dakota based in Brindisi in Italy, landed on an improvised runaway and picked up the engineer, who had made the investigation, two Polish politicians and about 50 kilograms of the most important parts of the mechanism of the missile. It should be added that the Polish engineer, after making his report in London, returned immediately to Poland, where he was arrested and executed.

All in all, the Polish Intelligence Service came to play an important rôle, not only because of the concrete results mentioned, but just as much because of the series of other messages which were transmitted on troop movements, production, political conditions etc., as well as important meteorological reports. In all, fifty of the Polish parachutists had been specially trained, in special training camps, in intelligence work, corresponding to about 10% of all the parachutists sent from the Free Polish Forces. It may be added that it was from Poland that the free world first received concrete information on the German extermination camps, and the German crimes against the Jews, both in an official account published by the exile Polish Government,[66] in frequent messages to the Press, and also in statements by Polish politicians and diplomatic representatives. That this information was received with scepticism, is another matter.

THE SOVIET UNION. The Supreme Soviet Command gradually reached the point where it was just as well supplied with information on enemy dispositions, even in considerable detail, as were the Western Powers. We have already described how the Polish intelligence was sent eastwards, although to a limited extent, and this was obviously of vital importance when the battles of 1943 approached Polish territory or – in 1944 – took place in Poland. But the decisive sources for the Soviet Supreme Command's Intelligence Service were the Russian partisan forces, who sent in a stream of information. These forces began to gather as early as the summer 1941, and their numbers increased without a break as long as great sectors of Soviet territory were occupied.[67] The principal tasks for these partisan units were not intelligence service, but sabotage and guerilla activities behind the front lines of the Axis Powers; but accurate knowledge of the positions of enemy troops and their movements, etc., were a matter of life and death for every partisan unit. Simply in self-defence, as well as in the planning of actions, they had to obtain information on enemy strengths, concentrations and intensions. But all the knowledge which the various partisan units succeeded in obtaining, on practically every imaginable type of enemy disposition was naturally of vital interest, not only for the units themselves, but also for the Soviet Army Staffs in "the great country", and here too it became an independent Resistance duty to obtain as full and precise information as possible, and then to get this from the hinterland to the Soviet Staffs on the other side of the front lines.

Here again it should be pointed out that the first stage of the process – the actual acquisition of information – cannot have been the main problem. The Axis Powers' forces found themselves here in an especially unfavourable situation, where they had to concentrate, re-deploy, set up depots, build runways, etc., in an extremely hostile area, and transport, re-deployment, etc., could not take place without being observed by the local population, or by one of the numerous great or small partisan units which operated behind the back of the Axis forces, and which were in close contact with the local population. The main problem was at first to get the mass of information brought through the Axis lines to the Russian Army units, or to the Supreme Command in Moscow. The establishment of regular connexions[68] became just as much of a duty for the military, State and party authorities in unoccupied Russia as it was for the partisans themselves, and in the first months of the War, communications were necessarily sporadic and occasional. This was connected with the unforeseen speed of the Axis forces' advance, which disrupted the communication system set up, previously, between the fighting Soviet Army and the captured hinterland. This rupture was all the more serious in that it was part of the Russian strategy that during a possible retreat, depots of weapons should be left behind, with units specially trained to form and lead partisan groups. The primary task of those so-called "destruction"-battalions was to complete the scorched earth policy and then to form partisan units. It seems moreover that in the first months of the war there was a tendency to call upon partisan units to unite with the regular armies. A proclamation from the political administration of the front in north-west points in that direction: " Form partisan groups! Cross the frontline! Unite with the Red Army! Become leaders of partisan groups! Organise fighting groups able to cross the front! Fight your way to the east, to the main forces of the Red Army".[69] In many places this might in fact have been possible. The battle areas were so enormous, and the terrain in places so impossible to guard, that in many regions there was no fixed front, and this made it possible for couriers from the hinterland to slip through to the unoccupied areas, from soon after the German aggression and up to the time when communication between occupied and unoccupied Russia was thoroughly organised.

When the confusion of the first months was over, however, and no blitz victory had been won, communications between the partisan formations and "the great land" became established and continually improved. Here there was a difference, if not in principle, then in practice, between the intelligence situation in northern and western Europe and in the Soviet Union. While in the North and West, there was a question to some extent of one-way communication, in that the Intelligence organs collected information and sent it on in the hope that it would prove useful, and also that it would be made use of, in the Soviet Union there was a question of two-way communication in that close co-operation developed between the partisans and their activities – including intelligence – and the regular Army units' fighting activity. On no other battle fronts was there such a close tactical relationship between the Regular Army's operations, and the activities of the Resistance. The background for this was partly the purely geographical situation, that there was no sea dividing the partisans from the fighting troops, and the partisans operated behind an open front, whereas in the west, on the other hand, no corresponding front existed until 1944. Another cause, however, was that partisan warfare in Russia was based upon deeply rooted traditions, which stemmed from the Napoleonic War, and the years of revolution after 1917, and the Soviet Supreme Command operated with partisan warfare as an integral part of the whole conduct of the war. This was established as early as 29 June 1941, in a directive from the Central Committee of the Communist Party.[70] This directive was addressed to the Party and Soviet organisations in the communes in the front lines, and was quite clear: "In the areas captured by the enemy, partisan units and sabotage groups shall be established, to fight against the enemy army units, to (make) partisan war break out far and wide, to destroy bridges, roads, damage telephone and telegraph communications, to burn down depots, etc. In the areas occupied by the enemy, intolerable conditions shall be created for the enemy and all his helpers, they shall be hunted and destroyed at every step. Their precautions shall be torn apart." The directive was launched in a speech by Stalin on 3 July, and further developed in more concrete orders in a resolution in the Central Committee on 18 July.

Contact, and commanding control were therefore established with the most important partisan units as quickly as this could be done, and regular and reliable communications were set up – of equally essential importance on both sides of the Front. In unoccupied parts of the Soviet Union, special organisational groups were trained, who were then dropped in the occupied hinterland, with the duty of linking up the existing partisan units with the regular Army Staffs, and with the Soviet Command organs in general. In May 1942, this work became centralised. A "Partisan Movements Central Staff" was created in Moscow, under the leadership of the Secretary of the Communist Party of White Russia, P. K. Ponomarenko[71] – in some respects a corresponding body to the British SOE and the American OSS – and this staff had the duty of co-ordinating the actions of the partisans with the Regular Army's actions, organising their supply services and training cadres for activity in the enemy-occupied hinterland. A special department was set up to safeguard the supply service, materially and technically. The partisans received extensive duties to act as intelligence sources for the Soviet Supreme Command, or for the various Army units' Staffs, and communications were established in various ways. The courier possibility still existed, but first of all, through the organisational groups or the specially trained agents who were dropped behind the lines, the partisans received plenty of radio material, as well as the necessary coding equipment, and special Air Forces were appointed to the "Partisan Movement's Central Staff",[72] so that it became possible not only for telegraphists with radio material to be dropped, but also for Russian aircraft to land on improvised airfields in areas which had been freed, at least temporarily, by partisan forces. In this way an effective two-way communication was established, which was in high degree useful to the Soviet Intelligence Service – quite apart from its operational importance, to which we shall return later.

Intelligence units were attached to the major partisan units, as well as special reconnaissance forces which, when the system had been developed, were able to keep the Soviet Supreme Command quite accurately informed on the re-deployment of Axis troops, on fortifications, depots and airfields, etc. This information on the enemy forces' re-deployment acquired a "regular and concrete" character, and served a treble purpose: first to keep the Soviet Staffs informed on what was happening in the hinterland, second to make co-ordination possible between the partisan units' operations and those of the Regular Army, as occurred for instance before the battle of the Kursk-Orel Bulge in 1943, and before the Soviet Army offensive in White Russia in 1944; and lastly to co-ordinate the movements of the various partisan units during operations by the Occupying Power against those units.

All in all, it must be registered that even if intelligence was not the prime duty of the partisan units, it became, nevertheless, an important part of their field of activity, partly because intelligence was a condition for their own security and activity, partly because they were able, to an exceptional degree, to get a clear idea of the enemy's dispositions, and to keep the Regular Army informed on what was going on in the hinterland.

GREECE. It is true of all occupied countries that a certain interval had to elapse after occupation, before intelligence from the occupied areas could reach the Allies, and have political or operational meaning. This was particularly the case in the Balkans, Greece, Albania and Yugoslavia. None of these countries were in the front line in 1941–42 as possi-

ble concentrations areas, and they were therefore relatively more isolated than the countries we have been considering, until the Mediterranean areas became a central theatre of war, from the end of 1942. Until
then, very little indeed was known in the Allied camps – and this refers
particularly to the Western Powers, who were directly engaged in the
Mediterranean theatre – on developments in the Balkans after their conquest by the Axis Powers.

Before the occupation of these Balkan States in April and May 1941,
SOE had had offices in Belgrade and Athens, and agents in Hungary,
Bulgaria and Roumania, where they had been engaged in preparing underground activities in all the Balkan territories,[73] but generally speaking
these attempts did not go beyond the preparatory stage, and the rapid
conquest of the whole of the Balkans took them by surprise, and led to
such a hasty evacuation that there was neither time nor thought for
leaving so much as the germ of an intelligence service behind. For a time,
what happened in these countries was generally shrouded in darkness,
and no information was received on developments in these areas, which
were geographically suited and traditionally ready for guerilla warfare.

In the case of Greece, the situation was that the British authorities –
either SOE or the British High Command – at the last moment before the
retreat to the Peloponnese and the rapid evacuation from there, had
made a hasty arrangement with two individual Greek patriots in Athens,
who undertook to maintain contact with the exile Greek Government and
the British authorities in Cairo. In 1942, one of these, a young Naval
Officer, Koutsoyiannopoulos, with the code name "Prometheus", succeeded in establishing indirect radio contact with Cairo,[74] although his
radio set had so little transmitting effect that his messages had to be
re-transmitted from a relay station in Turkey, and were therefore sometimes delayed. "Prometheus" had also succeeded in establishing periodical courier connexions with various partisan groups which were in the
process of rallying during 1942, in the west and north-west mountain
districts[75] of the country. But the exile Greek Government and the
British High Command in Cairo, even in the summer 1942, had only the
vaguest information on the size of the partisan groups' operations, and
their political character, or on the general situation in Greece, or the
details of the positions of the occupying forces.[76] They knew, through
the thousands of refugees from the Greek islands, and through the International Red Cross, that particularly in the winter 1941–42 there was
famine in the country. During that year, safe conduct was given to ships
to bring emergency supplies to Greece,[77] such as Canadian wheat, partly

through Turkey and partly through the Swedish Red Cross. But the information from "Prometheus" on the military and Resistance political situations was extremely sporadic. The partisan movement came into being in the mountain districts, whilst "Prometheus" lived in Athens.[78]

A radical change in this situation was brought about at the end of September 1942, however, when the Cairo department of SOE, in co-operation with the British High Command, decided to send a hastily improvised British Military Mission to Greece. The Command of the Mission was entrusted to Brigadier-General E. C. W. Myers, with Major C. M. Woodhouse as his Second-in-Command. The Mission, which carried money, radio material, explosives and weapons, consisted of twelve men in all, dropped in three teams in the mountain district of Rumelia near Delphi.[79] Via the fragile "Prometheus" contact it was arranged that the teams would be received by local guerilla groups, an agreement which was not kept, owing to sudden arrests and a breakdown of communications between Athens and the mountain groups, but the three teams, after a vain search from the air, were dropped "blind", although in the guerilla area. After some time the teams succeeded in making contact both with each other and the local guerilla groups, and an important sabotage operation of the Salonika-Athens railway, which was the primary object of their mission, was carried out successfully.[80] What was more important, however, was that both this mission and subsequent British parachute teams established permanent contact with the most important guerilla organisations, and, after some time spent in experiments, also radio contact with Cairo. The result of the latter success was that at Christmas it was decided in Cairo that the plan to evacuate Myers and some of his comrades, leaving Woodhouse and the others in the country, should be cancelled. Those to be evacuated were to have been picked up by U-boat off the west coast of Greece, north of Corfu, but the U-boat did not appear. Instead Myers received a request, which in the circumstances amounted to an order, to remain in Greece, with the task of establishing agreement between the guerilla organisations, which were in open conflict with each other, and so improve their possibilities for operational activity on the side of the Allies. However, the fact that Myers was given this mission meant also that a British Intelligence Service was established in Greece.

It turned out that quite an effective, if slow, internal communications network existed in Greece, linking one district to another, and that large sectors of the country, particularly in the mountain districts of Rumelia, Epirus, Thessaly and Macedonia were more or less securely in the hands of partisan groups, while the Occupying Power generally speaking only controlled the larger towns, with support points along the transport routes, particularly the Salonika-Athens railway. Up to then, these facts had not been known in Cairo, nor were the partisan forces' political views known, nor the mutual rivalry which bordered upon civil war.[81] But with the establishment of the British Military Mission, followed up by continued dropping of British, American and Greek liaison and radio men in various parts of the country – in all about 200 W/T operators were dropped, out of a total of about 1100 agents dropped[82] – a steadily increasing amount of intelligence was received in Cairo on the military and political situation in the country, and in addition there were good possibilities for mediating between the conflicting parties. The trump card in this mediation was the threat to break off the stream of supplies to the various areas or organisations. The decisive factor for the Intelligence Service which was built up was, as elsewhere in Europe, the regular radio contact which was now established. This was no easy matter, even though there were no direction-finders here to struggle with, but only technical difficulties. In the autumn 1942, there was one failure after another to get the sets, which had been damaged in dropping, to work. But from January the difficulties had mostly been overcome, and one dispatch after another was transmitted to Cairo, and dispatches from Cairo – often very long and detailed – came in regularly. In his book on the work of the Military Mission, "Greek Entanglement", Myers returns again and again to the work and difficulties of the telegraphists, and at the same time he emphasises the progress noticeable from the spring 1943, and stresses the work done by the New Zealand telegraphist, Bill Jordan.[83] "Since his arrival in January Bill – a New Zealand press correspondent in peace time – had raised the standard of our communication from a state of almost continuous failure to obtain contact with Cairo to one of the highest efficiency. He was now assisted by an able staff-sergeant, Stan Smith, and two other operators who had been dropped at different periods in the early spring. The daily, and often twice daily, schedules with Cairo worked so regularly that it was possible to maintain an extensive flow of traffic both ways on each schedule".

Myers' words on the unsuccessful efforts should be supplemented with the fact that in spite of all the difficulties, contact had already been made periodically during 1942, and that Myers had, for instance, received the comprehensive instructions mentioned above from Cairo at Christmas. But the essence is that regular contact was not established until about the New Year 1943. Myers mentions that from then on there was contact with Cairo every day, and sometimes twice a day, with messages both outward and inward, on economic, political and military questions, including frequent meteorological bulletins, which were extremely important for the aircraft flying personnel and supplies into Greece. It may be added that communication between members of the mission on the march in the various mountain districts was achieved with Cairo as relay station. Dispatches from Epirus could get through to Thessaly or Rumelia without much delay, and without straining the long courier route, hazardous as it was, in spite of all internal communication.

It leaps to the eye, that in the case of Greece the Intelligence Service was established essentially on British initiative, even if in the first phase they had been able to build on the contact with "Prometheus", which was cut off, however, in the winter 1942–43, when Koutsoyiannopoulos was arrested. By then, however, the British contacts had been established and the High Command in Cairo had a clear idea of the political situation of the Resistance in Greece. That the messages were fairly unanimous in reporting a republican feeling in Greek Resistance circles, and that the Foreign Office recoiled from drawing its conclusions from this concensus of opinion is another matter.[84]

YUGOSLAVIA. In many respects, the development of the Intelligence Section in Yugoslavia came to ressemble the developments in Greece. Here too the military collapse in April 1941 came so suddenly that neither SOE nor any other British authority managed to arrange for any contact in the country, before their precipitate evacuation. Not so much as a radio transmission set was left behind, and when later a new fumbling start was made, it had to be from scratch. Nor did the Yugoslav Government – which under King Peter, who was hardly more than a boy, and with General Dusjan Simovic at its head, sought exile in Great Britain – leave behind any form of agreement which would allow it to keep even slightly informed on developments during the Occupation. A black-out descended over the country and its fate, and remained there for a long time. In the Allied world – and this applies to both Great Britain and the Soviet Union – no precise information came through for months, as to what was happening behind the Axis curtain. Until well into the late summer of 1941, one could only build upon unconfirmed rumours, which trickled out via Istanbul and through the American and Turkish consulates in Belgrade, and which told of a national rising, apparently under the leadership of a certain Colonel Draza Michailović, a Serbian Staff Officer of Serbian nationalist and royalist views. For the exile Yugoslav Government, these sporadic messages, however vague they were, were of immense importance, and the information was passed on to the British Government. However, this first vague information contained only a part of the truth of what was happening in Yugoslavia, and only what was known in Belgrade. The reality was different, and far more complicated, although there was an element of truth in the rumours. It was true that a Resistance organisation had been created around a Colonel Michailović, who depended upon the Serbian nationalistic Cetnik organisation, and it was true that there was wide-spread sabotage and guerilla activity in the country – in reality a broad popular revolt was spreading like a prairie fire – but this activity was primarily inspired by the Communist Party, and led by the General Secretary of the Party, Josip Broz (Tito). And even though in the summer and autumn 1941 there was still a certain co-operation between the two organisations, and the Cetnik groups gave local support to the Tito movements, there would soon be a rupture and direct conflict between the two movements.[85] The rumours agreed, however, with experience from the First World War, when there had been Serbian guerilla activity behind the Salonica front, and the British Government, understandably enough, considered them fairly credible. On 25 August 1941, Winston Churchill wrote to Hugh Dalton,[86] the political Chief of SOE: "I understand from General Simovic that there is wide-spread guerilla activity in Yugoslavia. It needs cohesion, support, and direction from outside. Please report briefly what contacts you have with these bands and what you can do to help them."

At this stage, Dalton had nothing to report. He and SOE had no direct contact whatever, and knew just as little of Yugoslav affairs as anyone else outside the borders of the country. How far he was from the actual events is evident from a statement in his hand-writing at the time – August 1941:[87] "The Yugoslavs (the exile government) the War Office and we are all agreed that the guerilla and sabotage bands now active in Yugoslavia should show sufficient active resistance to cause constant embarrassment to the occupying forces, and prevent any reduction in their numbers. But they should keep their main organization underground and avoid any attempt at large scale risings or ambitious military operations, which could only result at present in severe repression and the loss of key men. They should now do all they can to prepare a widespread underground organisation ready to strike hard later on, when we give the signal".

This policy corresponded quite well with Michailovíc's way of thinking. It corresponded to that of the exile Government. It had nothing to do with Tito's policy or – as it would prove – with the reality. The words illustrate Dalton's lack of knowledge of the real situation in Yugoslavia at this stage.

In September 1941, however, SOE took the first initiative towards establishing contact and obtaining reliable information on what was happening. The initiative was to suffer a miserable fate. It took the form of the landing from a U-boat on the coast of Montenegro of a British Captain William Hudson, who had worked previously in Yugoslavia as a mining engineer, with two officers from the exile Royal Government.[88] Hudson's mission was one of reconnaissance. He was to contact, investigate and report on the situation in the country, and naturally get an idea, particularly of which groups or organisations were offering resistance to the enemy, and to what extent. SOE could not act in a vacuum, but needed information as a basis for further decisions. Certain, but misleading information was now received. At about the same time as this landing, the outer world obtained a slight connexion with the country. On 29 September, Michailovíc succeeded with the aid of an amateur radio set in achieving the first radio contact with Malta,[89] and sending the first facts out of the country, as he saw them, and this contact was maintained, with long pauses, throughout the autumn. From this moment, Michailovíc was no longer an anonymous possibility for the outer world, but a figure of flesh and blood. But the impression received was to have a mythical character, far from the world of reality.

Later on it was to be proved beyond doubt that the information received via Malta was misleading. Even before the talks with Tito in autumn 1941 had come to an end, Michailovíc had opened negotiations with German and Italian authorities and had decided on open warfare against the communist partisans, if possible with German or Italian aid. Of course neither Tito nor the British knew anything of this.

The task which Hudson faced became extremely complicated by the confused situation in which he landed – or stranded.[90] After his arrival, he quickly made contact with the guerilla groups which he and his comrades had come to find. There was indeed a guerilla force in existence in Montenegro. It proved immediately, however, that it was not Michailovíc it rallied to, but a leader quite unknown to Hudson: Tito. Through the partisan district in Montenegro Hudson was now brought to Tito's headquarters, which at this period was set up in the town of Uzice, about 125 kilometres south-west of Belgrade. During his travels and on arrival in Uzice, Hudson became aware of four facts: that there had actually been a national rising in July; that after the temporary suppression of this rising, a nation-wide partisan movement was coming into being under the leadership of Tito, and therefore of the Communists; that it was true that there existed a national Serbian Resistance organisation under Michailovíc's leadership; and lastly – and this was probably the most important fact in the situation – that there was an extremely tense relationship between Tito's and Michailovíc's movements. The Michailovíc movement was already known, also to Hudson. It was supported by the exile Government, and there was a little contact with it via Malta. Tito and his movement were unknown factors.

For Hudson, an immediate appreciation of the situation was extremely difficult. He found himself confronted with the existence of two movements, and further, when he arrived negotiations were in progress between the two parties on the creation of a united front.[91] In accordance with his instructions, to contact, investigate and report, he proceeded from Tito's headquarters to Michailovíc's headquarters in the town of Ravna Gora, only a day's journey to the north-east. Here he could confirm a promise which Michailovic had already received over the B.B.C., of British support to his movement; but he had no opportunity to follow or exercise any influence on the negotiations which were in progress between the two opponents. Tito wished him to take part, but Michailovíc opposed this on the grounds that this was an internal Yugoslav matter. Added to this, Michailovíc had just received the news on the B.B.C. that he had been made a General, and War Minister in the Yugoslav exile Government, which strengthened his opinion, which was correct, that at least from outside Yugoslavia he was regarded as the actual leader of Yugoslav Resistance.

All this had an unfortunate effect on his negotiations with Tito. These broke down finally in December 1941, and instead of co-operation, civil war followed, as Michailovíc's forces started to attack units of Tito's partisan army. The basis for this whole unhappy situation was to be found in both political and tactical differences. Michailovíc was a pure royalist, and as such he could not but detest and fight the Communist Tito movement. But added to this, whereas Tito looked on the immediate and nation-wide rising, with the liberation of the country and the introduction of a Communist state as his primary object, and in the name of this object was willing to disregard the losses of the partisan army and the consequences for the civilian population, who were really hostages and who had to suffer all over the country for the actions of the partisan army, Michailovíc regarded the situation from quite a different point of view. For him it was a question of keeping the Chetnik forces intact, until they could play a rôle during a military collapse of the Axis Powers and possibly an Allied invasion of the country, and re-establish the royalist government,[92] and in addition he was not willing to pay the undeniably high price which an immediate national fight would demand. It was this standpoint, in connexion with Michailovíc's pronounced anti-Communism, which made negotiation impossible. On the contrary, he turned to military confrontation with the Tito forces, and, impelled by his anti-Communist views, and his desire that his forces should survive, he compromised himself and his movement hopelessly by negotiating and making agreements with both Nedic's puppet government in Belgrade, and with Italian and German garrisons; and what he did not do himself, was done by his district leaders, who were far from always under his control. The final result was collaboration and civil war.

All this was still in the beginning stages, in the last months of 1941, when Hudson stayed, now at Tito's, now at Michailovíc's headquarters, and an appreciation of the situation must have been more than difficult to make. On the one side, negotiations were in progress between the parties. On the other side, sporadic fights were already taking place between them. On the one side there were tendencies which indicated a hesitant policy on Michailovíc's part, on the other side Hudson could actually note that his forces did occasionally carry out sabotage operations.[93] The picture was not clarified by several Cetnik groups or individual Cetnik members joining Tito's forces, while others seemed to be fraternising with the enemy. Hudson's mission to reconnoitre and report became extremely difficult in these circumstances, and in addition there were the almost obligatory difficulties with radio transmissions. He states himself that he was sent in with the "most antiquated radio set one can possibly imagine". It weighed 55 lbs, had to be transported by mules, which could not keep up with his day's journeys, and it could not function without electricity, which was not normally available in the mountains. A reserve battery transmitter could only reach Malta, and only in transmissions from Montenegro, and it also quickly burned out, and reserve batteries could not be obtained. With one thing and another, only occasional scattered information could be sent by this channel. In spite of everything, Hudson came to the conclusion that Tito's forces were dominating, and that from the Allies' point of view they were the ones who should be supported; that a civil war was developing; and that Michailovíc ought not to be supported. He managed to get a few telegrams to this effect on the air, before Michailovíc, from December 1941 and for several months thereafter, prevented further transmissions from Hudson. Michailovíc's Malta connexion continued.

How much or how little Hudson managed to send, and how far his transmissions were received, has been hotly debated. The decisive point was, however, that in Cairo and London his opinion was not used as a basis for assessing the situation in Yugoslavia. On the contrary: in Michailovíc one had found the colourful figure who so to speak personified the Resistance that one was looking for in Europe. He was the brave Serbian Officer who had stayed behind, in the well known Balkan tradition, to carry on the fight in the wild mountain regions. He was patriotic, loyal to his government, which had appointed him War Minister, and he was in communication with Malta and could occasionally supply Malta with his version of developments. If nothing else, he fitted very well into the propaganda picture of the typical guerilla leader. The outlines of the picture were drawn by the Prime Minister Simovic in an interview with the "Sunday Times" on 7 December 1941: Great regions of Yugoslavia were under Michailovíc's leadership under partisan control. His forces constituted a regular army, his soldiers, according to International Law had the right to be treated as regular soldiers, and roads and railways to Belgrade were constantly being cut off. 400 depots and 200 bridges had been destroyed. This was the tone, and PWE and the B.B.C. decided to give him the greatest publicity possible.[94] For many months he was built up as a mysterious figure for the outside world and for occupied Europe. But he was not only a propaganda figure. He also received material support, although to a very limited extent. On the basis of insufficient information and incorrect and historically conditioned conclusions, he not only received the highest priority, but an actual monopoly of the very meagre supplies which SOE could allocate to Yugoslavia.[95] Here the Intelligence Service failed for many months, with very damaging results both militarily and politically.

In the spring 1942, during Hudson's silence, SOE did make eight attempts to obtain more precise information, but they all failed.[96] At this period, there were only two aircraft available for SOE's flights to the whole Balkan region, and weather conditions and accidents also hindered SOE from obtaining thorough information. Two teams were lost, one team fell into the hands of the Ustace forces, and five attempts had to be cancelled. Throughout the whole year 1942, one lived – although with growing uneasiness – with the fiction that Michailovíc was the Yugoslav trump card, and that Serbia was the hot-bed of the Resistance. There was no concrete information on the situation in Dalmatia, Croatia, Bosnia or Slovenia, or on Tito's desperate struggle. It also contributed to the situation that one was caught in ones own propaganda, and that the Foreign Office at least had to consider the exile Yugoslav Government.[97] It was after all they who had broken with the Axis Powers in 1941, and had brought Yugoslavia over to the Allied camp.

From the autumn 1942, however, the situation in Yugoslavia received increased strategic interest. The Allied offensives in the Mediterranean theatre accentuated the necessity, for General Alexander in Cairo, that Michailovíc should now demonstrate his effectiveness in earnest. That was the reason for supporting him. In particular it was important that attacks should be made on the Yugoslav railway connexions with the rest of the Balkans. Doubts as to the Michailovíc myth were now beginning to assail SOE's Cairo leaders, and the British High Command. Both in order to obtain first-hand knowledge, and to press Michailovíc into action, an official mission under Colonel W. S. Bailey was sent to his headquarters. This mission arrived there on Christmas Day 1942.[98] Bailey's information got through, and totally altered the picture. Perhaps, but only perhaps, Michailovíc had support in some parts of Serbia, but the question of whether he had support in the rest of Yugoslavia was shrouded in darkness, and must in Bailey's opinion be investigated in detail by independent missions sent in, each to his own "sphere of influence". Michailovíc's activities must also be investigated. Added to this, Hudson now had the opportunity to transmit, and his stream of telegrams – 201 in all – now reached Cairo. Here a completely new picture appeared – a picture of a man who not only remained passive, but also, both himself and through his district leaders, collaborated with the Nedic government and the Occupying Powers – whatever his motives were and to whatever extent he was acting under the law of necessity. Hudson also reported that the Cetnik organisations were directly fighting the partisan units, who had taken up the fight against the Occupying Powers; and Hudson's concluding remark was that Michailovíc must now be forced to declare himself openly for active Resistance effort, and put such an effort into effect, and that in the event of his failing to do this, all support of him should be withdrawn. This, together with Bailey's information, destroyed the romantic picture which had been cultivated so assiduously, and for the first time attention was drawn to the partisans.

With these reports in their hands, both SOE and the British High Command in Cairo made a new appreciation of the situation. One had evidently acted blind, on misleading and insufficient information. A new orientation was therefore needed. After negotiations with London, where by no means all circles were pleased at having to make a volte-face, against the wishes and interests of the exile Government, and their own mistakes, the result was that both SOE's top leaders and the Foreign Office in March 1943 sanctioned SOE's Cairo department in sending a reconnaissance team into the partisan area. This must be a random dropping, since up to then contact had not been established with Tito's forces, and it was not even known where his headquarters were. The first group of two men – both Croatians – was dropped blind on 21 April in Croatia, and a new group led by a Canadian Major Jones followed immediately afterwards, also dropped blind, but in Slovenia. Both teams achieved quick contact with the local Tito leaders, which in itself was a proof of the movement's breadth and strength throughout the country, and a request to Cairo to send a British Mission to Tito's own headquarters followed immediately. A radio message from one of the pilot teams was to the effect that the Yugoslav partisans' headquarters agreed to receive a Liaison Mission, and "consider co-operation with the Allies as logical". Other messages made it clear that the partisan movement did not consist of scattered groups, but that it was a question of a coherent organisation under a Central Command, and SOE's Cairo leaders did not hesitate to get a mission put together and made the necessary arrangements by radio for the reception of the team.

This mission, led by Captains Stuart and F. W. Deakin, were dropped near Mount Dormitor in Montenegro on 27 May 1943, and from now on, doubts in Cairo had to evaporate. The Deakin team was dropped, incidentally, just as a violent offensive was launched against the partisans by Axis troops, Ustace troops, and Cetnik troops,[99] and the team, one of whose members – Stuart – was killed during the offensive, became acquainted at a few hours' notice with the true situation in the country, and took part in bloody fighting and a retreat into Bosnia. Deakin then reported that Tito's partisans were fighting a battle of life or death, and had a desperate need of all material help which could be given them; that the movement was under experienced fighting leadership, and extremely effective; and that Michailovíc and his Cetnik forces were deeply compromised in collaboration with the enemy. The Deakin team recommended withdrawing all support from him, and appointing an official British Military Mission, directly attached to Tito's Headquarters, as military and political liaison groups. From the end of June, the first, still almost symbolic dropping of material began.

In the decisions which now followed, Churchill intervened

personally.[100] For him it was decisive, particularly in view of his deep interest in the Mediterranean Front, and his strategic visions of an advance against Lubljana and Austria, which of the two parties were actually fighting. This party must be supported, regardless of political considerations, and in July 1943 he insisted that a British Liaison Mission should be sent to Tito, under the command of Brigadier-General Fitzroy Mac Lean, so that practical agreements could be made as to how the British could best support Tito's forces. The Foreign Office received the concession that one more mission should be sent at the same time to Michailovíc. One had still not given up hope of getting the latter drawn into the right harness. He was still the exile Government's War Minister, and this could not be completely ignored. Both missions had the duty of reporting and recommending as to how the Yugoslav Resistance could best be intensified.

It was Mac Lean's mission which proved to be the important one.[101] He was dropped with his mission of in all four British Officers, in Bosnia, near the town of Jajce, in September 1943, and from now on the intelligence situation in Yugoslavia was no longer uncertain nor the service ineffective. The partisans were constantly on the move, exposed to one offensive after another, but both their moves and dispositions and those of the enemy could now be followed quite closely, so that a co-ordinated military co-operation of considerable extent now became a reality. No more mistakes in dispositions occurred caused by a lack of intelligence service. A British Military Mission to Tito was a fact;[102] a permanent radio connexion was a fact; British Liaison Officers attached to the district leaders of Tito's forces were facts; and a mission appointed by Tito, attached to the British High Command in Cairo and led by the Zagreb lawyer, Vladko Velebit became a fact. In May 1944, Velebit carried out negotiations in London on behalf of the partisans.[103] In August Tito met Churchill in Naples. By the end of the year 1943, contacts were increasing from week to week, and as regards intelligence, Yugoslavia became an open book for the Allies.

In contrast to Greece and Yugoslavia, Albania had only peripheric strategic interest. But here too, a partisan movement came into being, partly under the influence and on the instructions of Tito's movement, after Tito in 1942 sent two of his officers into the country to urge the creation of a movement on the Yugoslav pattern. This took place, and might possibly have taken place without incitement from outside, and Albanian groups in the border areas were often in contact with Greek and Yugoslav groups. The movement here could not have any great military importance, but on the other hand, it had far-reaching consequences for the country's political development. The country and the movement were important enough, however, for the British also here to decide to send a Military Mission into Albania in 1943.[104] This was led by Colonel Niel MacLean. He was equipped with radio material, and could keep Cairo informed of his co-operation with, amongst others, the former opposition party leader, Balli Kombetar, and with the Albanian Communist Party under the leadership of Enver Hodja. Another piece in the Intelligence pattern was placed here, even if it was a less important piece.

It is worth noting that for a long time the lack of a sufficiently clear intelligence service was damaging to the British dispositions, and therefore to the Allied cause in the Balkans. This is particularly striking in the case of Yugoslavia, and there has been no lack of criticism from the Yugoslavs of British dispositions vis-à-vis Tito and his movement. To some extent this criticism seems justified. But it also seems worth noting that the intelligence service in this part of Europe, to the extent that it was established, was created predominantly on British initiative – in contrast to the situation in the rest of Europe. And it can appear somewhat strange that a movement like Tito's, which was in all other respects extremely effective, did not on its own initiative and at a very early stage establish the desired intelligence contacts with Great Britain, as the dominating power in the Mediterranean. Other movements, in spite of being very cut off, managed on their own initiative to establish long courier routes and announce themselves. One explanation – but it is hardly an adequate defence – can lie in the ideological orientation of the Tito movement towards the Soviet Union, and Tito's decision to turn Yugoslavia into a Communist State. This must at least have contributed to his turning his back upon the exile Government, and with it also upon London and Cairo, and directing all his attention eastwards. From August 1941, through a transmitter in the possession of Vladko Velebit, there was radio contact between Tito and Moscow,[105] but Tito's wish for material support from there had to strand, on geographical grounds if no others, and what was more, Moscow supported the co-operation between Great Britain and Michailovíc. Moscow, too, recognized the exile Yugoslav Government for a long time, and strongly recommended Tito to co-operate more closely with Michailovíc. For Moscow the creation of a people's front and not a one-sided Communist movement was the aim which Tito should strive for. It does not seem to have been obvious to Tito, for all his political gifts, that all material help must come from the

Allies on the Mediterranean Front. This is the only possible explanation for his waiting for a British initiative, and for his bitterness that this came so late and only after it had first been offered to his arch-enemy, Michailovíc.[106]

5. The Home Fronts and the Fronts Abroad

The Creation of a Resistance Mentality

RADIO BROADCASTS FROM THE FREE WORLD. In wartime and in times of crisis, political awareness becomes more acute. There will always be a desire for news, but during wars and crises, this desire changes character and direction. From being regarded as a journalistic feature, or perhaps even a diversion from everyday life, news becomes a vital question, possibly a matter of life and death, and the desire for news becomes a hunger. There is a tendency for interest in local, everyday questions to fade in proportion as interest in the overriding factors behind the war or the crisis increases in intensity. Both war and crisis call for adjustments in ones sense of proportion, and adjustments of this kind, towards reassessment of values and awareness of ones own political and human commitment were indeed features which marked the peoples of occupied Europe during the Second World War.

Here we are approaching the paradox that the peoples of Europe have seldom, or perhaps never, been more politically aware, more politically engaged, and in the case of the best men and women, more politically active and self-sacrificing than at the period when the Occupation settled over the European communities, with orders for censorship, isolation, passiveness and obedience, and when this same occupation decreed the most severe punishments and reprisals against all who did not obey these orders. Taken as a whole, the Occupation, with its opposition to or prohibition against all political activity other than that which served the interests of the Occupying Powers, released an eruption of political activity which, regardless of all ideological differences, at least had one thing in common – that it was directed precisely against the interests of the Occupying Powers. Of course there were districts which were only slightly affected, and people who quietly carried on their daily lives, even if in changed circumstances, but these were very few in comparison with the enormous numbers for whom politics ceased to be newspaper stuff, and became a personal question which went deep into their lives, thoughts and actions. Millions became involved and committed, and for millions, political developments became a matter of life and death. Even "unaffected" districts became affected, and even uncommitted persons became committed. They were all subjected to a propaganda which, on the background of the daily realities, forced them to make up their minds, and in countless instances to act. Contrary to the wishes of the Occupying Powers, Europe became politically aware, and politically active, and as we have seen, in the majority of cases active against the interests of the Occupying Powers. This is one of the paradoxes of the years of occupation, all the more remarkable because the Occupying Powers, particularly Germany, with the German Propaganda Ministry under Josef Goebbels' leadership, had elevated propaganda to an independent arm, and had mobilised all the forces imaginable in the effort to obtain influence and support through a propaganda success which completely failed to materialize. The means used included one-sided Press and radio services, control and censorship of the Press and radio of the occupied countries; extensive financial assistance to the Press and activities, such as meetings, of the Nazi Parties; support to the parties, unions and gatherings which were willing to promote an attitude friendly to the Axis. All this, which could be under-pinned during the years 1940–41 by an unbroken series of Axis military triumphs, drowned in the growing animosity of the occupied countries, and their resentment against the invaders and their behaviour. "German propaganda", notes Goebbels' British opposite number, R. H. Bruce Lockhart,[1] "may have inspired fear of Germany. I do not believe that it made a single friend for Germany, apart from Germans."

Such a categorical statement may not hold, perhaps, if one picks out the scattered instances where the exception proves the rule. But if one considers the statement in the way that it was intended, as a general observation, it can be applied generally. The propaganda of the Axis Powers in the occupied territories, in the neutral countries and in the Allied world, in the U.S.A. and in Latin America, was a catastrophic fiasco. There are multifarious reasons for this, and we shall here simply point to a few of the causes which were important in regard to the occupied countries, first of all the actual situation of occupation, and the ruthless and short-sighted occupation policy to which all the occupied countries, sooner or later, were subjected. All Axis propaganda, however clever it was and however credibly it could build upon obvious military victories, must fade in the war-ravaged countries which had daily to bear the lack and sufferings brought about by these victories and the merciless conduct of the victors.

To this was added a fundamental fact which in the context calls for special attention. As the Axis Powers extended their alliances and their occupation, finally covering most of Europe, and establishing apparent mastery over an enormous territory, which – exploited to the full – could have become a gigantic advantage, they found themselves increasingly isolated in relation to the populations of those territories.

The German conquests did not break down barriers – on the contrary, they created barriers, between the captors and the captured. The soldiers of the Axis Powers could strut around triumphantly in Warsaw and Paris, in Oslo, Zagreb and Athens, but in the midst of the crowds, and in spite of occasional and often doubtful acquaintanceships, they were strangely lonely, surrounded by an invisible wall of enmity.[2] In open country they could feel themselves not only lonely, but also afraid. Enmity lurked everywhere, and the Occupying Powers could only hold it in check so long as they possessed the military forces to do so. It was predictable that this would be the case in eastern Europe and in the Balkans, where the occupation policy was utterly ruthless: but that it was also the case in northern and western Europe, where the Occupying Powers for a time kept to correct behaviour, brass bands and attempts to refurbish cultural ties, is perhaps the best proof that the conquerors' isolation in the midst of victory was absolute, also when it was a matter of making a favourable impression upon others than the few collaborators. Not even the most efficient propaganda could bridge the gulf here. It was more likely to have the opposite effect. Every impulse which bore the stamp of the Occupying Powers, every piece of news or commentary issued by the propaganda of the Occupying Powers was suspect in advance, even when the news was correct or the commentary meaningful. The longer the Occupation lasted, and the more the prospects of the War altered, the deeper the Occupying Powers buried themselves in complete isolation in relation to the human masses over which they had gained purely physical control.

In contrast to this isolation was the lively contact which the peoples of the occupied countries, underneath the surface of apparent submission, established with each other and with the free world. Although no hint of romanticism should be allowed to colour our views, it is an astonishing fact that the peoples, who according to the statutes of the Occupying Powers were to be kept strictly isolated from any external influence, and to be forbidden access to internal or neutral intercourse and particularly to normal political activity, worked their way out of the intended isolation. Internal intercourse, both intercourse within the illegal circles, and intercourse between them and the surrounding population, became livelier and more intense than ever, and the imprisoned peoples were bombarded from abroad with information and commentaries to such an extent that Europe's millions became more politically oriented and more politically aware than in normal times. This was true of the many who were politically aware already, as well as the large groups who had lived hitherto with their family, trade or local horizons as the essential framework of their lives. The fisherman in North Norway, and the mountain peasant in Bosnia were just as sure as the prelate in Cracow or the lawyer in Nantes as to who was friend and who enemy, and what the world looked like. The War and the course it took, the Occupation and its consequences expanded all horizons and involved everyone, since everyone, to a greater or lesser degree had to bear these consequences, and there was no lack of information.[3] The radio stations abroad made sure of this, as well as the Illegal Press and the maelstrom of rumours. The ironic situation arose, where the Occupying Power – which was present – was isolated, whilst the Allies – who were absent – achieved enormous possibilities for contact.

The information and influence from abroad came first of all from the British B.B.C.; from the summer 1941 also from Radio Moscow; and from 1942 also from American radio stations. News on neutral radio stations also had a part to play. But in this spectrum of possibilities it was nevertheless the broadcasts in many languages from the B.B.C. which dominated the ether. Radio Moscow's greatest importance was in relation to the Russian population and the Russian partisans, even if Radio Moscow also engaged in broadcasts to the European peoples in their own languages. But neither the broadcasts from Moscow nor those from American stations were ever to play the dominating rôle which the B.B.C. broadcasts acquired. The explanation is quite simple. Great Britain was in the War from first to last; it was here that the exile governments sought asylum; it was here that intelligence from occupied Europe was sent; and the British stations had both the transmitting power and the geographical position to cover the European continental regions. There is no doubt that the B.B.C. gained decisive influence on the formation of public opinion in most of Europe, even in the Axis countries. Mussolini had no illusions as to this, when he wrote in 1942:[4] "The appearance of America confused the weaker souls and increased the already large number of listeners to enemy radio by many millions." Enemy radio – that was the B.B.C. In the psychological warfare which the German Propaganda Ministry had begun, with the radio as the principal agent, Goebbels and his assistants from 1940 met a superior opponent.

From the very beginning of the War, the British had already laid great weight upon psychological warfare, which was to play such an important part in the development of the European Resistance Movements. The B.B.C. had expanded its broadcasts in foreign languages with immediate effect, and in the winter 1939–40, Great Britain had given priority to influencing the German population, dropping leaflets in German over German territory.[5] This had had no demonstrable effect, and with the great conquests of the Axis Powers during the years 1940–41, British interest in propaganda was increasingly directed to the peoples of the occupied countries, although belief in propaganda as a weapon lived on. We have seen that propaganda was included as an element in the ABC-1 programme,[6] and the B.B.C. maintained its broadcasts to Germany and Italy; the British also continued to produce and tried to smuggle in propaganda material in German and Italian via the occupied countries. They also continued to drop material of this kind, sending it over Germany by balloon, when weather conditions favoured this method. It should be added that during this period, up to 1942, British propaganda suffered from two serious handicaps. First, these years were marked by the military triumphs of the Axis Powers, and Great Britain's corresponding lack of conspicuous military success, and this undeniably made stimulating propaganda difficult. The bombastic proclamations of victory from the Axis Powers could only be countered with realistic appreciations of the seriousness of the situation, and with factual information to correct the exaggerations of the Axis propaganda, for example in respect of numbers. The only bright spots – apart from the Battle of Britain – were the temporary success in the Libyan Desert. But it was in this very period of difficulty, and just because of this sobriety, that British propaganda won a name for credibility, which was denied to the Axis Powers – even though British propaganda could also miss the mark now and then. A certain amount of wishful thinking helped the British propaganda on its way, at least in the occupied countries. This was, however, one handicap. The other was that up to the summer 1941, British propaganda had no centralised leadership, but came under the control and direction of the Foreign Office, the Ministry of Information and the Ministry of Economic Warfare, and the British Chiefs of Staff and the War Cabinet also insisted on taking a hand. This state of things was brought to an end when, in the summer 1941 as already mentioned, the commanding organisation for all British propaganda, the Political Warfare Executive (PWE) was created, with the former Ambassador to the exile Czechoslovak Government, R. H. Bruce Lockhart as Director-General.[7]

The task of the new organ has already been described: To undermine and destroy enemy morale, and to support and create the will to resist in the countries occupied by the enemy. The instruments for carrying out this ambitious project were leaflets and all kinds of smuggled foreign language publications, also and especially the radio, and here in the front line, the B.B.C., although "black" transmitters also came into the picture. Arrangements were also made with the R.A.F. for its assistance in dropping the first category of propaganda material; and with the leaders of the normally politically independent B.B.C., so that PWE received political control of all broadcasts to enemy or enemy-occupied territory. Arrangements were also made with SOE as regards the training of parachutists specialising in propaganda duties.

In the composition of the staff of the new organ, Lockhart naturally drew heavily upon the personnel which had been maintaining the propaganda service ad hoc. But others joined them, and all in all it was a very colourful, but also an all-round team of propagandists who were to formulate Great Britain's broadcasts to occupied Europe. The staff included professional soldiers, civil servants from the ministries, journalists; businessmen, advertising experts, school masters, writers and other literary men, farmers, trades union men, lawyers, stockbrokers, psychologists, university lecturers from all the faculties, and one landscape gardener, as well as a majority of women whose professions were not specified, some of them leaders of individual national sections, some in the administration. In the British organs, which like PWE or SOE had the task of cultivating untraditional contacts with the untraditionally fighting Resistance organisations in Europe, untraditionally thinking amateurs played a dominating rôle.

PWE had their hands full. Every day and night, 160,000 words in 23 languages were sent out into the ether. Every piece of news, every commentary and every talk was carefully studied and its probable effect closely calculated before it was allowed to reach the microphone. Daily meetings of PWE's top leaders and weekly meetings in every national section made sure that nothing unintentional and – as far as this was possible – nothing incorrect was broadcast. Honesty without reservations was the fundamental principle, also during reverses, and the broadcasts sought to appeal to common sense and to critical thinking. If there was a question of serious reverses for the Allies, this was not covered up, and facts of this sort often reached listeners before the German propaganda machine could blare out the sensation. In this way, the wind was often taken out of the enemy's sails.

News received first priority, without commentaries disappearing nor being weakened for that reason. On the other hand, ideological tirades were unpopular, so that the B.B.C. broadcasts received a somewhat sharp, concrete form. Bruce Lockhart writes on this:[8] "One of my first efforts was to eliminate an undesirable eagerness on the part of our experts to indulge in wordy warfare with the German Propaganda Ministry. However entertaining and occasionally useful it may be to score off the enemy, propaganda is not and should not be a duel of dialectics between the political warriors of the rival propaganda organisations. It should be addressed to the masses".

A year later, Goebbels seems to have realised that there was truth and sound British common sense in this. He writes in his diary in April 1942:[9] "By questioning English prisoners of war in St. Nazaire[10] we find that our propaganda in England has had much greater effect than we had thought. The English lay greater weight on news than on arguments. I conclude from this that all our broadcasts in foreign languages, particularly those which are intended for England must be fundamentally changed. This is no longer the time for long discussions. Just as during the National Socialist fight against the republic there came a moment where posters and leaflets were no longer effective, so the moment has now come where arguments are no longer effective. I am inclined to think that our broadcasts in foreign languages should mainly contain news, but in such a way that the right tendencies are mixed with them."

Out of the total mass of the B.B.C.'s information, 78 % of the material went to the occupied countries, as PWE believed that it was there that the broadcasts had the best forum. "We were appealing", notes Bruce Lockhart, "to friends who were eager – sometimes, indeed, too eager – to listen to our broadcasts".

Nevertheless, broadcasts to enemy countries were by no means forgotten. The German Section consisted of more than 100 people, and the daily broadcasting time to Germany in 1943 was 5 hours, while that to Italy was 4½ hours. The length of broadcasts was carefully calculated according to the presumed importance of the country to which the broadcast was sent,[11] and in evaluating this and the contents of the broadcasts, PWE worked in close collaboration with the exile Governments, national committees, etc. in London. Here the size of the country, and its presumed military importance played a part, and outstanding

Resistance countries such as Poland, Holland and France had the opportunity of sending independent broadcasts, controlled by the exile organs in question. A great deal of foreign talent was mobilised, both here and in the B.B.C. broadcasts in support of the common struggle, and de Gaulle received the special treatment that the B.B.C.'s microphone was regularly put at the disposal of the Free French Forces – a privilege which gave both him and other Free French the opportunity to speak on the British radio to France. The best known spokesman for de Gaulle's views was Maurice Schumann.[12] The Free French under de Gaulle also made themselves partially independent of the B.B.C. by establishing a radio station in Brazzaville, in French Equatorial Africa, which was later moved to Algiers. But it was the broadcasts from the B.B.C. – the Free French as well as the British – which were listened to most closely in France.[13] Broadcasting times to the individual countries varied in 1943, as we have mentioned, according to their size and importance, with a ¼ of an hour to countries such as Luxembourg and Albania, 1¾ to Norway and Yugoslavia, 2¼ hours to Poland, 2½ hours to Holland and 5½ hours to France, of which only 10 minutes were reserved for the Free French broadcasts. The remaining countries were grouped in the time table according to size and importance. There was also room for neutral countries, Sweden receiving no less than 1¾ hours daily.

Over and above the actual propaganda activity, but included in the time table given above, there were the special coded messages which kept the Allied Headquarters in operational contact with the Resistance organisations, in support of all their underground activities. This had originally been a vulnerable point, but it gradually developed into routine. In operational respects, any question of the isolation of Resistance elements among the European populations was also eliminated, as soon as these systems were developed. The code messages were primitive at first, but they gradually became more sophisticated, so that they could be both unambiguous and short. They did not only have operational value, but also psychological effect, particularly upon the Staffs of the Occupying Powers, who were informed of the cryptic messages which came in hour by hour, warning them of underground activity with support from abroad, but who could only grope in the dark as regards the actual meaning of the various messages.

The contact between Europe and the free western world was thus a reality in two senses. The Europe Resistance organisations were in routine contact with the British and American support organs, for instance through the B.B.C. code messages; and people in continental

Europe, whether they were Resistance-minded groups or simply ordinary men and women, could tune in to London and – on long, medium or short wave lengths, and without the jamming stations being able to do more than make the process difficult – listen to what they believed and hoped would prove to be the truth. In London, extremely satisfactory reports were constantly received on the vast extent to which British broadcasts were heard. They received these reports in many ways, though refugees, via the neutral countries with connexions into occupied Europe, through organised opinion polls, and particularly through intelligence service reports. All these sources, in spite of occasional criticism, gave the same answers. People listened intently to the B.B.C., and the information they heard was spread far and wide, also to people who for some reason or another were prevented from listening themselves. As an extra confirmation, there was the direct proof which was implied in the energetic jamming, in prohibition against listening, in the confiscation of radio sets, and in the severe punishments which the Occupying Powers inflicted upon those who, in spite of all precautions, were caught listening.

Parallel with the radio broadcasts of the B.B.C., PWE established the "black" transmitters already mentioned. These transmitters apparently broadcast from occupied territory, but in reality operated from British soil.[14] Here, for obvious reasons, speakers were used from the country to which the broadcast was addressed, and on these "black" transmissions there was freer play for propaganda than on the B.B.C., which kept a firm hold on the sober tone and unvarnished presentation of the news which was the basis for the B.B.C.'s credibility. On the "black" stations, agitations and appeal to feelings were allowed to a greater extent than on the B.B.C. How much effect these "black" transmissions had, it is not possible to estimate. But they were included, for better or worse, in PWE's field of operations.

The same can be said of the widespread activities of PWE in printing and distributing leaflets, miniature newspapers and miniature books. It is possible, however, that this side of PWE's activity was far more important than the "black" transmitting stations. On the other hand, it cannot in any way be compared with the importance of the B.B.C. broadcasts. Nevertheless, PWE paid a good deal of attention to this activity, and the miniature editions, printed on paper as thin as silk, or directly on silk, turned up all over Europe. Bruce Lockhart mentions, with understandable surprise, an edition of Churchill's speeches, reduced to the size of a lady's handkerchief, and publications of this kind appeared quite frequently in northern and western Europe, where they supplemented the illegal Press, and by virtue of their character and origin alone, were an intriguing and desirable complement to it. The difficulty in this side of PWE's activities lay not so much in production – although this made considerable technical and typographical demands – as in distribution. The publications could either be dropped blind, in which case there was no certainty that they would reach the potential readers; or they could be smuggled in through the neutral countries – a process which was often both difficult and uncertain, quite apart from the hazards which smuggling entailed for the willing messengers, skippers or sailors. Distribution by this roundabout route was also slow, and the messages from London, when they finally reached their destination, were often out of step with the actual situation.

To some extent, PWE co-operated with SOE in this field, as the latter organisation undertook both to make aircraft available and to train special propaganda experts, who could have other supplementary duties such as that of arranging for distribution of propaganda publications made in Britain or British films for illegal showing, or of carrying out opinion polls, for instance on listening in to the B.B.C., attitudes to sabotage and Allied bombing, etc. This co-operation between PWE and SOE reflected the reality that propaganda from 1940 was an important agent for Great Britain in the combined conduct of the war, and that propaganda was increasingly addressed to the occupied countries, whose illegal struggle it was SOE's mission to support. But co-operation was far from always without friction. In PWE, high priority was naturally given to propaganda, whilst in SOE one was more concerned with the possibilities of intelligence, sabotage, arms supplies and the creation of underground armies. The point could be reached where SOE agents directly sabotaged the efforts of the British propaganda organisation. Two striking examples of this can be quoted from Denmark.[15] Here a container stuffed with top quality British propaganda material was thrown into the sea in August 1943, at an irritated order from the local SOE agent, who led the reception and would far rather have found a container full of explosives or weapons; and in the same country, in the spring 1944, two parachutists, specially trained in propaganda work, who were dropped in the belief that it was propaganda they were to engage in, were sent out by the local SOE chief on sabotage work, with definite orders to keep miles away from anything in the nature of propaganda. However, in the same country, a success can be mentioned, when a number of Copenhagen cinemas succeeded in showing British films, such as "The

Lambeth Walk" and "Desert Victory", which had been smuggled in through Sweden. Saboteurs blocked the exits of a cinema in the middle of a film, took over the operator's room and showed these British propaganda films to a closely packed audience, which included German military personnel – a daring and imaginative action which was rewarded with publicity in the free world. But an action like this one was an exception. British films also reached other occupied countries, but here they could only be shown to closed circles, which had necessarily to be small and hand-picked.

It almost goes without saying, but still deserves to be said, that propaganda from London and the whole of the free world was inextricably linked with the Intelligence Service. Energetic and reliable propaganda depended upon the propagandist, whoever he was and regardless of the means he utilised, being accurately and quickly informed on conditions and developments in the countries for which the propaganda was intended. It was especially stimulating when news from the country in question was correct and complete. If it could report fresh developments, this was an extra advantage, for it demonstrated for friend and foe alike the quick connexion between the occupied area and the free world. The Polish station, "Swit", which actually broadcast from England, but which seemed to be coming from Polish territory, thanks to a tremendous amount of intelligence work was able to bring "hot news" practically every day.[16] For instance, in the evening programmes it was able to bring news of the situation in Warsaw the same day – German decrees, the events of the day, etc. A special possibility was offered by the daily paper, published by the Occupying Power, "Nowy Kurier Warszawski". This appeared at 1 o'clock in the afternoon, but the proofs were already in the hands of illegal circles in the morning by 8 o'clock, and the contents were radioed to London so that they could be used as the background for a commentary the same evening, only a few hours after the paper appeared. The more reliable the information became, and the more listeners could check up on the news given from their own country or province, the more confidence was inspired generally in the rest of the information given. Contrariwise, incorrect or insufficient information undermined people's confidence and willingness to co-operate. London received confirmation of this fact again and again from the Resistance organisations in the various countries. The British Officers who were dropped in the Yugoslav partisan areas in 1943 came to experience this, in its severest form. Here, information had failed, and the Yugoslav partisans met these officers with bitter reproaches that people in London had cultivated the myth about Michailović, and had completely over-looked Tito's partisan movement. A wound of this kind took time to heal. Similarly the unfortunate effects can be mentioned, when the British propaganda and Press in March 1941 gave considerable publicity to an Anglo-Norwegian raid on Svolvær in Lofoten, in enthusiastic terms, when the enthusiasm was outweighed by widespread bitterness among the Norwegian men and women, who had to pay the price of the raid in brutal German reprisals.[17] The commando raid was planned and carried out without the knowledge of the Norwegian Government or their sanction, and led to the exile Norwegian Government thereafter being included in the planning of similar operations. This was another example of propaganda which was out of step with the European reality. But examples of this kind were the exception rather than the rule. In its information on developments in the occupied countries, the B.B.C. was subjected to extremely critical and always professional revision from the mass of listeners, and therefore sought by every means to ensure itself against inaccuracies and to tune its propaganda to local feeling. These were some of the reasons for the general confidence which the B.B.C. succeeded in building up around its broadcasts, and an immediate cause was the ever-increasing stream of intelligence material which reached London from all the occupied countries, at an ever-increasing tempo. In 1940–41, accurate information on conditions and feeling was in decidedly short supply, but gradually, as the intelligence organs developed a regu-lar routine, and particularly after they succeeded in establishing radio contact, the B.B.C. became an extremely reliable source of information, with constantly increasing credibility.

The U.S.A. created its own propaganda organ, corresponding to the British PWE, the Office of War Information (OWI), which in 1942 began broadcasting to the occupied countries of Europe on a line with the British stations. The organisational development in the U.S.A. took a parallel course to the British, even in imitation of the British model. In June 1941, President Roosevelt called for one of his close friends and colleagues, William Donovan, and persuaded him to establish a new organisation, built up under Roosevelt's direct control. Donovan had the title of "Co-ordinator of Information" (COI),[18] and his task was loosely described: "To collect and analyze all information and data which may bear upon national security, to correlate such information and data, and make the same available to the President and such departments and officials of the Government as the President may determine, and to carry out when requested by the President such supplementary activities as may facilitate the securing of information important for national security and not now available to the Government".

At this point, the U.S.A. was not at war, but with her help to Great Britain, was standing with one foot in the Allied camp. As early as 1940 Donovan was sent on a reconnaissance tour to Europe, first of all to Great Britain, to investigate the Commonwealth possibilities for surviving the crisis, and her material and economic needs, if the war was to be won. During this tour, and during a close collaboration with the Canadian director, William Stephenson, who had been sent to the U.S.A. by Churchill, to win over the American Government and the American people to the British cause, and to counter German infiltration in the United States, Donovan – and therefore Roosevelt – awoke to the fact that the U.S.A. was completely unprepared as regards intelligence, for the possibility of entering the war, with all the complications this could bring with it. It was this realisation which in June 1941 brought Donovan the task of building up the COI. But even the broad terms of reference of the organ indicated that the work might go beyond intelligence duties, and enter the field of a subversive and offensive character. The consequences of this were taken in June 1942, when COI was split up into OWI, which was to undertake the propaganda work,[19] and OSS, which took over the leadership of the actual undermining activity, including operational duties in connexion with support to European and Asiatic Resistance Movements. SOE thus received its American parallel in OSS while PWE received its parallel in OWI. The ideas were British – originating partly in SIS, partly in SOE – but the support to the Resistance Movements became gradually marked by the American contribution. It was the U.S.A. that had the vast resources.

As far as propaganda was concerned, it was still the British, however, who set the tone for the European countries. The American broadcasts could not compare with those from London. For one reason, the distance was so great that reception of the broadcasts was not good, and for another, the intelligence service which should be the basis for the broadcasts had not been developed, as was the case between London and Europe, so that news and commentaries normally lagged behind the constantly changing situations. A third reason was that OWI's staff lacked both experience in psychological warfare, and the British sense of its importance, and in addition, European conditions were somewhat foreign to the American commentators. Fundamentally, this difference in standpoints as to the importance of psychological warfare and the more orthodox views of the U.S.A. were connected with her vast resources of men and materiel. Here, Great Britain had memories of the blood bath in the trenches of the First World War, and had to face the fact that as far as numbers were concerned her armies could not come up to the level of the armies of the Axis Powers, and must therefore economise with their resources in men. She therefore laid great weight upon the possibilities offered by the undermining of enemy morale, and the support which could be expected, both at once and also – especially – in the long term, from the occupied countries. The U.S.A., with her great population and almost unimaginable resources, had a more massive view of waging war, and in this view, the support from the occupied countries only played a modest part, as a distant possibility. A certain shift occurred, however, towards the greater nuances of the British view, under the impression which the Americans gained of the importance of the feeling among the populations where they found themselves fighting – the first time, when the American Armies landed in French North-West Africa, and were forced to recognize the difference between resistance and welcome. In Italy and in France, also, the Americans acquired a growing understanding of the British views, and increased their efforts in psychological warfare to a corresponding extent, and their co-operation with the Resistance Movements. In a sense, the positions were reversed. In 1940 the British had laid great weight upon propaganda and upon building up co-operation with Europe's active Resistance, and of necessity had ignored the possible political consequences of a Resistance revolt which could take an uncontrolled political course when victory was in sight. They became more politically conscious, however, as regards the incalculable consequences of a too far-reaching European revolt. It was Great Britain who lay closest to a politically changed Europe, and who was most familiar with the complicated political conditions on the Continent. The U.S.A. was more distant and more foreign as regards these conditions, and politically more carefree in her engagement in whole-hearted support of all Resistance Movements, when once she had accepted the usefulness of these movements. But in the propaganda war, the American contribution had only secondary importance. Their contribution acquired importance, particularly in the form of increasing material support. For all other warring countries in Europe than the Soviet Union, London, Cairo and Algiers were the places from where information, encouragement and special messages were broadcast.

The Western Powers, however, were not alone in the arena, where psychological warfare was concerned. The Soviet Union also let her voice be heard, directly on Radio Moscow, and indirectly through the

Communist leaders who were intensely active participants in the Resistance struggle in the European countries, often as illegal veterans, and always so deeply entrenched in Communist ideology that they could act, if necessary, without direct specific orders. The war in the Soviet Union was fiercer, however, than in the West, and the situation of Russia was quite different from that of the Western Powers. Communism's fatherland was a militarily Great Power, in head-on collision with the Axis Powers, and a great part of her vast territory was quickly occupied by the enemy. Russian interests were therefore primarily to make contact with and issue directives to the Russian partisan armies, which shot up like mushrooms, as early as the summer 1941. This was the immediate consideration. Attempts to undermine enemy morale and to counter enemy propaganda came second, and interest in the more distant Resistance Movements in Europe outside the Soviet Union had a lower priority. This was particularly the case up to the New Year 1943, when the battle raged in the very heart of Russia, and when the Soviet Government and the Soviet Staffs had their backs to the wall, with other and closer problems to solve than strikes in Holland, illegal newspapers in France, or sabotage in Greece.

Soviet propaganda was adapted to these conditions. It reflected the will of the Central Committee of the Communist Party to demand the total mobilisation of all the Russian people's forces, at the Front, behind the Front, and in the hinterland conquered by the enemy. In their efforts in this regard, radio and printed matter were to play their part, which in certain respects corresponded exactly to the rôle which the corresponding instruments played in the West. The rôle was simply less subtle, and did not differentiate to the same extent as in the West, between the special circumstances and character of the different countries. Radio Moscow broadcasts were more in the nature of orders and directives, and were addressed first of all to the Soviet Unions' own citizens in the partisan armies, who were carrying on the struggle in the conquered hinterland. It became Radio Moscow's most important task, in relation to all its people west of the front lines, to ensure contact and operational co-operation between these partisan armies and the actual front line forces. Longterm questions, regarding building up an underground army which in a given situation would intervene in support of possible invasion, were irrelevant here, because the Front and the fight were already there, and because the partisan war, from the Front in the east to the Soviet borders in the west, was a reality and a part of the struggle, from the start of the war in Russia. The first directives on starting the partisan war were issued, as we have seen, as early as June and July 1941.[20] From then on, Radio Moscow established an increasingly firm grip on developments, and by special messages which were quite similar to those broadcast from the British radio stations, co-ordination between those fighting on both sides of the front line was secured.

Even though calls from Moscow had to be addressed primarily to the Russian partisans, however, Moscow naturally also sent out calls to the Communist parties outside the Soviet Union, and propaganda to all who managed to hear through the interruptions of the jamming stations and catch the faint and often wavering signals from Moscow. The main call from there was quite simple. It aimed without differentiation at the creation of the greatest possible resistance against the "occupants", as the Communists called them; the establishment of a People's Front with the Communist Party co-operating with all who would fight "occupants"; and the broadest possible co-operation with the Allies. Stalin struck the keynote in a radio speech on 3 July 1941:[21] "One cannot regard the war against Fascist Germany as an ordinary war. It is not only a war which takes place between two armies. It is also the entire Soviet people's war against the Fascist troops. This people's war to save the fatherland, against the Fascist oppressors, has not only the object of destroying the danger which burdens our country, but also of helping Europe's people, who groan under the yoke of German Fascism. Our faithful Allies in the great war are the people in Europe and America, including the German people who are enslaved by Hitlerite leaders. Our war for our own fatherland's freedom is united with the people's fight in Europe and America, for their independence and their democratic rights. It will be the united front of the people who join the fight for freedom, against slavery and the threat of slavery from Hitler's fascist armies." In November Stalin repeated this view in a further speech: "The Soviet Union, far from being isolated, has acquired new allies: Great Britain, the U.S.A. as well as the countries which are occupied by the Germans", and lastly he stated in November 1942 that "the liberation of the enslaved nations and the re-establishment of their sovereign rights" was an essential part of the Allies' plan of action.

In this rhetoric there lay not only an appeal to national Russian feeling, and an appeal for a popular rising behind the actual fronts, but also a confirmation of the Great Alliance of the Allies and an emphasis on this alliance including the European people in their fight against the Occupation. The central task for the Soviet Union must be the military struggle against the aggressors, which alone could create the conditions where the partisan struggle and the resistance struggle could have any possibility or meaning, as the supplement it could become. And it can certainly be said that the Soviet Union fulfilled this task with catastrophic consequences for the Axis Powers. However, until 1944, the Soviet Union was not in a position, either geographically or materially, to give much concrete support to Europe's multifarious Resistance organisations, and the Communist parties in North and West Europe and in the Balkans found themselves in the situation where immediate support must be obtained from the Western Powers. It was also the Western Powers' radio, and particularly the B.B.C.'s stations, which day in and day out informed the populations and appealed for their resistance, while Radio Moscow could only address public opinion in Europe to a modest degree. "As long as the (German) armies kept a great deal of the Soviet territory occupied, Stalin's primary hope was to lift morale in the population and in the Red Army," states the French historian Henri Michel,[22] and adds that general directives were issued on the radio to the Communist parties outside the Soviet Union, which did not touch public opinion directly in the occupied countries. The fact that broadcasts from Moscow only came through faintly in large parts of Europe and could only be heard with difficulty contributed to this. It was simply easier to catch the words of the B.B.C.

For the Communist leaders in the resistance organisation, this bond with the West was no problem. They were sufficiently schooled in Marxist thinking to be able to act both with and without directives. To the extent that it could be done, the Soviet Union maintained secret contact with Europe's Communist parties, and influenced the development of resistance in this way. But until the New Year 1943, while the Soviet was perforce on the defensive, and while the battles were fought deep in the heart of Soviet territory, the development of resistance in Europe was a distant phenomenon which had only marginal interest for the leaders in Moscow. The situation altered from the moment that the Soviet Union took the offensive in 1943, and the fronts were pushed further and further westwards towards the European countries. Then the attention of the Russians was drawn to the development of resistance, particularly in the Eastern European countries. Radio Moscow increased the number of foreign language programmes, reaching a total of 32 languages,[23] and special stations were set up for news and propaganda broadcasts to Yugoslavia, Bulgaria, Slovakia and Poland.[24] Both directly and indirectly the Soviet Union began to contribute to the psychological warfare, which helped in the promotion of European resistance. The Soviet influence became marked, less as the result of Radio Moscow's rôle than owing to the Communist leaders' independent initiatives and convinced ideological attitude.

The fact that the European Resistance Movements were strongly influenced from without, and that their activities depended to a great extent upon connexions – particularly radio connexions – with the free world, does not by any means imply that they were the product of outside influence. They were first and foremost the home-grown reaction to the actual situation in which the peoples of the occupied countries found themselves. They had stranded in the middle of a world war, the course of which affected them just as much as anyone else, if not more. For millions of people, its course was a question of life and death, and it was not even a simple question of the final course of the war, but of a quick or slow course. For one country after another, it was a question of national dependence, geographical dismemberment, political despotism and social and cultural oppression. It was no wonder that the peoples of Europe did not wait, as silent onlookers, when the battles raged on the open fronts. They were geographically cut off from the free world, but they were at the same time involved both spiritually and physically, and participants in the Resistance Movements which grew up in their midst felt the solidarity with and duty to the millions – often their own fellow countrymen – who were fighting on the open fronts. This solidarity could be rooted in many motives, national, religious, political, or simply human considerations, but whatever the motive, the will to make a contribution in the common struggle and the faith that it would be of value, were common to the whole of occupied Europe. For the leaders, it was imperative to convince the greatest possible number that even after military conquest, the struggle was a moral duty, a political necessity and a physical possibility.

One of the principal instruments in this war effort was the illegal Press.

THE ILLEGAL PRESS became a universal phenomenon. Regardless of what forms of action were developed by the Resistance Movements of the various countries – and this must depend upon a complex of factors, such as their geographical or political situation, their social and cultural conditions or tradition – the development of an illegal Press was common to them all. In most of the occupied countries, the appearance of an illegal Press was also the first warning of the underground struggle which was approaching. During the first months of occupation it was impossible, in most of these countries, to predict what form of action would develop, what possibilities would present themselves, and what means would be available when the possibilities finally arose, but it was not difficult to see the immediate possibility of undermining the Axis propaganda both without and within, and breaking the stranglehold of the censorship. The Occupation was therefore not many weeks old before the first illegal paper saw the light of day. In Czechoslovakia, the first leaflets had already appeared before the outbreak of the War, on 1 September 1939:[25] in Poland, as mentioned above, they were already being distributed in the streets from October 1939;[26]and in the midst of defeat, they had great psychological importance, as tokens that the fight had not yet ended, but rather it had now begun in earnest. These first illegal publications were short, and at first either contained general appeals for opposition to the restrictions of the Occupation, or to co-operation of all kinds, or they contained information on what was announced on the B.B.C., which became the most important source of the news.[27] This was the B.B.C.'s position as regards the whole stream of illegal newspapers which appeared in one country after another, where the Axis Powers entrenched themselves, and strangled official news agencies. By so doing, they paved the way for unofficial news agencies, which received a far more powerful effect than that achieved by the official news agencies.

A common psychological factor came into play here. In normal conditions, the day's paper and the day's radio news were certainly read and heard, and to a great extent believed, but censorship completely destroyed their credibility, as far as news and commentaries were concerned. This was particularly noticeable in the years of the German victories – 1939–41 – when the legal Press could bring a stream of just the triumphant – often true – bulletins which the occupied peoples least of all wished to read. It was quite another matter with the priceless typewritten or duplicated slips of paper, which sowed doubt as to the truth of what was stated officially, or in its commentaries countered the claims and views in the official flood of announcements. Here, in a primitive and exciting form, was all one wanted to know, simply because, if one was to bear the situation, one needed confirmation of ones secret hopes. For ever-increasing multitudes from Europe's millions, it was vital to their very existence that they could suck up the secret encouragement, and let the official stream of news pass them by, unheard or not believed. The propaganda of the Axis Powers, which in those years, 1939–41, could still grind out quantities of new and factual triumphs throughout Europe, drowned in a massive wishful thinking which clung to the few bright spots which a primitive paper, a rumour or a statement picked up on the radio could smuggle into their lives. Life had to be bearable, and it became a necessity to listen and believe everything that one was forbidden to believe. The illegal Press could address a circle of readers which made every effort to turn their backs to the flaming headlines and victorious bulletins, but who on the other hand read, re-read, reported and listened to the crumbs of comfort which escaped the censor, and which in an incredible, yet psychologically comprehensible way came to shape public opinion. In the fight for opinion which took place, all the official words and all the print were powerless against the little secret messages which went from hand to hand and from mouth to mouth. With astonishing speed and with an astonishing uniformity, the victorious Axis Powers and their local helpers lost their expected influence on public opinion in every country their armies overran. That this should happen in countries like Poland, Yugoslavia, and the Soviet Union, which were bombarded with threats from the start, and ravaged by terror, is quite understandable. But the surprising and most significant fact is that it also happened in countries which – at least for a time – were given relatively milder treatment, including concession, persuasion and exhortation – although accompanied by threats – and where the Occupying Powers tried at first to keep a vision alive of a new Europe under the leadership of the Axis Powers, but with vague promises to sympathising and therefore favoured countries and population groups. Their propaganda faded, therefore, as the victories showed themselves to be brutal conquests, and in the agitation there arose an absurd disproportion between the agitators' possibilities and their results. On the one side there was a gigantic propaganda machine, with control of all the Press and radio, with millions at its disposal and free access to every imaginable form of pressure, such as meetings, parades, concerts, sports rallies, flag waving, symbols and banners with golden promises – all with the guarantee of power behind them. On the other side, small, persecuted groups, anxious meetings, small means scraped together, and, at least in the beginning, small insignificant leaflets, challenging the massive mesmerism. And if the disproportion was absurd, when one considers the outward means, it was no less absurd when one considers the results. The legal and favoured was bankrupt, the forbidden triumphant. Legal newspapers were interesting to the extent that they could bring advertisements on where one could buy second-hand children's clothes, or where an alert reader, reading between the lines, thought he could detect that a successful re-grouping at the Front perhaps covered the reverse for the Axis Powers in which he wished to believe. Contrariwise, the little duplicated leaflet that was pressed into his hand, at his place of work or by a camp fire, became a true message, which he could believe absolutely. It was the Axis Powers themselves who created the foundation for this absurdity, with their ideology, which ignored everything except their own interests, and with the mentality of the "Master Race" broke with all humanist tradition and all human consideration, and thus became their own propaganda's worst enemies. Because the Occupation, with its humiliations, compulsion, terror and censorship was the dominating fact of life, and because the liberation from Occupation became the dream that was cherished, every official publication was reduced to wrapping paper, whilst the forbidden leaflets became heirlooms, smuggled from hand to hand in an invisible fellowship. To the extent that the official Press and radio identified themselves with or simply allowed themselves to be intimidated by the Occupying Power or collaborating organs, to that extent they lost their credibility.

There was also everyday psychology in the fact that the heirloom value was certainly greatest when the leaflets were rare, clumsy, and technically primitive. The illegal news sheet was like an antique. The fewer there were, the greater their value. And the illegal leaflet certainly began its hidden existence as a rare and primitive article. The first of them were often type-written letters, with carbon copies, which wandered out like chain letters into illegality. What a little group or – occasionally – a lonely person sat and wrote one night, could be known after a few days by thousands, and asked for by still more thousands. But on the heels of this form of illegal news sheet came the duplicated papers, published at irregular intervals and distributed in countless ways, dealt out secretly, dropped here and there, or posted to chosen or random addresses with camouflaged or no sender address. Step by step the illegal Press worked its way towards ever great perfection: regular publication, larger editions, printed papers, better news service for the editors, full commentaries and attempts at more sophisticated presentation. In many cases the local editions were linked up with the nation-wide illegal Press, and thus multiplied the editions, as well as publishing local news to supplement the general information and comments.

The developments of this side of the resistance struggle was naturally very different in the different countries, just as there was a considerable difference in the rôle which the illegal Press was able to play in the very different milieux they addressed. It goes without saying that their rôle was more important in Athens, Lyons or Amsterdam than in the mountains of Montenegro, or in out-of-the-way Norwegian hamlets; and that it reached its readers more easily in the great cities than in inaccessible regions far from the "head offices" of the papers. And here the problem was not only one of distribution. Many other factors affected the situation. It was in the cities more than in the countryside that one found a newspaper-reading public, communication was closer and quicker, and it was often here that the purely material consequences of the Occupation were felt most acutely. Here lay the great garrisons, here rationing and restrictions of every kind were particularly, and severely, effective, and on the average, the population of the towns had met the war and usually also the terror at close range. Europe's material and spiritual black-out was certainly general, but it was felt most bitterly in the cities, particularly in the industrial districts. Where the war – also the partisan war – did not hit the villages direct, existence was more bearable than in the metropolitan areas, and it was mostly in the metropolitan areas that the illegal Press was published. The exceptions to this generalisation were the actual partisan areas.

Even when all the differences are taken into consideration, however, there are still common features, in this field also. First of all, there was the ever-accelerating development in the output of papers. The few news sheets became many, the small papers became large, the editions grew, the numbers of pages increased, presentation improved, and as the months passed, publications from near and far poured in upon the peoples of Europe. Rivalry arose between the papers. If, for obvious reasons, there could be no rivalry as regards total numbers of readers, there could at least be rivalry as to contents and presentation. The influence of the paper depended largely upon its prestige, and this in turn depended upon contents, presentation, and especially regular publication. All resistance activity gathered speed, and Europe's illegal Press accelerated its activities at the same pace, if it was not ahead of developments. For even if there were areas where the partisan war was a matter of course, and printed matter only an auxiliary, the situation in most places was that the illegal Press was first on the field with its information and its appeals. The militant forms of action which followed were the consequences of these appeals.

The acceleration was general, and so were the practical problems. As soon as developments had passed the point where an individual sat down at his type-writer in the hope of starting a series of chain letters, practical problems thrust themselves upon him: How could he get hold of a duplicator, or later, a printing press? How could he get hold of paper, envelopes, stamps? Where was the money to come from? Where could one get reliable information? Who was to do the writing, and who was to lick the envelopes? What editorial line should one take? How could the distribution be arranged? Who would be courier? How could one protect oneself from a suspicious police or a zealous Occupying Power? Problems of this kind must be common property, whether the papers saw the light of day in Cracow, Oslo or Marseilles. One can confine oneself to registering that they were solved with the same rapid acceleration, but one can also draw some conclusions from the facts without much hesitation. The first conclusion must be that the publication of illegal papers compelled those involved to form organised groups, with concrete tasks to perform, in the publication of this or that paper; that as the papers expanded, these groups had themselves to expand constantly, not only with helpers from many sides, but also with feelers in many directions; and that the work had to be developed with increasing differentiation between the various tasks. Another conclusion is that the expansion of the papers was inconceivable without a considerable amount of support in the community to which the papers were addressed: there were the few or the many who put money into the affair; there were those who got hold of paper, at a time when paper was in short supply, and theft, or dealings on the black market for illegal purposes were punishable with death; there were the type-setters and printers – normal or secret – who took the same risks; there were the journalists or amateur writers who wrote the articles, there were the editorial staffs, authorities, managerial staffs, or other initiates who let information leak out, there were couriers who travelled with loads of papers; and there were the countless anonymous persons who were active at one or another of the links in the distribution chain. If a paper was to be national or simply regional, effective distribution must involve a very large public, hungry for news, who were more than willing to pass on the papers until the ground was practically covered, and in the whole chain in which the legal and illegal were intertwined, only a few knew each other or each others functions. No one asked questions. Much was implied and tacitly understood, but the most important point seems quite clear. The papers' constant growth entailed a fundamental illegalisation of society far exceeding the framework around those directly involved.

Other pieces of common property for the whole of the European illegal Press were investigation and punishment. It goes without saying that the Occupying Powers watched with anxiety and soon with alarm, as the forest of illegal papers sprang up all over Europe, and did their utmost to bring this unforeseen growth to a stop. Both directly and through the local police authorities in more or less voluntary co-operation, the Occupying Powers intervened with interrogations, arrests, confiscation and punishment of editors, publishers, distributors and readers. The punishments were severe, although they could vary from one country to another, and from one case to another. But death sentences and deportation were common, particularly in the early phases, where there was still hope of damming the flood with preventive measures, and where the work of an illegal Press was still the predominant resistance activity. Later, there were more serious matters to attend to, and as the newspaper forest continued to grow, the occupying authorities were forced to slacken their hunt in this immense area, where so many were compromised that effective intervention became completely insuperable. Before the occupying authorities began to give up in the face of this massive growth, tens of thousands had been hit by punishment – imprisonment, deportation and the death penalty. The figures are given for the victims in Belgium, where the existence of about 650 illegal papers cost about 3,000 dead, or about 30% of those directly involved.[28] The figure permits the statement that about 10,000 men and women were engaged, in Belgium alone, in illegal Press activity, and the Belgian Press was not larger than the illegal Press which circulated in Poland and in the countries in northern and western Europe. In Poland about 1400 newspaper titles were registered, in France and Holland about 1200, in Norway about 500, in Denmark about 550 – although it should be added that a newspaper title is not synomous with regular publication, constantly maintained. Various papers had only a short life-time, others appeared at irregular intervals, and often with varying editors, and also, papers sometimes merged with each other.

In the Soviet Union and in the Balkans the situation was somewhat different. Here illegal publications were only auxiliaries in the fight, not forerunners of it, at least in the partisan areas. Illegal papers based on Kiev or Athens only reached the partisan camps very occasionally, and had primarily local influence.

When arrests, seizure of editions or printing presses, and punishments which even included the death penalty were part of daily life for the illegal Press, one might have expected the papers to have wasted away. This was what the Occupying Powers anticipated in the early stages. But the constant increase in the numbers of papers and editions, and in their distribution, themselves bear witness to the miscalculation in this assessment. Here as in other resistance activities, there were hidden reserves to draw upon. No sooner were the editors of a paper arrested, or a printing press seized, than other men and women took their places, and with few exceptions, the paper reappeared, very often in the same or a larger edition, and quite obviously with the same tone and attitude on the editors' part as before the catastrophe. This too became a common feature, and was part of the background for the Occupying Power having sooner or later to abandon their attempts to bring the illegal Press to its knees. It is too categorical to assert that illegal Press affairs became trivial matters, but the statement is valid, that their importance must gradually be reduced, as the occupying authorities lost control of this field of investigation. It was impossible to deal severely with readers, when there were millions of them, and when being a reader was no offence, in the sense that the reader could not refuse to receive the paper. The representatives of the Occupying Powers were themselves zealous readers, and were flooded with illegal papers of every kind. The same rule applied here as with extensive strikes and demonstrations. The more people were involved, the more difficult it was to pick out those responsible, and the more arbitrary and therefore psychologically damaging were possible reprisals. The great triumph of the illegal Press was that it established itself as a normal phenomenon, so to speak, in an abnormal state of existence. On the other hand, it had to pay for this, with the triviality which sank over it when it became an everyday affair. The price of outward expansion was a corresponding weakening of intentness in reading. The course of the War also contributed to this. The more certain people became of the final defeat of the Occupying Powers, the less they needed the encouragement and the incitement which issued from the columns of the illegal Press. Imperceptibly, the papers changed their character to a corresponding degree. Post-war problems appeared side by side with the topical material and the revolutionary instructions of the Resistance.

It is true of all illegal papers that they could not deal with daily news. Most of them were monthly publications, and nearly always the date of publication oscillated under the pressure of practical problems which had to be solved. There were organs which tried to live up to the ideal of a daily paper, particularly the illegal news agencies which were set up successfully in France, Holland, Poland and Denmark,[29] but the daily paper had to be the exception, it had to be small-scale, and its distribution had to be limited. The periodical, usually a monthly publication, became the rule – and a rule which was subject to the pressure of circumstances. In acute situations and locally – as for example during a strike such as that which took place in Copenhagen in June 1944, or during risings such as those which took place in Paris and Warsaw in

August 1944, or in Milan and Turin in 1943, 1944 and April 1945 – illegal new sheets, or perhaps even hastily produced mini-newspapers, kept pace with, and exercised influence upon developments. But as far as the great mass of illegal papers was concerned, it was impossible to give first priority to news items. Here the radio took first place, especially when it was a question of news on the progress of the War. This did not mean that the supply of news disappeared altogether from the columns of the illegal papers. Local papers, particularly, had the possibility of publishing local news which did not find its way into the larger papers or on to the radio. But it did mean that agitation, commentaries and instructions were the main fields upon which the illegal papers had to concentrate, and in deciding on their material, editors could assume that concrete news was already known. For the early papers the situation was that the very fact that they appeared, almost regardless of the quality of their contents, was a stimulating encouragement. For all who could get hold of them, or who heard about them on the overworked rumour network, they bore witness to the fact that there evidently must be people around them who had not given up hope, but were prepared to resist. The contents, which in the introductory phases nearly always consisted of quite commonplace general appeals, or out-of-date repetitions of what the B.B.C. had broadcast, were therefore relatively unimportant. The stimulation lay in the very existence of the paper.

When agitation, commentaries and instructions were the fields on which the illegal papers had to concentrate, it should be stated that both the tone and the contents had to be adapted to the situation, the mentality, and the possibilities for resistance which applied or would apply in the future for the country in question. Here the illegal Press was held in a vice, and although it could take the lead when there was a need for proclaiming resistance or revolt, its effectiveness and possibilities and therefore also its growth and influence depended upon its not outdistancing the prevailing feeling and the realistic possibilities of the moment. The danger for a paper getting out of control or off course was also present, and it became a vital editorial duty – in a society which was debarred from all open exchange of opinion, and where editors could have no direct contact with their readers – to feel their way as to what the situation could bear. An appeal which was not followed was worse than no appeal. This was one form of adjustment. The other was that the paper must harmonise, both in tone and reading matter, with the editors' political, national, religious or other ideological views.

In this connexion, it also made a difference for whom the paper was intended, for many papers addressed themselves to special professions or groups, workers, university people, farmers, doctors, women, etc., not to mention the papers which were intended for partisan groups. The illegal papers – in spite of all the fellowship – had both political colour and viewpoints, decided from the editors' cellar or attic. The illegal Press therefore became both monotonous and vastly differentiated, at one and the same time.

They were monotonous in the sense that a number of main themes were common to all, and occurred again and again. This applied first of all to the War. It was important to state clearly that the War was not at an end, that the Axis Powers would not win, that their defeat was inevitable, and that the occupied countries' populations had their meaningful tasks to fulfil, in order to achieve victory. The reasons could be different, but the theme was the same. In 1940 the task was to state clearly that Great Britain would not let herself be conquered; in 1941 that the armies of the Axis Powers would become bogged down in the Russian vastnesses; in 1942 that the resources of the U.S.A. were inexhaustible. The main theme was the constant denial of the possibility for victory of the Axis Powers. A corollary to this was the persistent demonstration that everything that the propaganda of the Axis Powers blared out was one gigantic fraud. Not one Axis bulletin reached the public unchallenged. It was a matter of principle for the whole illegal Press to refute or play down all the victory fanfares of the Axis Powers, to explain away all the Allied retreats, and perhaps especially to uncover holes and inconsistencies in the Axis propaganda. On the same lines, the Resistance papers waged an unremitting war against every person or movement which – to a greater or lesser degree, directly or indirectly, and regardless of motives – supported the Occupying Powers. If the Occupying Power was an enemy, collaboration was a deadly enemy. No war is more merciless than civil war and if the illegal Press fought the enemy with all the words and arguments at its disposal, it was ruthless on the question of eliminating treason. The most savage words of the illegal Press can be found when it concerned itself with fellow-countrymen in the pay of the enemy, or simply in opportunistic co-operation with the enemy. Here too, all the illegal Press could agree. Another common theme was the persistent appeal for resistance in the ways and with the means to which the various countries at the given moment were suited. It was particularly in this field that the illegal Press had to beware of appeals which exceeded what the immediate situation could bear. Demands and instructions to their unknown readers could only be intensified one step at a time, and with an intuitive feeling for what was psychologically sound, and what was physically and technically feasible. But the general demand for resistance, and the claim that the peoples of Europe had a moral duty, as well as the practical possibility, to take part in the struggle were the constant, underlying theme of the illegal Press.

Commentaries and instructions must of necessity be more differentiated than agitation. Each country had its own situation and its own possibilities and problems, and commentaries in the one had little to do with those in the others. Every editorial staff followed developments with an eagle eye, in the country and the milieu in which they lived, and their comments were decided not only by nationality or the special problems of their particular corner of Europe, but also to a considerable degree by the views on this or that subject held by the editors in question. In spite of all the likenesses and all the fellow feeling, there were decisive differences between Communist, non-political, religious, professional, nationalistic and many other varieties of publications, not to mention the papers of the previously legal political parties. Here the unity and unison ended, particularly during the often stormy discussions which developed on post-war problems and especially during the last years of occupation, when victory was in sight and the problems of the present began to give way to those of the future. Both this fact and the increase in the number of papers contributed to the fellowship of the early years of the War gradually giving place to greater divergencies between the papers, and also to greater depth in the debate.

That the debate must go deep, and often take on a revolutionary character, was closely connected with the fact that the War had radically altered a great many of the conditions which had existed in pre-war Europe, and that the Occupation had forced normal political developments to mark time, at a moment where the foundations for many customary beliefs had disappeared. A simple return to 1939 was unthinkable, even in countries with established political and social conditions. Quite basic social problems were up for discussion, and in many places the 1939 solutions were out of the question. Monarchies were under debate, constitutions were under debate, frontiers were under debate, relations between exile politicians and their own countries were under debate, and everywhere social and economic problems were under debate. Towards the end of the War, all this stamped an illegal Press which had begun life with roughly the same mottoes, and which had maintained these mottoes in spite of all political differences and party lines as long as there was a common goal for all war efforts, and necessity bound together all those engaged in the struggle.

Commentaries could show up different shades of opinion, and even considerable divergencies. But instructions had to be general. It was permissible to indicate the general attitude which was desirable and the possiblities for resistance which existed for the population as a whole. Specific instructions to specific groups with specific duties were necessarily confined to those in the know, and to the extent that newspaper men were in the know – and they often were – they had to keep their knowledge to themselves. This meant in practice that the illegal Press could be instructive, and often give directions, when there was a question of the possibility of collective action on the part of large sections of the population, such as before demonstrations and during strikes, or when collective reactions were possible to many of the measures taken by the Occupation authorities, such as conscription for forced labour, actions against the Jews, restrictions, etc. Here instructions were not only useful but necessary, and there was a categorical demand that the newspaper men of the illegal Press should stick together and give similar, unmistakable directions. Disagreement or even lack of definite directions could create uncertainty and confusion, and injure the concerted action which was so necessary. The same applied to similarity in the directions of the illegal Press and those broadcast by the radio services from abroad. Here too, unanimity had to be achieved as far as possible. Where this did not occur, confusion resulted, or what was worse – despondency and distrust.

Since the numbers of papers ran into thousands, and the numbers of copies into millions, there can be little object in listing their names and figures in an account which deals with more than one country. The attempt would be a failure from the start. "Vrij Nederland" or "Het Parool" in Holland – Yes, but why not the Communist "De Waarheid" from the same country, or scores of other papers? From 1940–45 a total of about 1200 illegal publications saw the light of day for longer or shorter periods.[30] "La Libre Belgique", with a title from an illegal paper of the First World War – Yes, but why not the labour paper, "Le Monde de Travail", also from Belgium? – or scores of others. "Combat", "Libération", "Défense de la France" or "Résistance" in France – Yes, but the Communist "L'Humanité" had just as much right, or more. Or scores of others![31] "Rude Pravo" from Czechoslovakia – but why not some of the many non-Communist papers from the same country? Or other papers!

"Frit Danmark" – but why not the Communist "Land og Folk", also from Denmark? Or many others! "Rzeczpospolita Polska" or "Biuletyn Informacyny" from Warsaw, or "L'Italia Libera" and "L'Unita" from North Italy. Even a catalogue of the bare titles would exceed the bounds of this book, and by itself would be quite meaningless. Behind each paper was its origin, its development, its tragedies and triumphs, and neither titles nor numbers open up here for the continental drama which was played out. What is more important than columns of titles or figures is to establish that, although it can be discussed how much importance can reasonably be attached to the psychological war waged by the illegal Press, it is beyond discussion that the illegal Press, coupled with the radio service, and keeping pace with the progress of the War, captured the dominating influence on public opinion in the occupied European countries, and thereby contributed essentially to making the resistance struggle possible. In some countries this would hardly have been possible without the pioneer work of the illegal Press. Part of their contribution was also that they became recruiting centres for a great many other illegal activities. Members of a paper group often took action when there was a call to realise the ideas of resistance for which the paper argued, and this was especially the case in the first phases of occupation, when resistance-minded men and women did not differentiate sharply between one form of resistance activity and another. In the later stages, a definite separation took place, which improved security in the work, and which also improved the quality of the illegal newspapers which became more and more professional, also because great numbers of journalists joined the illegal Press.

In the partisan regions in the Soviet Union and in the Balkans publications did appear, printed illegally or smuggled in, but amid the stern realities of the fight in those Countries illegal papers played only supporting rôles. Incitement to resist came not so much from appeals from an illegal Press as from the brutal occupation policy which the Axis Powers laid down, in the case of Yugoslavia with the support of the Ustace movement. This policy, the daily struggle to survive and escape reprisals or forced deportation were the most important incitements behind the recruitment to the partisan armies. And where there could be long discussions, in the north and west, as to what forms of resistance were workable and appropriate, the forms were dictated here by geography, tradition and bitter necessity. The most obvious form and often the safest shelter were the partisan camps in the Soviet Union, their ideology was a matter of course. The publications which reached these camps from outside or were printed in the areas involved in the partisan war were unanimous in following the orders of the Central Committee of the Communist Party, and in the partisan regions in Yugoslavia and in Greece the same orders were predominant. Here the cause was not simply the struggle with the Occupying Power, but also a show-down with the old regime and the monarchy, and propaganda for Communist ideology. In both these Balkan countries the monarchy was under attack, not only because the Royalist Governments had chosen or had been forced to choose exile, and with it the gulf all exile created between the exile governments and the home country,[32] but also because before the War the monarchies here had resorted to different forms of dictatorship. The official Press had been censored even before the Occupation. Now the illegal Press, whether it was based upon conservative circles such as "Eleftheria" or Communist circles such as "Rizopastis" in illegal freedom in Greece, questioned the pre-war social system.

For the partisan groups in the Soviet Union the position, as we have seen, was that they were in close contact with the High Command in "the great land" on the other side of the Front, from 1942 channeled mostly through the "General Staff of the Partisan Movement". From there a steady stream of printed matter reached the partisan regions in the form of posters, leaflets, newspapers, etc. Sometimes such publications were simply dropped blind over the occupied area, sometimes they were smuggled in through the fronts, and sometimes they were landed on improvised landing strips cleared by the partisans. In addition, paper groups were active in the occupied regions, and the various partisan units had their own independent production of papers, leaflets, news sheets and other illegal publications. For the larger partisan formations it was a matter of prestige as well as being a practical task to develop such an illegal publishing activity parallel with the partisan war, and their purpose was for the most part the same as for all other illegal Press: to counter the propaganda of the Occupying Powers, to give information on the situation at the Front, and bring commentaries and instructions for the actual struggle, including analyses of the Occupying Powers' measures as regards economic exploitation and forced labour, and instructions as to how these and other challenges of the Occupation could best be met. In addition, propaganda should naturally stress the power of the Soviet regime, its moral and material strength, and underpin the connexion between the Soviet Armies' and the Soviet Government's struggle, and the general national interests. This emphasis on nationalism was a recurrent theme in agitation from Soviet radio and Press during the War;

the word "patriotism" was high-lighted, and this agitation appeared with the same strength in the illegal Press, which was an ideological echo of the voice of Moscow. There was no varied political debate here, such as developed in a large part of the main European Press. A monotonous panegyric of the Soviet regime was not only the main theme, but the sole political theme. Whereas the Resistance Movements in many parts of the rest of Europe took on a revolutionary character, sometimes of an extremely violent type, the largest of these movements – the Soviet – retained an ideologically unchanged character. The Soviet regime was not exposed to critical views, but was held up as the pattern and the ideal, also outside the frontiers of the Soviet Union.

Precise statistics of the illegal Press in the occupied regions of the Soviet Union are not available, but some figures have been given.[33] In the Ukraine about 20 larger papers appeared in 1943, and in White Russia in the same period about 40 papers were published, two of them covering the whole region, but most only distributed locally. The important active, strongly partisan Kalinin *oblast* could announce in November 1942[34] that during the year about 360,000 pieces of printed matter of various kinds had been distributed, some of them Stalin's speeches, some appeals to the various population groups; and that from July 1942 a special number of the *oblast* paper, "Proletarpravda", was published weekly, with 18 numbers in all and a total number of copies of about 390,000. Other papers came out in the Baltic areas, and generally speaking the distribution of news sheets, local papers and other publications, as already mentioned, was a matter of prestige for all the partisan formations. The very fact that underground papers were published enhanced the reputation of the divisions and units and for their readers were a symptom of their capacity, and a proof of their connexion with "the great land". In practice, however, the deliveries of papers by air from the unoccupied region, which by 1943 was fully organised, was just as important, and here the figures are concise.

In the first six months of 1943, 900,000 copies of papers and periodicals were delivered in the Ukraine alone, and about 6½ million smaller leaflets. In this, and in the fact that the partisans held open meetings in the villages they occupied temporarily, there is an obvious difference between the situation in the Soviet Union and that in the rest of Europe. Publications from the West did reach most of the occupied countries, but only in small quantities, in comparison with the illegal national publications. It should be emphasized, however, that even if deliveries by air in the Soviet Union outnumbered the locally produced papers, their actual appearance was an encouragement, in the same way as papers in the West had encouragement value. The confusion in opinion, and the doubt as to aims and means which of necessity assailed large sections of the populations in the occupied territories of the Soviet Union during the "blitz" victories of the Germans in 1941, were soon replaced by faith in victory and in the Soviet system's vast capacities. The Axis Powers never seized the obvious possibilities for influencing public opinion in a positive or even in a neutral direction, although these possibilities were present, in the wake of the military victories; and here again, the Axis Powers lost the psychological war, and collided with a massive, ideologically solid resistance.

A principal cause can be found in the German Occupation policy. From the start, this was dominated both in theory and practice by the representation of Soviet citizens as "sub-humans", weak-willed cattle, spoilt and degenerated through the Soviet propaganda and regime, and for that reason alone the inferiors of the Nordic Germanic "master race" – and therefore outlaws, defenceless victims of the conquerors' whims. This led to terror, to proclaimed and therefore commonly known maltreatment of millions of Russian prisoners of war; to ruthless conduct towards civilian populations, particularly by the so-called SS-Einsatzgroups; and to a merciless war upon all partisan activity. Willingness to negotiate or even neutrality was out of the question under such conditions. "The people in the occupied areas were obliged to choose" writes the American historian Alexander Dallin,[35] "and in the inevitable polarization that ensued, their choice was influenced at an early date by various facets of German policy and practice, the more important of which included, in addition to the treatment of prisoners of war, the behaviour of the German Army, the activities of the Einsatzgruppen,[36] and the German attitude toward incipient partisan warfare". A more moderate and human attitude on the part of some of the German Army units, and later subdued attempts to repair the damage that had been done, had no effect. "Deep and irreparable damage had been done," writes Dallin.

The German historian, Eric Hesse, is in agreement with Dallin in that respect. He, too, emphasizes the damaging effects of the short-sighted German policy of occupation and concludes: "With their measures in the occupied areas the German authorities very effectively paved the way for the activity of the communist agitators".

Often the last or only possibility for both army units which had been split up, or for the civilian population, was to take refuge with the partisan movement, and the Axis Powers lost the psychological battle even before it began. It is on this background that the Soviet propaganda, flown in or produced locally, should be seen. It did not need, as did the illegal Press in many Western countries, to argue for the struggle, because its necessity and character was created by the enemy himself. Its task was therefore rather as an encouraging supplement in the fight than a necessary introduction to it.

It would be an impossible task to establish with certainty what importance listening to the radio and the illegal Press had on developments in the occupied countries. That the Axis Powers ascribed great importance to both is proved, however, by their drastic and widespread countermeasures to combat the damaging effect they evidently expected: jamming stations, the ban of listening to foreign radio stations; confiscation or radio sets; the ban against foreign – even neutral – newspapers; police action against all illegal Press, merciless punishment of anyone caught listening in or reading them: publications, distribution and reading; open countermeasures against all illegal propaganda in the news organs controlled by the Axis Powers. Goebbels published a statement in "Das Reich" and polemized on the German radio against the B.B.C.[37] and Radio Moscow; "Völkischer Beobachter" published statements; the organs friendly to the Axis or controlled by the Axis published statements throughout Europe. The losing battle of the rotary press against the duplicators is certainly a fact. It is also an established fact that none of these measures prevented the illegal news agencies from capturing European public opinion, to such an extent that illegal news and illegal commentaries acquired a monopoly in representing all truth and all justice. The situation itself contained a glaring contrast between black and white, and the news agencies had the opportunity and the ability of outlining developments so sharply that they appeared only in black and white, without a hint of light or shade, or blurred contours. In the midst of the tragedy there was an ideal situation for all propaganda directed against the Axis Powers, and the situation was used with talent and skill. Radio and Press together could mark up incontestable successes in the psychological warfare – to the extent of its value. The question as to which had the strongest effect – the radio or the illegal Press – must be a matter of speculation. It can be stated definitely, however, that they came to supplement each other. The illegal Press tapped the free radio, and the free radio was hungry for illegal news, and used it diligently whenever possible.

When registering the success of the illegal Press, one must also remember that an illegal Press did not in itself constitute a resistance movement, even if it could function as a forerunner for one. It could give moral support, contribute to undermining enemy morale, pave the way for other form of action, and now and then intervene in developments with instructions and directions. At the same time, it could demonstrate the attitude in the occupied territories to the free world, and thus appeal for support and liberation. Its very existence was one of the proofs of the mobilisation of the conquered countries, and therefore one of many of the motives for the free world's fight. Apart from Poland, where there was manifest fear of the Soviet Union in large sections of the population, no Allied soldier stepped undesired on to the soil of occupied Europe. The illegal Press could only be a direct threat to the Occupying Powers, however, when its words were followed up by deeds. When this occurred it became dangerous. And because it occurrred, and occurred with growing intensity, it was dangerous.

The War was decided on the battlefields by the Armies – millions strong – of the free world. In these were included small contingents of free forces from the occupied countries – in the case of France and Poland, considerable forces. But side by side with this, the decisive battle of undermining activities were stubbornly carried out behind the back of the Axis Powers, and contributed, day in and day out, to exhausting the fighting power of the Axis, and influenced the course of the War decisively, both in the material, and perhaps even more in the psychological sector. To the extent that the conquered territories were an advantage at all, the advantage was at least reduced. The history of the War, therefore, is not only the history of great battles, but also the history of an undermining process. This War was a total war, both in the sense that the warring parties took the step of total mobilisation, and also in the sense that the conquered nations refused to recognize that the military defeat was final. Large sections of their peoples therefore regarded themselves, with the strength of free will, as committed partners in the total war. This was one of the differences between the Second World War and previous wars. The British historian, Hugh Seton-Watson, has expressed this fact in the words:[38] "It was usually accepted in European wars of the last century that in territory occupied in war the conquering power established a system of government with recognized rules, which were obeyed by the civilian population. To obey them was not treason to the lawful government, and there was no obligation to undertake sabotage or armed warfare against the occupying forces. The change is due to the 'total' nature of modern war and to the ideological nature of the Nazi German regime".

In these circumstances, the vertical front lines which could be marked on a map were supplemented by horizontal front lines, which cut across the vertical, and could weave their untraceable course into every corner of the occupied territory, where uneasiness and latent danger became factors which had constantly to be reckoned with, on government levels, on staff levels and out in the ranks. It was the victories of the Armies of Liberation which gradually restored official freedom of speech and freedom of the Press to most of the European nations. But in actual fact this had been restored long before in the illegal Press, which had no respect and showed no respect for aught but what the many editors chose to respect. Perhaps continental Europe has never possessed a freer Press. Censorship proved itself powerless under the conditions of the Second World War.

SABOTAGE AS A POSSIBLE FORM OF COMBAT. One of the concrete tasks which must naturally present itself to a group or an individual who had decided to take the responsibility and the dangerous step from words to deeds was to carry out sabotage. Literally from the first days of occupation, in all countries under its yoke, there were desperate or simply courageous people who embarked on sabotage actions. Ones first action, impulsive and unprepared as it must be, could only be extremely modest in the damage it caused. It might be a trivial act such as giving incorrect information, or a more definite act such as cutting telephone wires, minor incendiarism, or perhaps the theft of weapons, when the opportunity arose. In general, for capitulating army units to conceal their weapons was in itself an act of sabotage against the demand for total surrender of weapons. So long as sabotage remained on the level of chance, improvisation, seizing opportunities as they arose, and lack of organisation, planning and necessary material, it could only be an irritation factor at best, and perhaps a symptom which the conquerors found worth watching and taking immediate and severe measures to stop. Quite a different situation arose when sabotage became well organised and widespread. Then it could become a dangerous weapon, and a weapon which was adapted to Allied interests and strategy.

The potentials of sabotage were less obvious in 1939, however, than they were in 1945. In the intervening years sabotage broke through in earnest as a tool in the military and political struggle. The concept of sabotage was by no means unknown when the War broke out, and sabotage had been used sporadically long before 1939, and at least as far back as the Industrial Revolution, when desperate workers had tried to destroy the machines which they believed would take away their jobs. The Syndicalists had recommended and used sabotage as a means in class warfare; during the Irish rising against England in 1919–21, sabotage was used sporadically; and during the German fighting in the Ruhr in 1923, sabotage, together with strikes and passive resistance, had been a principal weapon.[39] T. E. Lawrence had used railway sabotage militarily with great success in his leadership of the Arabs' fight against the Turks, during the First World War.[40] But sabotage on the scale and with the advanced methods and means which were used in the Second World War, were, if not an innovation, at least a form of combat of which the extent and effectiveness took both the Occupying Powers and the saboteurs equally by surprise. Both parties were familiar with the phenomenon, but neither of them had realised that sabotage could play such a decisive part in the national political struggle as was the case. For the saboteur there was a period during which they needed to gain experience, both in the technical and organisational fields; and for the Occupying Powers there was a period in which they gradually had to register their increasing powerlessness against the phenomenon, and come to the recognitition that political methods, severe punishment, and even savage reprisals – after a time at random and in the dark – could not stem its flood. On the contrary it increased week by week in size and sophistication, and evidently had support not only among the iron-willed saboteur circles, particularly the Communists, but far into the ranks of ordinary citizens. Recognized sabotage, which left its mark in fires and explosions, continued to be an everyday experience. Information of new episodes announced its presence hour after hour around the clock. Depots, production and transport were constantly threatened targets.

Guarding threatened objectives was the first solution. But when all objectives were important, and all were threatened by sabotage, this possibility crumbled away. And in any case, experience proved that even closely guarded objectives could be attacked by the saboteurs. Here again, we meet the general, recurrent situation that through their first military victories the Axis Powers had gained possession of enormous territories, which in material resources, manpower and base areas, they wished to exploit to the last drop in support of their aggression, but which were not won over politically to the Axis Powers' wishful thinking, and could not be politically controlled. The opposite occurred. Politically, the conquests were a fiasco, and political control became an illusion. The Occupying Powers' own forces had thinned out, there were fewer and fewer trained personnel to control the occupied areas, and the auxiliary forces upon which the conquerors had to depend were insufficient, and were also branded, in the eyes of the conquered peoples, who gave their sympathies and their support to the activists. Even in countries where the Axis Powers found persons who either by conviction or through opportunism were ready to act in the rôle of collaborator, they themselves had the deepest suspicions of these collaborators' ability and will to give effective support to the Axis cause, and at heart they had no faith in the collaborators being able to contribute politically to that cause. Quisling, Mussert, Nedic and their fellows were kept on a short rein, and were closely watched and held in check by the Reich Commissars and the commanding Generals. Even influential politicians, who were eager to collaborate, met suspicion and rejection. In his book, "Vichy France", the American historian Robert O. Paxton has proved beyond doubt how eager prominent French politicians like Laval and even Pétain were to come to terms with the Germans, and how they were rebuffed. It seems likely that they never understood their rôles as mere puppets, and that all their hopes of achieving important national gains through genuine collaboration proved to be illusions. In such a climate, the possibilities for the saboteurs increased steadily. Sabotage was no longer regarded as a crime, but as a patriotic act, recognized as such by public opinion and often carried into effect with the approval and understanding of the factory managers or technicians in the know, or perhaps even with the help of accomplices among the guards.[41] A contributary cause in this situation was the realisation that sabotage could serve as an alternative to more destructive bombing. Even highly placed authorities could act with tacit approval of what was taking place. In such a climate the Occupying Powers could not rely upon anyone, and the saboteurs, on the other hand, could reckon with the sympathies and support of many outside the narrow circles of activists, while developments in this respect followed the course: few – many – more – most.

However, this climate was by no means a foregone conclusion, simply because the Occupation was a fact. Effective sabotage demanded more than a simple decision to take up the sabotage weapon. Many necessary conditions had to be fulfilled, if sabotage was to be more than the resolution of angry men to declare war on the Occupation. First of all, this climate had to be established, at least to the point where saboteurs could count on understanding and support – if possible from the majority of the population. This in itself entailed considerable problems. Respect for property and production were naturally ingrained, not only among property owners, but also in the populations generally, for whom production, employment and transport were the basis of daily life, however austere this might be under the conditions of occupation. But quite apart from natural, ingrained respect for property and a corresponding aversion to destruction, sabotage was a two-edged sword. Very few firms worked for the Occupying Powers alone. By far the greatest number were important to the community at large, in one way or another – production, deliveries or wages. Stoppages or limitations in production must inevitably bring difficulties, shortages and injury, at worst unemployment, and behind these unpleasant fact lurked the greater danger that in a given situation, Germany could take over the manpower available. In several countries[42] considerable "occupation psychosis" was needed before the majority of the population could tolerate or gradually sympathise with sabotage as a necessity, or as the lesser of two evils.

The pioneers of sabotage had other psychological considerations to take, however. One of these concerned the type of sabotage. Sabotage was most easily understood when it clearly hit the Occupying Power alone. Examples of this were military equipment, or enterprises which were solely engaged in deliveries to the Occupying Powers. But even here there were psychological considerations to be taken into account and the possibility of arbitrary reprisals. Would the population understand, and bear the consequences? The problem became acute when it was obvious in advance that successful sabotage would hit the civilian population, directly or indirectly. The saboteurs, who in February 1944 laid a time bomb in the ferry which was to transport a cargo of heavy water across the Tinnsjø in Norway, had to act in the painful knowledge that besides the militarily important cargo, the ferry would be carrying unsuspecting innocent fellow countrymen. And every saboteur who blew up a bridge knew that in addition to obstructing the traffic of military supplies, they were contributing to preventing necessary supplies from reaching the country's own factories, and their own countrymen. Every saboteur must know that explosions could unintentionally cost human lives. All in all there was a considerable psychological barrier to cross, before sabotage was understood, respected and finally approved. The times and the general occupation terror played their part here. What had been unacceptable in 1940 could be acceptable and even desired in 1944. The effectiveness of sabotage was also psychologically important. As long as this was sporadic and amateurish, many people could find it meaningless provocation, which could only help to make life more burdensome that it was already. It was different when sabotage became effective, and could be seen to be a co-ordinated link in the general conduct of the War, especially in countries where it appeared as an alternative or a supplement to Allied bombing. Here the Resistance Movements made every effort to argue, at home with the population, and abroad with the Allies, for the obvious advantages of sabotage – all things considered.[43]

If this view was to be accepted, however, sabotage had to be skillfully organised, and this again depended upon many factors: knowledge of the dispositions of the Axis Powers; their exploitation of the occupied countries' production machinery and transport networks; the formation of the necessary groups possessing technical know-how; courage and determination and thorough planning, which often depended upon advance infiltration into the objectives in view; and the presence of the technical means for carrying out the sabotage action. Every sabotage group, like any other military unit, had its supply problems to consider. Last but not least, it was important that sabotage did not hit indiscriminately. All sabotage was important, if for no other reason than that it served to lift morale on the home front, and to create irritation, uncertainty and disquiet in the enemy camp. This consideration was given high priority – particularly among the Communist groups – by those who wished to escalate the struggle, but the best sabotage was adapted to the wider context, and preferably co-ordinated with the strategic plans of the Allies so that it could be seen to support their operations, and it was best of all when it flamed up before or during invasion battles.

In none of the occupied countries were all these conditions present in the early days. In most countries a process of ripening was needed, during which the psychological, organisational and technical conditions had to be built up, and attempts had to be made to co-ordinate the fronts at home and abroad. This last condition, particularly, demanded intense, detailed communication between the home front and the front abroad. It was only possible to establish such communication gradually, and this was always fragile, and often too slow and unreliable for the Allies to be able to believe in the obvious possibilities of sabotage. Seen from abroad, it was a welcome supplement, but never an alternative. If one wanted a bridge blown up, a railway cut, or a factory put out of production, these objectives could be hit either by sabotage actions or by air bombing of the targets in question. Both methods had their advantages and their disadvantages. Sabotage could often be more effective and particularly more differentiated, in the sense that partial destruction could be sufficient with later rebuilding in view, and most important, sabotage, if skilfully done, involved less risk of the unintentional loss of civilian life which almost inevitably accompanied bombing. The saboteurs' risk of their own lives and of reprisals were possibilities which must be reckoned with, but the risk of unengaged civilian lives, all things considered, was less with sabotage than with bombing. On the other hand, from the Allied point of view, sabotage was subject to uncertainty. Would there, at the given time and place, be saboteurs who were willing to take the risk? If so, who were they and how skilful would they be – these unknown, anonymous men? Could one then count on the action being effective? Would the operation take place at the right time? These questions – from the outside point of view – were always subject to doubt. Such doubt did not exist, when it was a question of bombing – or it had a different character. Here an immediate order could be given, and the order would be obeyed, even if the bombing might not be effective. If it was not effective, however, it could be repeated, whereas unsuccessfull sabotage could hardly be repeated. The closely co-ordinated connexion between sabotage and bombing was an ideal which was never achieved, even though persistent efforts were made through the co-ordinating, co-operating organs, to establish the communication system and the reciprocal trust which were conditions for fitting sabotage into the collective strategic plans. This was no easy task, technically, strategically or politically, but there was a distinct difference in the presentation of the problem, and its solution, in East and West. In the Soviet Command, there was unanimity from the start on the importance of the partisan war – and therefore of sabotage – as parts of the collective strategy. There was a central unified command, which could effectuate its dicisions, without risk of argument or friction, to give united support to the partisan war and sabotage with all available means. Political complications such as obligations to exile governments or to large Reşistance organisations, which were politically conscious and even politically divided, did not come into the picture – at least not so long as the struggle took place on Soviet soil. Added to this, strategic bombing, which was given a high priority by the Western Powers,[44] was not such an important part of the Soviet conduct of the war, in which the air arm was mostly used tactically – a logical consequence of the fact that here, regular front line battles were in progress.

Conditions were far more complicated for the Western Powers. First, there were two Great Powers who intended to agree on all decisions, which in itself meant endless discussions. Next, consideration had to be given to exile governments and to de facto Allies in the European Resistance organisations, where members could be far from agreeing politically between themselves, with their exile governments, or with the Western Powers with whom they had to co-operate. If there were not more links in the decision-making hierarchy – and this will not be discussed in this context – these links at all events could be far from each other as regards starting-points, points of view, interests and obligations, and the groups involved were often not on speaking terms with each other. This applied particularly to Great Britain, which was the Western Power with the greatest number of foreign obligations, and which had the greatest interests to safeguard in rebellious Europe. The British historian, Elisabeth Barker, in an account of British decision – making vis-à-vis Yugoslavia and Yugoslav Resistance describes the complicated situation as follows:[45] "There were four main factors in British decision-making: the Foreign Office, SOE under its various names, the military (that is, the Chiefs of Staff, the Commanders-in -Chief, Middle East and the Supreme Commander, Mediterranean) and finally Churchill himself. There were also two or three jokers in the pack-by which I mean, quite respectfully, Brigadier Fitzroy MacLean, Colonel F. W. D. Deakin and also, at one point, Randolph Churchill – who influenced decisions as individuals rather than members of organisations. On the fringe of decision – making there were two other organisations – the BBC and PWE".

After a short description of these last two organisations, which were intended to be instruments for a policy, but in reality acquired a certain influence in formulating the policy which they were supposed to be safeguarding, Elisabeth Barker continues: "Between the various organisations there were bound to be tensions and frictions".

On the background of the complicated situation described, it is understandable that an ideal co-ordination, between the Western Powers and the European Resistance organisations with whom they co-operated, must be difficult to achieve. This applied also to the special but vital question of assessing the burden of sabotage as against the responsibility of bombing. Generally, the situation seems to have been that from the outside, there was a tendency to overestimate the effectiveness of bombing,[46] whereas contrariwise, the possibilities of sabotage were underestimated. This was the opinion in France, particularly, which was subjected to more bombing than any other occupied country, especially before the invasion in Normandy in June 1944. But similar observations were also made in saboteur circles in other parts of Europe, where saboteurs were very likely apt to overestimate the possibilities of sabotage. Their basis for assessment was always concrete – the object destroyed – but their views must needs be limited to the local area and the local success, Furthermore, their observations were quite naturally influenced by their knowledge of the unintentional destruction and losses which bombing entailed.

The time factor, the Western Powers' view of the Resistance Movements' rôle, and the general strategic situation in the West were also important. Both for military and political reasons, the Western Powers were uneasy at the idea of releasing violent activity too early. As far back as the ABC-1 plan in 1940,[47] resistance activity had been conceived as a supplementary part of a coherent strategy. This concept included building up the Resistance organisations which would in their various ways contribute to the immediate struggle, but which primarily should be prepared to intervene with support in the event of Allied offensives after invasion, whereever this might take place on the European continent. This did not prevent the Western Powers from heartily welcoming Resistance actions of every kind, including sabotage operations, as these gradually developed and accumulated, nor that they did not support such actions. SOE/OSS sent off one team after another of trained sabotage experts,[48] and ordered their Chiefs of Missions to support sabotage and establish the closest possible co-operation with local sabotage organisations. But the long term perspective remained, throughout, to keep the Resistance organisations intact until the actual moment when an Allied offensive should call for a co-ordinated Resistance effort, which could quickly be underpinned by the Allied Armies. However, for a long time there was no open front in the west, and this caused a tendency among the political and military leaders of the Western Powers to rein in the zeal for resistance. They were afraid of the Resistance cadres which had been built up so systematically being torn apart; they were afraid of reprisals followed by probable psychological reverses; and they were particularly worried at the thought of mass risings which they were not in a position to support. In addition they had political worries. To a great extent, time and developments had outstripped these theoretical considerations. Under the pressure of the Occupation, resistance activity and sabotage activity took on dimensions which could not be foreseen in 1940; and added to this, there were influential circles in the complicated military hierarchy of the Western Powers, which by definition were almost bound to work against the theory. This was especially the case for SOE/OSS, whose duty and interest it was to press forward with the development of resistance, and demonstrate its strength, simply but not solely to get access to the resources they were needing. It was more important, however, that an uncompromising fighting spirit developed in the occupied countries themselves, and this to some extent must topple the theoretical strategic reasoning. Here too, however, one must differentiate.

There were, quite naturally, large numbers of people who, regardless of all the hatred of the Occupying Powers, simply hoped that the storm would blow over, and that the lightening would not strike in their own locality or in their economic sphere, and who therefore looked with disapproval on every action which could provoke misfortunes which could perhaps be avoided. The instinct for survival was strong, and attachment to the life to which they were accustomed, and to its values, was deeply rooted.

But even in resistance-minded circles, there were divisions between extreme activists, who wanted action on the spot regardless of consequences, and other groups who advocated a waiting attitude, and imagined that there could be a static period where in comparative peace and quiet, they could prepare for later actions when the time was ripe. This could apply to very active Resistance men, who were building up intelligence networks, escape routes, etc., or who were engaged in long-term plans for forming cadres for a future activised Resistance army. The differences here were not as to resistance or non-resistance, but as to time, methods and situation. This was a general European attitude, because the attitude was rooted in the general complex of human feeling and thinking, but there can be no doubt that the mentality which advocated a waiting attitude was more common among the agricultural communities than among town dwellers; it was more outspoken in areas which were little affected by the physical occupation than in the junction points, where people had the enemy troops in sight every day; it was more common in conservative circles than in labour circles; and it was stronger in countries which had moderate occupation conditions than in those which were so to speak forced out into immediate action. But this can only be regarded as a schematic generalisation, and can only be valid after many modifications. The Communists, and behind them large labour circles, insisted after 22 June 1941 on the demand for immediate sabotage action; but conservative groups also supported this at an early stage; in Greece the partisan movement was recruited principally from the agricultural population; sabotage became extremely popular in Denmark, where the conditions of occupation were tolerable; intelligence people worked best when things were comparatively quiet, and would have liked to consign all sabotage to limbo, but they diligently supplied intelligence on the effects of sabotage, etc. A great many varying factors made themselves felt, and only one thing seems certain: that sabotage went from strength to strength wherever resistance arose. It can surprise no one that the Communists came to play a leading rôle, in this development. From June 1941 they were political outlaws, to a special degree, and both from their own ideological convictions, and under the impression of orders from Moscow, they took up sabotage as a quite logical weapon. Communist orders were for immediate support to their fighting comrades in the east, and a rejection of any hesitation in attitude or in action. To this basic view was added the built-in political effect which sabotage contained. The more fiercely the fight escalated, the more revolutionary its character became. Where tactical consideration was over, and technical problems had been solved, the Communists could be found in the foremost ranks of the sabotage front. The French historian, Henri Michel, believes it to be a fact[49] that this attitude to sabotage was a political rather than a military decision. And there is no doubt that neither their own danger nor reprisals kept the Communists from being the leading advocates of sabotage at all levels and with all available means.

Since, in order to be wide-spread and effective, sabotage had to be based upon a climate of general acceptance of its value and necessity, it could not be started on a large scale until public opinion as a whole had passed a fairly high threshold of bitterness, desperation or expectation of victory. The sabotage groups were faced with the same problem as the illegal newspaper groups. They could seize the initiative and go into action, but considerations of security alone set a limit to the extent to which they could outstrip current average opinion. Where the threshold lay between what was generally accepted and generally condemned, depended upon many factors: the course of the war; the actions of the Occupying Powers; the geography of the country and structure of its society; the traditions of the population, and much more. There were countries where the threshold was low, and where sabotage was a lesser action in comparison with the direct fight against enemy troops which at a day's notice could become the most important action. This was the case in the partisan areas of Europe. But there were other areas where the threshold was higher, and where sabotage became the most extreme form of action, at least until the moment where an all-embracing popular rising could be considered. Such conditions meant that sabotage-minded groups had to keep close watch on the attitude of the society around them, and calculate carefully when and how sabotage should be started. If it came too soon and was too amateurish, and if it became unpopular, it was correspondingly difficult to realise effectively. Popular support may not perhaps have been an absolute condition, but it was certainly very important. Another decisive condition was the availability of the necessary means for carrying out sabotage. These should preferably be effective, functional and sufficient. Small sabotage actions could be carried out with a little petrol and a box of matches, a pair of pincers, or perhaps a little gunpowder or other explosive which could be procured. But when it was a question of organised and powerful sabotage attacks, more was needed. Here too there was an inevitable interplay between material and psychological factors. Primitive sabotage, carried out with insufficient means and by inexperienced sabotage groups, were not convincing. For many people it must seem that the risks and the possible consequences were out of proportion to the results. Then there were many who would react negatively and sceptically, simply on the background of the poor results. This situation changed as sabotage advanced further and further from the introductory, experimental stage, towards an almost professional phase, where experienced groups with effective explosives could achieve results whose importance to the War was convincing. Then the original waiting attitude could be replaced by a wave of feeling in favour of sabotage.

Politics and Supplies

It was therefore vital, for many reasons, for the sabotage organisations of Europe, the partisan formations and the underground armies, that they receive the right tools to carry out their tasks, including hardhitting sabotage – and that they receive them in sufficient quantities. Both for this reason and because it was important to achieve the desired co-ordination between the home front and the front abroad, it was essential for the Resistance organisations that they were able to communicate with organisations in the free world, on the other side of the front, who were prepared to procure and deliver the means – in the form of all kinds of explosives, weapons, etc. – which could promote and maintain the fight and effective sabotage. Dependence upon help from abroad was not absolute. In many places, weapons were hidden when armies capitulated, or army units in the Soviet Union and in the Balkans which had been split apart formed or joined partisan units. In the Balkans, the possession of arms was a matter of course in many places, and a good deal of materiel could be procured by capture from the enemy, home manufacture, purchase, theft or in other ways. The early groups had to build upon their improvised activity with these possibilities, but in the longer view, the greater part of sabotage and partisan activity depended upon supplies from outside. Before proceeding to a closer examination of sabotage, partisan war and the formation of underground armies in more or less waiting position, it will be necessary for us to consider the supply services which in east and west, in north and south, were built up from the outside front to the home fronts.

THE SOVIET UNION. A central supply service of this kind was established in the Soviet Union with the creation on 30 May 1942 of the "Central Staff of the Partisan Movement",[1] a military and political organ, which was under the Soviet High Command, which again received its directives from the State Defence Committee, set up by the Central Committee of the Communist Party, a Soviet counterpart to the Western Allies' Chiefs of Staff Committee. The Chief of Staff was the Secretary of the Central Committee of the Communist Party in White Russia, P. K. Ponomarenko. Communications downwards to the partisan units in the hinterland behind the enemy was thus defined, and immediately after the German aggression in June 1941, Ponomarenko had been active in creating partisan groups and larger partisan units within his sphere of responsibility in White Russia.[2] Thus Ponomarenko already had experience as partisan leader behind him by 30 May 1942, an experience which the leaders of the British-American supporting organisations lacked for a long time.

The creation of this central staff in May 1942 should not be misinterpreted to the effect that it was only now that the question of the partisan units' position in relation to recruiting, communications, arming and strategic importance was taken up to consideration on a high level. What was needed now was to create an organ to co-ordinate and supplement the support and direction of all partisan activity, which had been playing an important rôle right from the first weeks of the war in Russia – for example in co-operation between partisans and the retreating army units – and that the Central Committee should contribute to creating the best possible co-ordination between the struggle of the partisan units and the war at the front.

It was almost a foregone conclusion that the partisan struggle had to play an important part in the War in the Soviet Union. The causes for this lie in the tradition of the country, its geographical conditions where the size of the vast territory which was quickly occupied, and its suitability in many places to guerilla warfare with its enormous, thinly populated forests and marshes, and the mountain districts of the Crimea, played their part, as did the German occupation policy. Added to this, scorched earth policy, in connexion with the start of guerilla warfare, was part of the Soviet Union Government's strategic thinking. In a directive of 29 June 1941, promulgated by the Ministerial Council and the Central Committee of the Communist Party, and supplemented by a new and more detailed directive of 18 July,[3] orders were given for the scorched earth policy to be put into effect, as the introduction to total partisan war. Where the enemy advanced, the exploitation of the conquered territories should be obstructed by all available means. Both these decisions were of enormous importance, and it would be pointless to try to weigh the effects of one against the other. Together they created immeasurable problems of quite unforeseen dimensions for the Occupying Powers and their warfare on Russian soil.[4]

The decisions in the directives as to the scorched earth policy were carried out to an extent which took the aggressors completely by surprise. The whole Soviet machine park was brought to safety in the east, depots were destroyed, dams, transport installations, mining installations, etc. were blown up or flooded, rolling stock was removed, etc. etc. Wherever the enemy came, the electricity supplies, coal supplies, transport services, harbours, mines, etc. were in a state of chaos so great that all the optimistic plans for economic exploitation of the conquered territories' resources came to nothing. A contributing cause was the fact that as regards engineers, technicians, skilled workers, administrative personnel and specialists of every kind, the Occupying Powers found a vacuum which could only be filled with difficulty or not at all. These categories of manpower had been transferred to the east, at the same time as the material was moved. The mass transfer was systematic.[5] As early as 24 June 1941, an Evacuation Soviet was set up, to organise the evacuation of material, whilst a sub-committee appointed on 26 September undertook the transfer of manpower. From July to December 1941 a total of about 2500 factories and works were transferred, and re-established far to the east in the Volga region, in the Urals, West Siberia, Kazakstan, Central Asia, and even in East Siberia and Transcaucasus. The number of evacuated persons exceeded 10 million, and 2,3 million head of cattle were moved. After this came the destruction of installations and material which could not be moved.

This whole process wrecked the German plans for exploiting Russian territory and its supply potential for Germany in helping to counteract the British blockade. This hope had been one of the main reasons for Hitler's plans of conquest in the East, and German strategy had been conceived largely with the aim of ensuring the material prizes which were now lost. A memorandum drawn up in 1941 by the German *Wehrwirt-schaft-und-Rüstungsamt* on the subject of the exploitation of Russian resources contains the following statement on immediate plans:[6]

"With regard to the first months, relief for Germany will take place in the supply sector as well as the raw materials sector, if a rapid operation is successful in:

a) preventing destruction of stocks,

b) capturing the oil fields in the Caucasus in undamaged condition

c) solving the transport problem."

The authors of the memorandum also envisaged great material advantages in the long term for Germany, as soon as the problems of transport had been solved and the co-operation of the population had been ensured. None of this could be realised after the vast Russian programme of destruction and evacuation had been carried out.

It became an enormous task for Germany to get hold of replacement material, raw materials and trained personnel to repair the damage and get even a minimum of mining and industrial production started again, and to get the transport network to function at all. The task was in fact so vast that supplies from the Soviet Union of the most important raw materials never reached the amounts which the Soviet Union, before 22 June 1941, had been able and willing to deliver. The balance was negative, and it was a major problem to keep the occupied areas just economically alive enough to supply the most immediate needs of the Occupying Power as regards transport, repairs and basic necessities.

A glimpse given by the German Armaments Minister, Albert Speer, illustrates the situation in Soviet territory in the winter 1941–42. Speer had been given the task of rebuilding the Russian industry after the great evacuation and destruction. In January he made a tour of inspection in the ravaged territory, and in Dnjepropetrovsk, the main centre for electricity production in the Ukraine and the Donetz Basin, he had to register a hopeless situation:[7] "My 'Baustab Speer' – as this large group of technicians called themselves – had found primitive billets in a sleeping car. Now and then a locomotive sent some steam through the heating system, to prevent it freezing up. Conditions in a restaurant car, used as an office and mess, were just as miserable. The re-establishment of the railway lines proved more difficult than we had imagined. The Russians had destroyed all the stations. There were no repair shops anywhere, no frostfree water tanks, no station buildings or intact sidings. The most elementary questions, which at home were dealt with by ringing up a subordinate official, became a problem here, even if it was only a question of getting hold of a nail or a little wood. It snowed all the time. Rail and road traffic were completely cut off, and the runways on the airfields were snowed up."

One can certainly assume that conditions for this important group of experts were as favourable as they could be made. It goes without saying that conditions for other groups, and particularly for the soldiers at the front – and for the civilian population – were even worse.

In addition to the problems created by the scorched earth policy, there were the problems which the partisan units created, after a few weeks of fighting, and these units established themselves and increased rapidly. What had been left behind and what was rebuilt, partly in the transport sector, was soon subjected to incessant attack in the occupied hinterland, where the Occupying Powers could never feel themselves in safety. The directives of 29 June and 18 July were followed to the full. These directives had decreed the formation of partisan units and sabotage groups everywhere in the hinterland behind the enemy lines, and everywhere these were ordered to attack enemy columns, depots, strongholds, etc., and to cut off all traffic on the railways, roads, telephone and telegraph networks so that – in the words of the directives – "intolerable conditions should be created for the enemy". The directives did not only give instructions as to how this should be done in the areas already conquered, it also gave instructions as to how best partisan activity could be prepared in the regions threatened by occupation, but which had not yet been overrun. The result was a hectic organisational activity both in the occupied and the threatened areas, and it was a matter of course that the Central Committees of the Communist Party in the republics and districts involved took the decisive initiatives. On many levels (kolkhos – rayon – oblast – town) large and small partisan formations were set up and the effort was made, in the midst of the unavoidable confusion,[8] to establish co-operation between the formations, whether they were small sabotage groups or a more military type of fighting units, such as those in the Leningrad district, which could be so large that they could take the title of "Partisan Brigades" and "Partisan Regiments". Much of this organisation had to be carried out after the Occupation was a fact, but in many places arrangements had been made before the enemy entered the area. Thus in the Ukraine, at the end of June 1941, a conference was held between the potential leaders of the coming partisan committees, and both here and in the other republics, veritable underground schools and courses were started for training in partisan and sabotage technique.[9] It is estimated that in the Ukraine alone about 4500 men received crash courses before the Occupation, and other groups were sent through the Front to support activities. Everywhere, support was to be had from veterans from the days of the civil war in the years 1918–22, and the influx of soldiers left behind in the captured hinterland, in large and small units, constituted a further complement. These soldiers remained behind, either because they were forced to do so, after their units had been overrun by the enemy, or by design, in order to promote and stimulate partisan activity. As early as the end of July, the first German military reports began to come in, on increasing partisan activities, and already then these activities were described as dangerous.[10] After this the situation deteriorated constantly. On 6 March 1942, Goebbels noted in his diary:[11] "An SD report informed me on the situation in the occupied part of Russia. It is after all more unstable than believed at first. The danger from the partisans increases every week. They control large areas of the occupied regions, and carry out terror. The national rising is also greater and more daring than first believed. This applies to both the Baltic countries and the Ukraine".

The partisan units grew rapidly in almost the whole occupied territory – with less growth in the Baltic provinces and practically none in the thinly populated regions of Karelia – and this growth was the result both of methodical organisation and improvisation. Recruitment embraced all categories of the population: peasants, factory workers and intellectuals, men and women, Communists and people outside the party, all the nationalities involved, all ages – in brief, a wide section of the population to the extent that it had not been evacuated. During 1941, the numbers of partisans increased steadily, and by the end of 1941 about 2000 commando units had been formed, with nearly 100,000 men actively fighting, besides the sabotage groups and an unknown number of helpers and sympathisors.[12] During the battles outside Leningrad well-organised partisan units played an important rôle, and during the battle of Moscow this occurred again. Fighting groups were in action in the actual Moscow district, as well as in Smolensk, Kalinin and the Orel sectors. It is estimated that about 30,000 men took part in the fighting behind this front, and General Guderian, the Commanding General of the German armoured forces who reached the furthest point to the east, can be quoted for statements of the difficulties regarding transports constantly cut off, extensive mining, and the necessity for ceaseless safeguarding of the hinterland, all of them tasks which posed hitherto unknown problems for the German Armies. Important districts in the "occupied" hinterland became quite simply liberated districts, where the partisans could harrass or periodically completely block German movements. Even during the 1941–42 campaign, "partisan pockets" were already being formed, and the German Occupation increasingly took on the character of a "strongpoint occupation", in the sense that although the most important junctions and other vital points were firmly in the possession of the Axis Powers, between these and everywhere on the intermediate stretches, the danger lurked of transports being cut off or ambushed, or subjected to more massive attack.

In the first phases of the War, when a great deal of improvisation was necessary, conditions were particularly difficult for the partisans, and they suffered great losses. But as soon as this was possible, efforts were made to bring the partisan war into the collective strategy through ever-increasing contact between the various partisan staffs, between these and the partisans Staffs in the High Commands of the various armies, and with the Supreme Command in Moscow. Detailed plans were gradually worked out, not only for the partisans' definitely military operations, but also for their sabotage activities. In this account it is not possible to draw any sharp dividing line between what is here referred to as "definitely military operations", and sabotage. In countless instances, sabotage actions were the principal task for partisan units, and these could only be put into effect through "definitely military operations" by large partisan units. The two forms of resistance activity inevitably overlapped each other, depending upon opportunity and circumstances. The dominating factor was attack on the transport system,[13] and this was due to the fact that the farther the Axis Powers penetrated Soviet territory, the longer and thinner, and therefore more vulnerable were the supply lines which they had to protect – a task which proved impossible – and this situation owed a great deal to the remarkable success of the scorched earth policy. For this reason alone, there was a limit to the objectives for sabotage, even in the most thickly fortified industrial regions. The transport network must of necessity be rebuilt, however, as an absolute and primary condition for further military operations, and both roads and railway lines had just as necessarily to pass through long stretches of partisan-infested regions, which were very difficult to guard. Again and again, therefore, the transport network became the most obvious target for attack, each time it was rebuilt. The problem of the vulnerable supply lines was recognized, for example, by Guderian in 1941. It continued as long as Axis troops remained in Soviet territory. There is a typical statement from 1943–44 from a German Officer, Colonel H. J. Ludendorff:[14] "The presence and activities of the partisan forces, amounting to about 15,000 men, in the Uschatsky area south-east of Polotzk, resulted in the Third Armoured Army being unable to use the Lepel-Beresino-Parafianov road and railway . . . from the winter 1943 until late in the spring 1944. This was the only line leading westwards from the Army area through the enormous trackless regions, full of forests and swamps, near what had been the Russian-Polish frontier. This was of vital importance for the Army, as the enemy either cut off the only other supply line (the railway and road Orscha-Vitebsk), and this was a constant danger during the winter battles of 1943 to February 1944 practically every day, or when the armoured Army was finally forced to move its front some kilometres to the west, and the road and railway mentioned was no longer available for supplies. Sufficient troops to force open this vital route, as a precaution, were not available before the end of 1943, in spite of the vital necessity of opening it and keeping it open." Here we meet all the elements of the problem: the distances, the terrain, the necessity, the partisan opposition, the lack of sufficient covering troops. And the German Officer's words correspond with those of the official "History of the Soviet Union", Volume X, where the position is summed up: "An effective fighting form became mass diversions (diversion = sabotage) against the main railway and road communications. On instructions from the Central Staff and the local partisan staffs, the leaders of all large units created a great many sabotage groups. These were trained in the technique of mining and supplied with materiel . . . The change-over to the tactics of mass sabotage against railway lines and roads by small groups was a great success."

Recruitment to the Partisan formations increased to a remarkable degree during 1942 and 1943, and not only the German coercive measures and terror were dicisive here, but also the victories of the Soviet Armies, which from the New Year 1943 crushed the myth of the invincible German Armies, and strengthened faith in a final Soviet victory. The psychological effect of the changed political and military position was bound to contribute, at an accelerating pace, to greatly increased recruitment to the Partisan forces. These now went over increasingly to the offensive, often in long marches of conquest, across the German lines of communication. During the marches, and indeed in general, the growth of the Partisan forces was almost explosive, and the German historian

Erich Hesse remarks that recruitment often exceeded the numbers for which arms could be supplied. The Partisan forces thus found themselves forced to create unarmed reserves, or where this was possible, to pass the surplus recruits through the front lines to service in the regular Soviet Armies. As in other Resistance Movements it proved that the supply service determined the extent of recruitment.

All this partisan activity, which increased with tens of thousands in the course of 1942, although the steppes of the Caucasus to the south seem to have been excepted, obviously had its own supply problems to solve. When the improvisation phase was over, it became a central long-term task to get the supply services organised, partly through co-operation between them and the partisan staff in the regular army, and lastly, from May 1942 under the co-ordinated command of the "Central Staff of the Partisan Movement". This occurred here as elsewhere principally with the help of deliveries which were brought in by air, either with agreed organised droppings of weapons, explosives and other materials, including radio equipment and articles of clothing, as well as foodstuffs, or by landings in the hinterland behind the enemy on improvised airfields. The more effective the partisan formations became, and the larger the areas they were able to control,[15] the safer the possibilities became, and the larger the deliveries of every kind, not only of materiel but also of trained technicians and instructors, and political commissars.

As to organisation, the "Central Staff of the Partisan Movement" was divided up into a network of subordinate departments, each with its own sphere of responsibility. Inwards this meant supply organisations, intelligence organisations and propaganda organisations, and outwards it meant the partisan units behind the fronts in the various republics or districts – Leningrad, the Baltic provinces, White Russia, the Ukraine, the Crimea, etc., or the smaller units in the various guerilla zones in the occupied hinterland. The main purpose of this work was to create the closest possible communication between the partisan staffs and the Central Staff, and between this and the Soviet Army units whose operations the partisan movement was to support. The ideal was a centralized controlling organisation, and greater weight can hardly have been placed in any other country on effective co-ordination between resistance activity and the operations of the regular armies. This did not and could not exclude the scattered partisan formations – whether they consisted of small groups or of larger, firmly established paramilitary units – having to be in possession of such independence that they were able to act on their own initiative in decisions on details, in accordance with the possibilities or the demands which the changing situations and opportunities could present. This was particularly the case in the first stages of the War,[16] where the partisans had to act in isolation, and therefore on their own responsibility, on the basis of the actual conditions in their own zone of operations, and with enough self-interest as to secure the groups' survival. Gradually, and in fact from the creation of the "Central Staff of the Partisan Movement", a new phase began, with more systematic leadership of the partisan war.

Here it was important that the Central Staff was created at a stage of the war where the first defensive mentality was giving way to an offensive mentality in the Soviet Army Command. The war had taken them by surprise, in spite of all the warnings, and in the beginning phase the overriding task for all partisan activity was to delay, harrass or block the enemy's advance. In the summer 1942, the Axis Powers were on the offensive, it is true, but during the winter Battle of Moscow, before the summer battles of 1942, and particularly while these battles raged, the Soviet Command looked forward to the offensive phase. After the many reverses, this was to turn the retreat, so that it would not only be possible to recapture lost territory, but also to advance across the Soviet Union's frontiers into Poland, into the Balkans, and finally into the enemy's own territory. Here the Partisan forces were entrusted with new different tasks, and at the end of August and the beginning of September 1942, a conference took place in the Kremlin,[17] with the object of specifying these tasks. In addition to the leaders of the "Central Staff of the Partisan Movement", members of the Central Committee of the Communist Party, representatives of the Defence Ministries, and representatives of the Politbureau took part, as well as a great many partisan leaders, flown in to Moscow from the partisan regions. The conference was concerned with the new extended fighting tasks, which would arise when the planned Soviet offensive began in earnest. The results of the conference were formulated in a special directive of 5 September 1942, with the title "Concerning the Tasks of the Partisan Movement". This decreed that the Partisan struggle should be expanded to total war, which should support the coming offensive, both operationally and politically. It was important that the lost regions should be recaptured, but it was also essential that the liberated areas should again be brought under the direct control of the Party. This had occurred to some degree in the areas which were more or less permanently under Partisan control. Here Soviet power and, as far as circumstances permitted, economic and political life had been reestablished, but now it was a question of the final liberation of all the territory which had been temporarily outside the direct control of Moscow. The decisions in the directives were not empty words. During the offensive which the Soviet Armies began from November 1942, and which continued during the years 1943–44, the Partisan Movement was intensified and became an important support to the advancing Soviet Armies, which in many places could advance through territories which had already been liberated.

In this war within a war, the problem of communications and supplies played a decisive part, as we have seen. Without supplies from outside, much activity would ebb away, and the Partisan Movement would not have had the great weight that it received. At the beginning of the war in Russia, where, after the unforeseen, rapid advance of the Axis Powers' Armies, there was inevitably considerable confusion and uncertainty in the captured hinterland, the earliest partisan units had to base their activities to some extent on the secret depots of weapons, explosives and other materiel which the retreating Soviet Armies had left behind, with a view to the creation of partisan activity. In addition, as time went on, there were the supplies which could be collected on every battlefield, either by the partisans themselves or by the population – an operation which illegal active groups and organisations tried to arrange. It should be stressed that the Soviet partisans, like all other partisans, needed and received support form the surrounding population, partly as regards provisions and information on enemy dispositions. In addition, another important source of supplies was the capture of materiel from the enemy – a possibility which naturally increased with the growing strength of the Partisan organisations, and which in time became an important factor in the supply service of the partisans. It became an everyday matter that the partisans captured rail transports, or surprised and plundered depots, ambushed road transports. These captures could be considerable, and as regards White Russia during the years 1942–44 have been calculated as follows:[18]

c.	550	motor vehicles and motor bicycles
c.	250	guns and mortars
c.	1,600	machine-guns
c.	2,000	automatic weapons
c.	15,750	rifles
c.	25	ammunition depots
c.	3,500	horses
c.	1,000	vehicles
c.	25	radio stations

Very considerable quantities of equipment thus came into the hands of the partisans, but it should be pointed out that these figures are for a period of 30 months; also that the materiel had to be shared and was shared out through an "exchange centre" to the formations which consisted of tens of thousands of partisans; and lastly that it is not clear, when this equipment became available – whether it was in the beginning or in the final phase. Supplies by this channel were far from sufficient. The basic supplies had to come from unoccupied Russia, and Russian calculations seem to show that even if captured weapons in some district could amount to 25% of the supplies from the other side of the Front, it was the latter which constituted the bulk. It should further be stated that a captured weapon was far from synonymous with a suitable weapon. What was acquired in this way could be a matter of chance, and it was by no means certain that captured materiel answered the particular needs of the partisan formations, which were decided, both as to weapons and sabotage materiel, by their mobility and special tasks. In primitive terms, a captured weapon without corresponding ammunition, or *vice versa,* could be useless.

The task of acquiring and delivering the supplies which the partisan units needed, and delivering them in sufficient quantities, was put into the hands of the Central Staff of the Partisan Movement from May 1942, as stated above. For this purpose a special department was set up for material and technical service, and parallel with it, special Partisan Staffs were attached to the Army Groups. The fact was that owing to the enormously long front lines, and in very many places also the nature of the terrain, the partisan units in many places in Russia were not physically isolated from the regular armies to the same extent as was the case in other countries. Close co-operation could often be established direct, therefore, between Army and Partisan units. Considerable infiltration through the front lines was possible, so that the partisans were not only recruited locally. In the "free" regions, formations were created up to Brigade strengths, which then went through the front lines and joined the existing Partisan units in the hinterland. The opposite naturally took place also, when Partisan groups near the Front broke through to join the regular Army as reserves. During the Soviet advance in 1943–44, these advancing armies were supplemented to a great extent by Partisan forces ready for action, in just the same way as Free French Forces were strengthened considerably in 1944 by the enrolment of French partisan forces into the regular armies. In some places in the Soviet Union, "Partisan Gates" were created, in weakly guarded sectors of the Front, through which men and materiel were channeled to the partisan operations in the hinterland. There could be a question of considerable quantities of materiel, which was successfully passed through to the occupied regions. There are no total or comparative figures for the whole of the supply service, but as examples of the figures calculated for such a "gate" about 100 kilometres north of Sjitomir, through which in the period December 1943 to January 1944, while the "gate" was open, we can quote the following quantities passed:

c. 1,200 automatic weapons
c. 135 light machine-guns
c. 85 anti-tank weapons
c. 35 mortars
c. 15 45 mm guns
c. 7 76 mm guns

in addition to c. 3,5 million cartridges and other equipment.

The front lines, thinned out in some places or in some types of terrain practically non-existent as they were, could not block deliveries by horse-drawn vehicles, and it was fairly easy for couriers to pass through the lines, eastwards or westwards. Cutters from the Black Sea Fleet were also used occasionally for supplies to the partisans in the Crimea.

All in all, there was a decisive difference between resistance organisations in the Soviet Union and corresponding organisations in the rest of Europe. The Soviet organisations were operating on the mainland with the forces of the regular front, whereas the Atlantic, the North Sea, the English Channel and the Mediterranean were barriers for the resistance organisations in the rest of Europe, which were forced, for geographical or political reasons, to seek support from the Allies in the West. In addition the Central Staff of the Partisan Movement was only established with a view to supporting partisan war on Soviet territory.

Even if the possibilities for infiltrating through the front lines contained certain openings for bringing supplies to the Russian Partisan units by land, however, it was by air that most of their supplies were delivered. For the Partisan forces which operated far from the front lines, delivery by air was the only possibility. Up to 1942, when the units were still relatively small, and the Soviet war machine was still working in low gear, the possibilities for large air deliveries were limited, but from 1942, larger air forces were made available to the Central Staff of the Partisan Movement, and to the special staffs in the various sectors of the Front.

The air forces which already existed were supplemented with ten Air Transport Regiments, and an Air Transport Division supplied with long-range aircraft, permitting flying great quantities of materiel to the partisan units in the large liberated pockets behind the enemy lines. As far as the Air Transport Divisions were concerned (up to September 1943 designated as "Flying Groups for Special Missions") the number of flights to the partisans were calculated as 4,335 in 1942 and 1,350 in 1943, with deliveries of 5,904 tons and 1,116 tons of materiel respectively. In addition, in the period in question, 1,250 instructors and technicians were flown to the partisan areas, and 499 persons were flown back to the free zone. The total figures were considerably higher. In 1943 the total air forces which were engaged on long-range operations carried out about 2300 flights with a total of 1,700 tons, flew 5,810 persons to the partisan areas and 2,210 persons out, mostly sick and wounded, in addition to flights from the forces at the Front, for which there are only scattered figures.

Deliveries were adapted to the partisan needs, and here radio communication was decisive even if couriers were also used in cases where the Partisan units did not operate too far from the front lines. Where a Partisan unit was in need of supplies, it telegraphed its requirements to the Central Staff of the Partisan Movement or to the nearest front sector, after which the deliveries could be adapted to the requirements stated, to the extent that material and transport possibilities were available. These requirements could involve not only weapons, ammunition and explosives or other sabotage equipment, but in high degree also necessities of life such as clothes, boots, provisions and medical supplies. Here delivery capacity by air was often insufficient, and needs of this kind had largely to be infiltrated through the front lines to the Partisan units in need. For certain areas there are total figures, for example, deliveries through the front lines on the west front zone in 1942 the following quantities of provisions were delivered:

Bread	c. 57,000 kg
Rusks	c. 28,000 kg
Groats	c. 1,300 kg
Tinned meat	c. 7,000 tins
Tinned fish	c. 2,300 tins
Sausages	c. 5,300 kg
Sugar	c. 7,300 kg

Similar deliveries although in minor quantities were made to the Ukraine Front and the Leningrad Front. Articles of clothing such as boots and clothing of various kinds were also delivered.

But deliveries by air remained the most important group, particularly in the question of distant partisan areas. For the years 1942–44 the centrally directed air deliveries of weapons from the Soviet Army depots were reckoned as follows:

Rifles	c. 53,000
Automatic weapons	c. 48,000
Pistols	c. 10,400
Light machine guns	c. 4,500
Heavy machine guns	c. 25
Anti-tank weapons	c. 3,000
Large calibre machine guns	c. 10
Signal pistols	c. 2,500
50 mm mortars	c. 1,900
82 mm mortars	c. 525
45 mm guns	c. 20
76 mm guns	c. 10
Replacement rifles	c. 2,750

In addition there were considerable quantities of ammunition, sabotage equipment, mines and other materiel. Plastic explosives of Western origin, delivered by Arctic convoys, found their way to Russian Partisan units.

From 1943, as the Soviet Armies gradually advanced farther to the west, the corresponding figures and the size of the partisan areas were reduced, and at the beginning of 1944 the Central Committee of the Communist Party took the consequence of the changed situation and dissolved the Central Staff of the Partisan Movements, after which the command and supply of the remaining Partisan units were put into the hands of the Central Committees of the various Republics and the remaining local staffs of the Partisan Movement within the various army units. The Central Staff of the Partisan Movement thus only retained the functions of a supply centre, and the functions of the supreme co-ordinating organ within the Partisan Movement as far as Soviet territory was concerned. Its sphere of activity only reached the Soviet Union's western frontiers. When the Soviet territory was liberated, and the Soviet Armies entered into contact and serious co-operation with the occupied eastern European countries such as Poland, Czechoslovakia and Yugoslavia, they there met the Resistance Movements which for years had been deeply involved in co-operation with the supporting organisations of the Western Powers, the British SOE and the American OSS. The problems were no longer predominantly questions of supply, and the meeting was not without its complications.

SOE/OSS. SITUATION AND FUNCTION. For the Resistance Movements in Europe, apart from the Soviet Union, London – for the Balkans, Cairo – was the place where efforts were made to co-ordinate Resistance operations. It was also the place from which the Resistance organisations, from the North Cape in the north to Crete in the south sought and received support. Up to June 1941, there was no other power to which Resistance activists could turn but Great Britain, and London became the centre for their attention and their hopes. Long after June 1941, the Soviet Union was under such pressure from her own immense problems, and after the loss of vast territories so far away from the rest of Europe, that London and the British Headquarters in Cairo must be the focus points for Resistance hopes, and the nearest possible starting points for supporting services and for the co-ordination of forces.

The British counterpart to the Central Staff of the Partisan Movement was the SOE. If one compares the two organisations, however, one fundamental difference stands out at once.[19] The one organisation functioned solely on home ground and had the function of supporting compatriots, whose situation and fighting forms were more or less uniform. The other functioned solely on foreign soil and in co-operation with Resistance Movements of a great many countries in utterly different situations, and therefore with very varied fighting forms and political aims. It is immediately obvious that the two organisations must be quite different in structure and function, but they had one thing in common – that they both had to base themselves on the fact that resistance against the Occupying Powers behind the lines could be decisively important for the course of the War, and that it must therefore be stimulated and supported, morally, politically, and technically with supplies.

This was immediately possible in the Soviet Union, where the value of partisan war must occur at once to the leaders of the country, when the war broke out in Russia and enormous regions were lost. The concept must be a matter of course, given the size of the territory, the nature of the terrain, the traditions of the country and the ideological attitude of the regime.[20] Great Britain's possibility behind the creation of an organisation which was to promote and support European resistance organisations, were undeniably very different from those existing in the Soviet

Union. And yet there were certain common factors. With the Axis Powers in possession of most of the European continent, one common factor was the vast size of the territory, and another, which existed in certain places, was terrain suited to guerilla warfare. Where this was not the case, other methods had to be used. On the other hand, Great Britain did not have the Russian traditions of guerilla warfare[21] and her ideological basis was undeniably different from that of the Soviet Union.

Great Britain, perhaps more than any other great power, as the Mother Country of the vast Commonwealth, and with strong conservative elements among the leaders of the country, hesitated at letting revolutionary forces loose, and this was precisely what occurred, when organisations were set up which were both to call for and support insurrection. The revolt was, of course, directed against Great Britain's enemies, but for those thinking on traditional lines, and particularly the Foreign Office, it was quite evident that such a revolt in politically unstable countries might well take on a further and undesired address,[22] as happened in Greece, Albania, Yugoslavia, and after September 1943, Italy. Revolt also threatened to create political complications in France and Belgium. Only remorseless military necessity could outweigh political risks. In the summer 1940, when SOE was started, such remorseless necessity was present.

SOE was not put under the British Supreme Command, nor politically attached directly to the British War Ministry. It became an independent organisation, politically subordinate to the Ministry of Economic Warfare, and its activities – always depending upon the support which the other services and the other military and political British organs were willing to give it – were based from the start upon the hypothesis that these activities could become a valuable supplement to the regular conduct of the war. "Set Europe ablaze," were Winston Churchill's concluding words, when on 16 July 1940 he sent brief instructions to Hugh Dalton for the tasks of the new organ.

Its sphere of activity was thus, in brief, "Europe", when the organisation saw the light of day, though not of publicity. For most of the war years its remained a mystery, even to those most in the know, what SOE actually stood for, what they were engaged in, what authority they had and what support they should therefore be given. The words on the Europe which was to be set ablaze referred primarily to the Europe which was occupied by the Axis Powers, and in July 1940 this included Czechoslovakia, Poland, Denmark, Norway, Luxembourg, Holland, Belgium and France.

In April 1941 came Yugoslavia, Albania and Greece, and from September 1943, the part of Italy which had not been liberated by Allied troops. Apart from this there was infiltration in the neutral countries of Sweden, Switzerland, Spain, Portugal and Turkey, which was an extension of SOE's activities in the occupied territories, and the much weaker possibilities existing for SOE activities in the Axis Powers' own territory. A final desperate possibility was that of SOE activities in an enemy-occupied Great Britain. The Soviet Union lay outside the SOE's sphere of activities. SOE operated up to the eastern frontier of Poland. The only exception to this was an unsuccessful attempt, which was never repeated, to drop a single agent in Estonia on 25 October 1942.[23] But this hopeless attempt, which ended tragically for the agent, was an absolute exception. Both the flying distance and the political situation ruled out any repetition.

When in December 1941 the War escalated to embrace the Far East, SOE's field of activity was also expanded to include Far Eastern countries, but since this account is confined to conditions in Europe, this must only be mentioned *en passant*.

This was what lay in the word "Europe". But what lay in the words "set ablaze"? No final nor complete answer to this question could have been given clearly in July 1940.[24] SOE's visions and experience would one day supply the answer on the basis of known results, and these again must depend upon initiatives and developments in the occupied countries. It was the men and women who were prepared to resist who would decide. London could neither give orders nor achieve the final answer. In this respect, the situation in London was different from the later situation in Moscow. It was clear that there was a wide register of possibilities which could be played upon. But what was realisable in this register, and in what strength, could only be a matter of speculation in July 1940. This did not exclude one from grappling with plans for psychological warfare, intelligence, strikes, sabotage, assassinations and farthest in the future, the creation of underground armies, which if and when a regular powerful British Army returned to the Continent, supported by "free" national forces, could support or even be a condition for such a military return and liberation. As we have seen, British Chiefs of Staff were operating with perspectives of this kind, even before the collapse of France.[25] More detailed plans were drawn up in a memorandum by the British planning staff in June 1941,[26] but recognising the fact of the enemy's numerical superiority, this memorandum made it clear that a number of conditions would have to be met before such plans could be considered to be realistic possibilities. Apart from the formation of resistance organisations, which in 1941 were still in embryo, the principal conditions were the following: the actual dispersal of enemy forces, a decisive weakening of his morale and his material strength as a result of propaganda, blockade, bombing and – possibly – sabotage, strikes and other underground activities, as well as mastery of the air and sufficient attacking forces. In December 1941 – after the U.S.A.'s entry into the War – Churchill, on his way to America in the battleship "Duke of York", prepared a memorandum[27] on the coming Western Allied strategy, in which he operated with the secret arming of underground armies in the occupied countries, and their insurrection in connexion with the return of Western Allied armies to the European continent. The idea of building up underground armies became superfluous to a certain extent – but only to a certain extent – with the entry of the U.S.A. into the War and the tapping of the Axis Powers' fighting strength on the East Front, in North Africa and in Italy. But once it had been formed, the idea lived on. The U.S.A., also, saw its value. The European underground armies became realities, for the very reason that the European Resistance organisations themselves decided to form such armies and even – as in Yugoslavia – threw themselves into open warfare with the Occupying Powers even before the Eastern Allies had started their offensives on the Continent. But here too, there is a clear difference between East and West. Whilst State leaders in Moscow could at once order their fellow-countrymen to go out in an open partisan struggle in support of an open front, the Western Powers could not do so, for various reasons. First of all, for a long time no open front existed which demanded immediate support, and it was also regarded as a golden rule in the strategy of the Western Allies that possible risings on a large scale could only be justified militarily and humanly, if they were linked closely with an Allied advance, which could quickly bring relief and liberation. Lastly the Western Powers were not appealing to their own countrymen, but to volunteer allies in the European resistance world. The Western Allies could support them morally and materially, but they could not give orders to them, much less demand efforts and sacrifices which they regarded as strategically indefensible. On these and on complicated political grounds, the Soviet Union's orders, methods and tempo must have a different character from those of the Western Powers in regard to the European Resistance Movements.

Many of the European countries which constituted SOE's field of operations were very different from each other in geography, political situation, political and social structure, national, religious and ideological attitude. SOE's activities had therefore to be much more elastic than the corresponding Soviet organisations' activities. In country by country, SOE had to adapt its functions and its ambitions according to what was politically desirable, technically possible, and geographically feasible. SOE had also to adapt itself according to numerous considerations, some of them arising from the Resistance policy, situation and possibilities of the various countries, some of them arising from Great Britain's resources and political and strategical aims. The structure of SOE was partly determined by circumstances. Its Headquarters were set up in London, with a branch in Cairo. For external affairs, sections were established for each country, with connexions to exile governments or other exile organisations;[28] for internal matters, a system of training centres was built up for instructors from the various countries; and liaison was also established with the traditional military staffs – Army, Navy and Air Force – with the Foreign Office, the BBC, PWE, special production sectors and, where there was a question of decisions on principle, with the War Cabinet.

Great Britain's connexions with the occupied European countries now became two-stringed. The exile governments of the countries in question, or the corresponding exile organisations such as the French National Committee, set up by de Gaulle, had the usual diplomatic connexions with the British Government through the Foreign Office; but parallel to this, SOE made secret contact with Resistance organisations throughout Europe, and very often the exile representatives were either not informed or were informed insufficiently in comparison with what they themselves wished.[29] Thus an operational and political dialogue ensued between SOE and the many Resistance organisations, and as these organisations gradually gained strength and self-confidence, and therefore value to the Allied strategy, it was this latter string from the Resistance organisations via SOE to the British Governments, that could replace formal, but often waning diplomatic relations. In this way, SOE gradually squeezed itself into a politically influential position. The same development was to take place to some extent with regard to the U.S.A.

Up to 1942, the U.S.A. had had no counterpart to SOE, but in June 1942 a parallel American organisation, "Office of Strategic Service" (OSS),[30] was established under the leadership of William J. Donovan, a New York lawyer in close touch with President Roosevelt; and the two organisations were soon attached to each other under the initials SOE/SO. After this, such close co-operation gradually developed between them, both operationally and as regards resources, that the collaboration almost became a fusion. British and American officers sat side by side on the Staff, and British aircraft often carried American materiel and vice versa. To sum up briefly, it can be said that the British had the experience, while the Americans, especially from 1944, could supply the greater deliveries of materiel. Although conditions varied from one country to another, there was a general tendency for the Resistance organisations to maintain independent communication with the Western Allies via SOE/SO, which was far from always being in harmony or even in contact with the existing exile organisations. These were often unable to keep up to date with developments in their home countries, or they perhaps directly disapproved of these developments, as they gradually received news of them. This was the case, for example, with the Greek and Yugoslav exile governments, and after September 1943, with the Royal Italian Badoglio Governments. It was the fate of all exile organisations that because they lacked close contact with their home countries and developments there, which were often rapid and drastic, they were in danger of lagging behind the feeling and standpoints which arose under the pressure of occupation. It was in the nature of things that the Resistance organisations thought and acted independently, and were unwilling, or simply refused to be directed by distant exile organisations, which knew nothing of the conditions of the struggle, nor its possibilities. Generally speaking, but with reservations, the normal tendency was for the Resistance organisations to be more activist and politically more radical than the exile organs, simply because they could assess the possibilities for action and the politically radical currents which were results of the Occupation. It was only natural that the double SOE/SO organisation, whose members had their finger on the pulse of Resistance, became the advocates for the extreme standpoints of the Resistance organisations, and they had the possibility and the will to plead their cause vis-à-vis their respective governments. Thus SOE/SO became a radicalising factor in the military and political hierarchy of the Western Powers, and this could give rise to tension – sometimes acute – between, for example, SOE and the Foreign Office.[31] The order to SOE and later SOE/SO was to set Europe ablaze, and the very words immediately suggested sabotage. The creation of underground armies entailed perspectives for the future, with many complications which must first be dealt with, but burning down or blowing up factories and depots, unrest, protest and strikes were the most obvious and immediate replies to the order. Its realisation demanded co-operation with the Resistance organisations in the occupied countries where, when, and however these appeared, and inde-

pendently of their political standpoints. Such organisations must be supported with instructors, means of communication, and sabotage material.
It was SOE's and later SOE/SO's task to procure and deliver this material. Their task was also one of propaganda: to incite. It was one of
guidance: to instruct. Of co-ordination: to negotiate. The task was also to
supply. Regardless of how far the Resistance organisations could manage
with the means at hand, with what could be seized, stolen, manufactured
at home or obtained in other ways, it was clear that sabotage would gain
considerably in effect when supplies were delivered from abroad, partly
because such supplies could be adapted to the special needs of the sabotage groups for suitable weapons, effective explosives, and other sabotage material which was simple to use. The light sub-machine gun was
obviously a more suitable weapon for the sabotage groups than a traditional military rifle; that the small hand grenade, no bigger than a duck's
egg, was more suitable than a home-made bomb; that plastic explosives
of high blast effect were easier to use than the dynamite which could be
stolen in a coal mine or a stone quarry; that specially constructed magnetic
mines were extremely welcome for sabotage of shipping; that specially
constructed detonators in the form of time pencils were greatly prefera-
ble to home-made fuses, etc., etc. Quite apart from the number of sabotage operations carried out with materiel from abroad, its quality was far
superior, in that the materiel from abroad was manufactured with a view
to the special needs of the sabotage groups.[32]

For Great Britain, the U.S.A. became the great arsenal, and for the
European Resistance organisations, Great Britain became the great arsenal, from which, as time went on, special equipment of both British and
American material was delivered. As regards its supply of expertise and
materiel the joint British-American organisation SOE/SO[33] received the
same function in the main European territiories as the Central Staff of
the Partisan Movement received in the Soviet regions.

Here, however, the similarity ends. SOE/SO faced far more complicated problems, because their domain included just as many situations as
there were countries or simply areas. What was geographically possible
in one place was perhaps impossible in another. What was politically
desirable in the one was perhaps undesirable in the other. And what was
technically feasible in the west and north could perhaps be unworkable in
the east and south, etc. etc. In every case, the sea separated the supply
base from the receiving country, and there were many more factors of
separation: language, political standpoints, technical and geographical
conditions, and the constant consideration of what at each stage could be

268 · Politics and Supplies . SOE/OSS

psychologically opportune. All kinds of complications presented themselves: the choice and training of suitable instructors, who spoke the language of the country in question and preferably were familiar with the country's conditions of occupation and with the latest restrictions; considerations of whether one Resistance activity or another should be promoted at a given moment; the continuous and often hampering negotiations with exile organs; corresponding negotiations with the Chiefs of Staff of the traditional services; problems of communication with the countries and groups; flying distances; internal supply difficulties including particularly the difficulty of making a sufficient number of suitable aircraft available. In this last field, especially in the beginning phases of the War, there was a question of a vicious circle. The sabotage groups had to demonstrate their effectiveness before the R.A.F. were willing to allocate aircraft for the particular occupied region, but effectiveness was difficult to demonstrate until these air deliveries were large enough for the sabotage groups to be able to achieve the proofs demanded. It took some time to break the vicious circle, but right up to the end of the War, there were traditionally-minded Staff Officers among the Commanders of the Western Allied Air Forces who retained their doubts of the rationality of using available air forces to help the European Resistance organisations, and who regarded bombing as more effective than dropping weapons.

This attitude is very clear from a remark made by the British Air Marshal Charles Portal to one of the leaders of SOE:[34] "Your work is a gamble which may give us a valuable dividend or may produce nothing. It is anybody's guess. My bombing offensive is not a gamble. Its dividend is certain – a gilt-edged investment. I cannot divert aircraft from a certainty to a gamble, which may be a gold mine or may be completely worthless."

The problem would not have existed, if first Great Britain and later the two Western Powers together had had a surplus of aircraft capacity, but this was not the case until the end of the War. In 1940–41, all that SOE could wring from the R.A.F. was two Liberators, rebuilt for their special purpose.[35] If further aircraft were needed, SOE had to go begging. In addition, there was a limit, in the first stages of the War, to what flying distances and what load capacity the planes could cover, and here there was a question of inverse ratio. The greater the flying distance, the smaller the load. Matters did not improve until the big four-engine aircraft went into mass production and were made available. The original loads of three or six containers could then be increased to twelve and twenty-four containers – depending on the flying distance. But until this occurred, there were large numbers of reception teams all over Europe who watched in vain for materiel – and the quantities of materiel – they so badly needed. To the last, the demands were never satisfied.

In this connexion, one should remember the enormous development in flying technique during the War. Increasingly larger and faster aircraft were built, and this development was certainly accelerated by the War. If this applied to flying technique, it applied no less to navigation technique. A single dropping of one or two instructors with radio material was a complicated and dangerous operation in 1941, which could take weeks, perhaps months, to plan. Failure to find the reception points, and long return flights were the order of the day. Later the order of the day became mass deliveries and precise droppings.[36] But it should not be forgotten, here, that the conditions of 1941 were totally different from those of 1944, as to quantity as well as quality. In addition to the improvement in materiel and technique, experience was a decisive factor – also the experience of both flying crews and reception teams.

In spite of all the difficulties, from 1941 onwards instructors and deliveries of weapons were successfully sent over even to distant regions of rebellious Europe. But before we look more closely at the type and quantities of these deliveries, it will be relevant to make some general observations on the methods used in bringing deliveries to their destinations, from London and Cairo. Roughly speaking, three methods of delivery were in use: 1) infiltration through neutral countries; 2) deliveries by sea; 3) air deliveries. This third group could again by divided into droppings by parachute or landings of materiel on improvised runways in the occupied areas. Of the three main methods, the first was of less importance, quantitatively, and was only used where miniature deliveries were needed, such as crystals for radio sets, microfilm with codes and signal plans, small objects such as time pencils, and occasionally propaganda and similar material. The second method – deliveries by sea – was only feasible for certain countries and regions, such as Norway, Denmark, Brittany, South France, Greece, and for a short time during 1943 Yugoslavia. This method was naturally out of the question in the case of far off countries like Poland and Czechoslovakia and normally also out of the question for neighbouring countries which lay quite close to Great Britain but which were densely fortified, such as Holland and Belgium. However, deliveries by air were feasible for all the occupied countries, and it was this type of delivery which was to dominate developments.

Even here, however, there were severe limitations, partly owing to the very limited allocations of aircraft for these special operations, and partly owing to flying distances and therefore determined by the geographical position of the various countries. The flying distances to Poland and Czechoslovakia, for example, were so long that deliveries were far below what was desirable, and besides this, if the aircraft were not to fly over strongly fortified territories, they had to make long detours. The problem was eased somewhat after 1943, when the Allies could use air bases in Brindinsi in South Italy. Flying distances were considerably shortened, and flights could be carried out over less closely fortified territory, thus making direct routes possible.[37] The problem remained, however, particularly with regard to Poland. For deliveries in Yugoslavia and Greece, the bases in Bari and Brindinsi were of the utmost importance. When an Anglo-American naval base was built on the Yugoslav island of Vis, in the Adriatic,[38] this became an extremely important centre for deliveries by sea to the coastal regions of the Adriatic.

Flying distance was one problem, geographical situation was another. It was far easier to carry out deliveries by air to thinly populated countries such as Norway, or certain parts of France, than to Holland, for example, where it was difficult to find suitable terrain for dropping, and almost impossible to clear runways for landing. The density of the German anti-aircraft batteries, and the strength of the German fighter defences naturally also created great difficulties in the countries bordering the North Sea and the English Channel. The method of landing on improvised airfields was practically speaking only used in France, and after 1943 in Yugoslavia – and only after the Resistance organisations had won so much elbow room for their operations that they were able to establish and secure suitable runways. Here the factor of distance played a part: the shorter the distance, the better the possibilities. For this type of flying, to France, Lysander aircraft were used, as these only required short runways for landing and starting, but they were slow and vulnerable, and of limited range.[39] In Yugoslavia, where after 1943–44 large areas had been liberated, larger aircraft had to be used. This method was naturally far more effective than dropping by parachute, first of all because men and materiel could be flown out of the country. Even in distant Poland, this method was used occasionally. After months of preparations and planning, Dakota aircraft landed on Polish territory in April, May and again in July 1944,[40] this last operation being to fetch the components of the German V.2 missile mentioned earlier. But these three operations in Poland must be regarded as the exceptions that prove the rule.

POLAND. The problem of long flying distances was greatest in the case of Poland, because the Polish Resistance Movement gathered an extremely large underground army, the Armia Krajowa, which needed considerable supplies. The problem of distance was thus coupled with a problem of quantity, which proved impossible for SOE and later SOE/SO to solve, to the extent which was hoped and planned for. This situation was made more acute by the political problem, that Great Britain had special res- ponsibilities towards Poland, and by the strategic situation, in which Poland had special possibilities for sabotaging the German war effort. These possibilities increased after the German invasion of the Soviet Union in June 1941, when Poland became a concentration area and a thoroughfare for the German Army to most of the East Front. The spe- cial political responsibilities arose from the fact that the British Govern- ment had signed a guarantee of Poland in the spring 1939, had then made a military pact with the Polish Government, and lastly had declared war on Germany on 3 September 1939, after the German invasion of Poland three days before. The German invasion of Poland had thus been the *causus belli* for Great Britain, and Poland therefore had a special place in British thinking. In addition, very considerable contingents of Free Polish Forces served on the Western Allied fronts, and this further strengthened the British feeling of special responsibility towards Poland.

For SOE this responsibility was particularly pressing and difficult. The exile Polish Government laid great weight upon the creation of a Polish Home Army, under the command of the exile government, and regarded this Home Army and its actions as Poland's principal contribution to the Allied war effort, and as their guarantee of political independence in post-war Poland. An essential condition for this ambition to be realised, however, was the establishment of close contact between the Polish Command in London and the Home Army Command; and a further condition, which was just as important, was that necessary – or at least the most necessary – supplies could be brought in from abroad, that is to say through SOE, to the Home Army. The Polish Command in London set up the "Bureau VI" which had the duty, in close co-operation with the Polish Section of SOE, of establishing the necessary communications for dealing with both intelligence and supply questions.[41] The difficulties were formidable, however.[42] With the detours which were necessary in order to avoid the German air defences, the flying distance amounted to 3500 kilometres, and added to this, flying had always to be fitted in with the moon and the weather, and favourable conditions for the reception groups. The season of the year was a limiting factor in itself. In the summer months, the light nights precluded flying, and this left the spring, autumn and winter, but in the cold weather the danger of icing up increased. Conditions for meeting all the technical and meteorological requirements were seldom present simultaneously, and time after time, flights had to be abandoned, or the aircraft had to turn back because of unforeseen changes in the weather, failures in orientation, intensification of German air defences, etc. etc. Many aircraft were lost on these dangerous flights.[43]

In principle, SOE met similar problems everywhere else, but the problems increased progressively with the distances. In addition, as we have seen, Great Britain's technical and material resources were more than modest in 1940–41, and SOE's share of the limited resources had a low priority, so long as there was still doubt as to how valuable Resistance activity behind the lines of the Axis Powers might prove to be. At the start, Polish operations had to be undertaken with rather unsuitable Whitleys and Wellingtons – both adapted to the purpose – and it was only after 1942 that four-engine Halifaxes, with greater range and load capacity, could be used. The Polish desire for the creation of a special Polish air force for deliveries to the home country was only partially fulfilled, when in July 1942 the Polish Government was given three Halifaxes, which operated with the special British 138 Squadron,[44] which had the task of supporting SOE's actions. This was only when there were no other more pressing demands, however, and even then, it was the R.A.F. who made the final decision as to when and where aircraft should be sent. This was the position, also after a special Polish group was set up within the framework of the 138 Squadron, and Polish crews with thoughts of their home country often had to operate with droppings in countries far from Poland – Norway, Denmark, France, etc. In 1943 the Polish Government asked the U.S.A. for help, and three Liberator aircraft were put at their disposal,[45] the British Government insisting, however, that this delivery must not influence the American-British deliveries. Even so, the aircraft for flight to Poland were quite inadequate. These few lines on the flying situation are included, amongst other reasons in order to emphasize the general situation, where the problem of supplies to the Resistance Movements, not only in Poland but everywhere else, was first of all a question of flying capacity, and only to a lesser extent one of materiel. Here too, however, there could be problems of various kinds: type of materiel, packing, suitable parachutes, etc. Right up to 1944, however, flying capacity was still the bottle-neck in the supply question, and even in 1944, Poland – and Czechoslovakia – were especially unfavourably placed.

In spite of all the obstacles, however, SOE began attempts to fly to Polish territory at an early stage. A flight planned in December 1940 with a Whitley aircraft was cancelled at the last moment because it was realised that the aircraft's range was not adequate, but in February 1941 a further flight – also with an adapted Whitley – partially succeeded. As related earlier,[46] three men were dropped, and although the dropping was made too soon and they landed in an area annexed by Germany, they succeeded in reaching the High Command of the Home Army in Warsaw, bringing a radio set. The rest of the materiel dropped was lost, but nevertheless, the first contact was established and the first experience gained. Although this was not encouraging, the attempts continued. The six months of light nights in 1941 were ruled out, but twenty flights were planned for the winter half-year 1941–42, and of these 12 were carried out, 9 successfully. For 1942–43 the corresponding figures were higher: 100 flights planned, 65 attempted and 42 successfully accomplished. In 1943–44, 500 flights were planned, of which 381 were attempted and 208 accomplished successfully.[47] Measured in tons, these deliveries amounted to 2, 50 and 263 tons in the three periods. 313 instructors were dropped, with considerable amounts of money in gold, dollars, German marks and Polish money. From the end of 1943 it was possible to use the bases in South Italy, and this, as mentioned earlier, was a great advantage. On the other hand, the transfer from British to Italian bases entailed certain delays in the programmes planned.

The instructors dropped were specially trained at Polish training schools,[48] where training – apart from parachute jumping – included signals training, the use of special weapons, sabotage technique, intelligence, propaganda and the other branches of underground warfare. In all 579 instructors were trained, out of whom 345 reached Poland before the end of October 1944.[49] But although the number of instructors dropped was fairly satisfactory, the deliveries of materiel lagged far behind what was planned, and what was needed by the Home Army. The quantities delivered up to 1 August only amounted to about half of what a small country like Denmark received during the War, although over 90% of the Danish deliveries were dropped after August 1944; but the deliveries were far less than the quantities successfully delivered to countries such as France or Yugoslavia. The figures must have been depressing, both for the Poles and the British, and must have underlined the military impossibility for Great Britain to assist the Polish cause. It also proved impossible for the British Government to give the political support to the exile Polish Government vis-à-vis the Soviet Union, which must have been desirable from the exile government's point of view. British attempts at mediation stranded, among other reasons because of the exile Polish Government's persistent refusal to accept the Russian demand for a radical change of Poland's eastern frontier. The military consequence for the Polish Home Army, however, was that Poland lay in a region where developments were determined by Soviet strategy; and as regards supplies, the consequence was that only a minor part of the Home Army materiel came from Western Allied deliveries. The rest had either to come from hidden stocks, be seized, or be home-made. This last group was very large and added decisively to the striking power of the Home Army.[50] The value of the help received from abroad should hardly be calculated in bare numbers, however. For one reason, these deliveries included vital special equipment, and for another, assistance from abroad was an important psychological stimulus. On the other hand, the Western Allied deliveries may have contributed to maintaining a dangerous belief, in the Home Army and among the members of the exile Polish Government, that the Western Allies still had strategic interests and possibilities in Poland – and this was an illusion.[51]

The Polish Home Army, in spite of all efforts, was inadequately supplied with weapons and other material, when the real supply crisis arose, with the mass rising in Warsaw, on 1 August 1944. The Soviet Army had by then completed a violent offensive through White Russia and Eastern Poland, had reached the Weichsel river in places, and after an advance of 400–500 kilometres had stretched its supply lines to the utmost. In the Warsaw sector, the foremost units were so near the city that the sound of their cannons could be heard here, and the Soviet Air Force had here superiority over the German Air Forces over Warsaw. At the end of July, Radio Moscow urged the inhabitants of Warsaw to rise in active fighting[52] and prophesied that final liberation would be hastened by such a rising. The appeal did not come from the Soviet Government, but from Polish Communists, who at that stage formed a Communist led "National Liberation Committee", which gradually took control of freed Polish territory, as the Russians advanced in Eastern Poland. All the signs pointed to a complete collapse of the German Eastern Front. When General Guderian was appointed Chief of General Staff of the German forces on the Eastern Front during this crisis, he described the prospect as dark indeed:[53] "After my appointment, the whole front – if it can be called a front – was hardly more than a collection of the remnants of our armies, which attempted to retreat to the Weichsel line. 25 divisions had been wiped out completely."

During this offensive, Polish partisan units in the region east of the Weichsel river had given the advancing Soviet armies what support they could, partly in co-operation with Soviet Russian and Communist Polish partisan units,[54] and the phase of the Polish Resistance struggle designated "Burza" (= wide-spread armed diversion activity) was thus in full progress. Now the Home Army Command decided that the time had come for a general rising of the Armia Krajowa's forces, as far as Warsaw was concerned. They gave orders to the underground forces in the city and to the population to this effect. The decision was taken by the Home Army Command, which could refer to a mandate given to them on 26 July by the exile Polish Government:[55] "At a session of the Government of the Republic it was unanimously decided to empower you to proclaim the insurrection at the moment which you decide is most opportune." It seems certain that the decision was political. At this moment there were two political poles for Polish politics, the exile government and the National Liberation Committee, and Warsaw's Home Army was not only loyal to the exile government, it was also under its political leadership. The decision also had a psychological background, as General Bor-Komorowski has emphasized:[56] "In an atmosphere of such intensity there was grave danger of an outbreak of less disciplined elements, whether through deliberate provocation or merely some accidental circumstance, leading to the unleashing of an unplanned rising." In the final analysis, the rising was principally a political decision, and here it was a catastrophe that the Polish Home Army was attached politically, and in regard to organisation and supplies to the exile government, and through them to the Western Powers, whilst Poland lay geographically within the Soviet Union's operational sphere. Without co-operation with the Soviet Supreme Command – and no such co-operation existed – the rising must be a hazardous attempt to establish an exile Polish and therefore anti-Soviet power centre within the Soviet sphere of operations.

The rising and the battle of Warsaw which followed it was bloody. More than two months were to elapse before the German Occupying Power had mopped up the last pockets of resistance in the great city, and this led to violent collisions of political character between the exile Polish Government and the Soviet Government, as well as acrimonius ex-

changes of opinion between the latter and the Western Allied Governments. These controversies and their political consequences lie outside
the framework of this book. Here it is our task to examine the supply
situation of the Home Army during the rising, and the material support
which the Western Allies brought the beleaguered Polish Resistance
Forces, whose supplies at the beginning of the rising were only sufficient
for a short fight of one or two weeks.

Regardless of what political or military assessment the governments
and staffs of the Western Powers made of the Polish Home Army rising,
they felt themselves bound, together with the Polish Air Force, to bring
what help they could. Poland was an Ally, and about 150,000 Polish
soldiers were fighting on the Western Allied fronts in the south and west.
The help was brought, and could only be brought by air from the bases in
southern Italy, and after extreme pressure from the exile Polish Government, both the British and American Air Forces agreed to attempt the
dangerous flights to the besieged city and its immediate neighbourhood.
The flights in August and September 1944 had quite a different character,
therefore, from anything attempted previously. The scattered night
flights to suitable reception points and under favourable conditions were
one thing; these flights – or attempts at flights – concentrated as they
were, both geographically and as to timing, were a very different matter.
The number of Polish aircraft in any one action was only nine, although
the number of Polish crews was higher.[57] The great bulk of flights, therefore, had to be carried out by British and American crews – and the
decision on this was only taken after extreme Polish pressure had been
brought to bear upon the governments of the two Western Powers. Professional opposition to the decision was also extreme. The Supreme
Commander of the R.A.F. in the Mediterranean war theatre, Air Marshal
J. C. Slessor, was direct and to the point when he reported to London on
3 August:[58] "I consider the operation of droppings over Warsaw so
dangerous and without prospect of success that I refuse my consent to its
execution by the air forces under my command. I have not changed my
opinion". Slessor then adds that he has agreed to flights with Polish
crews, under pressure. Later the political pressure became so great that
Slessor had to give in. In those desperate weeks, the number of aircraft
which left the ground was about 300, and the number of droppings carried out was about 200, of which, however, only 75 were received inside
the Polish battle zone, which was shrinking day by day. This zone included the city centre, but in the beginning had also covered two adjacent

forest districts, Kampinos and Kabacki. All in all there was a glaring disproportion between the stakes and their results.

The droppings had to take place over a city district, where German and Polish forces were so hopelessly entangled in bloody street fighting – or in fighting in the city sewers – that it was impossible for the pilots to know whether their loads fell into the hands of one party or the other. In addition, the German Air Force had temporarily regained air mastery over the city, which increased the dangers of the flights. The amount of materiel dropped exceeded what actually reached the fighting Poles by considerable amounts, however. In the city area itself, the droppings began on 4 August and continued until 14 August, after which there was a long pause until 10 September, when aircraft crews again succeeded in making droppings in the heart of the city. A last intense effort on 18 September was especially tragic. Whilst the dropping operations on 14 August had consisted of 26 aircraft, with 11 droppings, of which 10 were received by the Poles, on 18 September no less than 110 aircraft were sent in, which dropped 107 deliveries of which only 15 fell inside the diminutive area still in Polish hands. 92 loads fell into Germans hands that day, and the Poles had to watch containers falling out of reach. Having established that great quantities never reached the fighting Poles, we can turn to the actual figures of the materiel which in spite of everything did reach them. Apart from about 10,000 first aid packages, these were as follows:

  13 mortars with 325 grenades.
  150 light machine guns with 1.4 million cartridges
  300 sub-machine guns with 1 million cartridges
  230 anti-tank weapons of the "Piat" type with 3,450 grenades
  130 rifles with 28,000 cartridges
  950 revolvers with 36,000 cartridges
13,300 hand grenades, 3000 of which were for anti-tank operations.

The total figures for all the weapons dropped was far higher,[59] and simply as an example: a total of 3,085 sub-machine guns were dropped, most of which fell into the hands of the Germans. Less than 10% reached the beleaguered Polish forces, and of these 10%, two-thirds were received in the forest district of Puszza Kampinoska, a little to the northwest of the besieged city, from where the Army had hoped for reinforcements. Only 100 sub-machine guns reached the hard pressed forces in the centre of the city. The figures for the other categories of weapons were not quite so tragic.

There were several causes for the catastrophic result of this large-scale air action: first that the Soviet Air Force did not succeed in breaking the German air superiority over the city, and second that Soviet authorities refused permission for the aircraft of the Western Powers to land on the Russian airfields for tanking up and for possible repairs. Such a possibility was present, and in fact this was already a routine. The American Air Force, after long negotiations, had obtained Russian permission in June 1944 to carry out "shuttle bombing", in which American bombers, after attacking German targets, were allowed to land on Russian airfields, for example at Poltava and Mirgorod, to fill up with petrol and bombs and carry out further bombing over Germany on the return flight to England. This was conditional, however, upon Russian approval before each operation. When the rising took place in Warsaw, however, the Soviet Government shut the door upon this possibility. The official Soviet reason given[60] in the case of the Warsaw rising was that the Soviet Army, after its offensive through White Russian and East Poland of 500 kilometres, had reached the utmost limit of its military and supply capacity[61] and was therefore unable to force such a serious barrier as the Weichsel river, and capture a large town west of the river; that the rising in Warsaw had been started without previous arrangements with the Soviet authorities; that it was an irresponsible venture, which should not be supported; and that the Western Allies' attempt to come to the assistance of the fighting Poles was therefore no concern of the Soviet Government. In addition, the Soviet Government had no responsibility towards the Polish Underground Army, which was fighting under the command of an exile Polish Government with which the Soviet Union had broken off diplomatic relations, and with which it could not reach any agreement, for instance on the future Polish-Russian frontier. It was just at that time, when the rising broke out, that the exile Polish Government's Prime Minister, Stanislaw Mikolajczyk – who in 1943 had succeeded the Prime Minister General Sikorski after he had been killed – had been in Moscow for fruitless negotiations with Stalin. The proposal for an agreement discussed here was refused by Mikolajczyk's colleagues in the exile Cabinet in London, and after that, Polish-Soviet relations remained as cold and sterile as they had been ever since diplomatic relations had been broken off in 1943.

The Soviet Government could thus claim both military and political reasons for refusing immediate help to the fighting Poles in Warsaw, and the Soviet Government thus took the risk of a formidable political deterioration in relations with the Western Powers. The political consequences of the Soviet hard line, emphasized particularly by the Russian Air Force's passivity and the refusal of access to the Russian airfields could have been far-reaching, and Churchill particularly pressed Roosevelt to take the opportunity for a confrontation with the Soviet Government. He made the proposal to him that American aircraft, with or without Russian permission, should land on the Russian airfields; and on 4 September the British War Cabinet discussed the extreme measure of stopping deliveries via Murmansk-Archangel. Roosevelt refused to go to such extremes, and the Polish Warsaw Army fought to the death, until its remnants, on 5 October, were forced to capitulate.

At the end, the Poles did not fight entirely without Soviet help. On 12 September, while Polish pockets were still holding out, the Soviet Government changed course. It gave permission for American landings on the Russian airfields, which made the massive flight of 18 September possible, and from 14 September the Russian Air Force began flying over the Warsaw area, while at the same time Soviet forces, supported by Polish forces which had been trained and armed in the Soviet Union, attacked the suburb of Praga on the east bank of the Weichsel river. After four days, the suburb was cleared of German troops, and from 14 September the Soviet Air Forces began dropping weapons over the last of the Polish Resistance pockets on the west bank of the Weichsel. The Soviet figures[62] for this dropping are given as 156 mortars, 505 anti-tank rifles, 2667 automatic weapons and some amounts of food stuffs. How much of this reached the besieged Poles is not known. At this stage, the Polish Resistance pockets had been so greatly depleted, and the conditions for the beleaguered Poles were so hopeless, that the help came too late.

The Polish losses during the rising are calculated as 150,000 to 200,000 persons killed in action, in German attack, artillery bombardment of town districts, and in mass executions. The Warsaw rising was the bloodiest and most tragic defeat of the European Resistance Forces. Here the Resistance Forces engaged in a regular battle, without strategic agreements or co-ordination, under the most unfavourable conditions, and thus abandoned the principles of mobility, the element of surprise, temporary numerical superiority followed by dispersal, which were otherwise the characteristics of partisan warfare. Had it been co-ordinated with Soviet strategy and therefore with Soviet support, the rising might perhaps have succeeded. In the event, this support was withheld or it came too late, and the tragedy followed.

With the Warsaw rising, the Armia Krajowa bled to death. Those leaders of the organisation who survived were taken prisoner by the Germans, and the organisation itself ceased to be a political factor.[63] The Polish Communist Party had been building up another parallel Resistance organisation, however, ever since 1943 – the people's army or Armia Ludowa. Side by side with groups from the Armia Krajowa – although not without mutual suspicion and friction – groups from the Armia Ludowa began sabotage actions against the Occupying Power, and during 1944 the activities of both organisations gradually changed to partisan warfare in East Poland, and particularly in the case of the Armia Ludowa to close collaboration with Russian partisan units and co-operation with the advancing Soviet Armies. When the Polish Liberation Committee was set up in Lublin on 22 July 1944, the organisation of the Armia Ludowa was brought under the command of the Liberation Committee,[64] and as East Poland was liberated by the Soviet Armies, recruitments of its forces into regular Polish army units began. In addition to the First Polish Army, which had been set up and armed in the Soviet Union, a Second Polish Army was formed by recruitment from the Armia Ludowa and with volunteers from the liberated areas. This development corresponded to the similar development in France in 1944, where, as their districts were liberated, Resistance forces joined the regular units and supplemented them. The supply situation for the Armia Ludowa and for the regular forces which were formed in the liberated regions of Poland was obviously very different from that suffered by the Armia Krajowa. Here the sources of supply were nearby and were not hindered by the long flying distances or the presence of the Occupying Power. At the end of 1944, the Polish Armies numbered about 285,000 men,[65] supplied by the Soviet Union with 700,000 rifles and sub-machine guns, 15,000 machine guns and mortars, 3500 cannons, 1200 aircraft and 122 trucks.

CZECHOSLOVAKIA. Geographically, Czechoslovakia was in the same situation in regard to Great Britain as Poland, or perhaps in an even more unfavourable situation. The flying distance to Czechoslovakia was also a negative factor here, and all flying had to take place over strongly defended territory. The parallel between the two countries can be carried further in the sense that for Czechoslovakia too, the creation of air bases in southern Italy by the end of 1943 brought a certain improvement in the situation. Here the parallel ends, however. No British guarantee existed for Czechoslovakia, there was no military alliance, and very few Free Czechoslovak Forces.[66] The political situation was that after the Munich

Agreement in 1938, the President of Czechoslovakia, Eduard Benes, had sought political asylum in Great Britain, where in December 1939 he formed a Committee of Eight, which in July 1940 was recognized by Great Britain as a Provisional Czechoslovak National Committee. In July 1941 this was changed to a full recognition of the Benes government as the legal government of the country, by the Soviet Union, Great Britain, the United States, China, etc.[67] Neither Great Britain's obligations to nor her interests in Czechoslovakia went so far as they did in the case of Poland, however. Furthermore, the shadow of Munich hung over British-Czechoslovak relations both then and later, in that Great Britain reserved her position as to Czechoslovakia's frontiers after the War.[68]

Added to this the exile Czechoslovak Government, unlike the Polish, had no illusions as to the possibilities for creating a large and powerful home army. In fact it was not in favour of too much sabotage activity. There were several reasons for this. One was geographical, since Czechoslovakia and particularly the important regions of Bohemia was not considered suited to guerilla activity, and Czechoslovakia was not a transit territory for the German Armies marching eastwards, as was Poland. Another reason was political, in that control of large home forces could easily fall into the hands of the activist Communist groups – and this actually occurred to a great extent, when in the course of time partisan groups formed, nevertheless, first in Slovakia, where the possibilities for partisan activity were best, and later in Moravia and Bohemia. Lastly there was the military reason, that the exile government, advised by a group of Intelligence Officers who after 15 March 1939 had flown to Britain, where they established excellent intelligence contacts with colleagues at home,[69] gave predominance to the maintenance of the intelligence network. They did not wish this to be compromised by sabotage or other militant underground activities, and both they and the exile government believed that it would be possible to prepare the quick re-establishment of a Czechoslovak Army under the control of the exile government in the event of German collapse. Benes aimed at national unity. But his methods were diplomatic, not revolutionary. He had no illusions as to Czechoslovakia being able to liberate herself by her own efforts, or even as to the Czechoslovakian people being able to make any important contribution towards the liberation of the country. He believed that the restoration of Czechoslovakia would follow the results of the War, and he regarded it as the government's most important task to achieve the best possible relations with the warring Allied Great Powers. He saw clearly – more clearly than the Polish

Government – that the Soviet Union would emerge as a Great Power after the War, and that her attitude would be decisive for Czechoslovakia's political position. In spite of his political ties with the Western Powers, therefore, he sought and obtained friendly relations with the Soviet Government. In December 1943 he signed the Czechoslovak-Russian Treaty of Friendship and Co-operation in Moscow. He regarded himself as a possible bridge builder between East and West, and believed that by diplomatic agreement with the Soviet Union he could ensure the restoration of an independent democratic Czechoslovak state at the end of the War, and also the return of the exile government. In this way, the exile Czechoslovak Government's position would be different from that which threatened the Polish, Yugoslav and Greek Governments, and – in Benes's words[70] – the way would be open for "a clear and logical continuation of the first republic".

Benes hesitated, however, at drawing political consequences of his policy and particularly of the situation at home as regards resistance. In both open and secret messages to the population and the national Resistance organisations with which he was in contact, he advocated a waiting position, also after the German invasion of the Soviet Union. From his point of view it was a question of preserving calm as long as possible, avoiding provocation and unnecessary sacrifices. Considerations of humanity and a realistic political assessment of Czechoslovakia's possibilities were behind this attitude, but Benes separated himself, as did so many exile politicians, from the realities in feeling and standpoints which the Occupation created.

The real situation was different, and it was brought about by the Czechoslovak Communist Party. Soon after the German invasion of the Soviet Union in June 1941, the party's Central Committee issued an appeal to the Czechoslovak people.[71] The appeal referred to the Soviet Union's "firm stand" during the Munich crisis, prophesied victory for the Soviet Union, and called on all Czechs to "gather around the backbone of the nation, around the working classes . . . which at the moment of receiving a signal, will bring to the bloody regime the first powerful blow. At this moment maintain calm and maximum of vigilance". This appeal was the start of the Communist Party's energetic efforts to escalate sabotage activity and later partisan activity, and to establish a network of "National Resistance Committees" throughout the country, whereever this could be done, in factories, offices, parishes etc. Formally speaking, these were National Resistance Committees, but in reality they were usually led by the Communists, and it was the Communists who took the lead in activising Resistance developments, first through a noticeable increase in sabotage, later in the creation of partisan units.[72] The General Secretary of the Czechoslovakian Communist Party, Klement Gottwald, agitated on Radio Moscow for ever-increasing activity, and the work was urged on by Czechoslovak instructors, trained in the Soviet Union and dropped by Soviet aircraft in Czechoslovakia. In all about 125 partisan units were formed, most of them in Slovakia, where the nature of the country was best suited to partisan activity and lay nearest to the Soviet front. To some extent, the sabotage groups and partisan units sought co-operation with conservative circles, as the task was not only sabotage and the preparation of a massive popular rising, but also political agitation, and this entailed activity outside the party's own ranks. Under the pressure of this activist development, and pressed also by Czechoslovak Communists in exile in the Soviet Union, with whom he negotiated during his visit to Moscow in December 1943, Benes changed his hesitant course, and in February 1944 he made a speech on the B.B.C. in which he struck a new note:[73] "The moment is approaching", he concluded his speech, "when our all-national struggle on all our territory at home and abroad must begin. An opening of the Second Front, a general attack on Germany from all sides and the proximity of the Soviet front to our frontiers is a signal for this struggle. To this struggle I am calling you all". The reaction in the mother country to this appeal was generally speaking negative, apart from the Communist groups, and the Foreign Minister of the exile government, Hubert Ripka, had to send a long message in code to the national Resistance leaders at home, in which he tried to explain that the appeal was not meant to be taken literally, but was sent solely on account of Communist wishes or pressure. Ripka admitted to the sceptics at home that it did not correspond with the facts and the concrete possibilities, and that it was as psychologically unfortunate as it was politically necessary.

This, briefly, was the political background for SOE's activities in Czechoslovakia. It will be obvious that the task must be far less ambitious than it was in the case of Poland, for the sole reason that Czechoslovakian Resistance was confined for a long time to intelligence, passive resistance, and at the start sporadic sabotage which helped to reduce Czechoslovakian production.[74] In the first phases, the main task was to send radio telegraphists, especially, to Czechoslovakia, to support the Intelligence Service and possibly to prepare the ground for later activity – a task which was far less demanding than mass deliveries of weapons and other materiel. In this task SOE could co-operate with officers from the exile Czechoslovakian Government's Intelligence Service, in the same way as the Polish Section of SOE co-operated with the Polish Officers from the Sixth Bureau. The first radio telegraphist was dropped in April 1941,[75] after which there was a pause owing to the light summer nights, and two specially trained parachutists were dropped in December 1941. These two men's special mission was to carry out the assasination of the German SS General Reinhardt Heydrich, who had been appointed "Protector" of Bohemia-Moravia in September 1941. Heydrich was known for his unheard-of brutality, and it was for this reason that the decision had been taken, after many deliberations between the exile Czechoslovakian Government and the British authorities, to liquidate him. The mission was accomplished successfully. The two parachutists were admitted to the Czechoslovak Resistance network and in May 1942 succeeded in assassinating Heydrich. But Heydrich's death brought terrible reprisals. The towns of Lidice and Lezaky were wiped out and their inhabitants murdered – in the case of Lidice possibly also because the Germans had traced a radio broadcast from there – and a wide-spread round-up in the Czechoslovak Resistance network followed in the wake of the assassination.

This very limited and much discussed success had lasting influence on the work of SOE. The reprisals could not but contribute to restraining any tendency towards too much provocation, and many people in the hard pressed population turned from the thought of sabotage or other form of militant violence, on the grounds that this was difficult to carry through in Bohemia, thickly populated as it was; that its military value would be doubtful; and that reprisals would be out of proportion to results. We have already seen that the exile government was thinking along the same lines, and the hesitation of SOE was not only due to considerations of this kind but also to the fact that Czechoslovakia lay outside Great Britain's strategic operational area, and that developments in the country had only marginal interest, at least for the time being. From 1942 to the beginning of 1944 only a few flights were therefore carried out, and these only with telegraphists. Contributory causes were the difficult approaches and the number of accidents which resulted in only one seventh of the flights ending with successful dropping operations.[76] From april 1944, however, some teams of parachutists trained in sabotage were sent into the country with special sabotage equipment, and they succeeded in carrying out a number of sabotage actions against German depots and an airfield, and against the transport network. After successfully completing their missions they joined the partisan units. The extensive sabotage which was SOE's principal aim was not realised under the leadership of SOE, however. The initiative passed to the Communist groups, supported by instructors and materiel from the Soviet Union. The reasons have been given: the exile government's attitude to SOE's plans, which were always far-reaching, was generally speaking negative; the attitude in the circles with which SOE co-operated were generally speaking sceptical; and the technical difficulties were of such magnitude that the SOE plans had to be very considerably reduced. Apart from the assassination of Heydrich, although this echoed around the world, SOE operations remained largely at the experimental stage.

A considerable cleft arose in Czechoslovakia, therefore, between the Communist and non-Communist Resistance circles. The Communists were extremely active and became the leaders of the Czechoslovak Resistance struggle, particularly through their control of the National Committees. They carried out sabotage, set up partisan units and prepared a general popular rising. Their activity culminated in the popular rising which broke out in Slovakia in August 1944, after the Soviet Armies in April 1944 had reached the frontiers of Czechoslovakia.[77] Slovakia was in a peculiar situation. When Czechoslovakia was dismembered in March 1939, Slovakia was declared to be an independent state, in fact a German satellite. Slovak army units were therefore sent into battle on the East Front under the German High Command, and the revolt in Slovakia therefore took various directions. Some Slovak army units went over to the Soviet forces, others joined the partisan units. These had reached a strength of about 75,000 when they started the revolt, and for a short time gained possession of large Slovak areas. The partisans only had one airfield at their disposal, however, and this was in such poor repair that it did not permit the landing of sufficient Soviet help. The revolt had long been prepared by a Slovak National Council, set up in 1943, and had been discussed with Soviet Staffs in advance, although no definite arrangements had been made, and Soviet advice was rather to step up partisan activities. The German reaction here, as in Warsaw, was immediate and brutal, and after some weeks the revolt ended in a bloody defeat for the rebels, although they succeeded in maintaining partisan pockets in the mountains.

This Slovak revolt had many similarities with that of Warsaw.[78] The two revolts occurred in the same period; they both depended upon quick Soviet intervention; the underlying strategic situation was almost identical; and in both cases the Soviet Armies, after a long advance, were separated from the rebels by a barrier, in one instance the Vistula river and in the other the Carpathians. Other common factors were that it was technically impossible for the Western Powers to bring effective relief,[79] and that both revolts ended in bloody defeat. The differences are just as obvious, however. There was no open political disagreement between the Soviet Union and Czechoslovakia of any acute character, and the Slovak revolt was started after the Soviet authorities had been oriented and consulted, and even though the Soviet authorities had expressed doubts as to the possibilities and value of a general rising, and had recommended expansion of sabotage and partisan activity as a better course, the Soviet Supreme Command here took the consequences of the rising in that they started a violent offensive against the German positions in the Carpathians, to relieve the rebels, and flew in considerable quantities of materiel. The German positions in the Carpathians proved to be such an obstacle, however, that help came through too late, and the revolt was crushed with bloody losses for the rebels. The two eastern European insurrections, therefore, illustrate three decisive themes: first, that guerilla formations were very dependent upon outside support; secondly, these formations were badly hit when they abandoned the guerilla "hit and run" tactics and engaged in regular battles; and thirdly, it was out of the question for the Western Powers to support eastern European countries effectively, when' they were situated too far away for a sufficiently massive help to reach them by air, in situations where the Resistance forces broke the laws of guerilla warfare.

The position was quite different for the countries in the north and west, and along the Mediterranean, which could obtain decisive support from the Western Allies.

SCANDINAVIA. After Czechoslovakia and Poland, the Scandinavian countries, Norway and Denmark, were the next to be exposed to German occupation. The Western Powers' possibilities for bringing help to these countries in the form of instructors and materiel were far greater than in the case of Czechoslovakia and Poland. The flying distances were shorter and the approaches were over the open sea, and in addition, deliveries could be brought both by sea and by air, and limited quantities could be smuggled in through neutral Sweden. In particular, a valuable courier route was established with Sweden as transit country. Much of Norway's long frontier with Sweden lay in wild districts which could not be guarded effectively, and in the case of Denmark, up to 1943 there existed the possibility for many Danes, especially businessmen, civil servants and politicians, to obtain German exit visa for legal journeys to Sweden – a possibility which was extensively exploited, and from 1940, organised.[80] From 1943, illegal sea routes were established across the Øresund and the Kattegat, all based permanently in Sweden. These succeeded in maintaining continuous illegal sea traffic in both directions. A common factor for the Scandinavian countries' Resistance Movements was also that their final political aim, generally speaking, was the re-establishment of the pre-war constitutional monarchies and pre-war democratic and social conditions, although a desire for improvement, particularly in the social domain was a ground theme for many Resistance circles in both countries. Here the similarities end, however. Both politically and geographically, the situations of the two countries were very different.

Norway was at war, and had a strong exile government in London, with a very extensive mandate from the Norwegian Parliament to carry on the war, and the exile government had important possibilities for this. First of all, after the military capitulation in June 1940, the exile government still had what could be considered an extremely large merchant navy at their disposal, including particularly modern tankers which could give Great Britain decisive help in the critical years before the U.S.A. entered the war.[81] For that reason alone, Norway was an important ally, and in addition Norway had a strong financial position in all her negotiations with the Allies. This meant that SOE's operations in Norway, which in the first months of the War were marked by British interests and standpoints, had later to be carried on in understanding with the exile Norwegian Government and the Norwegian Home Army Command, Milorg. In the Norwegian General Staff in London, a special section was set up for Norwegian underground activity (FO.IV), and in December 1941 a British Norwegian co-operation committee,[82] was established, consisting of members of this section and representatives for SOE. SOE's operations, as well as other British and later American OSS operations in Norway, were prepared and effected from that date in understanding with the Norwegian Government and the Norwegian Home Front.

Denmark's political position was quite different. Denmark was not at war, was not an Ally, and had no exile government or other organ which could take the place of an exile government. Denmark had resigned herself to the Occupation as a *fait accompli*, and a legal Danish Government with broad parliamentary backing functioned in negotiations with the German Occupation authorities under the fiction that Denmark, in spite of the Occupation, had retained her neutrality, her territorial integrity and her political independence. In terms of international law, the Danish position was supposed to be a "peaceful occupation" (occupatio pacifica) – a concept which had no clear definition, because practically no precedent existed.[83] In May 1942 a leading Danish politician, Christmas Møller, escaped to London,[84] but neither he, the Danish Minister in London nor the Danish Council, constituted by London Danes, could claim any political mandate whatever. As regards Denmark, SOE could act without previous consultation with formally responsible Danish authorities.

Geographical conditions were quite dissimilar in the two countries. Dropping operations over Norway were to some extent facilitated by the geography of the country. The large waste areas were very suitable dropping terrain, but internal transport from the waste, trackless areas to the districts where the targets for sabotage were, was very difficult. Added to this, the pilots had to be very precise. A few seconds' delay in releasing containers could mean that a dropping intended for one valley could land in the next valley, on the other side of a mountain range. Even the rocky ground where the parachutists had to land could give serious risks. The first telegram received in London after the First dropping was brief:[85] "Landed on a rock. both safe." As a matter of fact, one of the two parachutists landed on the edge of an abyss. On a later occasion, a team landed on a step glacier, and four men drowned during a landing on a lake where the ice was too thin. In Denmark the situation was the opposite. Here most of the country was built up, but on the other hand, internal distribution in a country criss-crossed by the road network posed fewer difficulties, even though these distribution problems could be serious enough, and required organisation with many ramifications. The problems of localising the reception points, owing to the many bays, inlets and lakes, was less difficult, and soil was of such a type that landings entailed a minimum of risk. In both countries, but particularly in Norway, summer nights were too light for dropping operations to be carried out on a large scale, but on the other hand, also winter weather and lack of visibility often made such operations impossible. It was not until an improvement in navigation technique took place, and particularly from 1944 when the Eureka instruments were taken into use, that the climatic difficulties were partly overcome.

It was decisive for both countries, however, that they lay within reach of the Western Allied Air Forces, so that deliveries to both countries were technically possible, to the extent that the Western Powers were interested in the deliveries. As regards both countries, D Day 1944 was the turning point. It is true that both instructors and m had been sent to both countries up to that day, but nevertheless, priority as concerns supplies was still low. The greatest quantitie supplies were delivered after the liberation of France, when British-American resources, both in material and flying capacity, were made available for areas such as the Scandinavian, which until then had been marginal regions in the Western Allied strategy. The idea of an invasion in Norway had certainly been in the air for a time in 1942, operation "Jupiter" as it was designated,[86] but the idea never passed the preliminary stages of deliberations, and was not realised, and the discussions between the Allies on bringing Sweden into the War remained at a similar stage.[87] Deliveries to Scandinavia were therefore limited until the summer 1944, but this does not mean that the deliveries which were made were not important. Considering that Scandinavia never became a battle area of the war, and that the materiel delivered in the last nine months of the War was only partially taken into use, it can be stated with good reason that the early though limited deliveries were most important. They made it possible to effectivize sabotage at a relatively early stage; they constituted a material and psychological stimulus for the active members of the Resistance; and they were especially a disquieting element and therefore a factor of uncertainty for the German Occupation authorities. Norway, particularly, was regarded as a threatened invasion area.[88] In January 1942 Hitler described Norway as the "fatal area" of the War, and during 1942 the German forces there were reinforced month after month until, in June 1942, they numbered a quarter of a million fighting troops. At the same time, the main body of German ships were transferred to Norwegian ports. The whole of this unnecessary shift in strength, at a stage which was critical for the German Armies, had naturally first of all its roots in the belief in a possible Allied invasion, but uncertainty was increased by British raids and by the obvious cooperation between the Allied front abroad and the Norwegian Home Front. Here as everywhere else, it was not certain how far Norwegian-British co-operation went, and what elements of danger were involved in a systematic build-up of Resistance forces. It was possible to register this build-up, but not to assess how much weight should be given it. In this connexion the perspectives of the early deliveries were far greater than their size.

Both instructors and materiel could be sent by sea to Norway throughout the War, and to Denmark from 1944. On the Shetlands a Norwegian-British naval base was built, operating with transit routes between Britain and small Norwegian ports, which were already in use in 1940,[89] and here at first Norwegian fishing cutters were used, and other small ships which escaped in great numbers from South-west Norway to the Shetlands or to harbours in Scotland, whilst from 1943, fast submarine chasers were employed for transport. In the case of Denmark, transport by sea was carried out with meetings in the North Sea between British and Danish fishing vessels.[90] But even if this sea transport increased to a considerable extent, it was nevertheless the deliveries dropped by parachute which were predominant in the final count. For both countries there was an important transit route through Sweden. Couriers slipped through on this route with vital correspondence, usually in the form of microfilms; light material could also be channeled through this route; and lastly, thousands of compromised Resistance people and others threatened by the actions of the occupying authorities such as Jews, found asylum in Sweden, where from 1943 the able-bodied from among the refugees formed brigades equipped with Swedish weapons,[91] ready for action in their respective countries in the event of a final battle in Scandinavia. By the end of the War, the refugees numbered approximately 50,000 Norwegians and approximately 20,000 Danes, while the strengths of the two brigades were about 10,000 and about 4,500 men, all in a high degree of military training and well equipped with weapons from the Swedish arsenals.

The total of SOE's and later SOE/SO's stakes, in proportion to the size of the two countries and their strategic importance, was quite considerable. Both instructors and material were sent into the occupied areas by the various routes. In Norway the first instructors trained in sabotage had already arrived in 1940,[92] either from the Shetlands base or smuggled through Sweden, while the first dropping operations took place in January 1942.[93] The primary task for these first instructors, here and in Denmark and in all the European countries where SOE operated, was to establish the illegal telegraph service which was an absolute pre-requisite for effectiveness in all later operations. Other tasks were sabotage and co-operation with local Resistance organisations, with a view to setting up underground armies and arranging for their operations to be co-ordinated with those of the main Allied Front – tasks which were not at first accomplished without controversies and crises in confidence, which were usually rooted in general ignorance of possibilities, methods and objectives.[94] In time these disagreements were replaced by mutual understanding, and all in all, the Scandinavian sphere

of activity became relatively free of problems for the supporting ơ
sations of the Western Powers.

The deliveries from the West were of decisive value for the deve,
ment of resistance in Norway and Denmark. They determined the effe
tiveness and extent of sabotage, they were the main source of weapons
for the underground armies, they contributed to the expansion of the
intelligence services, and gradually linked the Home Front to the front
abroad in close collaboration. In the case of Norway, deliveries by sea
amounted to about 310 tons, about 150 tons carried out by small Norwegian ships and about 160 tons by the submarine chasers mentioned
above;[95] about 9700 containers were dropped by parachute as well as
about 2500 packages, in all slightly more than 1000 tons of deliveries. The
total material deliveries sent thus amounted to nearly 1350 tons.
Total shipments were a little higher, which may probably be due to extra
cargoes being added at the last moment. The number of instructors and
specially trained saboteurs, telegraphists etc., was about 425 men, most
of them dropped by parachute, although some teams were brought in by
boat. In addition, about 350 persons were sailed out to the Shetlands
base, many of them returning as specially trained instructors. This last
group of figures does not include the many who escaped on their own
initiative, and not through any organisation, and reached the north of the
England, the Orkneys, the Shetlands, and Scotland. The material delivered.– with the exception of radio material – was mostly sabotage material and light weapons suited to sabotage or guerilla activities. The totals
can be given for the months January to April 1945, when they consisted
of 25 tons of plastic explosives with detonators etc., 5 million cartridges,
2,250 light machine guns, 17,500 automatic rifles and 2000 carabines.

The overall picture for Denmark was much the same, although the
figures are a good deal lower.[96] Here too, the first instructors with
equipment for radio transmission arrived in the spring 1942, and with the
next teams and the first material deliveries in the spring 1943, developments gathered speed, and greatly influenced the increasing sabotage
activity which had begun. In all about 50 instructors were sent to Denmark, while the total number of containers dropped amounted to about
7000 plus about 700 packages – a total of about 700 tons. In addition, the
deliveries across the North Sea amounted to about 100 tons, and a considerable amount of material was smuggled by various routes through
Sweden. Particularly important deliveries were made by fast British
motor torpedo boats[97] which fetched cargoes of Swedish ball bearings in
small harbours near Göteborg, and from the autumn 1944 brought in

cargoes of weapons for Denmark, which the illegal Danish escape routes, operating between Swedish and Danish harbours, were able at this stage to take on to their destinations. In Denmark too, considerable amounts of special equipment and light weapons for sabotage were delivered. In both Denmark and Norway, some quantities of anti-tank weapons were also delivered.

The figures for both countries refer to the amounts of materiel which actually reached the Resistance groups. The number of flights which did not succeed, owing to climatic difficulties in the Scandinavian countries was considerable; and many aircraft were lost. In the case of Norway, this figure is 23 British and 5 American planes. The corresponding figure for Denmark is not known.

As far as Denmark was concerned, special conditions resulted in deliveries for Jutland, and to some extent for the island of Fyn, being easier to carry out than deliveries to Zealand. This was due partly to the longer flying distance, partly to the purely geographical situation, and also to the facts that Jutland was more thinly populated than Zealand, and that flying in took place over the open sea. The result was that Zealand, and therefore the capital, Copenhagen, were under-supplied in comparison with the rest of the country. This was balanced to some extent, however, when from the summer 1944 it proved possible – with the understanding of the Swedish authorities – to purchase 3000 modern Swedish submachine guns of Husquarna make, which were then smuggled to Zealand harbours by the illegal Danish escape organisations.[98] These Swedish weapons were a valuable supplement to the deliveries which reached the Danish Resistance organisations from the West. By the end of the War, a further 10,000 sub-machine guns were ready for shipment, but the German capitulation made this delivery superfluous.

HOLLAND, BELGIUM, LUXEMBOURG. SOE's deliveries to Holland, Belgium and Luxembourg were not hampered by flying distance. On the contrary, these countries lay nearer to Great Britain than any other occupied territories except North France. Nevertheless, there were quite special difficulties in connexion with these deliveries, which were partly due to the density of the built-up areas, with limited possibilities for finding suitable dropping points, although in all three countries there were agricultural and forest regions which could be used for the purpose. Even greater difficulties were caused by the very massive German occupation of the area, which was naturally regarded as particularly threatened by invasion, and the strong German defences made the deliveries very dangerous. This region was packed with German anti-aircraft batteries and radar installations, and well covered by German fighters,[99] also because British-American bomber formations very often flew over the area on their way to strategic bombing in Germany. Thus, for all flights connected with operations in these countries, the German defences had to be forced. There could be no detours.

In Holland a further serious difficulty arose, which must be mentioned briefly here. For a period in 1942–43, SOE's operations over Holland met with a series of disasters which were unique in SOE's history. These were due to accidents and to a very cleverly arranged German infiltration of the whole SOE organisation's Dutch Section, and for a time it threatened to disrupt the whole SOE organisation and work – which had never been fully accepted by the traditional military staffs – to such an extent that the possible advisability of stopping its activities altogether had to be considered by the British High Command and the British Government. The German designation for this affair, so critical for SOE, was "Englandsspiel".[100]   At the beginning, everything went according to plan. A Dutch Section of SOE was set up in the summer 1940, and after the first training course was completed, the first team of two men, one of them a W/T operator, was sent into the country on a reconnaissance mission, landed from a British motor torpedo boat on the Dutch coast. In November 1941, a new two-man team was dropped, consisting of an organisation leader, Thijs Taconis and a radio telegraphist, Hubert Lauwers. Taconi's task, as leader of the team, was to make contact with the Dutch Resistance organisation, "Orde Dienst", made up of ex-officers and non-commissioned officers, who regarded it as their first duty to build up a Dutch underground army for action during a German collapse or in the event of invasion, but who were for that reason against any immediate activity in the form of sabotage, etc. The organisation was conservative in attitude, and in accordance with its name, was prepared to maintain law and order in the event of chaos.[101] In the same way, as already mentioned, the Dutch Intelligence Service had sent some radio telegraphists into Holland,[102] among others the telegraphist van der Reyden. He was arrested, however, in 1942, and this arrest was the start of the disasters. During a brutal interrogation he was forced to give certain information, but did not give full details on his code system, and in particular he did not divulge his security check, that is, the mistakes which it was agreed he would include in his transmission in the event of his being under German *force majeure*. However, the German counterespionage, "Abwehr", which was led by two skilled officers, Joseph

Schreieder and H. J. Giskes, obtained considerable insight into the British code systems, transmitting places, frequencies employed, intervals between transmissions, etc., both in this way, and by systematic direction-finding of illegal transmissions.[103] The situation became even more serious when, in March 1942, they succeeded also in arresting the telegraphist Lauwers, while he was transmitting. In the interval before the next transmission, they forced him to transmit under German orders, with the Abwehr officers so to speak "ordering" a new dropping operation of men and materiel. Lauwers acted in good faith, as he too used the security check, and could therefore conclude that London was warned. However, unfortunately and quite incomprehensibly, this passed unnoticed, or was misunderstood in London, and on 27 March a new dropping operation was carried out in north-east Holland, in which two more men, including another telegraphist, fell into the hands of the Germans. The latter made sure that those receiving them acted their parts as Dutch Resistance men, and procured false illegal lodgings and identities for the new arrivals, so that these instructors and telegraphists did not realise that they were playing the Germans' cleverly planned game.

Now followed a series of droppings, followed by camouflaged arrests, through which the Germans could work directly with the Dutch Section of the SOE, who – still unaware of the thorough German infiltration of the Dutch Resistance network – sent over a number of teams, in May, June and July. These were immediately arrested, and the material they brought was expropriated or was woven into the German double game. Here the consequences were particularly serious, because first Taconis, and then a specially trained instructor, George Louis Jambroes had received instructions in London to co-operate with: "Orde Dienst" and with its help to build up a secret Dutch underground army – a plan which was approved by the Dutch Prime Minister, Gerbrandy, although he had nothing to do with the actual planning. This was in the hands of SOE. Here it became a problem for the Germans that "Orde Dienst" had ceased to exist at that stage, and that the telegraphist had to ask for permission to co-operate with other organisations.

The game went on for a long time. From June 1942 to May 1943, no less than 35 instructors were thus caught, and either arrested[104] or misled by the German *Abwehr* leaders. All the deliveries fell into German hands, and a number of aircraft were shot down as they flew in or flew away. Hundreds of members of the Resistance were arrested. The Germans completed the illusion by carrying out relatively harmless sabotage actions and reporting these to the unsuspecting SOE Headquarters in London.

This fantastic "England game" finished at the end of 1943. SOE had already stopped dropping operations in May 1943, however, disturbed at the disproportionate number of arrests of leading Dutch members of the Resistance, and also disturbed at the suspicious increase in the losses of aircraft engaged in the operations. The decisive moment came when, in August 1943, two of the instructors who had been arrested, Pieter Dourlein and J. B. Ubbink, succeeded in escaping from prison and finally making their way to Switzerland, where they immediately contacted the British representatives there. Their first telegrams on the situation in Holland were not actually believed, because Schreider had warned London that the two escapees were German spies, in the hope of keeping the "England game" going, but after a month or two, it dawned upon London what had been happening, both because of the messages from Switzerland and also because of the other facts in the case – the many arrests, the glaring number of aircraft shot down (about a third were lost) and the obvious lack of Resistance activity. From the beginning of 1944, the organisation programme for Holland was completely revised, and the game was up at last. A sarcastic telegram to the Dutch Section of SOE added insult to injury on April Fools' Day 1944:[105]

"messrs blunt bingham and succs ltd london in the last time you are trying to make business in netherlands without our assistance stop we think this rather unfair in view our long and successful cooperation as your sole agents stop but never mind whenever you will come to pay a visit to the continent you may be assured that you will be recieved with the same care and result as all those you sent us before stop so long."

The "England game" was over. In addition to the losses in men and material, and the German infiltration into important political, military and Intelligence Resistance networks, it had brought the Germans insight into the character of the whole of SOE's work, recruitment, training, aims and orders. Nevertheless, the "England game" did not fulfil the German *Abwehr* Officers' expectations entirely. When the game was at its height, they had hoped to obtain information on Allied invasion plans, particularly as to time and place. This they did not achieve.

When the "England game" was at an end, a complete re-organisation of the leadership of the Dutch Section of the SOE was carried out, and

296 · *Politics and Supplies . Holland*

the work which was then started[106] was co-ordinated with a newly formed Dutch office under the control of the exile government, the "Bureau Bijzondere Opdrachten" (Office for Special Tasks). The Dutch Major-General J. W. Oorschot was appointed leader, and in August 1944 a new start was made. At this point, the Dutch Resistance groups which had managed to survive were extremely poorly supplied with even the most elementary weapons and other materiel, but new Resistance organisations were formed nevertheless, and were ready for action when the weapons arrived. The most important of these were the organisations "Knokploegen" and "Raad van Verzet", which were combined during the autumn 1944 with the remnants of the "Orde Dienst" into a joint organisation, "Binnenlandse Strijdkrachten" (BS). Co-operation was now perfected in London, and in all about 100 new instructors were sent into the country with total final deliveries of weapons and explosives for approximately 35,000 men – rifles, sub-machine guns, carabines, hand grenades and anti-tank weapons, as well as ammunition. These considerable deliveries were carried out in about 600 flights, of which only about 200 were successful, however. The weather alone, during the winter months, forced many aircraft to turn back. The result of the deliveries was widespread sabotage, particularly in the northern and eastern provinces. In the densely populated central region around the large towns in the west, the Occupation was so massive and the food situation in the famine winter of 1944–45 so desperate, that effective resistance was almost unthinkable. Strategically, the sabotage had modest value, because the Allied offensive came to a stand-still after the reverse at Arnhem; but when the Allied offensive started again in March 1945, and Canadian troops advanced northwards in the direction of Groningen, the Dutch Resistance forces could and did give them valuable assistance.

Apart from the many individual tragedies which the "England game" brought with it, the affair led inevitably to a general crisis for SOE as a whole. What certainty could they have that similar crises were not developing elsewhere where they were working? The general problem of security in this secret work, and the advisability of using considerable resources for promoting the work must inevitably present themselves right up to the top of the British military hierarchy. How much weight should one place in this Resistance political work with many nations throughout the whole of Europe, over which one had only limited control, and of which one did not even have precise knowledge? In spite of the catastrophe in Holland, the leaders of SOE did not doubt – or they conquered their doubts. But in military circles with orthodox mentality, on the other hand, there were serious doubts at high levels. The British General R. H. Barry, who was serving as Chief of Staff under General Gubbins, and in his capacity as Planning Chief of SOE was responsible for liaison between SOE and the regular Army Staff, has made some general observations on this situation:[107] "In a normal military organisation the Commander or the Chief of Staff directing the war knows a certain number of things: he knows his commanders; he knows his units; he knows what is a good unit, what is a less good unit; he knows how those units are armed; he knows the security of his communications to those units; and most important of all, really, he feels that he has a direct chain of command to those units which is, so to speak, set in the concrete of the military discipline of the force concerned. Therefore from his point of view he knows, or think he knows, at least half his equation. That other half – which is what the enemy is doing – he hopes he knows enough about in order to make sense of his mathematics. Then you transfer that to Resistance. Now he cannot *know*, as far as one can see, the commanders; he cannot know the units; he has to take the say-so of people – with respect – like General Gubbins and myself, and we may be exaggerating; he does know that communications are perhaps somewhat tenuous; arrests may be made which may, from his point of view, result in the disappearance of the unit, and he does not know it has disappeared; reports of results may come in, yet he doesn't know that that set is not being operated by the enemy; and he has no feeling of a direct chain of command with the discipline of a military unit at the end of it. There may be that military discipline, but he cannot get that feeling".

Briefly, then, this was the scepticism which Barry met in his consultations on SOE's behalf with the military staffs, on whose good-will and confidence SOE depended. As my readers will have noticed, there was a clear reference in these observations to the "England game". Nevertheless, the leaders of SOE succeeded in retaining confidence in the work of the organisation. Perhaps it was important in this connexion that just at that period, when the facts of the "England game" were realised in London, the leader of SOE's work in Denmark, the parachutist Flemming B. Muus, happened to be in London for consultations on further work in Denmark. At all events, he was kept back in London for some weeks, and in December 1943, before the green light was given for his return to Denmark, he was closely questioned in the War Office by a number of high-ranking officers from the military departments, as to whether there could be a similar situation in Denmark. The Chief of the Danish Section of SOE, Lieutenant-Commander R. C. Hollingworth, took part in the interrogation and analysis. The investigation, which lasted several hours, ended positively. Muus could maintain that the SOE work in Denmark had not been infiltrated in any way, and this examination may have contributed to SOE surviving the crisis of confidence, which the "England game" obviously involved for the organisation. The British must certainly have tried to verify their facts in other ways, but the above examination is documented[108] and together with other investigations must have carried weight. SOE was allowed to continue its activities and in fact to expand them on an ever-increasing scale, and the crisis was short-lived.

In Belgium arose, in the course of the Occupation, a great many Resistance organisations,[109] which more or less independently of each other sought to fulfil the tasks at hand – intelligence, the creation of an illegal Press, the organisation of strikes, the establishment of escape routes, help to those who evaded forced labour, sabotage, the organisation of paramilitary activities, etc. SOE and also the Prime Minister Pierlot's exile government recognized how unpractical this plurality of organisations was, and tried to co-ordinate them, but without their efforts ever fully succeeding. The many organisations continued their separate existences, and only aimed in the same direction in the sense that, in their various ways and with the means at their disposal, they worked against the Occupying Power. It was a feature in this multi-coloured picture that there was opposition between the Flemish and Walloon elements in the Belgian population,[110] and there was also opposition between those who approved of King Leopold's military capitulation at the end of May 1940, and his continued presence in the country, and those who like the exile Belgian Government disapproved of the King's conduct. However, there were two Belgian organisations which numerically stood out above the others: "L'Armée Secrète" and "Front de l'Indépendance".[111] The first of these was founded in 1940, under its original name, "Légion Belge", and was recruited mostly from among ex-officers and non-commissioned officers. The movement was non-political, and had more of a military character than the other organisations. "Front de l'Indépendance" was founded in 1941, and had a central committee with a representative for each of the political parties, although Communist influence increased the most during the Occupation. It was these two movements which were to benefit especially from the co-operation with SOE and with the Pierlot government, and which therefore received the bulk of the British-American supplies. The two movements were different in character. The "Front de l'Indépendance" aimed at immediate action, gave high priority to sabotage, and procured the means for this by raids on German depots, by seizing materiel, from factories and mines etc., and establishing partisan groups in suitable districts. "L'Armée Secrète" corresponded more nearly to the Western Allies' idea of an underground army. Although they were not inactive as to sabotage and other underground activities, they concentrated on establishing a military force which would go into action at a given moment, and according to plan, in co-ordination with the strategy of the Western Powers, and in addition, would maintain law and order after the disappearance of the Occupying Power.

The Pierlot Belgian Government tried in 1943 to distribute the tasks of resistance between the two organisations,[112] so that "L'Armée Secrète", which was the larger of the two, should have a kind of monopoly of the military tasks which could arise, while the "Front de l'Indépendance" should take over the other very numerous tasks, including those immediately required. The boundary between the two organisations was not clear, however, and could not be maintained. Both organisations were thus given sabotage duties, the idea being that the one should have responsibility for military and the other for industrial sabotage. But this division of responsibility was impossible to realise in practice. As the Belgian historian, Henri Bernard, puts it: "Where did civil resistance end, and where did military resistance begin? Did there in reality exist a difference between 'military' sabotage and 'industrial' sabotage during total war? Or rather, is not all sabotage military?"

The schematic division was London's invention, and represented an attempt to bring some system and priorities into the assistance which could be given to the many Belgian Resistance organisations – of which twelve, apart from the intelligence groups, were officially recognized as Resistance organisations after the War.[113] It was difficult to set up priorities for the one reason that there were divergencies of opinion in the exile government as to which organisations should be supported, or given priority. Up to 1942, there was thus outspoken scepticism as to "L'Armée Secrète", which was regarded by several of the members of the exile government as royalist, and as an organisation whose primary aim was to maintain law and order at the Liberation, whilst actions against the Occupying Power were only secondary.[114] This opinion, which was unfounded, and which showed itself to be so, led to a number of changes in the ranks of the Belgian Government, and in the "Second Section of the Belgian Ministry for National Defence", which in co-operation with SOE decided on plans and priorities for SOE's work in Belgium. After these changes had taken place, it was "L'Armée Secrète" which received the largest share of supplies, although the other organisations were not excluded from support on that account.[115] SOE's operations in support of "Armée Secrète[116] were started in November 1942, with the despatch of a team of parachutists, who succeeded in carrying out eight receptions in all, in the district around Tournai, in south Belgium, in the period January to May 1943. Other teams followed them in the course of the year, the droppings were moved to eastern and south-eastern Belgium, and by the end of 1943, nineteen droppings had been successfully carried out, with deliveries of weapons and explosives, to "L'Armée Secrète". Other deliveries were made to the "Front de l'Indépendance", but the exact number of dropping operations for this and other organisations is not known. The deliveries of materiel to the south-eastern areas of the Ardennes – the province of Luxembourg – were for the benefit both of Belgian and Luxembourgeois groups, and indeed, the Resistance groups were made up of both Belgians and Luxembourgeois in close collaboration. The traditional frontiers were broken down, for example in the province of Haunaut, where Belgian and French Resistance men operated side by side. Part – but only part – of the material dropped, after being received successfully, was later captured by the Germans in the depots where they were stored, and here as everywhere, aircraft were lost in action.

These first deliveries consisted of light weapons, hand grenades and – what was most important at that time – two tons of plastic explosives, which helped to promote the wide-spread sabotage which developed in Belgium during 1943. The 1943 deliveries naturally did not cover any reasonable arming of "L'Armée Secrète", which the British and the exile Belgian Government aimed at building up as an auxiliary force, for the moment when the battles should reach Belgian soil. In October 1943, the deliveries came to a halt, for one reason because of the winter weather, although other priorities, especially the now urgent need for deliveries to France, played their part.

From the spring and through the summer 1944, however, deliveries started again, and this time they accelerated rapidly. From 3 March to 1 September, with a short pause in June, about 85 droppings were carried out, bringing about 1200 containers, or about 100 tons, and in September mass dropping operations followed on each others heels, with a total of about 1800 containers, or about 170 tons. These last September droppings consisted solely of weapons and ammunition, and did not only include weapons for "L'Armée Secrète", but also for the other Resistance groups and for the Gendarmerie which was being re-armed. In addition to the deliveries of materiel, about 225 instructors were dropped, about 40 of them telegraphists.[117]

All in all, the deliveries to Holland, Belgium and Luxembourg were considerably more modest in size than those which, for instance, reached the Scandinavian countries. As already pointed out, great difficulties were involved in deliveries in these thickly populated and densely fortified countries. The pattern of delivery here and in Scandinavia, and also in France, reflected the Western Allies' complex of ideas as to co-operation with European Resistance organisations. As soon as circumstances and resources allowed, instructors – particularly telegraphists – were dropped, and then comperatively small deliveries of special sabotage material and other equipment for use in intelligence and sabotage. The organisation of the underground armies was in progress at the same time, and command contacts with their leaders were being established. Large scale deliveries of weapons for these underground armies were not made until it could be expected that they could release mass activity in connexion with the Allies' operations. This reasoning was based upon considerations of security, political standpoints, and consideration of logistics. The last was a particularly limiting factor in the British decisions. On the basis of a calculation by SOE, from May 1941, it was clear that even roughly arming the underground armies to a strength of approximately 200,000 men, would entail using the full capacity of all the British bombing squadrons over a period of six months, and the stoppage of strategic bombing.[118] The recognition of this quite unacceptable condition, at a time when strategic bombing was given high priority, led inevitably to the modifications mentioned, even for countries close to Britain. Nevertheless the early deliveries, though they were limited, had psychological and material importance. The groups felt their fellowship with the Allied world, they were enabled to make their sabotage more effective, and to prepare for the final struggle; and the Germans had to register both the fellowship and the increasing effectiveness, largely based upon British and later British-American infiltration. The results in Holland, Belgium and Luxembourg were many-sided, and relatively greater than the actual quantities could lead one to expect.

FRANCE. From the British point of view, and after 1941 also from the American point of view, France was the European country whose Resistance policy must arise the greatest interest, although the Balkans, especially Yugoslavia, were a focus point for Western Allied attention for a time in 1943–44. France was by far the largest of the occupied countries; up to the collapse in June 1940 she had been a cornerstone in the Allies' strategic planning; and owing particularly to the pressure of American ideas on a common Western Allied strategy, she again became a cornerstone for this strategy, even after the collapse. If the Western Allies were to invade the Continent and liberate Europe, the most obvious route was through France, regardless of all visions of supporting such an invasion with more or less secondary attacks via the Mediterranean coastal areas. If this fact was not fully recognized before, there could be no doubt on the question after the Teheran Conference in November 1943, where a promise given by the Western Allies of an invasion in North France, and a supporting invasion in South France, was a central point in the military conclusions reached by Churchill, Roosevelt and Stalin.[119]

Up to 1940, France had been a great military power, and even after the defeat in June 1940, France possessed important military trump cards, which must engage the most intense attention both of the Axis Powers and of the Western Allies, with reference to developments in the country. These trump cards included the French Armistice Army of 100,000 men, garrisoned in the unoccupied zone of France;[120] the large French forces in the French Empire, particularly in Syria and French North-West Africa; and particularly the powerful French Fleet. A very small part of this was stationed in British harbours at the time of the armistice, and the personnel either gave up their arms or could choose to carry on the struggle on the side of the British; quite a large squadron passively allowed itself to be demobilized in the port of Alexandria; a considerable French naval force was put out of action in a British attack on Mers el Kebir at the beginning of July 1940; and other naval units in more or less fighting trim stranded in West French or West African harbours. The main French Fleet however, based on Toulon, continued to exist, and with it, anxiety or hope as to what could be the possible future of this fleet. The anxiety was the Allies', the hope the Axis Powers'. Before the signature of the Armistice, it is true that the French Admiral and Naval Minister, François Darlan, had guaranteed to the British Government that this fleet would in no circumstances fall into the hands of the Axis Powers, which would have radically altered the naval balance in the Mediterranean. But what guarantee was there that Darlan could or would stand by this guarantee, particularly when in February 1941 Darlan was appointed President of the Council in the French Government, and during his period of office allowed himself so far in active co-operation with the German Government that France came perilously near to participation in the war on the side of the Axis. In Syria[121] it came to direct fighting – without any declaration of war – between French and British forces, when Syrian bases were put at the disposal of the German Air Force by Darlan.

But if, on these grounds alone, France was one of the occupied countries whose political Resistance development must arise the greatest and most intense attention among the Western Powers, the country's political situation was so complicated and intricate that the question of British-American co-operation with the French Resistance Movement was more than delicate. In the first place, France was not at war with the Axis Powers. The war had ended with the Armistice, but without peace being established, and without the country avoiding occupation for that reason. Three-fifths of the country and the majority of the population – about 28 millions – were subjected to German occupation, in the southeastern frontier areas to Italian occupation, and in the unoccupied zone to the rule of the so-called Vichy Government under the leadership of Marshal Pétain – a government which, after changes in the Constitution in the nature of a *coup d'état* at the beginning of July 1940, had formally received far-reaching powers to govern the zone, but was in reality at the mercy of the Occupying Powers. In their occupation of the greater part of French territory, in their internment of millions of French prisoners of war, and in the economic and administrative clauses of the Armistice, the Occupying Powers had an iron grip on this Vichy Government, formally led by an old man – in 1940 Pétain was 84, and as the war progressed showed visible signs of senility – but in reality directed by shifting Presidents of Council, Pierre Laval, Pierre Flandin, François Darlan and again from 1942, Laval. From the Allies' point of view, nothing could be more unstable than this Vichy Government, which had to balance between the warring parties, but which, particularly during Darlan's and Laval's periods of government, showed a clear tendency towards increasing collaboration with the Axis Powers, partly under the pressure of their thumbscrews, partly – and this seems true of both Pétain and Laval – because of a genuine desire to collaborate in order to obtain advantages for France in a final German victory. This latter motive is clearly established in Robert Paxton's work, "Vichy France".

Formally, the Pétain Government maintained the fiction of the country's neutrality, and quite a number of states, first among them the U.S.A., supported this fiction with ambassadors in Vichy.[122] In fact, however, the government swayed back and forth under many different influences, ranging from the supporters of a far-reaching collaboration with the Axis Powers, even to the point of direct participation in the War in the Axis camp, to the French patriots who, from every imaginable variety of motives, could see a future rôle for France as once more participating in the War on the side of the Allies. Between these two poles, there were many opportunists who saw the regime as a means of keeping France free, for the time being, of the worst of the evils of war and occupation.

France was not at war. France was not an Ally. France and Denmark were alone among the occupied countries in having no exile government which could continue the war from allied territory, and encourage resistance in the mother country. And yet France was in a sense an extremely active, and later an extremely powerful, Ally. This alliance rested upon a stubborn claim. During the hectic days when the French Armistice was concluded, the French General Charles de Gaulle, Deputy Minister of Defence in the retiring Reynaud Government, escaped to London. On 18 June, on the B.B.C. he made an ardent appeal to the French people to continue the struggle.[123] De Gaulle's military claim was that the War had not ended for France with the defeat on the Continent. The Empire survived, and could continue the struggle. The Fleet survived, and could continue the struggle. Frenchmen could try to get to Great Britain, and continue the struggle. But to these military claims there was soon added a political claim: that the Third French Republic had not ceased to exist, with the formation of the Pétain regime and the changes in the Constitution, but that this republic, and its possibilities for and duties of continuing the struggle on the side of the Allies, survived in and with the person of de Gaulle, and in the rallying under his leadership of all Frenchmen who, abroad or at home, would continue the struggle. With this aim in view he created a French National Committee in London, and achieved British recognition of this committee as the representative of the France which still fought, and of himself as Chief of the Free French Forces. De Gaulle's aims were both military and political. On 18 June his aim was still in high degree military: the War had not ended for France, and Frenchmen still had the right and duty to continue the struggle. But it would soon be evident that de Gaulle's aim went further – to a political demand to represent France. This appeared clearly in a manifesto which de Gaulle broadcast from Brazzaville on 27 October 1940. Here he challenged the Vichy Government's legitimate right to represent France, and he assumed that right himself:[124] "There no longer exists any real French Government. The organ situated in Vichy and which pretends to bear that name is contrary to the Constitution and has submitted to the enemy. In its state of slavery this organ cannot be and is not anything but an instrument, which is being exploited by the enemies of France against the nation's honour and interests. Therefore a new government must assume the leadership of the French contribution in the War. Events force this holy duty upon me. I shall not fail it. I will exercise my authority in the name of France".

Regardless of the fact that only a handful of Frenchmen, and out of the French Empire only French Equatorial Africa rallied to de Gaulle, with his action the opposing pole to the Vichy Government was created, and Vichy's reply to the challenge was dismissal, recall and – when this was not obeyed – sentence of death in absentia for high treason. Violent polarisation in French political life was the inevitable result.

The opposing poles became on the one side de Gaulle and the few who heard his appeal at all and acted on it from the start, and on the other side a number of minority groups in France, who worked very actively for authoritarian forms of government and France's whole-hearted participation in the War on the side of the Axis Powers. These minority groups were led by politicians such as Joseph Darnand, Marcel Déat and Jacques Doriot, who all, in spite of mutual rivalries, agitated for the introduction of Nazi forms of government; for anti-semitic measures; for France's participation in the War; for a "New Order" in Europe under the leadership of Germany; and later for French participation in the War against the Soviet Union. They all acquired considerable influence and they all became willing tools for the Occupying Powers' policy of suppression of the French Resistance Movement, Gaullist as well as non-Gaullist. With Darnand's creation of the "Service d'Ordre Légionnaire", from which sprang the French terror organisation "La Milice", which became notorious for its crimes against Frenchmen,[125] effective instruments were formed for combatting all French resistance, and a situation was brought into being in France approaching civil war. Between these two extremes stretched a spectrum of every shade of opinion, standpoint and action, themselves containing every imaginable nuance.[126] Here there is only room for some simple generalisations.

One of these generalisations is that at the beginning of the Occupation, Pétain and his Vichy regime enjoyed tremendous popularity, greatest in unoccupied France, where the government was a concrete and comparatively reliable screen, least in occupied France, where the French had the occupiers at close quarters. For a majority of Frenchmen, ever since Verdun, Pétain had stood as the saviour of France, who would know better than anyone else how to rescue France from the catastrophe. This popularity, which approached hysteria, declined drastically in the course of the War, with Great Britain's obstinate resistance, the Soviet Union's and the United States' entry into the War, the first Allied victories, and in 1942 the total occupation of the whole of France. It declined also as the powerlessness of the Pétain regime against the Occupying Power became apparent, as living standards deteriorated, as the regime showed its inability to check the German coercive measures in all their forms,[127] and as the Vichy Government engaged in the policy of collaboration with the Axis Powers, particularly under the leadership of Darlan and Laval. The growth of de Gaulle's influence was the diametrical opposite to this. In 1940 he was a comparatively unknown General, without any high-ranking position in the French military hierarchy,[128] whose stubborn stand for resistance was only known and appreciated by a relatively small minority of the French population, but whose popularity showed tropical growth when he had the opportunity and strength gradually to raise up a free fighting France, which step by step won greater and greater prestige in the Allied world, while his Free French Forces increased continually in numbers and in military importance. Under the influence of these factors, the France which had been paralysed and temporarily apathetic in 1940[129] changed to a predominantly Resistance-minded France. There were other factors also behind this development. A decisive factor was the Axis Powers' aggression against the Soviet Union in 1941. With this aggression, the French Communists were drawn into the ranks of the French Resistance from one day to the next, and here they were to play a dominating rôle. Other factors were the German reign of terror, economic exploitation, annexation of Alsace-Lorraine, retention of French prisoners of war, conscription of forced labour, incessant police terror and the traditional hostility to Germany, rooted in a long series of Franco-German wars, On this background, and encouraged by the appeals on the B.B.C. – appeals on the part both of the British and the Free French – resistance increased in France month by month, and the defeat's first bitterness against Great Britain, who was supposed to have failed the French, with insufficient military support in 1940, was changed to a feeling of natural alliance with this country, and with the Allies in general. The France of the defeat changed her mentality and at home as abroad re-entered the War with French vitality.

It is characteristic of the early French Resistance that it had two enemies. On the one hand there was the Vichy regime and its collaboration with the Axis Powers, its constitutional – or anti-constitutional – dissolution of the Third French Republic, and the long series of humiliating concessions to the demands of the Occupying Powers, and in connexion with them the bitter fight with the French persons and organs which were in the pay of the enemy. On the other hand there was the enemy – the Occupying Powers, first of all the German Occupying Power. In this state of things there is a clear parallel to the Danish situation, where the early Resistance Movement's primary aim was a political show-down with any policy of negotiation or co-operation. Also in the French Resistance Movement's first phase, a principal aim was a reckoning with the policy of the Vichy regime. As the months passed, however, and the impotence of the Vichy Government became more apparent, and as it became more apparent that its days were numbered, the principal task gradually became the direct fight against the Occupying Power and the French collaborating organs, and the French Resistance took on a more and more militant character. While the Free French Forces were being built up on the front abroad, home forces were being hastily formed – intelligence groups, newspaper groups, sabotage groups, a large French underground army, Maquis units and the whole spectrum of Resistance groups with differentiated tasks, which became well known to the Occupying Powers everywhere in Europe.

This was – in brief simplification – the background for the French-British-American co-operation which would be established of the Resistance Movement in France. It was the background for the work which SOE and later SOE/SO had to take up, partly in co-operation with de Gaulle, partly independently of him.

It is obvious that the SOE had to create a French Section. This took place immediately after the SOE was set up in July 1940, and the section was named F Section, or after urgent representations from the Foreign Office also the name "Independent Section" – that is to say, independent of the de Gaulle movement.[130] Practically all the staff and a great many of the instructors who were sent to France by this section during the war were British subjects, almost all of them bi-lingual, either because they had lived in France for many years, or because one of their parents was French. The section also used a great many French subjects, however, who volunteered for work in the section – often because these Frenchmen or Frenchwomen did not feel at home in the de Gaulle circles[131] – quite apart from the thousands of French people in France itself, who came to work under the leadership of the instructors of the section. The leaders of the section changed during its first months, but from the autumn 1941, Major Maurice Buckmaster, previously a director of the Ford factories in Paris, was appointed chief, and held the post until 1944.

Buckmaster knew France well from his work in Paris, and had a great
many contacts in the country. Buckmaster joined the work after an inter-
nal disagreement,[132] caused by a demand from Hugh Dalton that the
SOE section should make an approach to the leader of the great Trades
Union, CGT, L. Jouhaux. This demand had been the expression of
Dalton's irritation at noticing that the leaders up to then had been predo-
minantly conservative, and lacked reasonable connexions with the
French working classes.

This SOE section, like all the others, worked under the control of the
British Chiefs of Staff, even though the political leadership of the organisation was given to the Ministry of Economic Warfare; and like all the
others it depended upon co-operation both with the Army Command and
with the Chiefs of the Navy and Air Force. The section made a slow
start, as – again like all the others – it had to begin from rock bottom. One
of de Gaulle's nearest assistants, the leader of the Free French "Bureau
Central de Renseignements et d'Action", Colonel L. Dewavrin, who
worked as chief of this office under the cover name, Passy, writes on the
British unpreparedness:[133] "The British had left France without leaving
the least organisation which could inform them on the German preparations" and he adds that whilst the Poles and Czechoslovaks had left some
secret agents behind them, with radio sets, both the British and the de
Gaulle organisation first had to prepare the preliminary work: "As far as
we were concerned, we had nothing but our great good will". A few
attempts by the F Section to send instructors to France as early as 1940
stranded,[134] and it was not until May 1941 that the section succeeded in
getting an instructor dropped with the necessary radio equipment, and a
few days later a second instructor followed, Pierre de Vomécourt, who
was to start the section's work of organisation in French Resistance
circles, or else to arrange for this to be done. Vomécourt was the
forerunner for scores of instructors with similar missions.

If it is obvious that SOE had to create a French Section, it was no less
obvious that de Gaulle, like other exile politicians, wished to have a hand
in Resistance political developments in the occupied mother country, so
that co-operation between the organisations at home and Great Britain
and the United States would not be channeled mainly – and preferably
not at all – through SOE/SO. De Gaulle could certainly not claim the
formal rights or the consideration which an exile government enjoyed,
and both he himself and the Free French movement had especially great
difficulty in gaining American recognition of any monopoly whatever of
representation of France. The U.S.A. maintained normal diplomatic re-

lations with Vichy up to the end of 1942, and looked on de Gaulle as a man of great personal ambition, who could by no means claim immediate recognition as representing France. Nor could the Americans accept de Gaulle's view that he in his own person and with his movement represented the Third Republic, or that his Free French movement represented any continuity in the French conduct of the War, regardless of the Armistice. Unlike the British,[135] the Americans had never undertaken any kind of obligation towards de Gaulle, and for a long time they kept him at a distance.[136] A purely personal incompatibility between Roosevelt and the French General lasted throughout the War. In the beginning, the Foreign Office, too, was somewhat sceptical at the idea of binding Great Britain too closely to de Gaulle, whose future importance was far from obvious in 1940 and 1941, when many Frenchmen with definite anti-German views and who were quite prepared to resist, were just as hostile in their attitude to the rebel de Gaulle as to the defeatist Pétain. One result of this was that the F Section had orders not to work in the unoccupied zone of France, and instructions to work with great caution in the occupied zone.

Even though de Gaulle's Free French movement did not have any status as an Allied exile government, however, France was still such an important operational area for the Western Allies – also before the invasion in 1944 – and de Gaulle's growing authority was soon so apparent,[137] that he steadily won his way to ever-increasing influence in the Allied camp. This was true both of his political position and of the importance which his French Free Forces gradually acquired, and it was also true of the co-operation between the French Resistance organisations and support organisations in London and from 1943 in Algiers. As we have seen, it was natural that SOE created a British-led section through which the British authorities maintained close contacts, quite independently of de Gaulle, with French Resistance organisations and individuals. From his point of view, de Gaulle must regard the existence of this section with displeasure and irritation, in so far as British-French co-operation according to his political philosophy should be channeled through his organisation, and preferably through his organisation alone.

Frenchmen abroad as at home were not to be reduced to agents for Great Britain's and later the United States' interests, but should be regarded solely as comrades in arms in the continued struggle of free France under his leadership. It was another matter that this struggle took place in alliance with Great Britain and the other Allied nations. But added to this was the fact that it soon became clear, through reports from

France, that de Gaulle's popularity was increasing so steadily that effective SOE work in France was unthinkable without co-operation being established with the de Gaulle movement. In consequence of this, the question of the creation of another French SOE Section – called RF Section – was raised as early as the autumn 1940, and it became a reality during the spring 1941, from May 1941 with its own offices. This RF Section received the task of working closely with de Gaulle's Free French authorities. Its first leader was a younger British Captain, Eric Piquet-Wicks.[138] From the start de Gaulle had aimed primarily at raising a Free French Army abroad which could maintain French prestige and ensure French influence, including political influence, in the Allied coalition; but parallel with this he also aimed at gaining influence over and control of the Resistance Movement at home, and he entrusted the leadership in this work to the French Colonel L. Dewavrin. The latter received the task of preparing and carrying out all kinds of underground activities in occupied France, and particularly of setting up and organising a French underground army. The final target was an organised Resistance Movement under Gaullist joint leadership, and there were constant warnings against the anarchistic conditions which might result from activities of rival groups, perhaps in conflict with each other and without any form of firm joint leadership.

Dewavrin had served with the Norwegian troops fighting in Norway in the spring 1940. His description of his first meeting with de Gaulle and his appointment deserves to be repeated here.[139] After the short presentation, with military dignity, the swift questions shot out:

"Are you active or in reserve?
Active, mon Général.
Diploma?
No.
Origin?
Polytechnical School.
What did you do before the mobilisation?
Instructor in fortifications at the Military Academy of St. Cyr.
Have you any other training? Do you speak English?
I am a qualified lawyer and speak fluent English, mon Général.
Where were you in the War?
With the expeditionary corps in Norway.
So you know Tissier.[140] Are you older than him?
No, mon Général.

Good. You are Chief of the Second and Third Bureaus of my General Staff. Good-bye. We shall meet again."

Thus Dewavrin, He threw himself into the work with what de Gaulle describes[141] as "a kind of cold passion for his work", and after much re-organisation – of which there were many examples – the work was centralized in 1941, when the Bureau Central de Renseignements et d'Action (BCRA) was created. Close co-operation was built up between this organisation and the RF Section. The BRCA was the directing staff, the RF Section the operative instrument.

Two organs came into being, therefore, working parallel in support of the French Resistance. The work was not only parallel, it was actually uniform, since for both sections it was a question of stimulating activity in the Field by sending over instructors, money, materiel and directives, but it may be added that Gaullist-led work was always dependent upon the British, and later British-American support which could be obtained. No matter how determined BRCA was – and behind it de Gaulle – in demanding French independence of action, as regards material resources – first of all deliveries from the Allied depots and the allocation of aircraft capacity or naval support – BRCA depended upon the co-operation of the RF Section and with it the co-operation of SOE. Friction between the two parallel organs was inevitable, both at top level and out in the practical work in the Field, but in the long-term perspective it was never destructive. If the work in the two sections was parallel and uniform, there was nevertheless an essential difference in their views and their approach to problems. For the F Section the work was primarily military, with immediate purely military aims in view, whether it was a question of intelligence, sabotage, escape organisation or other underground activities. The section sought as far as possible to co-operate with the "réseaux" or "circuits" – small decentralised groups which undertook this or that quite concrete task within one of these fields of activity, on orders from London. The words "réseau" and "circuit" were the illegal French terms[142] for closed circles of persons who undertook, and in theory confined themselves to a clearly defined, limited task. The expressions were current in London, but became the accepted terms in illegal circles, also outside France. Usually a "réseau" or "circuit" was built up around an instructor who had been sent to the Field with a specific mission, and more or less restricted to its fulfilment, although from December 1941 it became the practice, on General Gubbins' decision,[143] that the teams sent over should consist of an organiser, a radio telegraphist at his disposal, and an assistant to look after the practical side of the team's work, procure materiel, arrange the actual operations, etc. It was characteristic of the work of the section that several hundred instructor teams of this kind were sent over to carry out such missions.

The RF Section carried out similar work to this, but under the leadership of BRCA, the section's instructors also had the no less important and definitely political mission to seek to form a coalition of the countless groups of the French Resistance Movement, so that French Resistance could be represented both at home and abroad with the political weight at which de Gaulle aimed. Immediate military action was also the task of the RF Section, therefore, but side by side with this there was the desire for the long-term organisation of a French underground army in harmony with and under a joint command,[144] by which de Gaulle meant a united movement under his own leadership. Here there was a clear difference in the questions both of aims and means: on the one hand, the immediate action and the decentralised and obstinately water-tight form of action and operation, on the other hand the long-term planning and creation of a centralised Resistance organisation under a joint command. The first of these was primarily a British wish and British tactics. The second was the aim of de Gaulle's movement. The F Section was afraid of centralisation and the inevitable round-ups which it brought with it, the RF Section had the duty of cultivating the idea of the centralised structure of all Resistance within one great superstructure. The inevitable overlapping and friction between the two sections' work was the price which had to be paid.

In this process, the ex-Prefect of Chartres, Jean Moulin was to play a decisive rôle.[145] From the start of the Occupation, as Prefect of Chartres, he had opposed the German authorities, had been arrested and had attempted suicide, but survived, after which he was dismissed from his position by the Vichy Government. After his dismissal he had taken on a number of false identities and had worked with determination to get to know as many as possible of the mass of Resistance groups which were growing up. He had formed the opinion that above all else it was essential to gather the countless men of good will into a joint French organisation – a concept which agreed precisely with the ideas of the BRCA and the inner circle around de Gaulle. He had also formed the opinion that such a joint French leadership must subordinate itself to de Gaulle's authority, and in the autumn 1941 he succeeded, with the help of an American Consulate, in getting to Lisbon and from there to London, where he met de Gaulle.[146] There he inspired trust in de Gaulle, and at the beginning of 1942 after a short parachute training he was dropped in South France as a kind of general representative for de Gaulle, with the mission as far as possible to merge the many Resistance organisations, with their very different views and their very different spheres of activity, into a joint organisation which recognised de Gaulle's leadership, so that the home front became united with the front abroad, or at least approached this union. The size of the task was gigantic, but it succeeded. His first success was in building up a co-operation between three great organisations: "Combat", "Libération" and "Franc-Tireur", led by Henri Frenay, Astier de la Vigerie and Jean-Pierre Lévy. Moulin then threw himself into the work of organising a French home army under General Delestraint who, after an illegal journey to London and a meeting with de Gaulle, was given command of this army.[147] Up to then, the work had been concentrated in unoccupied France, but after November 1942 it was extended to North France, where in May 1943 a home French "Conseil National de la Résistance" was successfully set up with Moulin as the first Chairman of the Council.[148] With this, the desired unity was well under weigh, but shortly afterwards Moulin was arrested, and died after intense torture, while he was being transported to Germany. The French National Council survived under the leadership of Georges Bidault, and de Gaulle's authority was considerably enhanced. It was thanks especially to Moulin, but also to the work of the BRCA, that the Resistance political development in France proceeded from chaos to order; and thanks to this development, de Gaulle could increasingly claim, both as to the front abroad and the home front, to speak on behalf of France. This belongs to the "official", well known history of the War, however, and will not be amplified here.

One of the main tasks, both for the F Section and for the RF Section, was to bring help in the form of instructors, money, telegraphists, explosives, weapons and other material to France. This was done by various routes and various means.[149] The least important deliveries were those brought over by sea, although both personnel and materiel was shipped both from South-west England to Brittany, and later from Algeria to the French Riviera. This took place in fishing boats, small ships, fast naval vessels, and occasionally submarines. However, deliveries by air were more important – both dropping operations and landings with Lysander aircraft on improvised landing strips. As mentioned earlier, the latter method allowed both for flying in and flying out. The dropping operations were predominant in the transport system, however. In all about

1350 instructors were dropped by the two SOE sections, to which should be added the important but unknown number who were either flown in, smuggled in by sea, or infiltrated by some other route – usually through Portugal and Spain. The instructors had very many and various missions. A great many of them were telegraphists, who formed the backbone of the organisation, others had organisational tasks either in the political or military sphere, others again had specific orders as to sabotage missions at specific places, and lastly there were those who had intelligence or propaganda missions. A number were liaison officers, attached to Maquis groups or to other branches of the Home Army, and many had the task of helping to establish or maintain the many escape routes which ran through France, and which made illegal exit from or entry into the country possible both for French members of the Resistance and for Allied pilots who had been shot down. Many of the instructors, when their missions were accomplished, returned to base in Great Britain, and many did the trip between London and France more than once. Stated as an overall generalisation, this can sound simple and straightforward, but it should be added that every mission had its drama and often its tragedies. Several hundred participants in the work were killed in action, or executed, or died in German concentration camps.

After the invasion in 1944, in addition to the instructor teams mentioned, "Jedbourgh" teams, as they were called, were sent over. These three-man teams were formed for action in all the countries into which the Allies advanced, and were normally dropped near the front line, as it was the task of the groups to co-ordinate the activities of the underground armies with the Allied advance. The groups usually consisted of a Britisher, an American and a volunteer from the country in question, and one of these was always a trained telegraphist. These Jedburgh teams were to act as small general staffs in the hinterland in the Allies' immediate line of advance. In the months of June and July 1944, a total of 93 Jedburgh teams came to France, a number of them to Brittany,[150] where the French Resistance groups – both Maquis groups and waiting groups – were particularly numerous, and where Resistance operations behind the enemy lines were particularly valuable in connexion with the American break-through from their Normandy bridge-heads; but a number of these teams also came down in the French Alpine areas, just before the landings in August in South France.

We have looked at the question of personnel, but material was another matter. SOE also began its activities in this area in 1941, although to a very limited extent, with 22 flights and a total of 1½ tons of material dropped, most of it radio material and sabotage material. After that, the graph of materiel dropped and flown in rose from one quarter to the next, although for the quarter October-December 1943 there was a marked reduction in deliveries, so that the general increase was halted for a short time. There were several reasons for this. One was the increased weight which the Allies attributed to the deliveries to Yugoslavia, where widespread fighting, which could support the Allies' operations in the Mediterranean, was in full progress. Another reason was the uncertainty as to SOE's work, to which the experiences in Holland had given rise at this period. Lastly there was the fact that SOE's and OSS's operations, during the preparations for the invasion in France, were subordinate to direct control by the Allied Supreme Command, and that the aircraft available to the organisation was put under the central British and American Bomber Command and the Allied Air Forces in the Mediterranean theatre. With the exception of this temporary check, the pace of the deliveries rose constantly. In 1942, 93 flights were carried out, with deliveries amounting to 23 tons of material in all for the growing sabotage; in 1943, 625 flights brought 586 tons across the channel, the figures for the quarters being 20 – 148 – 277 – 133. After the decline in the last quarter of 1943, the curve rose sharply. Immediately before the invasion, France received greatly increased strategic importance, and the British-American deliveries to the French Resistance organisations received correspondingly higher priority. In the six months, January-June 1944, 2728 flights were carried out, the deliveries totalling 3,627 tons; and during the invasion battles and the battles for the liberation of France the figure rose further to 4,030 flights, with deliveries totalling 6,248 tons. In these figures are included the quite extensive flights from North-west Africa; and the figures also include deliveries from both the F Section and the RF Section, which were more or less equally shared, with a tendency for the larger share to be that of the RF Section. Trial flights from North-west Africa had already started in the spring 1943, but they gained momentum in the spring 1944, and during the invasion battles. The total figure in tons for France reaches approximately 10,500, but it is noticeable that about 60% of this was delivered after the invasion had begun; and the figures are stamped by the new technique employed by the American Air Force during the invasion battless, of mass droppings in daylight of material for the Resistance groups fighting in the enemy hinterland. Massive dropping operations of this type took place on 25 June, 14 July, 1 August and 9 September, with 2,077, 3,780, 2,281 and 810 containers respectively.

Under the pressure of the needs of the situation, the composition of the deliveries also changed character. Up to the date of the invasions in the North and South – 6 June and 15 August 1944 – both weapons and sabotage material had been dropped, including radio and direction-finding equipment. After the invasion the deliveries consisted solely of weapons and ammunition, for which there was a crying need particularly when, in the wake of the conscription of French manpower to forced labour in Germany, a mass flight took place of tens of thousands of Frenchmen to the Maquis – actual guerilla formations which were set up in geographically suitable regions of France, such as the Alps in the South and South-east, in the central highlands and in Brittany, the Vosges and whereever the nature of the country and the sparcity of the population made the formation of Maquis physically possible.[151] The number of Maquisards, armed partly from secret depots, partly through the seizure of weapons and partly by the Allies, is reckoned by the British as 100,000, and by the French as 200,000 men.[152] Any figure must obviously be subject to considerable uncertainty, particularly as the Maquis forces swelled enormously after the invasion and immediately before and during the liberation battles. Further, there was a noticeable draught in the Maquis ranks. People could join the Maquis for a period and then find hiding places elsewhere, with their relations, friends, or by working under false names in comparatively quiet districts. But during and after the invasion battles, the Maquis succeeded in cleaning up and taking over large areas, especially in central and southern France and in Brittany. The areas in question were particularly the Alpine regions in the South and South-west, the great areas lying west of the Rhône and south of the Loire. The Allied armies did not need to enter this region. In this square, liberation was carried out entirely by the Maquis units – so states the French author Robert Aron.[153] These large Maquis forces varied a great deal in character and organisation, some of them loosely attached and varying in numbers, others welded into closely knit units with military discipline, many of these led by young officers,[154] others with a more political slant, often under Communist leadership.

All in all, however, these forces were to a lesser extent under the military and political control of either de Gaulle's Free French Movement or the Allied Supreme Command than were the systematically organised Resistance organisations. The French Maquis forces' often very independent and uncontrolled fighting, and their temporary take-over of local government and with it many bloody reckonings with documented or suspected collaborators, was an important element in the liberation struggle during the German collapse, and not without considerable tragedy. For example, a large Maquis rising in the mountain plateau of Vercors, south-west of Grenoble, which started too early in the expectation of conditions which could not be fulfilled, of mass landings of airborne troops, ended in bloody tragedy, while corresponding risings elsewhere, as already stated, were crowned with success.

For the Allies there was not only the problem of arming the Maquis forces, to the extent that this might prove possible. Beside the Maquis stood the French underground army, built up under the centralised leadership of the "Conseil National de la Résistance", formed by Jean Moulin – which in reality meant under the leadership of de Gaulle. On this council[155] there sat representatives of the various Resistance organisations, the political parties and the trades unions, with connexions to a network of liberation committees all over France, prepared to take over the national and local administration when liberation came, as quickly as this could be done. One of the main tasks of the Council was to co-ordinate and lead the various underground activities, including the formation of an underground army, a task which they sought to fulfil through a sub-committee – "COMAC" (Comité d'Action Militaire). In February 1944, this underground army had at last been welded together into a joint organisation, the "Forces Françaises de l'Intérieur"[156] (FFI), from May 1944 with General Koenig at its head, appointed Commander-in-Chief by General de Gaulle, although he was himself under the command of the Supreme Allied Command SHAEF. Equipment had to be supplied to these forces also – and especially – and one need not point out that the difficulties of the required mass deliveries of weapons and other equipment were enormous, and actually exceeded the possibilities of SOE's two sections, even with American help. To a great extent, the supplies from the Allies had to be supplemented with what could be procured locally in various ways – from hidden depots, capture and home manufacture – but neither the underground army nor the Maquis were ever adequately armed. Nevertheless, as already stated, the quantities which were delivered during the last months before the invasion and during the invasion battles were considerable. For the months February to May 1944, the figures in tons can be specified in some detail. In this period, the following quantities were sent over, with approximately equal amounts from each section:[157]

Sub-machine guns	approx. 76,000
Pistols	– 28,000

Rifles	–	17,000
Bren guns	–	3,500
Anti-tank weapons	–	900
Mortars	–	160

In addition to these, considerable quantities of ammunition were delivered. As stated, in June and July the deliveries increased considerably.

Even these comparatively large quantities could not nearly cover the requirements, however. The number of organised active members of the Resistance, and persons willing to join the Resistance, was everywhere greater than the quantity of weapons. Some figures calculated by the British illustrate this situation.[158] At the end of May, it was calculated that approximately 10,000 men were armed for serious fighting lasting several days, 40,000 were armed to a lesser degree. These 50,000 plus a further 60,000 organised Resistance members belonged to formations in more or less direct contact with the London organisations. A further 350,000 belonged to organisations without direct contact to London, and again another 350,000 had individual contacts with the London organisations. In addition to these, there were approximately half a million railway personnel and about 300,000 persons organised in trades unions and prepared to stop work, so that it was calculated in London that perhaps 3 million men would be in a position, in one way or another to help the Allied Armies.

The figures can only be approximate, and correspond as regards arms to the situation in May, before the great deliveries of June and July. But in regard to the disproportion between organised members of the Resistance and the arms at their disposal, the figures tend to correspond with the French figures for Brittany, where the organisation of resistance was well advanced, and Maquis forces were operating, and where there was great interest in a rising on the part of the Allies, and dropping operations were therefore massive. The comparative figures at the end of July 1944 were:[159] 31,500 combatants, of whom 13,750 were armed.

After the Americans penetrated into the peninsular, locking the German forces in Atlantic harbour towns on the west coast, the number of armed combatants rose to approximately 20,000, and in November 1944, two French Divisions were formed, mostly of men from the Resistance forces in Brittany.

Even though the deliveries of weapons lay far below what was wanted, therefore, these deliveries represented a major achievement from the Allied Air Forces, at a time when the air offensive over France was reaching its climax, and both materially and psychologically the deliveries were a stimulus to the French Resistance Movement, which supported the invasion not only in open fighting, but just as much in sabotage and especially by strikes, first of all in the transport sector. Here the unarmed supporter also had his chance.

The size of the Allied deliveries to France and also their rhythm seem to reflect the opinions held by the Allied as to the strategic rôle of the French Resistance forces. During the preparations for invasion in 1943, the Allied planning council, COSSAC (Chiefs of Staff to the Supreme Allied Commander) had already taken the definite standpoint[160] that during the coming invasion battles, the contribution to the actual attack of the French Resistance forces should be regarded as a supplement, rather than an indispensible part of the combined plan. This basic attitude was taken after a professional military assessment of the possibilities of these forces. Certainly, the French Resistance Movement, in all its forms and with its countless organisations, had grown stronger and stronger during the previous four years of occupation, but it was impossible to foresee with what strength it could go into action at a given moment, and what degree of confidence one could reasonably place in the assurances of the capacities of the Resistance in action. The Allied Staffs knew what could be set in motion from without, but could have no certain knowledge of what forces could be set in motion from within. Up to the invasion, France had not played the rôle of a guerilla country in the Soviet or Yugoslav sense. The geographical conditions for this were not present, in most of the country, and particularly not in the strategically important areas in the north. There were therefore no indisputable proofs of the capacities of these forces. On the other hand, the possibilities were there, and French Resistance forces – sabotage groups, the Maquis organisations and the underground army – could be sent into action with the expectation of important results, during the invasion battles, as long as the organisational machinery was in order, and great and small forces were ready to intervene where the situation had created the operational conditions for the optimum exploitation of the existing possibilities – strikes, sabotage and armed revolt. The moment arose in immediate connexion with the invasion, and particularly after the Allied breakthrough from the Normandy bridge-heads, and the invasion in South France. It was therefore in August 1944 that the French underground army received its greatest importance, during the battles, behind the crumbling German front, in the encircling operations around the remaining occupation pockets, especially in the harbour areas in West France, and lastly in cleaning up and guard duties during and after the Liberation. When the Western Powers forced the pace of the weapon deliveries just before and during the invasion battles, this reflected their view of the rôle of the French Resistance forces.

Political considerations also played a part. De Gaulle's stubborn efforts to achieve centralised leadership of all French Resistance, both abroad and at home were simultaneously an advantage and a complicating factor for the Western Powers. On the one hand they could not be interested in political dissolution in France, and must on the contrary wish for conditions of law and order as soon as possible after the liberation of the various districts; on the other hand, de Gaulle's demand for recognition as the sole representative for France was an unproved claim, and his Movement was so heterogenous in its composition, including as it did many different groups, organisations and parties, that only time and developments could show to what extent the Allies could count on a stable France under his leadership and authority. The Americans, particularly, reserved their position for a long time, and both before and during the invasion battles, both the British and the Americans insisted on their right to maintain their many contacts with independent French Resistance groups, and did not bind themselves exclusively to de Gaulle or to exclusive deliveries to the organisations under his control. Considerations of security had a very high priority here. On both sides of the Channel, in the late spring 1944, everyone realised that the invasion was imminent, but the time, place and method of the attack was kept a closely guarded secret, only known by a small inner circle of military and political leaders who had to be informed. De Gaulle did not belong to this inner circle. He was not orientated nor asked for the assistance he could give until the day before the invasion began – a situation which gave rise to a violent altercation between him and the Allied leaders.[161]

Developments would show that the French Resistance forces could and did make an essential contribution to the liberation of France, and that although in some places there was an approach to anarchistic conditions, de Gaulle's prestige was great enough for him to weld France together, and step by step to take over the administrative and political leadership of a liberated France. But it was only the developments themselves which were to demonstrate this. On the other hand, the value of the de Gaulle movement and its hold also on the French mother country were soon so evident that de Gaulle's influence in the Allied camp was noticeably altered in the course of a few weeks. During the invasion battles, he received his first invitation to visit U.S.A.

for confidential talks with President Roosevelt, and these resulted in Allied recognition that, as leader of the National French Liberation Committee created in Algeria in 1943, he was the *de facto* leader of liberated France, as the Liberation gradually proceeded. With this recognition, and with the recognition of the Liberation Committee as the *de facto* government, the country received both a new Chief of State and a Government which could gradually take over the political and administrative leadership of France.[162]

YUGOSLAVIA. SOE's and later SOE/OS's supply policy towards the various European Resistance countries was determined by a number of weighty factors: the resources available at the time in question, strategic considerations which allocated top priority now to one now to another area, and lastly to some extent political considerations, although these had in many places to give way to considerations of the fighting capacity which the various Resistance Movements could be found to possess. Under the pressure of the realities of the War, principles and long-term plans often had to yield, and it speaks for itself, and is actually typical for this situation that Churchill in March 1943 could instruct the Greek SOE Section in Cairo[163] that, as regards help to the Greek Resistance Movement, it should favour the groups which were prepared to support the King and his Government, but with the decisive addendum that this principle should be dropped in cases of "operative necessity". Principles and plans came into conflict with realities, particularly in the Mediterranean war theatre.

Up to the invasion in France in June 1944, the Allies' only open land fronts were those in the Mediterranean regions; from 1940 they included the British-Italian-German front in the Libyan Desert; from 1942 until May 1943 also the British-American front with the Axis forces in Tunisia; and then the front first on Sicily, from July 1943, and lastly in South Italy from September 1943. This purely geographically determined placing of the open fronts meant that the Mediterranean countries, Yugoslavia and Greece, lay high on the Allies' priority list up to the end of 1944, and had lain highest up to the end of 1943 – this in regard to SOE operations and therefore supplies.[164] In November 1943, the Balkans and North Italy had top priority, and France had only a third place, and it was not until the spring 1944 that supplies to France received first priority, the Balkans and North Italy still retaining a high priority. With the one exception that there were periodically exploratory discussions on an Allied landing in Norway – designated as Operation Jupiter – up to the spring 1944 North and West Europe lay outside the zone where the Western Powers had acute strategic interests. East Europe lay outside this zone, quite apart from the geographical and physical impossibility of bringing any large-scale deliveries to the East European countries.

Priority was one factor, but there were other factors, such as practical possibilities and political complications. As far as the practical possibilities were concerned, it must be repeated that up to 1943, the resources at SOE's disposal were at an absolute minimum, and they were not decisively increased until the American help arrived, and SOE – from 1943 – was merged with the American sister organisation into SOE/SO. The two organisations and their activities in the Balkans, particularly in Yugoslavia, drew the attention of the Allied Supreme Command, at the same pace as the battles in Italy received increased strategic importance. SOE had started its Balkan operations with two out-of-date Whitley aircraft,[165] and it was only in the summer 1943 that this situation was radically changed with the allocation of 32 bombers for deliveries to the partisan forces in the Mediterranean theatre, North Italy, Greece, and especially Yugoslavia. Even this proved insufficient, and before the year ended, SOE had to ask for the number to be increased to 56 – a request which was made just as SOE entered the crisis brought about by the "England game", and for that reason among others was not acceded to until the spring 1944. From then on, things improved. The situation was eased greatly when the supply base was moved from North Africa to Brindisi in South Italy, and in June 1944, a special "Balkan Air Force" was formed to take over the supply service to all partisan forces in the Mediterranean.[166]

From the practical point of view the year 1943 was thus a turning point, and just at this period – the autumn 1943 – Yugoslavia took the centre of the stage, as far as Allied attention was concerned. At the same time the political considerations as to whom the Allies should support – Tito and his Communist oriented partisan army, or Michailovíc and his Cetnik movement with its declared loyalty to the exile Yugoslav Government – was now at last and finally decided.[167] This took place simultaneously with an important increase in the strength of Tito's movement. At the Italian collapse in September 1943, Tito's Partisan Army seized large quantities of equipment from six Italian Divisions, as they capitulated, and two Italian Divisions joined the Partisan Army direct. It was thus at the time of the Allied landings at Salerno in September 1943, that Tito's army gained considerably in strength, and won control, at least temporarily, of a large part of the Yugoslav territory, parts of Croatia, Bosnia and Montenegro, as well as Istria and Dalmatia, including a number of the Dalmatian islands with many large and small harbours, one of these being the harbour town of Split.[168] The Tito army now seriously threatened the German concentration routes in Italy, and this occurred at a time when British Military Missions arrived at the final realisation as to which of the two conflicting Resistance organisations in Yugoslavia it was strategically advisable to support – a realisation which was unanimously in favour of the Tito forces. By the autumn 1943, these had reached a total of about 200,000 men in open warfare with the German Occupying Power, with control over approximately half the Yugoslav territory, and with widespread support among the population.

From now on, it would be strategic and not political considerations which would determine relations between Tito and the Western Powers. It should be emphasized that this new assessment was not an SOE decision, even though SOE and later SOE/SO was the instrument which from the start had to translate strategic and political decisions into operational action. The British SOE Missions gave their unvarnished assessments, which were then backed up on strategic grounds by the Allied Mediterranean Command,[169] then by the Allied Governments, first the British and then the American, and at the Teheran Conference in November 1943 by the three Great Powers jointly.

The political problem was greatest for Great Britain. The British Government was bound to consider the exile Yugoslav Government and the Yugoslav King Peter, who at a critical time for Great Britain, in the spring 1941, with a state coup had given the British Empire their support and their trust. The situation was identical to that of the Greek Government and the Greek King, and even after the revolutionary change-over in the autumn 1943, Great Britain could not simply drop both consideration and obligation, but had to attempt mediation. In the autumn 1943 Great Britain still maintained contact with Michailovíc with a last Military Mission,[170] but at this stage he was given an ultimatum demanding concrete actions against the Occupying Power, and the cessation of all attacks on the Tito movement. When these demands were not met by the end of 1943, all support was withdrawn from Michailovíc. The Yugoslav situation was thus clarified and immediate military consideration, and not long-term political expediency and strategic plans had proved to be the decisive factor behind the decisions taken. Attempts at mediation between republican and Communist-oriented Resistance leaders from

Greece, and representatives from the exile Greek Government, held in August 1943 in Cairo, achieved no results.[171] Here the political question was kept floating.

All this crossed the original aims of SOE in one sense, but they had contained the difficult contradiction that on the one hand, the European Resistance Movements were to be supported in their energetic actions against the Occupying Powers, while on the other hand they were to be held back from hasty actions which could lead to undesired reprisals and the round-up or total dissolution of these movements. SOE's desire and aim was the creation, everywhere, of an organised united front, and the formation of Resistance forces which – at the right moment and preferably under Allied Command – could be set in action in connexion with an Allied advance, or in the case of collapse in the Axis camp. These ideas as to SOE's role had their roots in the situation of 1940, and were applicable to some extent in North Europe and West Europe. In the Mediterranean theatre and particularly in Yugoslavia they were crushed by the realities. They were in sharp opposition to the Communist standpoint and tactics, demanding immediate partisan and other Resistance actions, and in Yugoslavia as we have seen, developments ran directly counter to the long-term view. For quite a long time, Michailovíc and his Serbian Cetnik movement could fit in with this concept of a carefully constructed and generally inactive Resistance organisation in a waiting position.[172] Tito and his Partisan Movement had quite a different view, both of the danger of reprisals, and the demand and duty to resist.

It was in high degree thanks to Winston Churchill's intervention that developments led to the British changing their signals, and wholeheartedly supporting the Tito movement, long before there could be any question of direct military operations by Western armies in Yugoslavia.[173] For Churchill as for the SOE representatives directly affected in Cairo and Yugoslavia, and also for the Allied Mediterranean Command, strategic interests were so paramount that political interests were inevitably swept aside. It should be mentioned that these decisions were taken in full recognition of the fact that by supporting the Tito organisation, the Allies were helping a Communist-led movement, in open, definite opposition to the exile Royal Government – a movement whose declared purpose was to convert Yugoslavia into a federal state on Soviet lines. Fitzroy MacLean, who was thoroughly acquainted with Communist thinking and tactics from his experience as Attaché in the British Embassy in Moscow, had made it quite clear to his Government from the start[174] that with Tito – with whom he had excellent personal relations, based upon mutual frankness and respect – there was no question of a guerilla leader in the Balkan tradition, but of a determined Communist leader, whose success would inevitably lead to wholesale upheaval in post-war Yugoslavia – an upheaval which would leave no room for the Foreign Office's hopes for the re-establishment of *status quo ante bellum* in this area. During the whole of SOE's lifetime, there was a contradiction between this organisation, which had been given the task of rousing or supporting revolt in occupied Europe and which therefore by its very nature would be revolution-minded, and the Foreign Office, which at least could hope that the Resistance upsurge in Europe would turn against the Occupying Powers without developing into a revolutionary movement against the familiar political patterns of the Continent. In the case of Yugoslavia this hope was an illusion, which collapsed as the Tito movement gradually gained a firmer grasp on developments in the country.

This, in rough outline, was the political background for the radical change in the supply service to Yugoslavia, which started in the autumn of 1943. Up to the summer, only minimum supplies had reached Michailovíc and Tito. In the two years from June 1941, when the national revolt broke out in Serbia, until June 1943, when the re-evaluation was taking place, a total of 23 tons of materiel was delivered to the Michailovíc forces, whilst only 6½ tons were dropped for the partisan forces.[175] The main reasons for this have been described, but it may be added that in the period in question developments in Yugoslavia were of only marginal interest in relation to the battles in the Mediterranean theatre of war. In 1942, Greece was more important, and the supply line Salonica – the Piraeus – Tobruk. From the summer 1943, however, a monthly delivery was aimed at of about 150 tons for the partisan forces, whose actions could now have direct influence on the Allied operations against Italy. Owing to the lack of effective contact with a partisan army which was just then constantly on the march, under the pressure of German offensives, this aim was far from being achieved, or even approximately achieved, from one day to the next, but in the period up to September 1943, the stream of supplies to the Tito army rose to about 145 tons.[176] After this, and particularly after the arrival of the MacLean mission, and the temporary liberation of the Dalmation coast, the stream of deliveries swelled to about 2050 tons delivered by sea and 125 tons dropped during the last quarter of the year. It became impossible, however, to deliver by sea during the autumn, when a German offensive led to the recapture of the Dalmatian coast, but later the partisans managed periodically to re-establish local control over the coast, and at the same time the Air Forces which took over the deliveries increased rapidly, after being placed under the operative control of General Alexander's Joint Allied Mediterranean Command. At this point it was decided to bring all support to underground activity in the whole Mediterranean theatre of war – North Italy, Yugoslavia and Greece – under joint leadership, so that the best possible co-ordination could be achieved in the whole of this great area in relation to joint strategic planning. SOE's task then became one of opening a breach after which developments reached such proportions that the over-all command gradually passed into the hands of the traditional military staffs. In June 1944, the Balkan Air Forces, referred to above, were set up with headquarters in Bari, with their own depots and with airfields at their disposal in Brindisi and Foggia, under the command of the British Air Vice-Marshal W. Elliot. This alteration, and the increase of the air force for use in Yugoslavia to 100 fighters and 300 bombers, meant not only increased dropping and landing operations in liberated Yugoslavian territory, but also the possibility of air support to the partisan forces' operations.[177] This air support was increased during 1944, and took on considerable proportions. In the quarter July-September 1944, approximately 9000 aircraft left the ground, some on bombing missions, some on dropping operations. During these flights, 8,700 tons of bombs were dropped, and supplies amounting to approximately 5,000 tons.

It became characteristic that the air operations and deliveries received ever-increasing importance during 1944, although the deliveries by sea still played a considerable part.[178] During the first quarter of 1944, no less than 6,400 tons were delivered by sea, whereas the air deliveries for that quarter were calculated as between 230 and 320 tons; but during the second quarter, the air deliveries increased to between 2,600 and 3,100 tons, whilst the sea deliveries were reduced to 5,600 tons. In the third quarter, the air deliveries became predominant. All in all, after the arrival of the MacLean mission, the deliveries reached proportions considerably above those in other parts of Europe. As the months passed, there was a clear tendency towards increasing air deliveries, and this tendency was intensified as the partisans captured more and more territory, and were able to provide landing strips, which not only opened up for increasing supplies by air, but also for flights to and from the partisan forces. Yugoslavs could thus be flown out for training as pilots, and for instruction at the Yugoslav training schools in South Italy for service in the special Armoured Brigades; and in addition approximately 12,000 wounded were flown out of Yugoslavia, and 35,000 refugees, mostly women and children, and old people.[179]   The situation now arose where Tito – in consultation with MacLean and hard pressed by continual German offensives, particularly one surprise German parachute attack on his headquarters in Drvar,[180] where he and several of his closest advisors narrowly escaped capture – was forced to move his headquarters to the Dalmatian islands of Vis. This was now turned into a permanent Yugoslav-Allied base, with harbour and aerodrome. Supplies could now be sent from here to the Yugoslav mainland, more than half of which was liberated by the partisans during the summer 1944; and also British air and naval forces could now make raids deep into the Dalmatian coastal areas. To a great extent, the regular operations on the Italian front were linked up with the continued, intensified partisan struggle in North Italy, Yugoslavia and Greece.

In the case of Yugoslavia, the deliveries for the year 1944 were calculated as follows:[181]

Sub-machine guns and rifles	approx.	100,000
Light and heavy machine guns	–	50,000
Mortars	–	1,380
Hand grenades	–	630,000
Uniforms	–	175,000
Boots	–	260,000
Radio sets	–	700

in addition, ammunition, food stuffs, medical supplies, special equipment and sabotage material were delivered.

The above supplies were only supplementary to the equipment of Tito's Partisan Armies, which came largely from home depots dating from the capitulation in 1941, from captures from the enemy which increased as the fighting developed, from home manufacture, and from the considerable equipment which the partisan armies seized at the collapse of the Italian Occupation Army in 1943.[182] The above supplies, taken together, made it possible to set up a hard-hitting Partisan force, which reached a total during 1944 of nearly 300,000 men, divided into 100 Brigades, which again formed Divisions and Corps. From 1943, British and American Liaison Officers were attached in increasing numbers to the Yugoslav Partisan units everywhere. These Liaison Officers had the tasks of arranging for deliveries of supplies; working as advisors to the local Yugoslav Commandants; and co-ordinating the Partisan Army's actions with Allied battle strategy. The operative command, however, both before and after the arrival of the Allied Missions, lay wholly and unconditionally in Tito's hands. Here in Yugoslavia there was no question of an underground army in a waiting position, in accordance with the original concept in SOE, but of a regular war in the enemy's hinterland, which was in high degree to the benefit of the Western Powers during their operations in the Mediterranean area; and this forced a contribution and a reconstruction upon the Western Powers which they had not foreseen. The leadership of the organisation of the supply service was in the hands of SOE/SO, but it was the Allied Joint Command in the Mediterranean that increasingly took control, when it was a question of the co-ordination of the Yugoslav struggle with the Allies' operations.

Parallel with this purely military co-operation between the Yugoslavs and the Allies, an important political development began, promoted partly by Churchill,[183] who now not only recognised the Tito movement as a valuable military ally, but also gradually accepted the movement as a political factor, which could not be passed over when the question arose as to post-war Yugoslavia. Churchill therefore worked strenuously for and also succeeded – partly through a personal meeting with Tito in Italy in August 1944 – in arranging for political negotiations between him and the exile Yugoslav Government, represented by a moderate Yugoslav politician, Doctor M. Subasić, who became leader of a reorganised exile Yugoslav Government in May 1944. This reorganised government broke completely with Michailovíc in August 1944, and dismissed him from the post of Defence Minister and Commander-in-Chief of the Army. The situation was that in November 1943, Tito had proclaimed the formation of a provisional government in the town Jajce, and at the same time had rejected any idea of the King and the exile Government returning after the War. The British – and the Allied – problem was whether to recognise this government, maintain recognition of the exile government, or attempt a compromise. It was the last course that Churchill aimed at. The problem was touched upon during the conference in Teheran, where Stalin rejected it as unimportant, and the question remained hanging in the air throughout the spring and summer 1944. In the meantime, the Western Powers arranged to send over a Soviet Military Mission to the partisan territory in Yugoslavia, and the Soviet Government thus also recognised Tito as the actual leader of the country's struggle for freedom and independence. Ever since the movement had started in 1941, Tito had maintained telegraphic contact with Moscow, but up to 1944 the Soviet Government did not have the physical possibility of bringing his movement the material help for which they were crying. In addition, the Soviet Government had long held to the political fact that it, like the Western Powers, had diplomatic relations with the exile Yugoslavian Government, and for that reason they continued to recommend co-operation with Michailovíc as the formal leader of the Yugoslav liberation struggle. Now this was changed, at the same time as the Soviet Armies advanced into South-east Europe and made Soviet-Yugoslav military co-operation possible, as well as extensive supplies to the partisan armies, still hungry for materiel as they were.

As the Liberation of Yugoslavia approached in 1944, a number of political possibilities for post-war Yugoslavia were theoretically open. Owing to the close military co-operation which had developed since 1943 between Tito and the Western Powers, the latter had considerable influence in the country, and what was more important, the Tito movement could point to the fact that liberation came not only as the result of the Allied victories in general and the Soviet victories in particular. The country, by its stubborn Resistance struggle, had contributed decisively to liberating itself, and stood, with the rights of victory, in a freer position than the other East European countries. It was the Soviet Armies which finally liberated Belgrade, but they did so in co-operation with a strong Yugoslav Partisan Army, and in accordance with a military agreement which Tito had made in the winter 1944–45, during a short visit to Moscow,[184] which guaranteed the withdrawal of the Soviet troops when victory was won and the country finally freed.

GREECE. There were various similarities between the situation and developments in Yugoslavia and Greece as regards Resistance policy, and the co-operation which came into being between the Resistance organisations and the Western Powers. Developments in both these Balkan states were of strategic interest to the Allied Powers. Both countries were represented in the Allied world by exile Royal Governments, which the Allies could not simply ignore. Formally, they recognised these governments' legitimate political rights, and therefore could not act without reference to them. Great Britain's political obligations were evident, but the U.S.A., according to the Stimson Doctrine of 1932, did not recognise territorial changes brought about by force, and therefore also had obligations towards the exile governments, and this was also the case for the Soviet Union, which had recognised both the Yugoslav and the Greek exile Governments. These were some of the similarities. There were others. In both countries a partisan struggle developed, and partisan forces liberated large areas and thus contributed to containing considerable occupying forces. Another common factor was the fact that in both countries internal conflicting Resistance organisations grew up, on the one hand organisations, groups or cliques which supported the exile Government in their activities, and thus collided head-on with other organisations which denied the exile Government's right to return immediately to its pre-war political position of power. There were also a number of geographical similarities between the two countries; their mountainous districts were impossible for the enemy to control effectively, and the Occupying Powers were forced to confine themselves in the main to controlling important traffic and strategic support points; their geographical position made it possible for the Allies gradually to be able to establish reasonably stable communication between the partisans and the Allied world; and it was possible to provide this communication, and material support, both through infiltration by sea, and by setting up an air lift, first in the form of dropping operations and later with improvised landing strips.

All this opened up possibilities for the Western Powers, in the first place for SOE, later for SOE/OS, and for the Allied Mediterranean Command and its operative instrument in Mediterranean territories, the Balkan Air Force. It also created some difficult dilemmas, however. Whom were the Allies to support, and to what an extent, and what would be the political consequences?

In the case of Greece, the situation arose where a large number of Resistance organisations or groups had formed, but out of the heterogenous mass two organisations stood out particularly on account of their size and effectiveness, and called for the special attention of the Western Powers.[185] One of these was the EDES movement, led by Colonel Napoleon Zervas, and with its field of operations in Epirus. This movement supported the exile Greek Government, although Zervas himself had republican sympathies. The other, larger organisation was the EAM, or "National Liberation Front". This movement was originally formed as a people's front with support from several parties, all of them republican, but it came more and more under the control of the Greek Communist Party, KKE. It was for this reason that Zervas, in spite of his republican sympathies, came into sharp opposition to the EAM movement – or perhaps the situation was rather the reverse, that the EAM movement again and again turned its weapons against the EDES movement, so that the Greek guerilla situation approached and periodically overstepped the threshold of civil war. The EAM movement, the military organisation of which was designated ELAS, was a stubborn opponent of the exile Royal Government, an attitude which was uncompromising, and which the movement shared with two other less important organisations, led by General Saraphis and Colonel Psaros – both of them organisations which broke down before the Liberation. In general, therefore, all important Resistance political groupings were republican in their political orientation, although the EDES movement was prepared to accept the exile government's return if its return, with British support, could prevent a Communist seizure of power, which in Zervas' eyes was the aim of EAM. This conflict between the EDES and EAM movements therefore became a dominating feature in Greece, and was in many ways similar to the confrontation between Michailovíc and Tito, although with the decisive difference that Zervas was a thoroughbred Resistance leader, for whom there was never any question of simply maintaining law and order in support of some post-war government, but of the immediate and uncompromising struggle against the Occupying Powers. SOE, therefore, had to navigate between two conflicts, the conflict between the two leading Resistance organisations, and the conflict between the Greek Resistance and the conflict between the Greek Resistance and the exile Greek Government.

The acute differences in the two countries originated in the fact that up to the War, both governments had maintained dictatorships, which had outlawed the Communist Party, and the Occupation itself had provided that party with elbow room for the political and military activity in their illegal forms which must suit a party which was already illegal. Here was the source of the irreconcilable hostility which became a dilemma for the Allies as soon as they tried to influence, support and profit from the possibilities which the Resistance effort offered in both countries. In both instances political and military considerations ran counter to each other, and here was a built-in situation of conflict between on the one hand the Foreign Office, which cultivated normal diplomatic contacts with the two exile governments, and on the other hand SOE and the Allied Army authorities in the Mediterranean area, who naturally wished the Resistance activity to be the strongest imaginable, regardless of which political group or organisation carried it out. It became the Military Missions' primary task to attempt to mediate between the parties,[186] but where this failed or only succeeded partially, the Military Missions took the part of the organisation or organisations which, from their situation, position of command, and knowledge of local conditions they considered made the greatest contribution to the struggle. In both these

Balkan countries, mediation was attempted as assistance was given, and in both countries military considerations were predominant as long as the struggle lasted. Here the similarities ended, however. In the case of Yugoslavia, the Allies reconciled themselves to the Tito movement's indisputable predominance, also in the political sphere, whereas Great Britain especially, with her great strategic interests in the Mediterranean theatre, was determined to support the return of the exile Greek Government, and if necessary counter the Communist threat to post-war Greece with military forces. In the Greek guerilla forces, the members of the Military Missions were known and respected, but their leaders were also aware of the difference between military interests and political considerations, which characterized the British attitude to Greece. The result, in 1944, was the Greek Civil War, in which the British, and later the Americans, intervened. But any description of this lies outside the framework of the present account.

As long as the occupation of Greece lasted, the predominant consideration was the military interest in maintaining the greatest possible resistance there. The Allies therefore supported both EDES and EAM/ELAS, although support was periodically withdrawn from the latter organisation, when it proved too politically intransigent, or even engaged in open fighting with Zervas' forces. From 1942 it was the task of the British SOE missions, and later the numerous British-American Liaison Officers with the Greek guerilla forces to put this thankless tight-rope act into practice.

The first personal contact between the Greek Resistance organisations and the Allies was established, as we have seen,[187] in the autumn 1942, with the Myers/Woodhouse mission. This remained in the country for the rest of the Occupation, led first by Myers, and after his evacuation to Cairo in 1943, by Woodhouse, and it came to play an important rôle both for Greek-British relations and for the development of the Greek Resistance. In the course of time, the mission was supplemented by a large number of British and American Liaison Officers, spread over the extensive Greek guerilla territory, from Crete in the south to Macedonia in the north, from the islands of the Aegean in the east to Epirus in the west. The primary task – at the start the only task – for these missions was of a military nature, to advise and support the guerilla forces with supplies, and particularly to fit their actions into the strategic plans of the Allies, but this military task inevitably brought a political task with it: to prevent mutual differences from developing into internal strife, to the detriment of the struggle against the Occupying Powers; if possible to create a united front; and lastly to work for understanding between the republican elements which were absolutely dominating in the Greek guerilla forces, and the exile Royalist Government, which in the eyes of a majority in the Greek population was intolerably compromised by the pre-war Metaxas dictatorship, and by the fact that the puppet government set up by the Germans in Athens was partly recruited from circles close to the exile Government and the king.[188] The Military Mission did not succeed in this political task,[189] but as mediator between the conflicting parties it played an important rôle in at least partially reducing the differences, and it succeeded in some degree in bringing the parties on to speaking terms with each other. This – to turn attention away from the bitter internal conflict to a joint effort against the Occupying Powers – was a necessary condition for the primary military task at least periodically to succeed.

The Military Mission met the conflict, especially as between EDES and EAM/ELAS, immediately after its arrival, but during the first impor-tant actions against the Salonica – Athens railway,[190] it succeeded in persuading the groups from the two factions to work together. Then, however, the internal strife burst into flames, and the mission had to attempt mediation. After several months of negotiations, in July 1943, this led to a sort of armistice agreement, which at that important stage temporarily halted the internal arguments and fighting. Myers achieved general support for a national guerilla agreement, which fixed the bound-aries for the operational areas of the individual organisations, established a joint headquarters for the groups under the leadership of the British Military Mission, and thereby pointed in the direction of a united front.[191]

In August, Myers was called back to Cairo, and seized the opportunity to take with him six representatives of the Greek Resistance organisa-tions, of whom four were EAM leaders, and one a representative for EDES, to a conference in Cairo between them and the exile Government as well as the British Authorities. The discussions, which were princi-pally political in character, proved fruitless.[192] The ELAS representa-tives made the demand that the exile Government should expand by co-opting representatives of the Resistance organisations, and that the King should give an undertaking not to return to Greece until a plebiscite on the future of the monarchy had been held. Strongly supported by Churchill, and by the Foreign Office, King George refused these de-mands and the delegation had to return home with its mission unfulfilled. The result was a fresh outbreak of internal conflict in Greece, the EAM leaders engaging in attempt to gain control over the whole country, in an attack on the other Resistance organisations, in which the July armistice agreement was broken, and only the EDES organisation survived the attack. After this the British Military Mission, now under the leadership of Woodhouse, succeeded in obtaining a new armistice, in February 1944. This armistice proved fragile, and did not last long. In the spring, the ELAS forces tried again to liquidate the other Resistance organisations, but this failed in the case of EDES, whilst General Psaros was killed and his forces were dissolved. In April, the EAM movement set up a "Political Committee for National Liberation" in an attempt to gain control over the whole of occupied Greece. This step had far-reaching consequences. Mutiny broke out in the Free Greek Forces in Egypt, in support of the committee, the Greek Government resigned, and King George gave a definite undertaking that he would make the monarchy conditional upon a free plebiscite after the War. These events led to yet another conference under British chairmanship, this time in Lebanon, in June 1944, between members of the Greek Resistance organisations and political representatives from the exile Greek world, led by the Prime Minister of a newly formed exile Greek Government, the anti-royalist Social Democrat politician G. Papandreou. The results of the meeting did not satisfy the "Political Committee for National Liberation" at home, and new meetings followed, until a re-organised Greek Government was formed, with the participation of six members of EAM, and the "Political Committee for National Liberation". When this had been achieved, all the Greek Resistance organisations at last recognised the exile Greek Government, who on their part put their forces under the command of the British General Scobie. These last agreements were made as late as September 1944 at a meeting in Caserta between Churchill and Papandreou and a number of the latter's ministerial colleagues.[193]

The question of the King's possible return was postponed for decision at a later stage, depending upon the wishes of the Greek people. However, in spite of all the agreements, the differences were so fundamental that they continued to threaten the united front, with its weak basis. Nevertheless, the mediation contributed to reducing tensions and thereby created the possibility for a more or less common effort against the Occupying Powers, and their Greek collaborators; and in spite of all the difficulties, the mediation provided a basis for a Greek Resistance effort which could rely in high degree upon the supplies and the technical advice which the Western Powers could put at the disposal of the Resistance organisations, regardless of their political positions. The British

Military Mission to Greece was originally flown into the Country with a concrete operative task. It turned out that there was acute political tension in the country, and that this was further complicated by the fact that there were corresponding acute tensions in the British organs of authority as to the right course to take vis-à-vis Greece in general. To put it very briefly, these consisted of the difference in standpoint between the Foreign Office, which uncompromisingly supported King George and his exile Government, and SOE and the Army Headquarters in Cairo, which was just as uncompromisingly in favour of supporting the Greek Resistance organisations.[194] Thus the military Mission acquired an undesired and unintended political task.[195]

This did not prevent the mission from fulfilling its military tasks in the country, although the continual political interference complicated their completion. Calculated in bare figures,[196] the Allied support from 1942 to the end of the Occupation in 1944 amounted to 5,800 tons, in addition to which a very substantial number of military advisors, instructors, and experts of various kinds such as telegraphists were sent in. During the two to three years in question, a total of 1,072 agents were either flown in to Greece or smuggled in by sea. Out of these, 435 were of Greek nationality, while the remaining 637 were either British, American or Polish, by far the most of them, however, British. Added to these, a very large number of crews, especially British, contributed to smuggling deliveries to Greek territory, or making quite large-scale evacuation possible from Greek territory – these operations being carried out mostly by sea, although improvised landing strips were also used in liberated areas. The number of air and sea operations in the period under consideration totalled about 2,100, or an average of about 65 per month, of which most were naturally during the last period. In all, no less than 82 British or British-American Missions were posted throughout the Greek guerilla territory in 1944, all of them supplied with radio equipment and all of them both in inter-communication by radio with each other, as well as in radio communication with Cairo, where the exile Government had its seat, or with South Italy, where the Allied High Command had its base from 1943. In this way, the desired co-ordination between the many scattered guerilla formations was ensured. Here as in Yugoslavia, deliveries by sea played an important part – in the case of Greece, a dominating part. No less than 4,100 tons were smuggled in in this way, partly to the islands and partly to the west coast of Greece, while air deliveries only amounted to 1,700 tons. The deliveries mentioned can be sub-divided into approximately

4,800 tons of food stuffs and clothing, particularly boots, whilst deliveries of explosives, weapons and ammunition amounted only to about 975 tons.

This distribution, with emphasis on vital necessities of life, was due to the fact that there was less lack of weapons in Greece – and also in Albania – than in most of the other European Resistance areas. Some reasons for this were that the Greek peasants who constituted a major part of the active guerilla traditions, were in possession of small arms; large quantities of weapons had been hidden when the Greek Army capitulated in 1941; and as in Yugoslavia, the guerilla forces seized considerable supplies of weapons at the capitulation of the Italian Occupation Army in 1943. On that occasion, ELAS, particularly, succeeded in capturing large supplies, and this also formed the background for one of the organisation's repeated attempts to put down the EDES movement. This led to the temporary Allied weapon boycott of ELAS, until the situation was re-established by the armistice agreement in February 1944.[197] All in all, the principal need in these areas was not for weapons, although these were welcome, particularly special equipment for sabotage, but for food stuffs, clothing, medical supplies and other special equipment. At the German troops' retreat in the autumn 1944, a great deal of their materiel was abandoned, and members of the Allied missions noticed a clear tendency for the retreating troops to make sure that the abandoned materiel fell intact into the hands of ELAS,[198] so that further possibilities arose for internal conflict in Greece, also after the Germans had evacuated the peninsula – a conflict which, as we know, developed into a long civil war.

NORTH ITALY. One more Resistance Movement came into being in the Mediterranean area, which the Allies, and especially the Western Powers had to consider, and with which they had to establish contact: the Resistance Movement in North Italy.

Mussolini's dictatorship had never been completely free from latent opposition.[199] Ever since 1922, an anti-Fascist exile opposition had existed, whose writings had been smuggled periodically into Italy, and distributed illegally. There had also been elements of both anti-fascist and republican opposition in Italy itself, among Communist, Socialist and Liberal-democratic circles. These also tried to make themselves felt through writings, printed abroad, for example in Paris, and circulated illegally. Under the conditions of the dictatorship, however, this opposition had been weak and scattered, and most of the opposition leaders had been put out of action. From 1927 to 1943, about 5,000 persons had been imprisoned on political grounds, whilst about 10,000 were deported, most of them to deportation camps on the Lipari Islands, whilst 29 in all were liquidated. Among these was the republican agitator Carlo Roselli, who from 1943 had tried to form a republican movement, which was destroyed by the regime. The Communists, under the leadership of Palmiro Togliatti, also attempted illegal activity, but their organisation too was destroyed, in arrests and death sentences. Togliatti himself sought exile in the Soviet Union. In addition, all opposition was closely watched by the Fascist Secret Police, which it is estimated had about 15,000 persons under constant observation. The scattered opposition had not represented any serious threat to the regime in the period up to 1940.

Italy's entry into the War in June 1940 changed this situation fundamentally, however. The war was unpopular in Italy from the start, and its unpopularity increased, as it gradually became clear that there was no question of its soon being finished, with a quick victory and cheap triumphs within easy reach. On the contrary, for Italy the War was marked by one military catastrophe and humiliation after another,[200] and it gradually developed in such a way that Italy became increasingly dependent upon and humiliated by her Axis partner[201] – and the Italian population had never cared for Germany as a nation. From the first day of the War until 1943, the Italian Army and the Italian Navy had been hit by defeat in France, Greece, North Africa, Russia, in the Mediterranean and in Italian harbours. At the same time, the population had been hard hit by rising prices, lack of commodities, mass conscription to military service, and the bombing of Italian towns. In these circumstances, quite new possibilities arose for a growing anti-Fascist opposition, which not only emerged from the civilian population, but made itself felt in the Army and even in the Fascist Party. The royal family and royal circles also began to favour getting rid of Mussolini, the Fascist dictatorship, and the partnership with Germany. In 1942, a "National Action Front" was formed, and the same year the illegal Communist newspaper "Unita" began to circulate. Through this paper the "National Action Front" appealed to "soldiers, officers, militiamen and honest Fascists" to work for a separate Italian peace.[202]

The climax came during the Allied invasion of Sicily in July 1943, when Mussolini lost a vote in the Fascist Great Council, and the following day was dismissed by King Victor Emanuel, and arrested. The King then called on General Badoglio to form a new government.[203] His collapse did not come as the result of the popular opposition which was now rapidly developing, but took the form of a *coup d'état,* carried through in the highest quarters of the State; but his collapse reflected the recognition among the leaders of the State that the position of the regime in the country was so undermined by distrust, bitterness and desperation, that a *volte-face* in Italian politics was both necessary and inevitable. Badoglio proclaimed the continuation of the war on the side of the Germans, but no one had any illusions, least of all the German Government, which immediately took measures to occupy Italy, and disarm the Italian Army units, where they were to be found, and where disarming was possible. During August 1943, Badoglio in all secrecy opened negotiations with the Western Powers, which on 8 September 1943 led to an armistice between Italy and the Allies, at the same time as Allied troops landed on the mainland of South Italy, both at Salerno and at Tarento. Added to this, from October 1943, the Badoglio Government obtained the status for Italy of a co-belligerent, in the Allied camp, although it was not possible to agree as to any long-term political decision on Italian affairs. For the time being it was established simply that the Badoglio Government had accepted the unconditional capitulation of all Italian forces which was demanded, including the Italian Fleet, and that a final decision on Italy's future position was postponed until the end of the War.

A completely new situation thus arose in Italy, with a liberated South Italy as co-belligerent, and a German-occupied Central and North Italy. The problem was further accentuated when a German Commando unit succeeded in freeing Mussolini, after which the latter established the so-called Salo Government, claiming that this "government" – in reality a German puppet government – represented a reborn and reorganised Fascist, republican regime.

For the Allies the events on and after 8 September totally altered formal relations with the Italian opposition. Up to that date, Italy both formally and in reality had been enemy country, and the opposition – in so far as one existed – only an opposition. But from that day, the central and northern Italian mainland was an occupied area, on a line with other German-occupied areas in Europe. The Resistance which arose against the Salo Government and against the German Occupying Power could therefore be considered a Resistance Movement on a line with other European Resistance Movements, in which the Allies were interested, and which they had political and moral grounds for supporting. One logical consequence of this upheaval followed immediately. The military leader of SOE's operations in Europe, General Colin Gubbins, at once established an Italian Section of SOE, with headquarters and base in Bari in South Italy, with Major-General W. Stawell as Chief, and with connexions to the various branches of the Services in the Allied Mediterranean Command.[204] It was the task of this section, within the framework of Allied Mediterranean strategy, to give support to North Italian Resistance organisations, according to the same directives as those under which SOE functioned in the rest of Europe.

The intention of the British and American military staffs was one thing – they, like SOE/SO wished to establish co-operation with a coming Italian Resistance Movement – but the practical and political possibilities for realising their intention was quite another matter. In the first place, some time must naturally elapse before the change-over from one extreme situation to its diametrical opposite could lead to concrete results. Many complicated problems were involved. At the start there was no reliable knowledge of conditions in North Italy, of the attitude of the population, or the extent of organised resistance, etc., and the communications which alone could bring the necessary orientation did not exist. In addition, there was a certain scepticism as to whether the Italian population, after many years of dictatorship, and the material and psychological hardships of the war years, would prove to possess sufficient vitality and organising experience to be able to build up an effective resistance. This scepticism could only be conquered gradually, as it became evident that the Italian population's passiveness towards the war and its outcome was rooted in deep aversion to the Fascist regime, to the Monarchy, and to the Army which had followed Mussolini's war politicies without a protest, and which, in connexion with the events of 8 September, had not even managed to issue clear directives to the Italian Army units scattered throughout France, the Balkans and North Italy, which were forced to act on their own initiative in a situation of hopeless confusion. Allied scepticism included also the Italian Army units in South Italy, which were now, like their fellow countrymen in the Resistance organisations in North Italy, prepared to join the fight for Italy's liberation. In 1943, they were allowed to function as supply troops, and it was not until the spring 1944 that they were sent into action in small fighting units, not in Divisions and never in any reorganised Italian army.[205] Confidence increased as the Allies through SOE/SO and with the establishment of communications with the Resistance organisations in the north – a process which necessarily took time – had the opportunity of registering the change in attitude in the Italian population. In their eyes, the struggle was no longer in support of the Fascist dictator and a hated war, on the wrong side, but against the German Occupation and the Salo Government. Contrary to expectations, effective resistance now grew up in Italy on roughly the same pattern as that experienced in other occupied countries, particularly Yugoslavia and Greece. This struggle had to be given support, and it became the task of SOE/SO, and through these organisations that of the Allied Mediterranean Command, to get this support to its destination. Here, as always, SOE/SO faced the inevitable difficulties of obtaining enough materiel and suitable personnel for an effective effort of support in Central and North Italy. It was at this period that supplies to Yugoslavia had received top priority and it took some time before the Allies received proofs that Italy, after 8 September, was quite a different Italy from the nation against which they had fought in North Africa and Sicily.

In addition to scepticism and practical difficulties, however, there were political problems and reservations which bore a striking resemblance to those involved in the British-American activity in Yugoslavia and Greece. The Allied military authorities – and this applied also to the Soviet Union[206] – had signed the Agreement with the Badoglio Government appointed by the King. For the time being, therefore, they – particularly the British Government, and especially Winston Churchill – felt themselves to some degree bound to this government which, hesitant in its decisions and vague in its commands, had after all kept its Agreement with the Allies. During a period of transition, at least, this government was the basis for Allied policy vis-à-vis Italy, and the best guarantee imaginable at the time for stable political developments in Italy. What direction the political currents would take in a possible future Italian Resistance Movement – possibly towards republicanism, possibly towards Communism – was an open question in 1943, and here the precedents from Yugoslavia and Greece were alarming, particularly for Great Britain, for whose foreign policy the political developments in the Mediterranean regions had vital importance. Regardless of what military advantages could be gained by supporting an Italian Resistance Movement – and the Mediterranean Command was far from unanimous as to this – there were also political considerations with long-term consequences to be considered.

The Allies in general, and in particular SOE had no thorough knowledge of the size and depth of the Italian opposition, when the armistice was suddenly proclaimed in September. No firm contact had been established, even though a single British Mission had been sent to Italy in December 1942, with the purpose of seeking contact with opposition circles, and even though OSS had sought similar contacts via

Switzerland,[207] particularly with a view to obtaining intelligence possibilities. This had had no real importance, however, and the *volte-face*
in July-September had no connexion with Allied activity in the country,
nor was it the product of a popular rising. Of course the strikes in the
spring 1943[208] had been an indication to the conspirators in the Army, the
party and the Royal Family of popular currents of opinion, but the actual
overthrow of the Government had been achieved from above as the
direct result of the admission of defeat and catastrophe. Nevertheless,
bitterness towards both the war and the regime was so intense and wide-
spread that a popular rising was in the making, and with the armistice this
broke loose throughout Italian society, in the Army, among the working
classes, among the intellectuals, in the Administration, in the villages.
Resistance groups began to form everywhere, at first naturally under
somewhat chaotic forms. Partisan units appeared where the terrain allowed, such as in the Apennines and the Alpine regions, and officers,
non-commissioned officers and soldiers from the Army rallied to these
partisan formations as situation and opportunity permitted. Refugees
reaching Switzerland could tell of this first reaction to the new
situation.[209] A first result and proof of conversion was wide-spread help
to Allied prisoners of war, who reached either neutral Switzerland or the
allied basis in South italy in thousands. Every escapee could report spontaneous helpfulness and will to resist in the Italian population.[210]

Simultaneously with the expressions of spontaneous unorganised resistance, however, the first organised movement was also forming. The
tendency to organise made itself felt on many levels – in army units
which had been dissolved, in partisan areas, in the factories, etc. – but
soon a central command arose, of nation-wide character. This took the
form of a national liberation committee, the CLN ("Comitato di
Liberazione Nazionale") which gathered in the summer 1943 around the
person of the former Italian Chief of State, Ivanoe Bonomi,[211] who in
1922 had tried in vain to gather the democratic parties in an attempt to
prevent the Fascist take-over, and who had been without any political
influence since that time. Now the unification which had failed twenty
years before, succeeded in illegality. CLN represented a number of
anti-Fascist groups of Socialists and Liberals, who athwart political differences united in the effort to gather the Italian Resistance into a joint
organisation, with the purpose of fighting against the Fascist regime, and
thereafter the Salo Government and the German Occupying Power; and
also to lead Italy back to democratic conditions. The Liberation Committee was formed illegally in Rome during the weeks just before and after

Mussolini's fall, but a corresponding committee for North Italy was set up in Milan, after which the two committees began the work of organising all forms of active resistance, with sub-committees throughout the occupied regions. For CLN relations with the Badoglio Government were a problem. For the majority of the members of the committee, both the King and Badoglio were so heavily compromised by the many years of collaboration with Mussolini that they regarded this government with deepest aversion – although the government was recognised by the Allied Great Powers as the provisional legal government of the country – while other CLN leaders reconciled themselves to the authority of this government and established contact with it. Bonomi himself had secret contact with the Royal Family before Mussolini's fall. The problem was solved to some extent after the Allied capture of Rome in June 1944, as King Victor Emanuel then abdicated in favour of his son, Crown Prince Umberto, who was appointed Head of State, whilst Badoglio was replaced as head of the Government by Bonomi, who formed a government with representatives of the country's anti-Fascist parties.[212] CLN's standpoint in this affair led to sharp criticism, however, in wide circles in North Italy and particularly in the Communist circles, and this resulted in the formation of another parallel joint Resistance organisation, the CLNAI ("Comitato di Liberazione Nazionale Alta Italia"), where the Communists especially came to play the dominating rôle, and where political views were more radical, and particularly more militant than those of the government in Rome. The situation in the north was different from the situation in the south. With the creation of great numbers of partisan formations, constantly in action, with the enemy at close quarters and in daily confrontation with terror, attitudes could not but become radical. Here as elsewhere, the Allies entertained wishful thinking as to a Resistance organisation which obtained intelligence and intensified sabotage, but otherwise confined itself to organising its forces for a general rising when an Allied offensive could bring immediate help, but which should not engage in regular fighting too early. This was very far from corresponding to the predominant feeling in North Italian partisan circles. One of the leaders of CLNAI, Ferrucio Parri, has expressed it as follows:[213] "The partisan headquarters . . . had no choice. A country to liberate, a democracy to found, an honour to be redeemed, called for a national uprising of a more marked and better defined nature". On the basis of this feeling, the partisan war in North Italy escalated from week to week.

The Allies had to watch this taking place, while at the same time they knew that the final Allied offensive would not come in 1944. The invasion in South France halted the plans for this, and consequently the possibility to come to the assistance of the partisans quickly – apart from the supplies which were flown in. The British Commander-in-Chief in Italy, General Alexander, left the partisans in no doubt as to the situation. On 13 November 1944 he issued a proclamation, addressing the partisans and CLNAI direct:[214]

"Patriots! The summer campaign is over and the winter campaign has begun. The coming of the rain and of mud necessitates a slowing down of the rhythm of the battle. Therefore your orders are as follows: 1) Cease for the present operations organized on a large scale. 2) Keep your arms and have them ready for new orders. 3) Listen as often as possible to the programme "Italy is fighting" transmitted from this General Headquarters, so as to be aware of new orders and changes in the situation".

How far this proclamation was in accordance with the actual military situation in Italy at that time, and however well motivated it was from a military point of view, it acted as a douche of ice-cold water on the heads of the partisans in the North, and the inhabitants of the big towns, who now had another winter to look forward to, with lack, suffering and increased terror. Both in relation to current feeling and in relation to the realities in North Italy, it was doomed to be received with bitterness among the millions of North Italy, and added to this, it could not be obeyed. No breakdown in confidence followed, however, between CLNAI and the Allied High Command or the Government in Rome. In November 1944, SOE/SO managed to smuggle out a delegation from CLNAI for long negatiations in Caserta in South Italy.[215] The delegation was led by the CLNAI leader the politician Ferruccio Parri, the founder of one of the anti-Fascist parties, the "Partito d'Azione". After difficult negotiations with the Allied High Command and the Bonomi Government, it was agreed that up to the Liberation, CLNAI should exercise all the functions of government in liberated areas, as well as the command of the North Italian underground forces, CVL("Corpo Volontari della Libertá"), whilst the Allies undertook to increase deliveries to the North Italian Resistance forces, the partisan forces and the groups in waiting position. On their side, CLNAI undertook to carry out their actions in accordance with instructions form the Allied High Command – where this should prove possible. Every one of the partisan formations had their tactical problems, under the constant pressure of the occupying forces and fascist Militia, and these problems naturally could not be assessed from a distant headquarters. These agreements, undertaken by CLNAI under the pressure of the situation and with deep uncertainty, contributed to creating co-ordination between the Bonomi Government and CLNAI, and between the latter and the Allies, but in fact they only confirmed the co-operation which was already established between North Italy and South Italy, and between North Italy and the Allies, and which the SOE/SO missions to the North Italian Resistance circles had especially worked to create.

It was important that the Bonomi Government, in co-operation with SOE, had arranged in August 1944 for the Italian General Raffaele Cadorna to be dropped in the neighbourhood of Milan, so that, in collaboration with CLNAI, he could take over the highest command of all the North Italian Resistance forces, and thereby create a joint command, in so far as this was a possibility.[216] In this way, and through the Agreements of November 1944, a stable foundation was created for the Italian Resistance Movement, in spite of all the inevitable tendencies towards independent action on the part of individual groups. Through its actions, and in co-operation with Cadorna, CLNAI paved the way for CLN's assumption of the administrative and political leadership in the North Italian provinces, as these were gradually liberated.

A feature which was common to nearly all Italian Resistance organisations was their predominantly or entirely republican standpoint, and this became a complicating factor for the Allies in their decisions as to the size and type of support it would be most correct to give the co-belligerent new-comers, but the political reservations faded as the Allies' ties to the Royal Family became weaker, and their recognition increased of the predominantly democratic viewpoint of the Italian Resistance Movement. Military support from the Allies increased steadily, as the political situation clarified.

In spite of all political reservations, the situation contained a military logic which convinced the Allied High Command that this Resistance partner should also be supported, in recognition of the great military value which an Italian Resistance Movement could bring to the Allied cause. This recognition was considerably strengthened from the summer 1944 by the experience gained by the Allies during the invasion in France of the importance of the French Resistance movement's contribution. On the other hand there was still a clear tendency on the part of the Allies to encourage activity primarily aimed at local sabotage, and to support all

initiatives, including partisan actions which could injure the enemy locally and diffuse his forces; whilst the tendency to anxiety was just as
clear, when there was any question of promoting and supporting large
joint organisations not under Allied control which, in the event of the
collapse of the Occupying Power, might be able to seize political and
possibly revolutionary control over the country.

These political considerations were in accord with a corresponding
military assessment. The Allied Military Missions, which had gradually
been posted throughout the Resistance areas in North Italy, tried as far
as their influence allowed to restrain the steadily increasing partisan
formations from engaging in regular battles, and persuade them to confine themselves to the classic tactics of partisan warfare – sabotage,
ambush, surprise attack and similar actions which allowed for rapid retreat to almost inaccessible districts in the mountains, or in the cities.
This standpoint often made it difficult to reconcile the technical and
military advice of the missions with the ambitions of the partisan formations and national temperament, also because advice of this kind was
often, and not without reason, interpreted as politically motivated. In
particular, questions of this kind were raised in the spring 1945, when the
problem of the right moment for a general popular rising presented itself.
Here both CLNAI and the local partisan units advocated an early and
total popular rising, while the missions tried to hold back.[217] However,
considerable co-operation was increasingly established between the Resistance forces and the Allies – a co-operation which was not without
friction, for one reason because the Allies sought control over the actions
of the partisans, whilst these, with understandable pride, maintained
their right to independence and freedom of action.

Co-operation did not make serious progress until the spring 1944, when
the necessary communications between the two parties had been established, even though in the nature of things, it could never be completely
satisfactory. Communications were provided in two ways. The first was
by SOE/SO dropping Allied Officers over the occupied areas, and the
other was by the Resistance organisations in Italy establishing contact
via Switzerland. Ferrucio Parri had already had negotiations in
November 1943 in Switzerland with the Britisher McCaffery and the
American Allan Dulles[217a] representing SOE and OSS respectively, and
here the main problem was already touched upon: Should the coming
Resistance Movement develop as a supporting organisation under Allied
command and with flexible tasks, carried out in accordance with Allied
strategy? Or should it develop as a national and independent liberation

organisation, under Italian leadership and with the political aim of liberating Italy before or at the same time as the arrival of the Allies, and restore the Italian State in accordance with the wishes of the people? This was the same presentation of problems as the Allies met everywhere in European Resistance circles. On the one hand there was a desire for help from and co-operation with the Western Powers, on the other hand there was a demand for independence in political decisions. Italy's position was more difficult than that of other European countries, however, in that Italy had been an enemy country up to September 1943. This must inevitably accentuate the problem for both parties. The Western Powers had to adapt themselves to the idea that the enemy of yesterday had become the co-belligerent of today – hardly a simple adjustment – and the Italian leaders had national honour and self-respect to re-establish.

During the conversations in Switzerland, the problem was not yet acute, although the underlying viewpoints were sharply defined. The Italian Resistance groups were still in the process of forming, they were few and scattered, and no immediate Allied help was offered. The groups had to content themselves with weapons and other materiel originating from Italian army units which at the capitulation had joined or formed Resistance units,[218] and with the wide-spread organisation which was taking place in the great cities. The units procured a certain running supplement by capture, but after this, Allied help began to make itself felt, and this was also a necessity for the Resistance Movement, which was growing so rapidly that by 1945 it numbered approximately 250,000 combattants, to which should be added the tens of thousands who supported or stood behind the movement. The Allied help for the period up to the Liberation in April came to constitute about half the materiel at the disposal of the Resistance Movement.[219] This help was mostly delivered in dropping operations, while only a lesser part was delivered by sea or was smuggled through the front lines. In all, the Allied deliveries for the whole period 1943–45 amounted to approximately 3,000 tons, and an important number of instructors, some Italian, some British and some American, were also dropped. In the months before and just after the capture of Rome in June 1944, and the Allied advance to the German defences on the "Gothic Line" through the Apennines, from Pesaro in the east to north of Pisa in the west, there were many deliveries – for the months May to August 1944 about 800 tons in all, of which a little over 500 tons was delivered by the British and about 300 tons by the Americans. The results of this could be felt, and the German Commander-in-Chief, General Kesselring, had to send urgent representations to Himmler and to the Salo Government to try to get the sabotage and partisan activities, which were constantly harrying all the German transports, halted. Attempts were also made to do this, by the creation of the "Black Brigades",[220] a Fascist corps with the special task of stopping the growing Resistance activity in the mountain regions, in the towns and along the transport routes. But all attempts proved fruitless, and Resistance activity increased. In October, Kesselring had again to record that partisan and sabotage activity was spreading, often with paralysing effect, that the Resistance groups were supported by the population, and that a wide-spread intelligence activity was flourishing behind the German front. "This 'pest' must absolutely be got out of the way", concluded Kesselring,[221] and he recommended a special anti-partisan week, with the merciless use of all means of oppression, parallel with a continued and intensified fight against the Italian underground. How pressed the Occupying Power was emerges, for instance, from the fact that the possibility was seriously discussed of bombing the factories in the large cities in the event of strikes. But nothing helped, and both the Occupying Power and the Italian police were gradually forced to give up, and in fact to acknowledge that measures of compulsion only pushed more and more people into the ranks of the Resistance, whilst large areas were lost and the unrest in the cities was underlined by repeated strikes.

At the same time, the Allied infiltration and help increased. In the period from August to September 1944, new Allied Missions came to North Italy, and the period could show total deliveries of approximately 1,000 tons of materiel, after which, in the months of January to April 1945, the droppings accelerated rapidly with deliveries totalling 1250 tons. These consisted principally of deliveries of weapons, ammunition and sabotage materiel, but here as elsewhere, there were also medical supplies, radio material, clothing, and various types of special equipment. These deliveries were the result of intensive activity on the part of SOE/OS. In the four first months of 1945, there were 856 flights in all, of which 551 succeeded, whilst 305 failed, in that the materiel did not reach the Resistance units and in some cases fell into the hands of the enemy. The accelerating developments were the result of many factors, such as ever-increasing Allied resources, a violent increase in numbers in the Resistance organisations, increased recognition of their importance, but it was also connected with constantly improving communications between north and south. In all about 150 missions were sent to North Italy in the period from September 1943 to April 1945. Most of these consisted of Italian Officers, often with Royalist views, but in April 1945 no less than 48 British Missions were posted throughout North Italy, in addition to a somewhat smaller number of American Missions. The missions were posted most thickly in the Piedmont and Venice regions, which held the greatest strategic interest from an Allied standpoint, but there was also close contact with the great cities and the Resistance leaders there, who were waiting for the moment for the great general rising. In Milan the Allies had posted the Italian-born Massimo Salvadori as their direct contact with the leaders of CLNAI and with General Cadorna. The task for these missions was multiple. First there was a question of advising the Resistance and partisan groups, including the often thankless and impossible task of damping down the tempo of recruitment and activity, until the actions could be co-ordinated with the general strategy. Next there was the question of organising droppings and directing the distribution of material, a task which inevitably had to be carried out in relation to what was feasible in practice, and which just as inevitably must lead to certain groups feeling themselves overlooked, and suffering from the suspicion that the distribution could be politically motivated.[222] It was also necessary to create an effective intelligence network, which succeeded to a great extent through co-operation with a special intelligence network which was set up by the Resistance groups, "Partisan Intelligence Service".[223] Lastly it was a question of achieving unity and balance in the movement's actions, so that one action supported the next, and all actions supported the Allies – and here the political work must be done to get the Resistance groups to accept the Italian Government's and CLN's authority. Friction was unavoidable, but no visible internal strife broke out such as that in Yugoslavia or in Greece. If the situation in North Italy can be characterised as civil war, it was a civil war between a largely united Resistance Movement and the Saló Government's Italian forces. Behind the unity there were certainly deep latent differences on the subject of the structure of post-war Italy, but the very fact that all Italian Resistance groups had a common foe in the Saló-Government, and a common political purpose in fighting the Fascist regime, contributed to maintaining unity in the struggle, athwart the considerable social and political dividing lines which also existed.

Support from abroad

In retrospect it can be established that all European Resistance Movements received psychological, political and material support from abroad.[224] They were all imbued with a feeling of being participants in a common struggle, in which they were not forgotten and would not be forgotten, and in which they saw their efforts as both important and appreciated. This feeling contributed vitally to strengthening them, and to neutralising the feeling of impotence and the isolation psychosis which, without support from abroad, could have been their fate. That this or that organisation, sector, district or country could believe that the support from abroad was insufficient, came too late or was compromised with political conditions or *arrière pensées*, was unavoidable. It was also unavoidable that there must be differences between the importance which the leaders and members of the Resistance organisations attributed to their own little war, and the rôle assigned from abroad to the Resistance organisations. The two parties, the home front and the front abroad, had two different perspectives for their assessments, the perspective of the worm on the one front, and the perspective of the bird on the other. From within, one had knowledge of the small and on occasion the remarkable daily results, and of the efforts, suffering and losses, which it cost to achieve these results, and it was natural that there was a tendency to over-estimate the importance of what one had wrenched from the enemy with such toil, and in such great danger. From outside, one could be ignorant of the results and status in the little war; one could also be unable to acknowledge the value of the total sum of single results; and lastly, from outside, one had to have an overall view which must operate primarily with the known military factors under full control of the various high commands, whose effects on the course of the War one could calculate to some extent. What took place behind the enemy lines could be and often was anonymous, incalculable, and to some extent unknown, although knowledge of it increased from month to month. There was also a considerable difference in feeling between the home front and the front abroad. The one group lived with the enemy, and the acute danger of Resistance, at close quarters, night and day, and looked for the understanding, support and final liberation from the other group, with understandable impatience. If understanding and support was lacking, or if progress was delayed, it was only a short step to bitterness. The other group faced the enemy, and, like the home front, had to live with strains, suffering and losses, but the efforts on the front abroad were achieved under conditions which differed from those of the occupied countries, in that here one did not have to look back over ones shoulder for the ever-present enemy.

The help from abroad, as regards extent, character and timing, depended upon a great many conditions, which varied from one country to another, where practical possibilities, strategic considerations and political opinion played their part. If it can be established that all European Resistance Movements received support from abroad of one kind or another, it must also be maintained that this help never reached the level of the hopes nourished by the Resistance organisations. This again was connected with many circumstances, but it can certainly be stated in general that abroad, the traditionally-minded military hierarchies did not recognize the full advantage of the Resistance organisations' activities until late in the War, and therefore gave a lower priority to the help than was perhaps reasonable – at least lower than the Resistance organisations expected. This applied particularly to the Western Powers, for whom the whole complex of problems of co-operation with the Resistance organisations in foreign countries was new, whilst the Soviet Union's support to the partisan war seems only to have been hit by purely technical limitations.

If one raises the question as to how the Western Powers regarded the help to the Resistance movements via SOE/SO, one must realise that the answer will depend upon who is to give the answer, and at what point in time the answer is to be given, as well as which country is being considered. For many people in the western decision-making organs, the work of the two organisations must seem more of a burden than a reasonable strategic investment. But the time factor also played a rôle. SOE was created in the summer 1940, when Great Britain stood alone with her back to the wall, and at that time SOE must appear a natural supplement to British strategy, if one was to think on offensive lines, and if one accepted the philosophy that lay behind the creation of SOE, regardless of its visions of intelligence, sabotage, undermining activity and the raising of underground armies, which could only be hypothetical. It was a different matter after the Soviet Union and then the U.S.A. entered the War. The importance of SOE and the support of the Western Powers to the European Resistance Movements must at that moment fade more into the background, in comparison with the greater strategic possibilities which presented themselves. SOE survived, however, and merged more or less with OSS, and in view of the experience of 1943 of positive help given by the European Resistance Movements, increasing understanding appeared, even among the sceptics as to the work of the two organisations and their importance. The countries themselves played different rôles. Yugoslavia would demonstrate this first, and then France. In both countries the movements made themselves felt to such an extent that their importance in decisive moments could not be overlooked. To the extent that they acquired strategic importance, to that extent also, the importance of SOE/OS's operations increased.

How much value can be attributed to the help from abroad, and how far the various Resistance organisations would have succeeded in their struggle without this help are open questions. In this connexion one can hardly assess these values simply in tons or containers or instructors dropped by parachute, and ignore the psychological effect, even though one instructor was an important psychological factor in himself, and one container was an important factor in itself. However, it is indisputable that all the Resistance Movements pressed the Allies to send them help from abroad, and that they all received help, in greater or lesser degree. When the French Resistance leader, Jean Moulin, after detailed discussions with large French Resistance organisations, came illegally to England in October 1941, and wrote a report in London on the Resistance situation in France, he could conclude his final section on the necessity of help from abroad:[225] "Without aid in all spheres of activity, the influence of the Movements LLL (LLL =Liberté, Libération Nationale and Libération) will be in vain. They have reached today the highest peak possible, with the means at their disposal and it is not at all certain that they will be able to maintain themselves at their present high level, even in the matter of propaganda, unless they receive some prompt and substantial help". Moulin then lists the areas where help must be given first: moral support, support for building up frequent, rapid and reliable communications between the home front and the front abroad, money, and weapons. He ends the report: "The three movements are agreed that it is up to the FFL to make the required effort". Moulin's words are not very different, in essence, from that Tito told the Chief of the British Military Mission, MacLean in 1943, or his forerunner Captain Deakin, nor from the representations made by the Polish or indeed every other exile government day in and day out to the British Government.

These observations correspond in intensity with that with which millions all over Europe listened in to the forbidden radio stations, and are on a level with the tense impatience with which tens of thousands of Resistance activists, at tens of thousands of reception points, strained to catch the sound of the engines of the approaching aircraft, which from some aerodrome or other out in the free world flew in over Europe with messages, helpers, money and materiel. In the event it is a hypothetical question, whether the movements could have survived and made their mark without support from abroad. But the question remains, whether

352 · *Demand for Contact*

the actual support which all the movements received was in reasonable proportion to the resources which could have been used for the purpose, or in proportion to the efforts which the movements actually contributed. There is no answer. Only an open question.

But no Resistance Movement was to work without help from abroad.

Internal and external communication

DEMAND FOR CONTACT. The absolutely decisive condition for being able to establish co-operation between Europe's home front and the Allied front abroad was that in spite of every obstacle, communication services were created between the prisoners in the Axis Powers' European enclosure and their helpers in the free world. This made possible the information service, intelligence service, supply service, the desired co-ordination of actions at home with the operations of the front abroad and interchange between the two fronts of political character, whether this took the form of conflict or collaboration.

For the prisoners, it was a vital necessity on both physical and psychological grounds to break down the isolation which was proclaimed and practised. The alternative could be resignation and passivity. The necessity was apparent for the Resistance activists, and its importance increased with the Resistance activity, but even the millions who were passive, who were not caught up in the organised Resistance work, but who chose, and with luck were able to choose, to try to live on unconcerned, were affected by the isolation and tried at least to get information where this was to be had – through the radio, the illegal Press or through rumours. No one could be completely untouched, when the Occupation hit hard with encroachments in the professions, in trade relations, and in normal daily life, and when its restrictions and special decrees had their effect in even the most distant regions, and upon those who were politically most indifferent.

Everyone was affected, and everyone could be involved at any moment in drastic events. Everyone demanded news with an urgency far beyond the normal desire for it.[1] For the helpers abroad, there were important reasons for attempting to break into the occupied areas and obtain a sphere of contact which might prove more or less useful, and might perhaps be of vital importance. Both at home and abroad, therefore, great efforts and immense sacrifices were made to establish an adequate communications service, in spite of all the prohibitions. The fact that it existed and functioned was in reality the indispensable condition for by far the greatest part of the Resistance activities. If it did not exist, Resistance initiatives could easily fade or be seriously weakened in their effect. Regardless of obstacles, the communications service had to be reliable, full, preferably regular and – most important – rapid. From the very beginning of resistance it was the establishment of this service which, with good reason, received priority over all other work. The first Resistance groups which gathered in Warsaw in October 1939, had as the first item on the agenda the problem of obtaining contact with the exile government, which had escaped to London, and of collecting all the scattered initiatives in Poland;[2] and the first instructors who were sent from Moscow or London to the occupied areas brought with them, as their most important piece of equipment, not weapons or explosives, but a radio transmitter with the necessary code. To the extent that the contact between the home front and the front abroad acquired the characteristics mentioned, to that extent did the Resistance work increase in effect and importance. It is not enough, therefore, to establish that the attempt to make contact was the first vital task which presented itself, as the indispensable condition for all further work. It must be added that the communications service had to be expanded constantly and effectivized as the Resistance work gained momentum and increased in size and strength.

Perhaps there were only a few who immediately recognized the immediate necessity to open some path or other to like-minded men and women, and to the world outside the occupied area; but as soon as some Resistance activity had begun, and even when it is was only in embryo, the desirability or the necessity of creating contact channels very soon presented itself as the link or the condition for any expanding, meaningful activity. This applied to groups which worked with intelligence, it applied to newspaper groups, and it very soon applied to sabotage and guerilla groups. At a later stage it was to apply also to all para-military groups, and indeed to every developed Resistance organisation, in all its branches. All reception of weapons depended upon precise agreements, and agreements depended upon contact in one form or another, normally radio contact. The contacts had to be created and strengthened before the Resistance could develop.

The background was the same everywhere. The Occupation brought censorship with it, with immediate effect, control of all internal communication and total suppression of all channels of communication from the occupied areas to the world outside the occupied regions. The unoccupied zone of France and Denmark up to 1942 and 1943 respectively had strictly supervised communications with neighbouring neutral countries,

Switzerland, Spain and Sweden, but these were exceptional concessions which, as mentioned previously, were later withdrawn. For everyone who did not indulge in resignation, passivity and submission to the conditions of the Occupation, such a situation must lead not only to the desire for contact, but hunger for contact. For quite a number of people, the demand presented itself to find a way out of the isolation of the Occupation with absolutely immediate effect. This was the situation for everyone who for any reason must have attracted the searchlights of the Occupying Power, such as Jews, persons who had sought asylum in the area, persons who had expressed themselves as declared enemies of the Axis Powers, or military persons who suddenly found themselves cut off and in danger of arrest, internment or something worse. As a typical example one can mention highly placed Polish politicians and officers after the defeat of Poland in September 1939, or British personnel stranded in France after the French collapse in May/June 1940, including also British pilots who had been shot down and – also as examples – German citizens who had sought asylum before 1939 in one of the areas which were later occupied. For people of such categories, a first way out of the emergency could be to go underground, to turn into a civilian, with or without identity papers, but the final solution must be to find any channels which might still be open to the outside world, or to create such channels themselves. It was men and women of categories of this kind who were the first to discover the loopholes in the barriers which the Occupying Powers erected as quickly and as thoroughly as this could be done. Their escape to freedom started the improvisation of the escape service which soon developed into an increasingly organised communications service with possibilities for smuggling out persons, messages and material. It should be added that neither the necessity for flight nor its conditions could be the same in the various occupied areas, or for the different persons involved. Both the geographical conditions and the conditions of occupation played decisive parts here, and the range of variations is so vast that within it there was room for almost every imaginary variant; but the strength of purpose, the imagination, the physical stamina, and the standpoint and conduct of the escapee and the local helpers, as well as money and connexions, and pure luck or accident could decide the results.[3] The urge for escape was common property.

INTERNAL COMMUNICATIONS. Before we turn to a more detailed account of the development of the communications network of the Resistance Movement, it will be practical to point out some general characteristics which came to stamp this development. In the first place it must be important to emphasize that building up an illegal communications network was not by any means only or even primarily a question of establishing communications between the home front and the front abroad. It was just as urgent, if not more urgent, and at least an absolutely acute problem to establish internal communications and connecting agreements in the various countries between these countries' Resistance groups and Resistance organisations, and with these again and the surrounding population, and where possibilities offered, between them and legal institutions, local or central authorities and administrations. With censorship and the risk of tapping of all internal communications, whether postal, telephonic or telegraphic, or crossing lines with built in control cutting off communication, and with the organisation of wide-spread illegal activity, it became an obvious necessity for lines of communication to be ensured, country by country, and screened as far as possible from all official control. This was the case even within the individual groups, and special arrangements flourished. At that or that time, he or she, in such and such circumstances could be found here or there. In this or that form, telephone calls could be made to one number or another, or if this or that agreement was known one could write to a given address using a special code. All this could only be done if, owing to arrests or other misfortunes, the information was not completely out of date, and the road ended blind or led straight into the jaws of the lion. These were the conditions, and one adapted oneself accordingly. The facts of the situation can appear so elementary that they are hardly worth mentioning, but any treatment of the communications service of the Resistance Movements would be amputated, if one did not make these fundamental conditions quite clear, before trying to describe the more sophisticated communications service between the home front and the front abroad. Illegal contact at home from person to person, from group to group, from function to function, from locality to locality, and from the Resistance world to the surrounding legal world, was so fundamental in its importance that it must come first in any account of the problems of illegality and in addition, it is worth a minimum of exemplification.

Intelligence work has been mentioned above as one of the first Resistance activities which were attempted. In this field, the importance of reliable internal lines of communication will be obvious. No observations in the realm of military intelligence were of the least use so long as they remained the private property of the observer. They must be forwarded, and this had to be done by established illegal channels and preferably in code form. Here as elsewhere in the Resistance organisations, normal channels and normal processes were out of the question. One used either previously agreed codes for forwarding messages, or the traditional courier system, or a combination of both. Newspaper editors also had to ensure their lines of communication. On the one hand they had to procure money, information, rooms, printing possibilities and paper, and on the other hand they had to develop a distribution network which perhaps in certain areas and for single despatches could be the normal postal services of society, but in others, and for larger deliveries and local groups, they had to resort to special agreements and arrangements. These functions, necessary as they were for the running of a paper, generally demanded communication with like-minded people in the illegal world and with sympathisers in the legal world, and these connexions had to be established and made to work in secret. Sabotage groups had similar problems. Apart from the most primitive sabotage, where individuals or single groups attacked local targets chosen at random, with the simple means to hand, effective and rational sabotage had to be based upon a fairly thorough knowledge of the target chosen, and its importance to the Occupying Powers' production or transport plans; it also depended upon information as to the situation – including the situation of guards and important machinery – at the target selected, so that before the action took place the saboteurs knew as much as possible about where the weak spots lay, both in the guarding arrangements and the production processes. Even at this stage, the sabotage group or – where it was a question of co-ordinating a series of sabotage actions – the sabotage groups were forced to establish a system of contacts in order to obtain the necessary orientation.[4] But this was only one side of the problem. The actual formation of the group and its functioning demanded the establishment of a closed system of internal communications between the members of the group and its supply service, requiring increasingly close connexion with the illegal organisations which came into being to take on the responsibility for all supplies of arms and sabotage material, for passing on instructions from abroad, and for bringing instructors to their destinations, etc. Here one meets yet another closed system. These organisations were forced, for obvious reasons, to build up extensive internal communication networks, with a special view to the problems of distribution, with which the organisations were faced after every delivery, whether it came from inside or – as was more often the case – from outside the country.

It need only be mentioned briefly that guerilla groups or guerilla organisations had also to develop closed systems of communication routes to villages or towns, and more extensive courier connexions which could cover whole regions, or better still, as in Yugoslavia and particularly in Greece, large parts of the occupied zone. The British Liaison Officers who in 1943 found their way to the Yugoslav partisan headquarters, were among those who discovered this to be the case. As soon as they had reached Tito's Headquarters, there was no difficulty in principle, apart from the physical demands with which they were faced, connected with their travelling throughout the country by the established underground channels, or with their being posted in different regions of the country at the local partisan headquarters. The internal lines, which criss-crossed the barriers of the Occupying Powers, had long been in use. The dotted lines of the courier routes connected one locality with another; the full use of the detailed knowledge of possibilities in every single locality had been thoroughly tested and systematized; and even though the danger from the occupation troops was their permanent travelling companion on these journeys, it was the difficulties and delays more than the dangers which characterized these often week-long courier journeys, in the teeth of all the watchfulness of the Occupying Powers. Fitzroy MacLean experienced this when in 1943 he travelled from Bosnia to the Dalmatian island of Korcula, and so did C. M. Woodhouse, on his many journeys from Epirus to Athens, and around the Greek partisan areas in general.[5]

Everywhere in Europe, therefore, networks of internal lines of communication grew up, in varying circumstances and with varying possibilities, and their members forwarded or carried information back and forth between illegal destinations, as well as despatches, orders, illegal men and women of various categories, refugees and material. Where there were barriers, ways were usually found to circumvent them, or to find the loopholes through which one might pass. The communication routes could not only occasionally, but horribly often be destroyed, but they were rebuilt constantly, more quickly than they were torn apart, and generally at a pace which corresponded with the demands of the moment. The acceleration in the work of the Europe Resistance had its effect in this vital sphere, and under the weight of the oppressive measures of the Occupation, and the attempt to control everything and everyone, a shadow world came into being, of more or less complicated agreements, arrangements and relationships, which became the *sine qua non* of illegality. This shadow world and its short or long lines of communication eludes any schematic or statistical treatment, characterized as it was by agreements on all levels within families, circles of friends, places of work, localities, organisations or simply between one person and another, and characterized as it also was by constant changes, uncertainty, continual improvisations and long series of purely accidental circumstances.

Special mention should be made in this connexion of the millions of connecting agreements which were engendered by the fact that an enormous number of people – perhaps millions – went underground. The maximum result of this could mean that they joined the partisan camps or gathered in refugee camps in partisan conditions, in suitable forest or mountain districts, while the minimum simply meant that they changed their place of residence, took a new name, a new identity and perhaps a new appearance, and by every imaginable means procured the necessary money, papers and material help to remain hidden. This naturally applied to the actual illegal workers, in the first place, although many of these maintained a legal existence side by side with their Resistance work. This could often be an advantage. But numerically this category included still more persons who felt themselves in danger for one reason or another – first of all Jews who had escaped the razzias and the ghettoes, and others who were threatened on religious, political or ethnical grounds. The group swelled especially, however, when the Germans prepared and began the conscription of manpower from the occupied areas for forced labour service in Germany. This measure became a boomerang. Not only did great numbers go underground, but it led to the creation of still more guerilla formations, where the geographical conditions permitted. The French and Belgian Maquis in the Ardennes, the Vosges, the Jura, the Alpine regions in the south-east, the Pyrenees, the Massif Central and Brittany were consequences of these measures. For the great Resistance organisations it became a principal task to help the many young men who now evaded working service and took to the mountains or the forests and other inaccessible areas. The task was not only to prevent Germany from exploiting the manpower which she needed so badly, but also to convert the objectors to combattants. With this in view, a special organisation was set up in France, the "Service National Maquis", which started the systematic organisation of the scattered Maquis camps which now shot up all over France and which gave the French Resistance Movement a powerful push towards a more militant attitude.[6] The German measures were an opportunity, from the point of view of the Resistance, which must not be missed, but exploited. Once those conscripted were brought to Germany, it was too late, and many recruits to the underground army or the underground armies were lost for the Resistance. Contrariwise, it was a short distance from the Maquis camp, with its special atmosphere, to open warfare. The general hatred of forced conscription played into the hands of the Resistance Movement. Even those who originally gathered in the Maquis camps to evade conscription soon became combattants. At first it was a question of defending oneself, but from there it was a short step to the thought of attack in guerilla style. It was by no means everyone who chose, or could choose, flight to the Maquis camps, however. Even more sought shelter underground, many in the country, many in the great cities.

Here statistics and systematization fail. It could be a question of persons who, without any organisation, went into hiding with family or friends, very often in places of residence and situations which could change very freguently.[7] It could be a question of persons who with or without organisational support found temporary shelter, with the intention of reaching the free world. It could be a question of illegal persons who were absorbed, with the help of an organisation, into an escape network of hiding places, to maintain their illegal activity, seek new fields of endeavour, possibly try to reach freedom abroad, or perhaps lie low for a time. For every single person who in whatever way took cover, the fact was that his or her decision and its realisation were conditional upon a certain measure of internal communication, perhaps simply the knowledge that this or that family could and would find them shelter, the necessities of life, and if possible false papers, and in by far the majority of instances, the knowledge of organisational possibilities for evading actual or potential danger. The peoples of the occupied countries developed an intensively quickened sense of solidarity, and where official connexions became uncertain, or broke down, a hidden network of underground communications developed, even if this only meant that the person threatened had some contact or other, who could come to their help in a crisis, via family, friends, fellow workers or organisations. In countless ways, people learned to sense, with more or less reason, where they could turn if the need arose, with reasonable hopes of response, and an undercurrent of uncontrollable lines of communication became a reality. All illegal work of organisation had to be based upon mutual trust, but those who led the organisation had to inspect volunteers thoroughly before they were attached to the organised work. If their judgement or intuition failed, misfortunes followed.

The number of those who went underground with greater or lesser consistency cannot be calculated, and any attempt at a catalogue would at once be nullified by the fact that the category of the countless persons who permanently or periodically disappeared from their homes, from the national registers and archives, was so heterogenous in its composition, situation and aims that classification is not possible. One can with some reason differentiate between those who were working illegally, those who were on the run, and were only being sheltered temporarily, and those who kept hidden simply because they wished to remain hidden. It was, incidentally, not unusual for people to go underground for a period and then reappear with some plausible excuse to explain their absence. However, if we confine ourselves to those who took cover without joining directly in illegal activity, the total is very large. In the case of France, it was thought possible in Free France circles to calculate[8] that at the New Year 1944 about 55,000 persons were living with the Maquis, whilst 200,000 more were living underground. In the case of Holland the number of those living underground – the "onderduikers" as they were called – were reckoned at 200,000 to 300,000 persons, and here there was an organisation, "Landelijke Organisatie voor Hulp ann Onderduikers" (LO), which had the special task of obtaining shelter, false papers, ration cards etc. for hunted compatriots.[9] In the summer 1944 this organisation distributed about 220,000 sheets of ration cards per month, and the number increased in the autumn 1944, particularly when the railway personnel went on strike, and had to join the "onderduikers" already in existence. A similar organisation came into being in Belgium[10] in the autumn 1942, after forced labour conscription for all men between 18 and 50 and all unmarried women between 21 and 35 was decreed; and after March 1943 when the Occupying Power began to call up the young men from the 1922–24 classes and later others, for conscripted labour either in Belgium or – mainly – in Germany. The organisation was called "L'Aide aux Travailleurs Réfractaires" (ATR), and it undertook similar tasks to those of the Dutch organisation. Considerable help was given to this organisation from September 1943, in that a sum of money in the million class was transferred via secret transactions from the Belgian Government in London to a Belgian bank, the Director of which arranged a distribution network for the money, which covered the whole country and supported the work of the ATR. It is estimated that only about 10 % of those called up ever went to Germany. The rest took cover in one way or another, either with certificates which stated that they were working in Belgium, or simply by their going underground, many of them in the Maquis camps in the Ardennes and in Luxembourg. Here too, forced conscription proved to be a contribution to the transition from passive disobedience to active resistance. The German Governor of the country,

General von Falkenhausen, could register the defeat, but he had to state in his reports that the tens of thousands who were missing could not be localised. In Norway, a number of attempts to mobilise manpower for war effort in Norway or in Germany resulted in a similar failure.[11] Here a special "Arbejdstjeneste-komite" (AT Committee) was set up to counter Quisling's plans for a mass mobilisation of Norwegian manpower. A decisive trial of strength came in May 1944, when a government decree ordered the registration of all male youths from the 1921–23 classes. The home front organisation had received news of the plans, however, and before the date of registration, instructions were sent out on the B.B.C. and in the illegal Press to refuse to register. The registration was thus a fiasco. In Oslo, 14 persons registered, whilst it was calculated that about 6,500 went underground, in addition to a large number who took to the mountains. These were called the "Boys in the Forest", and they faced a difficult existence in conditions of great hardship. Here as in West Europe, it was a great problem to find shelter, food and clothing for the disobedient, and even to make contact with them, but this too succeeded. Calculated in bare figures, the totals for the three classes amounted to approximately 70,000 men, out of whom the Occupying Power succeeded in getting about 300 to work. The rest disappeared. As far as the "Boys in the Forest" were concerned, the severe winter climate made it impossible to maintain camps of the Maquis type, and here escape was systematically organised to Sweden, where the men joined the Norwegian Police Corps which was being formed and expanded. From July 1944, approximately 150 took that road illegally per week, while others scattered, to work on the land or in the forests. No actual Maquis could be formed here, although attempts were made in that direction. In Denmark, the number of those who lived underground is not known. Here no conscription of labour was put into force. The Germans made preparations for such measures, but the Danish authorities succeeded in checking them by delaying tactics during negotiations and falsification of the statistics.[12] But for other reasons, there were tens of thousands who had to go underground. During a German action against the Danish Police on 19 September 1944, approximately 1700 men were arrested and deported, while the rest of the corps of 10,000 men went underground and were assimilated without much difficulty, and hidden within the community. The fact that about 8,000 extra men did not present any problems seems to indicate that the number of persons underground must have been very large. In addition there were about 18,000 who found asylum in Sweden. In Poland and Czechoslovakia, there were also tens of thousands who lived underground,[13] in addition to the unknown numbers who took to the partisan camps.

The number of persons underground seems to have been relatively highest in Holland, but one cannot project the figures given for the Dutch "onderduikers" up in proportion to the population figures for the other occupied countries. The Dutch population did not have the final possibility, as did the peoples for example of South France, Norway and Denmark, of taking refuge in neighbouring neutral countries, nor had they the possibility, as was the case in East Europe, large regions of France and in the Balkans, of joining the partisan camps. Since these possibilities did not exist, the only solution for the Dutch was to go underground, with all the dangers and hardships which this entailed.[14] One reaches a vast total if one tries to assess the number of persons in Europe who had to live underground, either owing to illegal activity or to escape persecution or conscription of various kinds.

The fact that countless persons throughout the whole of occupied Europe lived underground, under false names, with false papers and counterfeit or illegally acquired licenses of different types, reflects on the one hand the abnormality of the society of the period of occupation. On the other hand, however, the phenomenon also reflects a certain normality, maintained in spite of all the restrictions of the times. Without such normality it would have been out of the question to find cover and the necessities of life for the countless men and women who escaped pursuit, or fled the decrees. Normality was of course dependent upon the conditions of the War and the Occupation. Nevertheless, it existed. Outside the war-ravaged areas themselves, including the very extensive militarized zones, life went on in seemingly normal conditions, even though these were affected by the war. In the first place, existence in great agricultural districts appeared normal, at least in North and West Europe and in Czechoslovakia, whilst the Soviet Union, Poland, North Italy and the Balkans were hit more directly. In the towns, too, even those devastated by war and hit by bombing, life and the functions of society had to continue as "normally" as this was possible. Both in the country and in the towns, there were therefore possibilities for absorbing those who for short or long periods sought hiding. The enemy could not be everywhere, and could not see through everything that moved. This was only a surface normality, however. There was hardly a town, a village or a fishing hamlet which did not hide its secrets, and in most places, behind the closed surface existence was hidden the illegal passage of information, material, and men and women, so that even the most innocent-looking place could be, and often was, a link in a chain of internal communications, or more directly involved in some form of illegal activity. The many who lived underground also reflected another circumstance. Their problem was not so much one of safety for the first night, as it was the problem of the maintenance of life during a longer period. For this, papers and licences of various kinds were needed, least in the country districts, most in the towns; and the fact that these things could be procured in the quantities which were involved was not only a result of falsification and theft, in various centres of administration, it also contained a proof that society was permeated by illegality and irregularities right through the legal machinery of administration, in all the occupied countries. The Occupation authorities had to rely on the existing systems of administration, if for no other reason because of their lack of manpower, but at the same time they had to face the fact that collaboration could bring treachery with it. How much or how little this occurred, was conditional upon local conditions, individual actions and stages, but the fact that it did occur was often the condition determining the extent of the illegal possibilities. Collaboration in Europe was certainly often shamefully wholehearted, seen with the eyes of the Resistance, but nevertheless, it cannot only be painted black, for it contained every shade, from darkest treason, through grey opportunism, to understanding or straightforward help.[15] It would therefore be a gross simplification to look on the occupation of the European countries as a total seizure of power, which led to full control. The farther the Axis Powers stretched their conquests, the thinner their possibilities became for controlling the captured societies, when these turned against the Occupation in defiance, on the basis of the possibilities which might be present in each individual country.

A feature of the help which the Resistance organisations gave to the many living underground was the raids of Resistance groups on registers and card indexes, where they seized ration cards and exit permits, etc. They also set up special groups for large scale counterfeiting of the papers upon which life underground depended. The fact that this could be done on the scale required bears witness to the often astonishing capacities of the Resistance organisations.

EXTERNAL COMMUNICATION. Without underestimating the difficulties involved in the establishment of internal communications, which demanded solidarity and illegality, it must nevertheless be maintained that the difficulties of ensuring lines of communication between the front at home and the front abroad were far greater and more complicated. This work was started, however, almost as soon as the Occupation was a fact, and bridge-building between the two poles continued as long as the Occupation lasted, and was intensified as the Resistance work developed. This was also a necessity. As described above,[16] none of the Resistance Movements came to operate without stimulus and help from abroad, and the condition for this was first and last the necessary lines of communication. The work of expanding them progressed as experience was gained, and they developed into a speciality of the Resistance.

The first lines of communication were drawn by refugees who tried to get to the free world by land or sea, and the first motives for flight were either the desire to get to safety or the desire to join the ranks of the Allied armies or national auxiliary corps. After the German occupation of Czechoslovakia in March 1939, a stream of refugees began to flow out of that country, and the first task of the Czechoslovak Resistance organisation, UVOD, was to organise the frontier passages to Hungary and Poland, from where the refugees were sent on, some to the Soviet Union, others to the countries in the West, where President Benes had sought asylum. The most important were a group of officers from the Czechoslovak Army Intelligence Service, who escaped, with British help, to London, from there to build up intelligence contacts.[17] But this was only the beginning. The stream from Poland started in earnest in the autumn 1939, when thousands of Poles made their way out of occupation through Slovakia, Roumania, Hungary, Austria and Switzerland, either to the Middle East, where a Polish Brigade was formed in Syria, or to France, where another auxiliary corps was formed, recruited from refugees and Polish immigrant workers in France. After the fall of France in June 1940, the Syrian Brigade marched with all its equipment into Palestine, to join the British forces in the Middle East, whilst the corps in France was evacuated to Britain.[18] After the Soviet occupation of East Poland, a great many officers and soldiers were interned in the Soviet Union, thousands of others also came to the east, some voluntarily, others compulsorily, away from the German tyranny. This was the start of the stream of refugees which would be characteristic of Europe, as one country after another was overrun, and from 1940, when Denmark, Norway, Holland, Belgium and France were occupied, the flood of refugees increased. From 1941, when the Balkans were occupied, it swelled again.

The individual escape routes lose themselves in the shadows, as far as details are concerned, with the exception of the relatively few instances where detailed accounts are still extant, of the planning, the refugee help, and the chain of chance happenings which came to determine the route for the escape in question. Every escape had its drama and its hotch-potch of episodes which one can only trace – or try to trace – in very few cases, today. One example can be given from Danish territory, and this example is typical in that it leaves just as many unanswered questions as the solutions which a meticulous Danish investigation has been able to find.[19] This example refers to a Polish pilot, W. P. Wasik. After the Polish defeat, he escaped via the Balkans to the Far East, and in December 1940 reached France, where he reported for further military service. After this, at the fall of France, he escaped via Gibraltar and North Africa to Britain. Here he enrolled in the Polish Air Force, and took part in bombing raids over Germany, and on 27 April 1942, after a raid on Cologne, he was shot down over Belgium. He and five other members of the Polish crew succeeded in escaping to Switzerland, where they were interned until some of them, amongst them Wasik, again escaped, this time via South France to Spain. Here his flight ended temporarily in a Spanish Prison, but here too Wasik succeeded in escaping, via Portugal, and getting back to his Squadron in Britain. New bombing raids followed, and on 30 August 1944, after an attack on Stettin, Wasik was shot down over Denmark. He landed by parachute in a Jutland fjord, and now he was on the run again, until shortly afterwards he returned to Britain via Sweden. His escape through Denmark to Sweden has been traced and is known to the last detail. It is a story of its own, composed equally of luck and accidental happenings followed by organised escape assistance with nearly twenty contacts. A typical feature for his route through Denmark is probably the link-up of spontaneous help at the place where he happened to land, from inexperienced helpers, and then the channeling into the organised Resistance machinery. The way through Denmark has thus been examined. But Wasik's route through the Balkans to the Far East, from the Far East to France, from France to Gibraltar, from Belgium to Switzerland, from Switzerland via South France to Spain, from the Spanish prison to Portugal – here there are no details, just as there are no details behind practically every one of the thousands of escapes we are considering. We have a caleidoscope to deal with here, and must accept the fact.

Some main features can be pointed out, however. First it can be established that the early escapes were unorganised, so that the results depended entirely upon the energy, physical stamina, imagination and luck of the escapee. The British Wing-Commander B. E. Embry's nine-week escape through France and Spain in June-July 1940 can serve as an example here.[20] For him, as for them all, it was a necessity during his flight to find people who were willing to come to his help in one way or another. A successful escape was conditional upon a certain minimum of shelter, food, money, warnings, directions and most often transport, although miles of the distances were covered on foot or – as in the case of Embry – on a stolen bicycle. This involves, contrariwise, that the longer the Occupation lasted, and the more the level of illegal organisation rose, the less was left to luck, although this factor always had to play its part. Next, it is clear that the direction of the escape must be determined by the countries which were still neutral, and where either asylum or further transport could be obtained, to the Allied world – from 1940 in practice Britain and the Middle East, and from 1941 also the Soviet Union. The number of these countries was soon narrowed down, and from 1941 included only Sweden, Switzerland, Spain, Portugal and Turkey, and as a transit region and only up to November 1942, unoccupied France. If the escapee was determined to reach the Allied world, Switzerland was awkwardly situated, with few possibilities for those escaping to get through to the desired destination. This is especially true for the period from November 1942 to August 1944. Sweden offered better possibilities, even though there were few flights between this country and Great Britain in the first years of the War, and they only allowed for escapees with high priority.[21] From 1943, however, the possibilities for flying on from Sweden increased considerably, and leading Resistance members were in safe harbour from then on, once they reached Sweden. Out of the countries mentioned, Spain was further compromised as a destination or a transit region by the fact that Spain, although formally neutral, was close to the Axis Powers, and particularly under the Foreign Minister Serrano Suner, who filled the post until September 1942, balanced on the edge between neutrality and war on the side of the Axis Powers. Many escapees, after all their efforts and hardships, had to spend shorter or longer periods in Spanish prisons or internment camps. The Miranda camp in the Ebro valley was a severe experience for thousands of refugees,[22] even though the possibility for escaping from this or other camps and prisons still existed, thanks to the diplomatic and economic pressure which British and American authorities could and did bring to bear upon the Spanish Government, always in need of transfusions from overseas.

British and American embassies and consulates in Spain waged a constant feud with the Spanish authorities, to come to the relief of these refugees,[23] partly by organising Red Cross parcels for the prisoners in the camps, partly and especially to get them released and brought over the Portuguese frontier, back to freedom in the Allied world, and to a renewed war effort or recruitment in the Free French, Belgian, Polish or Czechoslovakian forces, etc. As regards the British-American military personnel who began to stream into Spain from 1940, argument was based upon the Hague Convention of 1907, Article 13, which obliged neutral states to set prisoners of war free. This argument gave results, in spite of stubborn obstruction on the part of the Spanish authorities. Thousands of escapees, who had crossed the Mediterranean or the Pyrenees, reached safety either – if they were lucky – by asking for help at British and American consulates etc., or – if they were unlucky – after shorter or longer terms in the camps in question. But this was not only a struggle for British or American personnel. The multitudes of refugees who escaped to freedom included also Jews, stateless persons, Poles, and particularly Frenchmen who were trying to reach de Gaulle's Free French Forces, as well as citizens of many other nations. Many measures were used – argument, bribes, threats to intensify the blockade – and in the years from 1940 to 1944, about 30,000 persons were brought in this way to safety in the Allied world. The stream was periodically so great that an annex had to be added to the British Embassy to house the many waiting further transport out of the country.

Another common situation should be mentioned. The flight eastwards was easier to establish than the flight westwards, although this situation generally only affected persons in the occupied parts of the Soviet Union. Particularly after the front between Germany and the Soviet Union was pushed hundreds of kilometres easwards, flight to the unoccupied parts of the Soviet Union was only possible in practice for the population in the occupied parts of the country. From all other countries within the occupied territories, Britain, the Middle East and North-west Africa were the places of safety sought after, or the areas where the escapees could again join the fighting forces or find asylum. Here it is a question of a purely geographical distinction. The route eastwards for possible refugees from the western parts of the Soviet Union, which involved the passage through the German/Russian front lines, although by no means easy, was at least more feasible than the route westwards.[24] There was no sea in the east to block the way, and the front lines were so extensive and the terrain in many places so inaccessible that effective watch on the whole front was out of the question. The opposite was the case for those whose flight was to the west, and these were by far the most numerous. Whether their final aim was Great Britain, the Middle

East or North Africa, there was a sea to cross, and every escape route had to end with transport either by air or by sea.

The exact figure for all these refugees, as we have seen, is unknown. The proportion is also unknown of those who escaped in order to continue the struggle as against those who escaped in order to reach safety. But it can be established that the figure leapt up by tens of thousands, and that any final figure must have six digits, and more. Next it can be established that the size of the stream of refugees was determined partly by the urge to escape and partly – perhaps particularly – by the possibilities for flight. It is obvious that it was easier to escape from Norway to neutral Sweden, where the frontier was more than 1200 kilometres long, and largely consisted of waste land, than for example to attempt the hazardous flight from Holland through Belgium and France to Spain and Portugal, or through Germany to Switzerland or Scandinavia. It is just as obvious that the possibilities for escape were greater for a Frenchman, particularly if he lived in the unoccupied zone of the country, than for example for a Czechoslovak or a Pole. The longer the escape route, and the more barriers it must pass, the more complications arose for the escapee. And the barriers were not only frontier barricades. Barriers could consist of lack of knowledge of a language, a population, the possibilities of the terrain, and the restrictions which could face the refugee on his or her path.

The urge for flight also played a part, and here several factors contributed. One of these was the Occupation policy. The more brutal this was – or became – the greater was the incitement to flight. For a person in Poland, where the Occupation policy reached a climax of brutality, the urge for flight must be greater than for example in Denmark, where the Occupation policy was relatively mild. But the problem did not end there, in the comparison between Poland and Denmark. The Occupation policy was never static, and where – even in Denmark – it changed to a more severe form, for example with the introduction of conscription of manpower, or the increasing use of hostage murder, as a coercive measure, etc., the urge for flight must become more intense. For all Jews, the thought of flight must be constantly in their minds, but here the possibilities for flight proved tragically few in proportion to the millions involved.[25] For hunted persons living illegally, flight could also present itself as a last resort. Here there were factors which called for flight, such as the desire to join the military forces in the free world. Free French, Free Polish and Free Norwegian Forces can be mentioned as examples of such military formations, which appealed for recruits from home.

Political tasks could also call for recruits from home. In the study of the European emigration to the U.S.A. in the ninteenth century, one operates with a "push" and a "pull" factor. There could be a situation to escape from and a situation to hope for. Both factors had their effect behind the stream of refugees which became a flood from Axis-occupied Europe.

The stream of refugees had to take countless different courses. Every flight involved its particular problems, and contained the components mentioned – plans, chances, luck, and after a time organisation. But even though knowledge of the individual's problems is not possible, simply because of their vast multiplicity, some main routes can be outlined. For the populations in the occupied areas of Russia there was only one point of the compass to which flight was directed – the east. Here the front lines must be crossed, but this could be done with support from the partisan organisations and the army units behind the front lines. Here, however, a closer possibility existed for the threatened civilian population – escape to the partisan formations; and this led at the same time to the recruitment to these formations, which was desired both by the partisans and by the Soviet authorities. For the populations in the Baltic countries there was a faint possibility for escape across gulf of Bothnia to Sweden.[26] For the peoples of Poland and Czechoslovakia, the way to the east was a geographical possibility, and this was used where ideologically motivated, but the main stream went westwards, either as mentioned, via the Balkans and Turkey to the Middle East, or by tortuous paths via Sweden or Switzerland to Britain. For the people of Norway and Denmark the main direction for refugees was obvious. They went to Sweden, and in some cases via Sweden to Britain; in addition, as far as Norway was concerned, a special route called "the Shetland Bus" was established, with its base on the Shetlands,[27] by which refugees and volunteers were shipped from South-west Norway direct to Britain. The start of the route was improvised on Norwegian initiative, and it became really effective when it was solidly organised with a permanent base on British territory. The Danish escape organisation developed in a similar way after 1943. It was only when it obtained a permanent base outside the occupied territory – in the receiving country, Sweden – that the possibility of escape became solid reality, with daily trips across the Sound.[28]

For the refugees in Holland,[29] Belgium and France, the main route lay to the south, to Spain, the passes in the Pyrenees being negotiable with the help of mountaineers who knew the terrain or professional French

ɔanish smugglers. The way over the Pyrenees was one of the illegal
̩e routes used most intensively in Europe,[30] and in particular it was
̗ıratively easy up to November 1942, when the Germans occupied
the hitherto unoccupied zone of South France and set up forbidden zones
along the whole mountain range. The route was never closed, however,
and practically every day, illegal travellers from various countries crossed the mountain passes into Spain, and if they were lucky went on to
Portugal and freedom. The possibilities of the route were already obvious in the summer 1940, when chaotic improvised escapes were carried
out by a great number of refugees, most of them trying to slip out of
France unaided – British Army personnel who had been stranded somewhere in France, Belgians, Poles, and persons who had sought refuge in
France previously, and of course Frenchmen or women on their way to
North Africa, or looking for a possibility to join de Gaulle's forces. Here
as elsewhere the history of the escapees began with chaos, but developed
gradually, becoming more and more organised, with numerous networks
of greater or lesser breadth and greater or lesser effectiveness.[31] It goes
without saying that the journey by this route was most obvious for people
from France and especially southern France, whilst the difficulties of the
route must increase progressively with the distance from the north,
where not only the distance itself but also the barriers, for example
between the occupied and unoccupied zones, contributed to the factors
of risk. With increased organisation, however, and with networks which
caught up the refugees and illegal travellers of every kind, these risks
were reduced. When once those trying to leave the country by this route
had made contact with the well organised escape route network, the path
lay, if not open at least prepared, through the work of these organisations, with hiding places, couriers, intermediaries and experts as to ways
and means. British and American consulates in Barcelona and Bilbao,
and British and American embassies in Madrid were all active during the
transit through Spain.

The possibilities for escape from the areas in West Europe which we
are considering were not limited to the mountain paths which had been
opened up in the Pyrenees. Escapes were attempted and carried through
successfully both from Brittany and from the French Riviera, and here
too the improvisations of the early days developed into the later organisation of the routes.[32] At intervals, fishing boats and small vessels from
Brittany contacted British ships in the western waters of the English
Channel – never east of the Channel Islands – and in such cases, refugees
could reach Britain direct, and persons and material could be smuggled

back in the opposite direction. Here, as with the "Shetland Bus", it was important for the effectiveness of the route that it had a permanent base on free territory, in this case South-west England. Similarly, small ships sailed out with refugees from the French Riviera, landing them in Spain, French North-west Africa or Gibraltar. Here too it was a question of sailing out with small vessels from French harbours, combined with meetings on the high seas with boats from British or French territory. The boats were often "feluccas", long narrow sailing boats, well known and therefore not likely to arouse suspicions in those waters, manned by French, British or Polish crews. Submarine crews also took part, fetching escapees in British or Free French submarines, and usually bringing them to Gibraltar. General Giraud was fetched from France in November 1942 in this way, and brought to Gibraltar.[33] For these operations off the French Riviera, conditions were made more difficult after the German occupation of South France in November 1942, but the traffic never quite came to a halt, it was only impeded. French submarines also operated with landings on Corsica,[34] and after the island was liberated in 1943, Free French Forces established a naval base there with a view to operations along the French Riviera. The infiltration into Corsica by sea was considerable. Out of 26 SOE instructors sent to the island before it was liberated, 17 were landed from the sea and only 9 dropped by parachute.[35]

Two more ways of escape were available for potential refugees. The most complicated, from a technical point of view, was evacuation carried out with British Lysander, Hudson and Dakota aircraft, for the first time in 1941. This method could not by very wide-spread. It was too complicated and dangerous for that. It required a landing strip, great skill on the part of the pilot, and a discretion which it was not always possible to obtain. Unloading and reloading had to be done very quickly – in a matter of minutes. In all, F Section carried out 81 such operations, smuggling about 260 instructors into and fetching about 435 persons out of France.[36] On these flights there was normally a question of persons of very high priority, French Resistance leaders who were flown out, and specially trained instructors who were flown in. Minor quantities of material could also be brought over in this way. But for ordinary refugees, this possibility for escape was not open, although a few women were flown out by this method. A last way out was to escape to Switzerland. Here the majority were people seeking asylum, however, not those motivated by the desire to join free fighting forces, and never instructors from SOE's F or RF Sections, who after their missions were accomplished, or if their organisation broke down, made their way back to British or North

24*

African bases. They were normally instructed to apply to the escape organisations for help to leave the country through Spain to Portugal.

In the case of the Balkans, the situation, as already described, was that Yugoslavia was practically speaking hermetically sealed as regards the free world, right up to 1943. On can wonder how it was that no escape routes out of Yugoslavia were found at an earlier stage, either by sea or through Albania and Greece to Turkey, or perhaps by more tortuous paths; but the explanation is probably partly that the Adriatic was a completely closed sea up to 1943, and that the German-Italian occupation of these two countries made the transit extremely difficult, and partly and perhaps especially that the partisan movement reached such a size, almost at once, that joining the partisan camps became the obvious alternative to flight. On the other hand, when the connexion with the Allies was permanently established in 1943, as we have seen,[37] mass emigration took place from Yugoslavia, but here it was a question of the organised evacuation either of the wounded, or of persons seeking special training in the free world, or those with political missions to carry out there. Evacuation of this kind was organised from outside and came at a stage where the demand was for fighting more than flight. This applied to Yugoslavia and it applied no less to Albania, whilst a considerable leakage of Greek refugees to the Middle East took place via the Greek islands and Turkey. Here organised escape routes were set up, operating in co-operation with Allied bases in Turkey, and ordinary refugees, recruits to the Free Greek Forces in Egypt from Greece, and instructors and materiel from abroad were sailed out and in by these routes. There thus existed an organised escape route from the Greek island lying nearest to Turkey, Chios.[38] The number of Greek refugees and escapees in the middle East amounted in the spring 1943 to about 12,000,[39] a figure which increased rapidly after that time, when a direct appeal was made from the Allied headquarters in the Middle East for the numbers of volunteers who might be needed. For this transport, "caiques" were usually used – small vessels which normally plied among the islands of the Aegean.

In the general stream of refugees from North and West Europe, there was one group of refugees which stood out, by virtue of the quite special importance which their escape and return to Britain held for the Allied conduct of the war. This group consisted of highly trained British and later American military personnel, particularly pilots and crews, who had been shot down during raids over German or the occupied territories, and either had been lucky enough to land by parachute in occupied areas, or after forced landings had succeeded in evading the immediate German hunt. Lastly there could be military personnel who escaped after larger or smaller commando raids, such as the raids on St. Nazaire and Dieppe in 1942, or after the airborne landings in 1944 at Arnhem, or it could be a question of escaped prisoners of war from all the Allied countries. In this connexion, mention should be made of the great numbers of prisoners of war in Italy who – helped by the Italian population – either reached safety in Switzerland or succeeded in getting through to the Allied front lines in the south and taking up the struggle once more. Many continued the fight in Italian partisan units. But from the military point of view, all the Air Force personnel were most important. They were not a large group as to quantity, but as to quality they were extremely valuable, owing to the long and expensive training of the group, and the experience of the pilot. It is a measure of the importance attributed in London to this group and the possibilities for their evacuation back to British bases that special missions of parachutists from the SOE organisation were sent both to Belgium and to France, with the task, in co-operation with the existing Resistance organisations, to help these escapees to get safely back to the British bases; or where this might prove impossible, to collect them in camps in suitable Maquis areas. The principal problem, every time a plane was shot down, was to find the survivors and to channel them in to the various escape routes. This became easier as recruitment to the Resistance organisations reached further and further out to more and more persons, who in a given situation knew where hiding places could be found, and where organised escape with couriers etc. could be carried out. The difficulties were naturally particularly great for refugees of this special category, simply because they did not normally speak French, Dutch, Danish, or whatever was the language of the country were they were shot down, but here as in all Resistance work, it proved that the results improved with the growth of the organisation.

The number of pilots who got back to base in this way was not unimportant, even if the final figure is not known. A multifarious collection of organisations – Belgian, French and British – worked with growing success to ensure the return of the pilots.[40] One Belgian organisation, formed by and for a long time led by a woman, Andrée de Jongh, which operated under the name Comète, in spite of very many round-ups followed by deportations and executions, had about 800 Allied pilots' rescue and return to its credit. Another Belgian, Albert Guérisse, who was landed on the south coast of France, was caught by the French police but succeeded in escaping from them, operated in France under the name of Pat O'Leary, and in the period October 1941 to March 1943 had the rescue of over 600 pilots to his credit and their escape either from the Riviera or through Spain. And a third organisation, Shelburn, maintained an average of pilots smuggled out of the country of slightly over 60 men per month. Most of these went over the Pyrenees, and in 1943, escapes by this route were a daily event. It was almost a matter of course that the Free French organisation must take part in this work. In 1942, Dewavrin created a special escape section within the framework of BRCA,[41] led by Flight-Lieutenant Christian Martel, who from April 1942 organised the crossing of the Pyrenees and by sea of several hundred persons, British or French military personnel. A good many Air Force personnel were brought back by the planes landing at night on the improvised landing strips, whilst others, as we have mentioned, collected in Maquis camps or joined the existing Maquis. This was particularly the case in 1944, when the escape routes through France were overstrained, owing to the great numbers of flights and the corresponding increase in planes shot down, and here the temporary solution was to collect the pilots in special camps. One such camp in the Ardennes had about 160 pilots in August 1944, and during the Allied advance they were able to cross the German lines, return to their bases and again go into action. Dutch help to the British airborne troops, stranded after the battle of Arnhem, wounded and not wounded, north of the battlefield, has already been described.[42] In the case of Denmark, a special investigation has been made of the fates of Allied pilots.[43] Of the survivors, about 300 were taken prisoner, whilst about 100 reached Sweden and returned to their bases in England. The investigation clearly shows the connexion between the level of the illegal organisation and the possibilities for rescue. Up to 1942, all the pilots were taken prisoner, in 1943, two were helped to get back to freedom through SOE channels, but from 1944, when the Resistance organisation had expanded, the great majority of survivors reached Sweden in safety and went to Britain. The investigation, in which every pilot's "fate" was followed in detail, confirms that spontaneous help was at hand, but it was of little use so long as an organised assistance service was not available. When such a service had spread a network throughout the country, however, the path from the illegal amateur to the illegal expert was not long.

Although we have established that precise figures for the refugees and escapees are not extant, and can probably not be calculated, simply because the words "flight", "fugitive", "escapee" and "refugee" are so common and cover such a large range of illegal travellers that they by no means cover all the wayfarers on their long, forbidden journeys, it should be added that certain numerical quantities are available, and these allow for some overall assessment of the dimensions of the process of escape. However, the numbers of those who fled to the east and reached safety from East Poland, Slovakia or from the occupied areas of the Soviet Union are quite unknown,[44] but we have seen that there existed many channels of communication between the occupied areas and the unoccupied Soviet Union to the east, so that evacuation of scattered military personnel, wounded from the partisan units, particularly exposed groups, etc. was not only a possibility in many parts of the front, but a reality, particularly as large regions were liberated by the partisan, and flights in and out of the partisan areas became regular practice. In addition, the front could sway back and forth, and this opened up escape loopholes for many. We have already seen that a mass evacuation of millions of Russians was carried out before the Occupation became a reality.[45] The number of refugees from Czechoslovakia was never great, and those who did escape were mostly Communist leaders who were politically active from Moscow, whereas there were large numbers of refugees from Poland. Many Poles reached the Polish Army units as volunteers, and were transferred to the western battlefields, but the incitement to flight declined when joining partisan units or Resistance organisations became a workable alternative to flight.

More precise figures exist in the case of Scandinavia. The number of Norwegians who stayed in Sweden, either in transit or for the duration of the War, reached about 50,000 in the course of the Occupation, whilst the corresponding number of Danes amounted to about 18,000. Both figures varied somewhat, as many were simply on their way to Britain, whilst others travelled back and forth at intervals between the home country and the country of asylum – some of them several times. In the case of both Norway and Denmark, the organisation of this traffic was in the hands of special escape organisations, based on Sweden, and with the requisite illegal contacts and branches in the home country. The easiest flight to arrange was that from Norway to Sweden, where the long, thinly populated frontier area was impossible to control effectively. The work here was concentrated on the organisation "The Spider",[46] which grew into a large movement with many ramifications, with hiding places, couriers, supply system, and connexions to people with local knowledge who acted as guides for those who had to leave Norway for whatever reason – or to return to Norway from Sweden. Most of these journeys were across the land frontier, but sea routes also existed. The Danish routes were all by sea. There were few escapes from Denmark up to the autumn 1943, also because the urge for flight under the milder conditions of Occupation was not strong, but in connexion with a German attempt to arrest all the Danish Jews in October 1943, a break-through occurred for the Danish escape organisations. Whereas in earlier attempts to cross the Øresund, canoes, rubber dinghies, etc. had been used, and a number of escapees were drowned in the attempt, now a large organised machinery was improvised, using fishing vessels, coasters and fast motor boats, and over 95 % of the approximately 7000 Danish Jews were successfully brought to safety in Sweden, where asylum had already been guaranteed for all Jews.[47] After this, the experience gained from the transport of the Jews was exploited, so that the improvised routes came into daily use, and constantly increased in the numbers of men and the quantities of material brought across the Sound.[48] The routes had their permanent bases in Sweden, they had their own ships both at home and in Sweden, and they now made the passage from Denmark to Sweden very reliable, as did the well-organised service from Norway to Sweden. The routes had their stations on the west coast of Sweden, and departures from Denmark took place from varying harbours and beaches. The services functioned mostly with what were called "half-way contacts" between the two countries, that is, persons, material and post were trans-shipped in the waters of the Øresund and the Kattegat. In the case of Norway it should be added that hundreds of refugees reached Britain via the "Shetland bus" or other small vessels from South-west Norway.

The problem was far greater in West Europe, and greatest in Holland. Nevertheless the stream of refugees, particularly from Belgium and France reached astonishing proportions. Whilst the number of Dutch nationals who escaped through the barriers of the Occupation – mostly to Switzerland – was extremely modest, the Belgian and French escape channels functioned very successfully by the routes referred to. A Belgian escape network, with supporting stations in the large French cities such as Lyons, Toulouse, Montpellier and Marseilles stretched through the whole of France with contacts and couriers, to Spain and Portugal,[49] and great numbers of Belgians managed to get to Britain by these long routes, or to the Belgian Congo. The precise number is unknown, but the number of Allied pilots who reached freedom by these routes at least gives a hint of the great capacities of the routes. As regards France, as we know, there existed both French and British organisations, which specialized in escape transport, while at the same time French citizens sought and found the way to freedom on their own initiative – either to asylum in Switzerland, the U.S.A., Ireland or Britain, or to enrolment in the Free French Forces. The stream of Frenchmen who made their way to these forces began quite soon after de Gaulle's famous radio appeal in June 1940. However, the influx after a speech which was only heard by a few, and received with scepticism or aversion by many who heard of it, was understandably enough only a trickle in the introductory phases of the organisation. "However, single volunteers came daily to England", notes de Gaulle in his memoirs, on the situation in June-July 1940,[50] speaking of the few who came in small vessels from North France or who managed to pass through Spain, evading the Spanish police. The key word here is "single", and the arrivals in the first phases could be counted in very small numbers. Later, however, individuals became scores, and scores became hundreds, and the stream swelled especially after the occupation of the "free" zone in November 1942 and the change in the fortunes of war. De Gaulle's authority was obviously one of the reasons for this, as was Pétain's declining popularity, and also the increasing reliability of the organisation of the escape routes. In the winter 1942–43, when a French military force was being created in French North-west Africa, and the conditions of the Occupation at home became more severe, the stream grew to thousands. For the period between April 1943 and August 1944, it is calculated that about 20,000 persons attempted the crossing of the Pyrenees, whilst others attempted escape to North-west Africa by other ways. In his memoirs, de Gaulle gives the number of refugees who reached the recruiting offices in the area by various routes as approximately 12,000 men.[51] In addition there were refugees of other categories.

Switzerland absorbed a great number of refugees. This took place in spite of the fact that Switzerland was in a very difficult position, when it was a question of receiving refugees in large numbers. Both the supply situation of the country and considerations of security influenced the Central Government, as well as the authorities in the various cantons, in the direction of a certain reserve on the question of giving asylum. But under the pressure of public opinion, several of the national newspapers, church communities and Swiss refugee organisations – pressure which became especially strong when in August 1942 it was known that the authorities had turned back and deported Jewish refugees from the "free" zone of France – the authorities gave in, and permitted a freer and more extensive immigration into the country.[52] Critics could point, with reason, to the Swiss traditions of open doors and humane attitudes, and in 1942 it was becoming generally known that the Vichy Government gave no protection to the Jewish refugees in cases of German demands for their surrender. Originally, the Swiss Central Government had fixed an annual maximum of 6–7,000 refugees – a number for whom they believed they would be able to find work and food – but by the end of 1942 the number of refugees had passed 12,000, and it would rise considerably in the period which followed. The climax was reached in September 1943, after the Italian capitulation, when a stream of refugees began, which included about 2,000 escaped prisoners of war – a figure which would later rise to 4,000 – with 200 to 300 men crossing the frontier daily, most of them refugees from the Italian civilian population, so that the total for the month was over 20,000 immigrant refugees. In spite of all the difficulties, some categories of refugees, particularly those who tried to get back to the Allied Armies, also made their way out of the country successfully. But in February 1944, in spite of this leakage, the number of refugees had reached about 70,000, of whom a large part were soldiers from the armies of various countries.

Another escape line in Italy ended in Rome, where the Vatican provided certain possibilities for hiding and taking care of fugitives and sluicing them on to freedom. This was a minor route as to numbers, but for those on the run, any route was important.

Looked at as a whole, it seems not unreasonable to conclude that the number of refugees in toto was nearly 250,000. Most probably it was higher. Considering the restrictions of the times, the figure is high and illustrates both the necessity which drove them, and the urge which drew them. At the same time the relatively high Scandinavian figures illustrates that it was the possibility for flight more than the desire for flight which in the last resort determined the numbers who escaped. It is also characteristic that the possibilities for flight increased with the growth of the Resistance organisations, and with the popular support which they could gradually count upon. Good will existed, the length of every one of the thousands of escape chains which stretched, criss-crossing over Europe – people who gave shelter and food, people who procured money, people who brought the refugees on to relations and friends, people who gave warnings, who obtained false papers, people who knew the loopholes in the frontiers, people in authority at all levels who shut their eyes and ears, and as the ends of the chains, skippers, smugglers and mountain guides. Many acted from idealism, a number from opportunism, and others also for gain. There were thousands of tragedies involved, when refugees were caught, and when the work of helpers ended in their arrest, deportation or execution. [53] Nevertheless, as we have seen, tens of thousands reached freedom. The condition for this was a work of filigree, composed of spontaneous help and organised planning.

In these pages, the words "flights", "refugees" and their derivatives have been used in describing the multitudes who tried to get away from the enclosures of the Occupation, out to asylum in neutral countries or to the countries allied against the Axis Powers. The word "flight" and its derivatives has only a limited validity in the context of this book, in so far as these words contain any invidious meaning. The refugee evades a dangerous situation and seeks safety and if possible security in flight. This certainly applies to thousands of those who took to the illegal escape routes of Europe, perhaps to the majority. But it does not apply to other thousands who crowded these routes with the determination to reach the points where they could make their active contribution in free fighting forces, to pilots shot down or escaped prisoners of war on their way back to base, or for the Resistance men and women who used the escape routes because these could be used for bridge-building between the home front and the front abroad, which was an important condition for the illegal work and co-operation between the two fronts.

Even though in many cases it was the refugees of the first category who opened the escape routes, and found their way to the loopholes which existed, in spite of all the barriers, and broke out of the isolation of the Occupation, these routes very soon acquired another, constructive importance. They became courier routes. Among the groups of refugees who day after day forced the barriers between the occupied areas and the free world, the actual refugees rubbed shoulders with the volunteers on their way to active service on the fronts abroad, and with active Resistance members, carrying despatches, reports and surveys of local conditions from the European Underground. In countless instances, men belonging to this last group were simply in transit, and after accomplishing their missions would return to the active illegal sphere. For them the escape routes were simply the means of advancing the illegal struggle, and therefore without safe destinations of any kind. It goes without saying that the Resistance organisations created their own independent courier routes. But it is difficult to differentiate between these routes and the other routes referred to. The ways and means were often identical.

The interplay between the home front and the front abroad had to be built up on endless series of minutely detailed agreements, which again depended upon detailed knowledge of the situation, circumstances, and particularly standpoints and plans in the other – always very distant – camp. Here the courier system had its place as an indispensable link in

380 · *External Communication*

the chain of communication. The word "courier" in this context must not be given too narrow an interpretation. It could refer to a person who arrived in a neutral country or an Allied country at war, from the occupied areas, to make his report in person. There are countless examples of this, both in east and west and also on neutral territory where long and portentous conferences were held by the members of the Resistance who had slipped out of the occupied areas and military and political leaders from exile governments and Allied governments. At a later stage in the War, when the courier system had become well established and was reasonably safe it was almost a matter of routine for Resistance leaders, SOE/SO instructors, partisan leaders and political leaders behind the Resistance Movements to be called to conference on free, unoccupied territory. Contrariwise, it was possible for Allied leaders to visit the occupied territories.[54] Examples of this have already been described.

But the courier routes did not only serve for smuggling people. First of all they were used for smuggling written material, often by one of the refugees or some helper in the escape chain undertaking the risk of smuggling out the material and forwarding it. Then the escape route became a postal route, and it was in this capacity that the many escape routes received their great importance for Resistance political development. Written material of every kind came through this illegally organised postal service to the Allied world, so that in a great many spheres the Allies could act with astonishingly accurate knowledge of what was going on in the occupied countries. This material could be intelligence, illegal press information, descriptions of the situation of the moment, reports on feeling, correspondence with military and political leaders in both camps – abroad as at home – or it could be technical agreements on resistance of every kind, especially agreements between instructors from the various support organisations in the outside world and their headquarters.

Precise and if possible complete information on what was happening in the occupied countries was of the utmost importance to the Allies. It was important for propaganda, for organising the Allied supporting services, and in the end for military operations, and there was hardly a detail which did not engage the attention of the fighting free world: troop movements of the Axis Powers, construction of fortifications, production statistics, alterations in the restrictions of the Occupying Powers, the reactions of the peoples, the food situation, rationing regulations, etc. All the knowledge was scraped together and joined up into a complete picture of the changing situation behind the enemy lines. Even apparently trivial details could be of the greatest importance.[55]

The advantage of this form of communication between the home front and the front abroad was that here it was a question of communication which allowed for long and if necessary spacious explanations and arguments, and that photographs, sketches, statistics, etc. could be sent in this way. Technically speaking it was usually material which was photographed down to microfilm, which could be smuggled out or in in camouflaged packing. In special cases, such as some correspondance between the Danish nuclear physicist Niels Bohr and the British physicist Professor James Chadwick, who belonged to the British inner circle of scientists dealing with the construction of an atom bomb, the letters were photographed down to a size where they could only be read under a microscope,[56] and Bohr's letters were further ensured by the messages being melted into a hole in an ordinary door key. In this case, Bohr's opinion was requested on whether or to what extent the Germans might be approaching the manufacture of an atom bomb, and certain important scientific formulas were also asked for. Here quite extraordinary precautions were naturally taken. Normally reduction to 8 millimetre size, and forwarding in, for example, a rectum container were sufficient, but indeed, every kind of more or less commonplace camouflage packing was used, such as tooth paste tubes, shaving soap, tins of food, etc. The disadvantage of written communication was that the method was slow, and in spite of all photographic technique and camouflage, it entailed the risk of interception. The disadvantage affected the intelligence material, which must be considered urgent but it also affected most of the exchanges of operative agreements. Information by this slow route became static in character, and could keep the outside world informed on developments which had already taken place; but it could only be used with difficulty, where there was any question of making arrangements as to future operations, etc. This naturally did not mean that the messages by this route, which were often quite copious, were not often very valuable. The route was only useless when there was a question for example of shipping movements, sudden troop movements, or mutual agreements regarding unforeseen situations.

In the first phases of the Occupation, the illegal postal service was generally speaking the only form of communication which could be established. It was the most obvious form, during the first stages. It should be added, however, that this comprehensive type of communication, with its advantages and disadvantages, was maintained as long as the

Occupation lasted. It was because of the possibilities it offered for providing detailed information, and in spite of all its disadvantages, that it remained an indispensable part of the communication system; and it became increasingly valuable as the Resistance Movements gradually reached a higher level of work and organisation, which entailed well organised and therefore more reliable courier services. Both the Resistance Movements and the Allied support organisations had to begin from rock bottom, however. The course of the War and the rapid occupation of enormous territories took the belligerents by surprise, in the west as in the east. It also took the peoples by surprise, when they found themselves suddenly placed in an unforeseen situation. Both the military and civilian categories had to find ways of improvising a service from scratch, which demanded, above all else, two-way communication. We have a typical account from Dewavrin, of his – and incidentally Great Britain's – situation, when in the summer of 1940 he received the task of building up contacts between de Gaulle's Free French Forces and the home country.[57] He was given an office and a task, but a minimum of aids. When he applied to de Gaulle for money and the wherewithal to establish these contacts, the answer was terse: "I have none. Make your own arrangements". Dewavrin adds that the British had left the Continent without arranging for any contacts, and that only the Czechs and the Poles had used their short stay in France to arrange for secret agents, with radios, to be left there, and they were therefore the only ones in a position to start work immediately.

Dewawrin's situation is very similar to that in which the leader of the Danish Section of SOE, R. C. Hollingworth, found himself, when in October 1940 he was called to London from Iceland to build up what was then a very doubtful enterprise in Denmark.[58] He too received an office and a task, but for the rest he was more or less left to his own devices. He describes his start, recalling the two trays for incoming and outgoing correspondance. They remained empty for weeks and even months. Later, the offices in London and in Cairo would buzz with activity, but this was not until contacts and connexions had been built up – from rock bottom.

Taken as a whole, the connexions between the occupied areas and the Allies increased steadily during the whole period of occupation, and as we have described, after a time the situation allowed for personal meetings between Resistance leaders and political and military leaders from the Allied camp, or from the various exile camps.[59] During such meetings it was naturally easier to thrash out problems in all their aspects and with all the nuances which even copious written correspondance could hardly cover. Here a few single examples will be given. As we have seen, Greek Resistance leaders met representatives of the exile Government at conferences under British auspices, first in Egypt and later in Lebanon, with a view to forming a coalition Greek government, establishing the relationship of the Greek Resistance forces to the Allied High Command, and making important technical Resistance agreements. In the autumn 1943, Tito decided to send a Yugoslav Military Mission, led by one of his close assistants, Vladko Velebit,[60] to Cairo to negotiate with the British Commander-in-Chief, General Maitland Wilson, and with the Chiefs of the British Air and Naval Forces. Later – in 1944 – Velebit went to London where in reality he acted as Ambassador for the Partisan National Committee vis-à-vis the exile Government and the British Government, and in 1945 he became Deputy Foreign Minister in the Yugoslav Liberation Government. In the summer 1944, after setting up his headquarters on the islands of Vis, Tito himself had an important meeting with Winston Churchill in Naples. North Italian Resistance leaders had meetings on Swiss soil with both British and American representatives, first the local representative of OSS, Allan Dulles, who was able to arrange a personal meeting in the Allied Headquarters in Caserta in South Italy with leaders from CLNAI and Allied military chiefs and representatives of the Italian Bonomi Government. A great many French Resistance leaders made their way to Algiers or London for conference with de Gaulle and the Allied leaders. Jean Moulin has already been mentioned as a pioneer in this traffic, but the list was long, and included such names as Gilbert Rémy, Charles Vallin, Daniel Mayer, Christian Pineau, Pierre Brossolette, Paul Simon, André Philip, all of them mentioned *en passant* in de Gaulle's memoirs. Altogether they represent a broad segment of French Resistance, from Corsica to the Pas de Calais and from the Communist Party to definitely Right Wing groups. From Belgium and Holland, Resistance leaders arrived at intervals at the British Headquarters, to work there or to co-operate with their exile governments.[61] Norwegian and Danish Resistance leaders reached Britain, and it was particularly on Swedish soil that Resistance leaders from these two countries could negotiate with Allied leaders, and in the case of the Norwegians, with representatives of the exile Government.[62] Mention has been made earlier of the general discussion in Moscow in August-September 1942, between Soviet partisan leaders and Soviet authorities, but as early as July 1941 a conference took place in Gomel between the founders of the partisan movements and delegates from Moscow.[63]

All in all it may be established that the Axis Powers never succeeded in cutting off the connexions between the occupied countries and the outside world. The occupied territory was too vast for that, the watch kept over them correspondingly inadequate, and the urge for contact with the outside world too strong. The barriers fell, both owing to initiatives from abroad in the form of infiltration of instructors and military missions, etc., and also to initiatives from home, through the creation of escape routes, courier routes and illegal postal services – these three forms merging to such an extent that they can hardly be separated from each other.

RADIO COMMUNICATIONS. In the whole question of interchanges between the home front and the front abroad, however, it was radio communication which was to play the dominating rôle, in spite of all the communications by land and sea. It has been claimed that the existence of radio was the alldecisive factor, which determined the effect of all other Resistance work, and that one can unhesitatingly equate the capacities of the radio service with the operative possibilities of Resistance work. The assertion is hardly valid if it is taken quite literally. The partisan warfare in the Soviet Union, Yugoslavia and possibly in other geographically suitable areas would probably have been realised in any case. Demonstrations and strikes were not directly dependent upon radio communication, although radio broadcasts affected public opinion and awareness of activity. But it is true that much Resistance work depended upon effective radio service, that all Resistance Movements took the radio into use; and that the radio more than anything else contributed to breaking through the occupied countries' isolation, to maintaining the morale of their peoples, and to spreading the calls and instructions of the Allied world. From the first, the establishment of a two-way radio service was a quite basic necessity for the Resistance organisations, as well as for the support organisations. Dewavrin expresses it in the following words:[64] "The creation and maintenance of communications and radio transmissions, it was these problems which for more than four years were not only always in our thought, but literally constituted the greatest part of our activity". He continues by stating that it was only possible to fulfil this task with British and later with American help, and that endless requests had to be made before the help was given to a sufficient extent, owing to the scanty British resources in this as in all other areas.

The radio had several functions. The first and most immediate was for the radio stations – first of all the B.B.C. in the west, but from 1941 also Radio Moscow in the east, and from 1942 also the American stations – to be able to keep the peoples of the occupied countries oriented on the development of the War, and with increasing success, counter the propaganda of the Axis Powers and replace it with their own.

Goebbels was forced to recognize the problem. On 25 May 1943 he notes in his diary:[65] "Our propaganda within the Reich does not seem to have the right spark, either, and this appears from a great many reports from Gauleiters . . . For example, reports come in from various Gaus that many are again listening in to foreign broadcasts. The reason for this is of course that our news service no longer gives people a general view of the situation. Our silence regarding Stalingrad and our missing soldiers' fate tempts families to listen to the Russian radio, since this always gives the names of German prisoners".

The radio was more than a tool for broadcasting news and propaganda, however. It became an indispensable instrument in the illegal struggle, and especially indispensable in the interplay between the home front and the front abroad. Broadcasts in a great many European languages were interspersed with cryptic messages of one kind or another, which served as announcements to the illegal groups who were listening, on coming actions, usually dropping operations, but also warnings, requests for directives, or simply the acknowledgement of some arrangement. The form of these special announcements could vary considerably, from innocent slight changes in the concluding sentence of a broadcast, to quite obvious code messages in numbers, prose or poetry. Behind every one of these special announcements lay complicated arrangements and long preparation on both sides of the fighting front, and very often, special messages meant nothing at all, but went out on the ether to cloak the real, meaningful special messages. In the earlier years of the Occupation there were few, scattered, special announcements, but gradually this material swelled to minute-long gabbles of what was incomprehensible nonsense for everyone but the initiated.

Behind every special announcement, then, lay a complicated arrangement. Originally, these arrangements had to be agreed via the courier network,[66] but soon the broadcasting stations abroad received their opposite numbers in transmission sets which were established in occupied territory. When the first parachutists began arriving in the occupied countries during 1941, and thereafter increased in a sharply mounting graph, their most important equipment was not sabotage material or weapons, but radio sets; and their primary task was not to set sabotage or any other illegal activity in motion – although this formed part of the task – but to establish communications between Resistance activities and the support organisations which were preparing for mass activity behind the enemy lines, SOE/SO in the west, the "Central Staff of the Partisan Movement" in the east. It was a question of the means before the target, and regardless of whether the actual activity was one of intelligence service, propaganda, procurement of weapons, sabotage, assassination, the creation of underground armies or partisan warfare, rapid and reliable communication between occupied and free areas was the absolute condition for the full development of illegal possibilities. Once this contact was made, countless possibilities opened up for the interplay between the home front and the front abroad. If it was not present, or if it failed, co-operation came to a stop or never started. The radio service thus became a key function in all illegal work. To mention two parallel and yet contrasting examples, taken from the intelligence work: In February 1942, the three German battleships, the "Scharnhorst", the "Gneisenau" and the "Prins Eugen", which had been kept back for months in Brest harbour, and had been the target for a number of British air raids, succeeded in breaking out of their enforced passivity and getting back to their German bases through the English Channel. Their departure was observed by a French intelligence man, who nevertheless was not able to get radio contact with London at the right moment, because at that time the radio telegraphist had no specially alloted time.[67] Exactly the opposite occurred in May 1941, when the "Bismarck" left anchorage in a Norwegian fjord to sail out into the Atlantic. Her passage through the Kattegat was announced by Danish observers and the departure from Norway had been observed and immediately announced over the radio to London by the SOE instructor Odd Starheim[68] – an announcement which started the hunt which ended a few days later in the sinking of the "Bismarck".

In certain situations, the presence of an illegal SOE telegraphist in the occupied area could influence both political and military developments.[69] In August 1943, the Italian General Guiseppe Castellano arrived secretly in Lisbon, for negotiations in the British Embassy with Allied representatives on an Italian armistice, and the wish of the Badoglio Government for powerful military Allied intervention in Italy and an Italian change-over to waging war on the side of the Allies. The negotiations, which were the introduction to the change in Italian policy, were led on the Allied side by the British General Kenneth Strong and the American General Bedell Smith, and gave mainly positive results. After these preliminary negotiations, however, a purely practical problem remained: how were Castellano and behind him the Badoglio Government, to maintain contact with the Allies during the coming weeks, for the final clarification of the complicated political and military situation? An attempt was made on the spot to instruct Castellano in the use of a radio transmitter, but the final solution was that the Italians set free an SOE telegraphist, Dick Mallaby, who was in prison in Milan, so that in the weeks that followed up to the landings in Salerno, he was responsible for all telegraphic communication between the Badoglio Government in Rome and the Allied headquarters in Algiers. "This was", writes Strong, "only one of the many occasions that I received help from SOE (and OSS) in Intelligence matters during the course of the War".

The transmitting set was one instrument. The code was another. However important it was that the transmitter should start working, it was just as important, naturally, that the messages should be incomprehensible to the enemy, even though he could always register the length and frequency of the messages, and with the use of direction finders often localise the transmitting place and time – all of it fundamental in combatting illegal radio traffic, but useless so long as the code was intact. In 1941, a war began in the ether, also in this field, which would be waged and would escalate as long as the Occupation lasted.

In wartime, technical development often accelerates considerably. The fight makes demands upon technical development which must be met, met quickly, and met before the enemy gets ahead. The British-American "Manhattan" project for the development of the atom bomb was one example of this, the development of radar was another, and the development of air navigation, with improved means for precise sighting of bomb targets a third. In the field of radio, developments were explosive, so explosive that one must keep in mind that conditions in 1940 were fundamentally different from those in 1945. In the field of technology, the course of the War was affected by a marked Anglo-Saxon lead over Germany, a lead which increased during the War, partly because both the military and political leaders of Great Britain and the U.S.A. were well aware of the importance of the technological and scientific possibilities. A well known physicist, Professor Lindemann, was a member of Winston Churchill's inner Staff of advisors, and the Anglo-

Saxon leaders were not limited in their views of technology by any form of dogma or ideology.[70]

In the German camp, things were different. Goebbels and to some extent Speer were aware of this, but they were powerless, in their admiration of and dependence upon Hitler's "intuitive" decisions. In May 1943, Goebbels could note the situation in his diary with resignation.[71] "Our technical development, both in the domain of submarines and that of air warfare are far behind the English and American. We now reap the reward for poor leadership of the scientific sector, which has not shown sufficient initiative to bring scientific men into collaboration with us. One cannot let an idiot[72] lead German science for years, without being punished for such folly".

The explosive developments in the field of radio had decisive effect on the situation we are considering – radio communications throughout Europe between the home front and the front abroad. Both as regards transmitters and codes, there were accelerating developments with increasingly improved equipment and more and more complicated code programmes, with built-in warning systems for the event of arrest or discovery of the code. Development in this realm, and preferably rapid development, soon showed itself to be necessary. The technique and personnel of 1940 were not adequate. Problems arose in great numbers in all the occupied countries, but first in France, when the first radio transmissions of French intelligence began in the first months of 1941. Several networks, with intelligence as their speciality, were then established, but their activity was naturally blocked to some extent, so long as they had no signals service, or so long as this was inadequate. The courier system mentioned was both unreliable and, particularly, slow, and could only bring over intelligence of a static character. In January 1941, the break-through began. Two British-built transmitters were successfully smuggled through Spain into France, and work was started immediately.[73] Just as immediately, however, difficulties arose. The transmitters were heavy and awkward to carry. They weighed about 30 kilo, they were about the size of a suitcase, and for these reasons they had been damaged during the long, primitive journey – quite apart from the damage which was often caused to later deliveries during dropping operations. The damage to the two transmitters in question could be repaired, however, and the first transmissions began after a week or two. Then new difficulties arose. First one component failed, and then another, and then difficulties arose in connexion with receiving transmissions, both in France and in England, on the frequencies chosen and during the sending times allotted. Security precautions demanded further dangerous moves to new transmitting points, and fresh damage occurred to the unwieldy and vulnerable sets. It was obvious at once that demands were being made in this field upon the British radio industry, both as to quality and quantity, but the problem was also that it was not only SOE and the affiliated organisations, but most important, the Army, Navy and Air Force who were making similar demands for continual improvements and deliveries, In addition, there was the demand for personnel, which radio connexions with many occupied countries must raise – technicians, telegraphists, code experts, etc. There was a long way to go, and many bottlenecks to pass before the Resistance Movements' signal service could become effective. Great Britain was not a magic box out of which every article desired could be conjured at a day's notice.

As the situation stood in the first months of 1941, Dewavrin, who was the first to be faced with the problem, decided to send a French radio specialist to France, so that he could get an idea on the spot of the character of the problem and what could be done to improve the situation, both on the short and long term. He chose a Captain of the French Engineers, Pierre Julitte, who was dropped "blind" in the unoccupied zone in May 1941, bringing a transmitter which he soon made to function.[74] He quickly made contact with a number of the existing networks, both in the unoccupied and the occupied zones, and his first reports contained a proposal that an independent radio organisation should be set up, independent of the Intelligence groups and other Resistance units, and attached to them through a fast-working courier system. His proposal met opposition in British circles, both from the point of view of security and on technical grounds, although these were not specified in detail. The British always had a horror of tendencies towards centralisation in the European Resistance world, and their ideal was a number of networks, screened from each other and with independent radio communication – an ideal which was somewhat unrealistic in 1941. As regards the technical objections, they probably served to cast a smoke screen over their inability to deliver, under the rain of demands for deliveries with which the radio industry was bombarded. Improvements in the equipment were in full progress and development, but it was not possible immediately to meet all the demands, however well founded they were. Radio transmissions from France and other occupied countries began, as far as circumstances permitted, but technique and organisation still left much to be desired.

In February 1942 Julitte returned to London, not as planned by fishing boat from Brittany with half a month's experience behind him, but through Spain, with more than six months experience at his back. It was now possible to make a thorough examination of the whole radio service, on the basis of fresh experience, and Julitte had plenty of opportunity to study the problems with the British authorities involved – SOE and SIS.[75] The difficulties and problems which Julitte could now put forward will be summed up briefly here. In the first place, smaller and lighter transmitting sets must be manufactured. Some progress towards this aim had been made in France, by separating the British sets into three components, current supply, receiver and transmitter. To British objections Julitte could show a rebuilt transmitter which he had brought back with him, of the size of a brick. Next, more sets must be made available. The problem was that the German direction finders were now extremely active, especially in the great cities, so that "safe" sending times were limited. They had therefore changed over to transmitting from distant places in the provinces, but German raids on the roads and railways made the transport of radio equipment dangerous, and for that reason alone it was vital that the size and weight of the sets be reduced, also to make camouflage easier. It was essential that the telegraphist should be provided with transport and guard personnel, so that he was not himself burdened with the risk of discovery during transport, but the transmitter was set up by others, after which the telegraphist took over the Morse key. It was also important that more transmitting places be found, so that transmissions were not made from the same house or locality twice running. This proposal could only be solved locally, but in 1941 it was difficult to solve because of people's fear of making transmitting points available. Next, more flexible transmitting systems must be found, so that the telegraphist could not only change location at regular intervals, but also frequencies, and have the possibility of choosing both frequencies and transmitting times. This demanded that detailed transmission plans be worked out. Julitte also critised the British home stations' procedure, particularly the demand for acknowledgement signals, which took up precious time, and this included criticism of the British telegraphists' efficiency. In addition, Julitte suggested that the British send code announcements "blind" to permanent listening teams, who could listen in without other risk than that generally connected with ordinary listening, and without compromising the actual illegal network with answering signals, etc.

Julitte's comments and criticisms were constructive, and contributed to considerable improvements, and they proved to be identical with criticisms reported from other occupied countries. This was the case in Denmark, where the radio engineer L. A. Duus Hansen, who in 1942 had helped to get the British sets dropped in Denmark into working order, and who had himself transmitted messages from the Danish Intelligence Officers, had a meeting in Stockholm with the local SOE representative in the summer 1943. His advice and suggestions were roughly speaking the same as Julitte's, but he went a step further in that he offered to construct a Danish transmitter, and teach Danich telegraphists the British code system. This suggestion was accepted, and almost at one stroke it revolutionized the radio service from Denmark.[76] Both out in the occupied areas and in Britain – with effect in Cairo – constant efforts were made to improve the radio service. Just as explosives and other sabotage material and weapons became more sophisticated and suited to the special needs of the Resistance groups, so were improved radio transmitters also taken into large-scale production, and this advance was noticeable from 1943. The transmitters became smaller, lighter, and easier to camouflage, their transmitting effect was increased, and transmitters were manufactured both for direct and alternating current, as well as being made for running on the accumulator of a motor car. The Danes changed over to automatic transmission, so that a telegraphist could record his telegrams on tape, after which whole series of telegrams could be played back at top speed and received on the Home station in London on a corresponding tape, and could later be replayed in slow tempo.[77] This method reduced transmission time and increased capacity to about ten times what was previously possible, sending up to 700 letters per minute. In favourable conditions, even better results were possible. From Copenhagen, where there was a free sighting to a sky scraper on the Swedish coast, an ultra-high frequency connexion functioned with a station on Swedish soil. Both stations were provided with transmitters and receivers, and automatic teleprinters for rapid telegrams, and they worked with direction antennae, so that transmissions could be screened against direction finders from land, and could only be localized from the sea, and only within an acute angle. In addition, a transmitter was set up in Sweden, so that signals received from Copenhagen could be transformed to long wave length and sent direct to England. The system was under remote control from Copenhagen, and the long wave length transmissions were naturally open to German direction finding, but only to the extent that it could be established that the station was situated in Sweden.

Technical expansion also involved organisational expansion. The ideal practice, which it was sought to arrange generally throughout the European Resistance, was for every telegraphist to have many transmitters at his disposal, and many transmitting points, so that he could often, and preferably always, change his field of operations. It was just as important that the telegraphist should have a group of helpers who could both transport the sets to and from the transmitting point, and also rig them, as well as serving as guards and warning teams. It was also important that a register be available of varying transmitting times and frequencies, and this with the time-consuming decoding work entailed considerable expansion of the personnel, adequate to the radio work, both out in the Field and particularly in London and in the Mediterranean Headquarters with their connexions with a considerable number of European countries. Added to all this, there were constant changes in code arrangements and signal plans. The difficulties increased when atmospheric conditions made transmitting difficult, and the telegrams arrived more or less distorted, at worst with such large gaps that the messages could not be deciphered. The difficulties were greatest for those transmitting, whereas reception was normally clear, because of the British stations powerful transmitting effect. Originally, as we have seen, it was the practice to demand acknowledgement of receipt of messages, but after a time a change was made to sending blind, with repetition of the transmission, so that one could be fairly certain that the code groups transmitted had been received. This was done to ease the burden of the telegraphist. It was he – or she – who was in danger.

There were naturally extreme poles in the long register of possibilities. First of all, there were the extremes of 1940 with meagre resources and lack of experience, as against 1945, with specialised equipment and a wealth of dear-bought experience. There were the extremes of a Captain Hudson, wandering in the mountains of Montenegro in 1941 with a transmitter weighing 30 kilos carried by mule, a day's journey too late, and the Copenhagen telegraphist Tage Fischer Holst in the spring 1945, who after battling for 1½ years with the German direction-finders, could now use automatic equipment, screened from the direction-finders, and helped by guards and with a special workshop at his back. Within this register from the primitive to the perfect, there lay every imaginable variety of situation, problem and solution. In Poland in 1941, there were the first attempts to get transmitters rigged up with the materials to hand, with a young Polish student as manufacturer, and without any previous acquaintance with the Morse key.[78] There was considerable anxiety connected with their first attempt to make contact, and this actually succeeded, when a courier from London came to Poland via Gibraltar, Cairo, Cyprus and Constantinople with the necessary codes, afterwards returning by the same route. Experienced radio amateurs were not to be found, as the Germans had immediately dissolved the Polish Radio Amateur Club, arrested all the members and sent them to concentration camps. The same year, a start was made in England of a special factory for producing small, light transmitters, which should be mechanically strong enough to withstand the impact on dropping. 400 transmitters and 300 receiving sets were sent to Poland,[79] the education programme of the exile Poles included training 75 telegraphists, and a special transmitting station in England gave a course for telegraphists in Poland, so that 300 Poles were trained in this way to join the radio work. Everywhere there were technical and organisational problems, but the final result was positive: a steadily increasing flood of telegrams out and in; no isolation, but soon daily routine communication, never without deadly danger for the telegraphist or the team of guards, but also never without the day to day contact which was the condition for their work. In favourable circumstances, the results were even better. In March 1945, when the R.A.F. bombed the German Gestapo Headquarters in Copenhagen, the report of the principal results had been received in London before the aircraft got back to base.

The technical and organisational expansion had its counterweight in a corresponding expansion of the direction-finders of the Axis Powers. All over Europe the Occupying Powers were working energetically to stop the illegal transmissions, and the direction-finding service was also developing rapidly, both as to technique and organisation. Both fixed and mobile direction-finding stations were used, and the Germans worked first to establish the transmitting frequency and then, by cross bearings, to localize the transmitting point and if possible to find out the telegraphist's time table. Where a telegraphist had to use the same place several times, he was in danger, and had instructions, if the worst occurred, to swallow a cyanide pill. The loss of a telegraphist was a human tragedy. But the disclosure under torture of his code and signal plans could develop into a catastrophe, as occurred in Holland during the "England game".[80]

It must first be emphasized, however, that the conditions for radio transmission and direction-finding were very different in the various parts of Europe. In large, inaccessible mountain districts, in very thinly populated areas, and of course in the actual partisan regions, these conditions did not exist. From there transmissions could be sent without much risk of immediate intervention by the Occupying Powers. The latter could register the fact of the transmission, and its length, but could not prevent it. Before the sabotage of the heavy water factory Vemork in Norway, the telegraphist Einar Skinnarland was dropped on Hardangervidden, near the factory, from where he maintained the radio communication which led to the sabotage.[81] After its completion, he remained in the wilds and continued radio transmission. The Germans combed the eastern part of Hardangervidden, using 2,800 men, without finding him or two of his sabotage comrades, and continued transmissions made a further sabotage action possible, as well as several dropping operations. The direction-finders were a problem in densely built up areas, and particularly in towns, when intense cross beam work could reduce transmitting time to a few minutes, or at a place which had been localized to less than one minute.[82] Distance and atmospheric conditions could also cause their own difficulties, however, so that even large areas liberated by the partisans could pose difficulties for the telegraphists to combat.

All in all, it can be established that the quantity of telegrams increased steadily from 1941–45, and that the stream of telegrams from all the occupied countries swelled from month to month. In general, in spite of considerable teething troubles, telegraphists were sent as required, and as the illegal activity increased, so did the number of telegrams. There was a clear connexion between activity and radio transmission, in that as a rule a radio contact was the condition for great activity, whilst contrariwise, increased activity called for an increase in the number of telegrams. The balance between the two factors naturally could not always be established in the most favourable sense. Telegrams could pile up, and important information could be overlooked, and it could happen that a cancellation from one part or the other could come too late, for example when an aircraft started for some reception point which was not ready for the dropping; or often the opposite was the case, and a reception team turned out to the reception point, where the fly-in could not take place owing to sudden fog, etc. Intelligence, too, could disappear in the welter of information. But on the long perspective, this connexion is quite clear. Of approximately 7,000 instructors sent to the Continent by SOE alone,[83] there were many hundred telegraphists, for example about 100 in France, where the number of telegrams sent in April 1944 amounted to about 2,600, while in May 1944 before the Invasion, the figure had risen to about 3,700, after which it rose further. Immediately before the Invasion on 6 June, almost 6,000 reports came in per day from French territory.[84] In Poland, there were periodically 100 stations working, and the illegally established stations here maintained contact between the various districts, with London as relay station.[85] In comparison it can be mentioned that about 45 telegraphists established themselves in Holland in the period from the autumn 1943 to September 1944, out of a total of instructors of about 100;[86] that the number of radio stations in Norway rose from 2 in 1940 to 69 in May 1945.[87] Thanks to automatic transmission, and the special transmission via the relay station in Sweden, Denmark was in an exceptional position. Here the number of telegraphists was only 15, but the number of telegrams was relatively large, calculated as about 10,000 telegrams during the period May 1944 to May 1945, or slightly over 100,000 groups of letters.[88] As regards the Balkans and later also North Italy, there was continuous contact from 1943–44, generally speaking as required.

Figures given in a necessarily confused hotch-potch of telegraphists, telegrams, groups of letters, reports received, etc. can only produce quantities which cannot be related to each other. A telegram could be anything from a short operational message of 20 letters to a political statement of over 2000 letters – these examples are from Denmark. The British General R. H. Barry, who served for a long period as Chief of Staff in SOE, and as planning chief and liaison of the organisation to the regular military forces, has summed up SOE's radio traffic in a statement that this reached an output of two million words per week, that it demanded the development of special equipment, procurement and distribution of frequencies, preparation of signal plans and the construction and manning of receiving stations on a very large scale.[89]

The problem was the same everywhere. Radio contact was difficult. If it failed, the possibilities for co-operation between the fronts at home and abroad failed with it. When, in the autumn 1943, after consultations with Tito, Brigadier Fitzroy MacLean reached the Dalmatian island of Korcula after days' marches through the enemy lines, and with partisan escort, with the object of arranging weapon deliveries to part of the Dalmatian coast which was in the hands of the partisans at the time, all possibilities broke down, because the radio set he had with him suddenly refused to work.[90] Only a few months later, however, there were scores of radio telegraphists posted everywhere with the district leaders of the partisan movement, as well as in Tito's Headquarters, and much more than the extensive weapon deliveries now became possible. With direct radio contact, tactical air support could be given to the partisan operations, and an increasing number of signals with political content were sent through. The number of instructors sent to Greece gradually increased to about 1100, in 48 Allied Missions, all with radio contact.[91] A corresponding number of Allied Missions, also with radio contact, were at work in North Italy in the spring 1945.[92]

The radio service became decisive for the supply possibilities and for the whole co-operation between the Resistance organisations and the Allied organisations and commands. Illegal transmitters therefore became instruments of political importance, also. One could stop the stream of telegrams and with it the supplies, or one could control who telegraphed to whom and what the correspondance contained. One could use persuasion as to the despatch or formulation of a telegram, or one could advise against or perhaps refuse its dispatch. One could support a telegram with recommendations or one could do the opposite. The majority of the Resistance Movements were home grown, and had a strong urge to show their independence, but with the increasing co-operation, they were all dependent upon the attitude of the Allies, and it was generally the Allied Missions who controlled the radio traffic. The partisans in the Soviet Union, EAM and EDES, in Greece, to some extent Tito, CNLAI in North Italy, all exile governments and their home forces, and the Resistance Movement without a government – Denmark – they were all more or less dependent upon directives, instructions, advice and often pressure from outside. At the same time, however, the Allies often met a political will in the European Resistance Movement which far from always harmonised with their or the exile governments' ideas of what would be the desirable development in the various countries when the Liberation came. A good many of the political dialogues which ensued between the fronts at home and abroad were directly or indirectly channeled over the radio network or other lines of communication, in and with which SOE's various Chiefs of Missions had insight or control. If one excepts the Soviet Union, where there was no ideological/political division between the ideas on each side of the front, and keeps to the SOE/SO alone, and the connexions of its organisations with the many Resistance Movements whose contacts with the outside world they came largely to manage, in some places and at times with a monopoly, another circumstance appears quite clearly. These missions and the Chiefs of Missions gradually, and in an unforeseen degree, were to influence the political decisions of the Western Powers, by their reports and actions. The British author, Patrick Howarth, has expressed this situation with the words:[93] "As the end of the War drew near . . . the political responsibilities of individual SOE officers increased greatly. Young men, who in some cases had originally been dispatched to occupied territories primarily as instructors in elementary forms of demolition, suddenly acquired consular or even ambassadorial responsibilities without either diplomatic experience or diplomatic amenities. In meeting these responsibilities they too, in the overwhelming majority of cases, showed the flexibility and adaptability which accounted for so much of the success of the whole organisation. In the twentieth century – in Britain at least – the influence of the young in public affairs has seldom been strong, but the operations of SOE provided an exception to this prevailing rule . . . They . . . were of an age which might have qualified them for important military and naval tasks under the younger Pitt, but which in most walks of life today would be considered appropriate only for a junior executive under instruction".

His words refer directly to MacLean, F. W. Deakin and C. M. Woodhouse. Of these, MacLean was the eldest. He was 32 when he was dropped in Yugoslavia. But they could have referred to many others. On grounds of physique alone, SOE instructors were young, and as Howarth pointed out, they were sent out primarily to fulfil a military task, but often met a political one. In the very complicated political situation which existed in many places in the European Resistance world, they became the experts, and they were therefore often the natural advisors to their respective government organs, often in disregard of traditional considerations and decision-making bodies.

Their control of communication became one of their instruments.

The price for maintaining the radio service was high. There can hardly have been any other Resistance group which ran relatively higher risks than the telegraphists. Out of the 100 French telegraphists mentioned, about 33 % were arrested, 6 were killed, 12 were wounded and several chose death at their transmitters. It was calculated in France that the average "lifetime" of a telegraphist was 6 months.[94] In Holland the same "lifetime" was calculated for working telegraphists. 17 lost their lives.[95] The telegraphists ran the extra risk that in the event of arrest they could be sure of severe cross-examination and torture in the attempt to force them to transmit on German orders. Their loophole was either the arrangement mentioned, with the Home station, by which an agreed mistake was inserted in the first group of letters – the security check which was overlooked during the "England game" – or the security contained in the fact that the teams at the Home station knew the individual telegraphist's "key-writing" and could therefore check as to whether the transmitter was actually being used by the telegraphist in question, and not by some outsider. It was possible to identify such "key.writing" with the same certainty as one can identify ordinary hand-writing, and therefore before a telegraphist was sent to the Field, samples of his telegraphic "key-writing" were always taken for identification checks.[96] It was only in Denmark, and by agreement with Duus Hansen that this practice was not followed, and only after many months' experience had established the certainty of his and his colleagues reliability.

It is clear that the radio service became important first of all when there was a question of urgent messages, and all messages which could be given in brief, with the use of the code arrangements. It was therefore decisive for the intelligence work, for arrangements regarding deliveries of weapons and for directives back and forth between the instructors sent to the Field and their home organisations. Discussions of more comprehensive character went mostly by the courier route during the first years, but as the radio service gradually became more reliable, telegrams were also used for detailed discussions on both political and operative questions. In many cases the teams of the radio service used closed telephone systems,[97] so that telegrams received in one part of the country could be forewarded to another district, and telegraphed arrangements could naturally also be sent on through the internal courier network. Where this last method had to by used, however, speed declined.

There were two instruments belonging to the radiophonic realm[98] which were used in the interplay between the outside fronts and the Resistance Movements. One of these was the "S" phone, a device used during dropping operations, which at relatively short distances enabled the reception team to converse with the aircraft flying in, so that the latter even in unfavourable weather conditions could be led straight to the reception point and be able to carry out successful droppings. Another device, even better adapted to this purpose was the "Eureka", an easily transportable combined wireless ultra-high frequency transmitter and receiver, which made it possible for the reception to maintain contact with the approaching aircraft during the fly-in, with very little danger from enemy direction-finders. Even in foggy weather, it was possible to lead the aircraft to the reception point, and with the aid of an "S" phone make sure that it was the right aircraft, before lighting the lamps on the point. The Eurekas were not only valuable at the points where they were functioning, however. Pilots making for other places in the area, or on their way to bombing raids could come in on the beam and use the Eureka for general orientation. The aircraft was equipped with the corresponding receiver to the Eureka, the "Rebecca", and the interplay between these two made it possible for the pilot to navigate with great accuracy, as the Rebecca could catch the Eureka signals at a distance of about 100 kilometres, and set course with a margin of a few metres. If several Eurekas were working they could be used by the pilots to take cross bearings. These Eurekas were therefore not only used during dropping operations, and not only as mobile equipment. Fixed Eureka stations were established, which the Western Allied pilots used for navigation during bombing raids and mine dropping over enemy territory. "S" phones and Eurekas were taken into use from 1943 onwards, but unfortunately their value was not sufficiently understood by many reception teams, who simply found these devices unwieldy and therefore failed to use them. But where they were used systematically they were of the utmost value. It is typical that a great many of the telegrams extant from the correspondance between London and Jutland, where three permanent Eureka stations were working from the autumn 1944, are on the subject of the functioning of the Eureka stations. Single instructions, many expressions of thanks to the operators, and now and then anxious enquiries, in cases where the stations were either not functioning or where there was atmospheric interference.

In a great many fields, then, the radio became one of the technical means which contributed to making possible the technical and political Resistance developments which characterized Europe during the Second World War. In 1940, one experimented with carrier pigeons;[99] in 1943 one seriously considered sending an aircraft in over Denmark simply to take up the signals from an "S" phone on the ground; and a year later, the Home station was receiving two million words per week. If one estimated a word as having an average length of six letters, this makes twelve million letters. They all had to be decoded. How many were sent from the Home station we do not know, but they were many, and they gave the Resistance organisations an enormous amount of work. In primitive conditions, the teams had first to put their own messages into code, and then decode the messages received. A Jutland Reception Chief, Anton Toldstrup, has given a close-up of conditions. In the winter 1944–45 he had about 200 reception points working, and received and sent on men and material from about 220 dropping operations.[100] "Anyone who is not familiar with the way in which coding and deciphering is done", he writes, "will find it difficult to imagine the enormous work connected with this. Sometimes all the office staff was in full swing, coding and deciphering, and could sit bent over this work for hours. When one considers that the fixed sending and receiving times had to be strictly adhered to, one can perhaps form some idea of the hunted atmosphere which sometimes held sway at Headquarters". The expression "Headquarters" can sound bureaucratic. It was a question of about ten persons, with a maximum stay at one place: 15 days! Those were the conditions here. They were worse in other places.

6. Paramilitary Forms of Action

Sabotage

The tasks which presented themselves to the Resistance Movements of the various occupied countries were bound to vary considerably. Geographical factors played a part, the economic and political structure of each country played a part, and lastly their changing position in the joint strategic whole played a part. What was possible and feasible in one country could be impossible and pointless in another. The time factor, also, had its effect. What was impossible or inexpedient in 1940 could be possible and expedient in 1943 or 1944. Circumstances changed in the course of a few years. War conditions changed, public opinion changed or stiffened, and organisations came into being which could both make fairly exact plans for the Resistance work, and create the conditions for their becoming realisable. Psychological mobilisation, the creation of groups, the establishment of channels of communication and the setting up of Intelligence networks were obvious tasks, but the forms of action which were then taken into use must necessarily vary. What became an extremely important question in one country could be a relatively unimportant Resistance question in another. In the occupied regions of the Soviet Union and in Yugoslavia, Albania and to some extent in Greece, the partisan war quickly became the all-important function, whilst the illegal Press, the communications service, the intelligence service, the procurement of weapons etc. became auxiliary functions. These functions, however, coupled with demonstrations, protests, strikes and passive resistance could be the most important in countries and areas which were unsuitable for the partisan warfare which became the severest form of fighting resistance. In countries like Poland, France, North Italy, a spasmodic movement can be registered towards partisan war and a general popular rising as the final function in the Resistance struggle, whilst other Resistance activities, including sabotage, were important but parallel functions on the way to this final aim. Similar tendencies can be registered in the cases of Norway and Belgium. Small, densely populated, urbanized countries such as Holland and Denmark never reached the partisan level, although here too, tendencies and ambitions in this direction can be registered. Cutting across all the differences, however, there was one weapon which was common to all Resistance Movements regardless of the limits which circumstances imposed upon their operations. This weapon was sabotage.

At the outbreak of the War in 1939, as mentioned previously,[1] sabotage was known of old as an idea, but not as a general, widespread phenomenon. Up to 1939, sabotage had been used sporadically, and at random. During the Second World War, however, sabotage became systematized and made effective with the use of new technical means and well developed sabotage organisations. In addition, during this four to five year period, sabotage was developed with expert support from abroad, as an integral part of a unified strategic plan, in which it had its place as a supplement. Sabotage must be considered as such, during the Second World War. Its rôle was not to bring about any form of decision in the struggle, but to contribute in various ways to its outcome. For the individual saboteur, sabotage was a primary task, but in the wider context sabotage received only a secondary, although far from unimportant, rôle.

A simple, uncomplicated explanation can hardly be given of the striking fact, that sabotage developed almost at a stroke into such a decisive factor, that from being an idea which was relatively distant or even unknown for most people, it became an everyday phenomenon with which practically everyone was to become familiar. One material reason is probably to be found in the violent polarisation which the Occupation generally and the policy and ideology of the Axis Powers particularly entailed. But a contributory reason was probably also that the course of the War in the years 1939–41 was such that vast regions were overrun at lightning speed, and that millions of people, who either were already or became hostile to the Axis Powers because of their aggression, suddenly and unexpectedly found themselves robbed of the traditional military possibilities for fighting the enemy. The alternatives were therefore submission, passive resistance or active resistance, and for those who chose the last – and they were many – there was only one possibility left: to fight the enemy on home soil. If geographical conditions did not allow for the more militant possibility of waging partisan war, sabotage was the obvious course. An action which was normally regarded as criminal acquired greater respectability in an astonishingly short time, because sabotage was aimed at objectives which, although they were really the property of fellow-countrymen, had become property which the enemy either partially or wholly made use of or expropriated.

A quite decisive factor, however, was the fact that not only strong appeals came from abroad, to use the sabotage weapon and develop it systematically as circumstances permitted, but also the instructions and tools which made it possible for sabotage to become an effective weapon. Appeals of this character came both from London and Moscow – most unequivocally from Moscow, although not before June 1941. For the Communists in the occupied countries, the period 1939–41, during which the German-Soviet Pact was in force, was a period of considerable difficulty. On the one hand there was the official slogan that this was an imperialistic war, and that German-Soviet co-operation existed. On the other hand there was rooted Communist hostility towards all Fascism – German, Italian or collaborational. That many Communist leaders and rank and file members were aware of the tactical character of the pact and prepared for the fight against the Fascist Occupying Powers is both obvious and a documented fact. The call to them to fight came in June 1941.

For the Soviet Union, the problem from then on was uncomplicated, and the directives unqualified. From the moment of the German aggression against the Soviet Union, the call to fellow countrymen and to Communists all over Europe was clear and unambiguous: the greatest possible Partisan activity, and with it sabotage activity, as soon as possible and as effectively as possible, disregarding all considerations but that of injuring the enemy to the utmost. Every obstacle, however small, which could be put in the way of the aggressors, was of value, and all could and should contribute according to their possibilities[2] – workers, peasants, office workers, store personnel, intellectuals, young and old, men and women, even prisoners of war and workers in Germany conscripted by force. The call to all was perfectly clear. Only one example need be given:[3] "Comrade workers, intensify sabotage against the enemy's production, destroy his machines. Set fire to his factories, form groups of saboteurs. Railway workers, with every means put obstacles in the way of trains with deportees, systematically put coaches and engines out of action, get trains derailed and railway bridges blown up". The French Communist Press was full of directives. Peasants were called upon by every means to hinder or at least delay compulsory deliveries, in cases of necessity only to deliver inedible cattle, to butcher for the local population, to hinder control and evade the rules, and lastly to hide and procure food for all who avoided conscription or for other reasons sought refuge in the country districts. As far as office staffs were concerned the task was to sabotage all administrative measures, destroy registers, produce false identity cards and ration cards, and for all intellectuals it was to refuse all co-operation with the enemy. If one could not carry out sabotage direct, one could refuse all co-operation and contribute to paralysing society. It was a Communist duty to help the Soviet Union in its struggle with all means which might be available. The calls from Moscow were made first of all directly to the partisans in the Soviet Union, but they were also addressed to Communists in the rest of Europe, who were cast at a day's notice into illegality, and whose only chance of personal and party survival was in the immediate struggle, regardless of normal consideration to persons or society, but not regardless of tactical considerations as to method, forms of action and tempo. What had begun as an "imperialistic war" became a righteous war for the peoples' freedom, and the attitude to the Western Powers was altered in consequence of their alliance with the Soviet Union. Bombing raids from the West, with inevitable loss of life, must be borne, and sabotage must take place on the same footing as bombing. Fernand Grenier, the representative of the French Communist Party among the leaders of de Gaulle's Free French Forces, could express the same thought to a British journalist in the words:[4] "What is the purpose of the R.A.F.'s attacks on our railways? Should what is permitted your pilots be forbidden our patriots"? Here and in general, references to the fact that sabotage could lead to reprisals were waved aside, and the Communist Press turned fiercely against any soft considerations as to risks, legality or normality. Sabotage did not only injure the Occupying Power materially, it could also contribute to arousing popular reaction of great breadth and strength, possibly for the very reason that it led to reprisals. Countering the view that premature actions could not only bring unfavourable psychological reaction, but also lead to arrests and round-ups which might injure the work of building up hard-hitting organisations which were to stand ready, when the strategic situation allowed for a mass uprising, the Communists' argument was the reverse: immediate action was the condition for the organisations to acquire the breadth and strength which raised hard-hitting organisations, ready for and trained in action. Quite apart from the military value of these actions, they could contribute to arousing feeling and a mass movement which in themselves offered a certain security. If sufficiently many went into action in one way or another, the mass movement would make counter-measures difficult, and it was a mass movement that the Communists aimed at. Thus the Communist action theory had not only a political touch. It was the expression of a political decision and standpoint.

The call from Moscow, then, was unequivocal, and the reply from the European Communists equally unequivocal.[5] They would help the Soviet Union in the struggle with every means available. In this way they also helped the collective Allied struggle, and hastened the moment when the occupied peoples could achieve the liberation they longed for.

It goes without saying that sabotage must become an obvious part of the partisan war which blazed up in East and South-East Europe. This must especially be the case in the occupied areas of the Soviet Union, where sabotage could be a supplement, either through the implementation of the "scorched earth" policy, or as a decisive means against the attempts of the Occupying Power to rebuild the transport and production machinery in the conquered areas. Even though the most important duty of the partisans was direct attack against the rearguards of the enemy and the occupation troops – and as opportunity offered, the periodical liberation of whole districts and the attempt to restore Soviet rule – the destruction of the enemy's transport system was naturally also one of the duties of the partisan units. Derailing trains, removing lengths of railway track, blowing up bridges, mining roads, cutting telegraph and telephone wires, attacking depots and aerodromes and blasting enemy material – all this was obviously included among the gains of the partisan war.

Appeals for all forms of resistance, as well as appeals for the use of sabotage were also broadcast from London. For Great Britain and therefore for SOE, the problem was far more complicated and less obvious. First of all, SOE had to deal with a great many foreign countries, each of them with its own special situation. The Occupation was common to them all, and they were all represented vis-à-vis Great Britain by exile governments, national committees or national councils. But apart from this they were very different from each other as to geographical, linguistic, political and social conditions. Great Britain and SOE were not appealing to fellow-countrymen, or to comrades in the Party, but to peoples whose attitudes included every possible variety of political, religious or other ideological character. From London there was no possibility for issuing simple, unequivocal calls and depending upon their being followed. Calls had to be adjusted pragmatically, according to experience gained of the development of public opinion in the different countries, and help had to be adapted to situations and standpoints which were in constant flux. Added to the complications arising from this, there was a fundamental dualism in the British view of the desirability, and to some extent the character of the European Resistance it was the intention to support – a dualism which made itself felt throughout the political and military hierarchy in Great Britain.

On the one hand, there was a desire – first of all, in SOE, PWE and the many forces and persons in the British hierarchy who believed in the possibilities of resistance – for Resistance Movements to arise throughout Europe, which could contribute in many ways including sabotage, to weakening the enemy and supporting the British conduct of the War, and British help to such Resistance Movements had been incorporated in the general strategic programme.[6] On the other hand, the decision could give cause for uneasiness, politically, at the possibility that a revolutionary movement was being animated, which could get out of control. Anxiety of this kind naturally arose in the Foreign Office, which must be a conservative factor by the very nature of its work, honouring obligations to pre-war governments and political conditions. But similar anxieties were felt among the many varied exile governments, where and when political resistance developments at home diverged from the objectives and interests of these exile governments. Among the British military staffs, scepticism could also make itself felt as to SOE and its operations, and matters were not made any easier by the fact that even very highly placed military staffs, owing to the very thoroughgoing secrecy surrounding SOE's work, for a long time could be strangely ignorant as to the character and perspectives of this work.[7]

It became the task of SOE to find a balance between the desirable and the undesirable. From the perspective of the War, the greatest possible disturbance behind the enemy lines was desirable, with demonstrations, protests, strikes and naturally also sabotage, as well as all forms of militant action, not only because such developments would weaken the enemy and contribute to diffusing their watchfulness and their strength, but also on purely political and psychological grounds, as the proof that the peoples of the occupied countries hoped for the liberation which Great Britain had proclaimed as her central war aim, and that they were themselves prepared to make sacrifices in their own cause. The effect on morale could be just as depressing for the Axis Powers as it was stimulating for the peoples of the Commonwealth, quite apart from the concrete results which could be expected. This was the basic concept of the founders and leaders of SOE, and on this background, the primary questions for SOE were technical and tactical, particularly the question of the right time or the right times for the desired activities to be set in motion.

Premature, unco-ordinated actions would be of little value, and they could also give repercussions.

Here too, the dualism appeared in the definition of SOE's tasks. As already stated, SOE was created either to foster or feed European Resistance organisations,[8] so that both on the short and the long term these could support the British conduct of the war. On the short term, this should be done by undermining the Axis Powers' mastery by passive resistance, propaganda, intelligence, strikes and sabotage, etc.; on the long term it could be done by building up and supplying weapons to underground armies, which could rise at the British return to the Continent, according to a plan and tempo to be fitted into the British strategy and adapted to the possibilities of the military situation. In reality, a serious contradiction was built into this objective. SOE should on the one hand animate and support immediate activity, particularly sabotage, whilst on the other hand SOE must beware that this activity did not develop in such a way that the long term task – the formation of underground armies – would be endangered. The danger was of inevitable arrests, round-ups and reprisals, which followed every escalation of activity, and it existed whenever and wherever activity threatened to develop into mass uprising, at times or places where Great Britain, and later Great Britain and the United States were unable to intervene at once. As long as no Second Front existed in Western Europe, so long were the possibilities absent for co-ordinating Resistance risings according to these ideal concepts, and so long did SOE suffer from the strategically motivated demand both to force the pace of Resistance developments, and at the same time hold back the urge for resistance. As far as Yugoslavia was concerned, SOE was faced with a *fait accompli*, since Tito waged war without reference to the strategic ideas of the Western Powers, as to the rôle of the Resistance Movements. Here SOE, and therefore the British High Command in the Mediterranean, as well as the governments of the Western Powers, adjusted themselves, although after some delay, and during the Warsaw uprising they were faced with a similar *fait accompli* and tried to help as far as they could. But in Greece, North Italy, West and North Europe, the British and later the British and Americans held fast to the underlying concept that Resistance actions should as far as possible be co-ordinated with the strategy of the Western Powers, because their maximum effect would be obtained in that way. Sabotage was welcome and was supported with instructors and explosives, dropped by parachute, but the supply of arms to the underground armies was decided according to the moment where it was judged opportune that they should be sent into action, and directives to them were to this effect.

Where, therefore, the appeals from Moscow for immediate action and unlimited sabotage rested upon a concrete and unchangeable doctrine, appeals from London were adapted in consideration to the many conditions, including the time factor and the varying possibilities which the times and therefore the development of the War involved. As regards sabotage, appeals were not made for this until London had tested the feeling in the various countries, and was convinced that the time was ripe.

In this question alone, as to the right actions at the right moment, there was a wide margin for every point of view, and decisions had not only to be adapted to the individual countries and to the resources in men and materiel available to SOE at any given moment. SOE was far from being autonomous, and was by no means free to make independent arrangements. Apart from the considerations as to British policies in general and to the exile governments, SOE was dependent upon various military chiefs who were often sceptical of SOE's visions. All SOE activity depended upon its leaders being able to convince them of the realism behind these visions. SOE's Chief of Staff, General R. H. Barry, has indicated this dependence with the words:[9] "It is necessary, however, to remember a number of factors which we in SOE had to take into account and wrestle with. Personnel, equipment of all kinds and methods of transport, particularly aircraft, were desperately short. We had to make a case for every man, every Sten gun and every aircraft sortie against the requirements of the normal Services who could at all times produce powerful arguments that they were more directly concerned with operations and were, quite naturally, sceptical of the contribution we could make until some proof of success was forthcoming, a proof which we could not furnish without the necessary equipment and facilities".

This was SOE's vicious circle. In pocket edition, and far out on the periphery, we meet the problem in Denmark, where, in the spring 1943, the Chief of the Danish Section of SOE asked the SOE leader in Denmark to send in lists of sabotage actions, couched in such terms that it was clear which of them had been carried out under the direct auspices of SOE, which were carried out by groups connected with SOE, and which had no relation to SOE.[10] The object was plain enough. SOE had to fight for its share of the necessary resources, and the Danish Section had its own fight for a share of the share.

These were not all the considerations with which SOE had to contend. The organisation had to operate with the greatest possible regard to the plans and expectations of the Resistance organisations, and even though SOE aimed in principle at activity directed by London, adjusted to the immediate tactical and strategic needs of the Allies, in actual fact, it had largely to leave it to the Resistance organisations themselves to direct developments in the various countries. The tendency here was that the stronger the Resistance organisations became, the more they demanded the right to decide on the framework of their activities. This tendency was intensified concurrently with the growing self-confidence of the Resistance Movements and with the efforts towards centralisation which made themselves felt in most of the occupied countries. Here a conflict arose which was actually unsolvable, since SOE had no possibility of divulging the strategic plans behind the organisation's directives and arrangements, and contrariwise, London could find it difficult to assess the possibilities of the Resistance. Members of the Resistance very often felt that they received too little support, or that the character of the support did not harmonise with their ambitions.

Generally speaking it can be stated that these ambitions did not only come up to the original SOE visions – they went far beyond the expectations of the creators of SOE. This is clear, if for no other reason, from the fact that SOE was created on the underlying hypothesis that Resistance Movements would probably develop, but it was impossible to foresee whether this would occur, and if it did, to what an extent. That it would occur everywhere, and that mass movements would arise in Europe, even the greatest optimist could not have counted upon in July 1940. No matter how much SOE expanded its activities, and this took place to a greater extent that had been imagined, particularly after the merger with OSS, the two organisations never reached the level of the demands made by rapidly expanding organisations throughout the whole occupied European continent.

A contributing cause for this has been mentioned: the fact that the regular military staffs in the West – in spite of the contributions of the occupied countries in the form of intelligence service, disturbances and strikes, and in spite of an unbroken chain of tens thousands of sabotage actions and other Resistance operations – never fully acknowledged, and were slow to acknowledge even partially, the value of the European Resistance.

Acknowledgement did gradually increase, however, and from the autumn 1943 when the dimensions of the Yugoslav Resistance struggle became evident, and it was obvious that it constituted a major contribution on the Mediterranean Front, and even more in 1944, when the

French, North Italian and Belgian Resistance struggles could point to indisputable results, understanding of the importance of the Resistance became more wide-spread, but up to then SOE had to fight its way through considerable scepticism. In this respect, there was a clear difference between the importance which the Soviet authorities attributed, first to the partisan war on Russian soil, and later to Resistance activity in the rest of Europe, and the recognition of importance which the many countries which co-operated with the Western Powers could count upon receiving. Considering the Soviet Union was only able to give material support outside its own frontiers at a very late stage, and that the great majority of the European countries therefore had to seek help from the west and south, this imposed a limit on the fighting possibilities of the Resistance organisations. These were never tested to the full.

An explanation of the fact that officers in the regular staffs found it difficult to free themselves from traditional thinking, and that they – or many of them – felt a certain aversion to the thought of irregular warfare, lies naturally in their training, which had only included manoeuvres and operations with regular units under normal command. But it can also be explained by the fact that resistance and its effects were naturally unknown quantities – seen from without. No matter how many proofs gradually piled up of the possibilities of the Resistance, in the concrete situations there was always a considerable difference between what the military leaders had under their direct command and control, and the unknown and anonymous quantities which might or might not be made to operate behind the front lines. In planning great, decisive operations, the Army Chiefs had of necessity to operate with known quantities, and forces whose effectiveness they could approximately calculate, because they knew their armaments and training, and because they could, from above, fix the times and places for their engagement. They had no corresponding knowledge or control of the Resistance forces, which must naturally be heterogenous in their composition, training and weapons, so that their engagement could turn out to be on a higher or lower level than that expected. It is not only understandable, it was inevitable that the responsible Army Chiefs had first of all to plan and lead their operations on the basis of concrete knowledge of and absolute control over specific forces. It may be added, however, that the closer the communications between the Staffs on the regular Front and staffs on the Resistance front became, the more the possibilities improved for calculating the possibilities which Resistance activities might offer, as a welcome supplement to military operations. Another element of uncertainty showed itself in the political deliberations as to what unrest, strikes, sabotage and possible revolutionary uprisings in the Axis areas would end in, politically. There were also divergencies of opinion in the Western Allied camp on this question, as well as a constant wish for control of Resistance Movements which quite openly declined any control, regardless of whether it originated with exile representatives or with the executive bodies of the Western Powers.

It may also be added that understanding for the important contribution which the activities of the Resistance could make to the War was greater in Great Britain than in the United States. Thanks to their far greater resources in men and material, the U.S.A. was in a better position than Great Britain to ignore the support which the Resistance Movements could give, both in the preparatory stages and in the final battles, and this meant that the U.S.A. had a less differentiated and more frontal view of the conduct of the war than Great Britain. The drain on manpower in the Royal Navy and the Merchant Navy, and the bitter experience of the trench warfare of the First World War must force the British leaders to search the horizon for forces which could ease the fight and the planned final offensive. Even with the help of the forces of the Commonwealth, Great Britain could never mobilise armies which could measure up in numbers to the great armies of the Axis Powers. And SOE and the whole British concept of co-operation with European auxiliary forces had their beginnings when Great Britain stood hopelessly alone, and co-operation with the U.S.A. was still a hope without any certainty. The distance between the British and American views changed gradually, however. And here both military experience and political considerations had their effect. From the time of the Western Allies' landings in French Northwest Africa in November 1942, the U.S.A. came to realise the difference between operating in a free, pro-Allied country and enemy country.[11] Experience here, and later in Italy and France, contributed to sharpening the American military chiefs' understanding of the important contribution which European auxiliary forces could make. Contrariwise, developments led to the situation where British leaders showed a tendency towards increasing anxiety at the obvious political influence of the Resistance Movements, whereas the American leaders did not feel the same uneasiness on the subject. It was noticeable that one of the Western Allies – Great Britain – was closer to the European situation and possessed greater interests in a stable, and as far as possible a reconstructed Europe, than the other more distant Western Ally, the U.S.A. In this respect, the exile representatives' viewpoints also constituted factors which must affect the British standpoints more strongly than the American.

Within the framework laid down for SOE's – and SOE/SO's – activities, there could also arise conflicting opinions as to proper methods and proper timing. These differences could have their roots in SOE itself, for it was far from being a homogenous staff with a final fixed doctrine as to conduct behind it, but on the contrary was a group of persons gathered *ad hoc* from many professions and with varied opinions as to how the changing situations could best help the organisation to carry out its missions. The staff was composed of many individualists, and the work was done with many changes of organisation, so that, particularly at the beginning, there was abundant scope for multifarious influences. There was never any question of a streamlined organisation with a fixed framework and consistent leadership.[12] This was out of the question, because of the hypothetical nature of SOE's beginnings, if for no other reason. What would ones agents meet, out on the Continent? How should one react in country after country, to what one met? How would parallel organs react to SOE's recommendations and requests? How far did SOE's importance go? Since this was the situation, and since SOE had to adapt its activities with respect to the resources available, to political situations, to psychological climates within the spheres of the organisation's activity, to advice and wishes which poured in from a great many Resistance organisations in a great many countries, discussions and conflicts must inevitably arise as to what was expedient in a given situation, and what was not. On the one hand there was a desire for immediate action – and until the invasion battles began this meant primarily intensified intelligence service and wide-spread sabotage – and on the other hand there was the concept of more long-term planning with the purpose of organising underground armies, which could be sent into action in co-ordination with the attacking Allied Armies, during an advance which so to speak rolled out stage by stage, according to the direction and strength of the attacks. If one wanted immediate action, the solution must be calls for concrete efforts and quick deliveries of supplies. If one wanted long-term planning, the solution must be calls for careful building up over a wide range, and deliveries at the right moment, that is when the supporting effort was desired. Too early deliveries of materiel for which there was no immediate need could only mean that there was a danger that the materiel fell into enemy hands, and too widespread a build-up could involve the danger of round-ups. The unfortunate part of it was that both these wishes were entertained, and the result was a dilemma which entailed many compromises. The calls came, for sabotage and particularly sabotage which could support the Allies as directly as possible, for example as a supplement to the Western Powers' strategic bombing, but at the same time, in agreement with various exile representatives, the brakes were applied to some extent to developments.

All this was built into the general instructions according to which SOE worked, but regardless of these, there was the quite decisive factor, that the initiative, particularly as to sabotage, usually passed to the Resistance Movements and their leaders, who became – impatiently – more and more sabotage-minded. Just as SOE had to work on the premises set down by British organs and authorities, so did it come to work on the premises of the Resistance organisations with which it was in contact, and with which it co-operated. It was to the actual realities in the European fields of activity that SOE had to adapt its work and its policies. SOE had its most direct connexions with the European Resistance organisations, through the instructors and missions it sent out, and when these met activist groups out in the Field, who had a crying need for supplies of every sort, their reports must put constant pressure upon SOE, no matter what long-term plans the leaders in London and Cairo might be grappling with. It should not be forgotten, in this connexion, that the instructors sent out were volunteers, who were already eager for action and had volunteered for that reason; and that they almost inevitably identified themselves with the often desperate situation in which they "landed".[13] If they had been sent out to advocate the viewpoints of the military staffs of the Western Powers, this mission was overshadowed, when they were confronted with the illegal realities, which may not have been very obvious to the staffs which had sent them out. The illegal climate – whether it was the climate in a partisan camp, among saboteurs in the great cities of Western occupied Europe, or in the central organs of the Resistance everywhere – had its own strength, and this inevitably infected the mission which was sent to the Field to report, instruct and explain. Normally the reporter became a member of the dangerous, hardpressed circles, and in sympathy with them, and normally he or she became just as eager an advocate for the interests of those circles as he or she was presumed to be for the Western Powers' Staff plans. If SOE was under the pressure of parallel and superior organs, it was under at least as heavy pressure from the illegal universe of the Continent.

Wishes from this universe were mostly for communications and supplies: Weapons, clothes and medical supplies to partisan camps, and explosives, special equipment and special weapons to the sabotage groups. These were in rapid growth, and acquired an increased and – in the eyes of SOE/SO – an insatiable appetite for the tools which effective sabotage demanded. We have seen that sabotage was not an activity which the Resistance groups could engage in immediately and without further consideration.[14] If sabotage was to be effective, a great many technical, organisational and psychological factors must be in order. The organisational framework was created by the Resistance organisations, and the psychological conditions were created as the violations of the Occupying Powers, and the agitation of the free radio and the illegal Press gradually became convincing. It then became the task of SOE to procure the technical means which could make sabotage effective, and here it was not a question of quantities alone, but also of quality, in the form of improved explosives, special equipment such as magnetic bombs, detonators, mines, and various explosive devices, frogman equipment, light hand weapons etc. In time, SOE was to have special factories at its disposal for the manufacture of articles intended for the occupied countries, and experiments were constantly carried out with new types of weapons and other tools for the promotion of technical co-operation with the Resistance.[15]

For the sabotage groups' equipment to be technically satisfactory did not only entail greater effectiveness and greater safety for the saboteurs. It was also a contribution to achieving greater understanding for sabotage, and it therefore had psychological effect in various ways. When the sabotage groups, in co-operation with the illegal Press and the radio services abroad, needed to convince the majority that sabotage was an effective means, and could become more effective in the struggle towards final victory, and that it could possibly take the place of the far more destructive bombing of industry and transport, with its heavy costs in human lives, a strange interplay appeared between psychology and technique. The more technically perfect sabotage became, and the greater the destruction it caused, the more understanding increased for it, in spite of the intensified reprisals and the consequences of various kinds which it developed for the populations. In this respect, a peculiar direct ratio existed between the effectiveness of sabotage and its popularity. The more effective it was, and therefore the more dangerous for the populations, the more its popularity grew – contrary to all logic. It naturally contributed to this development that confidence in Allied victory increased, and the conviction that the occupied countries had their important contribution to make to the Allied cause.

It is not possible to determine any specific moment at which sabotage achieved its break-through, finally to become a generally recognised element in the collective Resistance struggle. The course of development differed from one country to another, and even from one region to another. Sporadic instances of sabotage were already occurring in 1940, carried out by scattered groups or individuals, and often on the border line of demonstrative protest actions,[16] but it was not until after 1941, when for one thing the Soviet Union entered the war, and for another SOE began to spread its network, that sabotage began to be noticeable, and then rose on a steeply mounting graph. The Communists stood in the front line of developments. As long as the German-Soviet Pact was in force, they had so to speak hibernated in passivity, legally or illegally, with the slogan that the War was the imperialistic powers' responsibility and crime. Even in France, after the collapse in 1940, there was no sympathy in Communist circles for Great Britain's struggle or for de Gaulle's appeals. "Whilst England's capitalist supporters would orientate feeling among French people in the direction of chauvinism, we Communists will orientate it in the direction of brotherhood with the German people, whom we do not confuse with their momentary rulers", wrote the editors of a Communist publication for the first quarter of 1941,[17] and as far as de Gaulle was concerned, even in May 1941 the verdict was as follows:[18] "One must not believe that freedom could be brought to us on the points of the bayonets . . . We are just as far removed from Gaullism as from collaboration". Under the impression of the German-Soviet co-operation, the Communists faced a difficult and for many a confusing constellation, not only in France, but everywhere else.[19] Whilst they prepared for the possibility that this constellation could alter, they remained onlookers for a long time, critical of the nationally inspired Resistance organisations, which were beginning to form in the two-year period from September 1939 to June 1941.

From the moment the Germans attacked the Soviet Union, however, the picture changed totally. From now on, the Communists stepped forward into the front ranks among the opponents of the Axis Powers, and quickly proved themselves to be the most militant and often the best organised Resistance men. Agitation, strikes, sabotage, assassinations and where possible partisan warfare became their weapons in the fight.

The strength of the Communist influence in the Resistance organisations differed greatly in the various countries, but it was outstanding nearly everywhere. In Yugoslavia, Albania and Greece it was finally dominating, if not in command. In North Italy and France it became considerable, whereas it was less outspoken in Holland, Belgium, Den-

mark and especially Norway. Poland, with her traditionally strongly
anti-Russian attitude and after the Soviet Union's occupation in 1939 of
East Poland, was in a special category. The Polish Home Army, the
Armia Krajowa, was built up from the start under directives from the
exile Polish Government, whose aim was the restoration of pre-war Poland and therefore of Poland's eastern frontier, which involved a confrontation with the Soviet Union and a latent anti-Communist feeling,
and a strong attachment to the Western Powers. Polish Communists
turned when the opportunity arose to the Soviet Union, and built up the
Armia Ludowa as a counterpart to the Armia Krajowa, but the leaders of
the latter, which was numerically the largest Resistance organisation,
were national Polish, without the slightest touch of Communism.
Czechoslovakia was perhaps in an even more special category. Here
there was no outspoken antogonism towards the Soviet Union, but contrariwise great bitterness towards the Western Powers, who were responsible for the Munich Agreement in 1938. In spite of this, President
Benes sought exile in the West, and step by step achieved recognition as
the leader of an exile Czechoslovak Government, first from the Soviet
Union and Great Britain,[20] and later from the U.S.A. and a number of
other countries. He maintained communications from exile with
Czechoslovak Resistance groups, gathered in the collective organisation
UVOD (Central Command of the Resistance in the Home Country) and
hoped for the establishment of a Czechoslovak united front. Benes' attitude to the political Resistance developments was that in recognition of
the hopeless geographical situation of the country, until the Russian
offensives began during 1943, he recommended a waiting policy with the
gradual creation of a broad organisation with a widely composed command. Here, however, he met Communist opposition. The Communists
were building up their own hard-hitting groups, which engaged in active
sabotage and gradually took over a dominating position through systematic infiltration of a number of national committees, which had been set up
all over the country.

Regardless of the greater or lesser weight of Communist influence in
the various countries, the Communist motto was for immediate action,
partisan action where this was possible, and sabotage action where this
was most feasible, and for the rest, co-operation between all parties,
organisations and factions which were effectively fighting against the
Occupying Powers. The idea of the People's Front from the 1930's was
resuscitated. Appeals to national feelings were also made by the Communists, and in consequence of this, in May 1943 the Soviet Union

dissolved the international Socialistic organisation, the Komintern,[21] so that this should no longer be a stumbling block for the non-political co-operation which the Communists proclaimed, at the same time as they formed their own Resistance cadres and inspired and infiltrated others. The call for united action was generally speaking followed, and in spite of all ideological differences, co-operation became a fact, even if it was compromised by political differences of opinion.

The problem was further complicated by the fact that Communist influence did not only vary from one country to another, but also from one region to another, and from one activity to another, so that there could well be strong Communist influence in one region or within one activity, whilst it could be entirely absent in other regions or in other activities. Resistance activity was in no way a Communist cause, but a national, religious, democratic and humanitarian cause, including men and women of all types, from all parties, and from all walks of life. It was simply that Communists were defined as Resistance members *per se*, if they were registered Party members, or if they decided to obey the Party call. All others had more or less freedom of choice.

In the question of sabotage, the Communists separated themselves, in a sense, from the rest of the Resistance. Although they were by no means in control in this sphere nor in any other domain of Resistance – tens of thousands of sabotage actions were carried out by non-Communist groups – they were freer than others as regards the normal life of society, and they were held back less than other Resistance organisations by considerations of the long-term creation of underground armies, in a waiting position, or other demands for security which this work involved. For them the victory of the Soviet Union was the condition for liberation, and it was a Party duty to support the Soviet Union with all means and with immediate action. They therefore went in wholeheartedly for sabotage as a fighting weapon, the only limiting factors being technical possibilities and tactical considerations. From June 1941, the Communists entered the sabotage struggle, either to take it up or to intensify it.

At the same time, SOE's initiatives also began to make themselves felt to some extent, even though it took time before the organisation expanded to the point where it could make its real contribution. This contribution was however decisive for sabotage, particularly in the technical field. As far as technical possibilities were concerned, all the European Resistance organisations had to rely on their own resources or seek the support which was to be had from the Western Allies, in reality from

SOE/SO. This applied also to the Communists, until well into 1944, with the exception of the Russians and of the Polish and Czech Communists. Only SOE/SO had or received the necessary resources and the geographical position which made help possible, or less possible in the ratio of the distance from Great Britain or the Allied bases in the Mediterranean area. And outside support, if not an absolute necessity, was in high degree desirable and decisive for the effectiveness of sabotage. Even countries like Yugoslavia and Greece, which operated with mostly or completely Communist-led movements, were referred by Moscow to co-operation with the Western Powers – and this found expression for example in the recognition by the Soviet Union of the exile governments of these countries, and in Soviet directions to co-operate with the Western Powers.[22] Here lay the touchstone for the inner conflict of the Western Powers between military and political considerations. It was the military considerations which received first priority. As the reader knows, the help of the Western Powers to these countries and especially to Yugoslavia was very considerable and concrete, and it was in high degree Winston Churchill's personal intervention which was decisive in this respect, running counter to the political considerations. In this way he also ensured that both sabotage and partisan activity in the two countries were closely co-ordinated with the Western Powers strategically and tactically on the Mediterranean Front, as was attempted in other regions with success in France, North Italy and Belgium.

When the psychological background had been created, when the sabotage groups had been established, and when saboteurs either from home sources or – more important – with supplies from abroad had the practical tools in their hands, sabotage thunder began to sound, daily and many times a day, everywhere in occupied Europe. With improved technique and expanding organisation, and with the increasing illegalisation of society, the thunder claps were more and more frequent, and their effects became more and more felt. Factories, shipyards, ships, electricity supplies, telephone and telegraph networks, railways, roads, bridges, viaducts, defence installations and barracks, administration centres, cars and aeroplanes, manufactured goods, semi-manufacture and raw materials – they could all be the targets for sabotage, and no target was reserved. Naturally, a great deal of the sabotage must hit objectives which were of minor importance, often objectives which simply offered themselves because they were easily accessible, but for the Occupying Powers, the incessant sabotage, repeated day in and day out, meant constant anxiety and intensified guard duties. Even trivialities contributed to the disquiet. The effect of a single sabotage action could usually be written off without much anxiety, but no responsible leader of Administration, Army or Police could tolerate the accumulative effect of the everlasting repetitions and the ever-present risk that the saboteurs would hit targets of real importance. The crux of the problem was that even if the Occupying authorities engaged in counter-measures in the form of guards, police enquiries, punishments and reprisals, the wave of sabotage continued to increase, in most places in a rising graph. At no stage and nowhere could the Occupying Powers feel themselves secure, and they lived in permanent uncertainty as to where the next blow would fall, how it would fall, and how serious the consequences would be. The saboteurs were often extremely inventive, and experience showed that in practice it was a hopeless task to try to ensure oneself against their surprise attacks.

The dilemma was not diminished by the fact that both concessions, where these were occasionally tried, and the most extreme brutality proved to have precisely the same effect: increased sabotage. Concessions contained an obvious invitation, and brutality only resulted in bitter resolve. The Occupying Powers were therefore cought in a situation to which no solution existed, with the manpower available, when the political battle was lost.

The problem was of course rooted in the fact that to fight against sabotage, just as to fight against any other Resistance activity, was an almost bottomless labour, when the territory which had to be watched over was so vast as was the case, and when control and guarding were required of factories, depots, endless lines of communication, etc., at the same time as the task of searching out and if possible liquidating intelligence networks, illegal newspaper groups, radio transmitters, weapon receptions and military groups, and the duty of guarding frontiers, controlling internal transport, not to mention the considerable drain on manpower involved in fighting the partisan units. It is clear that the Axis Powers, and from 1943 Germany alone, did not have the men available – and certainly not the qualified men – to carry on these tasks. If the problem had only existed in a single country, and regarding a single activity, it would have been possible to cope with it. But since it was universal and multifarious, it could therefore only be solved partially and haphazardly.[23] An example right out on the periphery can serve to illustrate the problem. When, in 1943, the Danish railway sabotage threatened to increase, at a moment when the German High Command in the country had received an order from the Führer to secure Denmark against the possibility of invasion, and when the German authorities therefore confronted the Danish authorities with a categorical demand for effective safeguarding of the railway network, the answer from the Head of the Danish State Railways was that considering the length of the railway network, the demand was unrealistic.[24] Total safeguarding would require 800,000 men, or about 20% of the total population of the country. Granted, that this piece of statistics was also unrealistic, and was only dug out with the good intention of waving the German demand aside – the fact remained. When the rail and road networks in the occupied territories stretched over millions of kilometres, to safeguard every sleeper or every bridge, or even the water towers, turn-tables, yards or junctions, was something which simply could not to be done.

The example illustrates another important fact. When German manpower was insufficient, administrators and commandants had to turn to co-operation with local authorities, and by negotiation, persuasion or force to try to drag them into the struggle against the growing illegal activities. The attempt was full of pitfalls. Where there was a question of open honest collaboration, the collaborators were soon branded and isolated, and where there was a question of collaboration with authorities who simply functioned because society had to function, this collaboration usually sprang from tactical considerations, opportunism, or as the result of the pressure of the situation. Seldom from conviction. Never up to the possibilities of the area or the expectations of the Occupying Powers. And this administrative collaboration was never reliable.[25] It functioned, but all things considered, sluggishly, with delaying tactics, with obstruction, often under protest and in many instances in direct conflict with the interests of the Occupying Powers. Matters were delayed, information and warnings leaked out, directives were overlooked, etc. The enormous occupied areas with their vast possibilities for production and mobilisation were never the prize which they could have been in a favourable political climate. There were advantages, but there were also enormous burdens. Sabotage was one of them.

1943 was the year where sabotage broke through in earnest. It has been mentioned above,[26] how that year Goebbels, on the basis of reports from the German Intelligence Service on the East Front received a gloomy impression of the German possibilities for damming the growing partisan and sabotage activity there. There was no comfort in Poland or Czechoslovakia. There too, there was great and increasing sabotage activity. And the picture was no brighter in the West. Field Marshal von Rundstedt, who was responsible for the German forces in the West, described the year 1943[27] as "a serious turning-point in the internal situation in France . . . Organised supplies of weapons from England to France increased every month", and his headquarters received "an effective picture of growing danger for the German troops in the West . . . not only did murders and sabotage actions increase against members of the German Army, against the Army's installations, railways and supply lines, but in certain districts organised attacks multiplied, by bands in uniform or in civilian clothes, on transports and military units". And at the end of the year: "It is already impossible to send out single members of the Army, ambulances, couriers or supply columns to the 1st and 19th Armies in South France without armed protection." If one adds to this a violent wave of sabotage in Greece in the summer 1943,[28] the partisan war in Yugoslavia, the new Resistance activity in North Italy, and a sharply rising graph of sabotage activity in North Europe,[29] 1943 stands out as the year where sabotage activity at all points of the compass was running out of control. The year 1944 was to reveal itself in even darker hues.

Von Rundstedt's comments reflect an anxiety which reappeared in the German assessment of sabotage: worry over the British-American infiltration. It was one thing that local groups decided to take up sabotage, it was another and more serious matter when these groups were linked up with British-American activity. In this case, it was not only the local population, but the enemy abroad who was operating behind the occupying forces, and it was impossible to assess how deep the infiltration went. One could only register, through arrests, that the Western Powers' instructors and materiel were now employed everywhere. This, and the fear of Communist activity, more or less supported from Moscow, were the main anxieties with which the Gestapo had to struggle. When sabotage began to make itself felt in Denmark in 1942, although it was still in the experimental stage, sabotage experts were sent from Berlin to Copenhagen with the principal task of establishing whether this sabotage was taking place on British or Communist initiative.[30] When neither of these alternatives appeared to be applicable, the experts could give a reasurring report, which as far as Communist activity was concerned was misleading. A year later, a similar enquiry would have confirmed both questions raised.

It may seem pointless in an attempted collective account to calculate sabotage statistics, or in that connexion to try to make even a fairly reliable statement of the total damage done. The quantities involved, even if one disregards the psychological elements in the matter, cannot be compared with each other. They range from cutting telephone wires, or setting fire to a barracks or a goods wagon, to blowing up a major factory installation or destroying valuable military equipment, from cars to oil depots or aircraft. Thousands of actions were never registered, simply because it could be impossible to determine whether sabotage had taken place, or accident, or something else altogether. And sabotage was so much a part of the partisan war that as regards the partisan areas, no one could say where sabotage ended and where an action changed from a sabotage attack to an ambush, or a regular engagement. This excludes figures for such decisive areas as the Soviet Union, Yugoslavia, or North Italy, and as far as other areas are concerned, statistics are either incomplete or have no standard of comparison, depending upon whether the figures give losses in working hours, numbers of explosions or fires, or the amounts of explosives used. For example, the Belgian sabotage organisation "Groupe G" had four objectives on its programme:[31] 1) Industrial sabotage. 2) Sabotage of the Belgian canal network. 3) Sabotage of railways. 4) Sabotage of electricity supplies. The group worked in close co-operation with scientific and technical specialists in the various fields, often on the principle of hitting the sensitive spots in links in production or transport, without destroying them totally, which could lead to work stoppage for a factory and therefore to forced deportation of the manpower employed. It also worked with expert assistance to ensure faulty work, so that products manufactured were unusable in practice. A statement of the effect of an organisation such as this disappears, therefore, into the immeasurable. It has been calculated that its sabotage of high tension installations alone led to a loss of 20 to 25 million working hours for factories working for the Occupying Power. But the figure gives us no information as to what really could have been done during these millions of hours.

With these and various other reservations, a few scattered figures will be mentioned, simply as a general illustration of the dimensions of sabotage.

In the case of Poland, the figures for sabotage, with reservations as to incomplete statistical information, are given as follows[32] for the period 1940–44: about 1300 goods trains derailed; about 7000 locomotives blown up; about 20,000 railway carriages destroyed; about 4000 motor cars destroyed; about 800 administrative offices blown up; about 1100 petrol tanks and about 4700 tons of petrol destroyed. In addition, about 25,000 instances of minor sabotage. Apart from the direct destruction, this meant considerable transport stoppage for the German transports, which for the year 1943 are calculated at about 3,200 hours and for the first 6 months of the year 1944 to about 4,700 hours. Also evasion of compulsory deliveries by Polish peasants.

From April 1940, the German Governor-General of occupied Polish territory, including the Government-General of Poland,[33] notes that great numbers of ammunition depots are being blown up; that from 1943, trains on several railways only passed at special times under guard, or not at all; that railway sabotage rose in 1944 to more than 10 daily explosions. The German General Haenicke states in 1944 that "the railways and roads can no longer be considered safe, when it is a question of directing reserves to the East". Haenicke, who was Military Commandant in the region, states this explicitly in a reminder to his forces of October 1943:[34] "A large number of the Members of the Forces do not seem to have realised that when they find themselves in the Government-General area, they are not in the Fatherland, but in a region where the majority of the population is hostile to us and opposes us with violence."

So much for the figures available from the eastern territories. The figures for a southern area, Greece, are estimated as follows:[35] 117 derailments; 209 locomotives, 1540 railway trucks, 28 kilometres of railway lines blown up; 5 tunnels, 67 railway bridges, 800 automobiles, 17 ammunition depots, 16 armoured cars and 5 aeroplanes.

From a northern country, Denmark, owing partly to the milder occupation conditions and continued Danish administration, the figures are fairly precise.[36] The main groups here cover 119 derailments, about 2700 instances of industrial sabotage, about 1525 railway stretches cut, 58 locomotives, 31 bridges and various other railway installations blown up, and also military equipment, repair shops, cars, aircraft and naval vessels destroyed.

But figures in this connexion are bare. If one could number the episodes referred to, and thousands of other sabotage actions, one number would perhaps stand for an important railway bridge blown up at a critical moment, where another number might only stand for damage to a tyre. Anything and everything! It is no better if one obtains information that this or that concern was out of action after sabotage for so many weeks or months. The question arises at once: How many men were employed? How large a proportion of the production was intended for the Occupying Power? How important was it? Could it be replaced, and if so, how quickly? As regards sabotage of transport, especially, timing plays a decisive rôle, and can perhaps be summed up in the question: is this a reference to a reserve unit on the way to a hard-pressed sector of the Front, or is it a question of a movement from one training camp to another? But in industrial sabotage, also, the time factor could play a rôle. An example can be given from Norway. The production of iron pyrites from the Orkla Mines in Trondelagen were of some importance to the German production of explosives. The mines had therefore a high priority for Norwegian saboteurs, and a number of sabotage actions were carried out,[37] some of the supply of current to the mines, others of their transport installations. The first sabotage actions led only to a temporary stop in production. From 1943, the Germans had lost the supply of pyrites from the mines in Sicily, and the Orkla Mines therefore received increased importance. After this, sabotage was intensified until the Norwegians succeeded in stopping this essential war production altogether. July 1943 here represents the moment where a form of sabotage which was already important received increased importance. But in every examination of sabotage, one is blocked by the fact that the figures in themselves have no real power of information on the phenomenon.

The British historian, M.R.D. Foot, in his book "SOE in France", has tried to attack the problem via a cost/benefit analysis of production stoppages, production decline and direct destruction, caused by 150 of the larger SOE-inspired sabotage actions, which were carried out because the concerns in question were working partially or wholly for the Germans.[38] After the liberation of France, these 150 actions were assessed as regards method and effect by British authorities, with a view to establishing the actual results. The analysis covers places, firms, products, dates and results, and without any attempt at adding up the quantities, for which there is certainly little standard of comparison, arrives at a mainly positive result as regards the sabotage effect. Production stoppage lasting months, production decline of 50% or more, and the destruction of tons of materiel are common factors. On this basis, Foot states in an attempt to make a rough comparison between the results of strategic bombing in France and the results of sabotage that in the sabotage actions analysed, about 1.3 tons of plastic explosives were used or in Foot's comparison, about ¼ of the explosives in just one of the "Tallboys" (the largest British bombs in use in 1944), or in another comparison, less than the weight which one Mosquito fighter bomber could carry. Foot carries his comparison further. He refers to an air operation on 8 June 1944 against a railway tunnel near Saumur, an important junction near the Loire on the railway line Paris-Bordeaux. Its disruption was important because the destruction of the tunnel would prevent the move of a German Armoured Division from South France to the invasion area in Normandy. Nineteen Lancasters were used in the operation, with a Mosquito escorting them, manned in all by 135 of Great Britain's best trained and most experienced flying personnel from a special group, Squadron 617,[39] known from a number of special missions such as the "Dam-buster" attack in the Ruhr Valley, and the destruction of the battleship "Tirpitz". One "Tallboy" bomb hit the target and destroyed the entrance to the tunnel, whilst 18 bombs were scattered in the surrounding terrain. Foot then remarks drily that the same tactical result could have been achieved, with less risk, by sending in the SOE group which was operating in the neighbourhood, incidentally under the command of one of the many women SOE employed, especially in France. The remark cannot be substantiated, but it is made by a historian with full insight into the collective French sabotage. The French historian Henri Michel, on the basis of general considerations, reaches much the same conclusion as Foot in his analysis.[40] He quotes a request by telegram from the leaders of the merged organisation "Mouvements Unis de Résistance", sent to London from Geneva: "If you supply us with explosives, and IF YOU SPECIFY THE TARGETS, our groups are ready to take on whatever destruction is named, and to increase it. One can thus avoid the uncertain and costly bombing which injures the morale of the population," and he adds: "Its is certain that the Allies made a great mistake by ignoring such appeals and stubbornly continuing to bomb Europe – including their Resistance friends."

From Danish sources a scientific investigation can be quoted, which reaches a different and predominantly negative conclusion.[41] The Danish historian, Aage Trommer, has carried out a detailed examination of the actual interruptions of the Jutland railway network during the period 1944-45, when the majority of the 1525 railway lines were cut (approximately 8,400 explosions). Trommer's findings are that the interruptions only lasted a short time, that the actions were badly coordinated, and that the military effect of this extensive transport sabotage was therefore slight. He finds that the main reasons for the meagre results were a lack of direction both from Danish and Allied leaders, and insufficient contact between the intelligence service and the sabotage leaders. Here is not a question of a hypothetical commentary with hypothetical evidence, but of technical investigation, confined to the proof of the above facts in relation to the factors of place and time. Trommer emphasizes the technical character of his investigation and refrains from speculative evaluations, for instance of the psychological and political effect of the sabotage, which also implies that no attempt is made to assess its effect upon the German High Command in Denmark, or the possible reaction of the Western Allies if no sabotage had taken place.

Trommer ends his detailed examination with an overall reference to railway sabotage in both East and West Europe, basing his comments on German and Allied literature, and on existing Resistance literature. On this basis he reaches the approximate assessment that railway sabotage had greater tactical value in the East than in the West, and that its tactical value depended upon exact co-ordination between sabotage and the operational command of the regular battles, and he asks for detailed investigations, country by country and link by link, before final conclusions can be reached. In his own conclusions he collides with a number of accepted ideas, including the conclusion which Foot puts forward, as well as with official declarations from the Allied High Command[42] – whatever weight one should attribute to encouraging acknowledgements of this kind.

With the recognition of the desirability, from a theoretical point of view, of detailed investigations of the type suggested, it can be established that sabotage of the European railways, like all other sabotage, was such a widespread phenomenon and was so complicated in its effects – practical, psychological and political – that a total measurement, which can be checked point by point, is unthinkable, at least on the existing information. The writer wil therefore confine himself in this account to some general remarks.

As stated, sabotage was conceived as a supplement to blockade, air bombing and general undermining of the fighting forces of the Axis Powers. This applies, whether one is considering the original ABC-1 programme of the Western Powers, its elastic realisation through SOE and OSS, the general appeals broadcast from the Soviet Union Supreme Command, or the special directives from the Central Committee of the Partisan Movement.

It is incontrovertible that sabotage became such a supplement. Every instance of explosion or arson meant a contribution, and the accumulation of actions in tens of thousands, regardless of any doubts or possible revision of opinion as to the effect of single actions, must mean a corresponding accumulation of the collective mass of contributions. Their effect was intensified by the fact that where the Occupying Power attempted to forestall such actions, they often brought about consequences which, on the law of the vicious circle, intensified the activity against them.[43]

In addition to this psychological effect, there was also the material effect. As far as sabotage is concerned, it is the size of the single action which is subject to uncertainty and debate. Generally speaking, it can probably be said that the members of the Resistance, with support from the majority of the Resistance historians,[44] are inclined to attribute greater results to sabotage and, particularly, greater potential than the examination of realities can justify. This is especially natural for countries such as France, which were exposed to extensive air bombing, which could not but cause great losses in human lives and unnecessary destruction, and where the statement of account involved personal experience of sabotage versus bombing, and where the scales tipped in the favour of the more careful and, at its best, more differentiated sabotage. It was also in the Field that one was best able to recognize and be proud of ones own results, and feel sceptical and bitter over the costly bombing which often failed in its effect. Contrariwise, assessments from abroad were probably apt to underestimate sabotage, if not as to its documented effect, then as regards its potential possibilities. As we have seen, SOE and OSS – but not the Soviet partisan staffs – had to fight a stubborn fight to convince the traditional staffs of the possibilities of sabotage and the demands which should be met for greater support. This in itself implies a defence against traditional thinking.

A fundamental difficulty in any overall assessment lies in the fact that much of the sabotage was not recognized, and cannot be established with certainty. This applies to sabotage which consisted of slowing down production or reducing it, or in poor or faulty production. In local manufacture, in the building of German fortifications etc., and for forced workers in Germany there was abundant opportunity to slacken working tempo and cheat with materials and prices.[45] Here it was not even necessary to operate with appeals to slow down or prevent production. Such appeals were made, but their effects cannot be established. Often the appeal was left unsaid but was clearly understood, in collective consciousness. With or without appeals, however, the absence of the will to produce or deliver, and even strict adherence to working norms and regulations were enough. If one is to arrive at a final estimate, one must operate with unknown quantities, which could be defined as the total Axis areas' maximum production capacity, in the event of the maximum will to produce, and then compare this hypothetical quantity with the actual production carried out. As regards forced labour alone, it is certain that there would be a considerable distance between the two quantities. There was a demonstrable reduction, for example in Roumanian oil production, Czechoslovak and Belgian industrial production, in

French coal production etc., just as there were demonstrable delays in the whole European transport system.[46]

German production was accelerated after Albert Speer took over the leadership of German war production[47] and millions of foreign workers and prisoners of war were put to work, but the actual acceleration reveals nothing as to how great it could have been in favourable conditions. Only when this undeniably indeterminable factor is taken into consideration can one reasonably move on to the direct destruction caused by the sabotage of activists.

An example from Denmark, which was untouched by battles, and where the productive machinery was intact, and where up to 1943 more or less normal conditions prevailed, has already been mentioned.[48] This Danish example is given with no claim to its being typical, but in the belief that it reflects a tendency, and it seems likely that the incalculable lack of effective production must be an important item in a final statement of account. The construction of German fortifications both in Denmark and in other countries was hit by poor planning, delays and unserviceable work.

In this connexion it will perhaps be practical to make a short detour to a frontier area. In June 1941, Germany proclaimed a crusade against Bolshevism, and appealed to western and northern countries for mobilisation of volunteers to this crusade. The appeal was generally speaking a fiasco in spite of a considerable anti-Communist attitude in large sections of the populations – at least in 1941. Only minimum contingents volunteered and the results of the appeals had no relation whatever to the German wishful thinking that support was to be noticed in Europe for the campaign in the East. This was not sabotage, perhaps, but it was the muzzled expression of opposition, or at best passiveness, added to which the few who volunteered were stamped in their home countries as traitors to the national cause. Returning volunteers met anger and fights, and it has been mentioned above that the Church Authorities, in harmony with public feeling, refused to celebrate mass for the fallen. Both where production and mobilisation were in question, the Axis Powers had to reconcile themselves to the fact that at best they met animosity and passivity. Direct sabotage must be added to these considerable disadvantages.

When considering sabotage as a whole, the observer must resign himself to the fact that it will mostly be a question of studying and assessing a flickering mass of pin-prick actions. By far the greatest number of sabotage operations consisted of small local actions of very limited value, and with very restricted effects. The impact lay in their repetition, extensiveness and mass – and in the resulting uncertainty. Naturally, above the grey mass of broken windows, cut wires, fires, railway lines blown up and industrial stoppages, there rises a large group of far more serious sabotage actions, noticeable for their important effects, for the inventiveness in their planning, for the daring in their execution or for all these combined. But in all sabotage tables it is the many small actions that raise the total.

This hardly applies to the partisan districts. Obviously a great many of the larger and more co-ordinated sabotage operations took place in these districts, where destruction by sabotage was so to speak a by-product of the partisan war. If a partisan unit had possession of a captured piece of terrain, even temporarily, there were many possibilities for it to blow up or remove what might be useful to the enemy in the area in question, so that after possible, and usually probable, recapture it was stripped of everything that could make the place valuable, and in such a way that only the most primitive re-building was conceivable – and under the constant threat of new attacks and further destruction. These massive instances of destruction took place mainly in the largest partisan area, in the occupied part of the Soviet Union, but this high level of destruction is also to be found in other partisan areas, particularly in Yugoslavia, and periodically also in Poland, North Italy and certain parts of France.

The total figures for material destruction caused by partisan actions as calculated from the Soviet side,[49] is enormous, and illustrates the importance attributed to the partisan war by the Soviet authorities, as an integral part of the total conduct of the war. Very likely they contain much of the explanation for the slackening in the German offensive in 1942, and the obvious shift in the balance of power on the East Front which took place at about the New Year 1943.[50] The totals given are as follows: Trains derailed and destroyed: about 18,000. Locomotives destroyed: about 9,400. Railway trucks destroyed: about 85,000. Cars destroyed: about 42,000. Bridges blown up: about 10,000. Armoured cars destroyed: about 2,900 (figures only given for the Ukraine and White Russia). Aircraft destroyed: about 500.

These are the figures calculated for all partisan activity, and it must be a matter for assessment, whether one places them to the credit of sabotage or partisan warfare. A great deal of the destruction was naturally carried out in connexion with partisan attacks of a military nature. But whichever classification one chooses, and regardless of all uncertainty as to precise numbers of activities of this kind, the result is the same:

important undermining of the enemy's freedom of movement and the demand for continuous guarding of the captured hinterland, as well as counter-measures against the saboteur/partisans – a task which is estimated to have demanded between 20 and 25 German Divisions, besides the employment of SS and Police forces.[51] It can, of course, be difficult to give definite numbers for an area which was already full of reservists, forces in the process of redeployment, forces resting, etc. But it is a valid statement that there was evidently a question of too small a force, as the partisan struggle expanded from month to month.

The Soviet totals can be supplemented here with a few specified numbers, chosen at random, to illustrate briefly that the activity which is evidenced by the collective figures was spread over most of the area captured by the Axis Powers. From the Brjansk area, on the Central Front, the following numbers are estimated for the period January to May 1942: 32 derailments, 125 bridges, 44 aircraft, 42 armoured cars, 418 lorries, and 205 kilometres of railway lines sabotaged, and materiel captured in large, listed quantities. From the Smolensk area, also on the Central Front, from January to October 1942: 316 derailments, 800 armoured cars, 145 bridges, about 6,500 tons of fuel sabotaged. From the Leningrad Front in 1942: 113 bridges and countless railway lines cut. Lastly a "partisan march" through large districts of the Ukraine in the autumn 1942, the march lasting for 30 days, and the unit passing about 500 kilometres, with 67 engagements: during the march, 2 aircraft were destroyed, 2 locomotives, 102 railway trucks, 9 armoured cars, 3 cannons, 42 tractors, 2 radio stations, 3 transformers, 2 telephone stations, a repair shop for armoured vehicles, and 16 fuel stores sabotaged.

To add to the list would neither shake nor change the record in principle, of weighty partisan and sabotage support to the Soviet operations. The situation on the East Front was critically affected by sabotage activity, according to the German General Manstein, who stated during the Nuremburg trials: "I cannot give you the exact figures . . . but as an example I can say that I remember that in 1944 in the course of 7 hours in the Central Army sector, almost 1,000 attacks were carried out on roads and railways in the hinterland, and in the Crimea that sort of attack took place every single day."

The figures quoted are from the largest partisan area in Europe, but also in the areas and countries of Europe where sabotage groups had to operate in complete secrecy, without support in partisan bases and under constant observation, in an outwardly normal society, the figures amounted to thousands of greater and lesser instances of sabotage. The

Polish Resistance leader, General Bor-Komorowski estimates the number of sabotage actions in Poland to have been about 10,000 in the months October to November 1941, with another estimate in the form of a decline in production of about 30%.[52] The extensive bombing of the French railways from April 1943 to May 1944 led to the destruction of about 2,500 locomotives, whilst sabotage in the slightly longer period of April 1943 to July 1944 accounted for about 2,600 locomotives, of which about 800 were sabotaged during the first invasion battles.[53] The number of rails blown up amounted to thousands during the invasion battles, so that explosions, strikes and adherence to minimum rules, as well as the carefully planned negligence of duty paralysed all normal transport for weeks, and thereby seriously delayed or blocked important troop movements, and vital deliveries at a strategically critical stage. Threats of sanctions against the well organised French railway personnel and the transfer to France of about 25,000 German railway technicians could not prevent general chaos at a moment when reliable railway transport was more important than at any other time.[54] At the same time, telephone and telegraph communications failed constantly, roads were blocked, and columns and garrisons were constantly threatened with attack. The chaos spread to Belgium and at the same time, sabotage continued in North Italy, Holland, Norway and Denmark. In Norway, sabotage increased considerably from the late spring 1944 and onwards, and the escalation came after heavy pressure from activist circles in Norway and after a prolonged debate, both at home and abroad, as to the desirability of sabotage on a large scale in that country. The attitude in London was for a long time ambiguous, partly because SHAEF during the invasion period preferred passive rather than active resistance in the occupied countries outside France. But a permission was at last reluctantly given, and the Norwegian saboteurs did not hesitate to launch a major sabotage offensive, just as a major sabotage offensive was in progress in Denmark after a relatively quiet period, requested by London for the few months, in which the underground army was built up. A detailed description of the Norwegian debate and its outcome is given by Ole Kristian Grimnes in his book, "Hjemmefrontens Ledelse".

In the 1000 days or so, during which the organised sabotage effort developed, there were scores of daily sabotage actions, and often hundreds.

But whether one is considering one or another geographical or technical area, and whether one fixes upon totals or partial figures, and with every possible reservation as to the optimistic evaluations which Resis-

tance groups were apt to make of the value of their results, three fundamental facts remain: great destruction, the creation of uncertainty in the
enemy ranks, and considerable difficulties with regard to an unimpeachable assessment of the military importance of sabotage. The first is immediately obvious, the second has already been examined, but the third
fact requires some further general comments.

Whether one is dealing with industrial sabotage, the sabotage of shipping, of transport or of any other targets, the bare figures are insignificant
to any attempt to approach what is described above as unimpeachable
assessment. In this, sabotage has similarities with bombing. After bombing raids, photographs could record the number and positions of the
bombs dropped, and the extent of the fires, but nothing certain as to
reduction in production. Were the machines hit, because the machine
room was burnt out? Were the electricity supplies cut off, and could they
be restored quickly? Could works be moved quickly to new premises?
Similarly, every sabotage figure covers an action and an effect, and
almost always a drama, but the figures constitute a block of incommen-
surable magnitudes, from the cutting of a telephone wire to an instance of
major or minor destruction, for a longer or shorter period, of an industrial
installation, or from the burning down of railway trucks which were
perhaps worn out already, to the derailment of a fully loaded supply
train. Even within the individual categories, the figures cannot simply be
listed in the same statistical column. What value is one to give to the
blowing up of a bridge? A complex of supplementary questions present
themselves, which cannot be ignored. What bridge was it? At what time?
On what stretch of road? With what possibilities for diversion? For
repair? It is not a question simply of the size of the bridge or the extent of
the damage, but in a high degree of the position of the bridge in the
communications network, and particularly of the timing of the damage.
The total destruction of a large bridge behind a peaceful sector of the
front could be less important than partial damage to a smaller bridge,
behind an active sector of the front at a critical moment. Similarly, as
with every category of sabotage, a complex of questions will present
themselves which cannot be answered satisfactorily by bare figures. The
derailment of a train! Of what train? Of an empty train or a fully loaded
train? What was the effect? At what time? With what possibilities for
getting the train on the rails again? And if it was a fully loaded train, what
was the load? On what route? At what time? Behind a quiet or a critical
sector of the front? And industrial sabotage! What was the industry?
What was the degree of damage? What were the possibilities for

rebuilding? What were the possibilities for replacement? In the bare figures the large sabotage action with the small effect appears with the same weight as the small sabotage action with the large effect. Knowledge of the size and range of sabotage has therefore only limited value in the assessment of what importance it had for the War, and this applies also, if one tries for example to calculate the number of wasted man-hours of delays resulting from sabotage. Hundreds of wasted hours in one domain and at one time can be more important than thousands of wasted hours in other domains and at other times, and added to this, a man-hour under the prevailing conditions does not necessarily bear any relation to normal performance.

In general, however, there is reason to state that there are two particular factors of decisive importance which must be taken into consideration in any attempt to evaluate sabotage. One of these is the time factor, the other the co-ordination factor. It is obvious that the most effective sabotage was that which was carried out at a point in time where it had the possibility of impeding or delaying the Occupying Powers in a situation where they were in need of immediate manoeuvrability, and in a critical situation were deprived of this or hampered as the result of sabotage. To return to the above train of thought, the blowing up of a bridge, the derailment of a train or any other retarding action had far greater importance to the fight if it took place behind a front in movement and therefore with immediate supply problems, than if it took place behind a quiet sector of the front. Even a small action could have importance here, whilst contrariwise the large action behind a static sector could turn out to have limited effect. Here the factor of co-ordination enters the picture, on a line with the time factor. Where the sabotage action was adjusted to the general needs of the war situation, both as to timing and targets, its impact was heavier than when it was an isolated occurrence. This applies to transport sabotage. It applies also to industrial sabotage. If this was put into effect in spheres of production which constituted bottlenecks, and particularly in spheres of production which were the targets for bombing, it was more essential than if it hit more or less at random in spheres which perhaps were chosen only because they offered accessible targets for sabotage, and because of a general impression among the people that all damage was effective. Here again, the small action against a key target could prove more serious for the Occupying Powers than even the most sensational action against a sphere of production on the periphery of importance. Again, the time factor enters the picture. An action against a given target could hit it at a time when the production was more vital than at another time. For example this applies to ships and shipyards, whether the latter were employed in building ships or were repair docks. As long as there was abundant or sufficient tonnage available, sabotage against such targets had limited value, whereas sabotage – including strikes – made itself seriously felt as soon as shortage in tonnage began.

Simply for the reasons given above, a reasonably reliable evaluation of the importance of sabotage cannot be prepared without extremely complicated analysis of the concrete effects of individual actions or series of actions. This does not apply, however, to the psychological effect of sabotage, and it applies only to a limited extent to its political effect. In these respects, every action had an effect – to a greater or lesser degree. Where it was a question of co-ordination as to timing and targets between sabotage on the one hand and the operations of the regular armies on the other, this was most systematic on the East Front. It speaks for itself that the German historian Heinz Kühnrich, who has dealt in detail with the history of the partisan war, with emphasis on the partisan war in East Europe, devotes a whole chapter[55] to an analysis of the co-operation between the Soviet partisans and the Soviet Armies and their General Staffs. This co-operation was highly developed both when the Axis Powers were on the offensive, and the task was to hamper the force of their offensive, and particularly later, when the Soviet Armies were on the offensive and the task was the reverse, to pave the way for the advance of the Soviet Armies. The partisan war, including sabotage, was here of considerable operational value, perhaps especially in the offensive phase from 1943, when the partisan movement was thoroughly organised, and where the Russian advance was powerfully supported by large-scale partisan activity, with sabotage now as its primary task, now as a by-product.

It is not to be wondered at that the co-ordination level was high on the East Front, since, as we have seen, the efforts at co-ordination met fewer complications here than in the West. When the Western Allies landed in South Italy, however, and after a number of changes in structure achieved firmer contact with the North Italian, Greek and Yugoslav partisans, possibilities were exploited here also, for ever-increasing synchronisation between the operations of the regular armies and the growing partisan and sabotage activity behind the front. Synchronisation of this kind was particularly effective in France and Belgium, immediately before and also during the invasion battles in the summer 1944. In direct co-ordination with the invasion in Normandy in June 1944, the French Resistance Movement's highest military organ, the FFI, in consultation and co-operation with Free French and Allied military staffs, started a three-pronged sabotage plan,[56] the "Vert" plan, which included sabotage of the French railways, the "Tortue" plan, which included sabotage of the road network, and the "Violet" plan which included sabotage of the French telephone and telegram network. These carefully prepared sabotage plans were put into action on code signals on the B.B.C., and led immediately to chaotic conditions behind the invasion front. The German communications system broke down at a critical stage, and their reporting services were partially paralysed at the same time as troop movements from the east, south and south-west were delayed for days, and in several instances for weeks. Both the material and psychological effect of these co-ordinated actions were considerable, and supplemented the effects of the Western Powers' bombing of transport centres and military columns. On D Day itself, about 950 actions were carried through, out of a planned 1050, and German Divisions which relied upon railway transport were delayed in their movements towards the bridgehead in Normandy for up to two weeks, by which time the bridgehead had been consolidated.[57] In a special communiqué, the achievements as regards the "Vert" plan including the first week after the Allied landings, were honoured in the following words: "This Army (FFI) has carried out an extensive sabotage plan, which aimed at paralysing rail and road traffic and cutting off telegraph and telephone communications. In the majority of instances, these aims were achieved." It seems to be confirmed in this part of Europe, also, that the ideal sabotage was that best co-ordinated as to timing and as to targets, with the general strategy.

Sabotage was a campaign which lasted for years. But it was a campaign without visible fronts, without indisputable victories, and normally without sensational data. It is only exceptionally that one can point with certainty at this or that sabotage action, or series of actions, and establish their concrete effect. But exceptions do exist. The most remarkable exceptions are to be found in Norway.

Near the little town of Rjukan in the Telemark in Norway, Norwegian industry had laid pipes through the 100 metre long Rjukan waterfall, with its abundant waters, with a view to production of electricity. A large electricity plant, the Vemork works, was set up in the immediate neighbourhood of the town. However, a by-product of the plant was heavy water, and it was on this product of heavy water that the Germans based their otherwise somewhat vague plans for the possible production of an atom bomb, with heavy water as moderator. The Norwegian production of heavy water was therefore just as essential for the experiments of German technology as it must appear dangerous for the Allies, and it became a high priority mission to get this production stopped.[58] The factory was situated at the bottom of a deep, narrow valley, however, and the installations for the production of heavy water were placed on the lowest floor of the factory, protected by many layers of thick concrete. The target was thus difficult to hit by bombing and the first attempt to destroy it was made in a Commando raid, carried out on the basis of Norwegian intelligence report, by airborne British Engineer troops from the special organisation, Special Air Force in November 1942. The attempt was a catastrophe for the Commandos. The aircraft and their gliders hit a mountain during the fly-in, and most of those on board were killed, whilst the few survivors were executed. Extensive razzias in the neighbourhood of the factory, and guard reinforcements followed. Sabotage was then attempted, and in February 1943, nine Norwegian saboteurs, trained in England and dropped by paracute in the high mountains near the factory, succeeded in forcing their way down the ravine surrounding the factory, entering it, and without loss of life, destroying about 500 kilograms of heavy water and putting important sections of the factory out of action, so that the Occupying Power was deprived of a further 400 kilograms through production stoppage. For five months the production of heavy water was at a standstill. Physically, technically, and as regards planning, this sabotage operation was the ideal, in daring, ingenuity and self-sacrifice. During the summer, production began again, however, and the problem again became acute. In November 1943, 158 Flying Fortresses from the American Eight Air Force made a violent bombing raid on the factory, and a nearby installation for the production of nitrate. The result was mainly negative, as far as the factory's vital parts were concerned, but the attack led unavoidably to extensive loss of life and property in the little Norwegian factory town. Only 50 kilograms of heavy water were destroyed. The production of heavy water was therefore unaffected, and in February 1944 the Germans were ready to transport 600 kilograms of heavy water to Germany, a move which was to be ensured by every imaginable means. Again a Norwegian activist group resorted to sabotage, this time against the transport, and in co-operation with Norwegian engineers at the factory, as well as personnel in the know in the Norwegian transport network, they succeeded on 20 February in sinking the ferry which was to carry the priceless cargo over the very deep Tinnsjø lake to further transport by rail. Thanks to two sabotage actions, not a drop of heavy water ever reached Germany, and thus the German production was stopped and all German plans for experimenting and then making an atom bomb, based on heavy water, were shelved.

Another remarkable, if debatable exception can be cited from the opposite corner of Europe. In November 1942, a British SOE group in Greece, led by the Captain C. M. Woodhouse mentioned earlier, succeeded, in co-operation with local saboteurs from both the EDES and ELAS organisations in blowing up the important Gorgopotamos viaduct on the railway line from Saloniki to Athens, and thus cutting off the German deliveries via the Piraeus to the Axis Forces in Africa.[59] At the time, immediately after the British breakthrough at El-Alamein, the German-Italian forces in Africa were faced with enormous supply problems. The supply lines through South Italy and African harbours were exposed to constant attack from the British base on Malta, and the Allies estimated that about 80% of the supplies to the Axis forces in Africa were being sent via the Piraeus – a supply line which was now cut for quite a long period. During the final battles in Africa in the winter 1942–43, the Axis Powers had only the vulnerable supply line which had to pass a now reinforced Malta.

This sabotage operation has been cited in several quarters,[60] also by Woodhouse himself, although he is otherwise extremely sceptical as to the military value of the Greek sabotage,[61] as a piece of sabotage with demonstrable strategic effect. The official British account of Great Britain's strategy describes the strategic aim of the operation, and characterizes its execution as a success. The evaluation seems debatable, however, and since a clarification of this assertion involves the more important question of the value of the time factor, the sabotage action is mentioned in this context. If one takes Field Marshal Rommel's supply difficulties into consideration – and his supply situation was catastrophic[62] – and if one accepts the British statement that the Afrika Korps received about 80% of its supplies via Piraeus-Tobruk or other Cyrenaica harbours, it is obvious that to cut off the only existing railway line from Central Europe to the Piraeus must have fundamental strategic importance. It was therefore logical that the Myers/Woodhouse Mission[63] was sent to Greece on 1 October with the task of blowing up the viaduct over the Gorgopotamos, or other viaducts on the exposed railway line. However, understandably enough, the action was delayed, and it was not carried out until 25 November – five days after British troops had occupied Benghazi, and thereby secured control over

Cyrenaica. Tripoli and the occupied harbour of Tunis then became supply harbours for the Axis forces, and on the background of this shift in
the timing of the operation it is probably doubtful whether one can attribute operational effect to it, apart from the supply problems which it
caused the Axis Powers' occupying troops in Greece on Crete and
Rhodos. This example seems therefore to underline the time factor's
predominant importance for a strategically effective sabotage operation.

There is probably more substance in another exception, also taken
from Greece. In June 1943 the Greek Resistance groups, at the request of
the British Military Mission, began a series of extensive sabotage actions, mostly directed against the Greek transport system. The object of
this chain of sabotage operations was on a line with other misleading
actions, to contribute to giving the German leaders the impression that
the expected Allied attack on South Europe would set in in the Balkans, or at least partly in the Balkans. This sabotage series actually
resulted in two German Divisions, at that critical moment, being sent from
Italy to Greece from where they could not simply be returned to
South Italy, for one reason because a further stretch of the Salonica-
Athens railway had been cut off by the Asapos viaduct being blown up.[64]
These two German Divisions, one of which was an Armoured Division,
were thus locked inside Greece, while decisive battles were developing
in Sicily and at Salerno. Considering the fairly narrow margin, there was
in these decisive situations, particularly after the landings at Salerno,
between the two parties' strengths, the absence of considerable German
reinforcements was obviously a contributory factor to the final result.
Here no assertion is made that their absence had decisive importance,
but only that it had an effect.

As pointed out earlier, the geographical possibilities of the Western
Powers for closer co-operation with the Resistance organisations, as well
as greater understanding of the value of such co-operation, increased
after they had established themselves on the Continent. This was evident
in France and soon after in Belgium, and it was evident in Yugoslavia. In
August 1944, the British Military Mission to Marshal Tito prepared the
"Ratweek" plan,[65] according to which the Yugoslav partisans would
carry out a synchronised series of sabotage actions in the first week of
September, directed against the roads and rails which led from Greece
through Yugoslavia to Central Europe, first of all the railway from
Salonica to Belgrade, but also alternative railways. The object of the plan
was to hinder or delay a German retreat from Greece and South-east
Yugoslavia, and the plan, to which the Chief of the British Military

Mission, Fitzroy MacLean, gives a whole chapter in his book "Eastern Approaches", included a precise distribution of tasks between the partisan sabotage actions and Allied bombing raids, as well as extensive deliveries of materiel in support of the partisan actions. The area in question was divided into sections, each with its Partisan Chief and with its British or American Liaison Officer, and it was based on detailed agreements as to what the one party – the Partisans – should undertake, and what the other party – the Balkan Air Force – should carry out. Close radio communication linked the Allied Headquarters in Bari to every single Partisan Section, so that the latter could ask for air support or for the bombing of sectors or special targets which were too strongly fortified for the partisans to have a reasonable chance of sabotaging them effectively. The plan was approved by Tito, and the Allied High Command, and was an example of perfect co-operation between the regular forces' bombing and the partisans' sabotage. The German retreat which was begun on 1 September under the command of General von Löhr, became a chaotic rout, with enormous losses in men, and even more in materiel. Everywhere the German convoys were ambushed and exterminated, bridges and viaducts were blown up, trains were derailed and roads were mined, whilst important junctions were bombed to pieces. Some stretches of the railway were totally blocked for weeks, others were 75% blocked during the period September-October, and no stretches were untouched. This picture of chaos is very similar to the chaos which arose in the German hinterland in France in June and July, and would arise in the spring 1945 in the North Italian battle zone.

Wherever in Europe sabotage was allowed to become part of a larger whole, it gained in importance. The statement points, as do so many other factors, to co-operation with the outside world being of fundamental importance for the effectiveness of the Resistance Movements. The closer the co-operation, the greater the effectiveness. This applies also to the co-operation of the Resistance units with each other, as to their functions and their incorporation in a joint organisational pattern. The condition for an operation such as "Ratweek" was precise information on the time of the German retreat. This, too, was known.

Sabotage became a supplement to regular warfare, and particularly in North and West Europe to strategic bombing. Could it also have been an alternative? This problem must present itself insistently, especially in countries such as France, Belgium and Holland, which were "plastered" with bombs. But it must also present itself in countries in North Europe, which had to face the fact that they could be exposed to bombing, particularly in Norway, where the theoretical risk on repeated occasions turned out to be a reality. The bombing of the Vemork factory has been described and this was not the only example. A particularly glaring example was an attack by 167 American Flying Fortresses on the Norwegian Hydro factory in Herøya, near the densely built-up town of Porsgrunn, where many of the factory workers lost their lives. But there were other examples[66] which could nourish anxiety and cause the exile Norwegian Government and the Home Front to argue strongly for sabotage as the desirable alternative to bombing. In Denmark, too, the problem was discussed and the Resistance groups operated generally from the unconfirmed condition that extensive sabotage would be the lightening conductor which could avert bombing. In actual fact, Denmark was not exposed to strategic bombing. On the other hand, both in Denmark and Norway, British precision bombing was carried out in attacks on the Gestapo Headquarters in Aarhus, Copenhagen, Odense and Oslo. These attacks, in spite of loss of life among the civilian population, were not criticised by the Resistance, but on the contrary, welcomed, and they were undertaken on direct requests from the Resistance leaders.[67]

The problem of sabotage versus bombing was most acute after the Western Powers, at conferences in Casablanca in January 1943, Washington in May 1943 and Quebec in August 1943, had decided upon an enormous strategic bombing programme, and because U.S.A.'s and Great Britain's military staffs in this connexion insisted upon the necessity, especially before the invasion in Normandy, of maintaining and even intensifying bombing in France and Belgium. This decision was taken after weighty deliberations in the Staffs involved, and only after Winston Churchill, who was himself in deep uncertainty, had put the proposal to President Roosevelt for renewed deliberation and final decision. The cause of doubt was naturally consideration of the loss of human life in the Allied countries, especially in France, which such bombing would involve, and the open question as to how far strategic necessity justified measures which, on humane, psychological and political grounds must appear unacceptable. It was clear in advance that the losses among the civilian populations would be great. The pessimistic calculation was that losses would reach 120,000 wounded and 40,000 killed – figures which fortunately proved considerably higher than the actual losses. It was also realised that the political damage could be considerable. It was one thing to liberate these countries and to inflict the losses upon the civilian populations which inevitably accompanied direct battles. It was quite another matter to spread death and destruction in advance, over helpless friends behind the actual front. However, the strategic demands were specified by the military Staffs in the form of an ultimatum, and humane and political scruples, especially from the British, could not make themselves felt. After a long and complicated debate, strategic bombing of French targets was maintained as the condition for the successful execution of the Invasion.[68] In his book, "Crusade in Europe", General Eisenhower debates the problem[69] and gives the extremely pessimistic casualty figure of 80,000, but his conclusion even after the War, when he wrote his book, is unshaken: The bombing was necessary, and the losses calculated were never approved by the military decision-makers, who with the help of warnings and by modifications of the plan counted upon being able to reduce these very considerably.

It was obvious that in the face of this presentation of the problem, the Resistance and the exile governments must raise objections and put the question, whether sabotage could be an alternative which could replace and therefore avert the massive bombing, or if nothing else, limit it. In Resistance circles at least, it was the general opinion that the possibilities of sabotage were underestimated, and contrariwise that the Allies overestimated the effects of bombing – which post-war investigations have to some extent confirmed.[70] For many, therefore, the answer was definite: Sabotage could be an alternative, or at least it could be given a greater rôle than the Allies seemed willing to entrust to it. The conditions were sufficient supplies of materiel and sufficient information on the targets which were considered strategically inevitable. One is almost reminded of Churchill's appeal to the U.S.A. in 1940: Give us the tools and we will do the job.

At the end of 1943, French Resistance circles were operating with a "Plan Vidal",[71] in the expectation of mass uprisings of French Maquis forces and Resistance forces in the FFI, which before or simulataneously with the Invasion could liberate considerable areas of French territory, and thus allow for large-scale deliveries of arms, and possibly the dropping or landing in liberated base areas of airborne forces, so that the liberated areas could be entry airports for advanced Allied operations in the liberation of the whole country. The plan was conditional upon advance mass deliveries of weapons and other materiel to the French Resistance forces; it was conditional upon the Allied Staffs' confidence in the Resistance forces' ability to realise these ambitious plans; and it was conditional expecially upon the Allies being willing to divulge the main lines of the plans of the Western Powers, for carrying out the coming military operations, to the French Resistance leaders. The acceptance of such a plan would in reality mean a revision of the careful planning of an invasion in France, which the Staffs of the Western Powers had fixed during many months of work.[72]

In February 1944, the plan was turned down. There were many reasons. It contained an element of improvisation which was incompatible with the methodical staff work of the Western Powers. It operated with the French Resistance forces' capacities as an unknown quantity. It would demand mass deliveries and such employment of the Western Powers' Air Forces as would seriously limit their possibilities for strategical and tactical intervention. Last but not least, the plan was conditional upon the French Resistance leaders being informed at least partially of the invasion plans and the invasion timing, with the risk of leakage which this must involve. The military Staffs of the Western Powers did not trust the possibilities of the Resistance to such a degree, and these must be regarded as a supplementary advantage, and not as a basis for planning. During the long painful debates concerning the strategic bombing of transport targets in France, the deliberations were kept strictly within British-American circles. The Free French authorities were excluded from the debate. De Gaulle was not informed until the day before the Invasion in Normandy.[73] The release of French sabotage against the whole French communications network in connexion with the Invasion was welcomed and prepared, but the planning of the Invasion could not be based upon the greater or lesser possibilities of which such sabotage or military uprising could hold the prospect.

Whether sabotage actually could have been an adequate alternative has never been thoroughly tested. Too much was at stake. In Norway bombing, with few exceptions, was stopped, and the Allies relied upon the greatly increasing sabotage, particularly of transport and shipping sabotage.[74] In Denmark bombing was never used as a strategic weapon, and here the eagerness for sabotage was perhaps particularly strong because of the understandable capitulation complex in the country. But in the countries in the west, the Western Powers maintained the necessity of bombing, and confined themselves to operating with sabotage as a welcome and important supplementary prize.

In such a brief statement, the problem probably appears in a more simplified form than the realities permit. It should, however, in all fairness be stated that the question was not only extremely delicate but also belongs in the sphere where simplified answers are inadmissible. As to the aim, that the necessary strategic targets must be put out of action to the greatest possible extent, there was no disagreement, but the two parties' basis for evaluation were certainly very different. For the Resistance men on the spot, in addition to the human and psychological factors, the realisation of the often insufficient and unintentional effects of bombing influenced them, and they were also influenced by the fact that they were inspired by strong optimism as to their own possibilities, on the basis of successful actions. A successful action of this kind was an attack on the Peugeot factories, which delivered cars to the German Army, and which were first bombed by Allied Air Forces, without decisive effect on the production, after which the Resistance groups contacted the Peugeot family, who showed themselves to be pro-Ally and gave instructions as to how the essential parts of the factory could be hit by sabotage without unnecessary damage, and without loss of life.[75] On the basis of such experiences it was easy to reach the conclusion that sabotage must be the right answer to the problem. But the situation was not always so favourable as here. The Michelin factories had to be put out of action by bombing, and it is an open question, whether one could project experiences from the optimum of successful cases over to the whole field of targets generally.

For the Western Powers, the results which the Resistance could achieve were and continued to be subject to understandable uncertainty. One could send over materiel and issue directives, but would they be followed? In all circumstances? At the right time? It is quite comprehensible, if the military leaders trusted more to normal forces under their direct control, than to anonymous cover names far from the control panels of the Staffs. Another circumstance which has been mentioned also made itself felt. A detailed description of desired targets which could easily fall into the hands of the enemy, could give an important clue as to where and when the blow or blows would fall. And bombing had other advantages. It could be repeated, which was seldom the case with sabotage, and further, one could oneself decide the time for it, whereas sabotage often required a long period of preparation. All in all, one must probably confine oneself to recognizing that both standpoints had their conditional validity, and that neither of them could claim to represent the absolute right solution. That sabotage – properly led – could have played a greater rôle than it did is, however, more than probable. But here too, the Danish research into the effects of railway sabotage calls for caution in judgement, whilst contrariwise the Soviet railway sabotage and the French sabotage during the Invasion battles tell another story.

The history of sabotage is not only the history of destruction. It is also

– and particularly towards the end of the Occupation – the history of how the sabotage groups succeeded to a great extent in preventing planned destruction by the Germans. In this respect, sabotage tactics tipped in this direction as soon as liberation was or seemed to be approaching.[76] In many places this last task was included naturally in the guard duties which presented themselves before normal conditions could be restored, after the abnormality of the Occupation.

Sabotage was developed as a fighting weapon during the Second World War technically and organisationally, as never before. The years since 1945 have seen many sabotage and saboteur stories, all spiced with drama, and many with tragedy. But the history of sabotage, understood as an exact analysis of every action or series of actions in their whole context with all surrounding circumstances, and therefore a final, certain and unimpeachable evaluation of its total effect can probably not be achieved. Sabotage was too extensive for that, and the evaluation would be compromised by too many complicating factors. Figures and statistics can give some idea of its extent, but they can be just as misleading as instructive.

Assassinations

Sabotage was directed against material values. A tragic side effect was that, directly or indirectly, it could also hit human beings. The saboteurs had to face this fact and share the responsibility for it. One should not suppose that it was an easy burden.

Assassination – and attempted assassination – was a more severe fighting form. It was aimed directly at human life, and the Resistance man who undertook to approve, order or carry out assassination, had certainly to assume power over life and death, most often with the risk that it might involve the deaths of many, first the victim, and then those fellow-countrymen who might have to share the penalty. The assassin was in even higher degree than the saboteur confronted with the final consequences of the War. In many instances he knew the immediate victim in deed, appearance and behaviour, and it was a part of his job to pronounce a death sentence with or without approval from a higher court, and undertake the rôle of executioner himself. In a great many cases he must recognize that he would himself be the first victim of revenge, but unfortunately seldom the only one.

Assassinations took place in all the occupied countries and they must be dealt with as the individual fighting form which they constituted.

It is necessary here to emphasize the special situation in the Partisan area. Neither sabotage nor assassinations can be separated here in any way from the Partisan War itself. One cannot draw any dividing line between the Partisan battle, with many casualties on both sides, the surprise attack upon and extermination of an isolated enemy patrol or camp, and the shooting of a lonely sentry, perhaps in connexion with a sabotage action or a Partisan transport. In the Partisan area, assassinations were not only everyday occurrences. They were a routine function, secondary to and inseparable from the other Partisan activities. Here the price was paid in advance. Reprisals in these areas were a proclaimed fact for both Partisans and supposed accomplices, and neither the soldiers of the Occupation nor the Partisan gave any quarter. In the areas where the Occupying Power put up notices with the word "Bandengebiet", every vulnerable group or force on either side was in danger of death without warning. If a possibility for assassination presented itself in these areas, there was neither room nor need for considerations as to the expediency of the assassination, its possible psychological repercussions or its ethical justification.

And it is in these areas that we find the enormously high figures of Occupation soldiers or collaborators killed, by far the greatest number killed in actual fighting, many killed during an ambush, but also an unknown, but in comparison with the total, tiny number of victims of planned assassinations. The Soviet figures of what are described with the common designation, "fallen enemy officers, soldiers and traitors", killed in the Partisan areas, are estimated at over half a million, and if one adds the corresponding figures from the Balkans, Poland and Slovakia the number exceeds one million.[1] It is at once obvious that instances of assassination are included in this group of numbers, and it will also be obvious that any attempt to differentiate between assassination, ambush, and shooting during an engagement will be fruitless.

It was neither here nor in the Partisan areas in North Italy and France that assassination posed any problems of principle as a fighting form. These problems, of a political, psychological and ethical character, can only be referred to in connexion with the countries and areas of Europe where existence, in spite of the Occupation, continued under a more or less thin surface of normality.

Sabotage gained increasing popularity. Its practical and political value was increasingly recognized in far larger circles than those of the saboteurs themselves, and even if they could mean lack, severe counter-measures and violent reprisals, the majority reconciled themselves, openly or tacitly, with these consequences. In Denmark, where the conditions of occupation were the mildest in Europe, an illegal professionally organised opinion poll showed that from the autumn 1943, a majority went in for sabotage.[2] It was far more difficult for the majority to approve the reasonableness, justification or necessity of assassinations. Here viewpoints were tangled into a complex of practical, psychological, religious and ethical scruples, and here emotional attitudes were inseparably mixed in consideration, judgement or condemnation. Here it must be our task to try to isolate the various factors, knowing full well that these varied in force and weight from one person to the next, and that attitudes depended also upon which country and in what circumstances assassination was chosen as an extremely painful necessity, often after difficult deliberations on the part of those taking the decision, and inevitably also now and then, on a sudden impulse which by no means always justified the deed, and never the chain of consequences.

From a practical point of view, to shoot down some individual, perhaps at random – a soldier or officer – was meaningless, and this was the case whether it was a case of a chosen victim, a chance or perhaps a group – for example if a bomb or a hand grenade was thrown into a café which was particularly patronised by Occupation personnel, or perhaps into a marching column. Many responsible Resistance leaders and all exile governments recognized this and turned against actions of this kind. It should be mentioned, for example, that de Gaulle, in a B.B.C. broadcast, voiced his disapproval of actions of this kind, on the purely practical grounds that the population was in the power of the enemy, and that it was all too easy for him to take a bloody revenge in such circumstances.[3] The Dutch exile government addressed a similar appeal to the Dutch Resistance in February 1943.[4] But theory was one thing, practice was another. Particularly after a long Occupation period, and in towns and areas with large Occupation forces, it was quite unavoidable that fights started between the civilian population and the Occupation troops, and regardless of principle, it was a short step to the cudgel, the knife or perhaps the revolver. The result could be an unintentional killing, and once this was a fact, there was no certainty that the affair could be arranged peaceably, even if this could occur in quiet periods and areas. But even in such cases, there was probably a threat of reprisals of a serious nature.

An extreme case can be quoted from Denmark, where a German officer arriving in the Danish provincial town of Odense found himself unexpectedly mixed up in an acute situation there. After a series of disturbances and sabotage actions, there was a total strike in the town, and the German officer suddenly found himself face to face with a crowd of demonstrators. He lost his nerve, drew his pistol and shot into the crowd, after which he was overpowered and seriously beaten up and wounded. It was only an episode, but it seems to be substantiated that it was just that episode at that particular moment – in the middle of the Italian collapse – which was the last straw, which made Hitler, extremely unbalanced as he was, order an ultimatum to be formulated which led to the resignation of the Danish Government a few days later.[5] Here an episode of this kind had political effect. The episode is not typical, however, although it is a glaring example of the long-range consequences which attacks on Occupation personnel could have.

It was a far more serious matter, however, when there was a question of a planned assassination, where the consequences piled up in the ratio of the seriousness of the attack, and where the rank and position of the victim, as well as the timing of the attack could be decisive for the extent of the consequences. Demonstrations, strikes and sabotage brought reprisals with them. Everyone knew this and accepted it in the course of time. During demonstrations and strikes, elements of feeling were usually so predominant that the thought of possible consequences easily faded into the background, if it occurred to anyone in the throes of anger or rage. In the case of coolly planned assassinations, the psychological background was quite different. Here success depended upon cold-blooded calculation, although it must be added that assassinations also inevitably were carried out in spontaneous desperation, where a favourable opportunity offered, or where the assassination could be characterized by thoughtlessness. But the most important and predominant attempts at assassination were those which were carried out deliberately, in cold blood, and in full recognition of what the price might be.

That this price was high and normally higher than where there was a question of other Resistance actions was not only known. It was obvious. The Occupying Power, with the mentality which they openly exhibited and of which they gave daily proof, could not be expected passively or even rationally, from a juridical point of view, to tolerate violent or fatal attacks on their personnel, or on persons in the occupied countries who helped them. Their reactions could be foreseen – that they would progress through the range of martial law, arrests, deportations, executions, and shooting of hostages, chosen especially or at random. On this background, deeply serious psychological and ethical considerations must present themselves. These must include the probability that the burden of reprisals would be greater in the case of assassination than in reply to any other form of Resistance activity, so that both for the decision-makers and their agents, and for their fellow countrymen in the community in which they operated, it must seem relatively heavy in comparison with the advantages from the attacks or assassinations, and also because reprisals showed a critical tendency to increase in scale. Some scattered examples can serve to illustrate the problem.

On 27 August 1941, during a parade in Versailles of French volunteers for the East Front, an attempt at assassination was made against Pierre Laval, Marcel Déat and Jacques Doriot.[6] None of them were killed, but Laval and Déat were wounded, Laval seriously. The perpetrator, Paul Colette, was seized and sentenced to death, a sentence which Pétain commuted to life imprisonment. Here there was a question of an attempted assassination, but not a fatality, aimed against Frenchmen. Here the account, which was primarily an internal French matter, could have been settled with the would-be assassin. But the Occupying Power's reprisals followed. First 3, then 8 executions, and about 360 arrests. The German authorities reacted even more violently[7] when on 15 September the same year, a German officer was attacked in Paris, after a German sergeant a few days before had been wounded by a revolver shot, resulting in 3 hostages being shot. The reply this time was 10 executions of hostages. There was even more violent reaction, illustrative of the summary "justice" with which the German Army tried to check the risk of assassinations, when the German military Commandant in Nantes was shot on 20 October 1941.[8] Revenge came the day after, with the shooting of 50 hostages and the arrest of 50 more, who were sentenced to death by a military court, the sentence being made conditional upon the assassins being caught, after a reward of 15,000,000 francs had been offered for information which could lead to their arrest. A day later, a German Major was shot in Bordeaux. The reaction was a copy of that in Nantes: 50 hostages shot and 50 more arrested and sentenced to death, the executions depending here too upon whether or no the perpetrators were caught. Further reprisals were a curfew after 1800 hours for the whole occupied zone, and a fine imposed on the town of Bordeaux of 10 million francs.

The German reprisals gave warning of the course which the Occupying Powers would take in similar circumstances. None of those executed had had any hand in the assassinations, but were fetched from the towns where these had taken place. This was a clear proclamation that the German reaction would be the blind murder of hostages, and that the

Germans both here and as it would prove, elsewhere, employed what can be described as the principle of round numbers. The reaction was not police investigation, nor "an eye for an eye and a tooth for a tooth", but a large and – in practice – a varying number of hostages executed or shot down at random for every assassination. The practice reappears in Holland for example,[9] where in January 1943 a German soldier was shot in Haarlem. The German reaction was the immediate execution of 10 hostages, arrested in the Haarlem district, and the execution was in accordance with a directive from December 1941 to the German Army, that a minimum of 10 executions should be carried out for every attack on a German soldier. In Belgium a number of executions were carried out in the late summer 1941, and in September the German authorities let it be known that thereafter they would execute 5 hostages for every attack on a German soldier.[10] The principle of round numbers reappears in an even more brutal form in eastern Europe. For example in Poland, where the German Governor of Warsaw, Ludwig Fischer, ordered it to be announced on 4 March 1942[11] that 100 Poles had been executed after the killing of a Gestapo agent, and with the addendum that a further 100 Poles would be executed in every similar incident. It is also documented that reprisals on the same scale was meted out to the population of the Soviet Union. A decree from the German High Command of September 1941 also operates with round numbers:[12] "As the penalty for a German soldier's life, death sentences of from 50–100 Communists must in general be regarded as reasonable. The method of execution must increase the deterrent effect even further." It is well known that this order was obeyed in many places. When a German office in Minsk was blown up in September 1943, the reaction was the summary shooting of 300 hostages.[13] Even in a "mild" Occupation area such as Denmark, one can register the phenomenon. When the liquidation of informers in the pay of the Germans began in the autumn 1943, Hitler ordered the random shooting of 5 hostages for every victim,[14] an order which was modified, however, as to numbers by the local German authorities.

But all this was only the beginning, and it gives a faint outline of a rough principle which was supplemented by countless other measures – martial law, arrests, deportations, followed by fines, cutting of rations, the total stoppage of supplies, etc., etc. In Norway in April 1942, 18 hostages were shot as a reprisal for the killing of two German Gestapo men, and when two German soldiers were killed shortly after during a razzia in the little West Norwegian town of Telavåg, the reaction was the total destruction of the town, the deportation of all the male inhabitants, and the internment of all the women and children in the town – a total of 260 persons. All the houses were burned down, all the boats destroyed, all the cattle slaughtered.[15] The example points to a period which would follow, where the level of reprisals was raised very considerably, and where the occupying authorities tried desperately to hit blindly and either without principles of any kind or according to varying or random whims. When the French village of Oradour sur Glane was wiped out in 1944, it was one example among many which shocked the whole civilised world. Right up to 1945, the Occupation authorities could resort to the principle of round numbers. When an attempt at assassination was made on the German Chief of Police in Holland, Hanns Albin Rauter, in March 1945, 250 hostages were executed.[16]

The choice of hostages varied, also. Now, the Germans chose hostages among Resistance members under arrest, now they picked on victims in the civilian population quite at random; sometimes they were hostages from the same town, the same street or the same trade or profession as the victim of the assassination, sometimes they were leading, well known persons, sometimes quite unknown, and having nothing whatever to do with the attack. No one could feel secure, and no one could assess the consequences in advance.

If one considers that the total number of executions or haphazard hostage murders ran into thousands – quite apart from the mass extermination of the Jews and the mass murders in the partisan areas, where these numbered millions – and that a very large number of these reprisal actions were hostage executions after assassinations or attempted assassinations, the background is given at the same time for the ethical and psychological problems which must arise in connexion with assassination as a Resistance weapon.

The problem presents itself in two parts. On the one hand, there was the question of personal scruples as to guilt and responsibility, on which the decision-makers and assassins must make up their minds. On the other hand there was the question of more impersonal considerations as to the psychological effect an assassination might provoke in the community, which often had to suffer the consequences. In principle, there may not have been any decisive difference between sabotage and assassination, in so far as both forms, and indeed also other forms of action, called down reprisals. There was a gap, however. Sabotage was directed against material things and often carried out in conditions and with methods which, although they were aimed at causing destruction, were also intended to spare what could be spared. If the Occupying Power then engaged in reprisals and revenge, this was felt to some extent to be their fault and responsibility. Assassination was quite a different, immediately personal matter, where a living human being and not a piece of metal was the target of the action, and for many reasons it was more difficult to find understanding for this, outside the most active Resistance circles. There must be weighty reasons for taking up this weapon, and the decision was compromised by the fact that the weightier the argument might be for choosing a victim, the greater the risk became for quite unacceptable consequences.

It is necessary to add, however, that none of the above considerations as to actions and consequences had unequivocal validity. As regards the ethical objections, it is not unreasonable to stress that the assassins were quite naturally volunteers, or where chosen from among persons whose situation, ideological standpoint or character made them especially suitable to undertake such executions, and for them such ethical considerations could have little weight; and further, that the situation leading up to an assassination could be so loaded with feeling that ethical considerations had no validity whatever. The chance situation, accumulated unreflecting rage, or simple self-defence could lead to action. As far as the psychological considerations are concerned, it is probably not incorrect to state that approval was easier to achieve at a later stage in the War, when the brutality of the Occupying Powers was generally known, and in wide circles had provoked a feeling of "come what may", so that the psychological damage which might be a restraining factor from acts of this kind was declining in importance, because the level of revenge had reached such heights that it called forth approval of such acts in desperation. This applied especially in the hardest hit areas, such as the Soviet Union, Poland and Yugoslavia, where measures of force and terror could be reckoned with in advance. An understanding of the times demands an insight into the basic change in mentality which the long years of occupation, the daily lack and danger, the continual outbreaks of violence and blind terror produced, with their effects upon both standpoints and feelings, and the fundamental reassessment of accepted standards. As a generalisation, one can say that the conditions of the Occupation, even where they were mildest, led to a hardening process which also had a brutalising effect. Thoughts, feelings and acts which before the War would have been unthinkable and unacceptable became increasingly approved and widespread, as the Occupation continued. If reprisals provoked horror, they also provoked fury, and the fury often tended emotionally to outweigh fear. On this background, there were Resistance members who could say that the reprisals themselves demonstrated the brutality of the Occupation, and therefore had a favourable effect in promoting a climate of Resistance mindedness. In the free outside world, the reports of the reprisals certainly sharpened the will to victory, and thereby to the liberation of the oppressed.

The reference to the popular understanding of assassinations and their necessity forces one to recognize an elementary fact. It was far easier to gain understanding for the killing or – as it was often euphemistically called – the liquidation of a compatriot, who in one way or another had entered the pay of the enemy, than it was to find understanding for the killing of a member of the Occupation troops. Practical considerations as well as psychologically conditioned viewpoints lay behind this fact. From a purely practical point of view, the collaborator, especially when he co-operated with the Occupying Powers politically or in police matters, was far more dangerous than the Occupation representative who came in from outside, with the exception, however, of the highest echelons in the Occupation hierarchy. The man from outside was a foreign body in a foreign milieu, with no knowledge, normally, of the language, the customs, the traditions, the persons or the groups in a strange country. He had to seek assistance where he could get it, and even where the collaborator ranked low in political experience and influence, administrative ability or adequate insight, he was dangerous. It was obvious that highly placed collaborators were dangerous. The Occupation decrees and their administrative execution had an easier run when they were effected by collaborating organs, depending upon what prestige or influence these might have. But the anonymous nonentity was also dangerous. He had the possibility of infiltrating the illegal network as the foreigner or the man in uniform had not. The collaborator was also guilty in another sense, and on another level than the Occupation representative. The latter was at least there under orders and functioned with responsibility or loyalty towards the authorities of his own country – a moral backing which the collaborator could not claim. And lastly, the age-old contempt for the renegade and the traitor stuck to the collaborator and to his actions, so that all in all there were practical, psychological and emotional grounds for a reckoning with him being easier to accept than a reckoning with a person from the Occupation authorities, who after all functioned by reason of, even if not according to the rules of war and conquest.

In the European Resistance world, then, a clear distinction was made in most places between assassinations of members of the Occupying Power and of collaborators. Whilst attacks on the former were often repudiated on the ground that they were useless and that the consequences were out of proportion to any possible advantage, attitudes were different when it was a question of the liquidation of collaborators. This was clearly stated as early as September 1941, in the illegal French newspaper, "Défense de la France":[17] "The assassination of a collaborator is a liquidation, not a murder. In the absence of military courts, spontaneous justice must be meted out to traitors. It is not a question of civil war, but quite simply of war." The statement was made in an illegal newspaper of Catholic tendencies, and at a time when the illegal French Press almost unanimously condemned the assassination of German personnel. "We advise everyone to refrain from useless manifestations, which do not contribute to the deliverance of the country," and "We formally disavow the attacks on an officer of the Occupation Army which took place on the Underground station Barbés." The practical development in this spirit – with exceptions – was common to France, Belgium, Holland, Norway and Denmark. Special groups such as the Belgian "Groupe Mobile des Partisans"[18] undertook the bloody reckoning with collaborators, and the illegal Press and the leading organisations behind a number of the groups supported the practice. In Holland, the Resistance organisation "Raad van Verzet", took action against collaborators in the Police Force, but also leading members of the Dutch Nazi movement and rank and file members were hit by liquidations. The established counter-terror proved unable to stop these activities, which increased in numbers. In 1944 there were about 300 liquidations, in 1945 considerably more.[19] In Denmark, liquidations were carried out of informers in the service of the German Police, only, and here in the beginning of 1944 we find a statement from the Danish Freedom Council, corresponding to the French newspaper announcement from 1941:[20] "The Nazi-minded persons who have met death in recent times, or have been wounded, have not been attacked because of their convictions but solely because they have undertaken, for high pay, to track down fellow countrymen who are active in the struggle for freedom, and to give them up to the Gestapo. These informers have not been put out of action as a punishment, but because they have caused the imprisonment of a great many people, and the execution of several, and solely to prevent them from endangering even more by continuing their activities."

Added to all this, the liquidation of a collaborator was a blow against the Occupying Powers on their most sensitive spot. To shoot down some person or other from the Occupation Administration, Police or Army could give an outlet to accumulated anger, and, particularly if it was a question of a member of the Police, could give momentary relief, but one could be certain that he would be replaced immediately, and his successor might be even worse. A valuable collaborator could not be replaced so easily. The possibilities for recruitment were limited in this case, and the Occupying Powers, in spite of all the collaboration, remained poverty-stricken in useful assistants. For the members of the Resistance, the removal of a collaborator could be synonomous with survival. Where a cunning informer was at work, the consequences could be the rounding up of whole regions or whole categories of operational activity. When this was the case, the problem could present itself with the force of an ultimatum: the removal of the informer or the cessation of the struggle. A textbook example can be given from Norway, where the "Rinnan" group, which operated in the Trondhjem district under the leadership of the top informer Henry Rinnan, was responsible for over a thousand arrests,[21] of whom nearly 100 persons lost their lives, whilst several hundred were deported, many after prolonged torture. The consequence here was a practically total round-up of the whole district. In cases of this kind, the problem appeared quite simple. Either the danger must be removed, or the Resistance activity must come to an end, usually after the infiltrated organisation had uncovered the informer's activities through many painful losses. Liquidation then passed beyond all political, psychological and ethical considerations, and took on the character of a surgical operation; and consideration of possible consequences had to give way, simply because in such a situation one was in the midst of, or faced with, consequences in all probability of even greater dimensions and wider range. Confronted with reprisal terror, many members of the Resistance had to decide whether they would give up in the face of this terror and stop their activities, or whether, on their own and others' behalf they would be willing to pay the price and bear the responsibility. As a rule, the reply, in most of Europe, was an acceptance of the conditions, and therefore a continuation of assassinations with emphasis upon the liquidation of collaborators. A very clear example of this occurred in Denmark in April 1944.[22] After the execution of a twenty-year old Resistance man, the German Reich Kommissar, Werner Best summoned representatives of the whole legal Danish Press and made a statement which left no one in doubt. He described Copenhagen as a "European Chicago", and announced that he had more than 100 saboteurs in prison, and that these were all liable to the death penalty. If the country quietened down, one would refrain from executing them, otherwise there would be no mercy either for them or for an unspecified section of the population. It was up to the Resistance leaders to decide. If this was unequivocal, the reply of the Danish Freedom Council was just as unequivocal, in an open letter to Best a few days later. Here any idea of yielding to threats of this kind was rejected, and the letter ended: "You can burn, ravage and murder. You can carry out imprisonment and execution. But you can never break our will and ability to fight the power which had plunged the world into war, and robbed Denmark of her freedom." It could not be stated more plainly, that the year 1944 was not a year where threats of terror could subdue the will to resist or bring Resistance activity to an end.

Naturally, in all appreciations of this kind, there must be divergencies of opinion. The Communists took the front rank in the arguments for the necessity of assassination. For them, after June 1941, every form of immediate action represented a patriotic and ideological duty in general, and a duty towards the Soviet Union's struggle in particular.[23] "Our duty is to help the Soviet Union with all means" are words from the illegal French paper, "L'Humanité" of July 1941, and in October 1941 the same paper published the following: "To hasten the hour of victory for the Soviet Union, its Allies and the oppressed peoples, what is necessary? Action, and again action, and yet again action." Whatever the consequences, they must be accepted, and in August 1941, the argumentation was pushed to the extreme standpoint, that reprisals could even bring new vitality to the Resistance struggle: "The blood which paints the pavements red will cause new harvests to grow up." Here it was a question of more than rhetoric. It was a political standpoint, which both contained a protest against all caution that was rooted in psycho-political considerations, and the belief that the very sacrifices made would strengthen fighting spirit. The paper's standpoint was the same in 1943: "The struggle and political wisdom are one and the same thing." On the basis of this way of thinking, the French Communists even tried to argue for a belief that the interaction between assassination and reprisals could be reversed so that the immediate reply to the death of a Frenchman should be the death of 10 Germans or collaborators. The French Communist leader, Fernand Grenier, who was the representative and spokesman for the party vis-à-vis de Gaulle, turned against the latter's appeals for restraint, and the arguments they contained, that assassinations were practically speaking meaningless, and caused unacceptable hostage murders. "It is untrue", he said, "that the development of the activity of the 'Francs-Tireurs-Partisan' has moved the enemy to execute hostages. Untrue politically and historically. The first hostages were shot in Paris in July 1941, whilst the first groups of 'Francs-Tireurs' were established two months later."

The Communist point of view was quite clear, therefore, and clearly in accordance with the general directives which were broadcast in June 1941 from Moscow, with reference to communist conduct. In its most extreme form, however, it could not be maintained. The possibilities for assassination were and remained numerically limited, whereas the Occupying Power had free play with regard to extending its terror, and deciding the character of its terror. It is obvious that regardless of all statements to the contrary, an inescapable connexion did exist between assassinations and reprisals, so that even the most firmly rooted ideologist had to recognize this interaction, and its negative balance of account, and to give tactical consideration to psychological effects. And after stressing the Communist point of view, one must also recognize that Resistance circles outside the Communist camp also went in for assassination, where this might prove necessary, particularly as to collaborators, or might simply be considered justified. It has been mentioned already that opinion outside the organised Resistance sectors of the populations generally accepted some assassination activity, as a bitter necessity, even though this fighting form was the most difficult for many to acquiesce in. Up to the end of the Occupation, and even after it, assassination activity was a subject for doubt, scruples, fear and debate, laden with emotion.

In decision and execution there was a wide spectrum of possibilities, from the spontaneous action of an individual to the carefully planned assassination, ordered by legal or illegal governments. It was unavoidable that the decision often had to be taken quickly and locally, and without the liquidation group having direct access to a superior organ. But usually an attempt was made to bring this activity under control, and as a desirable minimum to make sure that it was in accordance with general instructions from the Resistance leaders who took the responsibility for Resistance activities. Here too there was a noticeable tendency towards the centralisation which characterised the Resistance Movements. Against this tendency, however, the fact remained that neither from Warsaw, Copenhagen, Brussels or Paris could one judge as to an acute necessity out in the local areas, and that such judgement was naturally out of the question as regards the great partisan areas. The attempt was made, however.

In Poland, assassination activity received its special stamp when the "Directorate for Civil Resistance" set up special underground courts, which endeavoured as far as possible to try each individual case before the decision on liquidation was taken.[24] The establishment of these courts rested politically on a special directive issued by the exile government in April 1940, and the procedure and verdicts were based as far as possible on the provisions of the Polish penal law. These underground courts began to function from 1943, and only after long negotiations on the juridical and moral aspects of the whole procedure under which highranking members of the Polish Judiciary expressed serious doubts as to the legal and moral validity of the whole concept of such special courts. The courts came into being, nevertheless. They consisted of three judges, of whom one was a professional judge or lawyer with corresponding qualifications. According to the normal court procedure in cases tried *in absentia,* there was a prosecutor as well as a lawyer for the defence, and every effort was made to obtain the relative evidence in the form of documents, statements of witnesses, photographs, etc. There were three possible verdicts: acquittal, postponement of a final verdict until after the War, or the death sentence. In the case of the last verdict, execution followed, and this was entrusted to special groups, with the proviso that in principle no one should be required to participate in more than three executions. Where possible, the condemned man was acquainted with the verdict before execution, but in most cases this had to take place without warning, most often on the streets. After an execution, emphasis was laid upon the verdict and the grounds for it being made public on the B.B.C., through the illegal Presss and by public notices, and publication was always introduced with the fixed formula: "In the name of the Polish Republic . . .", after which the judgement followed and its grounds. A large number of cases – about 90% – were postponed, by these courts for later decision, whilst in about 10%, or in all approximately 200 cases, the death sentence was pronounced.

Parallel with these liquidations, others took place when individuals or local groups took the law into their own hands, and to the extent that such actions were described as operations sanctioned by the above mentioned Directorate for Civilian Resistance or other superior Resistance organ, the leaders of these organs tried, through proclamations, to disassociate themselves from such unauthorised actions. An example of this was a joint proclamation from the Directorate and the Home Army of 15 September 1943. In less important cases, local political commissions could pronounce judgement on Polish citizens who had had dealings with the Occupying Power. Here as elsewhere, the effort was to avoid situations of anarchy and achieve a control which was unattainable. When after 1944 developments in Poland gradually led to actual partisan war, this effort obviously lost control.

Similar efforts to obtain some control over liquidations can be established in Belgium, Holland and France and Denmark,[25] but all things considered, all well-meaning attempts in this direction had their obvious limitations.

Whilst there were large numbers of assassinations of Europe's collaborators, and whilst assassination activities also regularly hit members of the Occupation troops, it was only exceptionally that assassinations were carried out of the highest Chiefs in the hierarchy of the Occupying Powers. Exceptions do occur, however, and just as sabotage has its famous cases, so does assassination activity have its special cases, and these drew an enormous amount of attention all over the world. The assassinations in Nantes and Bordeaux have been mentioned, as has the attempted assassination of Rauter in Holland. There were others, however. There was an attempted assassination in Paris in September 1943 of the German Labour Minister Sauckel's Deputy Commandant, von Ritter;[26] there was the successful and carefully planned assassination of the German SS Commandant in Warsaw, Frans Kuschera, in February 1944; a bomb was planted with the intention of assassinating the German Military Governor of Paris, von Schaumberg in October 1943; and there were a great many assassinations or attempted assassinations of less high-ranking German personalities. In France and Poland, especially, a number of fairly high-ranking persons of authority were the object of either assassination or attempted assassination. The killing of the German General Commissar of White Russia, Wilhelm Kube,[27] in September 1943 aroused great attention, when he was killed by a bomb planted in his bed by a Russian chambermaid.

The assassination which more than all others drew world attention and had far-reaching and tragic consequences, was the shooting in May 1942 of the German Reichs Kommissar in Bohemia/Moravia, the so-called "Protector" Reinhard Heydrich. Heydrich, before being sent to Prague in 1941, had advanced to the post of Chief for the German Security Police with the rank of Himmler's Second-in-Command, and with decisive responsibility for the SS organisation's terrorist methods, including the persecution of the Jews. On 26 May 1942 he was shot down in one of the suburbs of Prague by two Czechoslovak Resistance men, trained in England by SOE and dropped with this special mission in view in December 1941. The decision on this assassination was taken by the exile Czechoslovakian Government in close consultation with SOE, which undertook the practical side of the preparations, and the background for the decision was the wave of mass arrests following Heydrich's assumption of "protectorship".[28] The number of arrests ran into several thousand, and in addition, a campaign of terror was started on a scale hitherto unknown, with executions and killings of Resistance members, especially among the non-communist organisations.[29] This situation led to the decision to get rid of Heydrich. The assassination was successful. Heydrich was fatally wounded and died a few days later. The reprisals which followed were examples of bestiality which echoed around the world: martial law, the death penalty for anyone who helped the assassins or withheld information, compulsory registration of everyone in the country, and as a first immediate act of revenge, the execution of over 200 persons, including whole families, followed by more executions in June, so that the total number of executions by the end of June 1942 reached about 1300 persons. To all this was added the total obliteration of the two villages, Lidice and Lezaky, all the inhabitants of which were killed or deported. The assassination and the terrible reprisals which followed paralysed the Czechoslovak Resistance Movement for months, and produced a fairly long period of passivity. Both in Czechoslovak circles and outside these, in the midst of the indignation, the question had to present itself, whether assassinations at that level were reasonable or were in reasonable relation to the consequences.[30]

The reply, for many, must be a "No". The example could not but serve as a reminder that the idea of assassination of the high-ranking persons in the Occupation system should at least be considered thoroughly and usually rejected. At the beginning of 1943, the Dutch Resistance leaders and the exile Dutch Government rejected plans to liquidate the leader of the Dutch Nazi Party, Mussert; and in the spring 1944 the Danish Resistance considered but rejected a plan to assassinate the German Reich Commissar in Norway, Terboven, during his short visit to Copenhagen. In this tragic chapter of European Resistance history, there was a relationship between results and consequences which could not be set aside, and which no one could ignore. Among the staffs of the Resistance, in the illegal Press, and man to man, the question of the justification of assassination was constantly under debate, and agreement as to the principle – even in Resistance circles – was never reached in West and North Europe. Whilst sabotage – even outside Resistance circles – obtained a considerable degree of general acceptance, as the lesser of two evils, the same cannot be said of assassinations, particularly not where these were directed against the personnel of the Occupying Power. The situation was different when it was a question of a reckoning with collaborators, especially collaborators in the Police Force. Here there was a question of self-defence. And here the debate as to principle was often silenced.

Partisan Warfare

Every Resistance activity, of whatever kind, was a strain upon the Occupying Powers. It contributed to keeping up the morale of the peoples of the occupied countries, and to undermining morale in the enemy camp. It created uneasiness among the staffs and in the ranks, and it brought material losses to the Occupying Powers, as well as loss of lives. It consolidated the conviction in the free world that the struggle was for a righteous cause, and thus gained psychological effect, also abroad; and it was a daily supplement to the struggle of the free world and thus acquired material importance. If the Resistance had not existed, it would have been easier for the Axis Powers to wage war. The Resistance helped to diffuse the attention and forces of the Axis Powers. And it did this even with the first faint signs of the beginnings of Resistance activity, before it had become a concrete danger, or at least a factor which must be taken into account in all decisions, at many levels. It forced the administrators of the Occupation and their local commandants into unexpected and mostly sterile consideration as to how far they should meet the growing rebellion with the blind violence or with attempts at persuasion to cooperate. But the consideration came too late. It was crushed on its way up to the top of the hierarchy, and it simply uncovered the perplexity which struck the Occupation authorities, when the self-confidence from the months of victory was replaced by nervousness and senseless measures in the years of defeat.

In the Balkans, in France, in Norway and in eastern Europe everywhere, the Germans had imagined that conquest would eliminate the possibilities of the areas in question for resisting the will of the conquerors. They had not foreseen the continuation of warfare, with other means, and certainly not a constant stubborn increase in the effectiveness of this warfare. Quite apart from the fact that the strategic estimates and plans of the Axis Powers miscarried, it was a new, unforeseen and complicating factor that the War was not over when the victory was apparently won. The situation was rather that problems acquired greater dimensions when the campaigns were finished, and the seeming victory was gained. In Yugoslavia a campaign lasting two weeks was nothing to the second campaign which began when the first ended, and even if Yugoslavia is an extreme case, we meet the same phenomenon everywhere, in greater or lesser degree. Where the military victory was supposed to be a conclusion, it proved only to be a beginning to a struggle on a larger scale than a five weeks' campaign in France, a five days' campaign in Holland, and two hours' exchange of fire in Denmark.

The conquered territory became so vast, in the course of two years, and the populations so hostile and ungovernable that no real control could be established, either over single regions or over the countless functions of the communities which were threatened from within. The Germans lacked the requisite personnel for this, and no less the requisite qualifications among the Occupation personnel. They lacked support from qualified helpers in the Occupation areas. They lacked above all political possibilities for underpinning their conquests. To the extent that the Occupation Powers had any Occupation policy whatever, to follow up their victories, this was either unsteady and not thought out to its conclusion, stamped by improvisation and *ad hoc* solutions, or – in the case of eastern Europe – suicidal, in so far as it was based upon a primitive belief that the German "master race" would be able to subjugate and suppress the slave masses with the force of Army and Police alone. Poland was split asunder and robbed of every form of independent State leadership, and in the Soviet Union, where the State leaders and government survived, no attempt was made to drive a wedge between the Soviet Heads of State and the population, or even groups of it. It was only when it was too late that hesitant attempts were made here and there to co-operate with the local population. A comprehensive account of German policy in the East lies outside the province of this book, but detailed expositions of this subject have been made, for example by the American Alexander Dallin and the Germans Martin Broszat and Erich Hesse.[1] The main lines of this policy appear to be quite clear. The Heads of the German State, completely dominated as they were by the Nazi theories as to race, totally ignored every opportunity to appeal to national, anti-Soviet feeling, and by terror, coercive measures, ruthless plundering of the population, etc. forced them out into more and more definite confrontation with the Occupying Power. In the Soviet Union especially, this meant the constant increase of recruitment to the Partisan formations. This applied to the agricultural population just as it did to the urban population, where hunger, the black market and forced deportations were decisive incitements to joining the Partisans. In the first months after the German invasion of the Soviet Union in 1941, both in the Ukraine and in the Baltic countries there were still persons and groups who hoped for a German proclamation of their countries' independence and an appeal to national, anti-Communist feeling. But nothing of the kind took place, and Erich Hesse adds the brief remark: "The basis of the National Socialistic eastern policy would lead to a large capital of sympathy and willingness for co-operation and a new order, particularly among the national minorities, being completely unused." Whether it might have been possible to ease the burdens of the German Occupying Power by appealing to the local populations has only academic interest, since it was never attempted.[1] When the Germans rejected any attempt at political cooperation with the Poles and when they regarded such attempts as both unnecessary and undesirable, and when at the same time, on the basis of a philosophy of might, they confronted these peoples with daily proofs of a master-slave relationship, and permitted cruelty, terror and the hunting of human beings, the result could only be political polarisation. In this polarisation, peoples were welded together, in self-defence, athwart all special interests, with all the means at their disposal, and the basis was created for obstruction and partisan war. This laid great burdens upon the Occupation forces, administration, troops, police and SS units, and when one considers the size of the areas in question and the size of the populations, it is clear that the demands for guard duties could not be met. The Occupation became ineffective, with great areas liberated by the partisans and with repeated demands for the engagement of Occupation forces to control or clean up first one, then another area.

If one is considering the occupied areas of Europe as a whole, it can be established that the Axis Powers were not in a position either as to quantity or quality to meet the demands for control made by the Occupation, in order to deal with the growing Resistance disturbances. The strengths of the Occupation forces are difficult to determine at any given time in any given region, because one must in all cases include in the calculation the troops which were in transit or redeployment, lying in reserve or resting, or simply in "waiting" position in case of invasion. But there can be little doubt that the Occupation and its ever-increasing tasks contributed to making it difficult to supply the Front with fighting troops, and in critical situations did so to a dangerous degree. The thinning out of the Occupation troops and their concentration in garrisons, always in an actively hostile environment, was a consequence of the enemy's conquests, his obvious lack of an even moderately acceptable Occupation policy, and the resulting universal Resistance activity, coupled with the co-operation of the Resistance organisations with the free world.

It was this thinning out of the Occupation forces which in many places made the stubborn partisan war possible; and the converse was true, that this again contributed to further diffusion. On the East Front it could happen that fighting troops had to be withdrawn from the front line to meet attacks in the hinterland by partisans, or that battle troops and materiel here failed to reach the Front, or arrived too late and in reduced numbers. The same thing occurred during the invasion battles in France in 1944, and during the Allied offensive in North Italy in 1944–45. It occurred repeatedly in Yugoslavia. The possibility was also present in Belgium, Holland and particularly Norway. The very fact of the uncertain situation as to disturbances, invasion, or the combination of both, contributed to diffusion. During the critical battles in Russia in 1943, 380,000 men were held back in Norway, 360,000 in Yugoslavia and 40 Divisions in France, in addition to fighting troops and Occupation forces in Italy, Greece, Belgium, Holland, Denmark, Poland and Czechoslovakia. Everywhere there was a need for manning and guarding, and almost everywhere there was the risk of invasion and internal disturbances. Granted, that many of the Occupation forces were reservists, troops resting or in the process of redeployment. A great many of them must necessarily have been elite troops, and many were involved in local fighting with inevitable losses, which became less and less possible to replace. The size of the territory and the hatred of the populations became compromising factors for the Occupying Powers, from 1943 practically speaking Germany alone.[2]

It is impossible to give the size of the occupied territories or the numbers of their inhabitants. Both figures varied with the movements of the fronts, particularly the East Front, and the time at which a possible calculation could be made. From the New Year 1943, when the Soviet offensives began, these would seriously and constantly reduce the Occupation territory in Russia, but on the other hand, at that stage – in November 1942 – the unoccupied zone of South-east France was added to the occupied area, and in 1943 the Germans occupied most of Italy, while at the same time the Italian Occupation forces dropped out of the Axis Powers' credit balance, and the whole task of occupation fell to the

German State and its scattered auxiliary corps – a doubtful asset as to reliability and military effectiveness.

With reservations, however, some quite rough figures can perhaps serve to illustrate the dimensions of the problem of occupation density, as opposed to the diffusion of the Occupation forces. At the end of 1942, when the occupied territories reached their greatest extent, these covered – in Europe alone, without the Soviet Union – more than 2,000,000 square kilometres, with about 125,000,000 inhabitants. It is more difficult to calculate the territorial size and population figures in the case of the Soviet Union, because the fronts were constantly moving and the situation fluctuating, with large areas under the control of the partisans, and with the evacuation of millions of inhabitants, particularly the highly trained. But if one includes only one third of European Russia, one arrives at a figure, for the whole occupied area, of approximately 3,000,000 square kilometres, with a population of over 150,000,000. Whether one then calculates the density of occupation according to area or according to population, one arrives at overtaxing and unattainable quantities. With one soldier per square kilometre the requirement would be 3,000,000 men; with one soldier per 100 inhabitants, the corresponding requirement would be 1,500,000 men. These examples are not intended as an assertion that these theoretical requirements were met, still less that the Resistance Móvements held down forces of such dimensions. It is simply a recognition of the fact that fear of invasion, and lack of any Occupation policy which could animate to or make possible a qualified collaboration, and therefore the possibility for resistance or even revolt to an unknown degree, actually caused diffusion. It thereby thinned out the Occupation forces to an extent which contributed to weakening them seriously, and created uncertainty. There is wisdom behind the French Communist motto, "Every man his Boche". The Occupation soldiers were not the only people with weapons, and they knew it. The results of this was ever-present anxiety, both as to what was happening and what could happen. The fact was that the Occupation forces were the few among the many, and an omnipresent control was beyond the capacities of the Occupying Powers, and gave elbow room for all kinds of Resistance activities, including partisan activity.

An important *sine qua non* for this last activity was that certain geographical conditions were present, and here one is not only thinking of the nature of the terrain in the form of mountains, marshes, large forest districts, etc. Such geographical areas were obviously suited to the waging of partisan war, but also great trackless regions could supply this back-

ground, if the very size of the area and its inaccessibility prov
security against any constant physical enemy presence. Here
pation had to be confined to securing vital junctions, if pos
stretches of road and rail, whilst the surrounding country cou
overrun and consolidated, village by village, railway by railw̶̶, ̶ ̶̶̶̶̶-
sroad by crossroad. Such a task was insuperable, and large areas had
therefore to be left without the troops combing them, and without German supervision. If Occupation troops were to move out from their
barracks into such areas – often designated by the Germans with the
word "Bandengebiet" – one patrol or platoon was seldom sufficient, and
would often be at the mercy of the partisans. Mopping-up had often to be
a major military operation, with the use of considerable forces, and even
so, the results could only be temporary and inadequate. The partisan
forces could count upon their capacity for rapid movement into new,
clear areas, and could return when the situation allowed. Their weakness
lay in their supply service not only of arms but also of the daily necessities of life – a weakness which was remedied in time, although never
entirely so. Partisan life was normally hard,[3] marked by Spartan conditions, improvisation and constant danger, but it could be lived, and as
time went on, by more and more. The handfuls of men became companies and the companies became brigades, and the partisans, unlike the
Occupation troops, were not in enemy country, but were operating
among helpful compatriots who would give them warning when the need
arose.

If the geographical conditions were suitable, this did not necessarily
mean that Resistance activity always developed into partisan warfare. In
a mountainous country such as Norway, with vast wastelands and great
trackless stretches, there was no partisan war, even though towards the
end of the Occupation there were tendencies in this direction, in that
large groups of young men, the "Boys in the Forest" as they were called,
took refuge in the waste lands, to avoid labour conscription. Here, however, it was a question of a defensive measure against a Quisling decree
calling up the 1921–23 military service classes for forced labour service.
Here the civilian Resistance call was to refuse to report for duty, to
destroy registers, and seize ration cards, so as to supply those who
refused. This was so effective that most of these young men could return
home after a short time, or look for work on the land. Out of about 70,000
who were called up, the Occupying Power and their satellites only obtained about 300 men for work. About 2,000 crossed the border into
Sweden from their camps, and volunteered for the Norwegian Brigade,

and a few remained in the camps until the liberation and were enrolled in the Norwegian Home Army, Milorg's forces.[4] On the other hand, partisan forces could be found in areas such as the Crimea, Brittany, the Vosges, the Massif Central or the Ardennes, which certainly offered certain geographical possibilities, without being ideal for the purpose. From descriptions of partisan life one often receives an astonishing impression of how near the Partisans or Maquis could be to the Occupation troops, side by side so to speak, only separated by forests and warnings.

The great cities of Europe also offered certain possibilities, not in the sense that actual partisan formations were set up there, but in the sense that a great deal of Resistance activity was concentrated in or started out from Resistance centres in these cities, and in the sense that a great city was an impenetrable jungle which offered shelter for Resistance activities as well as latent danger for the Occupying Powers. If the inhabitants of a city reached boiling point, it could be difficult to keep developments under control, and in critical situations, cities such as Amsterdam, Copenhagen, Paris, Antwerp, Warsaw, Milan and Turin could become the hotbeds for mass activity, which could explode in popular uprising. Here sabotage actions could also develop into quite massive, open attacks by large groups of saboteurs, in which case sabotage actions could take on a character approaching partisan raids. Sabotage attacks in daylight against defended targets, and carried out by organised sabotage groups became a possibility; and when industries, transport and garrisons had to be safeguarded, and this had to be done from the North Cape to Crete, it entailed a drain on manpower which was more and more difficult to meet. Attempts to establish guards with local recruits proved to be of doubtful value. Suitable geographical conditions, therefore, were not the only factors behind the formation of partisan units, although they constituted the most important. Except for Norway, there was hardly a mountain region in Europe which did not house partisans, and in addition to these there were the partisans who operated in thinly occupied areas, or who prepared themselves in the great cities.

The partisan war became the most severe fighting form which the Resistance Movements took into use, and the fighting form which caused the Occupying Powers the greatest losses in men and materiel, and it was also the fighting form which engaged the largest forces in countering the danger behind the Front.

The partisan war was fiercest in the Soviet Union and in Yugoslavia, and this is not only explained by the geographical conditions or the tradition of partisan war in the two countries, but also by ideological conditions. In both countries, Communist ideology was the basis of their fighting spirit, and fighting form, and Marx, Lenin and Stalin had all established the theme of the ability of the broad masses, through popular uprisings and partisan war, to counter even superior enemy forces.[5] During the wave of revolutions in Europe in 1848, Marx had declared this in an article in "Neue Rheinische Zeitung": "A nation which is fighting for its liberty should not engage strictly in the ordinary methods of warfare. Mass uprisings, revolutionary methods, guerilla bands everywhere, these are the only means by which a small nation can hope to hold its own against an enemy who is superior in weapons and equipment. By these methods, a weaker force can defeat stronger and better organised opponents." And after the revolutionary surge in Russia in 1905, Lenin came to the same conclusion: "The tried and recognized methods of guerilla warfare – constant strikes and the exhaustion of the enemy in barricade fighting, here, there and everywhere – have proved to be extremely effective," and in his work, "The State and the Revolution", Lenin refers again and again to the possibilities of the masses to oppose exploitation, for example in the words: "The exploiters are naturally not able to hold the population down without having a very complicated machinery to perform this task. The population, on the other hand, is able to hold the exploiters down with a very simple 'machine', almost without a 'machine', without a special apparatus, with the aid simply of the organisation of the armed masses." The words were aimed partly at the State apparatus of pre-Revolution Russia, but they received new relevancy in the face of the exploitation which began in 1941. Stalin, too, can be quoted on the importance of revolutionary uprising, for example in a speech in 1923: "Do not forget, comrades, that if we had not had the so-called 'foreigners' behind Kolchak, Denikin, Wrangel and Yudenich – the oppressed people who disorganised these Generals' hinterland by their silent sympathy for the Russian proletarian comrades . . . then we would not have beaten one of these Generals. While we advanced against them, their hinterland was dissolved. Why? Because the oppressed peoples were forced into arming, while we held the banner of freedom aloft for these oppressed peoples. It was that which determined these Generals' fate. It is these factors which, although they are hidden by our Armies' victories, in the end turned the scales. This must not be forgotten." In a speech of Stalin's from 1934, the same tone is struck again: "It will be an extremely dangerous war for the bourgeoisie, because such a war will not only be fought at the fronts, but also from behind the enemy. The bourgeoisie need feel no doubt that the countless friends of the working classes in the USSR, in Europe and in Asia, to judge from all the signs, will stab their oppressors in the back." Stalin was also thinking of Asia. So was Mao-Tse-Tung in 1937, when he noted, in a book on guerilla warfare: "We must underline that the guerilla struggle which is being carried on today in China is a page of history which has no precedent. Its influence will not be confined to China in her present struggle against Japan, but will be of world-wide importance." The Communist ideology, supported by experience, was prepared to resist the aggression of the Axis Powers. The partisan war, first of all organised and practised by people of Communist convictions, would come to drain the Axis Powers of much of their manpower, and inflict great losses upon them. Tito, also, stresses in an article in the paper, "Kommunist" in October 1946, that the Communist ideology and the Communist Party's understanding of the possibilities of partisan warfare, their ability to organise it and their will to accept its sacrifices, were a determining factor behind their entry into the partisan war. Tito here rejects the belief that the principal explanation of the Yugoslav partisan war lay in the geographical conditions of the country, or that it was the expression of a policy of desperation or adventure. Tito finds the explanation in the hatred of the Fascist Occupying Powers, and the peoples' traditional love of liberty and independence, and then emphasizes as the most important factor, which made the struggle possible, the ability of the Communist Party to organise revolt, and to give it a correct and responsible leadership. He strongly stresses the Party members' unselfish attitude in the struggle, and their loyalty towards the Yugoslav people, and refers in this connexion also to the Yugoslav Communist Party's loyalty towards Socialist ideas and the Soviet Union.

It has been stated earlier in this book that the Soviet figures for the Occupying Powers' losses in the partisan war are estimated as approximately half a million men, and the losses in the Balkans were not much less.[6] In Poland, also, as well as in Italy and France, the Occupying Powers had to register considerable losses in men in the fight against the partisans. Faced with the partisan threat, they could be forced to send in forces of the magnitude of a Division, and often several Divisions. The problem of combatting the partisans was, then, greatest in the classic partisan countries, the Soviet Union, Poland and Yugoslavia, which could build upon old traditions in guerilla warfare,[7] but apart from these, as we have seen, there were partisan formations in Slovakia, in the French mountain regions such as the Ardennes, Brittany, the Vosges, the Massif Central, the Alps and the Pyrenees, in Italy in the Apennines and in the North Italian Alps, and lastly in Albania and Greece – to which should be added the conglomerations of Resistance groups in practically all the large and middle-sized cities. The Occupation was never and could never be total, and the problem with the partisan-infested areas increased with the length of the Occupation, and the development of the organisations. And if the Occupation was never total, it was never permanent either, because every attempt to clean up one or another area usually stranded on the partisan formations' enormous mobility, and the rigidity of the German military structure, with its dependence upon systematic preparation and the use of heavy materiel, which in the special geographical conditions could only be engaged with difficulty and often not at all. Where there was a question of counterattack on partisan forces in wooded mountain areas, armoured forces, heavy artillery and air superiority were unusable. The fight must be fought as an infantry battle, and the attackers must at least be physically equal to the partisans, and always have numerical superiority. In this running battle for the hinterland and supply lines, even a major offensive could hit at thin air. Now and then, encirclement might appear to have succeeded, but again and again, the detachments which had been encircled, in spite of severe losses had the strength to break through the pincer grip, to regroup and go into action again elsewhere. Light equipment, stamina, Spartan habits, knowledge of the terrain, and the terrain's own character, as well as support from the local population, gave a mobility which neither the Italian nor the German Armies were able to counter. And if an area was at last cleaned up, it was beyond the powers of the Occupation troops to keep their grip on the area, which could again become the operational base for returning partisan formations, supplemented by the constant stream of recruits, forced into outlawry either by the urge to resist or by bitter necessity – often a necessity created by the ravages which the mopping-up operations brought with them. Here the principle applied that water finds its own level.

In reality, both in the Soviet Union and in the Balkans, there were considerable areas where the partisans had actual control, and could reorganise or set up new communities of a certain austere normality, liberated islands in a hostile sea. One gets a vivid impression of this from reading any of the many accounts by instructors who were infiltrated from abroad into these partisan areas.[8] Once they had reached a partisan base, dropped by parachute, landed from a naval vessel or a fishing smack, or simply flown in to an improvised airfield, they could stay at or with the base, often on the march, often fighting, but also often adopted into a society which was only exceptionally, and with one single dramatic departure from the rule, in direct touch with the enemy without previous warning. The dramatic departure from the rule was a sudden German parachute attack[9] on Marshal Tito's Headquarters in the town of Drvar, in central Bosnia, at the end of May 1944, carried out at a moment when, after an unsuccessful German sixth offensive against the partisans, Tito and his closest advisors had believed the situation in Bosnia – with some reason – to be stabilised to such an extent that Drvar could be regarded as a permanent base for further operations, and for expanding the provisional Yugoslav Government's administrative control over large parts of the country. But this was the exception. Normally, the base was warned when the enemy prepared for mopping-up operations, and the partisan island was far from being isolated. Long journeys could be carried through, far behind the enemy lines, and deep into the Occupation areas. There was contact by courier and radio, from base to base, and from the Yugoslav bases to the Allied bases outside the occupied territory; and people were flown in and out in large numbers – instructors, political negotiators, wounded, specialized crews, or whoever or whatever the conditions might call for. This occurred in the Balkans, it also occurred in the Soviet Union, and to a lesser degree in France. When the instructor from the free world had adapted himself to the material conditions and the physical demands which life in the partisan areas offered, he could in a great many instances feel himself protected in a helpful world, which the Occupation soldier was afraid to enter. Directly and indirectly, the Occupying Power was forced to write off great areas and stretches of road as impassable, most directly, when the authorities found themselves forced to put up notices announcing that this or that area was a closed danger zone, only to be entered under adequate military escort: "Bandengebiet – Strasse Civida/Udine – Nur im Geleit befahrbar". In large areas the escort had to be of the size of a Division or more. Here political and military fiascos were printed and imprinted in black letters on a white ground.

It is true of the partisan war, as of all other Resistance activity, that it started from zero and developed with accelerating speed in more and more partisan areas, and larger and larger partisan forces. But whereas the partisan areas can be pointed out with some accuracy, and the reason has been indicated in the previous pages, difficulties pile up when one attempts to state or even approach a statement of numerical strengths. The partisans were not in a situation which encouraged the setting up of any registering bureaucracy, with records and card indexes; and in addition to the lack of reliable statistical material, other difficulties arise, such as factors of definition and factors of time. Both factors make statements of precise figures equally unreliable.

What is to be understood by the term, partisan? Who is to be included in the definition? Must he or she necessarily be supplied with a machine gun or a number of hand weapons? There were those who had joined the partisan armies without weapons, and those who were only staying with them temporarily. There were those who were waiting for weapons. There were those who maintained communications between the camp and the outside world. Should couriers be included, or those who give shelter and warning, or the man who tears up his last shirt to provide bandages, or who helps with a sack of flour or a pair of horses? Or perhaps even the helpful sympathiser? Questions of this kind must necessarily hail down when one tries to estimate numbers. This has been tried on many sides and in many ways. But the fact is that all partisan activity was inseparably bound up with assistance and support from the sections of the population not directly involved in action. Food, clothes, sometimes shelter and transport, and always warnings had to come from them, and no partisan unit could cut its lines of communication with civilian life outside the partisan camp, either during a temporary stay in permanent quarters or on the march to new quarters. Mao Tse Tung has given pregnant expression to this rule of conduct, with the well known and·often quoted words, that a partisan is like a fish in water: no water, no fish! The Yugoslav Resistance leader and historian, Vladimir Dedijer, has stated[10] that one of the Yugoslav partisan movement's greatest difficulties was perhaps defending itself against more recruits than were immediately required, so that the country retained at least so much normality that the partisans could exist at all. A country consisting only of partisans was unthinkable, as was a partisan unit without support in the civilian population.

When the East German historian, Heinz Kühnrich, who has devoted himself more than anyone else, to a study of the partisan war during the Second World War, in his large and abundantly detailed work, "Der Partisanenkrieg in Europe 1939–45", is so bald as to give definite figures of the strengths of the partisan armies in the European countries other than Norway, Holland and Luxembourg, the columns of figures[11] must be read with the reservations indicated above. Kühnrich himself seems to be aware of this. He gives the figure of 1,933,000 for the Soviet partisan forces, but adds in a note that the figure includes partisans and Resistance members. Understandably enough, Kühnrich does not attempt to differentiate, because differentiation is impossible. This dilemma as to differentiation appears even more clearly when Kühnrich enters the figures of 75,000 partisans in Belgium and 47,000 in Denmark, in his columns. Here there is evidently a question of organised Resistance members, and not of partisans in the normal sense of the term. In Belgium there was at the most only a question of a tendency towards partisan activity in the final phase of the War, and only in a limited degree, and in Denmark the Resistance struggle never reached the partisan level, even if here too there were intentions in that direction.

It must be maintained that the definition factor alone excludes any precise statement of the numerical strength of the partisan formations. This does not mean, however, that this is the last word, and the problem is shelved. Here too there must be a graduation from one country to another. When Kühnrich estimates the Yugoslav partisan force in the summer 1944 as 370,000 men, it is reasonable, considering the special forms which the Resistance struggle took in that country, to maintain that this figure is a believable and probable figure for actual partisans, as it corresponds quite closely with the number given by Tito himself, and the figure reported by the Western Allied Missions. However, if one takes Kühnrich's figure of 500,000 French partisans in the summer 1944, this must include at least two categories of active Resistance members, both the Maquis forces which had been in engagements with the enemy for months in certain areas[12], and also the larger forces of the "Forces Françaises de L'Intérieur" (FFI) which had been in a waiting position up to the invasion but were activised concurrently with developments at the fronts, and especially after the Allies had broken out from the bridgeheads in the north and south. The matter is further complicated by the fact that the word "waiting position" should not be misinterpreted. Many of those in "waiting position" were engaged in various forms of active Resistance work. The whole problem of numerical values becomes no simpler if one considers the estimated figure for the Polish Resistance forces. The strength of the Polish underground army which remained loyal to the exile Polish Government, the Armia Krajowa, is estimated by the Commander of this army, General Bor-Komorowski, as 350,000 men,[13] a number one finds in Kühnrich's figures, but out of these 350,000 men only a proportion were active in the partisan sense, others were in waiting position, and no engagement of the total force ever took place. During the uprising in Warsaw in August-September 1944, the forces in the city and the neighbouring districts were sent into action, and before then, forces from this army and Communist forces from the Armia

Ludowa were sent into open fighting in eastern Poland, but a general simultaneous engagement of all Polish forces was never a realistic possibility. How many of the 350,000 should be characterized, after this, as partisans in the actual meaning of the word must remain a question of definition. On this background, even a cautious estimate of the figures of the European partisans cannot be a basis for comparison. But the fact remains that the numbers were great and increasing.

If the definition factor sets narrow limits for precision as to numbers, however, the time factor also does this. Every statement will naturally depend upon the time to which the statement refers. One may say in general that the partisan forces, regardless of their character and the form of their organisation, were in rapid growth everywhere and indeed in accelerating growth. The longer the Occupation lasted, and the more likely the defeat of the Axis Powers appeared, the more strongly the desire to volunteer made itself felt, and the more rapidly the partisan forces swelled. It is true of all Resistance developments that the Allied victories on the open fronts were decisive stimuli. But in this development, other factors also came to play decisive parts – the growing Occupation terror, the fact that mass recruitment was only conceivable after a pioneer period, where the necessary cadres had to be formed, communications established, and intelligence service and weapon supplies organised. This last factor, especially, was a fundamental condition for effective growth, and to the last it was an element of limitation. The armed partisan was a real asset to a formation, an unarmed partisan could be a liability. Whether his weapons were captured, home made, or delivered from abroad was immaterial in this connexion. The decisive point was simply that recruitment should preferably take place at the same pace as deliveries of weapons. Where recruitment was undertaken in expectation of weapon deliveries, and these failed to materialize, all expansion must be an illusion or – which was perhaps worse – result in disillusionment.[14] One could, and in several countries was forced to operate with forming groups of unarmed Resistance volunteers, and therefore with numbers of potential partisan forces which had little relation to the effective strengths. But on the other hand, when weapons arrived, it was a short step to recruitment, up to or somewhat beyond the quantity of weapons. It is more than likely that a statement of the problem can be made to the effect that it was the quantity of weapons which determined the recruiting percentage.[15] Unfortunately the converse, that the possibilities for recruitment determined the supply of weapons, could not be practised. A typical exemple can be given from Yugoslavia. In the early summer 1943, Marshal Tito informed the first British Missions to reach his Headquarters that he had a partisan force of about 150,000 men at his disposal. But in September the partisans disarmed six Italian Divisions, and in addition two Italian Divisions went over to the partisans. The result was an immediate expansion of Tito's forces, so that in October a British Military Mission could report home that their numbers had reached about 220,000 men. From then onwards, British deliveries streamed in, and in February 1944 Churchill could announce in the House of Commons[16] that the Yugoslav partisan forces had now reached a total of about 250,000 men, a figure which rose during the summer 1944 to approximately 370,000 men, and later increased further. Here is a clear example of the relation between the supply of weapons and the strength of a force. The supply of weapons, however, was everywhere dependent upon the level of organisation, and particularly the organisation of deliveries from abroad – organisation which took time. For this reason alone the time factor becomes decisive for all statements of numbers, if these are to have any real meaning.

In the East conditions were somewhat different. From the New Year 1943, possibilities for recruitment were increased here, and this contributed to strong growth in the Partisan forces. From the same time, however, the Front was constantly pushed westwards, so that the basis for recruitment in the population gradually decreased, the two factors counteracting each other. Thus all figures for this area must be variable. The German historian Erich Hesse, in his book "Der Sovjetrussische Partisanenkrieg 1941–44", points out the explosive expansion shown in the figures established for the year 1943, and in the case of White Russia he reaches the conclusion that the numbers of partisans were more than doubled. In addition, there was a considerable contingent which was incorporated into the regular Russian Armies during the Soviet advance. He estimates the total at the end of 1943, for the whole area still under occupation, as about 250,000 men. Here, however, a variable factor must be taken into consideration. At this stage, large districts of what was previously partisan territory had now been liberated. A static, precise statement of a fixed number of partisans or members of the Resistance can only be understood as referring to a maximum figure of all those enrolled in the partisan forces, at whatever time or stage, or contributing in any way to the resistance against the Occupying Powers.

One principal difficulty in giving reliable figures for the Partisan formations, or indeed for any Resistance organisations, is that it is only possible theoretically to differentiate between actual Partisans attached to established Partisan camps and often, but not always, in direct engagement with the Occupation forces, and persons who declared themselves willing to take part in resistance when weapons had been procured, and the situation was also ripe for a general uprising, for example in connexion with invasion or with a collapse in the armies of the Occupying Powers. This was particularly the case in North Italy, and in West and North Europe, as well as partially in Poland and Czechoslovakia, where persons of this last category could be attached to the Resistance forces on paper, in all good faith, but otherwise could function in normal society under their own or assumed names, and simply await the moment for a general revolt, started by agreed directives. The problem is inseparably bound up with the Western Powers' concept of the structure of the Resistance and its strategic use. As early as 1940, SOE (later also SOE/SO) placed considerable weight upon the establishment of Resistance groups, who were to start action immediately in intelligence services, sabotage, reception of weapons, assassination activity, propaganda and other forms of undermining activity; but parallel with this, as we know,[17] work was being done to build up and supply underground armies, which would not begin to function until the general strategy and the battle situation made the engagement of these forces, in stages, reasonable and tactically defensible – in the opinion of London/Cairo. In accordance with this, supplies of weapons were also prepared, but deliveries were witheld until the Allied Staffs judged the moment for engagement to be approaching; and deliveries were not intensified until just before or after the revolt was a fact. Britanny is a textbook example of a region where this programme was followed according to the model plan. Here there existed both a Maquis and a considerable paramilitary waiting force. In connexion with the Invasion and no less with the breakthrough from the Allied bridgehead in Normandy, the signal was given for a general rising of both the Maquis and the paramilitary forces. These were supported by extensive dropping of weapons, landings of airborne Allied forces, and a large number of missions – the Jedburgh teams,[18] each consisting of three men, an American, a Britisher and a Frenchman, of whom one was always a telegraphist. The Resistance forces here, in co-operation with the American forces, which advanced into the peninsula after the break-through, were of considerable importance in the rapid capture of the whole region, and the encirclement of the retreating German forces in the large Atlantic harbours of Britanny.[19] On the other hand, an uprising at about the same time, in the mountain plateau of Vercors near Grenoble ended in tragedy, because here the rising took place without co-ordination with the movements of the Allied Armies, and at a moment and in an area which made it impossible for the Allies to intervene directly, apart from dropping supplies, this being organised after intense pressure from the provisional French Government under de Gaulle, from aerodromes in Algeria. The fighting began shortly after the invasion, and continued until the end of July, 3,500 Maquisards engaging a German force of about 20,000. But this could not, as in Britanny, have any direct influence on the invasion battles.[20]

Paramilitary underground armies of the "waiting" type were organised in North Italy and in Western and Northern Europe, as well as in Poland, and in Italy, France, Poland and to some extent in Belgium, these joined up with the actual Partisan forces. When Kühnrich, in his statement on the Partisan forces in these countries reaches a total figure of about 3.8 million Partisans, these quite considerable "waiting" forces are included, and it is not possible to establish the numbers of the actual Partisans in the Soviet or Yugoslavian sense, in these totals. This is quite clear in the case of Belgium and Denmark, where, for example, the number of saboteurs only represented a minor part of the total. In the same way, the Norwegian underground army, or "Home Forces", was an organised force in waiting position, and here as in Denmark, the forces only went into action in connexion with the German capitulation, after which these Resistance forces took over a number of guard duties. Although some of these Western and Northern European forces were engaged in reception of weapons and sabotage operations etc. before the capitulation, this makes little differnce to the fundamental fact.

If one omits East Europe and the Balkans, where Partisan life and Partisan activity were the predominant Resistance form in great areas of the territory, and if one adds that a somewhat similar state of affairs prevailed in parts of North Italy and France,[21] one must accept the doubtful validity of any attempt at differentiating definitely between Partisans and other Resistance activists. In addition, a considerable movement took place between the Partisan camps and the surrounding communities, and from one Resistance function to another. In critical situations, for example, where the danger of conscription of forced labour contingents for Germany was acute, the Partisan camp could be the nearest refuge. On the other hand, it could well be a stage on the way to the free world or to a life under a false name and with false papers, in normal society. And Partisan camps were never out of contact with this normal society or with other more or less markedly Resistance functions in this society. When tens of thousands were in flight, or living underground, and when existence was saturated with illegal abnormality, from the black market to the most idealistic efforts, it was difficult to maintain definite figures covering the enormous range, stretching from the Partisan, via the Resistance activist, the accomplice, the potential helper and neutral onlooker, to the turncoat and the collaborator. Whilst there is a certain real basis for the Partisan figure in the East and South-East, the situation is far more complicated in the West and North, with all their graduations.

At the same time it must be accepted that also in areas without partisans, the existence of an organised underground army in waiting position had an incalculable psychological effect, quite apart from the fact that in places there could be a question of recruitment on paper, where the contribution of the individual perhaps only consisted of a promise to be willing to fight when the situation was ripe for an uprising, and the necessary weapons had been procured, often as well as general physical training and occasional instruction on the use of the weapons available. The Occupying Powers were aware of the existence of such unidentifiable forces, that recruitment and organisation were in progress, and that the invisible troops who walked about innocently in civilian clothes on the streets and in the fields, and did their everyday jobs, were in close contact with the Allied world abroad, and also that both espionage and weapon deliveries were taking place. Actions of every kind were daily reminders. However, the Occupying Powers had to live with an oppressive uncertainty as regards the size of these forces, as well as the place, form and timing of the expected rising. This could not but create a feeling of insecurity among the military Staffs, and forced these to look over their shoulders for the danger which might be lurking in apparently peaceful surroundings. In the East and in the Balkans, where in many places the uprising was an accomplished fact, the Occupation troops knew with reasonable certainty what they were facing, but in the West and North, and to some extent in the South, the dimensions and timing of a possible revolt were elements of uncertainty for them, and it was also uncertain to what extent these waiting forces were co-ordinated with possible Allied offensives. It is therefore understandable that they tried to provoke these forces to premature action, so that they could settle the potential danger before it should become actual.

This was precisely what the Staffs of the Western Powers and the exile governments were afraid might occur. The Staffs in London and South Italy were constantly urging restraint upon the Resistance forces, until the right moment should arrive, which in strategic terms meant that these

Resistance forces should go into action in co-ordination with the planned Allied offensives. The Warsaw rising in August 1944 was a tragic reminder of the danger of a premature rising, and the rising in Paris in the same month was very close to being premature, and in fact forced the Allied Supreme Command, SHAEF, to change the direction of their attack and their planned military dispositions.[22] The railway strike in Holland in connexion with the Arnhem operation proved to be premature, when the operation failed, and it created immense difficulties for the provisioning of the Dutch urban communities in the last winter of the War. Western Allied strategy operated with a plan for a "rolling" engagement of the waiting forces, and aimed as far as possible at bringing them under Allied control with this intention.

These forces were preferably to be organised under Allied command in such a way that they were mobile, flexible instruments, which could be available, region by region and action by action, as auxiliary forces for the Allies' operations. This type of concept had its roots in strategic and political considerations. The Western Powers viewed the contribution of the Resistance forces as having the greatest strategic value if they were brought in as required, unit by unit, when the military operations reached the point where the Resistance forces could be expected to function successfully in close contact with the movements at the Front. This is reflected in the directives which the Western Powers tried to negotiate with the national Resistance leaders, in the many both general and differentiated messages to the Resistance groups which were broadcast on the B.B.C. or through the illegally functioning signal service, in which restraint was urged until action should be ordered according to the military developments. It was also reflected in the organisation of weapon deliveries, and in the arrangements made for instructors to be sent to the Resistance Movements. Neither the Western Powers nor the exile governments in London or Algiers had any desire for the Resistance Movements in the south, west or north, to develop politically in too high degree, into independent political organs which might take over the power to bring about radical changes in the accustomed traditional pattern. All efforts were aimed at the restoration of Europe, to the extent that this was possible, not at European revolution. Where revolt against the established order was a *fait accompli,* as in Yugoslavia, the Western Powers reconciled themselves to this, and gradually adjusted themselves to it, although the British Government tried to mediate between Tito and moderate exile politicians;[23] but where, as in Greece, this was only a threatening possibility, the Allies intervened with military forces. As far as Poland and Czechoslovakia were concerned, the Western Allies were largely powerless, and had to confine themselves to diplomatic attempts to influence developments. But in North Italy, France, Belgium, Holland, Denmark and Norway the Allies supported the Resistance Movements with the means at their disposal, and sought close co-operation with them, while at the same time working for political moderation in these countries' Resistance Movements. Support was therefore graduated, and both military control and political influence was therefore sought in these Resistance Movements – efforts which by no means always harmonised with the intentions and ambitions cherished by the Resistance Movements – or some of them.

Exile governments, provisional governments and national councils in the free world were pieces of more or less weight, in this game for influence and control. The problem was especially acute in France, where de Gaulle and his provisional government, both before and after the Invasion and Liberation had to carry on a tough struggle to win political control and military command over the large sections of the French Resistance Movement which were Communist-led, or for other reasons remained sceptical as to de Gaulle's visions of a united France under his leadership. But the problem of control of the armed Resistance forces was in fact general.[24] As against the desire of the Western Powers, especially Great Britain, to play upon the many strings of the Resistance Movements according to her own and the common needs, the self-assured will of these movements was to create centralised organisations with autonomous, independent control of the pace and direction of their activities. It should be added that considerations of security also influenced the Western Powers. Their staffs and support organisations preferred isolated groups, so that if one was rounded up, this did not involve catastrophic consequences, and the effects could be limited, whereas the Resistance Movements tended to create centralised organs with autonomous will and freedom of action. The co-operation between them and the Western Powers was often idyllic, but there was also a good deal of conflict, and in all the Resistance countries a more or less clear radicalization of political ideology made itself felt, as well as a tendency towards dissociation from the static view of social conditions of the exile governments, in the more dynamic views of the Resistance Movements. The Occupation had brought political currents which the exile governments had not experienced, and where exile politicians or pre-war politicians again returned to power, they had to recognize the distance between their fixed views of society, and the demands for reform of certain self-assured Resistance groups. A simple return to a pre-war political situation was nowhere the only aim behind the efforts of the Resistance Movements. On the other hand, the Western Powers, who had no desire to be embroiled in these internal conflicts, had the whip hand. It was from them that the vital outside help came. It was from them that the Liberation must be expected to come.

The problems indicated here can be illustrated by two typical examples, In connexion with the Allied Invasion in Normandy, SHAEF issued directives to the Belgian Resistance Movement, to intensify sabotage activities, first of all against the transport network and the telephone and telegraph systems of the country. The reply to this was an intense increase in the sabotage activity already in progress – for July alone calculated as 42 trains derailed, 800 railway lines blown up, and 65 bridges destroyed, as well as numerous parts of the communications network cut off. In August this sabotage activity was increased further.[25] This all led to delays and detours in the German troop movements, already hampered by transport sabotage in France, although the results did not come up to the optimum expectations of the Belgian Resistance forces or the Allies. But the Invasion directives did not include a general rising of the whole Resistance force. Not until 1 September, the day before General Montgomery's 21st Army Group, after the rapid advance through North France, crossed the Belgian frontier, did SHAEF issue the order for a general uprising in the country; and one principal result of this rising was that Belgian Resistance forces captured the strategically important harbour of Antwerp, intact.[26] Antwerp's most important Resistance groups had already gathered at the beginning of 1944 in a co-ordination committee for Antwerp, and had carefully prepared a joint action to secure the harbour installations – locks, cranes, bridges and access roads – and in co-operation with a British armoured spearhead, this vital capture was carried through successfully, at the same time as the German opposition in the rest of the country broke down under the double pressure of the Allied offensive and the Belgian uprising. The Belgian Resistance organisations could take the credit for about 35,000 prisoners and thanks to the rapid liberation of Belgium, the country escaped extensive destruction. Here was an example of a form of Resistance action corresponding exactly to the Western Allies' ideal of co-operation between the outer and inner fronts.

The Western Powers' desire for direct control of the Resistance groups, the partisan groups and the waiting groups, and their fear of premature action on their part is also reflected in North Italy. Here, in

November 1944 as has been recorded,[27] the Allied High Command under General Alexander had proclaimed the end of the summer campaign, and had issued directives to the North Italian Resistance organisations to reduce recruitment and activity, and to await the final general rising in connection with a new Allied offensive in the spring 1945. Organisation was the key word for the long period of waiting. But at the same time as the Allied High Command recognized in theory, and co-operated with the North Italian joint command of the Resistance groups under General Cadorna's leadership, and under the auspices of the North Italian Liberation Committee, CNLAI, they tried in practice, by sending out great numbers of small Military Missions to the scattered Resistance organisations and partisan formations, and by the graduation of weapon deliveries, to exercise a moderating and controlling influence, both on tactical and political grounds. As early as July 1944, the Allied High Command had informed CNLAI that it was their intention to issue directives direct to the various partisan formations via the Military Missions attached to them and from the winter 1944–45, several of these missions worked against too wide a recruitment, on the plea that such recruitment would be useless and dangerous.[28] The problem had its roots in various factors; the inability of the Western Powers to resume the offensive in Italy before the spring; the great expectations of liberation, with corresponding eagernesss for action in North Italy; and the physical and psychological pressure under which the population had to live. But as things were, the Allied attitude had to be far from unequivocal and clear. The target for the Allied High Command was two-fold and its parts were mutually incompatible. It was to exhaust the enemy by constant harrassing raids and sabotage, and simultaneously to build up a waiting force for collective action in connexion with the final break-through into the Po Valley. But the latter consideration, which was partly political, was paramount, and the directive for a general rising of all Resistance forces did not come until 25 April, when it was followed by a mass rising through North Italy. Here too, the German collapse, under the double pressure from without and within, was total and sudden.

Lastly, as a final example of the Western Powers' use of Resistance forces in their strategy, it can be mentioned that when the Battle of the Ardennes was in preparation and later in progress, and German units from Norway were brought south, Allied directives to Norway and Denmark were issued with a view to hindering or delaying these troop movements as much as possible, by attacks on Norwegian and Danish railways[29] and in Norwegian and Danish harbours, while it was a military task for the Allied forces of the Fleet and Air Arm to obstruct the transport over the Skagerrak and Kattegat. It has already been mentioned that the Allies here overestimated the possibilities of the Resistance, but the intention was in accordance with the basic Allied view: to use the Resistance Movements supplementarily where their use was considered reasonable in relation to the general strategy, and by directives and deliveries of materiel to try to get control of the Resistance actions placed as far as possible in the hands of the Allied Staffs. Here too, we meet a certain dualism. The Allies recognized the Resistance organisations' central leadership, but reserved the right to take over control and to direct them into their patterns of action in the various regions.

All Resistance hampered and reduced the hold of the Occupying Powers on the captured territory. But whilst their measures against such Resistance activities as the illegal Press, sabotage and assassination activity, had to be confined to intervention with police actions, with reprisals, and according to their capacity and the circumstances, with a certain military safeguarding, the fight against the Partisan forces demanded not only the large-scale commitment of troops, but also heavy losses. In addition to this, the fight against the Partisans, with obvious exceptions to the rule, was almost entirely a fiasco. Time, the development of the War, the Occupation policy and experience, as well as the intervention of the Allied support organisations on behalf of the Partisan forces, resulted in the constant growth of the Resistance forces; and where in 1941 the Occupying Powers either ignored the problem – and in expectation of a quick end to the War could allow themselves to do so – or confined themselves to sending in forces of the size of companies or battalions to fight the Partisans, during the battles of Leningrad and Moscow in 1941 and particularly from 1942 onwards, they were confronted with mass movements which demanded the commitment of forces of Division size or larger. The problem was greatest in the Soviet Union and in Yugoslavia, but also in Greece, France and North Italy they found themselves faced with Partisan threats which could not be pushed aside without the massive use of well equipped troops. In addition, the Occupation garrisons had to be over-manned – the result of a combination of the threat of invasion and the risk of an organised rising behind the back of the Occupying Power. If the latter risk was on a minor scale – and in the principal countries this was far from being the case – it constituted an unknown quantity, nevertheless, and thereby acquired the weight of the unknown. No Occupation authority could allow itself to ignore the risk, and every responsible Commandant had to make his dispositions in the knowledge that the risk existed, but in uncertainty as to how great it might prove to be in the event of a confrontation.

This was only one side of the question. It was more serious that even after sending in large contingents of troops, the Occupying Powers were never able to halt the growth of the Partisan forces, but had to take cognizance of the fact that this continued, and that the Partisans' fighting power increased steadily as their organisation became firmer, and they received a stream of supplies from abroad. Now and then, after a cleaning-up operation, an ephemeral victory could be registered, such as that in the action mentioned against the French Maquis in Vercors in July 1944.[30] But an action of this kind was costly, with the commitment of two German Divisions at a critical moment during the Invasion battles, and under the threat of new invasions. Approximately 20,000 men were sent in against a Maquis force of about 3,500 men, many of whom fell during the stubborn fight for the Vercors plateau. Many of these Maquisards succeeded in fighting their way through the encircling German troops, however, and joined others of the many Maquis formations which existed at that stage, or were being mobilised throughout France. Both before and during the Invasion battles, these set up bases from which they made sortie after sortie against enemy transport lines, depots and garrisons, until August, when the mass uprising swept over the whole French nation.

The great disparity in numbers at Vercors, and the fact that the action, in spite of a temporary and very brutal mopping-up of the district, was only a partial success, is worth noting and is not untypical. Faced with well organised, desperate, fighting Partisan forces, which consisted of volunteers who man for man had consecrated themselves to fighting to the bitter end, and for whom surrender was synonimous with execution or deportation, the Occupying Power was forced to muster numerically superior forces. They also had to prepare every major action in the often almost inaccessible partisan areas, where their opponents had the advantage of the terrain and knew it as an ally, with such care that this betrayed the action in advance, and prepared the partisans for what was coming. The latter could block the approaches for the attack, in terrain where the possibilities for using heavy materiel such as armour and heavy artillery were non-existent. They could secure junction points and prepare retreat to new partisan areas and new partisan bases, and again and again the attackers had to recognize that even the most carefully prepared offensive against the Partisan areas failed. They found to their cost that the Partisan forces, in spite of losses, which were quickly made good by new and increased reserves, had simply re-established themselves in new Partisan areas. This was demonstrated most clearly in Yugoslavia, where from 1941–44 the Axis Powers organised a series of costly offensives against Tito's Partisans, in the hope of shutting in the main body and forcing them to engage in regular battles, so that they could put an end to the Partisan danger once and for all. The total number of offensives against the Yugoslavs is given as 7,[31] of which, however, the first 5 were in the nature of mopping-up operations, whereas the struggle from the autumn 1943 took on more the character of constant fighting, throughout large sectors of the front. The first offensive was in Serbia in the summer 1941, and was at that time directed against both Michailović's and Tito's forces. The next, at the beginning of 1942 – against Tito's forces alone – was in Bosnia. The third was in Montenegro in June 1942. The fourth in Herzegovina at the beginning of 1943. The fifth in Montenegro in June-July 1943. The sixth in Slovenia and on the Dalmatian coast in September-October 1943. And the last was the parachute attack on Tito's Headquarters in Bosnia in May 1944. From then onwards, fighting became general all over the territory. All these offensives failed as to their main purpose, even though, again and again, large Partisan forces were barely able to fight their way out of well planned attempts at encirclement. Here too, the rule applied, that whilst an offensive against Partisan forces had to be prepared carefully and thus betray itself, a Partisan attack came as a bolt from the blue, without warning. And one cannot overlook the likelihood that the conscripted Pomeranian peasant or Sawon factory worker were both less tough and less eager for battle than the Yugoslav Partisan, who was fighting on home ground and for whom the result of the battle was a question simply of survival. Of all the tasks of the War, fighting the Partisans in distant, inaccessible areas were among the most unpopular and most feared. The rapid, easy conquest of Yugoslavia in 1941, made possible with slight losses by a motorized army, which in blitz tempo took possession of the strategic strongpoints in the country, but not the country itself, would therefore prove to be only the introduction to the real struggle.

Here too, the concentration of fighting forces had to be raised to dimensions which exeeded the numbers of the Partisans. In the autumn 1943, after three offensives had failed in various regions of the country, the German High Command estimated the Partisan forces at about 110,000 men – a figure which, as stated, was too low. At the end of September 1943, German forces under Field Marshal von Weichs started another offensive, directed against Slovenia and the Dalmatian coast, which after the Italian collapse and the disappearance of the Italian Occupation forces had immediately been occupied by Yugoslav Partisan forces.[32] In this offensive – the sixth since 1941 – von Weichs mustered 14 German Divisions, 2 SS Regiments, 5 Divisions of mixed nationality under German command, in all about 200,000 men, in addition to about 160,000 Bulgarian and Croatian troops – a total of 360,000 men. The superiority in numbers was thus considerable, and during fierce battles the Occupation troops succeeded in wrenching the coastal areas from the Partisans, and the Dalmatian islands with the exception of Vis. However, even though the Partisan armies were hard pressed, they retained bases throughout most of the country, with a temporary main base in Bosnia, and as we know, their growth accelerated considerably after this very offensive.

A similar, almost uniform repetition can be referred to in the Soviet Union, where the first Partisan forces were already making themselves felt in 1941, but where the weight of the Partisan attacks increased to such an extent that the German High Command found themselves forced to direct increasing attention and energies to combatting the Partisans, and securing the hinterland behind their front. According to Soviet calculations, about 350,000 men were deployed in securing the captured areas in 1942, and in direct fighting against the Partisans.[33] In 1943 the figure rose again. Soviet estimates of the commitment include about 250,000 auxiliary troops and 25 Army Divisions, apart from Police and SS troops – a calculation which like the estimate for 1942, must be a matter of opinion. The captured territory was as far as possible covered by Police, SS troops, Army units in redeployment and resting, and units in transit from the home country to the Front or from one front to another. How large were the forces engaged at any given moment in direct fighting against the partisans can probably not be stated precisely, but that the commitment was very large and demanding is beyond any doubt as to exact numbers. Here too, it applies that the efforts made were useless, in the sense that it was impossible to get rid of the pest. The best one could do was to check it. But the Partisan forces increased, became constantly better equipped and organised, and co-ordination between their actions and the operations of the regular Army became increasingly close.

This last point contains the most fundamental factor to be considered in evaluating the influence of the Partisan war on the course of the War as a whole. While it can be difficult or doubtful to calculate the numbers on both sides of the Partisan front in the West and the East, and while it can be a question for debate, how far the influence of the Partisan activities penetrated into the course of the battles, there is no doubt that this was greatest where it was best co-ordinated with the operations of the regular armies. The co-ordination level seems, understandably enough, to be highest on the East Front, in the co-operation between the Soviet Armies and the Soviet Partisan formations.

There were various reasons for this. First of all, the Soviet Army was on the same mainland as the Partisan forces in the hinterland behind the enemy lines, which made both communications and supplies easier, particularly when – as was often the case – the Partisans were operating quite near the actual Front. But even where this was not the case, the flying distance was usually shorter than the distances – often prohibitive – with which the Western Powers could be confronted. To put it briefly, one can perhaps say that from 1942, the Soviet Union Supreme Command had already reached the stage of development in its operational co-operation with the Partisan forces which the Western Powers only achieved from 1944. The Soviet Heads of State and the Army Command laid great weight upon partisan activity from the start of the struggle in 1941, and the Soviet Partisan formations often included a nucleus of the remnants of Army detachments, which after being caught in a pincer movement, had fought their way out and in accord with a previous plan, continued the fight and joined or organised partisan formations, so that these received an important supplement of trained Army personnel and therefore a more professional character than the Resistance groups and underground armies which formed in large parts of the rest of Europe, often improvised by civilians with no previous qualifications.

In this connexion, a brief marginal note seems to be called for. After the German victories in 1940, there were two regular armies in the areas under German control on the European continent, with trained troops and professional officers: the French Armistice Army of 100,000 men, and the Danish Lilliput army of 5,000 men. SOE was in contact with both these armies, and received much intelligence material from both of them. For a short time, SOE operated with the entirely theoretical possibility that these armies, in especially favourable circumstances, could come to play a certain supporting rôle, whilst German Generals in France and Denmark regarded the existence of these forces with suspicion, and wished them to be disbanded. SOE was not alone in cherishing illusions. It is well known that General Giraud in November 1942 operated with the idea of an Allied landing in South France, and a rising of the Armistice Army, and his hopes were shared by officers of this army, for example by Major-General de Lattre de Tassigny, who after his flight later became a leading figure in the Free French Forces' fight. Similarly, Danish Officers worked with illusory plans to prepare the mobilisation of Danish forces on the basis of the Officers Corps of the Danish Army. When the German and Italian Armies marched into South France in November 1942, and the French Armistice Army was dissolved without a fight, all such ideas evaporated on the spot, and from that moment the supporting organisations of the Western Powers worked exclusively on the basis of co-operation with civilian Resistance groups, although in both countries these co-operated to some extent with professional officers. It is striking, however, that in both countries professional officers regarded the possibilities for building up underground armies of civilian groups with the utmost scepticism; they remained sceptical as regards co-operation between SOE/SO and such civilian groups; they gave higher priority to intelligence work than to sabotage, which they considered ineffectual and injurious to the civilian population; and their scepticism was rooted both in professional and political considerations. As they saw it, armies of this kind would be ineffective and would easily become dominated by Communist elements.[34]

After this digression, if we turn to the co-operation on the East Front between partisans and regular Army Staffs, we must recognize that there were more important grounds than those mentioned for the close interrelation which came into being here. First of all, this was a Communist dictatorship, with a one-party system, and under Stalin's leadership it was an authoritarian regime, which left no room for doubt or discussion as to methods, directives, or issue of orders, or the final political objective. What the Heads of State decided to promulgate in the form of orders was indisputable law for all the authorities involved – the Army Command, the Foreign Commissariat, Radio Moscow, the Central Staff of the Partisan Movement, the Supply Service, the Air Force, etc. – and the calls which were sent out over the radio or through instructors flown in to the Partisans, and reached the most distant Partisan leader, were categorical and unequivocal. They demanded and were in a position to demand the conduct of the war according to the directives issued from above, and these directives had no need to take the intermediate authorities into account, such as exile governments or intervening staffs or ministries. They did not have the character of proposals or requests, but of commands, and left no leeway for the Partisan groups, except as regards tactical decisions, determined by local conditions and the possibilities arising from the actual situation. Further, there was a question of a Partisan Movement which was ideologically uncomplicated, and ideologically educated – and continued to be educated during the War – to follow the Communist ideology without question, and to regard themselves as a movement under superior command. The instructors had both a tactical and political task, and this was dual: to wage merciless war without other compromises than those which might spring from tactical and technical considerations, and to re-establish the Soviet State authority whereever and whenever Partisan forces achieved temporary or full control over one territory or another. Hundreds of meetings with tens of thousands of listeners were organised by the local party leaders, and millions of leaflets and newspapers, either flown in from "the great country" or printed on the spot, contributed to the ideological solidarity.[35]

Here in the East, compatriots were working with compatriots, and without barriers as to language or politics. The brutal Occupation policy had a profound effect upon their solidarity, as did the Soviet Government's calls for national loyalty, and the growing conviction that the Soviet Armies would win, and restore the Soviet State, with the increased strength which would be created by national solidarity during the War.

In these respects, the Western Powers were in a far more difficult position in their dealings with the many European Resistance forces with which they co-operated. Here there was not one State authority, but several State authorities, first Great Britain and the U.S.A., which had to establish co-operation. And quite apart from the fact that up to 1944 both these countries had been separated from their European partners by sea or ocean, and great distances, the Western Powers were not a firmly knit unit as was the Soviet State. All decisions in these two countries, with their democratic constitutions, appeared as the conglomeration of countless impressions and influences from many authorities – War Cabinets, Parliaments, Ministries and Military Staffs in the front rank, but also Departments, Parties, and finally individuals, who made independent decisions. Agreement was far from always present, and was often difficult to achieve. What the State Department thought by no means always harmonized with what the Foreign Office might think; and what they might agree upon could meet opposition in executive organs such as SOE or OSS, who themselves were not always in agreement with each other. What American Staffs considered right could collide with the opinions of the British Staffs, and even within a British Command, there could be effects from collisions between the Staff and the Governments at home or in the Dominions. Such agreement as could then be achieved between the many authorities could strand upon unwillingness in the

Army Staffs or upon technical or economic difficulties. It was one thing to achieve a political decision that this or that country should be given these or those resources – and here already, problems could present themselves. It was another matter whether the British or American Air Forces were thereafter ready to undertake their transport, or whether production would be given the desired priority. Basically, the Western Powers had both their own will and a certain autonomy, and there were running dialogues between the two armies and between the armies and their governments.

The situation of the Western Powers was further complicated by the fact that whilst the Soviet Union had only one front, although this was the front which inflicted the greatest losses on the Axis Powers, and contributioned more than any other front to their final defeat, the Western Powers had many fronts, each with its requirements in resources. For the Western Powers, the war was global, and the war at sea, in the Middle East, in the Far East and in the Pacific taxed the available resources both in men and materiel, seriously hindering a great many decisions, and having decisive influence in many arrangements.

All this was only one side of the question, however. Between the Western Powers and the Resistance Movements involved, stood not only the exile governments and the far-reaching considerations which must be taken in their regard, but also the movements themselves, and their demands and conditions. These movements were not, like the Soviet Partisan Movement, ideologically uniform, they were extremely multifarious and complicated quantities, with their own inner contradictions in their social, political, national and religious composition. In the first place, they were composed of volunteers, who did not recognize any other command than that accepted by them in circumstances where they considered a superior command or command from abroad reasonable, or perhaps simply expedient. The stronger the movements became, the more stubbornly they could behave. Tito's conduct was typical, when in the autumn 1944, without any previous warning to his Western Allied Liaison Officers, and without these having any other idea as to his whereabouts than that he had suddenly disappeared from the joint base on Vis, he flew to Moscow for negotiations with Stalin.[36] All the Resistance Movements displayed a tendency towards increased independence, however, often both in relation to their exile governments and to the Allied Western Powers.

These were the conditions for the Western Powers. If they agreed as to a measure in relation to France, the attitude of the provisional de Gaulle government could be the determining factor, whether the measure could be decided upon. If de Gaulle approved the measure, the local Resistance force's own decision and their own initiative could be the determining factor as to whether and how the decision would be effectuated. There could be no issue of orders in the Soviet sense, at best there must be requests and arguments, supported by promises and occasionally threats, and usually conditional upon the possibility that the stream of supplies could be cut off. The Western Powers had to feel their way, and in these circumstances, the Allied representative on the spot often received a wide margin for his arrangements. He arrived with a mandate which gave him considerable influence, but on the other hand this was reduced by the assessments which a complicated Anglo-Saxon hierarchy might make of his situation, work and personality. And his own personality could be decisive both for the reactions of the Resistance forces and for the dispositions he was able to argue for vis-à-vis his immediate superiors and the many decision-makers behind them.

None of this prevented close co-operation, and the Western Powers made great efforts to establish unity, but it gave the co-operation a character which was radically different from that which developed on Soviet territory, between the Soviet Army and the Partisan forces, on which the latter could depend before and during their operations.

This co-operation was a strategic factor in the Soviet Supreme Command's operative planning. In an exaggerated and paradoxical form, one can claim – and it has been claimed – that the Soviet partisan war constituted a second front, and that the final defeat of the Axis Powers on the East Front can be largely accounted for by their failure to secure the vast deployment areas which they had to seize and control before their decisive military collisions with the Soviet Armies, in the later stubborn defence of the strategically vital positions which had to be, and were, held. Leningrad, Moscow, Stalingrad are the extreme examples.[37] The Partisan forces were important in these frontal battles for many reasons. They created uncertainty in the ranks of the attacking armies and thus contributed to weakening morale, from the ranks up to the staffs. They attacked the transport system, depots, vulnerable garrisons and troops in redeployment, and therefore impaired the supply service, overstrained as it was already. Now and then they forced the withdrawal of fighting troops from the front lines for engagements behind their own lines. They caused considerable losses both to the defence forces and to the actual fighting forces, and in time, these losses could not be made good. All this took place during the constant development of the Partisan forces' fighting power, so that the balance between them and the Occupation troops was gradually shifted in favour of the Partisans. From being an irritant, they became first a risk and finally a danger.

The Partisan forces had thus an essential function in the long period up to the New Year 1943, while the Soviet Armies were generally speaking on the defensive. During this period, their actions contributed to reducing the manoeuvrability of the Axis Powers and the power of their offensives, even if the full weight of Partisan activity was not developed until after 1942 – increasing thereafter. Before the last German attempts in 1943 to seize the offensive once more in the operation "Zitadelle" at Kursk, the German High Command was forced first to put down the Partisan activity behind the German front. Here the German Army concentrated large armoured forces in a battle which ended in German defeat. This was a turning-point in the War, and the prelude to the long chain of Soviet offensives up to Berlin. Here too, the same law was in operation as we have seen in Yugoslavia, that the commitment of forces against the Partisans had to be massive, and out of all proportion to the unknown strengths of the Partisans in the forest regions around Brjansk. In this offensive before the offensive,[38] 3 German Divisions were employed, 3 Hungarian Divisions, 3 German Infantry Divisions, 1 Armoured Division, and 1 Armoured Grenadier Division, as well as 2 Regiments, which were already engaged in combatting the partisans. The offensive was supported by about 350 aircraft, and followed the usual course. Village after village was combed and burned to the ground, the inhabitants were killed or fled, whilst the Partisan forces withdrew, fighting, into the trackless forest regions, and even after the 4 weeks of fighting, were able to threaten and attack the German supply lines, when the actual battle began. But the delay in the "Zitadelle" operation placed the Soviet High Command in a better position to make the necessary preparations to counter the decisive attack. Here as in so many other instances, the tactical objective to drive the Partisans from the immediate positions succeeded, whereas the strategic objective, to destroy the Partisan force failed. For a High Command trained in Clausewitz's philosophy, the repeated realisation of the enemy's elusiveness and capacity for regrouping must have been a depressing series of experiences.

If the Partisan forces acquired great importance for the course of the fighting, as long as the Axis Powers were on the offensive, their importance was even greater, when the Soviet Armies, after the Kursk Battle, seized the initiative and went over from the defensive to the offensive.

By then the routine of co-operation with the Partisan forces was established, and every offensive was prepared with precise co-ordination with the Partisan forces in the hinterland, so that before the attacks, they engaged in series of planned actions, with sabotage and particularly with raids on the supply lines, which paralysed the German defence forces' efforts to keep the supply lines open. Besides this, the Soviet Armies were often able to advance through territories which were more or less liberated, and therefore immediately passable for quick surprise advances. It also meant a great deal that the Partisans were able again and again to secure the bridgeheads of the great rivers, or to keep open the few transport routes there were in the forest and marsh areas, so that these barriers were not the hindrance for the Soviet offensives which they had been for the Axis Powers, when these were on the offensive. This was one reason why the enemy was never able to establish a continuous front line, but instead, this zig-zagged deep into the whole battle zone.

As an illustration, the Partisan offensive will be mentioned here which preceded the Soviet summer offensive in White Russia in 1944. The Soviet Armies had continuous contact at this stage with about 150 Partisan Brigades or about 145,000 men, and an operational plan which distributed a great many preparatory tasks to the Partisans, before the actual offensive began.[39] On the night of 20 June, the White Russian Partisans blew up railways in more than 40,000 places, and this was the prelude to a wave of sabotage, with the derailment of about 150 transport trains and a general rising, with the Partisan forces continually joining up with the rapidly advancing Soviet Armies. In this, too, there was an important element. The Soviet Armies could make good their losses during the offensives, with trained and experienced soldiers from the Partisan forces. The actual attacks, after the Partisan preparations, started on 22 June, and the German Front collapsed, with the loss of 28 Divisions or about 350,000 men – a still greater defeat than at Stalingrad – whilst the Front moved about 500 kilometres westwards in the course of a few weeks, so that the Soviet Armies reached the frontiers of East Prussia, and arrived in one place at the Vistula River, establishing a bridgehead on its west bank. Here there was a question of a regular military victory, the size of which was due to several connected factors – faulty German dispositions, considerable Soviet superiority in men and materiel, or Soviet air superiority – and it would be just as unreasonable to credit the Partisan forces with decisive importance in this result as it would be unreasonable to ignore their contribution. Here as elsewhere, one must confine oneself to recognizing an unmeasurable but considerable share: most considerable where Partisan activity, as here, was co-ordinated with the operations of the regular Armies.

During these same weeks, the French Resistance and Maquis forces rose in connexion with the Allied invasions and independently mopped up the square area west of the Rhone and south of the Loire.

It does not seem unreasonable in conclusion to emphasize the military value of the Partisan forces, however these were organised, and however the co-operation between them and the Great Powers was established. How great the emphasis should be must remain an open question. For some regions their value seems indisputable.

It is understandable that the self-assurance of the partisans was great, everywhere. They bore the double burden of the Occupation and of the fight.

Conclusion

The reader has a right to demand a conclusion. And the conclusion cannot escape the question which was raised in the first lines of this account: Did the Resistance Movements in their entirety constitute a fourth arm, on a line with Army, Navy and Air Force – or did they not?

The British historian, B. H. Liddell Hart, seems to have no doubt on the matter, or does he simply avoid the problem? In his "History of the Second World War", in over 750 extremely competent pages he hardly mentions the Resistance Movements. The exceptions are a reference of three lines: "In addition, the Allies benefitted from the help of some 60,000 (Italian) partisans, who were producing much confusion behind the German lines and forcing the Germans to divert troops from the front to curb their activities" (in 1945), and eight words on "Tito's partisans" as comrades-in-arms in the Russian capture of Belgrade in 1944. The name de Gaulle appears *en passant* in two places, and in a negative context, Russian partisans in a subordinate clause, dealing with anti-Soviet partisans' assassination of General Vatutin. SOE and OSS are not mentioned. Intelligence, sabotage, partisan war and other Resistance activity are annulled with the strongest instrument at the historian's disposal – silence!

In Liddell Hart's account, the Second World War appears as a traditional war, the result of which is decided by the operations of traditional forces, sometimes in well calculated and sometimes in mistaken strategic movements. His description reminds one of an intellectual analysis of a game of chess, where white beats black because black omits to use his knight at a moment where this would have been possible, while white, however, gets the upper hand through a bishop-castle combination in the final movements. From the metaphorical to the concrete: the Axis Powers could have won with different decisions at the right time. The Allies could have won earlier than they did. There is no room for imponderabilia in this logical analysis.

One can follow Liddell Hart a long way. One can hardly deny that the outcome of the war was decided by the military and economic capacities of the Great Powers, and political and military leaders' clear-sightedness or short-sightedness, and finally by the Allies' superiority in materiel and population. The outcome of the war was therefore a product of the battles on the fronts on land, at sea and in the air. For a military historian with especial interest in technical, military theory, strategy, tactics, weapon technique, signal service and logistics, it can be reasonable to stop here.

But the way to a full understanding of the problem is longer and more tortuous than Liddell Hart's way. And these remarks cannot follow him farther than to this point. The Second World War was a total war, not only in the sense that it was global but also in the sense that it was not alone a question of moving front lines, and therefore a subject for those directly engaged, militarily, but a tragedy with profound moral, psychological and political aspects which affected millions outside the military fronts in daily life, outlook, future and existence. As in other wars, the course of the War can be illustrated with a series of sketch maps, of the shifts in the fronts, and the vertical lines on various pages of the atlas can easily illustrate the side of the total war with which Liddell Hart has chosen to occupy himself. But as these pages will have shown, there was another side to the War, which can hardly be illustrated with sketches, diagrams, tables or graphs, the effect of which upon the results of the War in their entirety evades precise measurements and reliable estimates. One could in theory – although this would be an almost insuperable task, which has seldom even been attempted – arrive at standardized and therefore comparable figures for intelligence reports, illegal papers, the material effects of damage caused by sabotage, the number of illegal telegrams, the size of partisan forces, and the numbers of refugees, etc., but these will often be calculated figures, and they will be compromised by uncertainty as to the basis of calculation. Added to this is the quite decisive fact that figures of this kind will only be indicators, without any indisputable final result. What use was made of the intelligence reports? How far did the distribution and argumentation of the illegal newspapers reach? What side effects did sabotage have? What did the illegal telegrams contain, apart from operational arrangements? Exactly what military influence did partisan activity have? Who was it that fled/escaped, and what importance lay in an individual flight? In a column of figures of refugees/escapees, does a Jean Moulin, a Niels Bohr or a Giraud appear on a line with a Polish soldier in General Anders' Army, a Dutch Jewess or a Belgian labour conscript? Interwoven with all this there is a long list of psychological and political circumstances, the effects of which elude absolute conclusions.

It must simply be accepted that whilst staffs and governments, after Midway and Stalingrad, could calculate results in resources, men, kilometres and strategic consequences, a corresponding calculation cannot be made in the case of a war without fronts.

Worse still – it is not only a question of establishing what positive effect the Resistance Movements may have had. It is just as much a question of estimating what the negative effect would have been on the Allies' conduct of the war, if they had not existed.

But with all these reservations, and omitting others, it must be permissible on the basis of the present account of the nature and activity of the Resistance Movements, to claim that they came to exercise a not unimportant influence on the course of the War – also militarily. Whether, on this basis, they can be and must be characterized as a fourth arm is a question of terminology. It would demand a certain rashness, or else a very sharply delineated subject matter, if one were to ignore their influence on the military course of the War.

It must be an obvious statement, that the movements had psychological importance. But where there can be doubt and discussion on the extent of the movements' influence upon military developments, in the psychological sphere there must surely be an obvious certainty of statement, the question remaining open as to how far the reader will go in conclusion. This open question only applies to extent, not to essence nor to the direction of influence. Psychologically, the Resistance Movements made themselves felt in three directions. They influenced the Occupying Powers, they influenced opinion in the Allied and neutral world, and most of all they influenced the peoples of the occupied countries. The Resistance Movements had a depressing effect on the Occupying Powers, gradually approaching resignation; they had a stimulating effect in the Allied and neutral worlds; and in the occupied areas, the knowledge that the fight had not ended, but that it was intensified with the commitment of home forces, had profound effect upon morale. Subjected to the hardships and dangers of the Occupation, the occupied peoples – the Resistance activitists especially but also the passive but increasingly convinced sympathisers – could draw moral strength from this knowledge. If there was an enemy in the country, there were also enemies of the enemy, not only on the other side of distant fronts, but very likely in the midst of the community in which the individual lived his daily life, and according to his means contributed his mite to liberation from those hardships and dangers. The Resistance could not include everyone, physically, and up to the last day of the Occupation there were persons in all the occupied countries who, according to their nature or circumstances, remained onlookers. But everyone was psychologically marked by developments and physically dependent upon them, and even the passive were unable to remain apathetic to what was happening around them. In all essentials, the influence of the Resistance at home had a positive character. When the war was not far away, but close at hand, political consciousness was sharpened, and the Resistance organisations stamped the attitude of the man in the street, and formulated the practical tasks which fell to the men of good will. In this way, morale was maintained in the midst of all the tragedies, and national self-assurance received increased strength.

No lengthly argumentation is needed to establish the fact that the Resistance Movements acquired political influence. The political picture of Europe was turned upside down between 1939 and 1945. Not only frontiers, but also standpoints were changed. This was caused by the general course of the War, but it was also caused, and to a considerable degree, by the Resistance Movements. If one excepts Poland and Czechoslovakia, where the Soviet Union's political domination was finally decisive for these countries' political development, the developments in the South-East, South, West and North were influenced to a considerable extent by the Resistance Movements. This applies especially to Albania, Yugoslavia, Italy and France, where the forms of government and the post-war regimes came to reflect the demands of the Resistance Movements and their results. But it also applies to Belgium, Holland, Norway and Denmark, where the pre-war forms of government were re-established, but where the defence policies of these countries were changed from neutrality to alliance, a change which was based upon the experiences of the Resistance struggle and revaluation of defence policies. In addition, there were changes in domestic standpoints. Greece was a special case, but even here, the Resistance struggle had long drawn-out political after-effects, first in the form of civil war, where the left-wing Resistance groups tried in vain to change the monarchist form of government.

These were the immediate political consequences, which generally involved a new generation of leaders in European politics. But it may be more important that the Resistance Movements had practised a form of warfare which had an infectious influence in the post-war world, mostly outside Europe.

A graduated evaluation is left to the reader, but the summing up must be that the Resistance Movements received military, psychological and political importance and influence. This must be maintained, regardless of the fact that these movements' participation in the struggle cannot be proved directly by victories which decided the war, and regardless of the fact that it must be left to the future to decide whether the achievements of the Resistance Movements can be measured demonstrably within a specific period. It was the ambition of the Resistance Movements to help to shorten the War, but their motivation was even more the determination to take part in the struggle, also on a small scale – on motivation which could be political, national, religious or humane.

The movements became universal. Their possibilities were dependent upon this universality. If only one country had raised a movement of this kind, the possibilities for resistance would have been small. As it was, they became formidable. And their universality had two dimensions. One was the geographical dimension, the fact that all the occupied countries rose. The other was the organisational dimension, the fact that the framework of operation was so wide, that it was not enough to combat one function, and to combat them all was an insuperable task.

The movements were unlike each other, in that their possibilities were determined by the geography of the various countries, their social and political conditions, and leading personalities.

The movements were alike in that within an operative framework, which included a wide spectrum of common possibilities for action, each country chose the forms of action which suited their situation. With the exception of the Partisan struggle, which required special geographical conditions coupled with extreme measures on the part of the Occupying Powers, most of the other forms of actions can be found, with variations, in one country after another.

The movements were supported from abroad, morally and materially, and this support from abroad had such decisive importance for their effectiveness that Resistance can only be evaluated in its interplay with the front abroad. To a great extent their actions were an integral part of the collective conduct of the War. For that very reason, any account of the Second World War must necessarily include the Resistance Movements.

To omit this is to renounce profound understanding of the special nature and depth of this war.

Notes

A Survey of Problems

1. Ref. Dalton's ideas see: M. R. D. Foot: "SOE in France", chapter 1 and especially pag. 9–10, Hugh Dalton: "Memoirs", vol 2, "The Fateful Years", pag. 336 ff. F. W. Deakin in "European Resistance Movements 1939–45 (Milan-report), pag. 100–101.

2. In the Government reshuffle in February 1942 Dalton was replaced by the Conservative politician, Lord Selborne. Winston Churchill: "The Second World War", vol. 4, pag. 77.

3. This literature is unusually copious. In addition to Winston Churchill's and Charles de Gaulle's fundamental memoirs, both containing general surveys of the course of the war, studded with contemporary documents, a number of leading officers – particularly from the Western Powers and Germany – have published memoirs and diaries. Amongst others British works by Alanbrooke, Cunningham, Montgomery and Tedder, American by Bradley, Clark and Eisenhower, German works by or on Guderian, von Halder, Kesselring, Manstein, Rommel, Speidel. Also B. H. Liddell Hart: "The German Generals talk" is important.

4. This search for documents has been organised in various ways in the different countries, but nowhere neglected. In France and Holland the work has been carried out by large special institutes, "Comité d'Histoire de la 2e Guerre Mondiale" and "Rijksinstitut voor Oorlogsdocumentatie".

5. John Ehrmann: "Grand Strategy", vol. V, pag. 326. The figure includes everyone who – in some way or another – was attached to resistance organisations, from the maquisardes (about 100 000) to sabotage groups and the "Forces Francaises de l'Interieur" – of whom only a minority was armed – down to resistance – minded trade unionists and strikers. Considering the great number of French prisoners of war in Germany and the mass of forced labour there, this figure would seem high – about 10% of the possible total. Excluding children, old people and – partly – women the percentage is of course much higher.

6. Heinz Kühnrich: "Der Partisanenkrieg in Europa 1939–45", pag. 239 states that figure.

7. BBC's systematic build-up of the myth of the Yugoslav Četnik leader, Mihailovic, as the typical partisan chief, worthy of imitation, undoubtedly became a certain stimulus to resistance-people outside Yugoslavia. A BBC-message about the setting up of a Polish Committee of Liberation had an impact at the formation of the Danish "Freedom Council". (Danmarks Frihedsråd, "Historie", ny række X, 2, 1973, pag. 243–61. Exposé by Jørgen Hæstrup).

8. This allegation should appear from the following account. See f. i. the chapters on Intelligence, delivery of arms, sabotage and partisan activities.

9. Frictions of this sort owing to muddles and confusion, jealousies and ambitions are common phenomena in every country – and every period. They increased during the first war years, for instance inside the British organisations set up to support the

resistance movements, especially SOE and "Political Warfare Executive". It was not until the latter was set up in 1941 that the fields of action between the two were finally defined: SOE to cover operations, PWE the propaganda. Cf. M. R. D. Foot: "SOE in France", pag. 10, and concerning PWE: Bruce Lockhart: "Comes the Reckoning", dealing with the task of this organisation in great detail: to undermine and destroy enemy morale and support the spirit of resistance in the occupied areas through radio and leaflets etc.

10. The Polish, Norwegian and Dutch exile governments had settled in London in toto. As to Belgium the government under Prime Minister Pierlot had gone to London, while King Leopold had remained at home. The problems of loyalty were somewhat complicated, although the Belgian Resistance quite logically supported the government's policy: To continue to fight. This would not – however – rule out that resistance people individually could remain loyal to King and monarchy.

11. The French Resistance organisations – "Les Mouvements" – did not spontaneously and unconditionally acknowledge de Gaulle as the Leader. This developed only little by little and only partly. See Henri Michel: "Les Courants de Pensée de la Résistance", pag. 222–235.

12. On "SS-Sonderkommandoes" and their brutal actions in the Sovjet Union see in general Alexander Dallin: "German Rule in Russia". The French Militia under Joseph Darnand was created by the Vichy government – on direct orders from Hitler – by an act of 30/1 1943 as a supplementary police force set up to fight the French Resistance. It developed into a terrorist band, hated and despised by the French people and – of course – the Resistance. Darnand was called "The French Himmler". See Robert Aron: "Histoire de Vichy", pag. 615 f. The Ustacemovement was an armed Croatian terror organisation under the Croatian chief of staff, Ante Pavelic. It engaged in campaigns of extermination against Serbs, Jews and other groups living in Croatia.

13. The network operated under the code name "Cleveland", later "Clarence", see Henri Bernard: "La Résistance 1940–45", pag. 60 f.

14. Charles de Gaulle: "Mémoires de Guerre", chapter "La France Libre". Cf. Henri Michel: "La Guerre de l'Ombre", pag. 81, where both the Sein-group and also another group of fishermen are mentioned.

15. Bor-Komorowski: "The Secret Army", pag. 21 ff. gives an account of the early phase of the set-up of a united organisation under formal command of the Polish exile government.

16. Illegal "lone wolwes" were rare – but could be found. The French Major of the Reserve, the civil engineer Michel Hollard was one of them. In 1942–44 quite alone – in a few occasions with a single assistant – he carried out important intelligence tasks. In the summer 1943 he discovered the first launching ramps for V-1 missiles and also that they were aiming at London. His reports with plans and drawings reached London, Hollard himself carrying them by bicycle to Switzerland. He formed no organisation, but worked quite outside the system under the cover name "Reseau Agir". See George Martelli: "Agent Extraordinary". After the war Hollard was decorated with the D.S.O.

17. Bor-Komorowski: "The Secret Army", pag. 60.

18. These and other Central Commands will be mentioned in detail later where relevant for the account. A typical example of a great Resistance organisation slow at joining a Central Command, but faltering doing so at a later stage, accepting the value of unification, is the French "Défence de la France". For a long time it refused to join the French

Central Command, "Conseil National de la Résistance". See Marie Granet: "Défence de la France", pag. 145 ff.

19. It was this service Winston Churchill first of all was thinking of when in July 1940 he visualized a future collaboration between Great Britain and the occupied countries: "It is of course urgent and indispensable that every effort should be made to obtain secretly the best possible information about the German forces in the various countries overrun, and to establish contacts with local people, and to plant agents. This, I hope, is being done on the largest scale, as opportunity serves, by the new organisation under M. E. W. (Ministry of Economic Warfare)". Here Churchill is refering to the SOE. Winston Churchill: "The Second World War", vol. 2, pag. 572.

20. Cf. the appreciation by Allan Dulles, Head of the USA Intelligence Service: "The Great Powers of Europe entered World War I with intelligence services which were.in no way commensurate with the might of their armed forces or equipped to cope with the complexity of the conflict to come". Dulles: "The Craft of Intelligence", pag. 32. Cf. F. W. Winterbotham: "The Ultra Secret", with a detailed account of the decisive breaking of central German codes by the British Intelligence Service.

21. Winston Churchill: "The Second World War", vol. 4, pag. 249.

22. That this was just a myth is elucidated in detail by L. de Jong in his book "The German Fifth Column in the Second World War". Cf. B. H. Liddell Hart: "The Other Side of the Hill", pag. 391–2, where General Blumentritt gives an account of the difficulties German espionage had to meet in Great Britain. B. mentions a very few but helpless German agents, a statemant Liddell Hart has been unable to have confirmed. B. H. Liddell Hart: "History of the Second World War", pag. 548, note. Cf. M.R.D. Foot: "Resistance. European Resistance to Nazism", pag. 30.

23. In Belgium and France several organisations were operating. In Poland and Denmark the work was centralised.

24. Conditions in France could serve as a typical example. SOE had a special section for France (section F) operating parallel with – but strictly seperated from – a similar organisation under de Gaulle. Both could have agents working abreast in the same region without knowledge of each others but with parallel tasks. Frictions became inevitable both in the field and in Head Quarters in London. Cf. M. R. D. Foot: "SOE in France", index: "de Gaulle's attitudes to SOE".

25. See above pag. 16.

26. A thorough analysis of the embarrassing position and ambivalent attitude of the French Communist party during the painful period of the Germano-Russian pact of August 1939–June 1941 is given by Henri Michel in "Les Courants de Pensée de la Résistance", pag. 557–79. It appears clearly from this analysis that the French Communists during this period definitely refused any participation in the resistance then in process of formation. Here only a short quotation from "l'Humanité" 30/9 1940: "Today as yesterday the Communists are opposed to the imperialistic war, still going on, and they do not want to see France joining it again as certain war mongers like Doriot and la Gitton wish – and also certain emigrants and other mercenaries". In a later copy of the paper the emigrant and mercenary is named: de Gaulle. Locally and individually deviations from this line could, however, be found. See "Resistance in Europe, 1939–45" (ed. Hawes and White), pag. 94 ff.

27. The only odd exception: The British Channel Islands. Conditions here are described in C. G. Cruickshank: "The German Occupation of the Channel Islands". And the oppo-

site: The resistance work on the Greek island Chios, cf. P. P. Argenti: "The Occupation of the Chios by the Germans".

28. Bor-Komorowski: "The Secret Army", pag. 73.
29. On these problems see below, pag. 247.
30. Cf. Fitzroy MacLean: "Disputed Barricade", pag. 128, where some essential telegrams are referred. The Sovjet government was at that time against the idea of a communist trend in Yugoslavia and recommended – also referring to cooperation with the Western Allies – a popular front and a policy of cooperation between the Tito-forces and the Cetniks under Michailovic, supported by the Yugoslav exile government. About this see below pag. 328–29.
31. The USA agreed in principle to such exchanges of views in June 1940, when the collapse of France was a fact. Initial Staff talks were developing in August 1940, and the work was wound up in formal conferences on General Staff level in Washington January-March 1941. Cf. W. H. McNeill: "America, Britain and Russia 1941–46", pag. 7 ff.
32. Bruce Lockhart: "Comes the Reckoning", pag. 157.
33. J. R. M. Butler: "Grand Strategy", II, pag. 211 ff.
34. The most copious account is given in M. R. D. Foot: "SOE in France", pag. 1–10. Cf. Hugh Dalton: "Memoirs" vol. 2, "The Fateful Years", pag. 366 ff. Cf. also Bickham Sweet Escott: "Baker Street Irregular", chapter 1–2 inclusive and F. W. Deakin in "European Resistance Movements 1939–45" (Milan-report), pag. 98 ff and J. R. M. Butler: "Grand Strategy", vol. 2, pag. 260–61.
35. M. R. D. Foot: "SOE in France", pag. 8. Quite a few of the originators behind SOE had a personal knowledge of the stated precedences.
36. Dalton: "Memoirs", vol. 2, "The Fateful Years", pag. 366 ff.
37. J. M. A. Gwyer: "Grand Strategy", vol. 3, pag. 42 ff. Here some short quotations: "In areas where the German power has become sufficiently weak, subjugated peoples must rise against their Nazi overlords. Such rebellions can only occur once. They must not happen until the stage is set, until all preparations are made, and until the situation is ripe". And further on: "At the chosen moment in each area, these patriots will seize such objectives as headquarters, broadcasting stations, landing grounds and centres of communications. They will attack officers, sentries, guards and alarm posts and, where possible, barracks, camps and aerodromes. They will destroy German communications leading to the theatre of operations". It is stressed that such rebels will need rapid reinforcement from outside, f.i. by "free" forces from abroad.
38. R. Bruce Lockhart: "Comes the Reckoning", pag. 125. The book gives an extensive account of the creation of PWE and its activities.
39. SOE established a headquarters here as well. Cf. Bickham Sweet-Escott: "Baker Street Irregular", pag. 43 and 70 ff.
40. In Belgium the paper "Libre Belgique" as one out of a number of minor papers. The Belgian historian, Henri Bernard severely rejects German allegations of Belgian "Franc-Tireurs" activities behind the German frontzones during the first World War. Henri Bernard: "La Résistance 1940–45", pag. 79.
41. Concerning this cf. L. de Jong's appreciation of the BBC activities in "Britain and European Resistance 1939–45" (Oxford-report). de Jong was the leader of the Dutch "Radio Oranje" station under the BBC, and gives the following statement: "I think it may be said that life in occupied Holland was simply unthinkable without the daily encouragement coming over the wireless". He mentions the German 1943 decree,

ordering all radio receivers to be confiscated, stating that 800,000 sets were delivered out of a million, while c. 200.000 continued to function. Jeremy Bennett: "British Broadcasting and the Danish Resistance Movement" gives a detailed account of the activities of a single sector of the BBC.

42. This event, called "Englandsspiel", is fully elucidated from a Dutch point of view in "Enquetekommissie, Regeringsbeleid", Boek v. Het England-Spiel, pag. 565–96. From the German side there is the account by the Abwehr officer, H. J. Giskes: "London calling North Pole". Cf. the Dutch tele-operator P. Dourlein: "Inside North Pole". See also below, pag. 293 f.

43. Problems were of course less acute for the telegraph operators in thinly populated areas than in towns. In areas under partisan control conditions were very different from those of Amsterdam or Copenhagen etc. The Germans were also there able to pinpoint the stations, but unable to interfere.

44. Losses cannot be precisely established. In M. R. D. Foot: "SOE in France", pag. 474 he states that the French country section operated with losses of 10% on receptions and 10% during transports after reception. For Denmark, where reasonable precise figures are available, losses were high in 1942, lower in 1943, and during 1944–45, when more than 95% of the deliveries came down, losses were well under 10%. Best result in the Danish Fyn-region with 34 receptions = 700 containers and losses at 0%.

45. On S-phones and Eurecas see M. R. D. Foot: "SOE in France", pag. 84 ff.

46. There were of course setbacks. For instance in Czechoslovakia after the assasination in May 1942 of the German "Reichsprotektor", Reinhard Heydrich, and the wave of terrorism following the killing. But this example is more of an exception than the rule.

Development and Background of the Resistance Movements

1. The Sovjetunion is an exception. Here partisan war was proclaimed and ordered immediately after the German assault 22 June 1941. See below pag. 000.

2. German historians have consistently used the word "Widerstandsbewegung" of the opposition against the Hitler regime inside the frontiers of Germany which finally led to the attempt on Hitlers life in July 1944. (Cf. f.i. Gerhard Ritter: "Carl Goerdeler und die deutsche Widerstandsbewegung"). The justification of the use of this word can be discussed. Germany was not an occupied area and the word "opposition" can also be found. (Cf. f.i. Hans Rotfels: "Die deutsche Opposition gegen Hitler"). In this account the German opposition is not regarded as being on line with the resistance movements of the occupied countries, its situation and opportunities being quite different from those of the occupied countries. The Italian opposition against the Mussolini-regime was different. From 1943 it assumed the character of a real "resistenza" with similar qualities to those of the other resistance movements. It is significant and decisive for any evaluation that the German opposition never received any political or material support from abroad.

3. Fitzroy MacLean: "Disputed Barricade", pag. 137.

4. See below pag. 372 f.

5. Winston Churchill: "The Second World War", vol. 4, pag. 678–81.

6. In his memoirs de Gaulle bitterly complain of these conditions, both in the summer 1940, after the occupation of Syria, and after the landing by the Western Powers in French North West Africa. See in general these memoirs.

7. Charles de Gaulle: "Mémoires de Guerre", vol. 1, chapter "La France Libre".

8. After the liberation of French North West Africa 116.000 men were called up, a further 13.000 came from Corsica, 12.000 escaped from France, and other "free" French Forces totalled 15.000. In addition quartermaster-general's branch personnel. The figures are stated by de Gaulle in his memoirs, chapter "Combat".

9. Concerning the formation of these "free" forces on Sovjet soil and their political consequences, see Peter Gosztony, treatise in "Revue Internationale d'Histoire Militaire", no. 33, 1975, pag. 75–98.

10. It should be noted that this allegation is far from being accepted by all French resistance men, although de Gaulle gradually increased his influence within the French Resistance. It was not shared by the French communists, although they sent delegates to represent them on the board of de Gaulle's movement, but also non-communist groups showed some reserve towards de Gaulle and his demand for absolute authority. Thus the resistance leader Henri Frenay, head of the "Combat", worded his opinion as follows: "The Resistance movement does not consider itself originating from the appeal of 18. June. (de Gaulle's appeal on the BBC). Its point of view is that two battles are fought against the same enemy, each following its own laws. It does not want to be an army of landed parachutists". (Henri Michel: "Les Courants de Pensée de la Résistance", pag. 228). Cf. Marie Granet: "Défence de la France", pag. 13 ff.

11. A detailed account of the Danish position is given in Jørgen Hæstrup: "Secret Alliance" I-III.

12. Typical and common are here developments in France and Denmark, where the pre-war politicians established negotiations, which logically would have a tendency towards collaboration and consequently compromising politicians as well as policy. In 1940 Pétain was hailed as the great saviour of the nation. But the policy of collaboration of Darlan and – later – Laval compromised both the two – and finally also Pétain. The homage of 1940 turned into the contempt of 1943–44. Danish politicians enjoyed 1940 considerable confidence, but by 1943 they too had completely lost grip of events, and the Cabinet had to resign under the pressure of a popular rising, rejecting all further negotiations and consequent concessions. The British Channel islands were in a peculiar situation. Here, too, a certain collaboration between the local administration and the occupying power became necessity, but the collaboration did not damage the prestige of the administration. See generally C. G. Cruickshank: "The German Occupation of the Channel Islands".

13. Quite a few of the persons mentioned we shall meet on the following pages although this account is not meant to deal with individual happenings.

14. See below pag. 90 f.

15. Considering the actual situation negotiations would necessarily lead to concessions, and the road onwards to a certain cooperation and then to wholehearted collaboration. This for instance became the fate of Pierre Laval and the Vichy government. Instructive accounts of this development by stages are given in Robert Aron: "Histoire de Vichy" and in Robert Paxton: "Vichy France". In Denmark a similar trend was interrupted by the resignation of the Cabinet in August 1943. Later on the leading politicians established a growing contact with the leaders of the Resistance, ending up with yielding a not unimportant support. An account of this in Jørgen Hæstrup: "Secret Alliance" II-III.

16. On the Mers-el-Kebir episode see Winston Churchill: "The Second World War", vol. 2, pag. 206–11. This affair led to the rupture of diplomatic contact between France and Great Britain and a French bombing attack on Gibraltar. Even de Gaulle spoke in a talk

on the radio 8. July "with sorrow and anger" about what had happened. He did, however, stick to a full loyalty towards what he named "our Ally" in that talk, Charles de Gaulle: "Mémoires de Guerre", appendix in vol. 1.

17. It is hardly possible to distinguish sharply between negotiation and cooperation. Both governments in 1940 found themselves in an emergency, calling for negotiation. But the Cabinet ministers held of course different views as to how far negotiating should be allowed to go – and also as to its purpose. But negotiation has a built-in element of inertia. As soon as capitulation and negotiation had been accepted it could be difficult to decide when there was a reasonable argument for refusing a minor demand. Negotiation unavoidably led to concession and could soon assume the character of cooperation, paving the way for direct collaboration. the principal problem in the proces was where to say no, and also what consequences a refusal might carry. Differing opinions regarding this split open a gap within Cabinets as well as in the people. When assessing the relations between negotiation-cooperation-collaboration one has to appreciate each individual case and problem seperately. Such appreciations are not included in this account.

18. In the Sovjet Union a communist central Command of the partisans was uncontested. Also in Yugoslavia and Albania communist central control soon became a reality, and communist influence was strong and obvious in Greece, Northern Italy and France. In the smaller countries of Western and Northern Europe communist influence varied from district to district and from function to function, but was felt also here. In Czechoslovakia communist groups developed side by side with non-communists, the former more active than the latter. In Poland the resistance organisation that remained loyal to the exile government in London was sceptical, sometimes hostile to the special communist groups. Ancient anti-Russian sentiment and the occupation of Eastern Poland in 1939 by the Sovjetunion played their part, and from 1943 came a diplomatic rupture between the Sovjet government and the Polish exile government in connection with the Katyn-affair. About this see below pag. 174.

19. Jozef Garlinski: "Poland SOE and the Allies", pag. 31.

20. S. Okecki: "La Résistance Polonaise", pag. 444 in "European Resistance Movements, 1939–45" (Milan-report). Okecki also states, that a few weeklies had a weekly circulation of about 50.000 copies. About 33% of the papers were printed, the remainder duplicated. Nearly 90% were published in the General-Gouvernement, while the Polish provinces directly incorporated in Germany were less abundantly supplied with a total of about 40 illegal titles.

21. Vladimir Dedijer: "Tito", Danish edition, pag. 84–85. Information by D.

22. In Holland there were about 60 illegal publications by the end of 1940, with a first "Bulletin", written in hand, issued the day after the capitulation. (Werner Warmbrunn: "The Dutch under German Occupation", pag. 222). In Belgium the first two publications, "Chut" and "Le Monde de Travail" appeared on 15. June. (F. Demany in "European Resistance Movements 1939–45" (Liege-report), pag. 164). In France quite a few publications were issued in 1940, especially in the occupied zone, amongst others "Pantagruel", "En Captivité", "Résistance", "La France au Combat". (Henri Michel & Mirkine Guetzévitch: "Les Idées politiques et sociales de la Résistance", pag. 5).

23. Such appeared in France, Holland, Denmark and Poland. In France the resistance leader Jean Moulin started his "Agences de Presse Clandestine". (Henri Michel: "La Guerre de l'Ombre", pag. 102). In Holland appeared "De Vrije Nieuwscentrale" (cf. Werner Warmbrunn: "The Dutch under German Occupation", pag. 243 f.) and in

Denmark the News Bureau "Information", maintaining daily contact with the "Danish Press Service" in Stockholm, from where up-to-date news from the Danish underground was circulated to all the free world (cf. Jørgen Hæstrup: "Secret Alliance" II, pag. 250 f.). Also the Polish News Bureau could boast its own special correspondents abroad. (Cf. Henri Michel: "La Guerre de l'Ombre", pag. 103).

24. The problem is dealt with for France by Henri Michel: "La Guerre de l'Ombre", pag. 102. The Scandinavian experience quite logically confirms Henri Michel's exposé.

25. The French historian and resistance leader, Marc Bloch, has analysed this problem in his book, "l'Etrange Défait", written during the war. Marc Bloch died in 1944 after arrest.

26. As to France Henri Michel recites "women, farmers, railway men, students, shopkeepers, young people, doctors, university men, maquisardes etc.", see "La Guerre de l'Ombre", pag. 105. But the problem is not limited to what readers the papers appealed to. The writers also must be taken into consideration. The style differed clearly if the author was a clergyman, an economist or a soldier.

27. A typical example is the German political attitude in Norway on 9. april and the following days. The German military operation "Weserübung" was prepared with plans and alternative plans in minute detail, but politically speaking the operation was completely unprepared. It was taken for granted that the Norwegian government would accept the military facts, and no plans were handy in case such accept failed. This brought to life a transitory "Quisling-government", proclaimed over the Norwegian broadcasting system without the German ambassador, Bräuer, knowing – let alone consenting – and promptly dropped again and replaced by total political confusion. (A short account of these happenings in Andenæs, Riste and Skodvin: "Norway and the Second World War", pag. 54 ff.). A similar political uncertainty prevailed in Denmark during the same days. Here the Cabinet accepted the military facts, but it was soon clear that the Germans had no prepared political plans to meet the demands of the peculiar situation of "occupatio pacifica". During negotiations – drawn out for months – a number of ad hoc solutions had to be found. (Henrik S. Nissen: "1940. Studier i Forhandlingspolitikken og Samarbejdspolitikken", pag. 590 ff. Resumé in German).

28. A very detailed analysis of the German policy of occupation in the Sovjet Union with penetrating light cast on internal strife for power within the German hierachy in Alexander Dallin: "German Rule in Russia, 1949–45".

29. On the German policy of occupation in Poland cf. Martin Broszat: "Nationalsozialistische Polenpolitik, 1939–45". Together with Dallin's book it gives an excellent account of Hitler-Nazism's East policy. The tensions and uncertainties as to policy were perhaps especially obvious in Denmark, where the formal conditions were most unclarified. Here quite official tension appeared between the German Special Envoy, representing the "Auswärtiges Amt", the High Command of the Army, the Heads of Police and the organs dealing with economic matters and administration. (Cf. Jørgen Hæstrup: "Til Landets Bedste" I-II). The wavering, quite opportunistic policy towards France is clearly exposed in Robert Aron: "Histoire de Vichy".

30. Just a commonplace example: On 1. June 1943 a minute group armed with a trifle of high explosive and one pistol sabotaged an engine shed in a Danish provincial town. 6 locomotives were damaged. Just a local affair of negligible importance and only one out of a local series of sabotage actions. However – the next day, the 2. June – the action was given a 2-column report in "The New York Times"! It might be typical that a Danish special monography of 515 pages on the resistance of that region deals with the

episode in 9 lines. (Aage Trommer: "Modstandsarbejde i Nærbillede", pag. 77). If a detailed account is required an American Newspaper must be consulted! The Danish newsbureau in Stockholm keeping up a daily illegal contact with the Danish underground was in 1944 able to force BBC to intensive use of Danish underground news. BBC was simply given the ultimatum either to use the news or not receive any at all. BBC capitulated. (Cf. Jeremy Bennett: "British Broadcasting and the Danish Resistance Movement", pag. 176–201). The examples are Danish, but could just as well be Polish, Dutch, French or Yugoslav, picked at random.

31. Henri Michel: "Les Courants de Pensée de la Résistance", pag. 94–95.

32. Ibid. pag. 95. Later on one more communist representative, F. Billoux, was appointed to the provisional French government in Algiers, both with rank of ministers, the former minister for the Airforce, the latter minister for liberated areas.

33. Comment to Maurice Schumann, reported by Henri Michel in "Les Courants de Pensée de la Résistance", pag. 94–95.

34. "La Marseillaise" 17/1 1943.

Demonstrations

1. As the first country to be occupied Czechoslovakia presented the first great demonstrations in Praha in October-November 1939. The occupying power reacted with disproportionally violent reprisals, arrests, deportations and death sentences. See "European Resistance Movements" (Milan-report), pag. 230.

2. On symbolic demonstrations in favour of the House of Oranje, see Warmbrunn: "The Dutch under German Occupation", pag. 43 and 103–04. Cf. Keesing 1940–43, pag. 4203.

3. The cross of Lorraine, a red cross on a blue background, was 5/8 1940 accepted by de Gaulle as the special emblem of the "free" French. Cf. Keesing 1940–43, pag. 4183.

4. Regarding the acts of demonstration etc., mentioned here and later, see Henri Michel: "La Guerre de l'Ombre", pag. 82–87. Here Michel gives a number of actual and also some anecdotal examples of refusal to obey to occupation. Michel also quotes a leaflet by Jean Texcier: "Advice to the Occupied", which was widely circulated, bringing good advice on how best to practise the principle of the cold shoulder. A similar type-written leaflet appeared in Denmark. See also Henri Bernard: "Histoire de la Résistance Européenne", pag. 215.

5. Printed in Andenæs, Riste and Skodvin: "Norway and the Second World War", pag. 69. A great number of Norwegian demonstrations against the occupying power and the Quisling party are mentioned in Sverre Kjeldstadli: "Hjemmestyrkene", pag. 26 ff.

6. Article from 25/4 1941, printed in the Danish composite work on the occupation: "Besættelsens Hvem-Hvad-Hvor", pag. 303.

7. Keesing 1940–43, pag. 5232.

8. Hartvig Frisch: "Danmark, besat og befriet" I, pag. 164.

9. Henri Michel: "La Guerre de l'Ombre", pag. 90, cf. Henri Bernard: "La Résistance 1940–45", pag. 34. The demonstrations in Paris in November 1940 gave impetus to widespread student demonstrations the following days. The Germans reacted by shooting some students and closing the university of Paris. (Keesing 1940–43, pag. 4335).

10. Keesing 1940–43, pag. 5243 and 5367.

11. Keesing 1940–43, pag. 4862.

12. The V-campaign was launched from January 1941 by "Colonel Britton", alias the

leader of BBC's European News Department, D. E. Ritchie, but the original idea emmanated from the Belgian Section of BBC, and Laveleye, the father of the idea, simply found out that the V-sign would be the easiest sign to paint on walls, hoardings etc. A general account of the V-sign campaign is given by Jeremy Bennett in his "British Broadcasting and the Danish Resistance Movement", pag. 38–42. Cf. Henri Michel: "La Guerre de l'Ombre", pag. 89 and Bruce Lockhart: "Comes the Reckoning", pag. 306.
13. This thoroughly organised civil resistance and its coordination with the military was characteristic for the Norwegian resistance movement. A very detailed analysis of the organisation of the civil efforts is given in Th. Chr. Wyller: "Nyordning og Motstand", to which is referred. See below pag. 000 ff.
14. This military resistance effort is in detail described by Sverre Kjeldstadlix in his book "Hjemmestyrkene".
15. Stefan Korbonski: "Fighting Warsaw", pag. 166–69.
16. Erich Hesse: "Der Sowjetrussische Partisanenkrieg 1941–44", pag. 134.

Protests

1. About this see Winston Churchill: "The Second World War", vol. 3, pag. 287–97. Cf. Charles de Gaulle: "Mémoirs de Guerre", vol. I, chapter "l'Orient".
2. On Darlan's negotiations on the Syrian problem, see Robert Aron: "Histoire de Vichy", pag. 432–35. Cf. Walter Warlimont: "Im Hauptquartier der Deutschen Wehrmacht, 1939–45", pag. 140 f. Cf. Robert Paxton: "Vichy France", pag. 117 ff.
3. See below, pag. 448.
4. The episode is described in detail by Robert Aron in "Histoire de Vichy", pag. 456–59.
5. Robert Aron: "Histoire de Vichy", pag. 474 ff.
6. This also applies to Denmark, where German authorities from April 1940 to August 1943 had alleged "normal" negotiations with a Danish government and from August 1943 with a Danish public administration. The flow of Danish objections and protests was constantly growing – especially after August 1943, but was more and more overruled. This contributed to growing political difficulties for the Germans and also to stimulating the will to resist. On this see Jørgen Hæstrup: "Til Landets Bedste" I-II, where a great number of Danish protests are described in detail along with a description of the constant controversies between Danish and German administration.
7. On the German Church policy in Poland, see Martin Broszat: "Nationalsozialistische Polenpolitik 1939–45", pag. 175 f. Cf. Keesing 1940–43, pag. 4709.
8. The Primas of the Polish church, Cardinal Hlond, escaped in September 1939 together with the Polish exile government. From his exile he collected information on conditions in Poland, which was passed on to Pope Pius XII and also published in London 1941 under the title: "The Persecution of the Catholic Church in German-occupied Poland".
9. On the following see Th. Chr. Wyller: "Nyordning og Motstand", pag. 19 ff. Cf. Keesing 1940-43, pag. 4513. The account of the reaction of the Norwegian Church is based on Wyller's work.
10. Regarding the ecclesiastical controversy in Holland see Werner Warmbrunn: "The Dutch under German Occupation", pag. 156–64 etc. and Keesing 1940-43, pag. 4742, 5123 and 5303. Also Walter B. Maas: "The Netherlands at War, 1940-43", pag. 81–84.
11. On the stand of the Belgian Church see Keesing 1940–43, pag. 5067 and 5278.
12. Keesing 1940–43, pag. 4899. On the philosophy and political doctrine behind the Pétain

regime see f. i. Robert Aron: "Histoire de Vichy", chapter "Revolution Nationale, Doctrine", especially 207–17. Further Robert Paxton: "Vichy France", chapter 2, "The National Revolution", with a detailed description of the philosophy and policy of the Vichy-regime. In the original program of this regime only trifles were unacceptable to the Church. Problems did crop up, however, in connection with concessions to German demands, causing an ideological and moral decline for the regime.

13. Keesing 1940–43, pag. 5365–66.

14. On such Catholic Movements and papers, see Henri Michel: "Les Courants de Pensée de la Résistance", pag. 121 and in general the index of these Movements and papers.

15. The conditions and fate of the Danish Jews is accounted of in great detail by Leni Yahil: "Test of a Democracy". Here also the attitude of the Danish Church is mentioned.

16. The Vicar and Poet, Kaj Munk, became famous far beyond the Danish borders. His attacks on the Germans were so sharp that they had him murdered in January 1944.

17. Pavelić was the leader of the Ustaće-movement, fighting for the detachment of Croatia from Yugoslavia. He was a wellknown terrorist, connected with the murder of King Alexander and the French Foreign Secretary, Barthou, in Marseille in 1934, and sentenced to death "in absentia". He enjoyed the right of asylum in Italy and had the support of Mussolini in 1941 to establish a Croatian satellite state with himself as leader. A detailed account of the Ustaće-movement is given in Ladislaus Hory and Martin Broszat: "Der Kroatische Ustaće-Staat 1941–45".

18. On the massacres by the Ustaće-movement and Stepinac's reaction, also the reaction of the Catholic Church in general, see Fitzroy MacLean: "Disputed Barricade", index.

19. Apart from large-scale killing, rape, burning down of churches etc. they had the form of massacres of whole villages, giving grace to neither children, women nor old age, and mass executions of the Serbian population. Cf. Ladislaus Hory and Martin Broszat: "Der Kroatische Ustaće-Staat 1941–45".

20. Stepinac was after the war – in 1946 – found guilty of numerous crimes against the State and sentenced to 16 years of penal service. He pleaded not guilty and during his defence he accused the Yugoslav State of suppression of the Catholic Church. He did not deny cruelties and use of force prior to conversions, but maintained that he found the main reasons for these measures in the general political conditions.

Strikes

1. On the profound changes in the economic life of France, see Robert Aron: "Histoire de Vichy", pag. 243–45. The dissolution of the great trade organisations came in 3 decrees on 9. November and included "Le Comité Central des Houilléres de France" (coal), "Le Comité des Forges de France" (steel), "La Confederation Générale du Patronat Francais" (industrial leaders). Also the trade unions "La Confédération Francaise des Travailleurs Chrétiens", "La Confédération Générale du Travail" and "La Confédération des Syndicats Professionels Francais".

2. The economic conditions in Denmark during the occupation, including the problems of the labour market, are reported on in great detail in Sigurd Jensen: "Levevilkår under Besættelsen". On the French ban on strikes by decree, see Robert Aron: "Histoire de Vichy", pag. 404–05.

3. This so-called "People's Strike" is described in Jørgen Hæstrup: "Secret Alliance" II, pag. 320–52 and in "Til Landets Bedste" by same author, pag. 417–532.

4. See above pag. 38 f.
5. Keesing 1940–43, pag. 4398. Cf. Werner Warmbrunn: "The Dutch under German Occupation", pag. 105 and 147 ff. The course of events accellerated when a group of professors in an appeal to Seyss-Inquart – the so-called "Scholten-appeal" – maintained that no Jewish problem existed in Holland. When Jewish professors were dismissed a professor of law in Leiden, head of the faculty, protested against this encroachment. His sharp speech of protest to the students resulted in the strike and was illegally circulated in thousands of typed and duplicated copies.
6. Robert Aron: "Histoire de Vichy", pag. 401. Aron rejects – supported by contemporary labour papers – a communist assertion from after the liberation, that this strike had a political character. This rejection could be challenged. If there had been political motives behind the strike this would – quite obviously – not be mentioned in the labour papers of the day.
7. Henri Michel: "Les Courants de Pensée de la Résistance", pag. 646.
8. Ibid. pag. 633.
9. About the February-riots see Werner Warmbrunn: "The Dutch under German Occupation", pag. 106–11. Cf. Keesing 1940–43, pag. 4504.
10. "Nationaal-Socialistische Beweging der Nederlanden", founded 1931, polling 4.2% in 1937, but loosing votes at the local elections 1939.
11. Leading in the propaganda were the Dutch communists. Their party had been dissolved but reorganised illegally, since November 1940 publishing the underground paper "De Waarheid", which in spite of the German pact with the Sovjetunion attacked the Nazis in general and – especially – the Dutch Nazi party. Now they acted – calling a general strike with duplicated newsbills. See Walter B. Maas: "The Netherlands at War 1940–45", pag. 65 f.
12. Werner Warmbrunn: "The Dutch under German Occupation", pag. 113–18. Cf. Keesing 1940–43, pag. 5956–57.
13. On the planning, action and failure of this operation see R. E. Urquhart: "Arnhem". In chapter 8 the author, who was commanding the British airborne troops in the operation gives warm recognition to Dutch resistance men for help during the attack and in the following weeks, when many survivors were helped back to their British bases.
14. On this and the following see Werner Warmbrunn: "The Dutch under German Occupation", pag. 138–46.
15. The Allies here found themselves in the same situation as the Germans in 1940. Breakthrough and advance were so sweeping, that the tempo took everybody by surprise, calling for improvising, where there often was no time for reconciling present action to earlier theoretical planning.
16. A ban on listening in to London was issued in 1940, but not obeyed. On 15. May 1943 Seyss-Inquart published a decree ordering the handing of all radiosets. This was caused by the previous strike riots. Out of 1 million sets about 200.000 are reckoned not given up. See Keesing 1943–45, pag. 5957 and L. de Jong in "Britain and European Resistance 1939–45" (Oxford-report), the section on Holland, pag. 2. L. de Jong states, that listening in was intensive both before and after the decree about handing in, but listening became more difficult from autumn 1944, because of break down of the electricity supply after the Allied occupation of Southern Holland and the coal mines there.
17. R. E. Urquhart: "Arnhem", chapter 8.
18. Starvation – and cold – during winter 1944–45 became one of the most serious ordeals of all those that afflicted the Dutch people under the occupation. An account in detail of

living conditions in the Dutch towns that winter is given in Walter B. Maas: "The Netherlands at War 1940–45", pag. 205–14. The author himself went through that long winter.

19. On this exile opposition, see Henri Bernard: "Histoire de la Résistance Européenne 1939–45", pag. 34 ff. The Italian exile world included both a number of politicians in Western Europe, especially France, and communists as Palmiro Togliatti, the Italian communist leader and a member of the Komintern, who on radio Moscow instigated resistance against the Fascist regime, most intensively after June 1941.

20. The founder in 1929 of the movement "Giustizia e Libertá", publishing illegal prints. A number of leaders of the movement were arrested and Roselli was murdered in an ambush in France 1937, carried out by French hired assassins.

21. On the spirit and reaction of the Italian home front see F. W. Deakin: "The Brutal Friendship", pag. 222–23 and Ivone Kirkpatrick: "Mussolini", pag. 463–64.

22. About this see Keesing 1940–43, pag. 4937.

23. Ivone Kirkpatrick: "Mussolini", pag. 484–85.

24. F. W. Deakin: "The Brutal Friendship", pag. 35.

25. On this March strike and conditions behind it see F. W. Deakin: "The Brutal Friendship", pag. 223–32.

26. Ibid. pag. 316.

27. As to these changes normally see the general accounts of the War History. The changes were so important that special references make no sense.

28. F. W. Deakin: "The Brutal Friendship", pag. 654–55.

29. Ibid. pag. 655.

30. Ibid. pag. 701–03.

31. The reference is here to SS-General Karl Wolff's negotiations with the Allies on capitulation. On these negotiations and their influence on the relations between the Allies see f. i. Winston Churchill: "The Second World War", vol. 6, pag. 387–95 and, more detailed, Allan Dulles: "The Secret Surrender".

32. Henri Michel: "Les Courants de Pensée de la Résistance", pag. 562. In this work Michel analyses the temporary isolation of the communist party in a seperate chapter, "Un Parti Isolé", pag. 557–79.

33. The ban hit "Conféderation Francaise des Travailleurs Chrétiens" (CFTC) and "Conféderation des Representations Professionels Francais". As a logical consequence followed a ban on all strikes.

34. Ibid. pag. 604–05.

35. Ibid. pag. 645–56, where the communist strike doctrine and its relation to political aims is analysed in detail.

36. This did not apply to France only, but to all countries of Northern and Western Europe, and especially to Poland, where it was not a problem of enticing but simply of conscription of forced labour for Germany. By the end of 1942 Polish labour in Germany totalled 1.2 million and in addition half a million of Polish prisoners of war, a very considerable part of the 4 millions of foreigners exploited in Germany. Concerning the Polish figures see Martin Broszat: "Nationalsozialistische Polenpolitik 1939–45", pag. 107 ff.

37. "Generalbevollmächtigern für den Arbeitseinsatz" (GBA).

38. Albert Speer: "Erinnerungen", pag. 234.

39. On these demands and the following negotiations see Robert Aron: "Histoire de Vichy", pag. 521 ff. Cf. Keesing 1940–43, pag. 5242 and 5365.

40. Robert Aron: "Histoire de Vichy", pag. 502.
41. Keesing 1940–43, pag. 5423–24, reporting on Laval's speech and the course of the previous strike. Laval's appeals should be seen in the light of the increasing unemployment and also of the great number of French prisoners of war in German camps – totalling about 1.850.000. (See Pierre Gascar: "Histoire de la Captivité des Francais en Allemagne"). Furthermore the very mass of P. O. W.s made any idea of "la Relève" totally unrealistic.
42. Keesing 1940–43, pag. 5421. Luxembourg was invaded on the 10 May 1940. The Grand Duchess Charlotte had asked for right of Asylum in Great Britain together with her government.
43. Keesing 1940–43, pag. 5635.
44. On the declaration and the following negotiation see Robert Aron: "Histoire de Vichy", pag. 612 ff. On Laval's attitude and responsibility in the question of French forced labour to Germany, cf. Robert Paxton: "Vichy France", pag. 367 ff.
45. A bit of "quid pro quo" was obtained by Laval. The departments "Nord" and "Pas de Calais" were transferred from the authority of the German High Command of Belgium to that of Paris, the line of demarcation between the former occupied and non-occupied parts of France was abolished, the letter service was free for all France and the prisoners of war in Germany were promised a state of "free" workmen.
46. Keesing 1940–43, pag. 5635.
47. Ibid. pag. 6225.
48. The French town population suffered severely from malnutrition and rising prices. In spite of a good harvest in 1943, allowing for an increase of the daily bread ration of 25 gr. The ration had dwindled to 850 calories per day in 1944. The ration of fat was 200 grammes per month, of meat 300 gr. Delivery of potatoes and vegetables broke down again and again and the same happened to milk, hitting hard the babies and children. 1940 to 1944 saw a rise of prices for the general necessities of 166%. The mortality rate followed pace. See Robert Aron: "Histoire de Vichy", pag. 591. Conditions in the British Channel islands were similary severe. See C. G. Cruickshank: "The German Occupation of the Channel Islands", chapter "The Islanders".
49. See below pag. 434 f.
50. Regarding the situation and importance of the Paris-region in summer 1944, see Robert Aron: "Histoire de la Libération de la France", pag. 350 ff.
51. Ibid. pag. 382–83.
52. On the police of Paris, their illegal organisation, strike and general strike orders, ibid. pag. 383–87.
53. About the antagonism between de Gaulle's representative in Paris, Alexandre Parodi, and local leaders of resistance, see Robert Aron, ibid. pag. 394 ff. Forced by the events in the city 12-19 August Parodi gave in and approved a general rebellion.
54. Dwight D. Eisenhower: "Crusade in Europe", pag. 332.
55. Ibid. pag. 332–33 Cf. Charles de Gaulle: "Memoirs de Guerre", vol. 2, chapter "Paris".
56. The strikes are analysed in great detail by Hans Kirchhoff: "Augustoprøret 1943". Essays on special subjects in "Historie", Ny Række VII, 2, 1969 173–224. A detailed analysis of the strike in Esbjerg by Aage Trommer: "Besættelsestidens første folkestrejke" in "Historie", Ny Række, 2, 1966, pag. 149–231.
57. Here SOE's operations in the country were of decisive importance. Cf. Jørgen Hæstrup: "Secret Alliance", vol. 1, reporting on the cooperation between SOE and

illegal development in Denmark 1940–43. The importance of British deliveries of materiel for the rapidly growing sabotage, leading up to the widespread general strikes is especially dealt with in the chapter "Sabotage".

58. On the German ultimatum and the policy of the government see Jørgen Hæstrup: "Til Landets Bedste", vol. 1, pag. 22–40.
59. Recognised as such by the Sovjetunion in April 1944 and as the temporary governor of the country by declarations from Eden and Cordell Hull in July 1944. A detailed account of this in Jørgen Hæstrup: "Secret Alliance" II-III. The continued existence of the civil administration is dealt with in his "Til Landets Bedste" I-II.
60. Keesing 1940–43, pag. 4833.
61. The following account of the struggle for the organisations is based upon Th. Chr. Wyller: "Nyordning og Motstand", analysing the civilian resistance in Norway which developed parallel to the military efforts, accounted by Sverre Kjeldstadli in his book "Hjemmestyrkene".
62. See Sverre Kjeldstadli: "Hjemmestyrkene", pag. 129 ff. From Allied side such an "Operation Jupiter" was actually considered, but never carried out. Cf. Winston Churchill: "The Second World War", vol. 4, "Jupiter" in the index.
63. "Les Alliés et la Résistance Tchécoslovaque" in "European Resistance Movements" (Milan-report), pag. 230 ff.
64. Henri Bernard: "La Résistance 1940–45", pag. 37–38. Ibid. pag. 39 with account of the above mentioned "go-slow" tactics, employed in the Belgian industry.
65. Keesing 1940–43, pag. 5067.
66. Jørgen Hæstrup: "Linz, en sabotageepisode" in "Festskrift til Axel Linvald", pag. 55–68.

Passive Resistance

1. Joseph Goebbels: "The Goebbels Diaries", 2/3, 23/9 and 17/11 1943. The diaries include numerous lamentations about conditions at home, the coalition-partners and collaborators.
2. Owen A. Davey in "Journal of Contemporary History", 1971, no. 4, pag. 46–71.
3. The desire for joining up was not any stronger in the other countries of the North and the West. A recruiting campaign in Denmark yielded only 450 in June 1941 and 315 in July. From then on the results were steadily dwindling. It was felt disappointing that only a minute fraction of the recruits were trained soldiers and only very few officers. (Henning Poulsen: "Besættelsesmagten og de Danske Nazister", pag. 283–84). Also in Norway, Holland and Belgium only minute units were raised.
4. "L'Humanité", 15/10 1943.
5. It is not quite impossible to measure this phenomenon. The author has himself in two volumes analysed the negotiations between Danish Civil Servants and the German authorities of occupation from August 1943 to May 1945. ("Til Landets Bedste" I-II). The analysis discloses numerous cases of passive resistance of any description, delaying, double crossing and later on direct support to illegal activities. Henri Michel gives his account of the same phenomenon in "La Guerre de l'Ombre", chapter "Le Refus de l'Occupation" (pag. 82–84) and more detailed in the chapter "La Résistance Passive et Administrative", pag. 215–24. The Intelligence Services received a constant flow of information leaking out the civil services of the countries, and quite a lot of sabotage

was planned and carried out with the help of employees of the sabotaged plants. The services of communication constantly received assistance from members of the railway, post and tele-services etc.

6. Keesing 1940–43, pag. 4733.
7. Account from Eigil Knuth, speaker in the Danish radio, (Danish National Arch.).
8. On the passive resistance of the French railway service and the German countermeasures see Robert Aron: "Histoire de la Libération de la France", pag. 226 ff. Cf. the French resistance organisation "Combat"'s setting up of a special organisation, "Noyautage des Administrations Publiques" for infiltration and exploitation of the French administration on all levels to the benefit of the resistance. On this see Henri Michel: "Les Courants de Pensée de la Résistance", pag. 302 f.
9. This especially applies to Poland and the Sovjetunion. For Poland see Martin Broszat: "Nationalsozialistische Polenpolitik 1939–45", especially chapter 3.
10. Fitzroy MacLean: "Disputed Barricade", pag. 161 f.
11. Th. Chr. Wyller: "Nyordning og Motstand".
12. Keesing 1940–43, pag. 5365.
13. See M. R. D. Foot: "SOE in France", pag. 119 f.:" . . . though the bulk of the lower police ranks inclined rather to favour than to disapprove resisters of all kinds. As with the mass of the French civilian population, the proportion who were prepared to support anti-German activities rose as the war went on and the chances of beating Germany improved. Some of SOE's earliest efforts in France depended on clandestine French police cooperation". The same was the case in Denmark, where SOE from an early stage of its activities within the country kept contact with cooperative police men. (Jørgen Hæstrup: "Secret Alliance" I, pag. 214–18). Cf. Also Werner Warmbrunn: "The Dutch under German Occupation", pag. 127, with an account of similar conditions in Holland and the disarming of Dutch police units in 1944 and 1945.
14. On this dissolution, the period without police and the illegal reorganising of the police see Jørgen Hæstrup: "Til Landets Bedste" II, pag. 55 and 142. The illegal reorganising is described in detail in Jørgen Hæstrup: "Secret Alliance" III, pag. 139–46. It was characteristic for the situation after the dissolution that reorganising of the illegal police took place with the assistance of the Ministry of Justice.
15. On developments in the British Channel Islands see generally C. G. Cruickshank "The German Occupation of the Channel Islands". Quotations on pag. 156–57.
16. Keesing 1940–43, pag. 5232.

Intelligence Service

1. Peter Fleming: "Operation Sea Lion", pag. 35 f.
2. Charles de Gaulle: "Mémoires de Guerre", vol. 1, appendix. The appendix gives the full wording of the speech.
3. Marie Granet & Henri Michel: "Combat. Histoire d'un Mouvement de Résistance de Juillet 1940 a Juillet 1943", pag. 28.
4. Where no other source is stated the following account of Frenay's work and the activities of "Combat" is based on the quoted book by Marie Granet and Henri Michel, a profound analysis of the person as well as the organisation, and a principal work in the history of French resistance.
5. Pétain's popularity developed during the first phases of the occupation into a cult, approaching a religious, often hysterical character. Portraits of him were spread all

over France. When travelling, church bells were welcoming him and he was constantly surrounded by people of all spheres of life who wanted to see him – if possible touch him. Mothers handed their babies towards him to be blessed by him etc. Cardinal Gerlier concentrated the general opinion in 4 words: "Pétain, that is France". On this see Robert Aron: "Histoire de Vichy", pag. 162–63. Cf. also Robert Paxton: "Vichy France", pag. 35 ff. with a short portrait of Pétain.

6. Cf. on this also M. R. D. Foot: "SOE in France", with information on the intelligence activities of the French Army and Airforce and pointing out the fact that this would impede the possibilities of the Armistice Army for entering in on "serviceaction" i. e. active resistance. A parallel problem appeared for the Danish army, delivering intelligence to Great Britain but for that very reason refusing all participation in active resistance of any other kind. In both cases priority was given to the intelligence work and that to such an extent that other activities, which might compromise the army and lead to its dissolution, were condemned and rejected. (Foot, quoted work, pag. 134. Jørgen Hæstrup: "Secret Alliance" I, pag. 120–27).

7. A great number of states – 32 in all – kept normal diplomatic relations with the Vichy-government, for inst. USA, the Vatican and the Sovjet Union. From the USA the ambassador from November 1940 was a personal friend of president Roosevelt, William Leahy, who had been given the special task to counteract and neutralize any attempt for promoting active French cooperation with Germany. The work of this mission is described by William L. Langer: "Our Vichy Gamble".

8. In a memo from the American Vichy-embassy, dated October 1941, it is estimated that 85% of the Staff of the Vichy Foreign Office were pro-Allied. (Henri Michel: "Les Courants de Pensée de la Résistance", pag. 449).

9. This happened under the auspices of SOE by the "Section F", accounted of in detail by M. R. D. Foot in "SOE in France". A short account of the work of the section is given by Foot in "Britain and European Resistance" (Oxford-report).

10. As mentioned de Gaulle's direct representative to the French resistance organisations and founder of the coordinating central body of the movements, "Conseil National de la Résistance". Arrested and killed after torture in 1943. A very personal description of Jean Moulin is found in Eric Piquet-Wicks: "Quatre dans l'Ombre". Also Henri Michel: "Jean Moulin l'Unificateur".

11. See below, pag. 408 f.

12. Henri Michel: "Les Courants de Pensée de la Résistance", pag. 447.

13. Henri Michel: "Histoire de la Résistance", pag. 77.

14. M. R. D. Foot: "SOE in France". It is stressed by Foot (pag. 57 of the quoted book) that it probably was a mistake that not all agents posted from London were trained W/T operators. He also makes a point of emphazising the fundamental importance of the radio service.

15. The British intelligence chief, general Kenneth Strong, sums up as follows: "As far as Intelligence was concerned, nothing that human ingenuity and care could do had been left undone. Perhaps never again will so much detailed information be available for an operation of this kind. Our Intelligence concerning the enemy's strength and defences proved to be remarkably accurate, except in one respect". Strong then mentions the only exeption – the 352 division, which was never definitely localized. (Kenneth Strong: "Intelligence at the Top", pag. 139). Cf. Frederick Morgen: "Ouverture to Overlord" telling about the constant stream of resistance people, bringing intelligence for the Staffs in London, preferably via radio.

16. Dwight D. Eisenhower: "Crusade in Europe", pag. 287.
17. On Zeller, his initiative and negotiations and the following military developments see Robert Aron: "Histoire de la Libération de la France", pag. 340 ff. Cf. Charles de Gaulle: "Memoires de Guerre", vol. 2, description in chapter "Combat" of the Allied landing in Southern France.
18. A short time before Zeller had been in on the fatal maquis revolt on the Vercors plateau. He had escaped the German surrounding and reached the Alpine region. From an improvised airstrip he came to Algiers. On the Vercors rising see below, pag. 483. On Soustelle and his work in the Gaullist movement see his memoirs: "Envers et Contre Tout".
19. Winston Churchill: "The Second World War", vol. 2, pag. 217.
20. Ibid. pag. 572.
21. J. R. M. Butler: "Grand Strategy" II, pag. 268–69.
22. The development of the Belgian intelligence service is described by Henri Bernard: "La Résistance 1940–45", chapter 9, pag. 60–78. Where no other source is stated, this account is based on that work.
23. See above, pag. 30.
24. On the work in London and the negotiations of the Belgian government with British Staffs see "Britain and European Resistance 1939–45" (Oxford-report).
25. Out of these 77 SOE agents 21 were posted by Political Warfare Executive for propaganda work and 17 to serve and promote escape routes through France-Spain-Portugal.
26. This final figure put in relation to the 233 agent missions tells its tale of the inevitable losses, caused by German investigation and punishment, mostly by execution of agents rounded up. It is estimated that c. 2000 members of the intelligence organisations were executed or died in concentration camps. (Henri Bernard: "La Résistance 1940–45", pag. 78).
27. On these barrings and their consequences see "Britain and European Resistance 1939–45" (Oxford-report), report by L. de Jong.
28. Concerning the following account of Dutch intelligence activities see the quoted report by L. de Jong in "Britain and European Resistance 1939–45" and Werner Warmbrunn: "The Dutch under German Occupation", pag. 209–13. L. de Jong's report is the more copious.
29. All exile organs had a need for contact with the political development at home, which quickly made the conceptions of the exile governments obsolete. The Beckman plan corresponds with a similar plan for Denmark. In June 1941 SOE invited a Danish social democrat politician, Hedtoft Hansen, and the conservative politician, Christmas Møller, to come to London. H. H. refused for reasons connected with internal politics, but Christmas Møller accepted the invitation. He arrived in London via Sweden in May 1942 to become the leader of the "free" Danish movement in Great Britain. On his escape to England see Jørgen Hæstrup: "Secret Alliance" I, pag. 132 f.
30. "Britain end European Resistance" (Oxford-report), pag. 6.
31. See below, pag. 293 ff.
32. Somer was officially appointed in July 1943 and his organisation was not affected by the consequences of the "Englandsspiel".
33. R. E. Urquhart: "Arnhem", chapter 8.
34. On conditions and reactions of the Dutch administration see Werner Warmbrunn: "The Dutch under German Occupation", pag. 121 ff.

35. A short account of the particular situation in Denmark can be found in the account "From Occupied to Ally", published 1963 by the Danish Foreign Ministry.
36. On Ebbe Munck and his cooperation with the Danish officers see "Skipperen", en Bog om Ebbe Munck" (ed. Jørgen Hæstrup) or Jørgen Hæstrup: "Secret Alliance" I-III, index.
37. On this episode see Jørgen Hæstrup: "Secret Alliance", vol. 1, pag. 110–13.
38. See on this correspondance and the V-1 missile below, pag. 381.
39. The intelligence work, before and after 29. August 1943 is in detail described in separate chapters in Jørgen Hæstrup: "Secret Alliance" I-III.
40. Sverre Kjeldstadli: "Hjemmestyrkene", pag. 354–55.
41. Information from cand. philol. Berit Nökleby. Cf. Olav Riste in "Motstandskamp, Strategi og Marinepolitik", pag. 37–39 and 138–57. An account by a participant in Sverre Midtskau: "London svarer ikke".
42. On the Katyn-affair and its British and Exile-Polish repercussions see Winston Churchill: "The Second World War", vol. 4, pag. 679–81. Churchill is here not committing himself directly as to the question of guilt, although he makes no bones of the fact that all indications are pointing towards the Russians being responsible. But his version of the affair does disclose the attitude of the British government to the Polish-Sovjet confrontation, both then and later on: Hoping for a mutual understanding of a matter where the Western powers could bring little influence to bear. He quotes his statement to Sikorski: "If they are dead nothing you can do will bring them back". And to Maiski, the Sovjet ambassador in London: "We have got to beat Hitler . . . and this is no time for quarrels and charges". More detailed analysis of the "Katyn-affair" in J. K. Zawodny: "Death in the Forest" and Louis Fitzgibbon: "Katyn a Crime without Parallel".
43. On this see Emanuel Halicz: "Partisan Warfare in 19th Century Poland, the Development of a Concept".
44. Sikorski wanted a Polish-Sovjet approach with Polish concessions of territory in Eastern Poland. The Katyn-affair and soon after Sikorski's death in July after an air-crash barred the way for such an approach.
45. Formally speaking only Great Britain – and France – were obliged, but these countries lost influence as the war went on. By the end of hostilities they were unable to exercise any major influence in Eastern Europe – both for political and for strategic reasons.
46. The following account of Polish intelligence activities is based on a number of accounts of Polish resistance: "European Resistance Movements 1939–45" (Milan-report), pag. 419–63, report by S. Okecki. Tadeusz Bor-Komorowski: "The Secret Army". "Britain and European Resistance" (Oxford-report), reports by Willetts, Raczynski and Kopanski, with following debate. Jozef Garlinski: "Poland SOE and the Allies". Cf. also Hanns von Krannhals: "Der Warschauer Aufstand 1944", introduction, pag. 11–66. In the mentioned the information is generally very detailed, but as to intelligence service rather scattered. Detailed notes will therefore only appear where especially important, and containing direct quotations.
47. According to Count Raczynski ("Britain and European Resistance" (Oxford-report pag. 2) 4 Polish divisions were being formed in France in spring 1940. Of these 2 were operational when the Germans attacked on 10 May. The personnel was drawn from Poles abroad, from the numerous Polish workers in France and also directly from Poland.

48. It is estimated by Okecki that illegal secret military and political organisations in the first period of occupation were exceeding 150. Later on fusions reduced the number to well under 20. Quoted report, pag. 424. According to Bor-Komorowski a unified movement and command was on the agenda at an early date.
49. Jozef Garlinski: "Poland SOE and the Allies", pag. 47–49. Cf. Bor-Komorowski: "The Secret Army", pag. 71. Both are stressing the psychological value of this first dropping.
50. Cf. the later report by general Kopanski (Cf. note 46). All told about 400 transmitters and 30 receivers arrived in Polish territory in that way. The number of approaches increased and is stated by Kopanski to amount to:
1941–42: 12 approaches of which 9 were successful.
1942–43: 100 planned, 65 carried out of which 42 succeeded.
1943–44: 500 planned, 381 carried out of which 208 succeeded.
During the rising in Warsaw approaches were much more frequent. See below, pag. 000 ff.
51. A corresponding phenomenon is known from Denmark, irrespective of the minor size of the country.
52. On "Swit" see Stefan Korbonski: "Fighting Warsaw", pag. 200–213.
53. S. Okecki in "European Resistance Movements" (Milan-report), pag. 424, note.
54. Bor-Komorowski: "The Secret Army", pag. 22.
55. Ibid. pag. 23 ff. Cf. Hanns von Krannhals: "Der Warschauer Aufstand 1944", pag. 25.
56. Cf. note 53.
57. See below, pag. 275 ff.
58. Hanns von Krannhals: "Der Warschauer Aufstand 1944", pag. 66, estimated at "a few thousand followers". Krannhals compares this organisation with what is called "the mass organisation" of the home army. Okecki mentions them coordinately in his report without giving any figures.
59. Okecki's wording.
60. The Chief of Armia Ludowa, general Michal Rola-Zymierski, was from 1944 head of the section for the National Defence of the "Polish Committee for National Liberation", known as the "Lublin Government" of predominantly communist observance. ("Revue Internationale d'Histoire Militaire", no. 33, 1975, pag. 78).
61. Okecki's appreciation in "European Resistance Movements" (Milan-report), pag. 435. Okecki gives instances of Polish intelligence, making possible Sovjet airbombing of new airfields inflicting severe German losses.
62. The Danish intelligence service was at that time asked for information on the experimental activities at Peenemünde. Target practice was going on in the Baltic and could occasionally be spotted on the Danish island, Bornholm. (Description of this in Jørgen H. Barfod: "Et Centrum i Periferien" with an English summary. See f. i. pag. 340).
63. Webster and Frankland: "The Strategic Air Offensive against Germany 1939–45", vol. 2, pag. 158–60 and 283–85.
64. Most copious description by Jozef Garlinski: "Poland, SOE and the Allies", pag. 150 ff.
65. Ibid. pag. 158–64.
66. Count Raczynski in "Britain and European Resistance" (Oxford-report). Debate, pag. 26.
67. A principal work on partisan warfare in general – and the Russian particularly – is Heinz Kühnrich: "Der Partisanenkrieg in Europa 1939–45". Dealing with Russian

partisan warfare alone is Erich Hesse: "Der Sowjetrussische Partisanenkrieg 1941–44". From the West is published C. A. Dixon and O. Heilbrunn: "Communist Guerilla Warfare". Further "Istorija SSSR", vol. X, section on partisan war by I. S. Karetjenko and I. I. Slinko, and A. D. Sjarikov: "The Great Country Supplies the Partisans" (Voprosy Istorii, no. 4, pag. 121–29) and information to the author by A. A. Kurnosov. It is borne out by all accounts that partisan units were being organised already in July 1941 and that they constantly expanded.

68. On the efforts during the first months for establishing a solid communication service see information by A. A. Kurnosov.

69. Kurnosov states that by October 1941 about 33.000 men were left in the Ukraine for such tasks whereas about 437 units and groups totalling 7.200 men were sent into White Russia in order to organise partisan activities and about 1200 for other sorts of illegal action. Kurnosov states that these organising groups became centers attracting thousands of patriots and bases for partisan warfare. A remarkable part in promoting partisan war was played by trained servicemen stranded in the region and refusing to surrender. They formed their own independent "war units" or joined others. Their battle experience, skill and training was of utter value to the partisan activities, especially in adapting military technique to the specific partisan fighting conditions. This description corresponds with Erich Hesse's description of the importance of the so-called "Vernichtungsbataillone" and isolated army units, choosing partisan activity for surrender. (Erich Hesse: "Der Sowjetrussische Partisanenkrieg 1941–44", pag. 62–67).

70. Quoted in both "Istorija SSSR", vol. X and in Kurnosov's information.

71. Mentioned and described by Kurnosov, Sjarikov and in "Istorija SSSR", vol. X. "The Central Staff of the Partisan Movement" was subordinated directly to the High Command of the army, which in turn came under the special organ for united command of the war (GKO), responsible to Party, Board of the Presidents and Ministerial Council. Members of GKO were Stalin, Vorosjilov, Molotov, Malenkov, Bulganin, Mikojan, Vosnesenski and Kaganovitch. Thus the "Central Staff of the Partisan Movement" was incorporated in the joint war-effort machine much closer than the corresponding organisations of the West (SOE and OSS). There were also Republic-and-Oblast-Staffs for the partisan movement and partisan staffs at the War Council of army groups and armies.

72. Information from A. A. Kurnosov, who also gives a statement on the setting up a system of air strips behind the enemy frontzones.

73. Bickham Sweet-Escott: "Baker Street Irregular", pag. 22 ff., 52 f. and 62 ff.

74. Cf. "British Policy towards Wartime Yugoslavia and Greece" (ed. Phyllis Auty and Richard Clogg), pag. 7–8, 10–11, 219 and 265.

75. At the capitulation of the Greek army large quantities of arms were kept by Greek soldiers and officers, estimated by the Greek historian C. Pyromaglou at 120-150.000 light arms with ammo. These arms formed the base of the early Greek partisan units. "European Resistance Movements 1939–45" (Milan-report), pag. 305–06.

76. It is stressed that the Greek exile government did nothing to leave behind any sort of illegal staffs or any other sort of subversive organism with a view to secure national unity in the country. (C. Pyromaglou in "European Resistance Movements 1939–45" (Milan-report), pag. 304–05. These critical remarks might be countered with the argument, that nobody in 1941 could foresee the possibilities of underground warfare.

77. On the famine and emergency supplies see Keesing 1940–43, pag. 5088, 5425 and 5696.

78. An appreciation by Major C. M. Woodhouse, mentioned below, states: "In the towns themselves, chiefly in Athens and Saloniki, Resistance took the form of intelligence, helping escaped prisoners-of-war, some sabotage, some passive resistance (especially against the conscription of labour), and various political activities, including liaison with the active forces in the mountains. There was almost no armed violence in the towns". ("Britain and European Resistance 1939–45" (Oxford-report)).

79. Regarding this mission and its future activity see E. C. W. Myers: "Greek Entanglement" and C. M. Woodhouse: "Apple of Discord", both giving detailed accounts of Greek conditions and the new established Greek-British cooperation.

80. See below, pag. 000.

81. On this see below, pag. 437.

82. The precise number totals 1072, 435 being Greeks and 637 Britons, Americans or Poles. In 1944 82 allied missions worked in Greece – all equipped with radio.

83. E. C. W. Myers: "Greek Entanglement", pag. 160.

84. Cf. a sharp criticism by C. Pyromaglou in his reports in "European Resistance Movements 1939–45" (Milan-report) and "Britain and European Resistance" (Oxford-report). P. is reproaching the British goverment in general – and the Foreign Office particularly – for being unwilling to realize the predominantly republican opinion within the Greek resistance – in spite of clear reports from SOE-missions. This attitude of the Foreign Office had its background in Great Britain's commitments to the Royal Exile Greek government. The British felt themselves obliged to this government, which loyally had cooperated with Great Britain in the fighting in 1941.

85. On the Serbian rebellion summer and autumn 1941 and the reciprocal relations between the 2 organisations at that time, see Fitzroy Mac Lean: "Disputed Barricade", chapter "Serbian Rising".

86. "Britain and European Resistance 1939–45" (Oxford-report), Deakin's report.

87. John Ehrmann: "Grand Strategy" V, pag. 77.

88. One of these, Major Ostojic, became Chief of Staff to Michailović and a zealous advocate of attacking the Tito partisans. (Fitzroy MacLean: "Disputed Barricade", pag. 150).

89. "Britain and European Resistance" (Oxford-report), report by F. W. Deakin. That the information was misleading is proved beyond doubt by J. Marjanović: "The Collaboration of D. Mihailović's Chetniks with the Enemy Forces of Occupation". The documents published here not only prove the actual collaboration, but also a very early start of collaboration. The first attempts are dated to October 1941.

90. "Britain and European Resistance" (Oxford-report), reports by Deakin and by W. Hudson himself. As to the Hudson mission see these.

91. On the situation at that moment and relations and negotiations between the two parts up to the final rupture see Fitzroy MacLean: "Disputed Barricade", pag. 145 ff and "Britain and European Resistance" (Oxford-report), all contributions and the following debate i. a. about Hudson's attitude.

92. This constitutes a certain parallel to the ideas of the Danish officers, from 1940 in charge of intelligence work. In 1942 they presented what they called a P-plan, based on the idea of secretly preparing the formation of certain armed units under command of the army officers, not for immediate resistance purpose, but ready to operate in case of a German break down and in order to support a legal Danish government. The idea was temporarily considered by the British government, but very soon after again

dropped. On this see Jørgen Hæstrup: "Secret Alliance", vol. 1, pag. 120–27. Similar ideas were active within the French armistice army, see Henri Michel: "Les Courants de Pensée de la Résistance", pag. 451. Such attitude has apparently been felt natural for regular officers, who had no confidence in resistance and distrust in the political consequences involved.

93. "Britain and European Resistance" (Oxford-report), Hudson's report.

94. See Jeremy Bennett: "British Broadcasting and the Danish Resistance Movement", pag. 77 with diverse notes.

95. In the period January-May 1942 there were four dropping opeɪations including radio equipment, arms, money and medicine. Cf. "Britain end European Resistance" (Oxford-report), report by J. Marjanović.

96. On these attempts see "Britain and European Resistance" (Oxford-report), F. W. Deakin's report and following debate. The discussion between him and the Yugoslav historian, Marjanović, is centered less on realities than on interpretation. Marjanović categorically rejects that the Michailović movement at any time could be considered a resistance movement – as maintained by Hudson i. a. He also utters great doubt as to the British being ignorant of the real facts – as maintained by Deakin. Marjanović appears to be somewhat justified in pointing out that Hudson already during his stay at Tito's headquarters was given plenty of opportunity to form a clear understanding of the partisan's superiority and greater will to fight it out. It should, however, not be ignored that Hudson's instructions were to contact the supposed leader at his time of arrival, autumn 1941, and that the position then was rather unclarified. At least Hudson had to inspect the other camp.

97. J. R. M. Butler: "Grand Strategy", vol. 2, pag. 519.

98. Regarding this and the following developments see "Britain and European Resistance" (Oxford-report), report by Deakin, who was a principal participant himself. Cf. Deakin's account of the full sequence of events 1941–43 in "Hilsen til Hæstrup", pag. 23–31.

99. Not the first but what is known as "The Fifth Offensive" against the partisans, like the former ones sanguinary but tactically speaking fruitless. A radio signal from the Deakin mission clearly explained this and the magnitude of the operation: "Have broken through German ring north across Foca-Kalinovik road near Jelec last night. Tito has extricated over 10.000 men. One division left in Montenegro in Piva area. Bitterest fighting witnessed." ("Hilsen til Hæstrup", pag. 28).

100. On the revaluation which now followed see John Ehrmann: "Grand Strategy", V, pag. 78 ff. Here the Deakin mission is given the credit for achieving a turning point in British appreciation, and Churchill's direct interference is stressed.

101. MacLean has described his mission and cooperation with Tito in his book "Eastern Approaches", a most personal, colourful and detailed account. He also deals with the activities of the mission in his book: "Disputed Barricade". Especially "Eastern Approaches" leaves a vivid impression of conditions in the country, partisan life and the circumstances the Allied liaison officers had to accept for their work.

102. MacLean returned after his initial talks with Tito to his British base for reporting and organising military help. He was then again dropped in Yugoslavia as leader of the mission. Entering and leaving the country was soon organised, both for Yugoslav and Allied personnel.

103. Bruce Lockhart: "Comes the Reckoning", pag. 308–09.

104. "Britain and European Resistance" (Oxford-report), report by J. Amery. An extremely anti-British and totally misleading version is delivered by Albanian historians in "European Resistance Movements 1939–45" (Milan-report), pag. 123–42.
105. Fitzroy MacLean: "Disputed Barricade", pag. 137 and following pages where some important signals are quoted.
106. For the period June 1941-June 1943 it is a question of rather negligible supplies. The rate of distribution is, however, most illustrating: 23 tons to Michailović, 6½ tons to Tito. (John Ehrmann: "Grand Strategy", V, pag. 79.).

The Creation of a Resistance Mentality

1. Bruce Lockhart: " Comes the Reckoning", pag. 154.
2. The world famous French short story "La Silence de la Mer", published under the pseudonym "Vercors", gives a masterly expression of the actual problem.
3. Even in Germany P. O. W. camps listening in to Allied stations was going on. See f.i. Marie Granet: "Défence de la France", pag. 121 f.
4. Mussolini: "Memoirs 1942–43", pag. 3.
5. "The Strategic Air Offensive against Germany 1939–45" I, pag. 100, 105, 135, 140.
6. See above, pag. 37.
7. On this new formation and the following account of PWE's activities see Bruce Lockhart: "Comes the Reckoning", sect. III, "Wordy Warfare", pag. 125 to the end.
8. Ibid., pag. 154.
9. Joseph Goebbels: "The Goebbels Diaries", 15/4 1942.
10. The British Commando raid on St. Nazaire 26 March 1942. (Winston Churchill: "The Second World War", vol. 4, pag. 106).
11. A table showing the times of transmissions for the different countries by Henri Michel in "La Guerre de l"Ombre", pag. 99. The transmission periods varied from France with 5½ hours to Luxembourg and Albania with ¼ hour.
12. Henri Michel: "Les Courants de Pensée de la Résistance", pag. 787.
13. Ibid. pag. 788.
14. See above the "Swit" station. Cf. note 16. A transmission in Flemish language belongs to the same category.
15. Jørgen Hæstrup: "Secret Alliance" I, pag. 236 ff and II, 255 ff. An apparatus, planned on very generous lines, was set up in both London and Denmark, but never became operationel, probably because RAF were unwilling to allocate the airplanes. RAF concurred with SOE's scepticism as to this work.
16. "Swit" and its link with Polish intelligence see Stefan Korbonski: "Fighting Warsaw", pag. 200 ff.
17. Sverre Kjeldstadli: "Hjemmestyrkene", pag. 61–62.
18. On COI and the Anglo-American cooperation on intelligence and on the support to the European Resistance movements including the formation of OWI and OSS see H. Montgomery Hyde: "Room 3603", pag. 174 ff and 190 ff. The quotation pag. 175. (Pocket-edition). On Donovan's tour to Europe in 1940: Ibid. pag. 152 f. The book contains a general analysis in detail of the Anglo-American cooperation mentioned here. Cf. Edward Hymoff: "The OSS in World War II", chapter 2.
19. The author Elmer Davis was appointed leader of OWI. He was a political commentator of the Columbia Broadcasting System. The idea of dividing the tasks was prom-

oted by the author Robert Sherwood, a near friend of Harry Hopkins, president Roosevelt's right-hand man. Ibid., pag. 190–91.

20. See above, pag. 000.
21. On these Stalin-quotations see E. Boltin in "European Resistance Movements 1939–45" (Milan-report), pag. 14.
22. Henri Michel: "La Guerre de l'Ombre", pag. 100.
23. In 1943 Danish became language no. 23. Cf. "Besættelsestidens Fakta" II, pag. 1288.
24. Henri Michel: "La Guerre de l'Ombre", pag. 100. For the countries mentioned here it was a station in Tiflis, "Free Yugoslavia", and the Polish station, "Tadeusz Kościuszko", run by Polish communists in exile.
25. "Britain and European Resistance" (Oxford-report), report by Korbel, pag. 5.
26. See above, pag. 185.
27. On this cf. Henri Michel: "La Guerre de l'Ombre", pag. 101. Michel especially mentions France and Holland as countries, whose early illegal press was based on the BBC. The titles of a number of Dutch papers directly included the word: BBC. Michel would have been entitled to add that this also happened in Belgium, Norway, Denmark and Poland. The Belgian historian, Henri Bernard, states that the BBC was listened to with "religious" zeal by Belgian patriots. Henri Bernard: "La Résistance 1940–45", pag. 42. Cf. Jeremy Bennett: "British Broadcasting and the Danish Resistance Movement".
28. Henri Bernard: "Histoire de la Résistance Européenne", pag. 197.
29. See above, pag. 67.
30. A summary survey of the Dutch press is made by Werner Warmbrunn: "The Dutch under German Occupation". The summary includes 38 pages and is mainly based on the principal work on this subject: L. E. Winkel: "De ondergrondse Pers, 1940–45".
31. It is probably rather illustrating, that the French historian, Henri Michel, in his comprehensive work "Les Courants de Pensée de la Résistance", which to a high degree is founded on statements from the French illegal press, totally desists from a detailed account of the more than a thousand papers. He confines himself, in pages 793–800, to a philosophical summary of the papers in general, discussing their value as a source for appreciating the political trends within French resistance.
32. This probably applies to the least degree to Poland, where the dominating resistance organisation, "Armia Krajowa", recognized the exile government and – on principle – its leadership of the struggle. But as to tactics the decisions often had to be taken in the homeland – without any possibility of consulting the government. There is a similar problem in Norway, where the Home army, "Milorg", in principle accepted the exile government as Norway's legal leaders, but still maintained and exercised a considerable amount of autonomy.
33. The numerical values in the following are stated by the Russian historian, A. A. Kurnosov, answering direct questions by the author.
34. V. I. Smirnov i.a. (edit.): "Stranitsy Narodnogo Podviga" (Kalininskaja Oblast v. Gody Velikoj Otetjestvennoj Vojny), pag. 100 f.
35. Alexander Dallin: German Rule in Russia, pag. 71. On German policy of occupation in general see this work, especially pag. 68–76. Cf. Erich Hesse: "Der Sovjetrussiche Partisanenkrieg", pag. 47–50.
36. Just to illustrate Dallin states that one out of 4 "Einsatzkommandos" during the first year of the war liquidated 90.000 men, women and children.
37. Contrariwise the BBC propagandists were ordered not to get involved in dialectical

polemics with German propaganda. Cf. Bruce Lockhart: "Comes the Reckoning", pag. 154.

38. Contribution by Seton-Watson in "Special Operations" (ed. Patrick Howarth), pag. 88.
39. On the struggle of the Ruhr, see "The Strategy of Civilian Defence" (ed. Adam Roberts), pag. 106–35.
40. Described by T. E. Lawrence in "Seven Pillars of Wisdom".
41. Here a few illustrating examples. After a bombardement of the French Peugeot works-partly a failure at a price of a great many civilian victims in the surrounding areas and without substantially hampering production – SOE – trained saboteurs arranged a most succesful sabotage with the pro-allied Peugeot-family. (Henri Michel: "La Guerre de l'Ombre", pag. 229). Sabotage of transport of the heavy water from Vemork in February 1944 was carried out in cooperation between the saboteurs and the head of the technical organisation at the Vemork works. (Sverre Kjeldstadli: "Hjemmestyrkene", pag. 221–22). Sabotage on a German mine sweeper being built in Denmark was realised in cooperation of saboteurs with an employee of the shipyard, July 1943. (Jørgen Hæstrup: "Festskrift til Axel Linvald", pag. 155–67). Many more examples could be mentioned.
42. The views stated here are – of course – of no importance in respect of the proper partisan zones.
43. Cf. for inst. Sverre Kjeldstadli: "Hjemmestyrkene", pag. 210–11. Also Henri Michel: "La Guerre de l'Ombre", pag. 229, refering to French and Belgian points of view. From Denmark resistance leaders directly asked for a bombardement of a target in Copenhagen in order to promote a better understanding of the necessity of sabotage as compared to bombings. (Jørgen Hæstrup: "Secret Alliance", vol. 1, pag. 177 f.).
44. As already stated the idea of strategic bombing constituted a vital component of what is known as the ABC-1 plan. (See above, pag. 37) and a particularly high priority was allocated at the Casablanca-conference, January 1943. Cf. Winston Churchill: "The Second World War", vol. 4, pag. 604–22. Webster and Frankland: "The Strategic Air Offensive against Germany", vol. 4, pag. 153 f.
45. "British Policy towards Wartime Resistance in Yugoslavia and Greece" (ed. Phyllis Auty and Richard Clogg), pag. 22–23.
46. This principal conclusion emanates from Charles Webster and Noble Frankland: "The Strategic Air Offensive against German 1939–45", I–IV, which clearly demonstrates the failing results during the first years of the war and also the decisive importance of strategic bombing during the later stages of the war.
47. See above, pag. 37.
48. A survey in detail of the sabotage groups dispatched by the SOE to France in M. R. D. Foot: "SOE in France", cf. the index of that book under "Sabotage". The growth of SOE permitted more and more dispatches. In his book: "Resistance, European Resistance to Nazism 1940–45" (pag. 140) Foot estimates the size of SOE-personnel to amount to c. 13.000 persons in spring 1944. He adds: "The influence it (SOE) exercised on the war was disproportionately very much greater".
49. Henri Michel: "La Guerre de l'Ombre", pag. 227.

Politics and Supplies

1. A. D. Sjarikov: "The Great Country Supplies the Partisans" (Voprosy Istorii, no. 4, 1973, pag. 121 ff.) Cf. above pag. 185.
2. "Istorija SSSR", vol. X, section on partisan warfare by I. S. Karetjenko and I. I. Slinko, pag. 56.
3. Ibid, pag. 54.
4. Cf. Alexander Dallin: "German Rule in Russia", pag. 406–07. Dallin states from a number of calculations that the economic exploitation of the occupied regions in the East only were of negligible value for Germany, much lower than expected by German leaders and western experts. He mentions that the total deliveries from the East region only accounted to about 15% of deliveries from France. Dallin concludes that this modest result was only obtained by introducing a brutal policy of plundering, contributing to uniting the population of the occupied regions in obstinate will to resistance. Correspondingly the plans of exploiting the Balkan States turned into a total failure for the Axis Powers. Since 1941 the German import from all Balkans were dwindling and dropped below the pre-occupational level. See Dietrich Orlow: "The Nazis in the Balkans", pag. 170–74. Orlow sums up: "The passive and active resistance of the Balkan countries was an absolute success" and "The result (of the German policy) was a total failure of the German economic policy in the Balkans".
5. Mass evacuations described in "Istorija SSR", vol. X, pag. 86–92, from where the figures stated emanate.
6. Erich Hesse: "Der Sowjetrussische Partisanenkrieg 1941–45", pag. 22–25. On the negative balance sheet for Germany in the exploitation of the conquered territory see Matthias Riedel: "Bergbau und Eisenhüttenindustrie in der Ukraine unter deutscher Besatzung 1941–45" (Vierteljahrhefte für Zeitgeschichte, 1973, instalment 3).
7. Albert Speer: "Erinnerungen", pag. 205–06.
8. All over the occupied countries of Europe early resistance organisation was characterized by a certain amount of confusion. This would of course also apply to the Sovjetunion. It should, however, be pointed out that confusion here was less acute because the struggle – sabotage and partisan warfare – soon found its natural shape and also because there was no or little political frictions between the groups. The fact that groups and formations were raised and welded together by the Communist Central Committees gave a unity of the movement from the very beginning, which in other countries had to be worked out gradually. There might have been frictions, if the Germans had tried to appeal to the national feelings in the Baltic and the Ukraine, but as no serious attempt was made in that respect and as the general German East policy destroyed all local attempts to ease the situation for the population, the Sovjet propaganda had an easy job. Cf. Erich Hesse: "Der Sowjetrussische Partisankrieg", for inst. pag. 152–161.
9. "Istorija SSSR" vol. X, pag. 54 f.
10. Cf. Dixon and Heilbrunn: "Communist Guerilla Warfare".
11. Joseph Goebbels: "The Goebbels Diaries", 6/3 1942.
12. The figures here and in the following are based on "Istorija SSSR", vol. X, pag. 56 ff.
13. Stressed to the author in information from the Russian historian, A. A. Kurnosov: "Strategically speaking the partisan operations against communications, especially the railways, were probably of highest importance. The definite transfer of the operational centre of gravity to communications happened towards the end of 1942 and in 1943. As a consequence the mobility of the German forces was reduced:" This cor-

respondends with the German transportation officer, Herman Teske's investigations add evaluations in the Sovjetunion. Cf. summary of Teske's research in Aage Trommer: "Jernbanesabotagen i Danmark", pag. 183 f., referring to Teske's works: "Der silberne Spiegel" and "Partisans gegen die Eisenbahn".

14. Quoted in Dixon and Heillbronn: "Communist Guerilla Warfare".

15. Such areas could – at least temporarily – be of considerable size. The German historian, Heinz Kühnrich, holds the opinion that about 60% of White Russia or 108.000 square kilometres was liberated or at least controlled by partisans by the end of 1943. To assess square mileage and population in that way is most difficult, both because the front lines were constantly moving and because a liberation by partisans could be of only temporary character. But even a temporary liberation opened a way for supplies being flown in. Heinz Kühnrich: "Der Partisanenkrieg in Europe 1939–45", pag. 234–35.

16. Cf. Information to the author by A. A. Kurnosov: "At the beginning of the war the partisan units obviously were guided much more by actual operational conditions, by the present possibilities and of own interests".

17. "Istorija SSSR", vol. X, pag. 239.

18. The figures stated here and in the following as well as information on organisation are based on the essay by A. D. Sjarikov: ""The Great Country" supplies the partisans". Considering that the author is speaking of "provisional calculations" the figures are rounded off. The author, Andrej Dmitrievic Sjarikov, is head of the section in the War Ministry's Historical Institute and a specialist on the partisan movement. His figures must be accepted as authoritative – as far as figures in that context can be.

19. A cooperation between the Anglo-Saxon support organisations and correponding Sovjet ones was never established. Apart from a very limited exchange of information and material they functioned totally independent of each other. See account by Major-General Colin Gubbins in "The Fourth Dimension of Warfare", pag. 102 and 109.

20. On the ideological attitude of communism to partisan warfare see below, pag. 00.

21. Cf. above, pag. 38.

22. An inherent controversy thus existed between SOE and the Foreign Office and SOE also met controversial feelings from the traditional military staffs. These were asked to allocate resources to SOE without sufficient knowledge or understanding of the contributions SOE-operations could render in the mutual battle. An expert account of SOE's difficult intermediate position is given by Major-General Colin Gubbins in "The Fourth Dimension of Warfare", pag. 83–110.

23. On the attempt and its tragic consequences see Ronald Seth: "A spy has no Friend".

24. Cf. Hugh Dalton: "Memoirs 1931–45" vol. 2, "The Fateful Years", pag. 366.

25. See above pag. 38 f.

26. J. M. A. Gwyer: "Grand Strategy", III, pag. 42–43.

27. J. R. M. Butler: "Grand Strategy", vol. 2, pag. 517–18.

28. Such contacts could be utterly fragile. Because of its special character of being a top secret organisation it was often most limited to what degree the exile governments were informed or consulted on SOE activity in the different countries. This could cause frictions as frictions could arise between SOE and the national resistance leaders. Cf. i.a. Sverre Kjeldstadli: "Hjemmestyrkene", pag. 174–90, accounting of a classic example of this sort.

29. This caused for inst. tensions between de Guelle and SOE's French section. A striking example can be found in Denmark, when the Danish exile politician, Christmas

Møller, as well as the Danish Ambassador in London, Reventlow, were completely cut off from information on SOE's activites in Denmark. Cf. Jørgen Hæstrup: "Christmas Møllers London-breve".

30. On OSS see Edward Hymoff: "The OSS in World War II" with comprehensive bibliography. Cf. H. Monotgomery Hyde: "Room 3603" and Corey Ford: "Donovan of OSS". There is here a clear British-American parallel. The men behind the creation both of SOE and OSS were predominantly civilians. This reflects the fact that the intentions were not the formation of a traditional, military set up.

31. This was thus the case when the SOE-OSS activities in connection with Greece evoked violent outbursts of indignation in the Foreign Office. The prominent Foreign Office civil servant, Rex Leeper, who was responsible for relations to the Greek exile government used strong words about the head of the SOE-mission to Greece, Brigadier Myers, describing him as "the perfect catastrophe", "an utterly dangerous fool" and "a fanatic". Cf. "British Policy towards Wartime Resistance in Yugoslavia and Greece" (ed. Phyl. Auty and Rich. Clogg), pag. 167–205. The quotations from pag. 173.

32. See Stuart Macrae: "Winston Churchill's Toyshop", describing in detail the developing of such equipment.

33. On the collaboration between SOE and OSS and the growing integration of the two see Colin Gubbin's account in "The Fourth Dimension of Warfare", pag. 107–08. As far as Western Europe was concerned a full integration was achieved, whereas in the Balkans American OSS personnel operated under command of the British Military Missions.

34. Donald Hamilton-Hill: "SOE assigment", pag. 103.

35. F. W. Deakin in "European Resistance Movements" (Milan-report), pag. 103.

36. For instance the dropping of 3 instructor agents in Denmark in April 1942 took 3 months of preparation and 7 approaches – the 6 unsuccesful. In 1944 mass deliveries at up to 36 dropping points in one night were successfully carried out – even in spite of unfavourable weather conditions.

37. Jozef Garlinski: "Poland, SOE and the Allies", containing maps showing the flight routes used on pag. 66 and 144.

38. Fitzroy MacLean: "Disputed Barricade", pag. 249 and Donald Hamilton-Hill: "SOE Assignment", in a number of chapters describing activities on Vis.

39. Planned Lysander landings in Denmark were shelved because of too long flying distances. Jørgen Hæstrup: "Secret Alliance", vol. 3, pag. 153–54.

40. See Jozef Garlinski: "Poland, SOE and the Allies", pag. 154–64, where the protracted preparations and the operational accomplishment of the three operations are described in great detail.

41. Account by general Kopanski in "Britain and European Resistance" (Oxford-report), pag. 3.

42. On these difficulties see Jozef Garlinski: "Poland, SOE and the Allies", pag. 62–70.

43. In two nights – 14 and 16 September 1943 – 7 out of 16 Halifaxes were shot down and the remainder seriously damaged, repairs requiring up to 8 weeks. Garlinski: "Poland, SOE and the Allies", pag. 70.

44. This squadron carried out a total of 2562 flights, dropping 995 agents, 29.000 containers, 10.000 packages, loosing 70 airplanes and their crews. Besides this squadron also the no. 161 squadron was operating for the SOE. Garlinski: "Poland, SOE and the Allies", pag. 68.

45. "Britain and European Resistance" (Oxford-report), general Kopanski's account, pag. 5.
46. See above pag. 179.
47. Jozef Garlinski: "Poland, SOE and the Allies", pag. 47–49. Cf. "Britain and European Resistance" (Oxford report), report by mr. Willetts, pag. 4. Garlinski ibid. appendix. Cf. quoted report by general Kopanski.
48. Kopanski ibid.
49. Ibid. pag. 4.
50. Bor-Komorowski: "The Secret Army", pag. 73 ff.
51. "Britain and Europe Resistance" (Oxford-report), account by Kopanski: "We had not been informed by the British military authorities that as early as August 1943 Poland was excluded form the Western Allies' plans for the invasion of Europe" (debate, pag. 3) and: "It is difficult to appreciate – without additional study of the problem – whether more aircraft could have been provided by the RAF in the different stages of the air supply to the Home Army. It is equally difficult to judge if the main reason was the lack of planes for long-range and dangerous flights, or the fact that Poland was not included amongst the main British strategical targets. Although the figures might be impressive, the final results in supply were not sufficient even for the increase of subversive activities" (debate, pag. 5).
52. Appeals from Radio Moscou quoted by Winston Churchill: "The Second World War", vol. 6, pag. 114. The appeals emanated from the Polish transmitter in Moscou, "Tadeusz Kościuszko", and were sent on 29. July. The appeal had a general form and was not especially addressed to Warsaw and it has been maintained that the command of "Armia Krajowa" overreacted to the appeal. (Jacques de Launay: "Major Controversies of Contemporary History, pag. 310).
53. Evidence given during the Nüremberg Trials.
54. This picture is too confused to allow for description within the framework of this book. There were local cooperation but also local frictions and even local confrontations between units of "Armia Krajowa", supporting the exile government and units supporting the communist Committee of National Liberation (CPLN). See for inst. Garlinski: "Poland, SOE and the Allies", pag. 136–40.
55. "Britain and European Resistance" (Oxford-report), report by Kopanski, pag. 10.
56. Bor-Komorowski: "The Secret Army", pag. 203–04.
57. Numbers stated in the following are from the account by general Kopanski in "Britain and European Resistance" (Oxford-report) and from Jozef Garlinski: "Poland, SOE and the Allies", supplement. The numbers from the two sources are on a whole concordant, Kopanski however stating the nature of the supplies dropped, Garlinski only reckoning the numbers of containers dropped.
58. Quotation by Kopanski, "Britain and European Resistance" (Oxford-report).
59. Garlinski arrives at a final total of 2.154 containers, 33% of which reached the Polish forces, stressing the unreliability of any estimate of quantity of arms actually received by the Poles.
60. On this and on the political controversy between the Western Powers and the Sovjetunion, i.a. about the "shuttle-bombing" problem see Winston Churchill: "The Second World War", vol. 6, pag. 113–28. John Ehrmann: "Grand Strategy", vol. V, pag. 370–76. Garlinski: "Poland, SOE and the Allies", pag. 197–203. Cf. Hanns von Krannhals: "Der Warschauer Aufstand", pag. 166, 178 and 187 f.
61. These views are supported by the British military historian, B. H. Liddell Hart, who

points out that the Russian armies, having advanced hundreds of miles "were suffering the natural consequence of overstretching their communications and had to bow to that strategic law". Consequently Liddell Hart finds the reason for the Russians coming to a halt in front of Warsaw to be of a military nature – not a political one. He, however, puts a question mark to the Russian refusal to allow "shuttle-bombing" operations. Liddell Hart: "History of the Second World War", pag. 583–84.

62. Account of E. Boltin in "European Resistance Movements" (Milan-report) pag. 20.
63. A British attempt in December 1944 to send officers to "Armia Krajowa" – groups in South East Poland failed. The officers were interned in the Sovjetunion. H. T. Willetts in "Britain and European Resistance" (Oxford, report), pag. 8.
64. "European Resistance Movements 1939–45" (Milan-Report), report by S. Okecki, pag. 428.
65. Numbers from "European Resistance Movements 1939–45" (Milan-report), account by E. Boltin, pag. 29. To judge from the numbers stated the forces were considerably oversupplied with arms. This perhaps in anticipation of a further increase in strength following the Sovjet advances.
66. The total in Great Britain was in July 1940 4000 men. Cf. Winston Churchill: "The Second World War", vol. 2, pag. 573.
67. On the recognitions see J. R. M. Butler: "Grand Strategy", vol. 2, pag. 263 and R. Bruce Lockhart: "Comes the Reckoning", pag. 118–21.
68. Eduard Benes: "Memoirs", pag. 109.
69. "Britain and European Resistance" (Oxford-report), report by J. Korbel, pag. 5 and 13.
70. Ibid. pag. 14.
71. Ibid. pag. 8.
72. Cf. "European Resistance Movements 1939–45" (Milan-report), in which an account on the Czechoslovakian resistance movement compiled by the Czechoslovakian Academy of History grants all honour and responsability for activism to the Communist Party. The "bourgois" groups are accused of reluctance, "attentisme".
73. J. Korbel in "Britain and European Resistance" (Oxford-report) stresses that Benes felt exposed to communist pressure both as to the idea of intensified activity and of the plan to let the national committees play their part as a groundwork for a provisional National Constituent Assembly for post-war Czechoslovakia, quoted account, pag. 11 and 15.
74. Korbel ibid. pag. 9.
75. On the dropping operations see "Britain and European Resistance" (Oxford-report), account by F. E. Keary, pag. 9–10.
76. Keary, ibid. pag. 10.
77. On the rising in Slovakia see "European Resistance Movements 1939–45" (Milan-report), pag. 235–36. Cf. "Britain and European Resistance" (Oxford-report), account by J. Korbel, pag. 17 and his contribution to debate, pag. 8.
78. Cf. a direct comparison by E. Boltin in "Britain and European Resistance" (Oxford, report), debate on Czechoslovakia, pag. 12–13.
79. OSS was operating for a short time in the area liberated by the partisans, mainly in order to evacuate American Airforce personnel. Cf. Edward Hymoff: "OSS in World Warr II", pag. 184 ff.
80. Cf. "Skipperen, en bog om Ebbe Munck" (ed. Jørgen Hæstrup), pag. 153–273, which also contains a survey of the establishing of a net of routes 1943–45.

81. The Norwegian merchant marine totalling about 5 million gross register tons in 1940 was no. 4 in size, 7% of the world tonnage and as to tankers even 20%. 5/6 of the total would be sailing for the Allies and not a single ship obeyed in April 1940 Quisling's orders to all Norwegian ships on the sea to go to Norwegian or neutral port. (Andenæs, Riste and Skodvin: "Norway and the Second World War", pag. 96).

82. Sverre Kjeldstadli: "Hjemmestyrkene", pag. 89–104 and particularly pag. 101–04.

83. From Denmark was referred to the position of Luxembourg during the First World War.

84. Jørgen Hæstrup: "Christmas Møllers Londonbreve", pag. 7–58 gives an account of these formal problems and of Christmas Møllers impotence in his relations to SOE and later SOE/SO.

85. Ref. this see account by Colonel Hampton in "Britain and European Resistance" (Oxford-report), debate on Norway, pag. 5.

86. Winston Churchill: "The Second World War", vol. 4, index "Jupiter".

87. Ibid. vol. 5, index "Sweden".

88. Sverre Kjeldstadli: "Hjemmestyrkene", pag. 129 ff.

89. Ibid. pag. 59. Cf. Account by Colonel Hampton in "Britain and European Resistance", debate on Norway, pag. 3.

90. Jørgen Hæstrup: "Secret Alliance", vol. 3, pag. 221–27.

91. An account in detail on the formation and development of the Danish Brigade is given by the Swedish historian, Ulf Torrell in: "Hjälp till Danmark" (English summary). Here is also information on the Norwegian Brigade, a forerunner of the Danish one.

92. The first acts of sabotage on Norwegian soil happened before the end of the German campaign in June 1940. Sverre Kjeldstadli: "Hjemmestyrkene", pag. 58.

93. Ibid. pag. 182.

94. Ibid. pag. 182 ff.

95. The figures are from the account by Colonel Hampton in "Britain and European Resistance" (Oxford-report), appendix to the account.

96. The figures for Denmark in Jørgen Hæstrup: "Secret Alliance" vol. I–III, where also time, conditions and magnitude of supplies delivered by the Western Powers is described in separate chapters.

97. On deliveries via Sweden ibid. vol. 3, pag. 205–21.

98. Only a fraction of the Swedish arms were immediately issued to the active sabotage groups in Copenhagen. This gave rise to serious frictions within the Danish resistance movement. This is described in detail in Jørgen Hæstrup: "Secret Alliance", vol. 3, pag. 111–19.

99. On the German Air Defence along the Channel and the North Sea see Webster and Franland: "The Strategic Air Offensive against 1939–45", pag. 397 ff.

100. A comprehensive literature is elucidating this "Englandsspiel". A most detailed investigation is found in the Dutch Parliamentery exposition of conditions in Holland during the war: "Enquetecomissie Regeringsbeleid 1940–45". From the German side: "London calling North Pole" by the German Abwehr officer, H. J. Giskes. From one of the Dutch operators involved, P. Dourlein, the book "Inside North Pole". A summary in Werner Warmbrunn: "The Dutch under German Occypation", pag. 204–05, and – based on all available material – by the Dutch historian L. de Jong in "Britain and European Resistance" (Oxford-report), pag. 5–8. Where other source is not quoted this account is founded on de Jong's summary.

101. On "Orde Dienst", see Werner Warmbrunn: "The Dutch under German Occupation", pag. 186–87.
102. See above, pag. 165 f.
103. Details on the very clever German investigation in H. J. Giskes: "London calling North Pole".
104. Most of them finished up in the concentration camp Mauthausen and were executed autumn 1944.
105. Werner Warmbrunn: "The Dutch under German Occupation", pag. 205.
106. On the reorganizing and following work see L. de Jong in "Britain and European Resistance" (Oxford-report), account pag. 9 ff.
107. "Britain and European Resistance" (Oxford-report), debate regarding French conditions, pag. 21.
108. Accounts by Muus and Hollingworth in the Danish National Archives concur as to time, conditions and the course of the cross examination. Further details in Muus's memoirs: "The Spark and the Flame".
109. Henri Bernard: "La Résistance 1940–45" gives a detailed account of a great number of these organisations and groups. See particularly, pag. 79–113, the chapter "La Résistance Armée".
110. The German authorities tried to exploit this controversy. A Flemish separatist movement tried with little progress to function, and a German decree in November 1940 allowed only Flemish newspapers to be published within the Flemish speaking parts of Belgium. Attempts to form a separate Flemish legion for operations in the East was an utter failure. Only very few volunteered. Keesing 1940–43, pag. 4180 and 4749.
111. Henri Bernard: "La Résistance 1940–45", pag. 91 ff and 99 ff.
112. Ibid. pag. 102.
113. "European Resistance Movements 1939–45" (Milan-report), account by G. Lovinfosse, pag. 264–65.
114. On those see "Britain and European Resistance" (Oxford-report), account by G. Lovinfosse, pag. 3 ff.
115. Henri Bernard: "La Résistance 1940–45", chapter X, "La Résistance Armée", mentioning the various organisations and their contacts with London, for inst. a drop of 15 tons for the group called G. (pag. 89).
116. Indications of time and numbers in the following are founded on information from "Centre de Récherches et d'Etudes Historiques de la Seconde Guerre Mondiale", Brussels.
117. "Britain and European Resistance" (Oxford-report), account by G. Lovinfosse, pag. 2.
118. J. M. A. Gwyer: "Grand Strategy", vol. 3, pag. 45–46.
119. Winston Churchill: "The Second World War", vol. 5, pag. 302 ff. Cf. W. H. McNeill: "America, Britain and Russia 1941–46", pag. 361 ff. Both works contain an account in detail of the course of events.
120. As stated about pag. 152 f., the French intelligence network had contacts within the Armistice Army and it maintained an open question, up to November 1942, whether this army might be turned into an element of considerable importance if conditions developed in a favourable way. In November 1942 events proved that such hopes were unfounded.
121. On the Syrian crisis see Robert Aron: "Histoire de Vichy", pag. 434 ff. Charles de

Gaulle: "Mémoires de Guerre", vol. 1, chapter "L'Orient". Winston Churchill: "The Second World War", vol. 3, chapter "Syria".

122. William L. Langer: "Our Vichy Gamble" gives an account in detail of USA's policy on the Vichy regime. USA maintained its Vichy contact for practical reasons, not for sympathy nor any faith in the effective possibilities of the regime for governing and truly representing France. The Washington government was hoping to counteract the Vichy tendencies of collaboration and considered the embassy an important observationspost.

123. Charles de Gaulle: "Mémoires de Guerre", vol. 1, text of speech in appendix.

124. Charles de Gaulle: "Mémoires de Guerre" vol. 1, text in appendix. On de Gaulle's struggle for maintaining that not the Vichy government, but he himself was the legal representative of France, see Henri Michel: "Les Courants de Pensée de la Résistance", pag. 40–50. As previously stated the French resistance world included persons and organisations who neither recognized the Vichy regime nor the exiled de Gaulle as authorised to speak on France's behalf. This obviously further complicated the problems concerning France's status as to constitutional and international law. De Gaulle only obtained the authority he claimed step by step.

125. On Darnand's activities see the publication "Les procès de Collaboration" (Procès contre Brinon, Darnand et Luchaire).

126. Most essential is of course the attitude of the French Prime Ministers during the occupation, Laval, Flandin, Darlan and – again – Laval. Principal works on their policy are Robert Aron: "Histoire de Vichy" and Robert Paxton: "Vichy France", the latter stressing the genuine wish of the whole regime to wholehearted collaboration.

127. Robert Aron: "Histoire de Vichy" emphasizes (pag. 184) a short period in 1940, when the authorities and troops of occupation showed a correct attitude. This however only lasted for a short while, then an increasing use of violence spread, first in the occupied zone.

128. This applies irrespective of the fact that de Gaulle during the 1930 years had been involved in the debate in France on military problems, by publishing books and articles (especially the book "Vers l'Armée de Métier") and lobbying for political influence-especially together with Paul Reynaud. For the great majority of Frenchmen he remained, however, unknown, and his ideas did not convince in military or political circles.

129. An analysis of the French defeat in 1940 in Marc Bloch: "L'Etrange Défait".

130. See M. R. D. Foot: "SOE in France", pag. 21. Foot's work is the principal source on SOE's activities in France and the most comprehensive work on SOE, including an account in great detail of the early efforts leading up to the establishing of SOE.

131. Charles de Gaulle's popularity and leadership had to be built up gradually. Many people maintained – although holding anti-Nazi opinions – an unresponsive, sceptical and wait-and-see attitude to him and his movement. Cf. Henri Michel: "Les Courants de Pensée de la Résistance", pag. 726 ff. Cf. Charles de Gaulle: "Mémoires de Guerre", especially vol. 1, stressing all the difficulties in the early phase of the movement.

132. M. R. D. Foot: "SOE in France", pag. 178–79. Jouhaux was arrested by the Vichy government before the inquiry reached him.

133. Passy: "Souvenirs", vol. 1, pag. 54.

134. de Gaulle's organisation seems to have got going a bit faster. In July 1940 fishing

vessels from Bretagne got some intelligence smuggled out, and the first fragile contacts were established. Cf. Passy: "Souvenirs", vol. 1, pag. 66. Passy states (pag. 54), that nobody in the "free" French circles had the slighest idea of how a secret service should work, and any notions of it were deriving from criminal or spy thrillers of more than questionable value.

135. In the beginning of August de Gaulle had a British authorization as leader of a "free" French movement, allowing him to recruit French nationals, wanting to join him. de Gaulle and his National Defence Council did however not enjoy any recruiting monopoly. Many French nationals preferred to join the British forces, see J. R. M. Butler: "Grand Strategy", vol. 2, pag. 264. Cf. Charles de Gaulle: "Mémoires de Guerre", vol. 1, pag. 80 ff.

136. Cf. Charles de Gaulle: "Mémoires de Guerre", vol. 1 and 2. His memoirs give numerous examples of his confrontations with president Roosevelt. Cf. especially vol. 2, pag. 235 ff.

137. M. R. D. Foot: "SOE in France", pag. 21.

138. Ibid. pag. 21 and Eric Piquet-Wicks: "Quatre dans l'Ombre", pag. 22 ff.

139. Passy: "Souvenirs", vol. 1, pag. 33.

140. Pierre Tissier, one of de Gaulle's first assistants in London.

141. Charles de Gaulle: "Mémoires de Guerre", vol. 1, pag. 129.

142. Henri Michel: "Les Courants de Pensée de la Résistance", pag. 119. Also M. R. D. Foot: "SOE in France", which continuously operates with the two terms.

143. M.R.D. Foot, "SOE in France", pag. 179. Foot's work is composed as an account in detail of the work and results of the different "Circuit" teams. See in general his account.

144. Henri Michel emphasizes that the great French resistance organisations became connecting links between the many "réseaux" and the desired united leadership. He differentiates "Réseau" from "Mouvement" and "Parti" in stepwise suceession. See his work: "Les Courants de Pensée la Résistance", pag. 119.

145. On Jean Moulin and his work see Henri Michel: "Jean Moulin, l'Unificateur". A briefer account in Eric Piquet-Wicks: "Quatre dans l'Ombre", pag. 39–148. Cf. also M. R. D. Foot: "SOE in France", index of names.

146. Moulin brought with him a comprehensive memo, dated October 1941, which also stressed the necessity of a united leadership to enforce disciplin, orders and plans for action and allocate material support to the widely dispersed groups and single persons. The memo is published as an annex to "SOE in France" by M. R. D. Foot, pag. 489–98.

147. Ibid. pag. 227.

148. Details on the formation, development and importance of the Council in René Hostache: "Le Conseil National de la Résistance". A detailed report from the opening session of the Council is found here, pag. 140–44. The Council included 8 representatives of the resistance organisations, 6 of political parties and 2 of the illegally reconstructed trade unions. Moulin was the first chairman. After his arrest he was followed by the resistance leader Georges Bidault.

149. As to method, time and quantities of deliveries in the following see – failing statement of other source – M. R. D. Foot: "SOE in France", and especially appendix C, pag. 470–77, giving a summary of the total supplies.

150. On resistance activities in Bretagne and cooperation with the "jedburgh-teams", see Robert Aron: "Histoire de la Libération de la France", pag. 177–222.

151. In his "Histoire de la Libération de la France", Robert Aron makes a distinction between 3 phases in the development of the maquis: 1) Earliest germs, sown during the very first time of occupation by people unwilling to accept defeat and joined by persons in immediate danger of deportation or execution. 2) A further influx after June 1941 by socialists, syndecalists and communists, joining up in order to evade arrest and because partisan activity had then been proclaimed a principal means of resistance not least by the communists. 3) After 1942 the maquis swelled when forced labour in Germany was introduced, and still more after the German occupation of the Vichy zone in November 1942.

152. John Ehrmann: "Grand Strategy", vol. 5, pag. 324. de Gaulle: "Mémoires de Guerre", vol. 2, pag. 252 f. de Gaulle underlines the vagueness of alle statements as to numbers.

153. Robert Aron: "Histoire de la Libération de la France", pag. 548. See also pag. 548–572, describing the battles in this region of the maquisards against the German troups of occupation.

154. Henri Michel: "La Guerre de l'Ombre", pag. 303.

155. At the decisive full meeting of the Council 27 may 1943 were 2 representing the trade unions, 8 from the principal resistance organisations and 6 from political parties. Cf. Henri Michel: "Histoire de la Résistance", pag. 48 ff, where the foundation and tasks of the Council is briefly described.

156. Ibid. pag. 102 ff.

157. John Ehrmann: "Grand Strategy", vol. 5, pag. 326.

158. Ibid. pag. 326.

159. Robert Aron: "Histoire de la Libération de la France", pag. 180.

160. John Ehrmann: "Grand Strategy", vol. 5, pag. 324–25. On Cossac's planning see Frederick Morgan: "Ouverture to Overlord".

161. Winston Churchill: "The Second World War', vol. 5, pag. 554 ff. Cf. Charles de Gaulle: "Mémoires de Guerre", vol. 2, pag. 222 ff. and D. W. Eisenhower: "Crusade in Europe", pag. 231 f.

162. F. S. V. Donnison: "Civil Affairs and Military Government North West Europe, 1944–46", pag. 54. On the talks in Washington. cf. Charles de Gaulle: "Mémoires de Guerre", vol. 2, pag. 235 ff. Donnison's work describes in detail the Allied planning of the invasions in Europe and thus the problems of the transition from military to civilian administration of occupied regions. The idea was to form a special organisation AMGOT (Allied Military Government of Occupied Territories) to take over civilian administration of areas outside the operational zones of battle. The justification of such an organisation could obviously be challenged in the question of liberated allied territory, where national governments claimed to exercise sovereignty, be it exile governments or locally established temporary governments. For France the question was who would be entitled legally to take over the functions of government, and when this could happen. The recognition of a French de-facto government under Charles de Gaulle therefore was of paramount importance for clarifying the French problems.

163. "British Policy towards Wartime Resistance in Yugoslavia and Greece" (ed. Phyllis Auty and Rich. Clogg), pag. 12.

164. John Ehrmann: "Grand Strategy", vol. 5, pag. 322.

165. "European Resistance Movements 1939–45" (Milan-report), account by F. W. Deakin, pag. 119. SOE's work from Cairo was also hampered by other factors, shor-

tage of staff, especially competent code experts, constantly changing the top people and the leading principles of command as well as vagueness as to sphere of competence. This went on right up to 1943. Cf. "British Policy towards Wartime Resistance in Yugoslavia and Greece" (ed. Phyllis Auty and Rich. Clogg), report from Bickham Sweet-Escott, pag. 3–21. It is stated here that SOE in spring 1942 was allocated 4 Liberator airplanes, which however were only rarely concurrently operational.

166. On the strengthening of the supply service see John Ehrmann: "Grand Strategy", vol. 5, pag. 273–74.

167. Independent of Great Britain and against earnest British representations USA still maintained a mission to Michailović until autumn 1944. (John Ehrmann: "Grand Strategy", vol. 5, pag. 275). On the change in British attitude to Tito see above pag. 197 ff.

168. John Ehrmann: "Grand Strategy", vol. 5, pag. 79–80.

169. The invasion of Italy was planned and directed by the Allied Supreme Command in Algiers who right up to summer 1943 was ignorant of the strength and importance of the Tito-movement, although this was well known in Cairo. The Allied Command was now informed and proper coordination established allowing for a strategic revaluation. See Bickham Sweet-Escott: "Baker Street Irregular", pag. 168 f.

170. The mission was headed by Brigadier C. D. Armstrong with S. W. Bailey as political adviser. On the negative result of this mission and the final British rupture with Michailović see "British Policy towards Wartime Resistance in Yugoslavia and Greece" (ed. Auty and Clogg), account by Bailey, pag. 81 ff.

171. Ibid. pag. 147–66.

172. It is emphasized by two of the English who had close contact with Michailović during the war, that a decisive motive for his disapproval of immediate action was his personal recollections of the enormous losses suffered by the Serbian population during the First World War. Ibid. pag. 249–50. This, however, did not refrain him from fighting the partisans, which from the autumn 1941 was his chief aim. See for inst. Marjanović: "The Collaboration of D. Mihailović's Chetniks with the Enemy Forces of Occupation", pag. 23 ff. quoting a statement by Michailović, November 1941.

173. "British Policy towards Wartime Resistance in Yugoslavia and Greece", pag. 39 f and index of names, Winston Churchill.

174. Ibid. pag. 252. Cf. Fitzroy MacLean: "Eastern Approaches", pag. 231 and pag. 247 regarding Tito's ideas of obligations versus reprisals. On MacLean's stay in Moscow see this work, chapter I–VII.

175. John Ehrmann: "Grand Strategy", vol. 5, pag. 79.

176. On numerical statements for 1943 ibid. pag. 79–80.

177. "Britain and European Resistance" (Oxford-report), account by F. W. Deakin, pag. 15.

178. John Ehrmann: "Grand Strategy", vol. 5, pag. 273.

179. "European Resistance Movements" (Milan-report), account by D. Plenca, pag. 485–86.

180. The attack described by Fitzroy MacLean in his book: "Disputed Barricade", pag. 256 ff.

181. Henri Michel: "Les Mouvements Clandestins en Europe", pag. 101–02. The numerical statements are most variable, Yugoslav information stating that reliable values are non existing. ("European Resistance Movements 1939–45" (Milan-report), account by D. Plenca, pag. 486). Plenca's estimates are, however, roughly speaking of similar

magnitude as the figures stated here. The supplies were undoubtedly very considerable, but great uncertainty prevails because of lack of reliable documentation and doubt as to how much was really received, compared with the quantities actually dispatched etc.

182. The Yugoslav historian Marjanović estimates this collapse as leading to the disarming of 10 Italian divisions except for their heavy equipment. ("Britain and European Resistance" (Oxford-report), account pag. 6).

183. On Churchill's attitude to the Yugoslav question: See Winston Churchill: "The Second World War", vol. 5, pag. 408–23 and vol. 6, pag. 79–84. Regarding the often protracted debate and highly differing opinions of British authorities as to the right policy to Tito and to the Yugoslav exile government see "British Policy towards Wartime Resistance in Yugoslavia and Greece", (ed. Phyllis Auty and Rich. Clogg), pag. 22–48.

184. Tito's talks in Moscow with Stalin took place in a rather tense atmosphere. Tito maintained the attitude that under no circumstances would the Royal Exile Government be allowed to return and also that the Yugoslav partisan armies in a future cooperation with Sovjet forces would refuse any Sovjet supreme command and any Russian civilian or administrative powers on Yugoslav soil. An outline of these talks, based on information from Tito himself is given in Fitzroy MacLean: "Disputed Barricade", pag. 281 ff.

185. On the various Greek resistance organisations see in general C. M. Woodhouse: "Apple of Discord". Cf. C. Pyromaglou in "European Resistance Movements 1939–45" (Milan-report), pag. 298–323 and also in "Britain and European Resistance" (Oxford-report), pag. 1–22 and contributions in debate.

186. The mediation became a double sided one – both an internal mediation between the opposed organisations and the mediation between home resistance and exile government. The first was mainly a responsibility of SOE, the latter primarily had the political authorities of the country involved as principal partners, even if SOE also had some influence here.

187. Cf. above pag. 188 f.

188. Cf. "Britain and European Resistance" (Oxford-report), account by C. Pyromaglou pag. 16–19.

189. The Myers/Woodhouse Mission arrived in Greece unprepared for a political task. It appears that the mission had not been informed in advance of the internal political contrasts in Greece, although these were well known, at least in the Foreign Office. See "British Policy towards Wartime Yugoslavia and Greece" (ed. Phyllis Auty and Rich. Clogg), pag. 170–71.

190. See below, pag. 437.

191. John Ehrmann: "Grand Strategy", vol. 5, pag. 85. Cf. Myers: "Greek Entanglement", pag. 130–31 and "British Policy towards Wartime Resistance in Yugoslavia and Greece", pag. 123–24.

192. John Ehrmann: "Grand Strategy", vol. 5, pag. 85–86, "British Policy towards Wartime Resistance in Yugoslavia and Greece", pag. 147–66 and "Britain and European Resistance" (Oxford-report), account by C. M. Woodhouse, pag. 7.

193. Winston Churchill: "The Second World War", vol. 6, pag. 248–49.

194. The contrast was precisely stated by the British Ambassador to the Greek exile government, Rex Leeper: "His Majesty's Government in their Greek policy were speaking with two voices. The political voice, i.e. the Foreign Office, was giving full

support to King George and his Government. The military voice, i.e. G. H. Q., Middle East, was giving support with arms and gold sovereigns to the King's worst enemies in the Greek mountains". The High Command, Middle East, also included SOE, who in Greece as well as in Cairo were sailing between Scylla and Charybdis. (Rex Leeper: "When Greek meets Greek", pag. 3–4).

195. Cf. C. M. Woodhouse: "Apple of Discord", Cf. C. Pyromaglou in "European Resistance Movements 1939–45" (Milan-report), pag. 321 and same author in "Britain and European Resistance" (Oxford-report), pag. 16.

196. "Britain and European Resistance" (Oxford-report), account by C. M. Woodhouse, pag. 4.

197. Ibid. pag. 7.

198. Ibid. pag. 9.

199. A brief summary of the Italian opposition is given by Henri Bernard: "Histoire de la Résistance Européenne – La Quatriéme Foree de la Guerre 1939–45", pag. 33 ff.

200. The war brought setbacks and defeats on all fronts where Mussolini's armies were engaged. Regarding the reactions of the Italian people and the ineffiency and passivity of the military Command see F. Parri and F. Venturi: "The Italian Resistance and the Allies" in "European Resistance Movements" (Milan-report), pag. XII ff. It is here stressed that the resentment against Mussolini's war policy was manifest already during the Spanish Civil War, where Italian volunteers joined the battle of the government against Franco-forces. They also emphasize the importance of the exile policy.

201. On this devellopment see F. W. Deakin: "The Brutal Friendship".

202. Ibid. pag. 224.

203. This is all described in detail in the mentioned work by Deakin.

204. Henri Bernard: "Histoire de la Résistance Européenne", pag. 40. Up to then Italian matters had been dealt with by SOE's Cairo branch. Cf. "Britain and European Resistance" (Oxford-report), account by J. Stevens, pag. 1. Cf. Bickham Sweet-Escott: "Baker Street Irregular", pag. 199–200 and 116, according to which an Italian desk up to 1943 was set up in SOE-headquarters in London, but that activities here up to 1943 were confined to a vague contact with Italians in exile.

205. On the Allied attitude and the change of feelings of the Italian people see F. Parri and F. Venturi in "European Resistance Movements 1939–45" (Milan-report), XIV–XV f. strongly criticising the Italian High Command and government for the way the capitulation on 8. September was arranged and thus motivating the Allied scepticism.

206. On 13. October the Badoglio Government declared war on Germany and with an American-British-Sovjet joint declaration the Badoglio Cabinet was recognised and Italy thus accepted as a "co-belligerent". On the lengthly negotiations on this see Winston Churchill: "The Second World War", vol. 5, pag. 167–75.

207. Henri Bernard: "Histoire de la Résistance Européenne", pag. 39. OSS had established a branch in Switzerland headed by Allen Dulles, which from 1943 was developing ever growing contacts with the Italian resistance movement.

208. See above pag. 110 ff.

209. "Britain and European Resistance" (Oxford-report), account by J. Stevens.

210. "European Resistance Movements 1939–45" (Milan-report), account by F. Parri and F. Venturii, pag. XIX. By the end of September about 2000 British soldiers, POW's had safely reached Switzerland together with a torrent of more than 20.000 civilian refugees. This influx continued with 2–300 passing the frontier every day. Cf. Keesing

1943–45, pag. 6018. This result was only obtained through the help of thousands of Italian civilians. See M. R. D. Foot: "Resistance. European Resistance to Nazism", pag. 225: "None of these or any other escapes in Italy would have been conceivable without the self-sacrifice and cooperation of hundreds of thousands of the Italian rural poor". Cf. Tony Davies: "When the Moon Rises" with details of an escape.

211. F. W. Deakin: "The Brutal Friendship", pag. 240–43, 340–41 and 477–78. Also Henri Bernard: "Histoire de la Résistance Européenne", pag. 40. Cf. "European Resistance Movements" (Milan-report), quoted account by F. Parri and F. Venturi, pag. XVII.

212. The Bonomi Cabinet was composed from communists on the outer left to the Christian democrats to the right wing.

213. "European Resistance Movements" (Milan-report), account by F. Parri and F. Venturi, pag. XXIX.

214. Ibid, pag. XXIV.

215. Ibid. pag. XXXIV. Cf. Allen Dulles: "The Secret Surrender". The arrangements for the journey of the delegation were made via contacts with Dulles in Switzerland.

216. Henri Bernard: "Histoire de la Résistance Européenne", pag. 42. On Cadorna's attitude and loyal cooperation with CLNAI, see "Britain and European Resistance" (Oxford-report), account by dr. Vaccarino, pag. 5.

217. See "Britain and European Resistance" (Oxford-report), account by dr. Vaccarino, pag. 1 and 7, where the Italian opinion is clearly expressed. Cf. "European Resistance Movements" (Milan-report), account by Parri and Venturi XXX–XXXI.

217a. Parri and Venturi, mentioned account.

218. The British liaison officer to the partisan organisation in Piedmont, Colonel J. Stevens, underlines the importance of Italian officers and particularly non-commissioned officers for running the partisan units. ("Britain and European Resistance" (Oxford-report), pag. 4.

219. The numerical values here and in the following are based upon an account of F. Parri and F. Venturi in "European Resistance Movements 1939–45" (Milan-report), pag. XLII–XLIII.

220. See F. W. Deakin: "The Brutal Friendship", pag. 696.

221. Henri Bernard: "Histoire de la Résistance Européenne", pag. 41.

222. This point is a common feature in "Britain and European Resistance" (Oxford-report), accounts and debate from British and Italian side.

223. Henri Bernard: "Histoire de la Résistance Européenne", pag. 42.

224. To this should be added the support to countries and regions as they gradually were liberated and partisan forces in great strength were transformed into regular army units. Poland, Czechoslovakia and Yugoslavia received substantial Sovjet support concurrently with the liberation. In the West the rearmament of French forces became a feature of major importance, Cf. "European Resistance Movements" (Milan-report), account by E. Boltin. Also Marcel Vigneras: "Rearming the French".

225. M. R. D. Foot: "SOE in France", pag. 489 ff.

Internal and External Communication

1. "From the sound of Big Ben the people took courage", reported the Mayor of the town Chios in the Greek archipelago after the liberation. (Philip P. Argentii: "Occupation by the Germans 1941–44", pag. 59). All radio sets had been liable to confiscation, but some had not been handed in and news spread from mouth to mouth.

2. Bor-Komorowski: "The Secret Army", pag. 19–21.
3. Here only one example: A Dane, J. Thalbitzer, reached in 1940 illegally London via Germany-Balkan-Turkey-Suez-Cape Town. He joined a "free" Danish fighter squadron as a pilot, was shot down over France in July 1942. Escaped from a German P. O. W. camp together with other British fellow prisoners and made his way to Denmark followed by a British friend, Wing Commander Buckley, both arriving in Denmark in March 1943. As a last step now remained only a 4 mile wide jump across the Sound to Sweden. The attempt to cross by kayak failed and both men drowned. Jørgen Hæstrup: "Secret Alliance" I, pag. 206.
4. Examples could be found from all countries and all sabotage groups. Just as a typical example reference could be made to the Norwegian saboteur Gunnar Sønsteby's book: "Report from no. 24", where all elements mentioned appear in great numbers: Contact with group comrades, contacts with cooperating groups, contact with sympathising helpers within the plants attacked, contacts with exile government and British authorities and coordinating the different operations in order to make one complementary to the next. Contact with and via neutral Sweden. As stated by the leader of the Norwegian home army, Jens Chr. Hauge, in a preface to the book it constitues" a source of major importance for a saboteur's daily life in occupied Norway on the usual round of everyday life and the trivial preparations of dramatic operations". One could just as well point out another celebrity amongst Norwegian saboteurs, Max Manus, and his account in "Underwater Saboteur". The two great saboteurs did occationally cooperate, but both of them had his own system of contacts, independent and seperated in the daily work.
5. See Fitzroy MacLean: "Eastern Approaches" and C. M. Woodhouse: "Apple of Discord", both giving illustrating close ups of travelling life in the jungle of lines of communication in the Balkans. Cf. George Millar: "Maquis", illustrating life in a French maquis-camp.
6. On development in France see Marie Granet and Henri Michel: "Combat", pag. 182 f.
7. An account – rich in detail – of underground life is given by Walter B. Maas, who experienced years of underground existence in Holland. (Walter B. Maas: "The Netherlands at War 1940–45", pag. 121–24.)
8. Keesing 1943–35, pag. 6225.
9. Werner Warmbrunn: "The Dutch under German Occupation" 1940–45, pag. 187 ff. Cf. Walter B. Maas: "The Netherlands at War 1940–45", pag. 222.
10. See Henri Bernard: "La Résistance 1940–45", pag. 55 ff.
11. On development in Norway see Sverre Kjeldstadli: "Hjemmestyrkene", pag. 275–301.
12. Jørgen Hæstrup: "Til Landets Bedste", I, pag. 198–225. On the action against the police ibid. vol. 2, pag. 55–83.
13. Here too resistance reacted against drafting to forced labour. Cf. Stefan Korbonski: "Fighting Warsaw", pag. 223–27.
14. The fate of the Anne Frank family was known all over the world when the Anne Frank diary was published. In this case the underground existence ended up in tragedy, but for thousands of people it saved their lives.
15. On administrative resistance, its possibilities and limitations see i.a. Henri Michel: "La Guerre de l'Ombre", pag. 214–24. For political causes and because of the special conditions of occupation, Denmark became the country where civil services were given most rope as to reducing, delaying or even stopping the measures taken by the

occupying power. Refusal of collaboration was also used. How this in fact worked out is described in Jørgen Hæstrup: "Til Landets Bedste" vol. I–II. During the periods of utter crisis direct contact was established between the civil services and the central leadership of the resistance movement, "Denmark's Freedom Council". A certain parallel can be drawn between the Danish administrative situation 1943–45 and the situation on the British Channel Islands, although the possibilities open for the administration of the islands were far more limited. (C. G. Cruickshank: "The German Occupation of the Channel Islands").

16. See above pag. 348 ff.
17. "Britain and European Resistance" (Oxford-report), account by dr. Korbel, pag. 5. The strength of "Free" Czech forces in England amounted in summer 1940 to about 4000. (Winston Churchill: "The Second World War", vol. 2, pag. 573).
18. Summer 1940 about 14.000. Ibid.
19. See Anders Bjørnvad: "De fandt en Vej", pag. 147–53. It is obvious from Bjørnvad's studies, that the chances for escape increased rapidly as the resistance organisations spread their net-work in the country.
20. The escape is described in Anthony Richardson: "Wingless Victory". Another detailed escape story – from Italy – can be found in Tony Davies: "When the Moon Rises".
21. Many Danish and Norwegian refugees got stranded in Sweden, although a few, select ones got through to London by that way. As from 1943 the flights between Stockholm and Great Britain got more numerous and regular ("Skipperen, en Bog om Ebbe Munck", pag. 212 f. Cf. Ulf Torrell: "Hjälp till Danmark", pag. 33 ff.)
22. Madeleine Duke: "No Passport", pag. 179–80 and George Langelaan: "Knights of the Floating Silk", pag. 177–90.
23. On the British assistance to refuges in Spain see Samuel Hoare: "Ambassador on Special Mission", pag. 226–38.
24. Cf. above on the occasionally close contact between front units and partisan groups.
25. See Henri Bernard: "La Résistance 1940–45", pag. 58, summing up percentage and absolute numbers for deported and executed Jews from numerous European countries together with an acoount of the fate of the Belgian Jews.
26. The numbers were small. In August 1944 there were 1500 Estonian refugees in Sweden, Kessing 1943–45, pag. 6649. The Polish refugees totalled about 1000.
27. D. Howarth: "The Shetland Bus".
28. Jørgen Hæstrup: "Secret Alliance", vol. 95 ff.
29. The chance of escape from Holland was particularly small. Mainly at the beginning of the occupation some young Dutchmen attempted escape across the North Sea to Britain. Only about 200 succeeded. See Walter B. Maas: "The Netherlands at War, 1940–45", pag. 69.
30. On the establishing and running of this route see M. R. D. Foot: "SOE in France", pag. 93–101 and 188 ff.
31. SOE's French RF-section (see above pag. 310 ff.) started in 1942 a special organisation, DF-Section for organising escape from France to Spain-Portugal. Ibid. pages quoted and pag. 155 ff.
32. Ibid. pag. 61–73.
33. General Giraud had escaped from German prison in April 1942 and arrived in unoccupied France. His escape caused widespread repercussions for the French prisoners of war. The exchanges of prisoners came to an end and prisoners were more closely

guarded etc. The Vichy government tried to bring pressure to bear on Giraud in order to make him return at his own will to German prison, but in vain. After long-winded talks Giraud signed a declaration of loyalty to Pétain, but nevertheless – after talks with the American representatives – decided to evade to Gibraltar-Algiers. Cf. Robert Aron: "Histoire de Vichy", pag. 513 ff. Cf. D. W. Eisenhower: "Crusade in Europe", pag. 122 f.

34. M. R. D. Foot: "SOE in France", pag. 68.
35. Ibid. pag. 358. In connection with the liberation of the island a complete French company of specially trained troups were brought to Bastia by French submarines.
36. Ibid. pag. 88 ff and 478–88, quoting special instructions for pilots involved in these operations. Cf. Passy: "Souvenirs", vol. 1, pag. 179, stating that the aircraft only needed a few minutes from landing to starting again, provided that the preparations required were in order.
37. See above, pag. 326 f.
38. Philip P. Argenti: "The Occupation of Chios by the Germans 1941–44", pag. 61 and 71.
39. Keesing 1940–43, pag. 5996.
40. See Henri Bernard: "La Résistance 1940–45", pag. 47–54. M. R. D. Foot: "SOE in France" pag. 156. Also Henri Michel: "La Guerre de l'Ombre", pag. 117–19.
41. Passy: "Souvenirs", vol. 2, pag. 32–33.
42. See above pag. 168.
43. See Anders Bjørnvad: "De fandt en Vej". (English summary).
44. Cf. Henri Michel: "La Guerre de l'Ombre", pag. 118.
45. See above, pag. 248.
46. Sverre Kjeldstadli: "Hjemmestyrkene", pag. 245–46.
47. On the transport of the Jews see Leni Yahil: "Test of a Democracy", chapter VII.
48. Jørgen Hæstrup: "Secret Alliance", vol. 2 and 3, especially vol. 2, pag. 94–98 and vol. 3, pag. 208–21. It is, however, difficult to point to special pages, a regular illegal transit Denmark-Sweden was an established fact at least from October 1943, so that this transit is mentioned in practically all chapters of the two volumes.
49. A schematic map of the network in Henri Bernard: "La Résistance 1940–45", pag. 46.
50. Charles de Gaulle: "Mémoires de Guerre", vol. 1, pag. 76 f. It was particularly difficult for Gaullists to cross Spain, and de Gaulle points out the Miranda camp and the unfriendly attitude of the Franco-regime. Cf. Passy: "Souvenirs", vol. 2, pag. 33, stating the difficulties especially for Gaullists, who were without any diplomatic support in Madrid.
51. Charles de Gaulle: "Mémoires de Guerre", vol. 2, pag. 246. Cf. Henri Michel: "La Guerre de l'Ombre", pag. 119. Michel puts the number of arrivals via Spain at 7000.
52. On the attitude and the problems of Switzerland see Keesing 1940–43, pag. 5614–15 and ibid. 1940–43, pag. 6018. On the route via Rome see Sam Derry: "The Rome Escape Line".
53. A great many examples of this in M. R. D. Foot: "SOE in France" and Henri Bernard: "Histoire de la Résistance Européenne". Corresponding cases could be found in all countries, the least affected, Denmark, not excepted.
54. Thus the leader of the "free" French organisation, BCRA, Dewavrin made a secret tour to France in spring 1943 in order to obtain a united command of the French underground army then under formation. Cf. Passy: "Souvenirs", vol. 3, chapter 3, and René Hostache: "Le Conseil National de la Résistance", pag. 46. Dewavrin who

was the London leader of the "free" French contacts to the resistance organisations at home, was here running an appalling risk.

55. As an example could be mentioned that SOE instructors dropped in Holland during winter 1941–42 had been issued with silver coins, which had been withdrawn from circulation for months and with clothes in such a poor state, that this alone was sufficient to raise suspicion. Such blunders originated from poor knowledge of actual conditions in the country. Cf. "Britain and European Resistance" (Oxford-report), contribution in the debate by L. de Jong, pag. 4–5. It is also stressed by de Jong, who was head of the transmissions over BBC of "Radio Oranje", that intimate intelligence on general conditions in the receiving country was of vital importance.

56. "Skipperen, en Bog om Ebbe Munck" (ed. Jørgen Hæstrup), pag. 209–10.

57. Passy: "Souvenirs", vol. 1, pag. 54.

58. Jørgen Hæstrup: "Secret Alliance", vol. 1, pag. 51–53.

59. Some of the examples mentioned have been published above.

60. On Velebit's mission see Fitzroy MacLean: "Disputed Barricade", pag. 242, 272 and 294 f.

61. A typical example: In December 1941 the Belgian intelligence and sabotage organisation "Luc" was rolled up. 10 of the leaders managed to escape to Great Britain. (Henri Bernard: "La Résistance 1940–45", pag. 68).

62. Some typical examples: In March 1944 delegates from the Norwegian government and home front met in Stockholm. Talks lasted from 14 to 28 March. (Sverre Kjeldstadli: "Hjemmestyrkene", pag. 230 ff.) In April 1944 the chiefs of the Danish SOE section met delegates from the Danish Freedom Council. The meetings began 11 April and lasted until 27 April including also negotiations with local Sovjet authorities. (Jørgen Hæstrup: "Secret Alliance", vol. 2, chapter "The Stockholm Talks").

63. "Istorija SSSR", vol. X, pag. 56.

64. Passy: "Souvenirs", vol. 2, pag. 141.

65. Joseph Goebbels: "The Goebbels Diaries", mentioned date.

66. This could take a long time and require much resource. A dropping operation in Denmark in April 1942 was laid on via the courier service to Stockholm. Messages were exchanged for 3½ months and a total of 7 approaches had to be made before the operation eventually – and only partly – was pulled off. This was due so slow communication by courier to Sweden. (Jørgen Hæstrup: "Secret Alliance", vol. 1, pag. 116–18).

67. Passy: "Souvenirs", vol. 2, pag. 182.

68. "Britain and European Resistance" (Oxford-report), account by Colonel C. Hampton (section Norway), pag. 1.

69. Kenneth Strong: "Intelligence at the Top", pag. 104 ff.

70. Winston Churchill's vivid interest in all technological progress is clearly brought out from his work "The Second World War", for inst. vol. 4, chapter, "The Offensive in the Æther", but also in general all through his work.

71. Joseph Goebbels: "The Goebbels Diaries", 14/3 1943. Cf. same diary a few days earlier: "We have missed a lot in our being unable to induce the scientists to support our new state. That a man like Planck is reserved – to put it mildly – in his attitude towards us, is Rust's fault, and it cannot be repaired". Cf. Albert Speer: "Erinnerungen", pag. 372 f.

72. Gobbels is hinting to the Minister of Education, Bernhard Rust.

73. Passy: "Souvenirs", vol. 1, pag. 172.

74. On Dewavrin's resolution and Julitte's work see Passy: "Souvenirs", vol. 1. pag. 172 ff.
75. Ibid. vol. 2, pag. 181–91.
76. Concerning Duus Hansen's function as the leader of the Danish W/T section under SOE see Jørgen Hæstrup: "Secret Alliance", vol. 1, pag. 199–208 and vol. 2, pag. 98–116.
77. The method was based upon an invention by the Danish civil engineer Harald Bille, well known both in England and Denmark.
78. Stefan Korbonski: "Fighting Warsaw", pag. 158 ff.
79. "Britain and European Resistance" (Oxford-report), account by general Kopanski i.a. about developments of W/T communication between Poland and Great Britain, pag. 4 and 6.
80. Cf. above pag. 293 ff.
81. See Sverre Kjeldstadli: "Hjemmestyrkene", pag. 218 ff.
82. In the actual case in Denmark the operator, Fischer Holst, realised that a direction finder was arriving in the surburban road, where the transmission was going to take place. The message being vital he still proceeded and had the message off within a minute.
83. Henri Michel: "La Guerre de l'Ombre", pag. 134.
84. Robert Aron: "Histoire de la Libération de la France", pag. 251. Cf. Henri Michel: "Histoire de la Résistance", pag. 7..
85. "Britain and European Resistance" (Oxford-report), account by Count Raczynski pag. 7 and of general Kopanski, pag. 6. Raczynski sums up the transmissions to 372.000 groups of 5 letters for August 1944 and in addition 98.000 groups to stations in Italy.
86. Werner Warmbrunn: "The Dutch under German Occupation", pag. 212. Cf. "Britain and European Resistance" (Oxford-report), account by L. de Jong, pag. 10.
87. "Britain and European Resistance" (Oxford-report), account by Colonel Hampton, pag. 6.
88. See Jørgen Hæstrup: "Secret Alliance", vol. 2 112–16. A British summary for the telegraphically speaking starved Jutland puts the estimate at 50.000 groups for that region alone.
89. Account by R. B. Barry in "European Resistance Movements 1939–45" (Liége-report), pag. 351–55.
90. Fitzroy MacLean: "Eastern Approaches".
91. Henri Michel: "La Guerre de l'Ombre", pag. 133.
92. "Britain and European Resistance" (Oxford-report), account by J. Stevens, pag. 7–8.
93. "Special Operations" (ed. Patrick Howarth), pag. XII–XLII.
94. Henri Michel: "Histoire de la Résistance", pag. 64.
95. "Britain and European Resistance" (Oxford-report), account by de Jong, pag. 13.
96. M. R. D. Foot: "SOE in France", pag. 109.
97. "Britain and European Resistance" (Oxford-report), account by L. de Jong, pag. 13. Cf. Jørgen Hæstrup: "Secret Alliance", vol. 1, pag. 194–95.
98. On S-Phones and Eureca sets see M. R. D. Foot: "SOE in France", pag. 84–86. Cf. Jørgen Hæstrup: "Secret Alliance", vol. 3, pag. 136, 157–61, 166–67.
99. Henri Bernard: "Histoire de la Résistance Européenne", pag. 17.
100. Anton Toldstrup: "Uden Kamp ingen Sejr", pag. 126.

Sabotage.

1. See above, pag. 236 f.
2. Henri Michel: "Les Courants de Pensée de la Résistance" gives in chapter 5, pag. 551–721 an exhaustive analysis of the communist attitude – also in countries other than France.
3. Ibid. pag. 640.
4. Ibid. pag. 634.
5. Already on 22 June 1941 the Executive Committee of the Communist Internationale met. Chairman was the General Secretary, Georgi Dimitroff, and the object: To formulate a watchword for the European communist parties under the changed conditions. The main tasks were defined as: 1) To organise a general campaign in the capitalist countries for support to the Sovjetunion and: 2) To call for a national struggle of liberation inside all the occupied countries and also in Germany-directed against German Fascism. The slogan now was that the Sovjetunion was involved in a just and patriotic war, and that victory was the first condition for liberty for all occupied nations. Dimitroff concluded: "It is vital to organise all peoples for active resistance against the fascist powers of occupation and motivate the national resistance movements for active measures like mass strikes, sabotage etc." (Heinz Kühnrich: "Der Partisanenkrieg in Europe 1939–45", pag. 412–13).
6. See above pag. 37.
7. Cf. "British Policy towards Wartime Yugoslavia and Greece" (ed. Phyllis Auty and Rich. Clogg), where this divergence of opinion and information between SOE and the Britiah-American High Command in the Mediterranean is explained in detail.
8. Cf. above pag. 261 ff. In a session of a great number of SOE-leaders in London in July 1943 it was placed on record that a proper "Charter" for SOE was non existent or – at least – was unknown even to high ranking Top leaders of the organisation. The main points are briefly stated by Hugh Dalton in his memoirs and can also be deduced from the instructions worked out by SOE for special missions and SOE leaders in the respective countries where that body was operational. Regarding the uncertainties about a possible "Charter", see in general "British Policy towards Wartime Yugoslavia and Greece" (ed. Phyllis Auty and Rich. Clogg). Cf. Sverre Kjeldstadli: "Hjemmestyrkene", pag. 356, quoting information from general Colin Gubbins, who states that SOE's programme was outlined in a letter from Churchill to Hugh Dalton, which in fact became the "Charter" of the SOE.
9. "European Resistance Movements 1939–45" (Liége-report), pag. 351.
10. Jørgen Hæstrup: "Secret Alliance", vol. 1, pag. 58–59.
11. This was already obvious during the planning of the landing, where the attitude of the French forces constituted a decisive problem. It was also demonstrated during the actual landing operations, where this problem more or less forced general Eisenhower to negotiate with admiral Darlan, who was considered the only man able to bring French defensive fighting to a halt. See in general Dwight D. Eisenhower: "Crusade in Europe".
12. Cf. for inst. Bickham Sweet-Escott: "Baker Street Irregular", giving a vivid picture of the procedure within SOE, and developments of the way work was carried out.
13. A typical example is the dropping of Captain F. W. Deakin in Yugoslavia in May 1943. Charged with the object of estimating strength and efficiency of Tito's partisan army he arrived at Tito's headquarters during a pitched battle, part of a general German offensive. From abroad the partisan strength had been estimated at 4–10.000. Deakin

could now establish the fact that there was a solid, hard core of partisans amounting to at least 70.000 men. And further on: "It was not only a matter of figures but of the impression gained of their superb morale and discipline which was conveyed to Cairo and London". (Deakin's report in "Hilsen til Hæstrup", pag. 30).

14. See above, pag. 238 ff.
15. Henri Bernard: "Histoire de la Résistance Européenne", pag. 25. Stuart Macrae: "Winston Churchill's Toyshop".
16. Keesing 1940–43, pag. 4180: On scattered sabotage actions in Belgium in July 1940. Werner Warmbrunn: "The Dutch under German Occupation", pag. 202 f.: On scattered actions in Holland in the summer 1940. "Danmark under Besættelsen", vol. 3, pag. 142: On scattered actions in Denmark. Sverre Kjeldstadli: "Hjemmestyrkene", pag. 26–28: On provocative demonstrations, flinging stones and scuffles. Bor-Komorowski: "The Secret Army", pag. 39: On the first scattered sabotage actions.
17. Henri Michel: "Les Courants de Pensée de la Résistance", pag. 562.
18. Ibid. pag. 614. Michel's work brings a penetrating analysis of the attitude of the French Communist Party during 1939–41.
19. Particularly for the Scandinavian Communist Parties the Sovjet attack on Finland in the winter 1939–40 was an additional strain.
20. The British recognition came on the same day as the Sovjetunion's, on the 18 July 1941, and was forced through by the Sovjet decision after prolonged British reluctance. Cf. R. H. Bruce Lockhart: "Comes the Reckoning", pag. 106–20.
21. The cancellation was decided 15 May 1943 by "Komintern's" executive committee, and was wellcomed both in the Allied and neutral press and by Allied and neutral governments. Cf. Keesing 1940–43, pag. 5789–90.
22. See above, pag. 328 f.
23. Cf. f. inst. Sverre Kjeldstadli: "Hjemmestyrkene", pag. 252 ff., describing the rounding-up caused by an informer, and which only hit and partly ravaged one single region and only temporarily.
24. Jørgen Hæstrup: "Til Landets Bedste", vol. 1, pag. 264 ff.
25. These elements stand out clearly in Denmark, where the German authorities 1943–45 were involved in constant tug of war negotiations with their Danish opposite numbers. A full exposé of the problem in Jørgen Hæstrup: "Til Landets Bedste", vol. 1–2. The problem was, however, universal. Cf. for inst. Marie Granet and Henri Michel: "Combat", pag. 90 and 151 f. and the general account. Werner Warmbrunn: "The Dutch under German Occupation", pag. 121 ff. Henri Bernard: "La Résistance 1940–45", pag. 60 f. The administrative resistance in Norway is mentioned above pag. 000.
26. See above pag. 251.
27. M. R. D. Foot: "SOE in France", pag. 233.
28. Cf. below, pag. 438.
29. Particularly the Danish numbers increased so much – for the year 1943 – that it gave rise to a stronger German effort all over Western Europe. See Sverre Kjeldstadli: "Hjemmestyrkene", pag. 268.
30. "Parlamentarisk Beretning til Folketinget", vol. XIII, pag. 654. (German text).
31. On "Group G" see Henri Bernard: "La Résistance 1940–45", pag. 87–91.
32. "European Resistance Movements" (Milan-report), account by S. Okecki, pag. 429–30. The numerical quantities stated agree to a large extent with the statements in Bor-Komorowski: "The Secret Army", and it is clear from both sources that the

numbers constituted a minimum and do not include destructions by sabotage connected with armed partisan attacks.

33. Henri Michel: "La Guerre de l'Ombre", pag. 231.
34. "European Resistance Movements" (Milan-report), account by S. Okecki, pag. 431.
35. "Britain and European Resistance" (Oxford-report), account by C. M. Woodhouse, pag. 9–10.
36. Account in detail with summaries in "Besættelsestidens Fakta", vol. 2, pag. 1203–49. The number of acts of railway sabotage is here given as 8400, whereas dr. Aage Trommer, who has studied Danish railways sabotage in "Jernbanesabotagen i Danmark" (summary in English) uses the term "line-cutting".
37. Sverre Kjeldstadli: "Hjemmestyrkene", pag. 160, 216 f. and 222.
38. M. R. D. Foot: "SOE in France", pag. 435 ff. Cf. appendix of this work, pag. 506–17 with a list of the analysed plants and the effects of sabotage on them.
39. On the actions and importance of this squadron see Paul Brickhill: "The Dam Busters" and Webster and Frankland: "The Strategic Air Offensive against Germany, 1939–45", index "Squadron", especially about the Tallboy bomb, see the latter work, vol. 3, pag. 181–82.
40. Henri Michel: "La Guerre de l'Ombre", pag. 233.
41. Aage Trommer: "Jernsabotagen i Danmark" (English summary). The work is based on the operational reports of the Danish State Railways and all relevant documentation on Danish resistance organisations.
42. See for inst. statements by general D. W. Eisenhower on French and Belgian support during the invasion campaign. (M. R. D. Foot: "SOE in France", pag. 441–42 and "European Resistance Movements" (Milan-report), account by G. Lovinfosse, pag. 274–75). Cf. statements by general L. Gerow on the support from Luxembourg groups. (Henri Bernard: "Histoire de la Résistance Européenne", pag. 211–12).
43. A most obvious example is the German Regional Commander, general H. von Hanneken's decision in 1943 to disarm the Danish army and navy because this handful of 5000 men were considered a menace for the German occupying forces in case of invasion – which never occurred. The disarming was complete after a surprise attack by night, although the navy managed to scuttle the ships. After this, however, the resistance accellerated and soon became a far more formidable menace and nuisance for the Germans than the regular, now disarmed forces had ever been. On this "Operation Safari" and its harmful effects politically as well as militarily see Jørgen Hæstrup: "Til Landets Bedste", vol. 1, pag. 49–72.
44. There were exceptions, for inst. the Dutch L. de Jong and the British C. M. Woodhouse, both highly appreciative as to psychological and political importance but sceptical as to purely military value. Cf. contributions in "Britain and European Resistance" (Oxford-report).
45. Cf. S. Okecki in "European Resistance Movements" (Milan-report), pag. 432 f. referring to sabotage made by Polish workers in Germany.
46. Keesing 1943–45, pag. 4379 and 5067. Cf. "European Resistance Movements" (Milan-report), pag. 195, 231 and 279.
47. Albert Speer: "Erinnerungen" describes Speer's efforts to maintain or increase production and, connected with that, his running battle with Sauckel and the possibilities and value of forced labour.
48. See above, pag. 132.
49. The following summaries and single numbers are based on the German historian.

Heinz Kühnrich: "Der Partisanenkrieg in Europe 1939–45" (pag. 162, 177 and 525). Like all figures in connection with this topic these must be presumed to be somewhat uncertain because of their illegal nature and the obvious impossibility of producing foolproof statistics. Their general credibility is, however, confirmed to the author by the Russian historian, professor Kan.

50. This is how they are appreciated by Dixon and Heilbrunn: "Communist Guerilla Warfare".

51. Dixon and Heilbrunn puts the figures at 20 divisions ("Communist Guerilla Warfare"), Kühnrich at 25 divisions ("Der Partisanenkrieg in Europe 1939–45"), Kühnrich concluding, that the forces engaged constituted about 10% of the total available to the Axis Powers.

52. Bor-Komorowski: "The Secret Army", pag. 65.

53. "European Resistance Movements" (Milan-report), account by M. Baudot, pag. 388 and 390.

54. On the chaotic French railway situation, The organisation of the French railwaymen and the efforts just before and during the invasion, see Robert Aron: "Histoire de la Libération de la France", pag. 225–35.

55. Heinz Kühnrich: "Der Partisanenkrieg in Europe 1939–45", pag. 366–78, "Über die Zusammenarbeit der Sowjetischen Partisanen mit der Rote Armee".

56. On this plan and its realisation see Robert Aron: "Histoire de la Libération de la France", pag. 225–39.

57. The official British work on the invasion of Normandy, L. F. Ellis: "Victory in the West", vol. 1, states the enormously important effect of the actual chaos in all traffic and communication on the German operations to stave off the invasion. He does not – however – attempt to appreciate to what extent this was due either to bombing or to sabotage. Sabotage is mentioned concluding that a full and precise appreciation is out of question. Cf. pag. 49–51 and 121–24.

58. On the attacks on the Vemork-plant and the neighbouring nitrate works see Sverre Kjeldstadli: "Hjemmestyrkene", pag. 169–70, 206 and 220 f. Cf. K. Haugelid: "Kampen om Tungtvannet", giving an account in detail. Cf. Also Richard Petrow: "The Bitter Years", pag. 236 ff.

59. The action is described in detail by C. M. Woodhouse in his book: "Apple of Discord".

60. See i.a. John Ehrmann: "Grand Strategy", V pag. 84 or Henri Michel: "La Guerre de l'Ombre", pag. 231–32.

61. Account by Woodhouse in "Britain and European Resistance" (Oxford-report), pag. 9.

62. See in general "The Rommel Papers" (ed. Liddell Hart), particularly pag. 294–95 on the situation just before the British offensive at El-Alamein.

63. See above, pag. 188 f.

64. On this chain of sabotages, its object and consequences see Winston Churchill: "The Second World Wat", vol. 5, pag. 472–73. J. Ehrmann: "Grand Strategy", vol. 5, pag. 85 and C. M. Woodhouse, account in "Britain and European Resistance Movements" (Oxford-report), pag. 5.

65. John Ehrmann: "Grand Strategy", vol. 5, pag. 285–86. A corresponding scheme for Greece, "Noah's Ark", met with great difficulties caused by internal disagreement within the Greek resistance.

66. On the Norwegian-British-American debate on the problem: Bombing versus sabot-

age and on the attack on Herøya and other targets in Norway see Sverre Kjeldstadli: "Hjemmestyrkene", pag. 200–211. Cf. Ole K. Grimnes: "Hjemmefrontens Ledelse".

67. The attacks on the Shell-House in Copenhagen and Victoria Terrasse in Oslo were carried out in densely populated areas. For that reason and because no alert was sounded and also because of bad luck, many civilians lost their lives in both operations. On the attack on the Shell-House see C. Næsh-Hendriksen and Ove Kampmann (ed.): "Shell-Huset 21/3 1945". Cf. a detailed account of the plan and operation on Robin Reilly: "The Sixth Floor".
68. The plan, code-named "Transportation Plan", is described in detail in John Ehrmann: "Grand Strategy", vol. 5, pag. 293–304, also reporting on the previous debate.
69. Quoted work, pag. 263 ff.
70. On relations between aims and actual achievements of strategic bombing in general see C. Webster and N. Frankland: "The Strategic Air Offensive against Germany 1939–45", I–IV. Analysing the effect of strategic bombing of Germany this work draws the conclusion that right up to 1944 there was a considerable gap between expectations and actual results.
71. Cf. John Ehrmann: "Grand Strategy", vol. 5, pag. 327 ff.
72. On this long term planning see Frederick Morgan: "Ouverture to Overlord".
73. Winston Churchill: "The Second World War", vol. 5, pag. 554–56.
74. This happened after talks between the Norwegian exile government-supported by the leaders of the Home Front – and British authorities. Cf. Sverre Kjeldstadli: "Hjemmestyrkene", pag. 210 ff. Acoounts in detail of Norwegian sabotage in Gunnar Sønsteby: "Rapport fra nr. 24" and Max Manus: "Underwater Saboteur".
75. Henri Michel: "La Guerre de l'Ombre", pag. 229.
76. Cf. Robert Aron: "Histoire de la Libération de la France", pag. 232. Sverre Kjeldstadli: "Hjemmestyrkene", pag. 232. Henri Bernard: "La Résistance 1940–45", pag. 87 f. Jørgen Hæstrup: "Secret Alliance", vol. 3, pag. 373 f.

Assassinations

1. Heinz Kühnrich: "Der Partisanenkrieg in Europe 1939–45", pag. 525.
2. Jørgen Hæstrup: "Secret Alliance", vol. 2, pag. 259 f.
3. Keesing 1940–43, pag. 4846. Speech on BBC 23/10 1941. In a following speech on 25/10 de Gaulle appealed for a 5 minutes strike.
4. Werner Warmbrunn: "The Dutch under German Occupation", pag. 208.
5. "Augustoprøret 1943". by Hans Kirchhoff, unprinted manuscript.
6. Robert Aron: "Histoire de Vichy", pag. 396 ff. Cf. Keesing 1940–43, pag. 4768.
7. Keesing 1940–43, pag. 4797.
8. Robert Aron: "Histoire de Vichy", pag. 456 ff. Cf. Keesing 1940–43, pag. 4846.
9. Werner Warmbrunn: "The Dutch under German Occupation", pag. 58.
10. Keesing 1940–43, pag. 5067.
11. Ibid. pag. 5232.
12. Alexander Dallin: "German Rule in Russia", pag. 76.
13. Ibid. pag. 219.
14. Jørgen Hæstrup: "Til Landets Bedste", vol. 1, pag. 321.
15. Sverre Kjeldstadli: "Hjemmestyrkene", pag. 155 ff.
16. Werner Warmbrunn: "The Dutch under German Occupation", pag. 60. Cf. Walter B; Maas: "The Netherlands at War", stating (pag. 146) that Rauter in September 1943

had decreed killing of hostages at a rate of 3 to 1. A number of well known Dutchmen were murdered as hostages according to this decree, such as the banker Walraven van Hall, who had been supplying the illegal organisations with capital, in agreement with the exile government and the Dutch National Bank. Walter B. Maas states bigger figures for the killings of hostages after the attempt on Rauter, about 400, of whom 117 were executed at the place of the attempt.

17. Henri Michel: "Les Courants de Pensée de la Résistance", pag. 289.
18. Henri Bernard: "La Résistance 1940–45", pag. 95 ff.
19. Werner Warmbrunn: "The Dutch under German Occupation", pag. 207.
20. "Frit Danmarks Hvidbog", vol. 2, pag. 190.
21. Sverre Kjeldstadli: "Hjemmestyrkene", pag. 154 f. and 252 ff.
22. Jørgen Hæstrup: "Til Landets Bedste", pag. 443 ff.
23. On the attitude of the communists to the resistance and their refusal of ideas of cautiously waiting for a favourable moment for action, see Henri Michel: "Les Courants de Pensée de la Résistance", chap. V, pag. 551–681, from where the quotations are taken.
24. The setting up and procedure of the Courts is described in Stefan Korbonski: "Fighting Warsaw", pag. 115–45.
25. Henri Bernard: "La Résistance 1940–45", pag. 96 f. Werner Warmbrunn: "The Dutch under German Occupation", pag. 207. Jørgen Hæstrup: "Secret Alliance", vol. 3, pag. 150–51. In France death sentences of collaborators were correspondingly passed by the resistance organisations and published on BBC, in the clandestine press or directly by letter to the culprit. See Robert Aron: "Histoire de Vichy", pag. 595 f.
26. Keesing 1943–45, pag. 6224. On Kutschera pag. 6292. In Poland attempts were planned on the Governor General, Hans Frank, and the Governor of Warsaw, Ludwig Fischer.
27. Alexander Dallin: "German Rule in Russia", pag. 219. Dallin makes the following comment on this attempt: "His death caused a new stir among the population. It terrified the collaborators, encouraged the anti-German activists, and helped to convince the fence-sitters that the days of German glory was past".
28. "European Resistance Movements" (Milan-report), pag. 230 f. Also "Britain and European Resistance" (Oxford-report), account by dr. Korbel.
29. This also applied to general Elias, who as acting Prime Minister during the German occupation tried to soften the policy of the Protectorate Government, simultaneous with keeping contact with President Benes. When Heydrick took over, Elias was accused of high treason, condemned to death and executed January 1942.
30. Bruce Lockhart – who until he took over the PWE – was accredited to the Czechoslovak Exile Government, had no doubts: "The assassination . . . brought no comfort to the Czechoslovaks and no value to the Allied cause". ("Comes the Reckoning", pag. 184).

Partisan Warfare

1. An analysis of the German policy in the Soviet Union in Al. Dallin: "German Rule in Russia". An analysis of the German policy in Poland in Martin Broszat: "Nationalsozialistische Polenpolitik 1939–45". Cf. Erich Hesse: "Der Sowjetrussische Partisanenkrieg 1941–44", pag. 148–52.
2. It is possible to raise a question as to the extent of the strain, but not as to the reality of

it. The extremes are represented for inst. by B. H. Liddell Hart: "History of the Second World War", where the partisan activites are completely ignored, and the opposite view represented by the resistance leader-Minister of the Interior in de Gaulle's provisional cabinet, Emmanuel d'Astier. He points out: "During the World War partisan movements played a decisive part. The revolt behind the frontiers of the European peoples or – at least the fractions of them, who shape history – now and then accellerated and determined the German defeats". d'Astier then polemically brands Liddell Hart's – the "intellectual expert"'s – opinion to be "ridiculous". Emmanuel d'Astier: "De la Chute á la Libération de Paris", pag. 77.

3. Henri Michel: "La Guerre de l'Ombre", pag. 293–96 describing in general life in the maquis, which is also described by many others, for inst. George Millar: "Maquis". Fitzroy MacLean and C. M. Woodhouse have given exhaustive descriptions of life in the Yugoslav respective Greek partisan camps. Conditions were generally different from locality to locality – from season to season. Cf. some description in Patrick Howarth: "Special Operations".

4. Sverre Kjeldstadli: "Hjemmestyrkene", pag. 294, 301. Cf. above, pag. 361.

5. The examples quoted in Dixon and Heilbrunn: "Communist Guerilla Warfare", in Josef Stalin: "Marxism and the National Question" and in Lenin: "The State and the Revolution". A more thorough investigation of the communist top men's attitude to and faith in the possibilities of partisan warfare as an instrument in the class war in William P. Pomeroy: "Guerilla Warfare and Marxism".

6. The numbers are estimated ones and are – together with their basis of calculation – deriving from the Eastgerman historian, Heinz Kühnrich's, very detailed work: "Der Partisanenkrieg in Europa 1939–45". It goes without saying that a liberal margin of error must be acceptable for such calculations. This does not, however, shake the fact that very substantiel losses were inflicted.

7. On the Polish tradition see Emanuel Halicz: "Partisan Warfare in 19th Century Poland. The Development of a Concept".

8. A number of accounts of this sort, all from Southern-and-Western Europe are collected in the book "Special Operations", ed. Patrick Howarth.

9. An eyewitness account of the attack and the disengagement from it in Fitzroy MacLean: "Disputed Barricade", pag. 260–63.

10. In conversation with the author.

11. The quoted book, pag. 536 and following pages.

12. Robert Aron: "Histoire de la Libération de la France" estimates on pag. 318 the total maquis strength, armed by the Western Powers at about 140.000. This is the "official" total to which should be added other forces armed with captured arms etc.

13. Bor-Komorowski estimates the strength at 40.000 in 1940, 100.000 in 1941 and a final strength of 350.000. "The Secret Army", pag. 49 and 69.

14. Denmark is a typical example of this. By New Year 1943–44 London had appealed for the quick raising of an underground army and promised arms and equipment. The military groups were formed at a hectic pace, but practically speaking no arms arrived until August 1944 when droppings on a considerable scale started and soon gained momentum. This delay caused much disillusion and criticism. See Jørgen Hæstrup: "Secret Alliance", vol. 2, pag. 164 ff.

15. Cf. Fitzroy Maclean, who in his book on Tito, "Disputed Barricade" quotes telegrammes from Tito to Moscow asking for arms: "We have great opportunities of mobilizing men for a Partisan and volunteer army. Through lack of arms we are unable

to accept thousands of volunteers" (26/8 1942) and "Hundreds come to volunteer every day, but we have not enough weapons" (8/9 1942). See mentioned work, pag. 191.

16. Winston Churchill: "The Second World War", vol. 5, pag. 420–21.

17. See above, pag. 263 f.

18. The dropping of "Jedburgh-teams" was planned for all regions where a relase of the resistance forces was decided by the Allies. The "teams" had been entrusted with the task of securing optimal coordination between the forces on both sides of the actual frontline. See above pag. 314.

19. See Robert Aron: "Histoire de la Libération de la France", pag. 176–222.

20. The battles at Vercors are only rather briefly mentioned by de Gaulle in his "Memoires de Guerre", vol. 2, pag. 282. An account in more detail in Robert Aron: "Histoire de la Libération de la France", pag. 282–316.

21. In his book, "De la Chute á la Libération de Paris", the French resistance leader, Emmanuel d'Astier, points out the existence of certain maquis formations quite a long time before the maquis took the shape of proper fighting units. He is pointing at the fact that quite numerous groups at an early date had to seek shelter in inaccessable regions, for inst. Jews, Stateless people, Spanish republicans, men from Alsace-Lorraine. Mentioned book, pag. 96.

22. Cf. D. W. Eisenhower: "Crusade in Europe", pag. 332 f. and Charles de Gaulle: "Mémoires de Guerre", vol. 2 pag. 300 ff. Cf. a detailed account in Robert Aron: "Histoire de la Libération de la France", pag. 349–59.

23. A principal character was the Yugoslav exile politician, Ivan Subasić, who in July 1944 provoked a reconstruction of the Yugoslav exile government and then got negotiations with Tito going, leading to Subasić in March 1945 taking over the post as Foreign Secretary in the intermediate cabinet headed by Tito. This arrangement lasted until October 1945, when Subasić resigned.

24. This problem presented itself also when the resistance units were being demobilized and when attempts were made to incorporate them into the regular armed forces after liberations. The resistance men had got accustomed to being armed and to the feeling of being powerful. It became a difficult proces to be subordinate to a normally established State, especially as long as their political aspirations remained fully or partly unsatisfied. Such problems appeared for inst. in France and Belgium, but tendencies of that kind could appear in other countries too.

25. The numbers are SOE summaries, made by general Colin Gubbins. (Henri Bernard: "La Résistance 1940–45", pag. 108).

26. "European Resistance Movements 1939–45" (Liége-rapport), pag. 257–83 gives an account in detail of the conquest of Antwerp. Cf. also "European Resistance Movements" (Milan-report), pag. 277 and Henri Bernard: "La Résistance 1940–45", pag. 115–23.

27. Cf. above, pag. 343.

28. "Britain and European Resistance Movements" (Oxford-report), account by dr. Vac carino.

29. Cf. Sverre Kjeldstadli: "Hjemmestyrkene", pag. 224–26 and Aage Trommer: "Jernbanesabotagen i Danmark" (English summary). Both stress the strategic interest of the Western Powers in sabotage against the net of communications. Trommer, however, concludes that the actual results obtained were not up to expectations nor to the suppositions of the Allied High Command in spring 1945.

30. Cf. above, pag. 317.
31. Cf. Seton-Watson in "Special Operations" (ed. D. Howarth). Seton-Watson does not here mention the offensive of September-October 1943, which was observed at close range by Fitzroy MacLean, but states that British officers were present at the first and fifth offensive. He must refer to Hudson and Deakin. Deakin was involved just as the fifth offensive was in progress.
32. Fitzroy MacLean: "Disputed Barricade", pag. 248–49.
33. The figures for 1942 and 1943 are based on Heinz Kühnrich: "Der Partisanenkrieg in Europe 1939–45", pag. 175 and 222.
34. On this attitude of the majority of regular officers – although not all – see Henri Michel: "Les Courants de Pensée de la Résistance", chapter "Le Giraudism", particularly pag. 474–76. Cf. Jørgen Hæstrup: "Secret Alliance", vol. 1–3, where the problem is illuminated in several chapters. The parallel between France and Denmark is obvious and conspicuous and has perhaps also a certain similarity to the Michailović-problems.
35. Details in Heinz Kühnrich: "Der Partisanenkrieg in Europe 1939–45", pag. 237 ff.
36. Vladimir Dedijer: "Tito". Cf. Fitzroy MacLean: "Disputed Barricade", pag. 279 f.
37. The British military historian, B. H. Lidell Hart, in his book, "The Sovjet Army", defines the main cause for the German setbacks at the gates of Moscow and Leningrad as being the stamina and ability to suffer hardships of the Russian soldier, hardships like the climate for which the Western soldier was untrained and unaccustomed. As another fatal cause he points at the poor Russian roads, transformed by rain into inaccessible quagmire, robbing the German army of power to keep a sufficient supply service going. This being the case, it became a decisive factor that all roads, which in spite of heavy odds were kept operative, were constantly exposed to attack from the rear. The very risk and the necessity to secure the channels of communications became a feature of importance.
38. Heinz Kühnrich: "Der Partisanenkrieg in Europa 1939–45", pag. 369. Cf. Erich Hesse: "Der Sowjetrussische Partisanenkrieg 1941–45", pag. 225–26.
39. Keinz Kühnrich, mentioned work, pag. 247, and Erich Hesse, mentioned work, pag. 248 ff.

Literature

(Only works mentioned in text or notes are included).

Amery, Julian: "Approach March" 1973.
Andenæs, Johs., Riste, Olav and Skodvin, Magne: "Norway and the Second World War" 1966.
Argentii, Philip P.: "The Occupation of Chios by the Germans" 1966.
Aron, Robert: "Histoire de la Libération de la France, Juin 1944 – Mai 1945" 1959.
Aron, Robert: "Histoire de Vichy 1940–44" 1954.
Armstrong Hamilton, F.: "Tito and Goliath" 1951.
d'Astier, Emmanuel: "De la Chute à la Liberation de Paris, 25 août 1944" 1965.
Barfod, Jørgen: "Et Centrum i Periferien" 1976.
Benes, Eduard: "Memoirs" 1954.
Bennett, Jeremy: "British Broadcasting and the Danish Resistance Movement, 1940–45" 1966.
Bernard, Henri: "La Résistance 1940–45" 1969.
Bernard, Henri: "Histoire de la Résistance Européenne" 1968.
"Besættelsens Hvem Hvad Hvor", ed. Jørgen Hæstrup, Henning Poulsen og Hjalmar Petersen. 1966.
"Besættelsestidens fakta" 1–2, ed. Niels Alkil, 1945–1946.
Bjørnvad, Anders: "De fandt en vej" 1970.
Bloch, Marc: "L'Etrange Défait" 1946.
Bor-Komorowski, Tadeusz: "The Secret Army" 1950.
Brickhill, Paul: "The Dam Busters" 1951.
"Britain and European Resistance, 1939–45". Report from congress in Oxford 1962. Published in duplicate by St. Anthony Coll. Oxford 1963.
"British Policy towards Wartime Resistance in Yugoslavia & Greece" ed. Phyllis Auty and Richard Clogg. 1975.
Broszat, Martin: "Nationalsozialistische Polenpolitik 1939–45" 1961.
Bruce Lockhart, R. H.: "Comes the Reckoning" 1947.
Buckmaster, M. J.: "Specially Employed" 1952.
Butler, J. R. M.: "Grand Strategy", bd. II, 1956–1972.
Butler, J. R. M. og Gwyer, J. M. A.: "Grand Strategy", bd. III, 1956–1972.
Cruickhank, Charles: "The German Occupation of the Channel Islands" 1975.
Churchill, Winston S.: "The Second World War", 1–6, 1948–1954.
Dallin, Alexander: "German Rule in Russia" 1957.
Dalton, Hugh: "Memoirs", bd. II, "The Fateful Years" 1957.
Davey, Owen A.: "The Origins of the Legion des Volontaire Francais contre le Bolchevisme", treatise in "Journal of Contemporary History" 1971, 4, pag. 29–45.
Davies, Derry: "When the Moon Rises" 1973.
Deakin, F. W.: "The Brutal Friendship" 1962.
Deakin, F. W.: "The First British Military Mission to Tito", treatise on "Hilsen til Hæstrup" pag. 23–31. 1969.

Dedijer, Vladimir: "Tito" 1953.

Derry, Sam: "The Rome Escape Line" 1960.

Dixon, C. A. and Heilbrunn, O.: "Communist Guerilla Warfare" 1954.

Donnison, F. S. V.: "Civil Affairs and Military Government North-West Europe, 1944–46" 1961.

—Dourlein, P.: "Inside North Pole" 1954.

Duke, Madeleine: "No Passport" 1957.

Dulles, Allen: "The Craft of Intelligence" 1965.

Dulles, Allen: "The Secret Surrender" 1966.

Ehrmann, John: "Grand Strategy", bd. V. 1956.

Eisenhower, Dwight D.: "Crusade in Europe" 1948.

Ellis, L. F.: "Victory in the West", bd. I–II, 1962–68.

"Enquete-Commissie, Regeringsbeleid 1940–45" ed. Staten-General, Tweede Kamer, Holland.

"European Resistance Movements 1939–45". Report from congress in Liege, Bruxelles and Breendonk 14.–17. sept. 1958. 1960.

"European Resistance Movements 1939–45". Report from congress in Milano 26.–29. marts 1961. 1964.

Fritz Gibbon, Louis: "Katyn. A Crime without Parallel" 1971.

Fleming, Peter: "Invasion 1940" 1957.

Foot, M. R. D.: "SOE in France" 1966.

Foot, M. R. D.: "Resistance. European Resistance to Nazism 1940–45" 1976.

Ford, Corey: "Donovan of OSS" 1970.

"The Fourth Dimension of Warfare" ed. M. Elliot-Bateman bd. I–II, 1970–74.

Frisch, Hartvig, Buhl, Vilh., Hedtoft, Hans og Jensen, Eiler: "Danmark besat og befriet", bd. 1–3, 1945–48.

"Frit Danmarks Hvidbog" 1–2, ed. Peter P. Rohde. 1945–46.

Garlinski, Jozef: "Poland, SOE and the Allies" 1969.

Gascar, Pierre: "Histoire de la Captivités Francais en Allemagne" 1968.

de Gaulle, Charles: "Mémoires de Guerre" 1–3, 1965.

Giskes, H. J.: "London Calling North Pole", 1953.

Goebbels, Joseph: "Diaries" 1948.

Gosztony, Peter: Treatise printed in "Revue Internationale d'Histoire Militaire" nr. 33, pag. 75–98, 1975.

Granet, Marie: "Défence de la France" 1960.

Grimnes, Ole Kristian: "Hjemmefrontens Ledelse" (Oslo 1977).

Halicz, Emanuel: "Partisan Warfare in 19th Century Poland" 1975.

Hamilton-Hill, Donald: "SOE Assignment" 1973.

Hesse, Erich: "Der Sowjetrussische Partisanenkrieg 1941–44" 1969.

Hlond, August: "The Persecution of the Catholic Church in German Occupied Poland" 1941.

Hoare, Samuel: "Ambassador on Special Mission" 1946.

Hory, Ladislaus og Broszat, Martin: "Der Kroatische Ustascha-Staat 1941–45" 1964.

Hostache, René: "Le Conseil de la Résistance" 1958.

Howarth, David: "The Shetland Bus" 1957.

Hymoff, Edward: "The OSS in World War II" 1972.

Hæstrup, Jørgen: "From Occupied to Ally" 1963, ed. by the Danish Foreign Ministry..

Hæstrup, Jørgen: "Secret Alliance" I–III. 1976–77.

Hæstrup, Jørgen: "Linz, en sabotageepisode", treatise in "Festskrift til Aksel Linvald", pag. 155–58, 1956.

Hæstrup, Jørgen: "Table Top", treatise in "Jyske Samlinger" Ny række V, 1961, pag. 357–420.

Hæstrup, Jørgen: "Tilblivelsen af Danmarks Frihedsråd", treatise in "Historie", Ny række X, 2, pag. 243–261, 1973.

Hæstrup, Jørgen: ". . . Til landets bedste". I–II, 1966–67.

"Istorija SSSR 1941–45", bd. X, ed. A. V. Kavasev 1973.

Jensen, Sigurd: "Levevilkår i Danmark under besættelsen" 1971.

"John Christmas Møller. Londonbreve" ed. Jørgen Hæstrup. 1974.

de Jong, Louis: "The German Fifth Column in the Second World War". 1953.

"Keesing, Contemporary Archives", 1940–45.

Kingsley Webster, C. and Frankland, Noble: "The Strategic Air Offensive against Germany, 1939–45" 1961.

Kirchhoff, Hans: "Augustoprøret i Vendsyssel 1943", treatice in "Historie", Ny række VIII, 2, 1969, pag. 173–224.

Kirchhoff, Hans: "Augustoprøret i 1943", 1978.

Kirckpatrick, Ivone: "Mussolini" 1964.

Kjeldstadli, Sverre: "Hjemmestyrkene" bd. I, 1959.

Korbonski, Stefan: "Fighting Warsaw" 1956.

von Krannhals, Hanns: "Der Warschauer Aufstand 1944" 1962.

Kühnreich, Heinz: "Der Partisankrieg in Europa 1939–45" 1968.

Langelaan, George: "Knights of the Floating Silk" 1959.

Langer, William L.: "Our Vichy Gamble" 1947.

de Launay, Jaques: "Major Controversies of Contemporary History" 1965.

Lawrence, T. E.: "Seven Pillars of Wisdom" 1935.

Leeper, Reginald: "When Greek meets Greek" 1950.

Lenin, V. I.: "The State and the Revolution".

Liddell Hart, B. S.: "History of the Second World War". 1970.

Liddell Hart, B. S.: "The Other Side of the Hill" 1951.

Liddell Hart, B. S.: "The Sovjet Army".

Maas, Walter, B.: "The Netherlands at War, 1940–45" 1970.

MacLean, Fitzroy: "Disputed Barricade" 1957.

MacLean, Fitzroy: "Eastern Approaches" 1949.

McNeill, W. H.: "America, Britain and Russia, 1941–46" 1953.

Macrae, Stuart: "Winston Churchill's Toyshop" 1971.

von Manstein, Erich: "Verlorene Siege" 1955.

Manus, Maximo: "Underwater Saboteur" 1953.

Marjanovic, J.: "The Collaboration of D. Mihailovic's Chetniks with the Enemy Forces of Occupation" 1976.

Marshall, Bruce: "The White Rabbitt" 1952.

Martelli, George: "Agent Extraordinary" 1960.

Michel, Henri og Granet, Marie: "Combat" 1957.

Michel, Henri: "Les Courant de Pensée de la Résistance" 1962.

Michel, Henri: "La Guerre de l'Ombre" 1970.

Michel, Henri: "Histoire de la Résistance" 1958.

Michel, Henri et Mirkine-Guetzevitsh, Boris: "Les Idées Politiques et Sociales de la Résistance" 1954.

Michel, Henri: "Jean Moulin l'Unificateur" 1964.

Michel, Henri: "Le Movements Clandestins en Europe" 1965.

Midtskau, Sverre: "London svarer ikke" 1968.

Millar, George: "Maquis" 1947.

Montgomery Hyde, H.: "Room 3603" 1962.

Morgan, Frederick: "Ouverture to Overlord" 1950.

Mussolini, Benito: "Memoirs 1942–43« 1949.

Muus, Flemming B.: "The Spark and the Flame" 1951.

Myers, E. C. W.: "Greek Entanglement" 1955.

Nissen, Henrik S.: "1940, Studier i forhandlingspolitikken og samarbejdspolitikken" 1973.

Orlow, Dietrich: "The Nazis in the Balkans" 1968.

"Den Parlamentariske Kommissions Betænkning" bd. XIII.

Passy (pseud.) André Dewavrin: "Souvenirs" I–III 1947–51.

Paxton, Robert: "Vichy France" 1972.

Petrow, Richard: "The Bitter Years" 1974.

Piquet-Wicks, Eric: "Quatre dans l'Ombre" 1957.

Pomeroy, William J.: "Guerilla Warfare and Marxism" 1969.

Poulsen, Henning: "Besættelsesmagten og de danske nazister" 1970.

Reilly, Robin: "The Sixth Floor" 1966.

von Rentsch, Hellmuth: "Partisanenkampf" 1961.

"Resistance in Europe 1939–45" (ed. Stephen Hawes and Ralph White) 1973.

Richardson, Anthony: "Wingless Victory" 1950.

Riedel, Mathias: "Bergnau und Eisenschüttenindustrie in der Ukraine unter Deutscher Besatzung", treiatise in "Vierteljahrshefte für Zeitsgeschichte", pag. 245–284, 3. hefte, 1973.

Riste, Olav: "Bak fiendens linier", treatise in "Modstandskamp, Sttegi og Marinepolitik", pag. 138–57, 1972.

Ritter, Gerhard: "Carl Goerdeler und die Deutsche Widerstandsbewegung". 1956.

"The Rommel Papers" ed. B. H. Liddell Hart. 1953.

Rothfels, Hans: "Die Deutsche Opposition gegen Hitler" 1958.

Seth, Ronald: "A spy has no Friend" 1952.

"Shell-huset. $^{21}/_3$ 1945" ed. C. Næsh Henriksen og Ove Kampmann. 1955.

Sjarikov, A. D.: "The Great Country supplies the Partisana" (original title in Russian) "Voprosy Istorii" nr. 1973, pag. 121–179.

"Skipperen, en bog om Ebbe Munck" ed. Jørgen Hæstrup. 1974.

Soustelle, Jacques: "Envers et contre Tous" 1970.

"Special Operations" ed. Patrick Howarth. 1955.

Speer, Albert: "Erinnerungen" 1970.

Stalin, Josef: "Marxism and the National and Colonial Question" 1935.

Stead, P. J.: "Second Bureau" 1959.

Sternstein, Wolfgang: "The Ruhrkampf of 1923", treatise in "The Strategy of Civilian Defense" ed. Robert Adams, pag. 106–135. 1967.

"Stranitsy Narodnogo Podviga" ed. V. I. Smirnov m. fl. 1974.

Strong, Kenneth: "Intelligence at the Top" 1968.

Sweet-Escott, Bickham: "Baker Street Irregular" 1965.

Sønsteby, Gunnar: "Rapport fra nr. 24" 1962.

Toldstrup, Anton: "Uden kamp – ingen sejr" 1947.

Torell, Ulf: "Hjälp till Danmark" 1973.

Trommer, Aage: "Besættelsestidens første folkestrejke", treatise in "Historie", Ny række VII, 2, 1966, pag. 149–231.

Trommer, Aage: "Jernbanesabotagen i Danmark" 1971.

Trommer, Aage: "Modstandsarbejde i nærbillede" 1973.

Urquhart, R. E. and Greatorex, Wilfred: "Arnhem" 1958.

Vigneras, M.: "Rearming the French" 1957.

Warlimont, Walter: "In Hauptquartier der Deutschen Wehrmacht" 1964.

Warmbrunn, Werner: "The Dutch under the German Occupation" 1963.

Wilmot, Chester: "The Struggle for Europe" 1952.

F. W. Winterbotham: "The Ultra Secret" 1974.

Woodhouse, C. M.: "Apple of Discord" 1948.

Wyller, Th. Chr.: "Nyordning og Modstand" 1958.

Yahil, Leni: "Test of a Democracy" 1967.

Young, Gordon: "In Trust and Treason" 1959.

Zawodny, J. K.: "Death in the Forest" 1962.

Zinner, P. E.: "Communist Strategy and Tactics in Czechoslovakia" 1963.

Further information has been received form:

A. A. Kurnosov, scientific member of the institute of general history, Moscow.
Berit Nökleby, cand. philol. Norge.
Centre de Recherches de d'Etudes Historiques de la Seconde Guerre Mondiale.

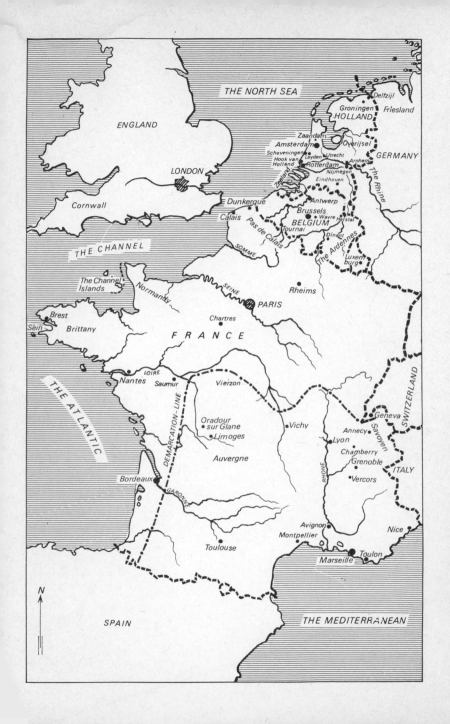

Odense University Studies in History and Social Sciences

(The prices do not include the Danish sales tax)

1: Anders Bjørnvad: *De fandt en vej. Den allierede overflyvning af Danmark under besættelsen* . . . 1970. 205 pp. Dan.kr. 40.00.

2: Jørn Henrik Petersen: *Aspekter af den økonomiske problematik i en centraldirigeret økonomi.* 1971. 311 pp. Dan.kr. 90.00.

3: Aage Trommer: *Jernbanesabotagen i Danmark under Den anden Verdenskrig.* 1971. 323 pp. Dan.kr. 30.00.

4: Henning Bregnsbo: *Kampen om skolelovene af 1958.* 1971. 236 pp. Dan.kr. 28.00.

5: Jørn Henrik Petersen: *Socialpolitisk teori. Bind I.* 1972. 135 pp. Dan.kr. 30.00.

6: Mikael Venge: *Christian 2.s fald. Spillet om magten i Danmark januar–februar 1523.* 1972. 218 pp. Dan.kr. 60.00.

7: Aage Trommer: *Modstandsarbejde i nærbillede. Det illegale arbejde i Syd- og Sønderjylland* . . . 1973. 515 pp. Dan.kr. 90.00.

8: Klaus Jørgensen: *Atomvåbnenes rolle i dansk politik.* 1973. 173 pp. Dan.kr. 20.00.

9: Erik Gørtz: *Measures of the Effects of Economic Policy.* 1973. 75 pp. Dan.kr. 30.00.

10: Leif Szomlaiski: *Yngre Sjællandske Krønike. Baggrund, tilblivelse og værdi.* 1973. 118 pp. Dan.kr. 40.00.

11: Aage Fasmer Blomberg: *Fyns vilkår under Svenskekrigene 1657–60.* 1973. 698 pp. Dan.kr. 100.00.

12: Ole Nørskov Nielsen: *Andagtslitteraturen og de gudelige vækkelser på Fyn 1820–1840.* 1973. 200 pp. Dan.kr. 40.00.

13: Niels Chr. Knudsen: *Production and Cost Models of a Multi-Product Firm.* 1973. 302 pp. Dan.kr. 50.00.

14: Jørn Henrik Petersen: *Socialpolitisk teori. Bind II.* 1974. 448 pp. Dan.kr. 120.00.

15: Erik Beukel: *Socialdemokratiet og stationeringsproblemet 1952–53.* 1974. 72 pp. Dan.kr. 20.00.

16: Carl-Johan Bryld: *Hans Svane og gejstligheden på stændermødet 1660.* 1974. 166 pp. Dan.kr. 30.00.

17: Tage Kaarsted: *Storbritannien og Danmark 1914–1920.* 2. udgave. 1975. 249 pp., ill. Dan.kr. 60.00.

18: Erling Ladewig Petersen: *'Alī and Mu'āwiya in Early Arabic Tradition.* Repr. 1974. 264 pp. Dan.kr. 60.00.

19: H. V. Gregersen: *Plattysk i Sønderjylland. En undersøgelse af fortyskningens historie indtil 1600-årene.* 1974. 393 pp. Dan.kr. 100.00.

20: Erling Albrectsen: *Fyn i oldtiden.* 1974. 152 pp. Dan.kr. 40.00.

21: E. Ladewig Petersen: *Veritas et honor regis.* 1974. 100 pp. Dan.kr. 25.00.

22: Hans Chr. Johansen: *Befolkningsudvikling og familiestruktur i det 18. århundrede.* 1975. 211 pp. Dan.kr. 60.00.

23: *Uppsalaoverenskomsten 1520.* Af Lizzie Wie Andersen [m. fl.] 1975. 208 pp. Dan.kr. 60.00.

24: Per Chr. Andersen: *Kristen politik. Kristeligt Folkeparti 13. april 1970 – 21. september 1971.* 1975. 128 pp. Dan.kr. 30.00.

25: Emanuel Halicz: *Partisan Warfare in 19th Century Poland: The Development of a Concept.* 1975. 220 pp. Dan.kr. 70.00.

26: Zygmunt Tkocz: *Klassestruktur og sociale forandringer i Østeuropa.* 1975. 194 pp. Dan.kr. 60.00.

27: Eric S. Einhorn: *National Security and Domestic Politics in Post-War Denmark.* 1975. 108 pp. Dan.kr. 30.00.

28: Finn Petersen: *Grønlandssagens behandling i FN 1946–54.* 1975. 130 pp. Dan.kr. 30.00.

29: Thelma Jexlev: *Fra dansk senmiddelalder. Nogle kildestudier.* 1976. 128 pp. Dan. kr. 30.00.

30: Hans Kryger Larsen: *Erik Arup. En historiografisk undersøgelse . . .* 1976. 72 pp. Dan.kr. 20.00.

31: Jørgen Grundt Larsen: *Modstandsbevægelsens Kontaktudvalg i Stockholm 1944–1945.* 1976. 184 pp. Dan.kr. 40.00.

32: Hans Chr. Johansen: *Studier i Da: ¬k Befolkningshistorie 1750–1890.* 1976. 214 pp. Dan.kr. 35.00.

33: Thorvald Ringsmose: *Rantzausholm Gods før og efter Svenskekrigene 1657–60.* 1976. 88 pp. Dan.kr. 20.00.

34: Jørgen Hæstrup: *Den 4. våbenart. Hovedtræk af de europæiske modstandsbevægelsers historie 1939–45.* 1976. 542 pp. Dan.kr. 120.00.

35: Jørgen Hæstrup: *Secret Alliance. A Study of the Danish Resistance Movement 1940–45. Vol. 1.* 1976. 326 pp. Dan.kr. 80.00.

36: Arne Bonvig Christensen: *Invasion i Danmark?* 1976. 200 pp. *Out of print.*

37: Jørgen Hæstrup: *Secret Alliance. A Study of the Danish Resistance Movement 1940–45. Vol. 2.* 1976. 398 pp. Dan.kr. 80.00.

38: Chr. Bo Hansen: *Retssystemet. En retssociologisk analyse.* 1976. 143 pp. Dan.kr. 40.00.

39: Sven Erik Larsen: *Militærnægterproblemet i Danmark 1914–1967.* 1977. 112 pp. Dan.kr. 30.00.

40: Klaus Jørgensen: *Hjælp fra Danmark. En studie i dansk u-landspolitik 1960–71.* 1977. 443 pp. Dan.kr. 80.00.

41: Jørgen Hæstrup: *Secret Alliance. A Study of the Danish Resistance Movement 1940–45. Vol. 3.* 1977. 422 pp. Dan.kr. 80.00.

42: Hans Snitker: *Det illegale Frit Danmark – bladet og organisationen.* 1977. 192 pp. Dan.kr. 45.00.

43: Per Kristensen: *Bønder og bebyggelse.* 1977. 246 pp. Dan.kr. 60.00.

44: Vello Helk: *Die Jesuiten in Dorpat 1583–1625. Ein Vorposten der Gegenreformation in Nordosteuropa.* 1977. 335 pp. Dan.kr. 80.00.

45: Emanuel Halicz: *Danish Neutrality during the Crimean War (1853–1856).* 1977. 251 pp. Dan.kr. 70.00.

46: Thomas Riis: *Les institutions politiques centrales du Danemark 1100–1332.* 1977. 397 pp. Dan.kr. 90.00.

47: Mikael Venge: *Når vinden føjer sig. Spillet om magten i Danmark marts–december 1523.* 1977. 179 pp. Dan.kr. 80.00.

48: Knud J. V. Jespersen: *Rostjenestetaksation og adelsgods. Studier i den danske adelige rostjeneste og adelens godsfordeling 1540–1650.* 1977. 330 pp. Dan.kr. 110.00.

49: Henning Nielsen: *Dansk udenrigspolitik 1875–1894 med særligt henblik på beslutningsprocessen.* 1977. 215 pp. Dan.kr. 40.00.

50: Jytte Jensen: *Organisering og finansiering af byggeriet på Ulriksholm i 1630'rne og 1640'rne.* 1977. 101 pp. Dan.kr. 40.00.

51: Hanne Eriksen: *Partiet De Uafhængige 1953–1960.* 1978. 197 pp. Dan.kr. 40.00.

52: *Chance and Change. Social and economic studies in historical demography in the Baltic Area.* Ed. by David Gaunt et al. 1978. 296 pp. Dan.kr. 100.00.

53: Haakon Bennike Madsen: *Det danske skattevæsen. Kategorier og klasser. Skatter på landbefolkningen 1530–1660.* 1978. Ca. 450 sider. Dan.kr. 80.00.

54: Per Sundbøl: *Dansk Islandspolitik 1913–1918.* 1978. 156 pp. Dan.kr. 40.00.

55: Jørgen Hæstrup: *Europe Ablaze. An Analysis of the History of the European Resistance Movements 1939–45.* 564 pp. Dan.kr. 120.00 .